MEDIA
AND
SOCIETY

FIFTH EDITION

MEDIA
AND
SOCIETY
FIFTH EDITION

MICHAEL
O'SHAUGHNESSY

JANE
STADLER

OXFORD
UNIVERSITY PRESS
AUSTRALIA & NEW ZEALAND

OXFORD
UNIVERSITY PRESS

Oxford University Press is a department of the University of Oxford.

It furthers the University's objective of excellence in research, scholarship, and education by publishing worldwide. Oxford is a registered trademark of Oxford University Press in the UK and in certain other countries.

Published in Australia by
Oxford University Press
253 Normanby Road, South Melbourne, Victoria 3205, Australia

National Library of Australia Cataloguing-in-Publication data

Author: O'Shaughnessy, Michael, 1951–
Title: Media and society / Michael O'Shaughnessy and Jane Stadler.

Edition: 5th ed.
ISBN: 9780195574340 (pbk.)

Notes: Previous ed.: 2008.
Includes bibliographical references and index.
Subjects: Mass media.
Mass media and culture.
Other Authors/Contributors: Stadler, Jane Megan.

Dewey Number: 302.23

Edited by Valina Rainer
Text design by eggplant communications
Typeset by diacriTech, Chennai, India
Proofread by Anne Mulvaney
Indexed by Russell Brooks
Printed by Sheck Wah Tong Printing Press Ltd

Contents

List of Figures

List of Plates

List of Tables

Case Studies

Acknowledgments

This book is very much indebted to the numerous scholars and teachers of media, cultural, and film studies who have developed the study of the media so fruitfully; we want to acknowledge their significant work. Our ideas and approaches owe much to them. We are also inspired by the wisdom and insights of our students. However, responsibility for the way these ideas have been presented here is ours alone.

The following people and institutions kindly agreed to give permission to reproduce photos and other textual materials, and we gratefully acknowledge their assistance and cooperation: '4000 Chemicals' anti-smoking advertisement, © Commonwealth of Australia, Department of Health and Ageing, reproduced by permission, courtesy of the National Tobacco Youth Campaign; Billiam the Snowman YouTube video image courtesy of Nathan Hamel and Greg Hamel of KOTAS; HBSC: Commodity/Luxury and Traditional/Trendy advertisements, © HSBC Bank Australia Limited; questions and analysis relating to Figure 9.2 (Dr Barnard) derives from work and images presented by Guy Gauthier in a package made up of slides and notes: Guy Gauthier, 'The Semiology of the Image', British Film Institute Education Advisory Service, London, 1976; Hammer and Coop MINI publicity image © 2006 Boris Vallejo and Julie Bell, photo provided by MINI USA; Hahn Loveboobs advertisement courtesy of Andrew Disley at Lion Nathan; *The Assassination of Jesse James by the Coward Robert Ford* film poster © Warner Bros. Entertainment Inc.; 'Blessed art Thou' painting of Angelina Jolie, courtesy of the artist Kate Kretz; 'Bloody Murder' advertisement for King of Shaves courtesy of Paul Irwin, Director of Creative Partners (Aust) Ltd; 'Thembo's Burger Hut' courtesy of Alex Latimer and Patrick Latimer, originally published in the *Laugh it Off Annual*; Queensland Transport antiterrorism culture jam courtesy of Holly Zwalf and Shannon Huber, originally published in *Heretical/Philosophia* 2006; 'African Mother Drop the Debt Image' reproduced courtesy of the photographer, Tif Hunter, and Red Cell; Disability Campaign images appear courtesy of the Disability Services Commission; the 'Monoculture' cover is reproduced courtesy of *Colors Magazine*; the 'Young Designers Emporium' image appears courtesy of Jupiter; the Nike email exchange is reproduced courtesy of Jonah Peretti; Avant Card images appear thanks to Nobody Denim and *Cosmopolitan*; 'Happy Wedding Day' advertisement 1994 reproduced with permission of Wedgwood, Barlaston, Stoke-on-Trent, England; newspaper headlines, 'WE DID IT' and 'Good v Evil', courtesy of the

West Australian; 'Well Hello Sailors' article courtesy of the *Sunday Times*; James Currey publishers for extracts from Ngugi Wa Thiong'o's *Decolonising the Mind*, 1986; Penguin UK for the extract from John Berger's *Ways of Seeing*, 1972; Pantheon Books for extract from Edward Said's *Orientalism*, 1980; Routledge for extracts from Richard Dyer's *The Matter of Images*, 1993 and O'Sullivan et al.'s *Key Concepts in Communication Studies*, 1994; the British Film Institute for the extract from Sylvia Harvey's *May '68 and Film Culture*, 1978. Thanks to Justin Nurse at Laugh it Off for permission to reproduce the Weapon of Mass Distraction, Diesel Desire and Black Labour images. Diesel generously allowed the reproduction of its advertisement Luxury Living in Today's Africa. The Corne Krige and Breyton Paulse rugby images are courtesy of Club Newlands. Guardian Newspapers granted permission to reproduce the 'Saudis Acknowledge Women Exist' article, and Getty Images/Touchline Photo permitted the reproduction of the boxer, Vitali Klitschko. The Oreo image is reproduced courtesy of DSTV MultiChoice Africa. The excerpts from *The Truth about Stories*, © Thomas King and the Canadian Broadcasting Corporation, are reproduced by permission of House of Anansi Press, Toronto. The extracts from *Big Ideas: The Wisdom Interviews of David Williamson* by Peter Thompson, broadcast Sunday 22 February 2004 on ABC Radio National, are reproduced by permission of the Australian Broadcasting Corporation and ABC Online, © 2004 ABC, all rights reserved.

Every effort has been made to trace the original source of all material reproduced in this book. Where the attempt has been unsuccessful, the authors and publisher would be pleased to hear from the copyright holder concerned to rectify any omission.

We would especially like to thank our research assistant Joanna McIntyre for her contribution to edition five and particularly for her analysis of Lady Gaga's significance in contemporary media culture. We would also like to thank those at OUP who have made publication of this book possible, particularly Karen Hildebrandt, Jessica Hambridge, Belinda Leon, Estelle Tang, and our copy editor Valina Rainer.

Michael O'Shaughnessy and Jane Stadler

Introduction: The Media-world

This book aims to explore the media and their role in contemporary society. In introducing readers to media studies, a discipline that has developed since the 1970s, we will explain many of the main concepts, approaches, and key critical terms used in this field.

Throughout the book we use the expression 'media-world'. This suggests three different ways we can think about the connection between media and society.

- First, 'media-world' invites us to think about the relationship between the media, their institutions, and the world we live in, how these two areas are connected, how the media affect society, and vice versa. We examine this most specifically in Part 1, Chapters 2 and 3. We are interested in how the media express or challenge society's dominant values and norms—its ideology—so our study and analysis of the media focuses on the social role of the media, especially in Part 3.
- Second, 'media-world' points to the idea that the media construct their own particular views and visions of society for us through their representations and their view of the world. We are interested in exploring these media viewpoints by analysing specific media examples and by giving general methods and guidelines for your media analysis; this is the major focus of Part 2 (Pictures), Part 4 (Stories), and Part 5 (Media and Identity). In Part 1 (Chapters 4 and 5), we explore how representing the world, primarily through language and images, is a particular process, a way of constructing reality.
- Third, the term suggests that the world we live in and the ways we live are now so heavily influenced and dominated by the media that we can describe this as a 'media-world'. Most people today, particularly young people, live in a media-dominated world and that is a major reason for writing this book: it is important and useful to understand the media that we are all living with. We consider this throughout, but specifically in Chapters 7 and 25.

We explore the media-world primarily by looking at media texts and stories, media representations—found in films, television programs, advertisements, news stories, and on the internet—and by doing textual analysis.

We examine how we read, watch, and listen to media texts, give methods for analysing and interpreting them, and explore the complex relationship between these texts and the 'real' world; in other words, the relationship between the media and society. We consider various aspects of the media, but media stories and representations are our main focus. The pleasures of these stories are what draw us to the media, they are the basis of our media consumption, so we think it is important to offer ways of understanding them. Our examples are mostly chosen from Australia, the USA, South Africa, and the United Kingdom as these are our areas of media experience.

Themes and influences

There are several themes that run through the book. These are partly the result of our own interests as authors and we think it's important to acknowledge how our personal experiences and histories have influenced our approach to the media, just as your experiences and histories will influence your approach. We do not write from an objective, neutral position. There are two of us writing this book and we sometimes write in the first person using the pronouns 'we', or 'us', or 'our'. Occasionally, when we write from just one of our positions we will use the pronouns 'I', or 'me', or 'my' and indicate whether it is either author's point of view.

We are both white, both grew up in middle-class families, have spent much of our working lives in education, and share a number of similar ideas. But we grew up in different countries, are different genders, and have some specific individual influences.

Four major influences have contributed to Michael's understanding of the media and the world. First, as a Western, middle-class, white male, I grew up in the UK deeply imbued with the ideology of liberal individualism. I believe in concepts such as democracy, freedom of the individual, and freedom of speech. I therefore saw the media as an arena for individual creativity and expression. Then, when I was in my twenties, I discovered the insights of Karl Marx and Marxism, and saw how Marx's work could be developed in understanding the media. This understanding showed me a world dominated by class struggle and economic necessity, a world in which individuals are determined by their class and social positions. I began to understand the media as one of the mechanisms through which the ruling classes try to maintain their domination over subordinate classes. At the same time, feminist thought and practice led me to look at gender issues and media representations of gender. I began to understand how the inequalities of class and race articulated by Marx were compounded by patriarchal oppression: the media could be understood as a site that maintained sexist and male-dominated views of the world. My initial focus on the oppression of women was followed by analysis of masculinity. Finally, an interest in Freud led me to the work of Wilhelm Reich and Carl Jung, to psychoanalytic and psychotherapeutic approaches, the growth movement, and the teachings of Native Americans. These gave me new insights into how people and societies work, and into the role of the media in our lives. All four strands have contributed to my perceptions and work on the media as shown here.

Jane's understanding of the relationship between the media and society has been influenced by living on three different continents. My experiences in Africa, America, and Australia made me more conscious of social inequality and cultural differences than I might otherwise have been; however, it was not until I enrolled to study philosophy and media, communication and cultural studies at university in Australia that I began to analyse my own assumptions about and understandings of the world, and to think critically about where these ideas came from. These experiences developed into an interest in researching and teaching about media and cultural studies.

The main themes of the book

The contradictory nature of the media

We see positive and negative aspects in the media and we try to show both of them. We also recognise that there are often contradictory arguments made about the media and how they work. We want to try to show a variety of perspectives so that you can understand the different ideas people have had about the media and then decide what your position is. We are not offering a definitive series of answers about how the media operate and what they mean, but an exploration of different approaches.

Aesthetic and social aspects of the media

We will present a variety of approaches that can be used for analysing and interpreting media texts. These will focus on two aspects: aesthetic and social concerns. Aesthetic concerns means looking at and evaluating the forms of media—for example, understanding how films communicate through processes such as cinematography and editing. Social concerns means looking at the social and political views that the media communicate to us in their content. The methods of analysis presented here can be applied to many other texts, for example novels, plays, and paintings.

Global and historical context

We want to understand how the media operate in the world as a whole. We can do this better if we have some idea of how they have developed historically, and how media disseminate culture around the globe.

Psychological concerns of the media

As well as thinking about the social aspects of the media we examine how the media relate to people's inner and psychological lives.

Different factors producing the media

We will explore why and how we get the kind of media we do, asking what produces or determines the media. There is no one answer but we recognise five distinct factors:

1   technological developments: the production of new media forms
2   economics: the need and desire to make money/profit
3   human creativity: the work of all those producing media content or media technologies
4   social controls: implemented by people in positions of power, especially governments, who attempt to control what appears in the media and what does not
5   audiences: who through their consumption of the media ensure its success or failure.

No one aspect dominates and they are often interconnected. We need to be aware of all of them as significant.

Ideology, discourse, and hegemony

There are three key theoretical concepts running through the book: ideology, discourse, and hegemony. We introduce them gradually, with many examples, so that readers can build up a full sense of what they mean.

Content

Most of the media examples we discuss come from 'popular' or 'mass' culture—the cinema, television, advertisements, photography, newspapers, and the internet. We have not chosen these either to celebrate or denigrate popular culture but because they are accessible, familiar, and, we argue, socially significant: many people learn how to think and feel about the world in which they live through popular culture. We are not saying they are great works of art that people will look back on in 50 or 100 years as very significant, but that they are important in that they indicate the social values of our culture. That said, we think that many of them have significant aesthetic value, which also makes them worth analysing.

Many examples relate to gender, the family, and ethnicity.

Gender and ethnicity are relevant to anyone who wants to understand their own identity. We all grow up and are positioned as gendered and ethnic subjects; that is, our identity is defined as male or female, black or white, and so on. Who we are is affected by this social positioning, and the health of society depends on how well we relate to each other from these positions. We invite this analysis of gender and ethnic issues in the media that can lead to a fascinating exploration and wider understanding of society, other people, and ourselves. (These concerns are addressed throughout the book, but gender and ethnicity are specifically considered in Part 5.)

Ethnicity and cultural identity are important in the way social groups define themselves and each other and are crucial in many of today's social and political conflicts within and between different countries.

Gender is significant in two ways. First, gender involves issues of social power and equality: it is not simply a question of the social oppression of women by men, but a more complex situation in which men and women are constructed and oppressed by the patriarchal, competitive, and heterosexist values of society. The media and their representations of gender play a key role in this.

Second, gender relates to sexuality, one of the key human drives. While in some ways sexuality is repressed in Western culture, it is often at the centre of media representations. Sex sells, and the popular media return to issues of sexuality time and time again, making it an important area to examine. Issues of social power and sexuality are often linked in complex ways and we expect that all readers, men and women, will be able to relate to these through their own experiences. These issues are also relevant in understanding the family, a major institution of society, and one that is undergoing significant change. So we look at many examples of media representations of the family, which again will connect with readers' own experiences.

Overall we are concerned with the political and social considerations of the media. Feminists began using the phrase 'the personal is political' when they realised how the everyday domestic lives of many women—staying at home, looking after children, doing poorly paid work—were part of the wider picture of women's political situation. All personal and social behaviour is political: the clothes we wear, the food we eat, how we work, what we do with our money, the media we consume, how we spend our leisure time, and so on. These behaviours are political because, through social and global interconnections, they relate to and affect how we and other people live in the world, which is what makes them worthy of analysis.

Media studies can be either an attempt at neutral and descriptive analysis that tries to explain, from the outside, how the media work, or it can be politically engaged and aim to challenge how the media work. Much of media studies has been idealistic—a part of the search for a more equal society—and this aspect has given it a political slant. Marx coined the phrase: 'The point is not to understand the world but to change it.' We see media studies operating in this broad political arena of developing and encouraging social change and debate about political issues but we also think there is a point to understanding the world. We hope that this book can help in your understanding of the media-world you live in.

We are aware that global warming and ethnic tensions are major social issues that are also linked to economic concerns. The media play an important role in how these are represented.

The book includes a model essay, illustrations, practical exercises, and suggestions for further reading. It includes theoretical overviews and detailed case studies. It encourages readers to reflect on their own identities and media usage. Each chapter includes an overview of the main topics for consideration, a glossary of key terms used, and case studies and summaries.

Guided Tour

Chapter overview

Each chapter begins with a short overview that outlines the subjects the chapter will cover.

Margin notes

Key terms are highlighted in bold and defined in margin notes. A glossary at the end of the book contains all the key terms.

Case studies

Extensive case studies apply the ideas and approaches presented in the book to specific topics, giving students a model for their own media studies assignments.

Discussion points

These exercises and discussion questions prompt students to debate issues among themselves and investigate how the media influences their own lives. These points are raised at the end of each chapter. They include exercises to consolidate, apply, and extend understanding of issues raised in the chapter.

Chapter summary

Each chapter ends with a short summary that lists the key skills and ideas that students should have acquired from the chapter.

Defining the Media

All of us who professionally use the mass media are the shapers of society. We can vulgarize that society. We can brutalize it. Or we can help lift it onto a higher level.
William Bernbach, founder, Doyle, Dane and Bernbach (DDB)

This chapter will
- outline the main characteristics of the media
- give a brief history of the media
- explore the media's key determining factors
- give a definition of the media.

Denotation

denotation
Denotation is what Barthes calls 'the first order of signification'. It is the most obvious level on which a sign communicates and it refers to the commonsense meaning of the sign. The denotative meaning can be expressed by describing the sign as simply as possible

To consider what a text denotes is to analyse it on a purely descriptive level without delving into what it might imply. It is simply to ask 'What is there?' **Denotation** attempts to describe without comment, evaluation, or judgment, the contents of an image. At this level, signs are as close to value-free as possible. On a denotative level the American flag, say, is a rectangular shape consisting of horizontal stripes of red, alternating with stripes of white, with a smaller rectangle of blue in the upper left-hand corner. The blue rectangle contains white star shapes, also arranged in horizontal rows.

Case study: The representation of cigarettes and smoking in film and television fictions

There is a clear belief among both tobacco companies and anti-smoking groups that tobacco advertising encourages people to smoke. Once Western governments realised that smoking was definitely harmful to health they decided to ban cigarette and tobacco advertising in most media; however, it is still possible for people to be seen smoking in films and television dramas. In thinking about the overall question of media influence we can approach this continued representation of smoking within screen texts in a number of ways: a quantitative content analysis to measure how frequently smoking is portrayed on screen; a qualitative analysis to assess what the situations and emotions are when people smoke on screen; research into the effects/influence of these images; and research and questioning as to how and why smoking is included as part of the scripts. As media researchers you can devise and carry out work in all these areas.

Smoking: Quantitative content analysis

Some people are concerned that the simple amount or quantity of onscreen smoking we see is significant.

An extensive content analysis study conducted at the University of California found that 'In films of the 1950s there was an average of 10.7 [smoking] incidents per hour. Pressure from lobby groups saw this figure fall to 4.9 between 1980 and 1982, but by 2002 the total had risen to 10.9'. The study suggested that the recent rise in 'smoking incidents' in films 'allowed manufacturers to overcome restrictions on tobacco advertising'. Additionally, Professor Stanton Glantz argued that 'This is particularly worrying in the light of research that shows that young people are taking up smoking because of what they see on the big screen' (Glantz 2004).

Discussion points

1. In thinking about popular culture and media products, would you argue that we get what we want, or we want what we get?
2. Do you think programs such as MasterChef are programs that are of the people or for the people? What examples would you argue fit into these two categories?
3. Look out for particular media events. How do the media construct them? How involved in these events are you?
4. How would you argue for and against forms of media censorship? What forms of censorship would you argue for (if any) and for whom?
5. Reflect on your experience of media coverage of events in Iraq. What arguments would you make for and against the way the media have covered events? As events continue to unfold, monitor how the media deal with them.

Summary

You should now be able to
- comment critically on the media's role in relation to some of the major crises and conflicts in contemporary society; for instance, discuss and comment on the media's coverage of the conflict in Iraq
- explain general principles of how the media function and discuss these principles
- consider the importance and effects of the media's need for popularity
- apply the acronym SEARCH to media representations
- discuss arguments about whether and/or how the media affect and influence people
- define and illustrate the terms 'embedded journalism' and 'product placement'
- discuss the pros and cons of media censorship
- analyse fictional representations of smoking.

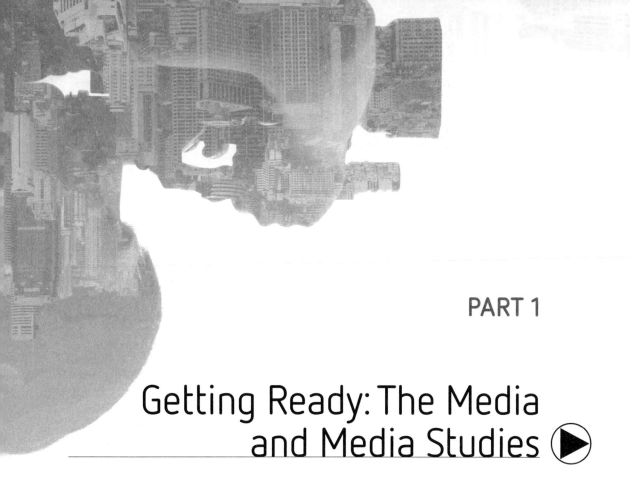

PART 1

Getting Ready: The Media and Media Studies ▶

Media is the nervous system of a democracy. If it's not functioning well the democracy can't function.

Outfoxed

OVERVIEW OF PART 1

Part 1 presents an overview of what the media are and what media studies is trying to do. It presents initial definitions, approaches, questions, and assumptions. Then it explores issues of representation, language, the social construction of reality, how we, as audiences, read media texts, and developments of new media technologies.

CHAPTER 1

Defining the Media

All of us who professionally use the mass media are the shapers of society. We can vulgarize that society. We can brutalize it. Or we can help lift it onto a higher level.
William Bernbach, founder, Doyle, Dane and Bernbach (DDB)

This chapter will
▶ outline the main characteristics of the media
▶ give a brief history of the media
▶ explore the media's key determining factors
▶ give a definition of the media.

What is 'the media'?

'The media' is a commonly used term, but what exactly does it refer to? The **media** include a whole host of modern communication systems, for example cinema, television, newspapers, magazines, advertisements, and radio. They also include video games, computers, phones and mobile phones, pagers, iPods, interactive multimedia, and most importantly, the internet. Defining the media is not easy because the media are constantly changing with the development of new forms and technologies (see Chapters 7 and 25), but there are a number of characteristics, historical developments, and determining factors that delineate what the media are, and these can lead towards a definition.

media
the technologically developed communication industries, normally making money, which can transmit information and entertainment across time and space to individuals and/ or large groups of people; they are literally in the middle of this process, the means for communication.

Media characteristics

- The media are human communication systems.
- The media use processes of industrialised technology for producing messages.

- The media generally aim to reach large audiences or to be used by many people and hence have been referred to as 'mass media' operating through 'mass production' leading to 'mass communication'; their success is often built on popularity.
- The media usually aim to facilitate communication across distance (and/or time) between people, or to enable communication in which the sender does not need to be present as the communication is recorded and then transmitted.
- The media are called 'media' because they are literally in the middle, or are the middle chain, of this communication (*media* means 'middle' in Latin); they are the mechanisms that connect the senders and the receivers of messages.
- The development of the media has been affected by commercial interests that recognise that the media are potentially highly profitable industries.

Media history

There are several important historical moments or periods in the development of the media.

1   The first major medium in Western culture was the Gutenberg printing press in the fifteenth century, which led to the reproduction and distribution of information and entertainment through pamphlets, books, and then newspapers. This meant information was made more widely available to many people. The mass production of paper increased media output.

2   During the late eighteenth and nineteenth centuries, the Industrial Revolution in Europe saw new forms of power and manufacturing lead to rapid developments in printing technologies. At the same time, there was a revolution in the road, rail, and water transport communication systems. Major social changes and new forms of industrial production led to a massive growth in urban populations and new patterns of work and leisure. Demand for rapid communication of information and entertainment increased, alongside rising literacy and population growth.

3   The last part of the nineteenth and the first half of the twentieth centuries saw a further explosion of communication systems and technologies that have affected our daily lives in numerous ways. The advent of photography, film, sound recording, radio, and then television alongside the development of the telegraph, the telephone, and the rapidly changing systems of travel, particularly the car and aeroplane, all combined to change the map of human culture forever. People living in industrial, developed countries began to accept all these as basic conditions for human life.

4   Since 1980 we have undergone—and continue to undergo—another major revolution in communications, thanks to the development of new technologies, particularly the computer chip and digital media. Satellite and cable communications, digital television, computers, video games, virtual reality, mobile phones, and the

internet are once again changing patterns of human behaviour, changing our modes of accessing knowledge, our entertainment, our ways of seeing the world and of interacting with one another.

For most people today the media are the main source of their knowledge and entertainment and are part of the very structure of their lives. According to A C Nielsen, Americans watch more than four hours of television on average every day. That's 28 hours each week, two months per year, or the equivalent of watching nine years of non-stop television over an average lifespan. Australians aren't far behind: a 2011 survey shows urban Australians watch 3 hours and 9 minutes of television daily <www.freetv. com.au>. We are also in the midst of a shift from television to new media and computer-mediated communication (**CMC**). Indeed, Americans spent an average of 32 hours per month on the internet in 2010, spending most of that time involved in social networking. According to 2010 statistics from Nielsen, sites like Facebook and Twitter now account for 22.7 per cent of time spent on the web; the next closest activity is online games, which make up 10.2 per cent <www.comscoredatamine.com>. People truly live in a media–world. It is important to note, though, that there is still a global split or **digital divide** (see pp. 117 and 465) between those people who have unlimited media access and those who do not.

This split can be experienced within one society where there is a big division between rich and poor or between different countries or different global regions. Figures from 2011 indicate that internet penetration in Africa is 11 per cent, whereas in North America and Australia it is about 80 per cent <www.internetworldstats. com>. To further illustrate the extent of the inequity, universal access to basic communications services is defined very differently in South Africa from in North America. In the USA, universal service is defined as 'access to a personal computer with a world wide web browser, a personal internet email address, and the capacity to make one's own information available via the Web' (Snow 2001, p. 21). The South African Department of Communications defines universal service as 'the provision of a telephone line within a reasonable distance of 30 minutes travelling' (Fourie 2001, p. 610). This is changing. South Africa is installing telecentres with access to phones, faxes, computers, electronic commerce, and government information in post offices and other community sites. In addition, mobile phones are found increasingly throughout Africa as they are in the rest of the world. It is estimated that globally there are already over 2 billion internet users—that's over 30 per cent of the world's population <www.internetworldstats.com>. Indeed, over 3 million new world wide web pages go up every 24 hours (Brown 2004). As media analyst Heather Hudson points out, 'Access to information is critical to development; thus information and communication technologies (ICTs) as a means of sharing information are not simply

CMC
Computer-mediated communication

digital divide
The increasing gap between those who have and those who do not have access to technology, access to content, ICT skills, and money to pay for digital services; most often used to refer to the difference between the developed and developing worlds' access to the benefits of digital technology.

a connection between people, but a link in the chain of the development process itself' (2006, p. 310). It remains to be seen whether the digital divide will continue as developing nations and underprivileged groups in developed nations leapfrog to new technologies (for instance, bypassing landline installation and going straight to mobile and wireless technologies without investing in outmoded infrastructure), but it is clear that information poverty is an inequity that is crucial to overcome.

Media determinants

In the Introduction (p. xviii) we mentioned five factors that are crucial in determining how the media develop. It is worth repeating them here and considering their interconnections. They are

1   technological developments: the production of new media forms
2   economics: the need and desire to make money/profit
3   human creativity: the work of all those producing media content or media technologies
4   social controls: implemented by people in positions of power, especially governments who attempt to control what appears in the media
5   audiences: who through their consumption of the media ensure its success or failure.

We do not think any one aspect dominates and they are often interlinked. We suggest that you be aware of all of them as significant.

Technology is central to the media but technological changes do not just happen magically. Media analysts need to ask: what brings about these technological changes and developments? The answer is that the media develop within specific economic and social frameworks, and from specific economic and social determinants.

Socially there are three significant factors relating to points 3, 4, and 5.

1   First, the role of human creativity, which includes inventors of new technologies such as Thomas Edison, and practitioners of these technologies, for example photographers, app developers, film directors, and composers.
2   Second, the role of people in positions of social power and control. These people can limit and control the media and they can help develop them. In relation to control, some governments, concerned about the potential power of the media, have sought to retain control either by actually running the media themselves or through strict censorship laws. President Robert Mugabe's government in Zimbabwe routinely prosecuted journalists who were critical of government policies and thus sought to control media information. In Western democracies there is a general principle known as 'freedom of the press', which suggests that the media should be independent of government control. Public broadcast systems in Australia and the

United Kingdom—the ABC, SBS, and the BBC—are funded by the government, yet are meant to be independent bodies who make their own decisions about program production and content. The private media (for example television Channels 7, 9, and 10 and the Fox cable networks) are funded by independent advertising and thus not linked at all to governments. All these media are bound to uphold laws of decency and acceptability, which are monitored through government legislation, for example censorship boards and libel laws, so there is still some overall control. Additionally, socially responsible citizens may set up watchdog committees or organisations to police the morals of the media.

Currently, there are interesting struggles going on about how governments and societies control the internet, which crosses all national boundaries. These relate not only to issues of sexuality, pornography, and particularly, paedophilia, but also to concerns of governments such as those of Burma and China, which may be worried about the propagation of Western ideas, values, and media products. When Google, the world's leading internet search engine, entered China in 2005, it had to comply with Chinese regulations including government censorship and surveillance initiatives. In effect, when people searched for topics the Chinese government deems to be sensitive or seditious, google.cn could not display the search result. In 2009, Google's YouTube service was banned and Gmail became unavailable when the Chinese government accused Google of spreading obscene content. In October 2010, Google refused to continue to comply with China's content filtering policy and its subsequent exit from China indicates democratisation and control of internet content within and across national borders has become a significant topic in media studies.

In relation to the development of media technologies it is important to note that in wartime, governments have supported the development of many new technologies for the military: developments in the First and Second World Wars, the Cold War, the Vietnam War and the Gulf Wars all contributed to innovations in the media. The development of early video-camera technology, for example, was related to its use for American military surveillance; internet, cable, and satellite technologies were all originally developed for the military. Other media technological advances are spinoffs from the decisions by US and Soviet governments to invest in space technologies. In efforts to find ways of sexually satisfying soldiers based in Iraq who are separated from their loved ones at home, sexual dildonic technologies, which allow partners to sexually stimulate each other over the internet, are now being developed.

3   The third social factor is audiences and consumers. Media success and viability relies on providing satisfaction for its audiences; if audiences aren't buying a media product it is likely to fail. In the history of photography, film, and video, for example, we can see how the (male) audience desire for pornography was a huge driving force in the development of all these technologies as was the way they were distributed and popularised. Many developments in the internet have similarly been driven by the pornography industry.

This last example and the significance of audience demand points us directly to economic factors. The distributors of pornography are not really interested in making their audiences happy and sexually fulfilled; they want to make money. Most media changes have occurred within **capitalist** economies, so their development has been hugely influenced by profit motives and we must understand that the media have been developed in the interests of making money. Media history shows that technological changes tend to be implemented when they are seen to be profitable. Thomas Edison, who developed the phonograph and the wireless, was at least as much a businessman as he was an inventor.

All this shows how closely the determining factors—technological, social, and economic—are linked. We want to stress the economic because in some ways it is the least visible or obvious factor, yet it is very important in the production of media. The popularity of reality television (see Chapter 18), for example, is obviously based on audience interest, camera technologies that make it possible to effectively capture the dance routines on *Dancing with the Stars*, and creative minds coming up with the concept. But note how the cheapness of the production of these programs as opposed to fictional dramas, which need writers, actors, costumes, and sets, is crucial in a time of increasing television competition and note how audience participation encourages audiences to use and buy the latest mobile phone and SMS technologies. These programs don't just make money for the telephone companies through the phone-ins; more importantly, they get audiences accustomed to using these technologies. As media analyst Bill Hammock has noted, the US telephone communication company AT&T invested in the development of the *American Idol* series to 'get Americans into the habit of text messaging' (Hammock 2004). We need to remember these economic factors. Because vested interests and power relations influence both the content and interpretation of media texts, questions about the relationship between media, profit, and ownership are important and constitute the basis for studying the political economy of the media (see pp. 22–5).

capitalism
The dominant global economic system, organised by workers selling their labour for wages, and investors making profit through interest and economic growth. Capitalism, which gradually replaced the feudal economic system from about 1600, is characterised by private ownership and control of the means of production (capital) by individuals and corporations.

Conclusion

While the complexity of the media makes definitions difficult, the following is a useful starting point: the media are technologically developed communication industries, normally making money, that can transmit information and entertainment across time and space to individuals and/or large groups of people; they are, literally, in the middle of this process, the means for communication.

This transmission of information is not one way. The recipients of media messages are also involved in the process of communication as part of a feedback loop that influences the production of media. While it is true that many media forms, such as television, radio, film, and newspapers, have an asymmetrical flow of communication from one sender to many receivers, the rise of more interactive media forms has changed this dynamic. But even in television, radio, and newspapers the audience has always contributed something to the communicative exchange (primarily through the process of constructing meaning, but also through ratings, research, SMSs, tweets, talkback, letters to the editor, Facebook pages, and other feedback mechanisms). The 'one to many' model of mass communication is also being transformed by technological advances, as the following chapters demonstrate.

This chapter has

- defined the media
- outlined key media characteristics
- outlined media history
- considered significant media determinants.

Discussion points

1   In what ways have media developments affected human societies in the last 500 years? Think of specific examples.
2   How much of your own life is currently engaged in media activities? How do the media impact on your life?
3   Can you find examples of the five media determining factors in relation to the development of specific media products? Which, if any, do you argue is most important? Why?

Summary

You should now be able to

- define terms such as 'the media', 'mass communication', and 'the digital divide'
- give a brief historical overview of how the media have developed
- explain the factors and different determinants that are relevant when considering the development of the media in general
- discuss how these determinants can be related to specific media texts.

CHAPTER 2

Media Studies

*They criticised me a lot and I appreciated that, because I used the media—even the
conservative ones—as a mirror from which I can see the image I'm projecting.*
Nelson Mandela, speaking about the South African press, 2002

This chapter will

▶   ask why anybody might want to study or teach about the media

▶   consider the pros and cons of the media

▶   put forward two historical views of the media

▶   explore fears about the media

▶   look at media studies as an academic discipline and consider different media studies
approaches.

Why study or teach about the media?

As a starting point for this chapter and your study we pose two basic questions.

Question 1

Why are you studying the media and what are you hoping to get out of this? Take time to think
about this and write down your ideas. There are no right or wrong answers to this question (or
rather, all answers are right). It's useful for you to record your position so you can compare it with
other people's and so you can look back on it later.

Commentary

Your answer might be about creativity and expressivity (you may want to make interactive computer games or television programs). It might be vocational (you want to be guaranteed a good job as a journalist), or financial (you see the media as an excellent way of making lots of money), or critical (you may want to critique the manipulative power of the media and understand its potential as a mechanism for beneficial social change). Or it may simply be curiosity—you may be fascinated by these technological communication systems that take up such a large part of so many people's lives. Your answer may include aspects of all of these positions, and it may raise many other points. It will probably change while you are studying the media. Keep your first response as a reference point to look back on.

Question 2

Do you think the media, in general, are good or bad?

1   Take time to make a list of all the arguments you can think of for and against the media, that is, arguments that posit the media as a good or a bad thing.
2   Ask yourself: Whose interests do the media serve? Who benefits from the production, distribution, and consumption of media texts and messages? When you answer these questions, try to include general statements about the media as well as detailed examples that support these statements.

This question goes straight to the heart of many common discussions about the media. You will probably find strong arguments for and against the media that reflect commonly held opinions that are part of our culture's common sense.

Commentary

The question about 'good' or 'bad' media is designed to reveal the contradictory ways people think about the media, and the different ways the media are used. It may also point out the difference between how the media could be used in society (their *potential use*), and how they are used in society (their *actual use*). Potentially, the media could be used in lots of different ways, for example to increase our understanding of global inequalities or as a means of democratic voting; actual use refers to the current practices of the media. The potential power of the media, their regulation and control, are of major concern for all contemporary societies.

The points in the table below suggest a number of different general positions for and against the media; they all contain some truth and highlight many of the concerns of **media studies**.

media studies
Media studies analyses the role of the media in society and studies media technologies, media institutions, and the production, consumption, circulation, and content of media texts.

Table 2.1 **Points for and against the media**

For	Against
The media's huge range of cultural information and entertainment contributes to the development of popular knowledge. People are more aware and better educated through the media than ever before.	The media offer people a repetitive diet of worthless trivia. Like bread and circuses, they cater to the lowest intellectual abilities.
The media can inspire and develop us, actively encouraging us to do new things in our lives.	The media make us passive observers—couch potatoes—whereby we lose the ability to think or act for ourselves.
The media help us explore and develop our understanding of sex and violence by depicting social attitudes and inviting critique of the behaviours that are represented.	The media corrupt and pervert us and our children, desensitising our feelings and emotions, and encouraging immoral sexual behaviour and violent acts. The media need to be heavily censored.
The media are truthful and informative and, as such, make a major contribution to democracy and social accountability by offering us a window on the world.	The media are a series of false constructions serving minority political interests.
The media are democratic in that they allow all people in the world a voice.	The media serve commercial interests and are totally controlled by multinational corporations and advertisers.
The media enable free thought and speech to be disseminated.	The media are in the business of controlling our consciousness, thereby controlling who we are and how we think. Access to the media is limited.
The media are shrinking the globe, uniting us and bringing us closer together, thereby creating a global village.	The media are making us all the same and destroying marginalised cultures.
The media give space to the voices of different social groups and cultures.	The media are a form of cultural imperialism, whereby dominant cultures impose their values on less powerful cultures.
The media are agents for social change.	The media maintain the status quo.

Two examples illustrate some of these arguments. Media analyst, Professor John Hartley, showing the 'good' side of the media, has noted how Nelson Mandela writes in his autobiography (Mandela 1995) about his visit to Canada, where many Inuit people greeted him and celebrated his arrival. They had witnessed his release from prison in South Africa on television. Mandela's freedom struggle connected with their own struggles in Canada for land and political rights, and it was television that made possible the connection between these different and geographically very distant people. As Mandela said, 'Television had shrunk the world and had, in the process, become a great weapon for eradicating ignorance and promoting democracy' (Mandela 1995, quoted in Hartley & McKee 1996, p. 74).

On the other hand, the 'bad' side, the media can be seen as part of a purely self-serving and profit-motivated consumerist culture. Consider the *Iron Man* films: *Iron Man* and its sequels have been heavily promoted and packaged for release to a new generation of film goers. An estimated $100 million was spent marketing *Iron Man 2*. This, combined with the system of film distribution and release and other marketing tools, made the release commercially successful, a veritable money-making machine.

The *Iron Man* franchise also demonstrates the money-making capacity of Hollywood films. According to Marvel, the surprising level of success of the first *Iron Man*, which earned an international box office of almost $600 million and sales of just over $160 million on DVD and Blu-ray, allowed the company to develop lucrative new partnerships and expand old ones for the sequel. *Iron Man 2* merchandise includes toys such as helmets and action figures, T-shirts, products and tie-ins with Diesel men's fragrances and Audi cars, a video game, a soundtrack that went to the top of the charts, as well as product placement deals with companies such as Dr Pepper. The original comic and the first film can thus be seen as a long advertisement for other goods. It could be argued that this was a form of economic exploitation that preyed on children and teenagers, who are often considered to be a very susceptible media audience. The youth market is very important to advertisers. Companies such as The Viral Factory do extensive market research in youth culture to identify emerging trends, and then use the media to market the **subcultural** phenomena they have 'discovered'. Their objective is to harness the aura of cool and create an association between it and a particular brand. Young people, whose incomes are not already committed to things such as mortgage repayments, are particularly vulnerable to such strategies because they are perceived to be impressionable and image conscious.

subculture
People who share cultural activities such as dress, leisure activities, and social beliefs, that are resistant or opposed to mainstream culture; used mainly in relation to youth cultures.

These cases are specific examples of arguments for and against the media. They help to flesh out the generalities evident in the statements in the table above. There are many other examples you could find. This idea about the potentially good and bad aspects of the media will be a theme throughout our discussions and analysis of the media.

Why do we teach about the media?

Some of the reasons Michael and I teach about the media are shared by many media teachers and researchers. These reasons demonstrate our contradictory view of the media, our love–hate relationship with them.

1   We grew up watching television and films, reading, and listening to CDs. We spent a lot of our leisure time consuming media products. The media were a source of

great entertainment and information. Today we still get huge enjoyment from the media, whether it's from spending time on Twitter and Facebook, finding clips on YouTube, accessing music and videos on iPods, iPhones, and iPads, watching *Dexter*, or seeing the Coen brothers' latest film at the cinema. We expect many students will also love some aspects of the media. Teaching about the media aims to enhance understanding, appreciation, and enjoyment of the media through understanding how they work.

2 We see the potentially positive social power of the media. Media communication systems are capable of sharing ideas across physical distances and of making them known, despite cultural differences. They are capable of making information and aesthetic forms available in a truly global form to all people, and can therefore, in this capacity, be called democratic. The media have also been termed democratic because, like a representative democracy, media can provide a voice for the people and can be used to represent the political views of minority groups as well as those of the majority of the population. The media are used to publicise political issues and events, making it possible for pressure groups to unite around a common issue or injustice, thus overcoming the disempowering effects of isolation in ways that would not have been feasible without mass communication. For the media to be able to fulfil these democratic roles in public life, freedom of expression is crucial. The media can contribute beneficially to the development of our future world, and it is important to demonstrate this.

documentaries
Films and television programs about real-life situations.

A good example is the **documentary** *An Inconvenient Truth*, which has shown the seriousness of climate change. It is interesting to note how many politicians and business corporations began to take the problems of climate change much more seriously just a few months after the film's release.

3 We are critical and distrustful of the ways the media are actually working. We believe that in key structural ways, these powerful means of communication are often misused by the people controlling them. Consequently, it can be said that through their use of the media these people are abusing us, contributing to many of the problems of our society and helping to maintain a status quo of global social inequality. Teaching about the media can raise awareness of this negative side of the media, and can develop ways of challenging and changing the media at the same time as celebrating their positive aspects. This social concern gives a critical agenda to media studies. It looks forward to social change and it means that media studies operates in a social and political framework.

Our love–hate relationship with the media reflects some of the contradictions of the media suggested above (p. 12). These contradictions make media studies a stimulating discipline. Understanding the media can help you to develop skills that will equip you to work creatively in the media, and can also lead you to a critical awareness of how the media function so you can engage as an informed citizen with the ongoing social debates about the media and the powers they have.

Two historical views of the media

The love–hate and good–bad views of the media are not new: since the advent of the printing press, commentators and analysts have put forward two contradictory views of the media: a utopian belief in the media's positive possibilities versus a fear of and wariness about its dangers. Every new medium has inspired similar debates. The distribution of information through printing supposedly threatened to corrupt, pervert, and destabilise society in various ways, for example in the nineteenth century by mobilising the working class, uniting them around common concerns, and facilitating the formation of trade unions and lobby groups. The emergence of the printing press also decentralised power by enabling widespread communication and distribution of information by organisations other than the state and the church. Some argued that these were positive qualities as they helped society become more democratic and equal. In the nineteenth century there was also concern about how the reading of romantic novels would influence the minds of young women, who were a huge market for such fiction; Thomas Hardy's novel *Jude the Obscure*, for example, was banned for its moral dangerousness. Others saw the broadening of women's minds as part of the move towards women's emancipation. We are seeing similar contradictory debates today over satellite communications and the internet, both of which can cross state boundaries and are difficult to police, or computer games that may be excessively violent, encourage teenage lethargy, or, alternatively, that may develop swift reaction skills, computer literacy, and engage people much more actively than does television. Currently, it is argued that the technology of the internet and mobile phone cameras allow the development of new kinds of journalism, through internet blogs, citizens' journalism, and cameras that can report images across the globe, that provide far more democracy and diversity within the media. The use of the social networking website Facebook encourages media participation, developing communication skills, and broadening horizons. Alternatively, it is argued that the internet is dumbing down our culture, is potentially dangerous in that it encourages internet stalking and surveillance, and brings with usage new ailments, such as 'internet addiction affliction disorder'. Media fears are based on the political, moral, and cultural damage of which the media are capable. The optimistic flip-side are hopes that the media will help solve all our social, political, and communication problems and lead us into a new utopia.

Current debates about the good and bad aspects of the media echo earlier arguments. Note how easily the following idealistic prediction about the telegraph in the 1840s could be used to describe today's hopes if we substituted 'the internet' for 'the telegraph':

> Universal peace and harmony seem at this time more possible than ever before, as the telegraph binds together by a vital cord all the nations of the earth. It is impossible that old prejudices and hostilities should any longer exist, while such an instrument has been created for an exchange of thought between all nations of the earth (quoted in Czitrom 1982, p. 10).

In contrast, here is the negative view, fearful of the dangers of the new media, from an 1889 article, 'The Intellectual Effects of Electricity':

> All men are compelled to think of all things at the same time, on imperfect information, and with too little interval for reflection ... The constant diffusion of statements in snippets, the constant excitements of feeling unjustified by fact, the constant formation of hasty or erroneous opinions, must in the end, one would think, deteriorate the intelligence of all to whom the telegraph appeals (quoted in Czitrom 1982, p. 19).

Once again there are similar arguments being used against today's twenty-first century media. We will examine these long-held fears about the media in more detail.

Fears about political use of the media

The fears about the political ends to which the media can be put relate to the way the media can be used by political parties to control people. While totalitarian fascist and communist states of the 1930s inspired these fears, political uses of the media also occur in democratic societies, where advertising can be seen as a form of propaganda and brainwashing that supports capitalist consumerism, as first shown in Vance Packard's book *The Hidden Persuaders* (Packard 1957). It is often argued that there should be controls placed over the media so they are not misused. Fear that the media may be used for political purposes is one reason many countries insist that the government should not own and/or control the media; this fear also lies behind many of the debates about who has the right to media ownership. Note, however, that media practitioners often see themselves as political watchdogs, and in this respect are referred to as the 'fourth estate'. The term 'estate' derives from the time of the French Revolution, when the judiciary, the parliament, and the Church were referred to as the first, second, and third estates respectively. The media, as the fourth estate, are a body who can comment on, criticise, and investigate, through free speech, what these other institutions do, which is why freedom of the press is so important. It was, for instance, the media that publicised the crimes against humanity perpetrated by the South African apartheid government, prompting the global community to impose sanctions against South Africa and to exert political pressure. The government explicitly blamed the press for giving the National Party a negative image overseas, and for drawing international criticism of the apartheid policy (Fourie 2001, p. 429). The political, cultural, and economic pressure exerted by the global community as a result of this bad press contributed to the downfall of apartheid. More recently, social networking media have been used to mobilise protesters and lobby for regime change and democracy in what has become known as 'the Arab Spring'. The 'Facebook Revolution' in Egypt is a noteworthy example: on the 'Revolution Day' Facebook page developed by Egyptian political activists, more than 85 000 people developed a list of demands for the Mubarak regime and pledged to attend antigovernment protests in Egypt in January, 2011.

Fears about the media's influence on morals and health

The moral fears arise from the concern that the media will be a corrupting force, particularly in relation to sex and violence. It is argued that people's values can be corrupted by the media they consume. This has led to moral panics and campaigns against too much sex and violence on television. Moral panic tends to focus on the effects of media consumption on young people because they supposedly have less experience on which to base sound judgments and less developed critical faculties with which to position fiction or other media content in relation to external reality. It has been suggested that the cumulative effects of consuming media that contains violent and/or sexualised content might be particularly harmful for young viewers, due in part to the tendency of young people to learn by mimesis (mimicking or imitating what they see and hear). Because interactive media forms such as video games require participation in the acts of violence they represent, they are considered to be especially worrying. Another perspective on this issue is that the prevalence of high levels of gratuitous sex and violence in the media naturalises such material, making comparable behaviour in real life seem natural, normal, and acceptable. The danger here is that the media might inadvertently legitimate unacceptable ethical positions, such as the use of violence as a method of conflict resolution, or a lack of respect for one's sexual partners (see censorship/effects, pp. 48–51). The flip-side argument in relation to sexuality would say that in today's media-world we are better educated and informed about all sexual matters than at any other time in human history.

Health concerns might focus on the messages conveyed by the media, such as the prevalence of junk food advertising for young people, and the media themselves, such as television and computers, which encourage a more sedentary, less active lifestyle.

Fears about the media's influence on culture

There are those who fear that the media devalue a society's culture because what they produce is so trivial or superficial. This is best illustrated in the debates around the relative importance of so-called high and low culture. High culture is supposedly the great art produced by a society, art that is morally uplifting, complex, and serious. It is said to be found in such cultural products as opera, painting, and literature, the understanding and interpretation of which require training and specialist instruction.

Low, or popular, culture, on the other hand, is what the masses consume; it is found in magazines, mass-market paperbacks, popular cinema, and on television. Critics of low culture deride it as morally degrading and simplistic.

Traditionally, low culture has been denigrated as inferior and potentially damaging, and the fact that it was a product of mass media was used to disparage it. Educators thought they needed to protect people against the damaging effects of low culture. The first teaching about the media was an 'inoculation' approach. Teachers would analyse mass media products in class, aiming to show students how corrupt, cheap, worthless, and harmful they were. It was thought that by giving students a little bit of low culture, they could be protected or inoculated against it, just as you inoculate against disease by administering a small dose of it. The high–low opposition still informs the way a lot of people think about the media.

Such oppositions are partly the product of class-divided societies—high culture is the province of the ruling and middle classes, the bourgeoisie; low culture is the province of the working class. But it's interesting to note that both right-wing conservatives and left-wing radicals have disapproved of low culture and the popular mass media: the right wing sees the media as offering a diet of cheap, tawdry, corrupt entertainments, the left wing sees these entertainments as a political sweetener, acting to distract the workers from their political grievances.

Since the 1970s there has been much study done of popular culture in media studies, mainly due to the need to understand the dynamics of the huge media audiences attracted to it—if so many people are consuming media texts, it is important to understand them—but it is also an attempt to validate popular culture itself, to see it positively and avoid labelling it as something inferior to high culture (p. 38).

Fears about contemporary consumerism and advertising

It may be that the media in the main simply reflect the dominant values of society that are based on the values of continual economic growth and consumerism. Advertising is a crucial media form that supports consumerism. Consider the following critique of advertising by musicologist Robert Fink:

> Because [advertising] *promotes goods*, it produces *materialism*; because it advocates through *incomplete truths* and *deceptions*, it creates *cynicism*. When advertising appeals to *mass markets*, it promotes *conformity*; when it appeals to *status*, it promotes *social stratification* and class conflict; when it appeals to *fear*, it promotes *anxiety*; when it appeals to *newness*, it creates *disrespect for authority*; when it appeals to *youth*, it *undermines the family*; and when it appeals to *sexuality*, it creates *erotic obsession* and dysfunction. Because it appeals to the *individual*, it makes people *selfish*; because it must be *simple* and easily understandable, it deals in *social stereotypes* and *debases language*. Because advertising is *emphatic* and repetitively *insistent*, it promotes *regression* and *irrationality*, putting consumers into a *hypnoid*

trance that leads to *compulsive consumption*, inability to defer gratification and disregard of future consequences; at the same time, because it *idealizes 'the good life'*, it creates *perpetual dissatisfaction* and feelings of lack (Fink 2005, p. 64).

It is not necessary to agree with everything in Fink's critique to acknowledge that the way advertising is linked to ever-growing consumerism is of concern and is worthy of note and discussion.

Media studies: Different approaches

The first serious academic study of the media began in Europe in the 1930s. Since then it has developed in different countries in various ways. We list here some of the most significant approaches and methodologies so as to give an overview of the whole media studies field. We think all of them have some value.

The Frankfurt School

The Frankfurt School is the name given to a group of Marxist scholars who first analysed the role of the media in Europe and Germany in the 1930s and then moved to consider American media in the 1940s and 1950s. As Marxists, they stressed the way the media functioned to subordinate the working classes and how they were determined by economic interests. After seeing the political dangers of the media in Nazi Germany, they defined the popular media in the USA as a **consciousness industry** that helped to control the masses. The Frankfurt School was important in that its members produced the first in-depth studies of the media and were the first to see the media as industries. It has influenced many subsequent media analysts.

consciousness industry
Term used by the Frankfurt School to describe how the media functioned to control the minds and feelings of the masses at the same time as making money.

Effects research

Different strands of research developed in the USA and Europe. In the USA most media research was conducted by sociologists and psychologists who were interested in trying to measure media effects. Effects research has been carried out extensively but its results have been contradictory because the effects of media are so difficult to measure. It seems that the only conclusion reached is that it is not possible to measure direct effects because the media are just one component of an infinitely complex chain of causal factors (such as the audience members' upbringing, social class, education, personal prejudices, experiences, and so forth). Nevertheless, researchers keep trying. But a major question remains: How do the media, even if they don't have direct measurable effects, influence the way we think, feel, and behave? Contemporary effects researchers are investigating indirect, cumulative, and long-term media effects that are important to understand. We will not examine effects research in detail in this book but will return to the central issue of media effects/influence (see especially Chapter 3) since it is of interest on so many levels, from gauging the social impact of controversial media content, such as stereotyping and pornography, through to more pragmatic, profit-driven questions related to advertising effectiveness.

Communication models

A significant field of media research (predominantly of American origin) is interested in explaining how communication in the media works by focusing on forms of media communication (McQuail & Windahl 1981; Fiske 1990, chs 1 & 2). Communications analyst Harold Lasswell worked out a formula (Lasswell 1960) that formed the basis for much subsequent work. It is still useful as a starting point for thinking about what communication is. Lasswell showed diagrammatically how the communication chain pointed to different areas of media research.

Table 2.2   **Areas of media analysis**

question	who?	says what?	in which channel?	to whom?	with what effect?
name of media element	communicator	message	medium	receiver	effect
type of media research	control studies	content analysis	media analysis	audience analysis	effects analysis

Source: Adapted from McQuail & Windahl 1981, p. 10

Our main focus will be on what is being communicated in which channel. To explore this we will use two academic disciplines: semiology and structuralism. Semiology analyses the way communication works through signs and codes; structuralism shows how the ways in which stories are told, their formal structures, are part of their meaning. We will examine these in detail in Parts 2 and 4. Harold Innis, Marshall McLuhan, and Walter Ong are three important North American thinkers who have theorised how the mass media work and communicate. They saw the media as significantly changing society. Innis' great contribution was to analyse communication systems in terms of how they change society's use of space and time, including analysing changing modes of transportation as forms of communication (see Innis 1951). He argued that the means of mediating and transmitting communications shaped history, and this argument was the genesis of the political economy approach to the media. McLuhan's well-known phrase '**the global village**' points to the way that media communications unify

global village
The phrase 'the global village' suggests that the globalisation of communication media has brought the whole world closer together, like a village in which everyone is interconnected.

the world (for further discussion of globalisation, see Chapter 25). Ong, taking a much wider historical view, looked at the way the print media have changed Western society from a spoken-word culture (an oral culture) to a society based on print and literacy. Ong's point is related to McLuhan's other famous catch-phrase, 'the medium is the message', which suggests that the medium or the technology used to transmit communication (whether print, radio, screen, web, wireless, or via mobile phones) is just as important, if not more important, than the content of the message itself.

Content analysis

Alongside effects research, the method known as **content analysis** was developed. Content analysis originated in journalistic research that relied on counting the occurrences of words or phrases. This research method was applied during the Second World War, for instance, to

content analysis
Quantitative measurement of media content.

analyse Nazi propaganda publications. Content analysis provides a systematic way to make inferences about patterns of images, printed words, or verbal data, in order to describe and quantify their meanings and interpret their consequences. The research method can be used to reveal cultural patterns, and to identify trends in media and communication content, as well as identifying where audiences focus their attention. For media and communication scholars, content analysis can be used to locate and measure patterns in what the media actually produce: so, for example, research on women and the media could look at how much content is given over to women or what roles women are portrayed as performing. In 2010 The Australian Sports Commission released a research report, 'Towards a Level Playing Field: Sport and Gender in Australian Media' that used content analysis to reveal that women in sport are under-represented in the Australian media. Key findings of the report are that women make up just 9 per cent of all sports coverage in Australian television news and current affairs and 7 per cent of other sport programming; furthermore, television news reports on female sport are shorter than all other types of sport news.

Another example is found in the documentary film *Manufacturing Consent* (a significant analysis of media power). In this film the linguist and philosopher Noam Chomsky looks at US media coverage of East Timor. He does a content analysis in order to support his view that the US media acted politically in the interests of the US government. Thus, in this film, Chomsky combines content analysis with a political analysis of who controls the media, their bias, and their self-censorship.

Chomsky argued that during the 1970s the Indonesian government carried out atrocities on the East Timorese that were equivalent to those perpetrated by Pol Pot's Khmer Rouge forces in Cambodia in the 1970s, but that the American media did not report this equally. His content analysis of *New York Times* coverage of these two events between 1975 and 1979, graphically illustrated in the film, is damning: there were 70 column inches of listings in the *New York Times* index referring to East Timor stories, compared to 1175 inches of index listings for stories on Cambodia. He links this disparity in coverage to the fact that the USA was involved with the Indonesian government and was implicated in arms sales to Indonesia, whereas Cambodia was not a friendly nation.

> The church and other sources estimated that about 200 000 people were killed [in the conflict over East Timor]. The USA backed Indonesia all the way. The USA provided 90 per cent of the arms for the conflict. Right after the invasion [Indonesia's invasion of East Timor] arms shipments were stepped up … There is no Western concern for issues of aggression, atrocities, human rights abuses and so on if there's a profit to be made from them … As the atrocities reached their maximum peak in 1978 when it really was becoming genocidal, [media] coverage dropped to zero in the United States and Canada (Achbar 1995, pp. 102–3).

Chomsky's work is very important in that it demonstrates the way political power can control the media—in this case, largely through not reporting events rather than misreporting—a finding that is related to study of the political economy of the media (see pp. 22–5); but he uses content analysis to support his argument.

Political economy of the media

This approach, derived partly from the Frankfurt School and theorists such as Innis, is concerned with the way the external forces of economics, ownership of the media, and political power impact on media production. The main argument put forward is that the media will serve the economic and political interests of whoever owns and controls them—whether this is private individuals interested in profit or governments interested in political control. The **political economy** approach involves conducting research into who owns and controls the media. It focuses on how industrial mechanisms and imperatives surrounding production, distribution, and exhibition affect the kinds of texts created, the kinds of audiences they reach, and the messages they send. It is often used to show that mass media products embody capitalist ideologies that are then consumed by the mass audience.

political economy Explains how the media are determined by a combination of economic, social, and political factors, particularly ownership and control of the media.

A simple example is the way in which the production output of the Australian and British film industries has been determined by the domination in the market of the American industry, a domination felt not just in film production but also in terms of distribution and exhibition. This domination has always had an impact on Australian and British cinema chains, which are more committed to showing American than home-grown products. In Africa the need for foreign involvement to finance feature films has led to debates about what African cinema really is. *Country of My Skull* (also titled *In My Country*), for example, is a film based on the South African writer Antjie Krog's story. Filmed in South Africa, it is about the South African Truth and Reconciliation Commission hearings, but it was funded with overseas money, directed by UK-born John Boorman, and starred Samuel L Jackson and Juliette Binoche (American and French actors). These foreign influences were deemed necessary to get the film a wide distribution, and to get it made at all. In many African countries it costs too much to produce local programs with high production values that can compete with the established, well-resourced American studio systems. The varying fortunes of these 'indigenous' industries can be charted in relation to government policies, tax incentives, and investment, rather than in terms of the creative output of filmmakers themselves. Similar studies can be made of Australian and British television productions, which also engage in an economic struggle with American products.

One of the major concerns of the 2004 Free Trade Agreement between the USA and Australia relates to issues of cultural production, particularly television, film production, and new media. Many Australians were worried that if Australia did not maintain some restrictions on American products, if it did not guarantee a certain percentage of television time and cinema releases for Australian products, then it would be swamped by American media. This would mean both a cultural loss in terms of seeing and hearing Australian stories, voices, and content, and an economic and creative loss in terms of losing an industry and outlet for Australian media creators. It has been argued that the great successes of Australian film and television since the 1970s were built on first, the 1970s restrictions that guaranteed that Australian television advertisements should be made by Australians in Australia, and second, the government support for the film industry. These factors gave the opportunity for many Australians to learn the necessary skills for filmmaking and make full-length features. This followed a period from the 1950s to around 1970 during which the Australian film industry virtually disappeared under the dominance of the USA. The 2004 Agreement has allowed that a certain proportion of Australian films and television must still be Australian; however, the same provision was not made for any new digital media communication systems that might evolve in the future and Australian critics of the Agreement fear that this will result in the further domination of American productions in the future and a furtherance of what is called American '**cultural imperialism**' (see pp. 464–9 for a full discussion of this concept). American formulas and format still provide the benchmark that local productions are judged by and try to imitate.

cultural imperialism
Imperial domination of the world maintained partly through the dissemination of cultural products. Argues that the globalisation of communication results in the domination of traditional cultures and the intrusion of Western culture and values such as consumerism.

Major concerns relate to the way media moguls such as Rupert Murdoch, Chairman and CEO of News Corporation, control more and more media outlets, and what political restrictions there should be on their media ownership. The concern is that their influence on media output is so great that it increasingly limits our information and gives them significant political power. Their companies have control over book publishing, other print media, television, and satellite outlets, as well as over news, entertainment, sports, and other non-media interests. Note how Murdoch has bought internet sites such as TeamXbox because he knows how important they are to young people. In Australia the new laws on media ownership, enacted in 2006, seem to permit even more media monopolies.

One of the ways satellite television has developed is by buying the rights to major sporting occasions: people who want to see these very popular events have to buy into satellite. Consequently, public broadcasting channels such as the ABC in Australia and the BBC in the United Kingdom start losing their audiences. Economic issues are also felt in relation to advertising, which is central in media production and threatens, through sponsorship, to exert more control over programming. Sports stadiums and competitions are now regularly renamed in relation to corporations and companies, so that television coverage of major events is always announced in terms of the sponsors, who also have to be acknowledged after matches by the winners. Consequently, audiences keep hearing the sponsoring companies' names repeated.

Television researcher, Professor George Gerbner, from the University of Pennsylvania, articulated the argument that market forces lead to a standardisation of product:

> It's a paradoxical fact that while channels proliferate, we have many more channels than ever before … at the same time ownership shrinks; so what happens is fewer owners own more channels and therefore can program the same materials across many channels; *therefore instead of more channels creating greater diversity they seem to be creating greater homogeneity, greater uniformity, greater standardisation and greater globalisation* … they can say [to overseas channels] we can sell you an hour's worth of programming for less money than it would cost you to produce your own … this proposition is economically so attractive … it's a standardised, marketing formula [our emphasis] (*The Media Report*, ABC Radio National, 29 August 1996).

media homogenisation
Financial pressures and other forces lead all media products to become similar, standard, and uniform.

There are two major arguments put forward against Gerbner's view that economic control leads to **media homogenisation**. The first is that the market spread of media actually allows opportunities for many different social groups to be heard. People have the opportunity to use the media to their own advantage as there is wider and cheaper access to media production and communication. The internet is regarded as having a huge potential for such democratic and diverse output.

The second relates to audiences: ultimately, the audience—the media consumers—have a big say in what gets produced. If they do not like a product it will fail, and this forces the media to produce acceptable material. Additionally, audiences can make their own meanings out of texts. They will not necessarily be brainwashed by what they consume.

In relation to the claims that media owners such as Rupert Murdoch have too much control, as shown in the documentary *Outfoxed*, John Hartley puts forward a contradictory argument:

> As for those who think that we have an evil empire, and it's run by that terrible Uncle Rupert, I'd ask people if they've ever heard of a chap called Panckouke and the answer is 'Probably not'. Nobody's ever heard of him. Panckouke was the most important media identity of the

French Revolution. Have we heard of this man who owned lots of Parisian newspapers and French media during the French Revolution, or have we heard of the ideas being promulgated in those media by such as Tom Paine and Marat and all the rest of them? The latter. We hear about the ideas, we're interested in the ideas. Ownership in the long run does not determine what it is that these media are capable of doing, they're ... historically outside of the control of the owners, who ride the waves of profitability and legislative opportunity for a while and then disappear. So yes, they're powerful in a business sense but I don't think they're as powerful culturally as people make out (*The Media Report*, ABC Radio National, 21 December 2000).

These debates about control, effects, and response are central to media studies.

Structural organisation of the media

The way media products are structurally organised affects the way they present information and this has also been an area for media research. Two of the key terms used in this context are '**agenda setting**' and '**gatekeeping**', terms most often used in relation to journalism, news, and current affairs.

Agenda setting refers to instances in which media coverage draws attention to an issue or event and puts it on the agenda for public discussion and debate. It can be understood as a form of media management or manipulation in which a public figure (such as a politician) might issue a press release about a particular issue, or include it in a policy statement or speech on more than one occasion, thus encouraging follow-up coverage by the media. This 'sets the agenda', puts that particular issue on the media agenda, raising its public profile. Media analyst Joshua Green, in discussing American presidential elections, has shown how clever campaigners specialise in negative advertising. He refers to the tactic of Republican political consultant Lee Atwater, 'that a campaign should frame its opponent before the opponent can frame himself' (Green 2004), and explains how, in 2004, the Republicans decided to try to 'frame' John Kerry as a 'flip-flopper', a man who was always changing his mind. They would run television commercials demonstrating this but they also put out similar stories to the media that would come out as news, not advertising. They would only need to get the story taken up by one important newspaper, and then they could

agenda setting
The process by which media producers set up the issues—the agenda—that the media will focus on and that audiences will subsequently perceive to be important.

gatekeeping
The process of controlling what gets included and whose voices are heard in the media, particularly in the news.

call all the network morning shows and say, 'Listen, there's going to be this big story coming out in *The New York Times* tomorrow morning. We'll give it to you at one minute after midnight, as soon as it goes on the web; we'll provide you with all the information'. And the result of that is, that come the next morning at 7am, at 8am, at 9am, not only will the story be on the front page of *The New York Times*, it'll also get blanket coverage on all the morning shows. And that *really helps set the day's news stories for all the rest of the media outlets who take their cue from The New York Times and the morning shows.*

It is important to see how different television channels and newspapers watch what their rivals are doing and often feel compelled to take up similar stories, similar agendas, so that they will not be seen as missing out on something.

In Australia, the prevalence of negative advertising in the media could be seen in the 2010 federal election as both parties addressed citizens' fears and anxieties. There were also attempts to frame the opposing parties and individual politicians, and fight the election on particular issues. Julia Gillard had just assumed leadership of the Australian Labor Party from Kevin Rudd, and the Liberals wanted to frame the party as mutinous and unstable, and Gillard as untrustworthy. On the other hand, Labor presented the Liberal leader Tony Abbott as old-fashioned and out of touch, and his party as greedily conservative.

The media also participate in agenda setting by giving extensive coverage to sensational or spectacular issues and events. A snowball effect can result, as the media coverage of the topic gains momentum and generates the perception that the issue is of great importance partly because it is getting so much press coverage. When, for example, cases of anthrax were discovered shortly after the World Trade Center and the Pentagon were attacked in September 2001, the media described it as a 'germ warfare scare that has engulfed Florida and spread to New York' (*Weekend Australian*, 13–14 October 2001, p. 1), despite the fact that there were only four people infected with the disease at the time the newspaper went to print. Extensive media coverage of the threat of biological warfare by terrorists in crop dusters created the perception that an anthrax epidemic was engulfing the population of the free world. When some people purchased gas masks to protect themselves from airborne diseases, the media reported that a wave of panic was spreading in response to the anthrax scare. Rather than reporting on a rising incidence of infection or an actual threat of escalating biological warfare, the media were creating a wave of panic by putting the issue on the agenda, on the front pages of national newspapers. Four cases of a disease do not constitute a remarkable increase in the risk of contracting the illness. In fact, what has increased is the reporting of the risk.

The notion that the structural organisation of media programs and journalism affects the way they present information involves showing how the media are often drawn to give more weight to the viewpoints of official institutions than to alternative viewpoints. The news is supposed to be **objective**, to provide a balanced account of issues and events, to air both sides of a debate, and include diverse perspectives. But the media often privilege certain voices, the agenda setters. This is not a deliberate conspiracy; there are various practical reasons for it: the fact that news is deemed to happen in parliament or the law courts, the reliance on

objectivity
Perceiving, reporting, or presenting things from an impersonal, neutral, unbiased perspective.

official spokespeople and experts to comment on events, and the use of journalists themselves (who select and present the news). All these factors are part of the gatekeeping process.

Many broadcasters, in the interests of keeping their costs as low as they can, rely on news-gathering organisations to supply their stories for them. Agendas are also set in advance: news is often old insofar as journalists go to the people and places where they know things are going to happen. People who are skilled in dealing with the media often arrange press conferences in which they attempt to have the media report their point of view: in the two Gulf War conflicts, for example, the military were very careful to make sure that they had as much control as possible over journalists (see pp. 55–8). Media access can also be denied: when George W. Bush visited Australia in 2004 he held a press conference with American journalists but refused to have one with Australians, thus avoiding having to deal with some potentially difficult questions. It is significant that the media have found it very difficult to get access to pictures and stories from refugee detention centres in Australia or at the Guantánamo Bay 'terrorist' camp. Election campaigns in the United Kingdom, Australia, and the USA are now mainly orchestrated by the political parties as media events at which politicians no longer meet the people. Instead, candidates do everything for, and in front of, journalists and cameras.

The way news is organised on a daily basis, with limited time and a need to maintain popular ratings, leads to simplification and sensationalisation of events. Consequently, audiences rarely receive a complex understanding of events with explanations that cover long-term causes: the focus is on what happened today and how the situation changes hour by hour so that each new bulletin will have something more immediate. In this sound byte era the use of striking headlines and good pictures predominates. The Tom Tomorrow cartoon (Figure 2.1) illustrates these features of contemporary news reporting.

Figure 2.1   Tom Tomorrow cartoon

Source: Dan Perkins, 1992

news value/newsworthiness
The elements of an issue or event
that make it important enough to
report on in the eyes of journalists.
Newsworthy features include conflict,
relevance, locality, prominence,
novelty, and magnitude.

News is also structured on the basis of what journalists call **'news values or newsworthiness'**, a set of values and priorities that have come to be accepted by journalists as common sense in what is regarded as important to be reported.

News values, or the features of a story that make it valuable and newsworthy, include calamity, proximity, celebrity, novelty, enormity or severity of impact, relevance, and visual appeal. For example, for the Australian media one person dying in a shark attack in Australia is far more newsworthy than a hundred people dying of cholera in West Africa. Stories with entertainment value, reports about positive breakthroughs or amazing achievements can also make the news.

Much news is bad news, that is, disasters, things going wrong, and problems are highlighted. As a visual medium, television privileges pictures: a story about a whale attacking one of its handlers at a theme park in America in July 2004 became an Australian news story, presumably because of its exciting footage, which was easily transmitted from America to Australia. In terms of political or social import this story has no importance and the man was not even badly hurt, but it looked good. The fact that today many daily events are recorded on video in America whereas many fewer are recorded in Africa simply adds to the preponderance and likelihood of including American news stories rather than African stories in the Australian media.

There is also a stress on individuals to personalise stories, which tends to simplify issues—the election campaigns mentioned above, with their excessive focus on the characters of individual leaders, illustrate this. Because of the underlying ethos of individualism in Western society, the media place great emphasis on individuals and often make use of the persona or image associated with media personalities (such as celebrities, politicians, and newsreaders) in order to encourage the audience to read something more into the story.

Textual analysis and cultural studies

Analysing the media's political, economic, and organisational structures is important but these approaches don't focus so much on the actual media texts and their meanings. A perceived problem with much cultural studies research examining narrative media is that textual analysis and case studies provide richly detailed analyses of style and meaning in small samples of texts from which it can be difficult to make well-founded claims about broader patterns or implications for other audiences, texts, or contexts. By contrast, empirical research methods, such as content analyses of large samples, may overlook specificity and detail, and the capacity to analyse meaning-making within individual texts and readers is weak. Content analysis draws attention to *what* is being presented in the media but its limitation is that it doesn't interpret *how* these events are portrayed or how individuals actually interpret and respond to them. This question has been explored more in European traditions of media analysis.

Whereas American researchers were mainly sociologists and psychologists, European work came from literary, historical, and philosophical studies, and from traditions of textual analysis. These traditions had typically focused on interpreting literature, theatre, painting, music, and so forth, trying to explain their meanings. In the United Kingdom this tradition was significantly developed at the Centre for Contemporary Cultural Studies (CCCS), the so-called Birmingham School. This brought together literary and historical approaches alongside Marxist, feminist, semiotic, and structural linguistic theories, combining a body of critical theory with political concerns.

Concurrently with a number of other institutions, the CCCS helped develop and spread the growth of cultural studies, which continues to be influential today. Like the political economy approach, it is interested in questions of political power and the social role of the media. A significant area of its work has been in understanding popular culture and issues of representation, alongside examination of the role and position of the audience, and wider contextual studies, so it has a wide scope in its analysis. **Textual analysis**—looking at the forms, language, signifying systems, and genres of the media—is one central aspect of cultural studies and this informs much of our work. Detailed textual analysis, sometimes called 'close reading', can take a number of forms. Aesthetic analysis attends to the style of a text, analysing language use, image construction, and the nuances of meaning produced by aesthetic choices such as the connotations of words, the composition of images, or the techniques used in sound design and film editing. Semiotics is an important method of textual analysis that is detailed in Part Two of this textbook. Narrative analysis is another type of textual analysis, which focuses on larger textual structures as discussed in Part Four. Media scholars frequently use textual analysis as a research method to reveal the underlying ideological meanings of media texts and the relationship between representation and reality, as examined in Part Three.

> **textual analysis**
> The process of interpreting and analysing any media text, typically focusing on its form and content, style, and structure.

Audience studies

Several of the above approaches are concerned with audiences, either assuming they are being influenced or affected in some ways or considering their place in the communication chain. Others focused simply on the media institutions and texts themselves. Since the 1980s many media researchers have argued that the audience area needed developing—they wanted to try to understand how audiences actually do interact with the media and considerable work has been done in this field. There is a variety of theoretical approaches to media audiences, which we look at in Chapter 6.

Media education

Since the mid-1960s, media study has grown in Australia, Europe, Asia, Africa, and America, in schools, colleges, and universities, so that it now stands as an important and popular academic area in its own right. It is possible to find a variety of media courses in tertiary education: mass communications, media studies, cultural studies, film and screen studies, multimedia, journalism, and so on. These are built, to different degrees, on an interdisciplinary method, and present a mixture of critical, practical, and vocational approaches. They use many of the approaches listed above but they add an important element—practical work in teaching people how to be scriptwriters, journalists, filmmakers, and so on. The methods listed above do not include this practical aspect. We believe in the value of practical media work alongside theoretical analysis and we hope that this book will be of as much value to students who wish to enter the media professionally as those merely wishing to understand the media.

Conclusion

In thinking about media studies and all the approaches mentioned above we define it as follows: Media studies is the study of

1   media technologies
2   media texts—their content, production, circulation, and consumption
3   the media institutions in which they are produced
4   the media's role in society.

This definition encompasses social questions about the media, how people use and understand them (their influence), and technical or aesthetic questions about the ways they communicate (that is, the language of the media). These two concerns—*sociological* aspects (thinking about the social and political roles of the media) and *aesthetic* aspects (looking at and evaluating the artistic merit of texts)—are central to our study. Audience studies, political-economic, and structural power issues are very important but we cannot cover all of these areas in one book so will not look at them in detail. From an Australian perspective, Cunningham and Turner's book, *The Media and Communications in Australia*, is particularly good (Cunningham & Turner, eds 2009) on some of these areas. Our focus will be on how to explore media texts, textual analysis, and their connection to society.

This chapter has

• defined media studies
• explored the contradictory (good–bad) aspects of the media
• considered historical views of the media and recurrent fears about the media
• looked at the development and different approaches of media studies, including the Frankfurt School, effects research, communication models, content analysis, political economy of media, the structural organisation of media, cultural studies, and audience studies.

Discussion points

1   What specific media examples can you find to support the argument that the media are good or bad?
2   Can you find any contemporary media news stories or reports that examine the role of the media? What arguments about the media do they put forward?
3   Do the media serve the interests of some social groups in favour of others?
4   How important is it to consider who owns and controls media output when examining its content? (As always try to give specific media examples to support your argument.)
5   *The Matrix* was made in Australia. Do you consider it an Australian film? Why?
6   Which approaches developed in media studies do you think are most useful? Why?

Summary

You should now be able to

- consider your own interest in the media
- understand and comment on positive and negative aspects of the media in general
- give your own specific positive and negative media examples
- explain some of the recurrent fears of the media that have been put forward
- define and illustrate subculture, cultural imperialism, content analysis, political economy, media homogenisation, agenda setting, gatekeeping, and news values
- explain briefly the different approaches that have been developed within media studies
- comment on the strengths, weaknesses, and validity of these approaches
- apply different approaches for understanding any one media text.

CHAPTER 3

What Do the Media Do to Us?
Media and Society

> *Movies don't create psychos, they make psychos more creative.*
>
> Scream

This chapter will explore the relationship between the media and society by

▶ giving an overview of contemporary society

▶ giving some basic guidelines about how the media work

▶ exploring how or whether the media affect and influence us

▶ looking at two specific media examples.

Contemporary society

Change and crisis

We live in a world that is undergoing huge social and political change and turmoil. Such changes went on throughout the twentieth century, so it is short-sighted to see this as something new. Nevertheless, the rate of change seems to be accelerating. Currently, we face the following global issues.

1   There is an ecological crisis of global warming, pollution, and diminishing natural resources.

2   There is a political crisis in terms of power struggles fuelled by ethnic, national, and religious differences, as well as social inequalities; these may fragment individual societies (conflicts in Iraq, Congo, Libya, Syria, Tunisia, and Egypt, for example) or be struggles between countries and cultures (Iraq and the Western bloc countries, Afghanistan and the West, Israel and the Palestinians, China and Tibet, for example), or be found globally as in the so-called war against terrorism.

3   There is an economic crisis of growth, consumption, and production. This crisis is, of course, linked to ecological and political power issues.

Inequality and difference

Looking at the world globally, and at individual Western societies, it soon becomes evident that there are major social inequalities. Societies consist of a complex network of groups with different—sometimes competing, sometimes overlapping—interests. Some of these groups are advantaged (in terms of such social goods as housing, education, and life opportunities) by virtue of their birth, their wealth, their class position, their skin colour, and their gender. Consequently, there are advantaged and disadvantaged groups in society, or, to put this another way, dominant and subordinate groups. Three major areas of social division are class, gender, and race, although in some contexts religion, age, sexuality, caste, and education can be equally divisive in ways that are often closely related to these three primary categories. Class, race, and gender frequently restrict or create opportunities for individuals and groups to flourish and to attain coveted positions in society.

Since the beginnings of colonial explorations of the rest of the world by Europe in the sixteenth century there have been major differences in wealth between different countries and cultures. While you might imagine that the world is becoming more economically equal in the twentieth and twenty-first centuries, the opposite seems to be true, as evidenced by the data from the website of *New Internationalist* magazine:

> Inequality is on the increase. In 1976 Switzerland was 52 times richer than Mozambique; in 1997 it was 508 times richer. Two hundred and fifty years ago, the richest countries were only five times richer than the poorest, and Europe only twice as rich as China or India (*New Internationalist*, <www.newint.org/index4.html>).

The gap between rich and poor is also huge and increasing within Australia, the United Kingdom, and the USA. It is estimated that, in Britain in the 1970s, 7 per cent of the population owned 84 per cent of the wealth; currently, it is estimated that 1 per cent owns 50 per cent of the wealth. While many wars and social conflicts are presented in the media as religious or ethnic struggles—for example Muslims against Christians, Tutsis against Hutus—these may be better understood as struggles caused by social and financial inequalities.

Maintaining consent in Western democracies

If Western democratic societies are full of social inequalities, why isn't there more social disorder and disruption? Why don't the disadvantaged and underprivileged rebel more often? Why do so many people seem to accept their subordination? There is, of course, some social disruption, particularly crime; however, crime is not usually understood as the actions of oppressed social groups who are struggling to redistribute wealth and who have a political agenda. Rather, crime is usually understood as, and presented in the media as, the actions of greedy, deviant, psychologically sick (or evil) individuals. In general, Western democratic societies have found ways to maintain social stability at the same time as maintaining social inequalities. They have succeeded in influencing the perceptions, beliefs, and values of many people, by winning their hearts and minds so they accept the status quo (see pp. 205–6). How is this consent maintained? Here are some initial suggestions regarding this complicated question.

- Western liberal democratic systems give everyone the right to vote (in Australia it is a legal obligation). In effect, voting entails delegating power to the political party that best represents and articulates your priorities, values, and beliefs. Because the politicians 'represent' the views of the citizens who vote for them, this system is termed a 'representative democracy'. Clearly, the media play an important role in the process of representing and communicating political policies, issues, and so forth. But in practice there are limits to democracy: in most democracies there are only two or three significantly powerful parties, so your voting power is limited to the policies and values they are willing to promote. Because of the need to appeal to the majority of voters, the views of the main parties will invariably be relatively conservative, mainstream positions that are often rendered even more general by the media's attempts to cater to the largest possible audience. In the USA only about 50 per cent of people eligible to vote actually vote at presidential elections. Do we conclude that 50 per cent of voters don't think it is worth voting? The general belief is that voting gives people a say in how their society works; thus the consent of the population is won because people have a sense that they have contributed to and participated in the decision-making processes that structure their society.

ideology
Ideologies are sets of social values, ideas, beliefs, feelings, and representations, by which people collectively make sense of the world they live in, thus constituting a world view. This world view is naturalised, a taken for granted, commonsense view about the way the world works.

- The West is built on an **ideology** (see Chapter 11) of individualism that stresses personal rights, freedoms, and equality. Such beliefs are often legally enshrined in statutory rights and freedoms. This is in contrast to the restrictions of communist countries, such as China, and other societies, such as Burma, which limit individual human rights in the face of collective social good. As individuals, you appreciate the freedoms that Western democracy offers you, and you are encouraged to believe they make the system just.

- Because Western societies are well developed economically, they are able to offer a relatively high standard of living: most people have access to, or possession of, a phone, a fridge, a television set, a DVD player, and a computer. These societies also have welfare systems: many people receive benefits (in Australia and the United Kingdom it is possible not to work and still receive some money to live on, although this is becoming more difficult) and health support. All these factors keep people relatively content and contribute to a belief that Western democracy is the best system available at present. Even if you do not believe in it, it is relatively easy to survive, and it is easier to go with the system than against it.

Such ideas and beliefs are also maintained through a number of social institutions, one of which is the media. The media are a central arena in which consent is won and maintained by representation, agenda setting, and other mechanisms that position certain values, issues, and attributes as being important, desirable, natural, or normal. This argument informs many of the points made throughout this book and will be illustrated in numerous examples. It is based around theories of ideology, hegemony, and discourse, which are explored in Part 3.

How the media work

The media show us what the world is like; they make sense of the world for us

The processes of representation, interpretation, and evaluation are absolutely central to the media.

Representation

The media—press, radio, television, cinema, and so on—have become the arenas through which people receive most of their entertainment and information about the world, so they are the primary sources for how we see the world. Most of us have, for example, some idea of what the Himalayas are and what they look like, but this knowledge is most likely to be gained not from our actual experience of going there, but through representations: reading about them, hearing and watching media stories told about them, and viewing pictures of them.

Interpretation

In their representations, the media give information, and then explanations, ways of understanding the world we live in. They take on an interpretative role, teaching people how to make sense of the world, of other people, and of ourselves.

Evaluation

In so doing, they consistently privilege some issues and identities while devaluing others, thus giving an evaluative framework, a judgmental view of the information about the world that we receive.

These three processes can be understood in relation to gender and ethnicity or race. The media teach us about masculinity and femininity, what it means to be a 'normal' man or woman; they teach us about race relations, about non-European and European cultures, about the supposedly typical characteristics of these groups. In the social roles that they assign to women and men, and people of different ethnicities, in the desirable and undesirable stereotypes that they continually present, they provide a structure, framework, and pattern for understanding ethnicity and gender issues. This is not to say that the media set out with this educational—teaching—agenda in mind, or that they are necessarily even conscious of what they are doing, but that the influence they have on us as we grow up, reading and consuming the media, is to give us these patterns that explain how we will see ourselves and others, how we will understand gender, race, and our own identities as men or women with particular national, cultural, and religious identities. This is the politics of representation. As film studies Professor Richard Dyer says, 'How we are seen determines in part how we are treated, how we treat others is based on how we see them; such seeing comes from representation' (Dyer 1993, p. 1).

identity
Refers to selfhood, to the characteristics and qualities that uniquely distinguish a person, a group, or a thing from others. The meaning of the term 'identity' is connected to difference (being identifiably unique) and sameness (being identical to oneself, having an essence or personality or qualities that do not change over time).

Of course it is possible for the media to give many different explanations of the world, many contrasting ways of making sense of masculinity and femininity and other aspects of **identity**, but this book argues that across the major media outlets there is a tendency to give broadly similar views of the world, what we will call later a discourse (see pp. 68–9) on masculinity and femininity that outweighs other viewpoints and which sets up a view of what 'normal' gendered behaviour is.

Media products do not show or present the real world; they construct and represent reality

Many media products represent the real world but these media products are not the real world itself; they are *representations* or *constructions* of the world. This point is also crucial and is explored in depth in Chapters 4 and 5. Media studies examines how the media constructs reality, and then explores the values, beliefs, and feelings that these constructions present to us.

The media are just one of the ways by which people make sense of the world

The media are not the only social forces to make sense of the world for us, nor do they have total control over how we see and think about the world. They combine with other forces of socialisation. Most significant for children will be the socialisation they receive through the family, religious, and education systems, which teach them how to understand and act in the world. As we grow up, other views about how to behave, about social morality, are disseminated through a whole range of legal, cultural, and political forces. The media provide just one arena in which these views are presented and popularised. The media generally act to reinforce values that are part of the whole society.

The media are owned, controlled, and created by certain groups who make sense of society on behalf of others

Those people who own, control, and create the media are media producers. They are not a totally separate social group, since they are also part of the audience and of society as a whole, but they are a small, elite group, a complex group of people that includes

- owners and business managers, who are concerned primarily with the need for the media to make profits
- creative personnel, such as writers, directors, cinematographers, and webmasters
- technicians who run the equipment and machinery.

Even these categories overlap in a number of ways; for example many technical jobs are also creative, some managers have creative interests and abilities, and most creators are aware of financial needs and constraints and need to make a living. But note that

- despite the fact that there is a small, limited number of media producers, they speak to, and on behalf of, the whole society (addressing a broad cross-section of the public)
- those people with most media power—particularly financial and creative power— are an even smaller group
- access to the resources required for media production is limited
- those groups who make sense of society on behalf of others are predominantly white, middle-class, and male. Without suggesting any conspiracy here, it seems obvious that they prioritise white, middle-class, masculine values as the norm, since such values are natural to this group. Consequently, the media have a tendency to make sense of the world from this particular point of view.

The need for popularity

As an antidote to the notion of a powerful elite in charge of the media, note that the media have to sell themselves successfully to large numbers of the population: they have to win big audiences in order to be economically viable and survive. This need for popularity complicates, and adds a twist to, the power of the white, middle-class males. If people do not like a product, they will look elsewhere for one, so the media must satisfy their popular audience, which is predominantly working-class and about 50 per cent female. When commercial television was first introduced into Western societies, audiences quickly turned to those channels that offered the entertainment they liked best, particularly game shows and soap operas. There was a major move away from public television stations—the ABC in Australia and the BBC in the United Kingdom—that offered many programs with middle-class and highbrow values. These channels have continually struggled with the need to maintain ratings and the need to present programming that satisfies their mass audiences. The ABC is still regarded by many as elitist because it privileges high-cultural texts, although it can also be seen to offer an important alternative to mainstream programming. (It also includes many British shows compared to the predominantly American content offered on commercial channels.)

Consequently, there may be an interesting contradiction between the values of media producers and their audiences' desires, a contradiction that is revealed in the course of satisfying the imperative to popularity; there is thus a recognition of the powers of the audience/consumers to determine which media products succeed. It could be argued that audiences influence, if not control, media output through their choices of what media products to consume.

To analyse the role and position of popular culture in a way that considers its products and the way audiences, or consumers, use them is complex. The media were described by the Frankfurt School as a 'consciousness industry' that performs a kind of social control in keeping the masses ordered, but some cultural studies critics see them as a potential source of democracy and empowerment for the people.

This contradiction is illuminated by two different ways of defining popular culture. The first defines popular culture as those cultural pursuits that are *of*, or *from*, the people, that is they are produced organically, by the people themselves (this definition was most often used when describing earlier folk culture activities such as songs and dances). In a modern context the notion that popular culture is the culture of the people rests on the idea that ratings and other feedback mechanisms ensure that the content of television and other media forms is at least partly determined by what the people (the consumers) want. The second defines popular culture as *for* the people, which suggests that something is handed down to them that they accept. There is a big difference between that which is of and from and that which is for the people, a difference that is useful in thinking about the power of the media and whether it lies mainly with the producers or the users/audience/consumers, whether the content of the media derives from the culture of social elites, or whether from the culture of larger social groups, the people. As usual, there is no simple answer in media studies; elements of both may be found bound together.

The acronym SEARCH

Looking at the social role of the media means being interested in the social values and beliefs of media texts—their ideology. The acronym SEARCH foregrounds social issues and social differences. Most letters stand for a way of socially categorising people, and each category usually includes both the socially advantaged and disadvantaged, as follows.

'S' stands for sex, sexual orientation, and gender. In comparison to women, men are a socially advantaged group in modern societies. Men have more social power and control than women, and there is still discrimination against women. There is also discrimination on the basis of people's sexual preference or sexual orientation—that is, whom they are sexually attracted to. Heterosexuality is seen as the norm, while homosexuality, lesbianism, transsexuality, and bisexuality are seen by mainstream culture as deviant, making those who are not heterosexual another disadvantaged group.

'E' stands for environment. Environment is an element that provides a broader context in which the key elements in the SEARCH acronym are all situated. Our society at present faces a global environmental crisis above and beyond purely human social issues. It's important to see how the media portray the environment today, how they encourage us to make sense of the world ecologically. The media seem to celebrate the natural and non-human world in many ways— notice how often animals are used positively in advertisements. Yet human growth continues to threaten the planet and the media often contribute to this by fuelling consumption. Media advertising encourages us to buy over-packaged, over-processed products that damage the environment, causing waste and pollution in the process of their production and consumption.

'A' stands for age. Society is made up of people of all ages, but many societies have ageist aspects to them in that the elderly and young people are treated as second-class citizens.

'R' stands for race and religion. The world is made up of different ethnic and religious groups; most modern societies are multicultural or multi-ethnic. Historically, however, some races or ethnic groups have dominated and exploited others, in particular through colonialism and imperialism. Racial inequalities and conflict persist, and we can see the existence of dominant and subordinate racial groups, as well as negative attitudes and stereotypes that are directed at some ethnic groups. Religious conflict is also significant in some cultural struggles.

'C' stands for class. Modern societies have been described as consisting of three classes: the upper or ruling class, the middle class, and the lower or working class. The upper or ruling class is the smallest in numbers and is the most socially advantaged or privileged, while the lower or working group is the largest in numbers and is socially disadvantaged. Definitions of class are usually framed in terms of the power (and wealth) and/or the cultural values of a person. These definitions are complex, and more difficult to use today than previously, as societies have become much more fluid in terms of social class. In other words, it is less easy to categorise people according to class. Nevertheless, it is worth noting that modern industrial societies, in the wake of increased and continuing high levels of unemployment, now use the term 'underclass' to describe a significant portion of the unemployed population, and it is clear that society still has broad divisions in terms of wealth, money, and wages as well as in terms of what are regarded as acceptable cultural values. So it is still useful to employ this category in understanding society. Australia is significantly different from the United Kingdom in relation to class as Australia aspires to an egalitarian ideal of mateship (though this carries an obvious masculine bias); nevertheless, there are still significant differences in terms of wealth and power between different groups of people.

'H' stands for handicap. Handicapped and disabled people (also known as differently abled people—note how different words and labels, *different discourses* carry different associations) are another social group who are disadvantaged or discriminated against in various ways. Systematic absence from media representations can also be a form of discrimination because it gives the invisible group the message that they are not valued or noticed by society, an attitude that is absorbed by most other people in society.

Other categories (height, weight, hair colour, for example) could be used as markers of normality or deviancy, but these six (sex, age, race, religion, class, and handicap) are particularly useful for drawing attention to social discrimination.

Using SEARCH

We use SEARCH as a tool to search for the assumptions underpinning many conventional views of the world, to wake us up to social inequality, and to the ecological problems that we must search for ways to resolve. You can use the acronym SEARCH to analyse media texts and to understand how you and others are socially represented, categorised, and positioned in the following way.

1   Consider how you are placed in relation to these six categories. How does it feel to be in these positions, and how well represented are you in the media?

2   How do the media represent the world in relation to these six categories? Ask the following questions of specific media texts/images, using SEARCH as an approach.

   a   How does each media text or image represent the environment, class, race, religion, age, gender, and (dis)ability?

   b   What would each media text or image look like to a working-class person, a person of non-European descent, an elderly person, a woman, a homosexual person, a handicapped person, and a person concerned with the survival of endangered species?

   c   Do the media give a privileged view of some groups over others, show some groups as advantaged, others as disadvantaged?

3   Look at Figures 3.1, 3.2, 3.3, and 3.4. What views of age and disability are presented in these four advertisements?

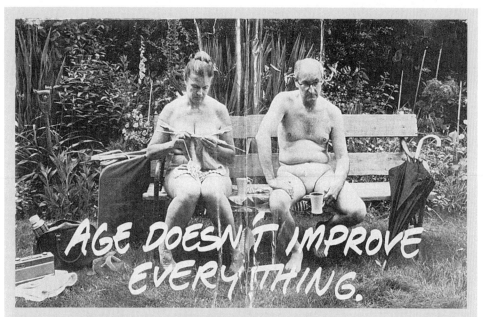

Figure 3.1   Advertisement for Levi's jeans, c. 1990

Source: Levi's Jeans

Figure 3.2   Advertisement for Grosby slippers, c. 1998

Source: Grosby Slippers

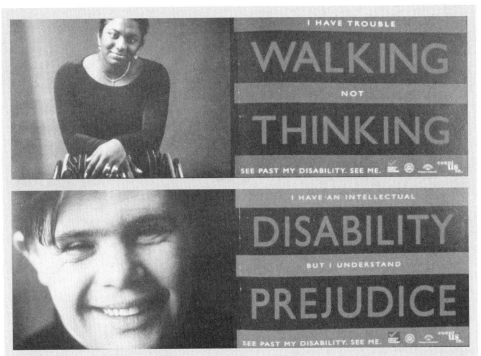

Figures 3.3 and 3.4   Campaign images from the Disability Services Commission. The slogans read: 'I have trouble walking, not thinking. See past my disability, see me' and 'I have an intellectual disability but I understand prejudice. See past my disability, see me'

Source: Disability Services Commission

Media and society

The big question we keep returning to is how, or whether, the media affect and influence us. We like the way Kerry Millard's cartoon in Figure 3.5 presents both sides of the argument.

Figure 3.5   Millard cartoon

Source: Kerry Millard 1996; published in *Australian Lawyer*, November 1996

Do the media reflect or affect the world?

Traditionally, two models have been suggested as ways to understand the relationship between media and society. The first suggests that the media reflect the realities, values, and norms of a society. Thus, if we want to study a society we could turn to its media—its films, novels, television series, magazines, and popular stories—which will reflect to us what people feel and think, how they behave, and so on. But the media themselves do not directly affect society; they simply act as a mirror of society, or a window on the world, that can be used as a resource to understand the society. The second model suggests that the media do affect what people think, what they believe, and how they behave. The media construct our values for us and have a direct effect on our actions. We will examine both models.

The media as a reflection of society

| Do the media change the world? | |

The main arguments against the notion that the media reflect the already-existing norms, values, and realities of society are that the media construct and change events rather than just reflect them. Think about events that happen in the real world but that are also presented extensively in the media—events such as the royal wedding of Prince William and Kate Middleton, the Academy Awards ceremony, and sports events such as the Olympic Games, the World Cup, and the Melbourne Cup. These events happen independently of the media, but the media build them into something more, into media events, constructing rather than just reflecting them (Wark 1994).

The Melbourne Cup is an Australian horse race that is celebrated nationally (and, more recently, internationally, thanks to worldwide media coverage) as 'the race that stops a nation'. It is presented in the present tense, as though it has always and will always be true. Historically, the race dates back only to the nineteenth century, but, more importantly, stopping the nation only became a real possibility once media communication could transmit this event live across the nation, through the telegraph, then radio, then television. At this point the media allow the possibility of a simultaneously shared, national event (the significance of the Melbourne Cup relates to Australia's search for national identity). Events that bring the nation together into what cultural analyst Benedict Anderson (1983) calls an 'imagined community' help Australians to define themselves and their culture. Two national character aspects celebrated in the case of the Melbourne Cup are the triumph of leisure over work and the pleasure of gambling. We can think of few other countries that make a horse race such a significant national event.

The media hype up the significance of such events. Newspapers, radio, and television networks start reporting and speculating on the Melbourne Cup several weeks in advance. (It fits neatly into the annual sports calendar by coming in early November after the Australian football and rugby seasons have ended, and before the cricket, tennis, and other summer sports seasons are fully under way, so there is plenty of media space available for it.) It becomes a feature on non-sports media programs, a major news event, so that, for example, ABC Radio National news programs actually broadcast from the race meeting. The speculation about who will win is linked to gambling and commercialism; participation in the event means being involved in some form of a bet.

Two points emerge from this media event.

1 'Stopping the nation' is only possible via the media, so we can say that the media construct this event rather than reflect it.

2 If you are a regular media consumer, you should 'naturally' be interested in this event, particularly if you identify yourself as Australian. Indeed, the media suggest that not being interested in the race would mean being un-Australian.

The second point relates to how the media construct and shape our actions, our sense of who we are, our daily and annual routines. This is an example of the way people live in the media-world. The media contribute to the construction of a calendar of annual events. Such constructions are not new: throughout history societies have organised themselves around cyclical events, mainly religious holidays and festivals linked in some way to the change of seasons and the practices and rituals of food gathering. These practices have changed with the process of industrialisation so that holidays and rituals are now organised to suit the needs of an industrial society. The biggest annual Western media event is Christmas, but other occasions have also become media events. Valentine's Day, Mother's Day, and Father's Day have all become part of the social and media calendar. These three days are commercialised through the buying and sending of cards and presents, so promotion of them through the media is important financially. Gradually, almost every week and every day of the year has become designated a particular event or linked to a particular cause, and the media are central transmitters of and publicists for them.

Christmas comes earlier each year, occasions such as the Academy Awards—a wonderful piece of media self-promotion and American cultural imperialism—are increasingly big media events. Note how they become part of everyday conversation—'Did you see the Oscars?' people ask. Knowing who the winners and losers are, what they wore, and with whom they attended become important pieces of social knowledge, a sort of cultural capital, for social intercourse. Not knowing threatens mild social exclusion. Increased coverage is facilitated by improved technology (satellite link-ups) that allows the instant and cheap transmission of perfect images and sounds from continent to continent in a way not possible only a few years ago.

A process of selection is at work here. Some events are not promoted—for example the African Football Cup of Nations, arguably the third most significant international soccer competition in the world after the World Cup and the European Cup, receives virtually no coverage or news reports in Australia outside SBS, the multicultural television channel. In contrast, American football and world grand prix motor racing receive extensive and increasing television coverage across the globe. Are these selections made on the basis of audience desires and choice, or on the basis of commercially driven interests? Motor racing was one of the last arenas still available to cigarette advertising and sponsorship in Australia. Why was it allowed to maintain this sponsorship? There are big commercial interest groups supporting and lobbying for media coverage.

While the media construct and promote events such as the Melbourne Cup, they also can change events. The simple act of recording an event will alter it. This is most apparent with the camera. The presence of a camera alters people's behaviour. It may alter in small ways, but it is nevertheless a factor to note. It has been a major concern for documentary makers who try to record real events objectively; many now recognise that their presence changes their subjects (see Chapter 18).

Media recordings have also begun to determine how and when real events will take place. The links between sport and media are significant; each lives off and supports the other, a relationship that means that sports tailor themselves to fit in with and benefit from media coverage. So, for example, when a goal is scored in Australian Rules football in televised matches, the umpires wait to see a light from the television channel indicating that the television advertisement is finished before restarting the game. Matches are also scheduled over the weekend to fit in with and maximise television viewing times. Olympic Games coverage is organised around getting good television coverage and being able to present this across the world for peak-time viewing (in the USA and Europe). Because of this imperative, the marathon has been run at times best suited to worldwide television audiences, rather than to athletes.

The media can become important players in more significant events. One of the most celebrated examples is the media coverage of the Vietnam War. Television pictures of American atrocities and injuries became a major factor in the development of the anti-war movement in the USA and Australia, resulting in popular protests that helped to end the war.

So far the arguments about reflection have considered how the media influence real-life situations; they cannot mirror or reflect them innocently since they become part of the events and change them. When we consider fictions, however, is the reflection model useful? Do fictions show outsiders what life is like in any particular society? Can we gain an understanding of the USA, Africa, or Australia by looking at their television dramas? The reflection model is unsatisfactory here because it assumes that media products transparently reveal the truth about any society. Media fictions will give us some useful information but that information will always be limited.

The effects model

What sort of influence do the media have on audiences?

Let's now consider the effects model. Part of the problem here is what words to use to describe what the media do to us. 'Effects' is often used scientifically to suggest there is a precise response triggered by the media: we watch something and it makes us do something. The word 'influence' is more useful in that it allows flexibility: we watch something and it encourages us to do or believe something. The term 'affect' is also useful as it can refer to change in a general sense, or can be used specifically to indicate the physiological dimensions of emotional responses (such as hair-raising fear or the hot flush of embarrassment or shame). The argument throughout this book is that the media can and do influence us in many ways, so we will prefer that term. We will also sometimes use the term 'effects' to indicate the direct or measurable 'results' of media consumption. We certainly need to be aware of this term because it is a key concept in the debates about the media's influence and power. The issue of media effects is also an important consideration in studies of media audiences. For this reason we revisit the media effects debate in Chapter 6.

Some media effects researchers have issued strong statements about the dangerous effects of violent media. Bushman and Huesmann, for example, write: 'The correlation between media violence and aggression is only slightly smaller than that between smoking and lung cancer' (Bushman & Huesmann, in Singer & Singer 2001, pp. 234–5) and it is stronger than the correlation between condom use and the prevention of sexually transmitted HIV. Even when carefully designed experiments have been done to back up such claims, it is important to bear in mind the difference between *correlation* and *causation*. A correlation suggests that two things usually occur together, such as excessive consumption of junk food and obesity. Statistically, people who eat more junk food are fatter than people who eat less junk food. This is a strong correlation between a high-fat diet and obesity, but the reason for someone being overweight could also be that they have a thyroid imbalance, that they lead a sedentary lifestyle, or that they are genetically and metabolically predisposed to have a fuller figure. A causal relationship only exists when it can be proven that out of all the variables that affect people, one variable can be isolated as the culprit that definitely has a particular effect.

The documentary *Super Size Me* attempts to establish a causal relationship between McDonald's, obesity, and other health problems by eliminating all other food from the filmmaker's diet for a month. In the case of the Columbine school shootings, Michael Moore's award-winning documentary *Bowling for Columbine* prompted reflection on the media's role in creating a trigger-happy population. Moore suggested that by showing so much violence and crime, the media influence people to perceive the world as being a hostile place, to live in a state of fear, and thus to be more likely to own and use guns. However, the media cannot be isolated from other social influences, such as family, community, education, and religion, and researchers have been unable to establish a direct causal relationship between media violence and aggression or other effects.

How is the effects issue popularly presented? In 1998, a story in the *West Australian* newspaper with the headline 'Cartoon Triggers Illness' reported that:

> Hundreds of children have been rushed to hospital across Japan after feeling ill while watching a popular television animation program on a nationwide network. The cartoon ... triggered convulsions in children ... when a bright red explosion flashed for five seconds on television screens (*West Australian* 1998).

There seems to be no doubt that this particular episode of a popular program (*Pokemon*) did produce responses in many viewers but the effects of the media in this instance are not related to the violent subject matter (the content of the television program), but rather to its form (the electronic transmission of light signals). Similar effects to those described in the newspaper report on the *Pokemon* episode are found to occur as a result of stroboscopic flashing lights, which can produce epilepsy in some viewers. Indeed, for this reason Gaspar Noe's rape revenge film *Irreversible* (2004) comes with an epilepsy warning as it includes nauseating pulsing lights and sound effects designed to make the audience experience the physical disturbance felt by characters in the narrative. There is also concern about the potential for recent 3D movies such as *Avatar* (2010) to trigger seizures in audience members with photosensitive epilepsy. This is an example of the way the media can affect audience members on a physiological level. Psychological and direct behavioural effects of media content are much more difficult to measure. Similarly, it is possible to measure immediate, felt reactions, such as laughter or the tendency to tense up during suspenseful action sequences, but not complex, sustained, emotional responses.

The media can also produce effects in our behaviour through their technological forms. Our daily habits and lives have changed radically through the increase of media communication systems. The development of the media has made our lives quicker, more sedentary, and more domestic: telephone and internet communication enable us to contact each other in an instant, mobile phones have given teenagers and businesspeople more geographical freedom by enabling them to easily contact and be contacted by friends, parents, or business associates when they are outside the home or office. We can deal with problems and communicate feelings across distances in a moment and people no longer need to be able to do simple arithmetic, as they have learnt how to use calculators. The use of word processors has had a major effect on writing practices, making it much easier to produce material that can easily be copied, changed, and rearranged. So the very pattern of our daily lives, in the media-world we live in, is structured differently due to media technologies. This is part of what American communications theorist Marshall McLuhan was getting at when he stated that 'The medium is the message' (McLuhan 1987, p. 7). Rather than concentrating on the content of messages, he wanted people to think about the media's technological forms and how they affected people.

But in relation to the question of effects, affects, and influence, it is the area of media content and the way it is presented that we now focus on in more detail. This is the area that raises most discussion and controversy. Another report in the same newspaper, with the headline 'Suicide Alert on Film', shows how this argument can be popularly presented:

> The suicide scene in the latest film version of *Romeo and Juliet* has prompted concerns among psychologists and counsellors that the film romanticises suicide … 'Anything that influences suicide [rates] to go up should be a big concern to society' (*West Australian* 1997).

The implication here is that the film can directly encourage teenage suicide. At the beginning of the twenty-first century Australia has one of the highest teenage suicide rates in the world, with a particularly high rate among young males, and consequently, Australian society is sensitive to this issue. Even so, moves to censor this film because of its portrayal of suicide would be profoundly misplaced. Youth suicide is the product of much wider social conditions, and it is these that need consideration. At the same time the media can be part of these social conditions. Watching news reports about AIDS, terrorism, refugees, global warming, and famine might conceivably make someone who already feels depressed and disempowered become suicidal for reasons that are easier to understand than being seduced by the glamorous representation of youth suicide in *Romeo and Juliet*. To use a more concrete example, one of the statistics of male teenage suicide in Australia is that many gay youth attempt suicide. It is argued that this is because of their distress over the way society treats homosexuality:

> Between 20 and 35 per cent of gay youth have made suicide attempts, the best available statistics show … Youthful gays often internalise negative stereotypes and images of themselves. And when you have been told that you are 'sick, bad, wrong for being who you are', you begin to believe it (Herdt 1989, p. 31).

Cultural theorist Alan McKee (1997) has argued that the media are implicated in this because they present so few positive images of gay youth. McKee sees popular representations of gays as a way of helping raise self-esteem and combating these suicide figures. Similarly, there is current concern about the number of super-thin models in the media who might encourage anorexia in young people. To combat this Israel has attempted to legislate against the media's use of models who are medically underweight, and some fashion houses also now won't use super-thin models. The relationship between media and society regarding these issues is complex, and the influences on audiences might not always be what is expected. There were, for instance, fears in the Australian tourism industry that Greg McLean's horror films *Wolf Creek* (2005) and *Rogue* (2007) would deter backpackers because they dramatise dangers to tourists in the outback, but following the films' release tourism to the regions of Australia depicted in the films rose significantly.

Should there be some forms of media censorship? If so, then who should make and control these decisions?

The effects issue is most often raised over questions of sex and violence. The simple hypothesis is that media violence encourages violent behaviour in the audience, and that sex portrayed by the media can corrupt the audience. Even though research about media effects is inconclusive, it is often suggested that criminal acts have been prompted by watching media violence or pornography, an argument that is sometimes used in law courts. The logical answer for many people is to limit what can be seen through the use of censorship; however, as the quotation from *Scream* that opens this chapter suggests, the media are not responsible for making people bad. While accepting that the media can influence people, and that society needs some forms of censorship, for example of child pornography, we make the following points against increased censorship and against the use of the effects model to justify it.

1   People have some autonomy (self-control and self-determination) in how they behave; while we may imitate some things we learn from the media—what clothes to wear, use of language, and social interaction—we know what it means to be violent towards someone and are careful about such actions. We are rational beings who can think about and reflect on what we see and do. We understand that media representations, stories, and images of violence are stories or fictions. We can make judgments about what we consume from the media; we do not respond automatically to what we see. We are adept at distinguishing between media representations that might contain simulated images of violence (using pig's blood and prosthetic wounds), and the real thing. Blaming the media is an excuse that denies our responsibilities (and is often used to argue for a lighter sentence for those charged with violent crimes).

2   It is important that people have access to information about real violence and sexuality because restricting such access and information can be socially and politically repressive. The Vietnam War is a great example of how media coverage can provide society with information that has political consequences. As noted earlier, media coverage of this war was a major influence in turning Americans, Europeans, and Australians against the war.

    We need to have full access to knowledge of events that have a direct influence on us. Since people rely on the media for information about distant places and events, control of media representations can be remarkably effective in promoting particular beliefs and attitudes: to a certain extent, the media shape our perception.

    There is also a question about how real violence is presented on television. Many people have raised concerns about so-called reality TV programs, such as MTV's *Teen Mom* and *Jersey Shore*, broadcasting their stars' physically aggressive altercations, and shows dealing with footage of actual police business and bad drivers have been criticised for the way they sensationalise violence.

    One of the things you will be aware of as media critics is how the language of the media—camera angles, music, editing, slow motion, and so on—can be used to present and manipulate events in particular ways; this language needs critical analysis.

3   The case around fictional sex and violence raises different questions. Censorship laws in Australia, the United Kingdom, and the USA all underwent extensive liberalisation in the 1960s. In South Africa such reforms had different implications and came later, in the 1990s. Explicit sex and violence have become commonplace in fictional media, helped by improved technology and special effects that have made graphic

portrayals, particularly of violence, ever more realistic and detailed. Reactions to this, and campaigns against media sex and violence, have been around since the 1970s, and debate about these issues continues. These developments raise the following questions: Do we need censorship? Are there limits to what should be shown? Who should be allowed to see what? What boundaries do we need to draw in order to enable audience members to make informed choices about what they wish to be exposed to without undercutting the political and artistic advantages of freedom of expression and freedom of choice? How do we define the kind of characteristics or landscape that we want the media-world we occupy to have? Who decides?

In the debate between libertarianism—giving people freedom of choice about what can be shown and seen—and state censorship and control of the media, Jane and I are inclined towards libertarianism. In an ideal world we would not need censorship, but this is not an ideal world; we need to protect people, particularly children, against images that abuse and harm them, or encourage such harm— we need some censorship and restrictions. Two arguments against censorship are made here.

1   The first relates to the value and importance of fantasy. Fictional stories, like dreams, allow us to explore and indulge in fantasies. Dreaming of attacking someone is not the same as doing it, yet many of us do dream of this at some time. Fictions allow us to explore and understand our sexual and violent feelings (see pp. 333–6). Child psychologist Bruno Bettelheim argues for the value of violent fairy tales for children. Although 'fairy tales underwent severe criticism when the new discoveries of psychoanalysis and child psychology revealed just how violent, anxious, destructive, and even sadistic a child's imagination is', Bettelheim argues that fairy tales allow a space for this imagination and that banning fairy tales, because they are monstrous and scary, would keep 'this monster within the child unspoken of, hidden in the unconscious … Without such fantasies, the child fails to get to know his [sic] monster better, nor is he [sic] given suggestions as to how he [sic] may gain mastery over it' (Bettelheim 1978, p. 120).

2   The second suggests that censorship of violence or sexuality won't work. Censorship reflects a belief that if we control media images, we can control human behaviour; if we stop showing violence, people will stop acting violently. But people act and feel violently towards one another for a variety of reasons. If people want to watch a lot of violence or anger in the media it may be because there is a lot of violence or anger felt in the real world (thus the media are reflecting these feelings). Anger caused by social oppression might be one such reason. The way to deal with such violence is not to censor the media, but to examine what is actually happening in society and try to deal with the deeper causes of anger and violence. Focusing attention on media violence and censorship distracts us from looking at the social problems that determine violence. If the violent feelings are really there, censorship won't make them go away anyway.

The same arguments apply to images of sexuality. In an ideal world we would spend time understanding people's sexual and emotional feelings rather than resorting to censorship. It is disturbing that people sexually abuse children or want to watch such representations, but the fact that they do points to the sexual problems in society. The media sometimes celebrate sexual feeling, but they also often point to the sexual problems and repression felt by many people. Censorship or fear of media images of sexuality draws attention to the need to look more closely at our sexual feelings, to deal with these openly in the real world. We might argue that there is too little sex in the media, too few programs that attempt to bring aspects of sexuality into more open debate.

The media effects debate is a contentious one because it becomes linked to political agendas. Many of those arguing that television violence has dangerous effects on its viewers are seeking to put forward conservative and restrictive censorship legislation. Civil liberty supporters are concerned about the possible erosion of democratic freedoms so they argue that there are no clearly proven direct effects that can be measured, that the media do not have a direct effect. The danger of following this second position is that we lose sight of the fact that in some way, media will affect and/or influence their audiences, though it may be hard to measure and quantify in relation to any individual viewer. Music therapy is an obvious example. It is based on the assumption that music (a form of media) can and will affect its listeners. In his book *The Mozart Effect*, Don Campbell explores many examples where music is successfully used to produce different feelings and states of mind (Campbell 1997). If music can change or create different moods and feelings for its listeners, it seems crazy to deny that audiences won't be affected by other media in some way. After all why do companies invest such huge amounts of money in advertising and public relations campaigns? We perhaps need to develop more subtle and sophisticated ways of studying and understanding media effects and influences. Some analysts have used the concept of 'compassion fatigue' to suggest that there is a cumulative effect of seeing so many news reports of world disasters, famines, and human suffering, which has resulted in our turning off some of our emotional responses—feeling compassion for these people and events—simply because they are too much, and there are too many, for us to cope with. Some people avoid watching the news because they feel they are affected negatively by its continual cycle of disturbing events, so it is evident that the media do affect us in certain ways (see Chapter 6 for a full discussion of audiences).

We conclude this discussion of the relationship between media and society with two examples: first, media images of cigarettes and smoking in fiction; second, real-life media images of war and terrorism from the Iraq conflict.

Case study: The representation of cigarettes and smoking in film and television fictions

There is a clear belief among both tobacco companies and anti-smoking groups that tobacco advertising encourages people to smoke. Once Western governments realised that smoking was definitely harmful to health they decided to ban cigarette and tobacco advertising in most media; however, it is still possible for people to be seen smoking in films and television dramas. In thinking about the overall question of media influence we can approach this continued representation of smoking within screen texts in a number of ways: a *quantitative* content analysis to measure how frequently smoking is portrayed on screen, a *qualitative* analysis to assess what the situations and emotions are when people smoke on screen, research into the *effects/influence* of these images, and research and questioning as to how and why smoking is included as part of the scripts. As media researchers you can devise and carry out work in all these areas.

Smoking: Quantitative content analysis

Some people are concerned that the simple amount or quantity of onscreen smoking we see is significant.

An extensive content analysis study conducted at the University of California found that 'In films of the 1950s there was an average of 10.7 [smoking] incidents per hour. Pressure from lobby groups saw this figure fall to 4.9 between 1980 and 1982, but by 2002 the total had risen to 10.9'. The study suggested that the recent rise in 'smoking incidents' in films 'allowed manufacturers to overcome restrictions on tobacco advertising'. Additionally, Professor Stanton Glantz argued that 'This is particularly worrying in the light of research that shows that young people are taking up smoking because of what they see on the big screen' (Glantz 2004).

Smoking: Qualitative analysis

What do you feel and think when you see characters in films smoking?

A qualitative analysis would look in more detail at who is smoking, in what situations they smoke, and how this is filmed. The point here is that it's not a question of how many times we see smoking, it all depends on how each smoking incident is portrayed. Anti-smoking advertisements might well, for example, show people smoking but in such a way as to link it with unpleasant behaviour or sickness and disease.

1   Who smokes? Is it the main characters or secondary characters? Men or women? Young or old? Healthy or unhealthy? Heroes or villains? Does it make a difference if the smoking character is a hero or villain? When Charlize Theron's character smokes in *Monster* it could be argued this is not harmful to audiences as she is playing a psychotic killer whom we are not encouraged to emulate, whereas if James Bond, or the Hobbits from *Lord of the Rings*, or Keira Knightley as Cecilia in *Atonement* smoke this is more dangerous since they are positive heroes whom we are encouraged to admire and identify with (though it's worth noting that audiences often admire villains too and Theron, playing Aileen Wournos, was, in a way, the hero of the film).

2   It's useful to examine what prompts characters to smoke, where and when they light up. Do pleasant or unpleasant things happen to people when they smoke? How are they feeling as they smoke? We see Nicole Kidman smoking as Virginia Woolf throughout *The Hours*, but her portrayal as stressed and mentally unstable might suggest a negative link between stress and mental instability and smoking. On the other hand, until Pierce (Chevy Chase) 'cures' her with hypnosis, we often see Britta (Gillian Jacobs) in season one of *Community* lighting up in moments of stress, but as a way of dealing with anxieties, and she is clearly identified as the positive heroine of the series. Audiences might link smoking with this positive character and see it as an action that can help in difficult circumstances. One of the most common clichés links smoking and sexuality and pleasure: sharing cigarettes can be a metaphor for shared sexual attraction.

3   How is smoking filmed? The way we see cigarette smoking presented will also influence us. It is quite common to focus on glamorous close-ups of cigarettes being lit, the flame of the match, the warm glow of the tobacco, or on the actual inhalation by beautiful lips. Smoking in these incidents is foregrounded; at other times it may be much more in the background. We often see the 'beautiful' visual effects of smoke drifting across the screen, illuminated by subtle backlighting. But we could see nicotine-stained fingers and teeth, an ugly mouth, or harsh lighting—the kinds of images used in anti-smoking campaigns (see Figure 3.6). Whatever techniques are used will associate different feelings with smoking, drawing our attention to it in different ways, giving it more or less attention.

All of the above elements need to be considered if we are to try to understand the qualitative associations behind representations of smoking rather than just quantify the incidence or prevalence of smoking in popular culture. Government public health campaigns, such as the public service announcement in Figure 3.6, actively work to counteract the influence of repeated representations of smoking and glamorous representations of smoking in the media. Such campaigns

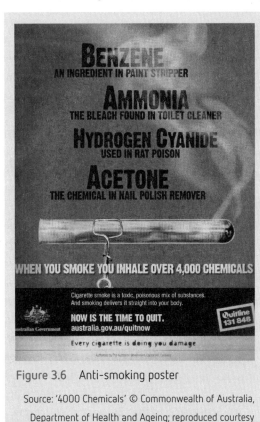

Figure 3.6   Anti-smoking poster

Source: '4000 Chemicals' © Commonwealth of Australia, Department of Health and Ageing; reproduced courtesy of the National Tobacco Youth Campaign provide factual information to audiences so that they are better able to make informed decisions about smoking.

Research into the influence and effects of seeing smoking on screen

This is an area of audience research and, as we have already discussed, it is very difficult to prove any simple and direct effects from seeing smoking on screen since there are so many variables to consider. It might be useful to look at smoking statistics to find out who is smoking and how much. It seems that despite the knowledge about the health dangers of smoking many young people (particularly a rising number of teenage girls) continue to take up smoking. It's also worth noting that from a marketing point of view cigarette companies would target young people as this is when most people actually start smoking and are at their healthiest, so they really want to make smoking seem attractive to this group.

Why do writers and filmmakers include smoking in films and television?

This is an interesting question. As potential writers and filmmakers, you might consider whether you would include smoking in your scripts. There are a number of possible responses.

1. Realism. Some filmmakers argue that if you are aiming to reflect and portray real life in your dramas then you have to include smoking since many people do or did smoke. Keira Knightley plays the character Cecilia in the film *Atonement*, which is set in Britain in the 1930s and 1940s. Most women of her age and class did smoke at that time. If you didn't show this, the film might seem unreal. Some filmmakers choose not to show smoking in order to be socially responsible. In Lauren Weisberger's novel, *The Devil Wears Prada*, smoking is an integral part of the heroine's lifestyle and character from page 2 of the book: 'Attempting to drive this $84 000 stick-shift convertible through the obstacle-fraught streets of midtown at lunchtime pretty much demanded that I smoke a cigarette … I raised a shaking hand to give him the finger and then turned my attention to the business at hand: getting nicotine coursing through my veins as quickly as possible.'

   What message does this send to young women reading this?

   In the film version director David Frankel made a positive decision not to have any of his characters seen smoking as he felt smoking on screen encourages audiences to smoke.

2. Money. A second and simple answer is that smoking on screen is a direct financial result of cigarette companies paying for **product placement**: they pay a film production to include their product on screen, thereby getting around the advertising ban and providing film companies with much needed funds for their ever-increasing costs. Sylvester Stallone has been quoted as admitting that, 'As I discussed I guarantee that I will use Brown and Williamson (B & W) tobacco products in no less than five feature films. It is my understanding that Brown and Williamson will pay a fee of $500 000' (Department of Health, Western Australia 2004). Similarly, 'Philip Morris paid $42 000 to have Lois Lane smoke Marlboro cigarettes in *Superman II*' (Department of Health, Western Australia 2004).

product placement
Companies pay film and television producers to include their products in a story as a subtle form of advertising.

Product placement for tobacco companies is now being banned but remains common for many other products. Some argue that it is more effective and more insidious than direct advertising; since audiences don't realise they are being advertised to, it is more subtle. As audiences increasingly find ways of bypassing adverts—switching the sound down, leaving the room, using video recording technology that leaves out the adverts—product placement is an excellent way for companies to continue advertising. Filmmaking is a costly business so you might well understand a filmmaker accepting this money. If a cigarette company offered to finance your film would you take the money?

3   Aesthetics and narrative codes. Smoking is used first as an *aesthetic*, second as a *narrative* device. Aesthetically, smoking has wonderful visual potential. The wispy, semi-transparent movement of smoke or mist across the screen has an enormous atmospheric quality: it creates movement, depth, and mood; it can suggest mystery, horror, or romance. Look at any films by Ridley Scott (or his earlier advertisements) to see how he uses smoke to create atmosphere.

Smoking can also be an excellent shorthand sign system for developing character and narratives. Since films started, cigarettes, cigars, pipes, and cigarette-holders have been used as props that tell you something about a character and contribute to a story's development. See how Helena Bonham Carter's character in *Fight Club* uses smoking to show her reckless, dangerous, sexual appeal. The predominant representations of smoking on screen in the past have shown it as sexy, cool, and glamorous; there is a culturally coded history, which many people have grown up with, that demonstrates this. The point we want to stress is that filmmakers may use smoking purely as an aesthetic and narrative device that has little to do with actual smoking. You may be against real smoking but in the narrative world of film, smoking is just a sign system; even non-smokers such as ourselves can enjoy Bette Davis and Paul Heinrich lighting up together at the end of *Now Voyager*.

Case study: The media in Iraq

The role of the media in its photographic and film or digital coverage of the violent events in Iraq raises many significant questions about

- the truthfulness and impartiality of the media
- whose viewpoint is given and how much media images are instruments of propaganda
- what images should be shown and what effect these images might have on audiences
- how screening and publishing these images has a direct impact on the political events that are being reported
- the impact and use of new media technologies.

There have been many significant media moments during this conflict that include the images of the toppling of Saddam Hussein's statue in Baghdad, the images showing his two sons after they were shot, pictures of Saddam in captivity and the unauthorised film of his execution, the photographs of George W Bush presenting a Thanksgiving turkey (that was actually a fake) for the American troops, the photographs of Iraqi prisoners being tortured and humiliated in Abu Ghraib, the fake photographs of British soldiers also torturing prisoners, the videos, screened on the internet, of hostages having their throats cut, and the continual shots of civil war in Baghdad. In 2011, protests against the Iraq government provoked violent reprisals against demonstrators and journalists. Iraq continues to be one of the most dangerous places in the world for journalists: 255 journalists and media workers have been killed in Iraq since the US-led invasion in 2003.

The extreme levels of violence and humiliation—murder, torture, and suicide bombings in which innocent civilians are killed—go beyond simple warfare. The ubiquity of media technology that can be used by anyone, not just the official media, has made these images more visible and more available than in any previous conflict. How can media analysts look at these issues?

It is commonly accepted that media images from the Vietnam War showing the 'realities' of US bombing and army practices, as well as America's own casualties, were a major factor in changing US and global opinion about the war and thus helped to bring it to an end. One of the most famous and disturbing images was of Vietnamese children fleeing a napalm attack.

In her book *Regarding the Pain of Others* (2003), cultural critic Susan Sontag has discussed the role of war photography and media coverage of war since the American Civil War and the Crimean War. Artists, photographers, and reporters all sent back media information and in all subsequent wars media have played a role. In more recent times the media have been involved in coverage of the two Gulf Wars. In these recent conflicts the media developed 24-hour television news coverage. The American government, aware of what had happened in Vietnam and of increased media broadcasting, was concerned to try to keep some control on what the media reported and showed.

In the first Gulf War this was achieved by trying to limit the access the media had to information and images, and by transmitting images that were monitored by the armed forces, which did give extensive coverage but from very limited perspectives, resulting in the impression that it was more of a video-games war. In the second war they were more open to journalists but encouraged the practice of **embedded journalism**, whereby a journalist would be invited to join a particular group of soldiers and thus get a first-hand view of the conflict. This view would inevitably see many things from the perspective of the US, British, or Australian soldiers and thus have a certain slant to it that would tend to present the soldiers' view of the war. In a comparison of embedded and non-embedded journalists' articles, sociologist Andrew Lindner observes that 'the physical, and perhaps psychological, constraints of the embedding program dramatically inhibited a journalist's ability to cover civilians' war experiences. While most embedded reporters didn't shy away from describing the horrors of war, the structural conditions of the embedded program kept them focused on the horrors facing the troops, rather than upon the thousands of Iraqis who died' (2008, p. 33). Lindner goes on to say that a variation on the original embedding program still exists today and 'Even journalists committed to depicting the Iraqi experience of the ongoing conflict, such as Jon Lee Anderson of

> **embedded journalism**
> Embedded journalism is when a journalist is allowed to join a group (such as a military troop) to gain access for reporting events; and consequently tends to see events from the group's point of view.

the *New Yorker*, have travelled on brief stints with Army units because it's one of the least dangerous ways to cover the insurgency ... In the case of a future large-scale invasion (in Iran or Somalia, for example), both Pentagon officials and media industry leaders have indicated an interest in reviving the full embedding program' (2008, p. 38).

The two sides of the media war are shown in the documentary film *Control Room*, directed by Jehane Noujaim, which looks at US and Arabic coverage of the war, focusing on the Arabic satellite channel Al Jazeera. It is noticeable that both sides see the other as a form of propaganda.

> Donald Rumsfeld: We know that Al Jazeera has a pattern of playing propaganda over and over and over again. What they do is, when there's a bomb goes down, they grab some children and some women and pretend that the bomb hit the women and the children, and it seems to me that it's up to all of us to try to tell the truth, to say what we know, to say what we don't know, and recognise that we're dealing with people that are perfectly willing to lie to the world to attempt to further their case (*Control Room* 2004).

Sontag (2003) asks what purpose it serves to look at images showing death, wounding, torture, pain. Do images from Iraq serve a purpose? There is a variety of arguments.

Some say it is important to show all images from the conflict, however violent or upsetting they may be. In this view, it is felt that people need to see these images because that is what is really happening, that we need to see them in order to understand the situation, to face up to the grim reality and to make sure governments and armies are accountable. Not showing them could be a form of censorship and protection for the armed forces. It is interesting that both the Australian and US governments give limited media access to detention centres.

On the other hand, the violent images are so shocking that they either should not be shown or should be shown with suitable advance warnings. In particular many people are concerned about children seeing these images, not only because such images may terrify or traumatise them, which is the main argument, but also in case they encourage the child's own levels of violence. There are concerns for adult viewers too, either that these images desensitise people (we have seen so much violence that we now don't care about it any more), or that they encourage our ghoulish, voyeuristic tendencies (these images are just objects of fascination for our consumption), or that they will cause us unnecessary pain and trauma. There has been considerable debate in the media itself about what it should publish. Television is concerned with its ratings as well as its social conscience. Television stations also knew that images from Iraq that were not broadcast were being made available on the internet. American businessman Nick Berg was the first man whose execution was broadcast in this way. One source on an interesting website that explores these issues tells us that 'Nick Berg' was the second most searched request on Google in May 2004, following *American Idol*.

There is a further concern that these images can affect what is happening in the conflict. When the first images of Western hostages pleading for their lives or about to be killed were available they were shown by the Western media, who, gradually, decided to show these images less frequently in case they were seen as helping the terrorists' cause or would encourage other hostage takers to perform similar acts. The military conflict thus becomes a media conflict.

The power of media images was perhaps most apparent in the circulation of the torture photographs in Abu Ghraib. It has been suggested that it was the graphic visibility of these images that brought the issue of torture and humiliation by US troops on to the front pages of the newspapers. Without this photographic evidence the issue might well not have surfaced. The power of the photographic image was crucial in the debate.

Out of all these issues there are two points worth elaborating. The first relates to the question of 'reality'. We are at pains throughout this book to stress the mediated, constructed nature of all media products. We are not seeing reality; we are seeing representations. As such, we ask you to question who produces media images, how they are constructed—camera angle, lighting, and so on—and what purpose they serve. There are two factors about the reality of the Iraq images: the first is that a lot of them were produced by media amateurs and, as such, are not well constructed and some, the video internet execution images for example, are low-grade in terms of sound and vision. But it is these very qualities of amateur, poor media quality that impress viewers since they seem to get closer to an unmediated reality. Given the public's cynicism about the truth of the media and our saturation with media coverage, these amateur videos and photos communicate more powerfully to us. The second factor is that they carry more truth value because they are produced by 'ordinary' people, not by media reporters, and because they were initially circulated by the democratic technologies of the internet or cell phones and were not official, authorised media outlets. We are not questioning that there are real events here and the camera does record something of this reality, but we need to remember they are still constructions and to consider them as such.

The second point is to ask whether these images do indeed help us understand what is happening. This is a point that Sontag has taken up. She makes distinctions between photographs and words:

> The problem is not that people remember through photographs, but that they remember only the photographs ... Harrowing photographs do not inevitably lose their power to shock. But they are not much help if the task is to understand ... Narratives can make us understand ... Photographs do something else: they haunt us (Sontag 2003, p. 89).

Sontag is not saying photographs are a bad thing, but she is questioning their ability to fully explain situations. Even though they clearly carry huge emotional impact, this may not always be helpful in determining future actions. Nevertheless, it is often photographic and film evidence, rather than written reports, that have triggered most public debate.

These two examples focusing on representations of smoking and of the conflict in Iraq illustrate that the media's influence on society is complex and multilayered. The media can influence behaviour and attitudes, and its effects need to be considered in terms of media ethics, control, and persuasive impact in addition to analysing media content.

Conclusion

We hope you are beginning to see some of the complexities of the media–world relationship and the issue of whether and how the media both reflect and influence society. We suggest that Figure 3.7 is a way of understanding this double aspect of the media. In this model, media producers, media texts, and media audiences are separated from popular common sense. The media producers, in constructing their images and stories, are reflecting various social ideas and beliefs that are held by different social groups. The audiences consuming these texts are partially influenced and affected by what they see. These influences then contribute to the overall social fabric of popular, commonsense ideas.

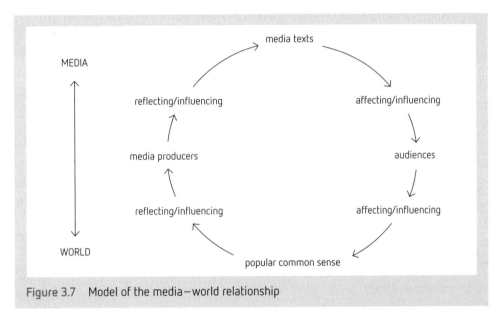

Figure 3.7   Model of the media–world relationship

But media producers, texts, and audiences are all part of the social whole; they are not separate entities. The media are one of the social forces that produce popular common sense, the general social beliefs and feelings of a society. In turn, these social beliefs and values influence the media, who reflect them. Like the chicken and the egg, there is no simple solution as to which comes first—media representations or popular common sense; the two are permanently intertwined. What is more, in today's media-world, media images and reality often blur together: we begin to see real events in relation to familiar media images. Thus, the Gulf War was said to look like a video game, and Associated Press news reports of the 2011 Japanese tsunami had headlines like 'Japan looks like "Hollywood disaster movie"', stating that the television images 'resemble scenes from a Hollywood disaster movie. Powerful waves, filled with debris. Uncontrolled fires. A ship caught in a massive whirlpool' <http://www.wbir.com/news/article/161163/2/Explosion-feared-at-Japan-nuclear-plant>.

This chapter has

- considered some of the conditions of contemporary global society
- explored how the media work through making sense, constructing reality, and being popular
- introduced the term 'SEARCH'
- considered whether the media reflect or affect the world
- explored effects models in media studies
- examined media representations of cigarette smoking and of Iraq.

Discussion points

1   In thinking about popular culture and media products, would you argue that we get what we want, or we want what we get?

2   Do you think programs such as *MasterChef* are programs that are *of* the people or *for* the people? What examples would you argue fit into these two categories?

3   Look out for particular media events. How do the media construct them? How involved in these events are you?

4   How would you argue for and against forms of media censorship? What forms of censorship would you argue for (if any) and for whom?

5   Reflect on your experience of media coverage of events in Iraq. What arguments would you make for and against the way the media have covered events? As events continue to unfold, monitor how the media deal with them.

Summary

You should now be able to

- comment critically on the media's role in relation to some of the major crises and conflicts in contemporary society; for instance, discuss and comment on the media's coverage of the conflict in Iraq
- explain general principles of how the media function and discuss these principles
- consider the importance and effects of the media's need for popularity
- apply the acronym SEARCH to media representations
- discuss arguments about whether and/or how the media affect and influence people
- define and illustrate the terms 'embedded journalism' and 'product placement'
- discuss the pros and cons of media censorship
- analyse fictional representations of smoking.

CHAPTER 4

What's in a Name? Language and the Social Construction of Reality

We don't speak language, language speaks us.

Martin Heidegger

All words are pegs to hang ideas on.

Henry Ward Beecher

This chapter will explore how language structures the way we understand the world by

▶   giving insight into the politics of naming

▶   demonstrating that language is not natural or neutral

▶   exploring the ways in which language is a changing site of power and struggle

▶   looking at examples of language in use in social contexts and in the media.

A central argument of this book is that media representations are constructions based on language. This chapter examines the nature of language and relates it to ideas about human societies as a whole and to the 'social construction of reality'. What we say about language in general can then be applied specifically to the media.

Here, in a nutshell, are our arguments.

1   Human societies organise and structure the world in particular ways.

2   In so doing they construct the world and they construct reality.

3   This reality tends to become normalised and naturalised so that it is taken for granted—'That's life'—by the people in that society.

4   We tend to forget that reality has been constructed or that it could be organised differently.

5   We learn about the world primarily through language; thus language is crucial in this construction and in the transmission of this construction to others.

It's very important to note that this argument means that, like the media, reality—the social world we live in—is also a construction. You can get an idea of how this argument works through the following hypothetical example. Suppose a group of people who are dissatisfied with the culture and society they live in decide to start a new community on a desert island. Once on the island they organise their time and customs in the following ways. They decide to have an eight-day cycle in which they work for five days and rest for three. The men will all eat and sleep together in one building with the children, while the women will eat and sleep together in a separate building. Once every 32 days they have festivals where they dance together all night. The women go out and grow the crops while the men do all the cooking.

This may seem rather far-fetched, but it draws our attention to the way any society will organise its time, its rituals, its work practices, and so on, in order to suit its needs. Anyone who travels from one culture to another often feels initial surprise at how differently the new culture organises things to the culture they're accustomed to. Travellers also often notice how the new practices become normal, so that when they return to their original culture it is their home culture that seems unusual.

Imagine the situation of any children born into our imaginary community. For them these structures would be the normal, natural, everyday structures of their world. As children, we accept the customs of our family and society as normal, and in so doing we lose sight of the fact that they have been socially constructed. This is crucial. The naturalisation of social construction blinds us to the fact of human agency in constructing the realities we inhabit. Throughout this book we ask you to be aware and wary whenever the terms 'natural' or 'normal' are used. These words are often used to naturalise forms of behaviour or social organisation so that people don't question them, but we argue there is nothing natural about the way human societies are organised. All our actions and behaviour are acted out in social situations and institutions that are the product of human cultures, not of nature. This is not to say that they haven't evolved in relation to natural climatic, cyclical, and geographic conditions, nor is it to say that there is something wrong with these practices, but they are not natural in the sense of being behavioural patterns that inevitably or necessarily arise from human physiology.

What's in a name? The linguistic politics of naming

Does language describe or interpret the world?

Language, as the primary means of communication, is the central medium used for the understanding, interpretation, and construction of reality.

It is necessary to consider for a moment the nature of language and the relationship it has to the world. There are two theories for thinking about the relationship between language and the world.

1   *Reflective or mimetic* This suggests that language simply describes the world, that it is a method used to name and describe what already exists. According to this theory all humans see the world in the same way, share the same basic concepts; language is simply a vehicle for expressing these concepts and the world that exists independently of it.

2   *Constructionist* This suggests that language doesn't describe a pre-existing world. Rather, it constructs the world through naming it, and constructs the concepts through which we understand life and the world. Thus different languages represent the world in different ways, and speakers of one language will understand and experience the world in ways peculiar to that language and differently from the ways of speakers of a different language. This is not to deny the reality of the material world, or that it pre-exists language, but to say that it is only apprehended, only understood, once it has been named, or constructed, through language. All knowledge of reality is mediated by language. Our experiences of the world take form only when presented through language.

Christian mythology illustrates the power of the word, of language, as a means of giving life and structure to the world: 'In the beginning was the word and the word was God.' One of Adam's first tasks was to name all the animals and plants, thus giving them substance or calling them into existence. The Bible tells us that language brings things into being. But there is not just one language, not just one way of describing the world. Anyone who has learnt a second language knows that the two languages do not correspond exactly, word for word. Different languages have different ways of describing or naming the world. Inuit language, for example, has as many as twenty-seven words for describing forms of snow, whereas English has just two or three (Hall 1997, pp. 21–44). Reality can be named by language in different ways.

Colour is a good example. Although the spectrum of colours is a continuum in which there are countless variations of colour, through language we name the spectrum and structure it in a particular way. We simplify the spectrum into seven colours, which enables us to handle and describe it, even though we might find it impossible to point precisely to the place where red becomes orange or orange becomes yellow. But the seven-colour system we use is just one possibility. We could break the spectrum into six colours, combining indigo and violet into purple, or nine colours, adding turquoise or teal, aqua or ochre, and if our language did this we would even begin to see the spectrum differently. So our words structure the world in particular ways in order to make sense of it.

If the reflective or mimetic method described above was correct then either there would be one universal language that perfectly described the world, or different languages that would correspond exactly so that there would always be exact equivalent words in every language. This is not the case.

Not only do different languages carry slightly different meanings, but there are also differences in such things as the way tenses are used and the use of verbs or nouns to describe things. Different languages structure the world in quite different ways. German, for example, is a gendered language with different words for 'the' depending on the gender, number, and case of the noun. (*Der* is the masculine, singular, nominative form of 'the' used for phrases such as *der Junge* (the boy); *die* is feminine or plural nominative and accusative; and *das* is neuter, singular nominative and accusative).

There is an anecdote about a Japanese company that wanted to mount an advertising campaign for selling razors for women to shave their underarm hair. The company used an American advertising agency. This agency devised a cartoon campaign that would feature an octopus shaving under its eight arms. When the commercial was ready the Americans showed it to staff of the Japanese company. These staff were taken aback and shocked, and refused to accept the campaign. The problem was that in Japanese culture an octopus does not have eight arms, it has eight legs!

This story illustrates the idea that whatever language we are born into will structure the way we see and understand the world. This is the basis of the Sapir–Whorf hypothesis:

> At the heart of the Sapir–Whorf hypothesis is the claim that the very words we speak and the grammatical structures we use actually influence or determine the way we think. In this light, language is not just a means of communicating ideas, it actually helps fashion them (Open University 1981, p. 72).

Do we speak language or does language speak us?

Our view of the world expands as our language capacity expands. We might say that we don't speak language, language speaks us. This, indeed, is one of the main tenets of the work of linguist and anthropologist Edward Sapir and his student Benjamin Whorf and of structural linguistics. The Sapir-Whorf hypothesis suggests that language constructs our identity, that we are a cog in the machine of language. This hypothesis has been interpreted in two ways:

1   our language determines our thinking
2   our language merely influences our thinking.

The second interpretation gives us a degree of autonomy. It is worth noting that if we discover new things or new feelings, we have to invent new words in order to describe them, and this gives us further autonomy.

We accept the constructionist position, as opposed to the mimetic position, and argue that language enables us to think and understand. It gives shape to our perceptions and feelings by giving them labels. It is a system of representation, a term discussed below (see pp. 75–6). The whole process of language is a naming or labelling process that carries profound social and political implications.

Imagine two people engaged in sexual activity. How would you describe or name what they are doing?

- They are making love.
- They have gone to bed together.
- They are having sexual intercourse.

- They are fucking.
- They are fornicating.

All of these describe what is happening, but each carries a different set of connotations, associations, and feelings; they construct different discourses (see p. 69). The first description emphasises the romantic feelings involved, while the second is euphemistic, letting us imagine what is actually happening. The third takes a clinical or medical view, while the fourth has a cruder, more derogatory feeling associated with slang. The last use of language has moral and biblical undertones, suggesting that the two people are unmarried and therefore what they are doing is bad. None of the descriptions is wrong; they all invite us to view and understand what is happening in different ways. There is no way of describing what is happening that does not carry a particular view of the actions. Language is not natural, neutral, or static. It is arbitrary, value laden, charged with power relations, and dynamic.

Names as an example of constructed identities

It may seem obvious to you that your name is part of yourself, but names are given quite arbitrarily, and different names may cause us to think differently about ourselves, to see ourselves in a particular way. I, Michael, was born in London, England and most of the kids at my school were white and English. My name, Michael O'Shaughnessy, marked me as an outsider because both my Christian/given name and my surname are particularly Irish. (Note that calling a first name a 'Christian name' places you in a particular cultural and religious tradition while your 'surname' probably identifies you with your father rather than your mother, thus structuring you into patriarchy.) At school I was called a wild Irishman (in a friendly way). This label, given to me by my English teachers and classmates, reinforced a stereotype of Irish wildness and Irish savagery, which gave me a sense of who I was. I saw myself as having a wild streak, and came to see myself as different, as an outsider. Such an identity allowed me to adopt a critical view of England and Englishness at the same time as being a part of that culture. Had I grown up in the same place but been named John Smith or Sebastian Courteney-Smythe, I suspect my character and my values would probably have been markedly different, and in many ways I am pleased with my non-English identity: because the Irish aren't seen as 'Pommies' it feels easier to be an Irish-Australian than an English-Australian (see the discussion on interpellation, pp. 185–6).

People often have a number of different names: first names, diminutives, surnames, nicknames, and so on. All of these construct us differently and are used by other people to construct our identity in their eyes. They also allow us a number of different personalities for each name. In work situations, hierarchical positions can be reinforced by the use of names. Because using someone's surname indicates formality and respect, those in junior positions tend to address those in senior positions by their surnames (although this is, of course, dependent on the culture of the organisation). Conversely, because using someone's first name is a sign of familiarity and informality, those in senior positions tend to address those in junior positions by their first names. Secretaries, for example, are often referred to by their first names. Consider how different names bring out different aspects of your personality.

Sometimes people change their names. Some immigrants to Australia from non-English-speaking countries change their names or adopt different names to fit in more easily. Our own experiences with Asian students in Australia have demonstrated that some adopt a new or Anglicised first name partly because non-Asians have difficulty pronouncing and remembering Asian names. In changing their names, they may also take on new personas, and may discard some of their traditional cultural practices. People who adopt a religious group or cult sometimes change their names to give themselves a different identity that marks them as part of their adopted group.

Ask yourself how many different names you have. In what ways do your names affect your personality? Think of other names you could have. Would these give you a different personality and identity?

In considering the significance of language we suggest the following guidelines.

Language is not natural

Language does not simply name the world as it exists, but it also constructs a view of the world. You may be already thinking that talking or writing about language is a complicated thing, because you have to use language in order to talk about it. As we write this we are aware of the different ways we could express things and the different meanings that would result. We are also aware that you, as reader, may want to take issue with some of the things we write. So we want to qualify what we mean when we say language is not natural. We don't mean that it is not natural for humans to speak. Indeed, it seems that one of the defining qualities of what it means to be human is to have an innate capacity for language. Children have a built-in propensity to learn languages. But there is no normal, right, correct set of words, or way of speaking, that describes the world. Some theorists describe this characteristic of language by saying that all languages are arbitrary, meaning that there is no necessary connection between the sounds and symbols that make up any language on the one hand, and on the other, the world itself. The symbols and sounds in the word 'thong', for instance, don't have any real relationship with summer footwear, except by convention. 'Thong' doesn't look like something that goes on a foot; it doesn't sound like the slapping noise a thong makes on your heel as you walk, and the letters 't–h–o–n–g' certainly don't smell, taste, or feel like the objects with which they are arbitrarily associated. In fact, different cultures use totally different letters, sounds, and words to represent similar forms of footwear: *sandalo* in Italian, *flip-flops* in South Africa and the United Kingdom, *jandles* in New Zealand, and *thongs* in Australia, where the thong has a privileged place as a recognised symbol of the relaxed, outdoor Australian lifestyle, to the extent that it featured in the 2000 Olympic Games opening ceremony in Sydney. But some cultures, whose peoples don't wear thongs, have no word to describe them at all. In other places the word 'thong' is used to describe skimpy g-string underwear that nobody would ever consider putting on their feet or, with the possible exception of a Brazilian samba carnival, associating with national identity. There are numerous languages that describe the world with their own particular inflections and biases. The idea of bias leads to the next point.

Language is not neutral

Language always carries some associations, connotations, or values with it. We have already seen this with the 'making love' example. Even ordinary words, such as 'up', 'down', 'top', 'bottom', 'left', and 'right', carry significant associations. They may be used simply to describe spatial positions. But 'up', 'top', and 'right' also carry positive connotations that relate to a culture that values right over left and is formulated on a competitive, judgmental ethos that compares us with others and grades us in hierarchical terms such that 'up' and 'top' are viewed positively, but 'down' and 'bottom' are perceived as negative terms. Even as a named part of the body, 'bottom' carries negative connotations in the way Western culture sees it. In Christian mythology the left hand is considered to be the sinister hand because of its Latin origin in the word *sinistral* (meaning left or left-handed), and because the devil is supposedly left-handed. The right hand is the superior, dexterous (derived from the Latin *dexter*) hand. These words are thus neither innocent nor neutral.

When it comes to more obvious political naming, it is easy to see how the terms 'terrorist', 'guerrilla', and 'freedom fighter' have been used by different political groups to refer to the same people. Similarly, the terms 'boat people', 'refugees', 'asylum seekers', 'queue jumpers', and 'illegals' have all been used to describe people coming from Asia to Australia since 2001, and each descriptive term refers to a different discourse for understanding who these people are and what 'we', the Australian public, should think about them. (Note how 'boat people' is not a term/discourse normally used to describe the arrival in Australia of Captain Cook and his crew, although it could be.) Consider the differences between 'climate change', 'global warming', and 'ecological time-bomb' as ways of describing what is happening to the global environment. In the immediate aftermath of the terrorist attacks of

September 11, the Western press and some politicians presented the event linguistically in terms of 'good' and 'evil' (see Figure 4.1).

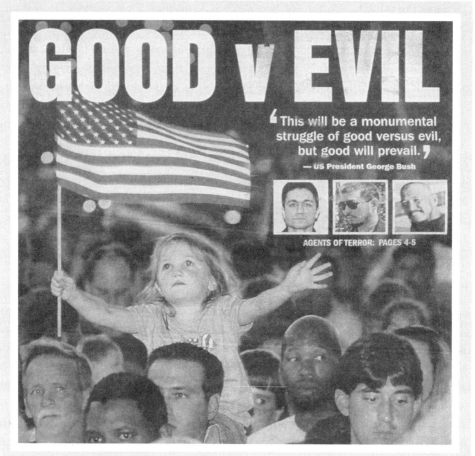

Figure 4.1   Headline from the *West Australian*, 13 September 2001

Note how these words

- draw on a religious and moral discourse
- construct real events in the same terms as Hollywood adventure films such as *Star Wars*
- tend to negate the possibility of any debate or questioning about the meanings and causes behind such actions by simplifying the issues into good and evil, black and white terms, thereby sending the message that the only right and logical action is to somehow punish, eradicate, or eliminate that which is 'evil'.

We're not arguing the political rightness or wrongness of these different labels but noting that the same people can be named in very different ways that have very different meanings, and that all such names carry a political position. The critical term 'discourse' is useful to help understand how language works (see Part 3).

Cultural theorist John Fiske argues that a **discourse** offers 'ways of thinking about a particular topic, set within a particular context'. He illustrates this in relation to the occasion when video footage was taken of a black man, Rodney King, being beaten up by four policemen in Los Angeles in 1991, but in court the police were found not guilty, which resulted in African Americans protesting on the streets.

discourse
Discourses are paradigms or ways of understanding that are communicated through texts and language use, and that organise knowledge and social power.

> You remember what went on in the streets of L.A. after the Rodney King verdict? Was that a 'riot', or an 'uprising', or a 'rebellion'? If we call it a riot, that puts it in one discursive frame which suggests that it was criminal, it was social disorder. If we call it an uprising, it suggests that it's another discursive frame, another discourse, there was a point to it, there was some organisation, it was against something and it wasn't just disorder. So the word 'riot' and the word 'uprising' come from quite different discourses, ways of talking about an event. So discourse is extremely important. No social event proscribes what discourse we use to describe it, it's our choice as users of language. And the way we make the choice of which discourse to put a particular event in, is an extremely important thing to understand (ABC Radio National, *Media Report*, 7 December 2000).

Consider these three ways of describing the area comprising Africa, South America, and much of Asia: the 'Third World', the 'underdeveloped world', the 'majority world'. There is a major difference between the first two terms and the last. The first two place that world in the negative: if it is third then it comes after the first two worlds—in the language of hierarchy and the language of competition, which structure much of Western thought, it comes below, it is a loser. Similarly, to be underdeveloped is to be less than, or the negative of, developed. So in this context 'underdeveloped' is a negative term indicating that such areas have failed to meet their full potential, to mature, or develop.

The point is that while the terms 'Third World' and 'underdeveloped' world are helpful in some ways in pointing out the discrimination against this 'Other' world, they remain negative and they give a view from the perspective of the minority world. They don't really challenge the structures of power involved; however, to name this area as the 'majority world' is to give a positive value to it, because in Western democratic thought majorities carry rights and power. Naming this area the majority world places the so-called developed nations in a minority position. Suddenly you might see the injustice of a world that is heavily geared towards materially satisfying the minority.

Language is a changing site of power and struggle

Language meanings and associations can change over time. We need to realise this so that in any language analysis we look at the meanings in a historical and cultural context. Feminist author Dale Spender has noted how, in relation to gender, language has a tendency to sexualise and denigrate terms used to describe women (Spender 1980, pp. 16–19). She considers the pairings of a number of oppositions, for example master–mistress, bachelor–spinster, king–queen, courtier–courtesan, lord–lady. Her findings are that as time passes either the female terms lose out in terms of their status and value—'lady' describes ordinary women, whereas 'lord' retains its powerful meanings; 'bachelor' is a social position with more positive value than 'spinster'—or else the terms come to describe women in terms of their sexuality (for example, over time 'mistress' and 'courtesan' have become words that describe women's sexual position in relation to men).

The label 'queen' has been used to describe and denigrate homosexual men, the implication being that for men to be feminised is a put-down. Note, though, that in the struggle over language, gay men, who first appropriated and reworked the meaning of 'gay' to validate and celebrate homosexuality, have now also reappropriated 'queen' and 'queer' as positive labels of description. 'Queer theory' is now part of media and cultural studies, and fashionable boutiques proudly use the media to advertise 'Queen-sized shoes'. In addition, many women have reclaimed and redefined the diminutive term 'girl' that has in the past been used to refer to mature women in an affectionate way that nevertheless diminished their social standing (by categorising them with children). Now the term *grrrl power*, said with a growl, leaves no doubt about the social standing of the women who use it to refer to themselves, their friends, and to media identities such as the stars of *Charlie's Angels*, Lisbeth Salander, 'the girl' with the dragon tattoo in Stieg Larsson's *Millennium Trilogy*, Baby Doll (Emily Browning) in *Sucker Punch*, and Uma Thurman as 'Kiddo' in *Kill Bill*. If grown women are being referred to with a word that means 'juvenile female', it seems that the term has literally been empowered and redeployed in an assertive way.

This shows that language meanings are not fixed and can be struggled over by different people and by different social groups. Historically, such struggles have been very important, particularly those that occur between different ethnic groups. These struggles over language are struggles for power and they are very common.

Who controls language?

In Britain in the eighteenth century, speaking Gaelic in Scotland was forbidden and made punishable. The English were seeking to maintain their rule—hegemony—over the Scots by wiping out Scottish culture and imposing English cultural values through the use of the English language. In Africa, the USA, and Australia indigenous languages have, at various times in the past, been banned as part of attempts to destroy indigenous cultures. The English language has been used as a source of establishing European power over indigenous populations. Even now the use of Singlish (Singaporean English) or Ebonics (African-American English) is considered to be improper and accrues penalties in academic institutions in Australia, the United Kingdom, the USA, and elsewhere.

African writer Ngugi Wa Thiong'o has described how language can be used in struggles for power between different racial or ethnic groups. He talks about how as a child in Kenya he was forced to learn English, on pain of punishment, in a way that alienated him from his own culture and people by depriving him of the use of his native language, Gíkúyú:

> English became the language of my formal education. In Kenya, English became more than a language: it was the language, and all the others had to bow before it in deference. Thus one of the most humiliating experiences was to be caught speaking Gíkúyú in the vicinity of the school. The culprit was given corporal punishment—three to five strokes of the cane on bare buttocks—or was made to carry a metal plate around the neck with inscriptions such as 'I am Stupid' or 'I am a Donkey' (Ngugi 1986, p. 11).

Ngugi shows how the use of English as the official language devalued Gíkúyú and made it inferior in the eyes of those for whom it was a native tongue. As they began to see and think from a European perspective, Africans became alienated from their own cultures and came to look down on fellow countrymen and women who had not taken up European ways and words. In this way European economic and political domination—imperialism, the establishment of empire—were supported through language control:

> Economic and political control can never be complete or effective without mental control … For colonialism this involved two aspects of the same process: the destruction or the deliberate undervaluing of a people's culture, their art, dances, religions, history, geography, education, orature and literature, and the conscious elevation of the language of the coloniser. The domination of a people's language by the languages of the colonising nations was crucial to the domination of the mental universe of the colonised (Ngugi 1986, p. 16).

This is not a form of economic imperialism, but of cultural imperialism (see Chapter 25). The final irony for Ngugi is that he became a great writer of English whose writing, which has become part of the English literary tradition, is not available to the majority of his own people, who cannot read English. The complications of language are illustrated by Ngugi's history: after his realisations about language and power as a successful writer in the 1980s he decided to renounce the English language, stating that 'This book … is my farewell to English as a vehicle for any of my writings. From now on it is Gíkúyú and Kiswahili all the way' (Ngugi 1986, p. xiv). However, he later moved to America and once again found English as his main language and the language that would reach a wider audience.

You can look at equivalent struggles over language between Australians of European descent and Aborigines, between non-English-speaking Australian immigrants and English-speaking immigrants, between African Americans and European Americans, between Native Americans and immigrant Americans. A key question in all these struggles is which language will survive. Even when one language triumphs, as English has done in many situations, there can still be struggles between different kinds of English spoken by different social groups, for example between cockney English and 'the Queen's English', between 'black English' (or Ebonics) and 'white English', between Australian English, Singaporean English, and white American English, and between English spoken by Aboriginal Australians and English spoken by non-Aboriginal Australians. These struggles are about having power through language; forms of 'deviant' English are often forms of resistance by oppressed social groups.

In 1995 a Canadian radio program about a conference for Native American peoples reported that the contradictions around language were keenly felt: there was an attempt to maintain traditional languages as a way of maintaining traditional culture—once the languages are gone, the culture will be gone, but there was also a recognition that English had become the language of many of those indigenous groups, so that in a sense it could be seen as their language. Moreover, English was the language that made shared communication between the different groups possible at this meeting (ABC Radio National 1995).

In the 1990s the South African government decided that its new national anthem should always be sung in the four main languages so as to equally represent the different social groups who make up South Africa.

A further complication arises when we consider that English is increasingly the language of mass communication across the globe (Chinese is the second-most used language). It is certainly the language that dominates computer-mediated communication, especially the internet. Therefore, in order to have one's voice heard in an international forum, being able to speak and write publishable and quotable English is becoming a necessity. Does this mean that the media contribute to the formation of a monoculture and that the globalisation of communication networks can only be seen in a negative light? We will return to this complex question in Chapter 25.

Language and social change

Can you change society by changing language?

Awareness of the above arguments about language (arguments that are really about the politics of naming) has led social groups to try to change language use in order to change social behaviour, particularly in relation to sexism. This begs the question: 'Does changing language lead to social change?' Will, say, using 'Ms' instead of 'Miss' or 'Mrs', or 'differently abled' instead of 'disabled', change how people think, believe, and behave? While changing language will make some difference, several critics have shown that word changes can be accommodated by mainstream culture without social changes taking place.

'Ms' was originally intended to be a parallel term to 'Mr'. However there are lots of studies ... which suggest that 'Ms' is not being used nor interpreted in this intended way. A study [in Canada] ... showed that people had a three way distinction: 'Mrs' was used for married women, 'Miss' was used for single women, and 'Ms' was being used for divorced women ... In Britain it's reported that 'Miss' and 'Ms' have sort of coalesced so the distinction now is between 'Mrs' and 'Ms'—'Mrs' signalling a married woman, 'Ms' signalling a single woman ... the distinction 'Ms' was intended to eliminate is still getting expressed but in a different way (Susan Ehrlich, quoted on ABC Radio National 1995).

In many cases it is not only language, but also the medium of communication that determines people's choices about how they represent themselves to others. Many forms that have to be filled out (particularly those requiring computerised data entry) either neglect to offer 'Ms' as an option, offer it as a restricted option for females over a certain age, or offer it in conjunction with 'Miss' and 'Mrs', rather than using 'Ms' as the default title to designate females as the term was intended to function (the equivalent of 'Mr', which designates all males, married or single, who do not have a specific title, such as 'Dr'). Additionally, it seems 'Ms' has now come to take on feminist connotations while the term 'feminist' itself has now taken on negative connotations for some young women so they do not want to use the term 'Ms' because they do not want to be labelled feminist (although they are clearly the beneficiaries in many ways of the feminist movement). A related phenomenon can be seen in the film *Hot Tub Time Machine* (directed by Steve Pink, 2010) in which Craig Robinson's character Nick Webber-Agnew is humiliated by his mates for having a hyphenated surname. The hyphenation of last names became popular so that women did not need to give up their own name when they married: they simply added their husband's last name to their own. When a man also adds his wife's last name to his own, however, this is considered to be emasculating.

This example shows that in order to eliminate discrimination against women, there has to be social change as well as language change. Without social change, changing language is fighting a losing battle. Nevertheless, language change and language awareness are important parts of raising our consciousness about bias and discrimination, and thus help us move towards social change.

Conclusion

This chapter has argued that social reality is constructed and that language, as a system of representation, is central in this construction. Language is not natural or neutral but carries certain values. It is also a site of political struggle.

The arguments we have made here about language can be applied to the media, even though the media don't always use words—they might use pictures, images, forms of camera movement, editing, or even structural strategies (for example, positioning information that is considered to be most important at the top of a webpage). The media's techniques can be understood as the language of the media; the discussion about language in this chapter is relevant to the conventions of journalistic uses of language as well. As critics, you can now begin to deconstruct the language of the media and the way stories in the media are written and structured.

This chapter has

- argued that social reality is constructed and that language is central in this construction
- explored the politics of naming
- shown how names can construct identity
- argued that language is not natural or neutral and that it is a changing site of power struggles
- considered language and social change.

Discussion points

1   Explain what 'We don't speak language, language speaks us' means. How would you argue for and against this idea?
2   Consider the differences between 'climate change', 'global warming', and 'ecological time-bomb' as ways of describing what is happening to the global environment.
3   Find examples of language that carry particular social or political meanings.
4   Explain and illustrate the term 'discourse' in relation to language use.
5   How many languages do you think will still be used in 100 years time? Which will be the main languages used?
6   Can you change society by changing language?

Summary

You should now be able to

- explain the concept of the social construction of reality and the role language plays in this construction
- explain the mimetic and constructionist theories of language
- give examples of how language constructs the world
- critically discuss the idea that language is not natural or neutral
- show how language is related to social power
- explain and illustrate the term 'discourse'
- discuss language as a site of social struggle with relevant examples
- consider whether changing language can change society
- argue about whether we speak language or language speaks us
- explain why an understanding of language is important in media studies.

CHAPTER 5

Mediation and Representation

There is no such thing as objective journalism. The phrase itself is a pompous contradiction in terms.

Hunter S Thompson

This chapter will

▶ examine the meanings of the terms representation and mediation

▶ give models to illustrate how the media communicate and represent reality

▶ question the truthfulness of media representational technologies and conventions such as objective journalism

▶ analyse some specific examples of media representation.

Representation

The last chapter argued that language constructs and evaluates the world and reality by naming it. The media constitute a language system, so what we say about language also applies to the media. Language and the media are both systems of representation. Representation is a key concept in media studies. It has three meanings:

1   to look like or to resemble
2   to stand in for something or someone
3   to present a second time—to *re*-present.

Language and media representations do all three.

We know and understand the world through language, through representations. This is not to deny that the real world exists—of course there is reality—but it is to say that all our learning about the world is mediated by language. There is a complex relationship between representation and reality. As Richard Dyer puts it:

This is difficult territory. I accept that one apprehends reality only through representations of reality, through texts, discourses, images; there is no such thing as unmediated access to reality. But because one can see reality only through representation it does not follow that one does not see reality at all … Reality is always more extensive and complicated than any system of representation can possibly comprehend and we always sense that this is so — representation never 'gets' reality, which is why human history has produced so many different and changing ways of trying to get it (Dyer 1993, p. 3).

What Dyer is suggesting here is that when we feel that language and representations don't do justice to our sense of reality, we have to find new ways of representing them, and indeed, this has been the history of human culture, constantly developing new modes of representation and discovering new ways of seeing reality. Here is another example of how we are not totally trapped in systems of representation, but can struggle to redefine language to invent new languages. But the central point remains that we still only know reality through representations: 'There is no such thing as unmediated access to reality' (Dyer 1993).

Can there be unbiased, objective representations of the world? Michael and I argue no. Because all representations come from humans, they come from a particular position. So they are relative; they will carry the bias of a particular person or group of people, just as this book carries our biases and positions. How true can representations be? In the end this is something you have to decide for yourselves. You may decide that one set of representations are true or that they are more true than others—in other words, that they are the best available so far. This is Jane's and my position. As we grow and learn, we find models that best fit how we see and understand the world.

As an example of different and developing ways of looking at the world (very literally in this case) consider the following maps (Figures 5.1 and 5.2).

Figure 5.1   Traditional world map

Source: *New Internationalist*, 1998

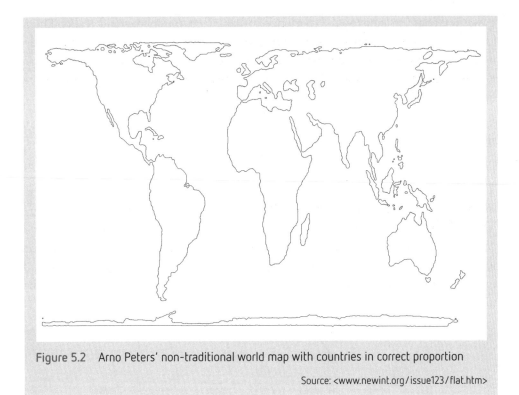

Figure 5.2   Arno Peters' non-traditional world map with countries in correct proportion

Source: <www.newint.org/issue123/flat.htm>

Which map appears most real to you? Which is most familiar and conventional?
What are the differences between them?

Commentary

Traditional maps have tended to show countries incorrectly in proportion to one another, to the advantage of the European colonial powers, while the southern continents are shown far too small. Europe, with its 9.7 million square kilometres, appears to be larger than South America, which is 17.8 million square kilometres, North America appears to be considerably larger than Africa, which is 30 million square kilometres, whereas, in fact, North America is smaller (only 19 million square kilometres). Scandinavia, 1.1 million square kilometres, seems to be as large as India, which is 3.3 million square kilometres.

The new map (Figure 5.2) provides a helpful corrective to the distortions of traditional maps—no less than our world view is at stake. By setting forth all countries in their true size and location, this map allows each one its actual position in the world (*New Internationalist* 1998).

The above points are crucial. If you can understand them you will be well placed for the rest of the book. Talk them through with other students and try to see how they relate to your own experiences of language, the media, and reality. These ideas lie behind the important statement given earlier (see p. 36): media products do not show or present the real world; they construct and re-present reality.

We will develop this idea by looking specifically at the media apparatus to see how it deals with reality.

The media apparatus

The word 'media' literally means 'middle'. The media are the things that come in the middle of or mediate communication. They are the means through which message senders can communicate to message receivers, or audiences. Anyone wanting to communicate chooses a medium to do so, whether it be spoken or written language, some form of pictorial representation (pictures, diagrams, photographs, films, and so on), or another medium. Figure 5.3 is a modification of Lasswell's formula (see p. 20).

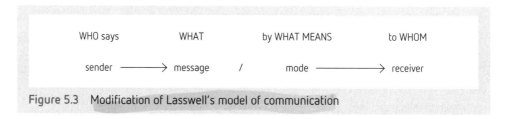

Figure 5.3   Modification of Lasswell's model of communication

In this formula the answers to 'WHAT' and 'by WHAT MEANS', in other words the messages and the modes, constitute today's media. In modern industrialised society, messages are transmitted through the technological means of the world wide web, print, film, digital technologies, mobile phones, computer systems, and so on.

We stress here the process of mediation: the media stand between us and the world or reality. We can understand our relationships to the world and the media according to the model in Figure 5.4.

Figure 5.4   Model of the media–world relationship, stressing the process of mediation

Note how the double arrows in this model recognise that the world impacts on the media and that audiences are active in making meanings—they don't just passively receive them.

In relation to the visual media of photography, film, digital cameras, and to the sound recording media it has been suggested that they are neutral mechanisms that simply mirror the world, giving us a window or an ear on the world (Figure 5.5).

Figure 5.5 Model of the media–world relationship, suggesting that the media are neutral mechanisms that simply mirror the world

Media studies rejects this model, stressing instead media construction, selection, and interpretation, to develop the concept of representation (Figure 5.6).

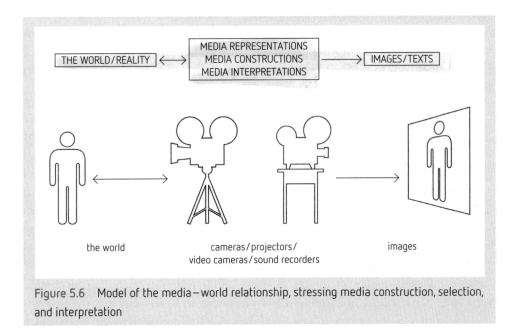

Figure 5.6 Model of the media–world relationship, stressing media construction, selection, and interpretation

We need to reiterate this point strongly in relation to the film-based visual media and sound recording media because of the particular qualities shared by photography, film, digital cameras, and sound recording.

The media and reality

Do cameras and media technologies show us the truth?

Many media and artistic representations refer to things from the real world. Novels, plays, poetry, painting, sculpture, photography, film, and digital cameras all aim to re-create objects and people that are part of the world we live in. But photography, film, digital cameras, and sound recording—media technologies—have a different relationship to the real world than other means of representation, such as language, painting, and sculpture. Cameras can reproduce reality in a mimetic way, and therefore appear to show us unmediated reality. These media use impressions from the real world, and then digitise them, or put them onto film, digital video, or MP3 recorders, to produce images and sounds. Unlike literature, paintings, or sculpture, which are produced by the artist's hands and imagination, photography, film, and digital cameras actually record the reality that is out there. So whereas these new technologies appear to be objective, human eyes, ears, and hands produce subjective renditions of the world. This has tended to make people believe in the realism of these technologically produced images so that we think that we really see or hear the truth when we see photographs and film, or when we listen to recordings. Because these media depend on a connection between the real world (the referent) and the way it impinges on celluloid or audio-tape, through light patterns and sound waves, there is some truth in this belief—but only some. It is crucial to be aware of the fact that these realistic media are constructed as well.

1   For a start we do not actually see three-dimensional reality; we see two-dimensional images of reality in film and television. When French filmmaker Jean-Luc Godard remarked, 'There are no just images, there are just images', he meant two things: first, he was making a political point that the dominant media images of Hollywood and mainstream media do not offer a fair or just view of the world in terms of its representation of class and social differences; second, he was saying that images are just that, images—they cannot give us reality, the real thing. Godard also commented that 'A photograph is not the reflection of reality, but the reality of that reflection' (Harvey 1978, p. 71). Belgian surrealist René Magritte drew attention to the illusory nature of images in many of his paintings, including his famous *This is Not a Pipe*. This painting draws our attention to the fact that the image is simply lines and colours that look like a pipe, that it is not the actual thing to which it refers.

2   Film, photography, and video images only give us a particular or partial view of what we are seeing. We only see from one angle, with one view and with particular lighting. We cannot encompass the whole of reality on the screen. There are numerous processes of selection and omission that lead to the way we are shown things and the way different shots are put together. Editing selects and omits material. Choices are made that produce a particular viewpoint, giving a particular meaning to what we see. Commentary accompanying images also explains in a particular way what is happening. Sound recordings are equally selective.

3   Images are linked together within bigger systems of narrative and genre, which also affects how we see them. In these systems the media have tended to hide their own processes of construction. By this, we mean that when they show mediated events they aim to make them flow smoothly without showing the construction that has gone on. All the paraphernalia of representation—autocue, lights, sound, camera equipment, and so on—are hidden from sight. Events seem to unfold naturally, as if they were happening before our eyes. This third point is not so true since the 1990s as previously. The media sometimes deliberately reveal their own processes of construction: popular television studio programs show the cameras and behind-the-scenes crew, thus revealing and referring to the recording and constructing processes. Audiences are far more media aware; they enjoy seeing behind the scenes, and they understand that a lot of media manipulation and construction goes on. The growth of media studies has contributed to this.

4   The technology for constructing reality keeps improving. It is now possible, through computer technology, to compose photographs that appear real but are not. Documentary theorist Brian Winston has commented that 'the technology for digital image manipulation is rapidly becoming a fixture in all newspaper and magazine offices' (Winston 1995, p. 5). The consequence is that 'by the summer of 1993, the status of the photographic image as evidence was becoming somewhat tattered' (Winston 1995, p. 5). The consequence of this ability to manipulate photographs is that media reality becomes even more questionable (Figure 5.7).

The rest of this chapter will analyse some specific examples of media representation to show how they construct particular views of the world.

Figure 5.7   Digitally manipulated image of American President George W Bush, circulated on the internet following the 11 September 2001 attacks on the Pentagon and World Trade Center

Case study: Families in photographs and paintings

Everyday family photos are media representations/constructions, and they are a fascinating source to examine. Our first example compares two representations of the family: one (Figure 5.8) is a family album photo taken in 1960, the other (Figure 5.9) is Thomas Gainsborough's eighteenth-century oil painting of Mr and Mrs Andrews (c. 1750). Both these images offer particular views of the family.

Figure 5.8   Happy families: a family snapshot

Source: Author's private collection

Figure 5.9   *Mr and Mrs Andrews* by Thomas Gainsborough

Source: National Gallery, London

Figure 5.8 presents an idealised story of the family. It stresses family unity within a patriarchal framework; the five people are working together but are marked out hierarchically in terms of height and age—the male figure, who also has the biggest piece of machinery, is the leader, while the rest of the family are progressively scaled down. The image celebrates the family and the bourgeois values of property ownership and work: there is evidence of the large garden and the process by which it is cultivated and controlled. The audience is invited to celebrate this process of ownership, to witness and congratulate a successful and happy family. It makes an interesting contrast with John Berger's analysis of Gainsborough's oil painting, *Mr and Mrs Andrews*, in one of the pioneering studies of media and representation, *Ways of Seeing*.

Berger (1972) argued that in the eighteenth century, oil painting, one of the key media of its day, was a way for the property-owning classes to represent and celebrate their power and ownership. The picture of Mr and Mrs Andrews implies a sense of power over the land that they own. It is a land for recreation—Mr Andrews goes hunting (his gun gives him symbolic phallic power)—and cultivation (we see corn and sheep). But clearly, the Andrewses take no part in this rural labour—they simply own and benefit from it. In terms of gender we see a subordinate female figure in terms of height, but also one who is established through costume as a source of visual pleasure and ornamentation.

Ownership and commission of oil paintings was only available to a small elite group who could afford to buy or commission one. Photography in the twentieth century has, in contrast, set itself up as a democratic medium in terms of its affordability to all and in terms of the skill required to do it— anyone can take pictures: 'You push the button, we do the rest', says one early Kodak advertisement. But photography is still being used to celebrate official family and property values, and is one of the key mechanisms for documenting a positive account of the family through snapshots of weddings, christenings, and holidays, preserved on the mantelpiece, in the family album, and on the hard drive.

There is an alternative view to the official reading of this family photograph and of the elements that the photographer has chosen to ignore. I, Michael, am in it, and I know the histories behind the image, the realities that were being hidden: the father was having an affair, within a year the parents would be separated, the children were extremely unhappy, and there was always an argument about the children having to do gardening!

What this alternative view reveals is the process of construction involved in what we might regard as the most innocent of photographs—the family snapshot: first, in the general ways family snapshots are constructed to celebrate family values, presenting a discourse of the family, and second, in the detail of any particular image. You should be able to see this very clearly when considering how you have been represented and manipulated in any media constructions since you will be aware of the realities and histories behind the constructions, and of the elements that the camera or the media text has chosen to ignore.

Case study: Representation of queer culture: The Sydney Mardi Gras

Our second example (Figure 5.10), a press photograph and report of Sydney's 1996 Mardi Gras Festival, is an example of mediated and constructed news.

What meanings are being communicated by the photograph, its caption, and the news story? We can divide this into three elements: the photograph itself, the caption, and the written report. Briefly, the photograph appears to celebrate the event in terms of humour and pleasure. Through the humour associated with men dressing up and dancing, it mediates what might otherwise be, for some, a shocking depiction of homosexuality and male sexuality. Media coverage of the Mardi Gras continually negotiates the risk of offending viewers by using humour to offset this danger. Yet while an essential part of the Mardi Gras ethos is to poke fun at male power and authority, this text seems to reveal a very different story. After the humorous caption and the positive opening paragraph, the selection of 'facts' to be reported depict the event in terms of criminality, danger, socially irresponsible behaviour (assaults, littering, drunkenness), and implied public cost (without mention of the huge boost to Sydney's economy that this event brings in through tourism). The reference to Clean Up Australia Day in the fourth paragraph (see text reproduced with Figure 5.10) can be read as a veiled moral point that suggests Australia needs to be cleansed of such events. This report thus becomes increasingly negative about and critical of the event, revealing an interesting example of selection and construction.

Well, hello sailors

A **RECORD** crowd of 600,000 watched Sydney's eighth annual gay and lesbian mardi gras parade last night.

Police said the massive crowd was generally well behaved.

There were two arrests. One man was charged with offensive conduct and another with four counts of assaulting police.

Fifteen people were taken to hospital and 13 treated for ailments ranging from chest pains to intoxication.

Tons of confetti, bottles and cans awaited council crews on Clean Up Australia Day.

Figure 5.10   News story about and photograph of the Sydney Mardi Gras

Source: *Sunday Times*, 1996

News reporting and objective journalism

Our third example (below) offers a much more detailed analysis of the way language is used in a short news story, developing our ideas from Chapter 4.

Many media students aim to enter the media industry and become journalists, so it is important to consider the news media in relation to the power of language. In addition to the politics of naming (see pp. 62–5), and the way reporters will present a story according to its news values or newsworthiness, we must also be aware of the conventions of news writing.

Journalists are taught to write from an objective (see p. 26) perspective. News reporters do not write from a first person perspective. In other words, they don't use the pronoun 'I' and they don't directly state their own opinion. In a hard news story a journalist will never say something like 'I think the new environmental policy is problematic'. This use of language makes it seem as though nobody is writing the story, suggesting that the story is a collection of facts that are presented in a neutral manner. The news does not seem to reflect an editorial policy or an economic imperative, or to be a particular journalist's ideas, words, or opinions. It seems to be 'the objective truth'. In this way the media, and the people in control of the media, speak for us all, as though their views are the natural, normal, and factual ones.

Journalists are also taught to avoid bias by presenting a **balanced** report. If a journalist is covering a story on a court case, they are obliged to interview the defendant (or somebody representing the defendant) and the plaintiff (or a spokesperson, such as their lawyer). Similarly, a journalist reporting on an environmental conference must interview politicians from the government *and* the opposition

> **balance**
> Balanced reporting entails the presentation of both sides of an argument, giving them equal space and time.

to find out about their policies. Representing both perspectives is intended to avoid presenting a one-sided story, which would be considered biased and might alienate readers and reduce sales of the newspaper. Conflict is newsworthy, so if the interviewees agree on environmental policy the journalist is likely to ask a prominent businessperson or a member of a lobby group for comment. It is assumed that impartially presenting opposing viewpoints creates a balanced report, which suggests that the truth is located in the neutral zone between two polarised opinions, and that there are only two important perspectives on any given topic. This is not always true: there may be many opinions and many relevant facts, and the 'correct' opinion might not be located in the middle ground.

In the process of writing objectively and giving a balanced account of the story, journalists include quotes from experts who are authorities in the field or who have personal experience of the matter in question. Quotes are reported in such a way as to clearly attribute opinions and ideas to the person who said them, and to clearly separate facts from opinions. If something is presented as a fact, the journalist is supposed to validate it by checking with two other sources to make certain it is correct.

Journalists and news reporters are taught to begin with the most important points first, with the climax of the story at the start, then, gradually, fill in the context, history, and background, thereby presenting news in the form of an **inverted pyramid**. Media practitioners know that most people don't have time to read a newspaper from cover to cover, or to listen attentively to every news report on the radio or watch news on television. Since readers skim the news, the most important and

> **inverted pyramid**
> Information is given in descending order of importance, as in a news report.

newsworthy information is presented first. The headline is usually an abbreviated sentence designed to capture attention in less than seven words. Unnecessary articles such as 'and', 'are', or 'that' are omitted from headlines to make them as concise, informative, and punchy as possible. The first sentence of a news story is called the 'lead'; it is a summary of the entire story. In a typical lead the journalist will try to answer as many questions about the story as possible in one short sentence. Sometimes journalists will attempt to capture the reader's attention using some other device, delaying the revelation of the story's main point. This technique, called the 'buried lead', is much more common in feature writing than in news reports. The main questions addressed in the lead are who, what, when, where, why, and how (often referred to as the 'five Ws and an H'). Thereafter, information is given in descending order of importance: the journalist fleshes out the story by providing additional details, quotes, and facts.

While the formula and conventions that journalists follow are designed to make the news as factual and fair as possible, we know that language can never be completely neutral. Analysing a news story can reveal how unintended bias can be encoded in the terminology and structure of a text, even if the author intends to be objective. Many of the features of the media text discussed below contribute to its meaning but would not necessarily have been intended by the journalist.

Case study: Analysing the language and structure of a news story

'Saudis Acknowledge Women Exist' is a report from South Africa's *Mail & Guardian* newspaper about gender, law, religion, and power in Saudi Arabia (Pilkington 2002, p. 18). The first sentences of this article read:

> Saudi Arabia is to gender what apartheid South Africa was to race. In public life a woman is almost entirely segregated from men: excluded from the workplace, penned in special 'family sections' in restaurants, taught in separate schools and colleges and forbidden to drive.
>
> Under the country's fundamentalist interpretation of Islam, her husband may marry up to four times, but an adulterous woman faces death by stoning. Outside the home she must wear the abaya, a black gown that enshrouds her completely, except for a slit for the eyes.
>
> There are signs, however, that the kingdom is reforming. It is not so much a wind of change as a puff, but it is significant. Women have been granted voluntary identity cards for use in banks and other public places. The card ends the iniquitous legal position in which a Saudi woman simply does not exist. As a child she is a ward of her father, as an adult the ward of her husband and as a widow the ward of her sons.

<www.mg.co.za>

Using our knowledge of the conventions of journalism and the power of words, we can analyse how the language and structure of the media text position the reader and encode a particular meaning or a preferred reading (see p. 102) laden with value judgments, rather than objectively informing the reader about recent legislative reforms related to gender equity in Saudi Arabia.

- *Context* In terms of its media context, the article is in the international news section of South Africa's national newspaper, a paper committed to political comment and positive social change. The social and political context of the news story is also important: Saudi Arabia is a monarchy that observes Sharia or Islamic law, which does not give women and men equal rights with regard to issues such as voting, having a licence to drive, or holding political office.

- *Intended reader* (see p. 97) Consider whom the newspaper wants to communicate with. The way newspapers are organised into national, regional, and international news, and the way the different sections are labelled does not invite us to see ourselves as members of the global community, or as residents of a particular suburb. In this case, the paper is addressing its reader as a South African. It is positioning us as South Africans, constructing a South African subject position. This way of communicating has been called 'interpellation' (see p. 185).
- *Othering* In doing so, the text is establishing Saudi Arabians as 'Other'. It divides people into two camps: 'them' as opposed to 'us'. The heading and the first paragraph reinforce the 'us vs them' dichotomy established in terms of national identity and context (see 'Binary oppositions', p. 282).

The headline of the story does not mention the new identity card that offers legal recognition of women's rights to money, property, and independence, which is what the story is about. Instead, the title alludes to the fact that the lack of such rights is similar to 'not existing' in the eyes of the law. The implications here are that the Saudi men must be pretty slow if they've only just realised that women exist. This is implicitly belittling the legal reforms, rather than celebrating them as a positive step. Overstatement of the problem is used to ridicule the new identity card and the legal reforms by making the progress towards a solution seem too limited. (This is a disguised perspective or an opinion, which may or may not be true. Because it is disguised in the language use, readers don't get a chance to question or evaluate it.)

The words that make up the headline were chosen from a **paradigm** of possibilities. By 'paradigm' we mean a set or selection of words that mean similar things and that could be substituted for one another. For example, in the headline 'Saudis Acknowledge Women Exist' the word 'Exist' was chosen from among many other possibilities. It could have read, 'Saudis Acknowledge Women's Rights', or 'Equity', or 'Independence'. Such a headline would have been more informative, but the headline printed in the *Mail & Guardian* was probably chosen to provoke the reader to read further.

Syntagm relates to the sequence of words. A different sequence of words would focus on a different aspect of the title as the main subject. Rearranging the sequence of the words, any of the headlines above could have started with the two words 'Saudi Women' (as in 'Saudi Women's Rights Acknowledged'). When we rearrange it like this, we realise that the original headline implies or assumes that Saudi Arabian citizens are all male and that it is the males who are the subjects making laws and decisions about women. In the original headline, women are the passive objects of the headline.

Can you think of alternative headlines that would encapsulate the most newsworthy points of the story effectively? Here are a few suggestions: 'Saudi Legal Reform Helps Women' or 'Progress for Saudi Women'. Analyse how each of the headlines above and your own headline **frames** the story in a different way, altering its emphasis and inviting the reader to focus on different aspects or **angles.** Now write your own lead for the story (use present tense, active voice, and avoid writing in first person perspective). Try to answer as many of the '5 Ws

paradigm
A set of terms, things, or ideas all based on a common theme or unifying system.

syntagm
Syntagm, like syntax, is a term that refers to the structure or pattern of words in a sentence or things in a sequence.

news frame
The selection and presentation of stories, issues, quotes, headlines, and images influences the way audiences make sense of the news. The processes of inclusion and exclusion, and the use of language, structure, and emphasis convey values, judgments, and perspectives that determine what the audience will consider to be important.

angle
In journalism the angle is the central focus or the main idea in the organisation and presentation of a story and its lead.

and H' questions as you can in less than 25 words, and keep the lead as snappy and interesting as possible to hook the readers' interest.

The lead (the first paragraph of the story) creates another analogy, using more oppositions to position the reader on the privileged side of a self–Other dichotomy.

Self	Other
Us	Them
South African	Saudi Arabian
Racism	Sexism
Then	Now
Good	Bad

In other words, the structure of the article encourages the reader to make a negative judgment about Saudi Arabians, and may lead to prejudice and discrimination. This is reinforced by the connotations (see p. 136) or associations of the terminology used in the article.

- *Language use* The clothing that Saudi women wear is described as 'enshrouding them completely'. The word 'shroud' has connotations of death, and of being wrapped up in a way that constrains movement. The words 'covering them completely' could have been less value laden. Another example of the loaded use of language is the phrase in the second sentence describing women as being 'penned' in sections of restaurants. Because it is usually animals who are kept in pens, this suggests that Saudi men treat women like animals, whereas the article could have said that women were 'restricted to special family sections in restaurants'.

- *Structure and hierarchy* Readers notice the headline first, and then they pay attention to the first paragraph. As mentioned above, information in news stories is often structured in order of importance (a hierarchy of meaning, with the least important details coming last). The quotes from Saudi men and women offering their own opinions about how the legal reform will affect their lives come near the end of the story, which gives them less chance of being read. News is supposed to give a balanced account of different sides of a story in order to maintain journalistic objectivity and perform the information/education function without bias; however, sometimes a story seems balanced because it includes different views, but it is biased because of the way it is structured.

This news story does offer two different perspectives on the significance and magnitude of the legislative reform. In paragraph three the journalist states that 'the kingdom is reforming. It is not so much a wind of change as a puff'. In paragraph eight Selwa al Hazzaa, a Saudi woman who is head of ophthalmology at King Faisal hospital in the capital, Riyadh, says, 'A huge jump has been made'. The non-Saudi perspective of the journalist is privileged due to its position closer to the beginning of the story.

Another important point, along similar lines, is that two different perspectives are offered about the reason for gender inequality. At the beginning of the article (top of paragraph two) the journalist writes, 'Under the country's fundamentalist interpretation of Islam, her husband may marry up to four times, but an adulterous woman faces death by stoning'. This statement creates a strong causal link in the reader's mind between Islam and the ill treatment of women in Saudi Arabia. In the very last paragraph of the story there is a quote from a Saudi woman talking about the Muslim faith: 'There is nothing in the Qur'an that says a woman can't drive or has to have her face covered. This is male domination—not Islam.' Again we have two different perspectives, but the one that comes first, which is implicitly privileged due to its placement in the article, is the only one that most people will read if they are skimming the newspaper.

The news report we have been discussing highlights important differences between what the media actually do and what they ought to do. **Normative theories** of the media are theories or approaches that offer an ideal view of the roles or functions the media ought to fulfil in society. The concept of objectivity discussed above includes a set of professional practices based on an understanding of the ideal role that the free press should play in a democracy. The conventions of objective journalism are designed to enable journalists to fulfil this ideal role. For example, the free press ought to cover both sides of an issue or debate in an impartial way and it ought to act as a watchdog that informs the public about what the government is doing, critiquing the government and sniffing out corruption or discrimination. The media ought to provide a voice for the people and feedback to politicians about what society wants, needs, and thinks. Due to factors such as accuracy, credibility, and diverse interpretations of information, the media's actual functions might be a far cry from the ideal normative theories. So, for example, in the news report critiquing the treatment of women in Saudi Arabia the intent was to inform the public about legal amendments and human rights issues, but the actual role that the media played may have contributed to divisive or discriminatory attitudes by creating a binary opposition between 'us' and 'them'.

> normative theory
> 'Normative' refers to assumed norms and standards of correctness; to ideal views about the role the media should play in society, particularly the functions the press ought to perform.

Through the use of language and the way the text is structured, Saudi Arabians are ridiculed, Othered, and vilified to a certain extent. The news story, which (according to normative theory) is supposed to objectively inform us about events in other parts of the world, has been used to make a religious and political criticism of another culture. Like many readers of this article we have never been to Saudi Arabia, as result of which our understanding of the religious and legal rules governing gender relations in that country is largely dependent on media messages. This means that journalists have a very responsible and important position in society because they have the power to frame the way we see or understand world issues and events.

Conclusion

As media analysts, it is your job to be aware of the processes of media construction, to ask how images are being constructed, what view of the world people are being invited to see, and to challenge the reality of these productions. In so doing, you are involved in the process of deconstructing the images and texts you look at.

Let's reiterate why this is important.

1   As potential media producers—writers, editors, camera operators, webmasters, and so on—you need to know the tricks or tools of the trade: how you can produce images and words that will move people to tears, anger, or joy. You deconstruct the media in order to know how to use cameras, lighting, editing, and so on, to produce particular effects and meanings. You are learning the aesthetics and technical methods of the media, the language of the media.

2 As critics, you enhance your appreciation of media products through understanding the way they work; you can then communicate this to others.

3 Through deconstruction you will be able to see the social and political views that are often implicit but not directly stated in media products. You thus reveal the ideological messages and meanings contained in the media, the ways they make sense of the world for people, through showing the processes of construction. This social, political, and ideological concern is at the heart of this book. Understanding that the media's views of the world are constructions is the key to ideological analysis.

This chapter has

- examined the term 'representation' and its relation to the real world
- emphasised representation as a form of construction
- illustrated the mediating aspect of the media apparatus
- looked at examples of representations of the family, Mardi Gras, and Saudi women.

Discussion points

1 Find different global maps. Consider and compare how they represent the world.

2 Watch any episode of a satirical current affairs show and note what examples of media construction it reveals.

3 Think of an occasion on which you or your friends or relatives have been represented by the media. Look closely at these representations and consider how you were constructed in this process. These representations may include visual images and words, either spoken as commentary or as printed text.

4 How would you argue for and against the notion of objectivity within media news reporting?

5 Apply the arguments put forward in the analysis of the 'Saudis Acknowledge Women Exist' news story to a current news story that interests you.

Summary

You should now be able to

- define the terms 'representation' and 'mediation'
- explain how the media communicate and construct reality
- analyse family photographs, news photographs, and news reports in terms of how they construct reality
- define the terms 'objectivity', 'balance', 'Othering', 'inverted pyramid', 'paradigm', and 'syntagm'
- explain the conventions of objective journalism and reflect on the way they impact on the construction of a news story and position viewers, listeners, or readers to respond to it
- analyse the language use and the formulaic structure of a news report.

CHAPTER 6

Texts, Meanings, and Audiences

We must get away from the habit of thinking in terms of what the media do to people and substitute for it the idea of what people do with the media.

James Halloran, *The Effects of Television*

This chapter will
▶ consider the different factors that affect how people read media texts
▶ examine different theories of media audiences.

Having looked at media and society, and at issues of representation, we can now start to look at media texts and how people read them. The term 'read' is being used loosely here to refer to any process of interpretation—viewing, scanning, listening, and other forms of engaging can all be termed 'reading'. By 'text' we mean any media item—photographs, advertisements, films, magazines, books, websites, television programs, newspaper articles, and so on. A text must be capable of being reproduced and subjected to analysis. To read or decode a text is to make sense of it, regardless of whether it has actual writing in it. Textual analysis is a central component of media studies.

| Do media texts have single or many meanings?

Later chapters present different critical approaches for textual analysis, but first we need a framework to answer the wider question of whether we can determine what texts mean.

There are two main concerns here.

1   Do texts have a single, essential meaning that analysts, readers, and critics are looking for or can numerous, different meanings be found in any one text?

2   What factors need to be taken into account in trying to establish what meanings a given text might hold?

Regarding the first concern, it is widely accepted in media studies that texts carry a number of possible meanings.

We suggest that

dominant reading
The meaning of a text that is accepted by most audience members and can be determined by examining its textual codes and social/historical contexts.

- there is a **dominant reading** or meaning for a text (Hall 1980, pp. 128–38)
- there are different meanings according to the different contexts, critical criteria, or personal perspectives used to approach the text.

These different meanings lead us to the second concern: who is reading the text, when or where they are reading it, what theoretical approach is being taken, and so on. There are four overlapping factors to take into account:

- texts—analysis of texts on their own
- production contexts—the study of how texts are produced
- distribution contexts—the study of where and when texts are sold or screened
- audience contexts—the study of how audiences actually use and make sense of texts.

Each of these contributes to the readings of what a text means. The more that is known about all four, the greater the potential to establish the different possible meanings of any one text and to give reasons or explanations for these different meanings and readings. Figure 6.1 illustrates this diagrammatically.

Figure 6.1   Model of the relationship between texts, contexts, and audiences

The text itself

Some people argue that while background knowledge and different contexts may be important, what ultimately matters is the text itself. In many instances this is all that is available. Anyone looking at a text without background knowledge (which is the case for many audiences) can only determine meaning by looking at the text. Textual analysis focuses solely on the textual content and the textual processes used—the language, the way it was photographed, the kinds of camera movements involved, and so on.

It is impossible to make full sense of a text (to give it a meaning) in isolation. Texts produce meanings by referring to the world outside themselves and by using pre-existing codes of representation. Audience members have to have knowledge of the real world to which the text refers and knowledge of the conventions of the text's medium (its photographic, cinematic, or televisual codes of representation).

The biographical film, *The King's Speech*, for example, will mean more to people who have some knowledge of the life and times of King George VI and the context of Britain's war with Germany in World War II. Similarly, Quentin Tarantino's *Inglourious Basterds* won't mean as much to people if they don't know details about World War II and the Nazi occupation in France. This film rewrites certain elements of history, yet some knowledge of the historical context is required to properly appreciate the changes that are made. Films also communicate by working with the codes and conventions of narrative films in general, such as the use of continuity editing, and the historical drama and the war film in particular. When you have some existing knowledge about these events and genres, you can make good sense of such films.

Interpreting the meaning of the text depends on this understanding. In acknowledging these factors that influence the ways in which a text might be interpreted, we are beginning to refer to the codes and conventions the text is using in its production. Knowing the meaning of the text is dependent on these knowledges. The text's context is also being referred to, but the focus is still primarily on the text. Semiotic and structuralist approaches work in this way (see Parts 2 and 3).

Contexts

Production context (background textual knowledge)

It is helpful to know about the actual processes of the making of a text; this gives clues as to its meaning and illuminates the text in a number of ways.

1   Begin by finding out about the acknowledged motivations of those involved in production. Who wrote, filmed, or photographed the text? What did they say they were trying to do? What have they said about the text? What other work have they done that is relevant? Where several people are involved—as in film and television production, which has producers, directors, cinematographers, editors, music composers, costume designers, and so on—questions can be asked of all of them to find out what interactions went on between them. Try also to explore their unconscious intentions by finding out important personal details of their lives to see if these illuminate the text. The **auteur theory** approach to film studies is an example of this way of reading media products; it focuses on the director as the key figure one needs to know about in order to understand the film (Caughie 1981; Cook 1985, pp. 137–46).

A film's director, considered to be the author of the text, is assumed to have creative control over the project. Over the course of their careers, some directors develop distinctive signatures, consisting

auteur theory
The theory that films are the creative products of film directors and can be interpreted as their personal visions, marked by a unique 'signature style'.

of characteristic styles, favourite actors, themes, narrative structures, or motifs that brand their films. For instance, dramatic lighting, expressionist imagery, and outsiders or alienated characters often played by Johnny Depp or Helena Bonham Carter, are recurring motifs in the films of Tim Burton, whereas in television the showrunner Matthew Weiner has become known for his fastidious attention to period detail and his control over art direction in *Mad Men*. The auteur approach to screen media helps to elaborate on the aesthetic or artistic qualities of screen texts and the context of production, but it neglects to fully acknowledge that screen production is a collaborative process involving creative input from many sources, including the scriptwriter, cast, and crew.

2   Look at the conditions of production. What was being aimed for? What financial or political constraints were involved? Who commissioned the work? Where was it made? What social, political, and historical factors influenced the text? All these factors may have determined the outcome of the final text. Political economy approaches stress these elements.

Distribution context

Does it make a difference where and when we read media texts?

Texts do not just appear on their own. They always exist in a social situation, distributed in a specific context. Because the context of a text influences its meaning, it is important to understand this context to do textual analysis. The two main contexts are space and time: where the text is being read and when it is being read.

Space

Every text appears in a specific media space and in a wider social space. A magazine advertisement appears in a particular magazine and is sold in a particular shop, in a particular location—town, village, city, and so on—in a particular society and country. A television program appears on a particular television channel, and is seen in a particular room—bedroom, hotel room, sitting room, lecture theatre, and so on—all of which are specific social locations. These different spaces can influence the text's meaning: whether a particular advertisement appears in a teenage girls' magazine or a men's soft porn magazine, each of which has a different implied readership and a different social agenda, it will take on a different meaning. The same program screened on SBS, the ABC, or Channel 10 in Australia will be affected by the differing ideals of each of these channels and their audiences: multicultural and experimental broadcasting in the case of SBS, social responsibility in the case of the ABC, and commercial success in the case of Channel 10. In the United Kingdom, the same program shown on BBC, ITV, Channel 4, or SkyTV would also be affected by the differing aims and cultures of these channels. In South Africa the three different SABC channels each target a different demographic and have a different flavour and emphasis in terms of language, age, and focus.

Texts are not presented in isolation but are surrounded by other texts—magazine articles, television programs, and so on—that will in turn influence people's readings. Popular television texts used in an academic course will be seen and read differently because of the new context they are placed in. You may be watching *South Park* at home with your friends for entertainment and relaxation while you eat a Big Mac. Alternatively, you may be watching it in a university lecture theatre as part of a course of study; you may even be taking notes. Programs will even change meanings depending on who they are watched with—on our own, with friends, with parents, or with a group of strangers.

The importance of context can be easily seen by thinking of clothes as a kind of text. The meaning of articles of clothing will change depending on who is wearing them (man, woman, child) and where they are wearing them (at work, on the beach, at a party). Meanings are affected by and dependent on their context.

Taking this further, it is important to look at the wider social context any text appears in: images of Paris Hilton or Britney Spears, found all over the world, will have different meanings in different countries. Teenage girls from different ethnic and racial backgrounds in America, Europe, Bali, or Iraq, with different religious, social, and moral codes, will make different readings of Paris and Britney's appearance, songs, and performances (Fiske 1989a, pp. 95–113), while teenage boys will make another set of readings. The social norms and conventions of any culture will engage in an interplay with texts and will produce different readings and meanings. So, the placement of texts within their social and spatial contexts, and their relationship to other texts need to be considered.

Time

It is useful to notice the time of day that people engage with media texts and consider how that forms part of the context in which texts are interpreted. Many texts are produced to fit specifically with certain times of the day and are consumed or interpreted at these times. Newspapers are focused on mornings (the time associated with going to work). Although there are matinee sessions, movies are usually watched by most people in the evening and mostly on the weekend, in the context of leisure time. Television schedules are organised around what are perceived as normal patterns of work and family life, so that programs aimed at women predominate during weekdays, children's programs are usually shown in the early morning, after school and early evening, adult programs are screened after nine o'clock, sport broadcasts dominate during the weekends, and radio news bulletins are programmed hourly, on the hour. Thus texts have a specific time context that contributes to their meanings. Note that the internet is not governed by the usual spatiotemporal conventions. Internet news bulletins, for instance, do not focus on local issues as they can be accessed anywhere in the world, at any time. In fact, many internet users log on at times when there is less traffic.

On another level, we must locate texts in the specific historical times in which they are produced and consumed. Alfred Hitchcock's *Rear Window* was made in 1954 and represents a study of spectatorship at that time. Hitchcock was critiquing the voyeuristic practice of movie going and comparing it to spying on one's neighbours through the back window: the protagonist in *Rear Window*, immobilised and confined to his apartment as a result of a broken leg, uses binoculars and a photo-journalist's camera equipped with a zoom lens to intrude upon the private moments of his neighbours. In this film the medium is presented as a powerful source of knowledge, but it is also seen as invasive and problematic. The social concerns in *Rear Window* revolve around privacy, reflecting the paranoia in the USA arising from McCarthyism. (In the late 1940s and early 1950s US Senator Joseph McCarthy instigated the persecution of anyone suspected of being a communist or being sympathetic to communist politics, so the fear of being spied on was very real.) When watching *Rear Window* in the twenty-first century, because so much time has passed since the release of the movie, the social concerns it showcases and the technology it uses to explore those concerns may seem trivial or clichéd, yet audiences may also derive pleasure and comfort from a sense of nostalgia as the story seems to come from a more secure and easier world than ours.

The ending of the film *Fight Club* did not provoke audience upset when the film was first released but after the events of 11 September 2001, television stations withdrew it from screenings because its ending looked so similar to the destruction of the Twin Towers.

You should by now be realising that study of any media text involves a potentially huge and ever-expanding area of knowledge in relation to understanding terms of the text itself and all the different contexts it might inhabit. Consequently, our readings are never complete; we must be open to finding new factors, such as new background information and different aspects of the social and historical context, which will affect our readings. The more information we have, the closer we get to understanding what a particular text could mean and how it is able to produce such a meaning.

Audience

How can we analyse and understand media audiences?

All our efforts at finding the meanings of texts may come to grief when we confront the real audience. Theories of the reader or audience suggest that because readers produce meanings, and all readers are different, it is possible to come up with many readings and meanings in a text. Any reading may only hold for particular individuals. Therefore, any attempt to discover a meaning for a text that holds for more than one reader must rely on generalisations, and runs the risk of becoming overly reductive. While we accept that audiences make different readings, it is still valid to explore texts through examining their textual codes and social and historical contexts in the process of textual analysis. In doing so, we can look for a text's dominant reading. While this is a valuable part of studying texts, it doesn't account for how audiences actually read texts, and since, in a way, media texts don't meaningfully exist unless they are being read by someone, this question must be considered.

A large body of work focusing on media audiences acknowledges that the contexts, practices, and processes of reception are just as important in generating meaning as the context of production, the text itself, and the medium by which the message is communicated. This branch of media studies is known as **reception studies**.

> **reception studies**
> The study of how audiences actively receive, read, consume, and interact with media texts.

The inscribed reader

When the way audiences engage with media texts is looked at, consideration needs to be given to what communication theorist Paul Willeman has called an '**inscribed reader**' (Fiske 1987, p. 62). The inscribed reader can best be understood as a receptive member of the target market to which the media text is deliberately addressed. When considering the nature of the inscribed reader of a particular text, ask yourself whether the message seems to assume that the receiver is male, female, wealthy, poor, highly educated, image conscious, young, old, a member of a certain nationality, and so forth.

> **inscribed reader**
> An ideal reader who is constructed by the text, or who is imagined/intended by the producers of the text.

The actual reader

There are a number of ways that actual audiences, or the **actual reader**, can be studied. We can engage in audience research, looking not at texts and the meanings they contain, but at audiences and the meanings they extract from or ascribe to media texts. We need to observe, interview, and interact with audiences as, and after, they read media texts, we need to watch them watching, or reading, or listening to media texts. We can also develop theories that understand and explain the process of being an audience. These theories examine what is happening when people read texts. You can study your own responses and readings and compare them with other people's as a way to understand this method. Audience research is a crucial part of media studies, as it completes the circle of text, production, and consumption.

> **actual reader**
> The real flesh and blood individuals who interpret or read texts.

Audience research and theories about audiences

Audience research has understood the audience in two different ways: in terms of effects and in terms of reception. Effects studies (see pp. 19–20, 45–51, 99) look at how audiences are directly affected by the media—the media are theorised as things that make them a 'vulnerable' audience. Reception studies, which emerged in the 1970s, look at how audiences are active: in other words, how they use and interpret the media (Cunningham & Turner 2009, pp. 74–6).

Media scholars are not the only people who conduct studies of audiences. Audience research is very significant for the media industries themselves. Companies such as Nokia, for instance, invest a great deal in research that indicates how media consumers might use their mobile phones, and organisations such as MTV use focus groups, ratings, and other forms of audience research as a way of finding out how successful they are and for testing new products. In youth media, the advertising executives who undertake effects research have become known as 'cool hunters', or 'merchants of cool', such is their investment in the science of defining, packaging, and marketing images that will brand their merchandise as cool in the eyes of young people. Research falls into two areas: quantitative and qualitative.

> Is it more important to know how many people watch a program or to know what they feel about it?

Quantitative research looks at numbers: for example, how many people watch a particular program (ratings research provides this information). Qualitative research is concerned with how people are actually responding to specific programs: why they like or dislike certain programs, what aspects they respond to positively or negatively, and whether they watch attentively or have media such as television and radio on for the sake of companionship and background noise. This type of qualitative research falls within the reception studies area.

The media try to perfect techniques for measuring the nature of audience response, which they then use as a guide to improving their products. They use preview audiences to test drive films. In these previews, audiences are asked to give their responses to the film. If some parts of the film don't work for enough people, then the producers can change them. The film *Blade Runner* is a well-known example. After initial audience previews it was decided to introduce a voice-over commentary and change the ending to romanticise and simplify the text. At the time, the revised version of the movie proved more popular with the preview audiences. Some years later the cult success of the movie prompted the release of the 'director's cut'—the version Ridley Scott preferred to that dictated by the producers. This is a common phenomenon now, one example being *Donnie Darko*, but the release of directors' cuts still has to be approved by the producers, and they are only released when it is expected that they will make a profit.

Political parties aim to make party political broadcasts that will win the support of the electorate. The preview process for speeches and broadcasts now measures audience response moment by moment, with audiences pressing buttons to indicate their responses when they are asked to choose between such given responses as pleasure/boredom, trust/distrust, and so on. A profile is built up of the most successful kinds of electioneering, and this profile is then built into the finished products. Market research is all about measuring the numbers of audience members or consumers, and their likes and dislikes. It is a way of winning markets, and so it can be said that audience research is part of the market economy of the media. Considerable money and effort are put into this work.

In contrast to audience research conducted by commercial interests, audience research conducted as part of scholarly media studies, which is considerably less well funded than its commercial counterpart, claims to come from a disinterested perspective. Effects research, mentioned earlier, devises experiments to test audience responses to programs, including direct measuring of brainwaves and physical reactions, and observation and measurement of actions and behaviour after watching programs. The findings from such research are inconclusive, partly because fear, surprise, and desire can generate similar physiological responses.

How can we understand the relationship between media and audiences?

There is a variety of ways of understanding the media–audience relationship.

1 *Direct effects* The **direct effects** model is sometimes also called the 'hypodermic model' or the 'magic bullet theory of communication', indicating that media producers inject or shoot their intended meaning directly into the audience. The audience absorbs the message like a sponge, or as drugs absorbed into the bloodstream. This reflects the belief that the media are capable of radically affecting people's behaviour and beliefs to such an extent that they can be used for the purposes of political propaganda. The direct effects model of media audiences assumes that media consumers accept the intended meaning encoded in media messages with relative passivity, and that the relationship between media producers and consumers is predictable and asymmetrical. There is a power imbalance: producers of the media messages have more control over meaning, and the transmission of information is largely one-way, with limited audience feedback or input. This view originated in the 1930s when the media were being used by the Nazis in Germany, by the communists in the Soviet Union, and by advertisers and political parties in the USA. This view suggests that if you have control of the media, you can control people's minds, beliefs, and actions according to the process represented in Figure 6.2.

> direct effects
> The direct-effects model of communication (also called the 'hypodermic model') suggests that the media transmits powerful messages to audience members, who absorb the meaning passively and are strongly affected by it.

all-powerful media ⟶ brainwashing ⟶ audience

Figure 6.2 Direct effects model of the media–audience relationship

reinforcement
The media reinforces ideas and feelings that other social institutions are already communicating.

2   *Reinforcement* The **reinforcement** model (represented in Figure 6.3) refines the direct effects approach by suggesting that the media work in conjunction with social forces to influence people when their messages coincide with ideas being produced elsewhere in society— through education, the family, the churches, and so on. Media theorist Paul Lazarsfeld's influential audience research suggests that the media are most effective when they work to reinforce existing beliefs, values, and behaviours (Lazarsfeld & Stanton 1949). Lazarsfeld's work indicates that people often tend to ignore or resist information that does not reinforce their existing experiences and opinions; however, the media can play a significant role in activating interpersonal channels of communication, especially when messages reinforce the beliefs of opinion leaders, who then pass on the media message to others within their sphere of influence, and so forth.

Figure 6.3   Reinforcement model of the media–audience relationship

cultivation
The media has a cumulative effect on audiences. Long-term exposure to media cultivates attitudes and beliefs through the persistent repetition of messages and images.

3   *Cultivation* A large body of research into **cultivation** suggests that it would be unwise to dismiss the long-term, cumulative effects of screen media on society. In an article entitled 'Cultivation Revisited', media researchers Jonathan Cohen and Gabriel Weimann state that:

> One of the more fruitful avenues of research has suggested examining the effects of television on viewers' attitudes and beliefs, rather than on their behaviors. According to cultivation theory, massive exposure to television's reconstructed realities can result in perceptions of reality very different from what they might be if viewers watched less television. In other words, the highly stylized, stereotyped, and repetitive images portrayed on television have been regarded as an important source of socialization and everyday information (Cohen & Weimann 2000, p. 99).

Note that different media texts and genres offer different images of the world. While the news, thrillers, and crime fiction may contribute to the development of a 'mean world' perspective, romantic comedies will do quite the opposite.

4 *Desensitisation* Another key effect that researchers think the media may have is **desensitisation**. Researchers predict that long-term exposure to certain types of media images can build up a tolerance to things that would otherwise be troubling. Repeatedly watching the combination of humour with graphic violence in films such as *The Killer Inside Me*, *RED* (*Retired Extremely Dangerous*), and *Inglourious Basterds*, for instance, might make us less sensitive to media violence, and less likely to have a shocked response to actual violence or to perceive violence and aggression as bad. Some researchers go so far as to link media violence to actual aggression in this way:

> The first exposure to violent media can make a person (especially children) anxious and fearful. Repeated exposure reduces these effects and leaves the viewer wanting stronger doses of violence ... repeated exposure to violent media, for example, a couple of hours a day for 15 years, causes a serious increase in the likelihood of a person becoming a habitually aggressive person and occasionally a violent offender (Bushman & Anderson 2001, pp. 481–2).

5 *Observational learning and cognitive scripts* One of the explanatory frameworks that currently holds most credence regarding the effects of the media on young audiences is the theory of **observational learning** of social behaviour and **cognitive scripts** (see Bandura 1994). This theory suggests that people learn how to behave by observing role models in action and by remembering the script that was performed so that they can play the part later, should a similar situation arise. A script is like a program or narrative that offers ways of behaving or dealing with particular circumstances; it can be derived from witnessing real or fictional interactions. Research indicates that 'Scripts for behaviour are also constructed early in development, and it is likely that continued exposure to media violence influences the development of aggressive scripts' (Dubow & Miller 1996, p. 136). The script is most likely to be retrieved, mimicked, and progressively reinforced if the situation an individual faces is very similar to the one seen on film or television, if the screen violence is very realistic, if the person identifies with the role model, and if the actor receives positive reinforcements or is perceived as having desirable characteristics, such as being attractive, wealthy, or powerful (Geen 1994, p. 157; Bushman & Huesmann 2001, pp. 236–7).

6 *Uses-and-gratifications* (Blumler & Katz 1974) The **uses-and-gratifications** understanding of the media–society dynamic (represented in Figure 6.4) is significant for bringing the concepts of pleasure and gratification into debate about the media, and it paved the way for more recent research that argues that audiences are not just passive consumers brainwashed by media products, but are active participants who make their own meanings.

desensitisation
Long-term exposure to media can make audiences progressively less sensitive or responsive to images and messages that made a strong impression when first encountered.

observational learning and cognitive scripts
People learn how to behave by observing how their role models act and by remembering the script that was performed so that if, later, they encounter a similar situation they can play the part.

uses-and-gratifications
Audiences use the media in unpredictable ways (through selection, interpretation, and integration with other everyday activities) to please themselves, not necessarily as media producers intend it to be used.

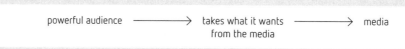

Figure 6.4 Uses-and-gratifications model of the media–audience relationship

Such qualitative studies are often carried out through ethnographic work, which explores audience responses through a mixture of direct observation, interviewing, and research. This model acknowledges that audience members often use television, radio, and other media as a background to everyday activities, such as cooking, domestic tasks, and studying. In such instances the audience might gain pleasure from using the media as a form of companionship, but they are unlikely to experience direct effects in response to media content as they may only glance or gaze at the television, scan news headlines, or listen inattentively or infrequently to the radio. The uses-and-gratifications model suggests that direct media effects are impossible to measure due to the infinitely variable, personalised contexts of reception.

Audience research based on an ethnographic model

Hall (1980), and then Morley (1992), worked with Hall's encoding/decoding model of communication. This model suggests that different kinds of decoding or readings of media texts are possible, including

preferred reading
Audiences accept what is being presented without questioning the meaning intended by the media producers.

negotiated reading
Audiences accept only some of what is being presented to them.

alternative/oppositional reading
Audiences interpret a text completely against the preferred reading.

polysemic
A sign that has more than one possible meaning.

- **preferred readings**—audiences accept what is being presented without question
- **negotiated readings**—audiences negotiate with the text's intended meaning and accept only some of what is being presented to them
- **alternative/oppositional readings**—audiences read completely against the preferred reading.

The word '**polysemic**' comes from the Greek words *poly* (many) and *seme* (meaning). 'Polysemic' thus means many meanings. While the polysemic nature (see pp. 145–6) of media texts does provide the possibility for multiple interpretations, these readings 'correspond to the reader's response to his or her social conditions not to the structure of the text' (O'Sullivan et al. 1994, p. 239). Fiske and media theorist Tim O'Sullivan give an example of how these three types of reading might occur in relation to one media text:

We might take potential readings of a series of advertisements portraying women as sex objects, clothes horses, or mother figures. A preferred reading according to the dominant-hegemonic code is to accept and agree with this portrayal as natural, accurate, and attractive. A negotiated reading may be produced by a middle-class career woman who broadly accepts the preferred reading, but 'for others, not for me!' She reserves the right to produce her own reading of the ads which corresponds to her social position as an independent woman. An oppositional reading might be produced by a feminist as insulting, degrading, restricting and proof of men's exploitation of women. The first reading could be produced by women who would buy the products, the second by women who might, if it suited their purposes, and the third by women who would not (O'Sullivan et al. 1994, pp. 239–40).

Morley was interested in seeing how social groups, rather than individuals, make readings, so he looked at trade unionists, young people, and people of colour, expecting to find that they would make readings that would support their own class, ethnic, or youth subcultural values.

The idea of researching audiences as social groups has been productive. An ethnographic approach has been developed by researchers who have studied women as audiences of soap operas (Hobson 1982; Brunsdon 1986). A considerable amount of work has been done exploring the way women read popular women's texts (such as magazines, melodramas, and romance novels) in a way that makes these texts meaningful to them (Ang 1985, 1991; Radway 1987). This work looked closely at the social circumstances in which women consume the media and how they relate media texts and technologies to their real lives. Fiske (1989a) has developed the notion of audiences being able to resist what is presented to them. He argues that audiences have considerable power over the texts they consume. Other researchers have explored audience readings of Madonna, particularly those made by young women, people of colour, and gays (Schwichtenberg 1993). Dyer and others have looked at how gay and lesbian audiences read the media, as in Dyer's analysis of readings of Judy Garland (Dyer 1987, pp. 141–94). Again, these studies show how audiences make use of texts from their particular perspectives. An extensive audience analysis is found in cultural studies theorist Henry Jenkins' *Textual Poachers*, in which he looks at a whole range of activities and ways of reading by different groups and people, particularly in relation to the *Star Trek* series (Jenkins 1992; Tulloch & Jenkins 1995). The poaching idea suggests more ways of readers altering the texts and becoming active rather than passive. In their efforts to understand how the media influence or affect us, media industries and social researchers will look for new ways of understanding and researching the text–audience relationship.

Audience projections

Do our individual personalities influence our media readings?

We want to introduce a final approach that draws on theories of **projection**. This is a term that was used by psychologists Sigmund Freud and Carl Gustav Jung. The central idea is that in texts audiences see aspects of themselves, which they are not consciously aware of, mirrored back. This relates to the wider concept that in everything

projection
People project their own unconscious feelings onto other people or objects; they see in objects and other people aspects of themselves reflected back.

we see around us we find a reflection of ourselves. Of course, this isn't literally true, but what is being suggested is that the way we see, interpret, and respond to the external world and to other people is a reflection of our own, unconscious, internal state. Another way of putting this is that we project ourselves onto the world and other people. This is a basic tenet of much work in the fields of psychology and psychotherapy.

I, Michael, realised this when I started listening closely to what I and others said when we were interpreting media texts. I understood that I was projecting myself, my view of the world, onto the text. In preparation for a course on melodrama, I watched D W Griffith's short film *Mender of Nets* with two friends. Discussing the film afterwards, each of us had a very different reading of the ending, in which the actress Lillian Gish is left on her own. One of us said with optimism, 'Ah well, she's learnt a lot. It will be better next time.' The second said despairingly, 'Of course, relationships never work.' The third reflected that 'All men are bastards!' The three readings (all of which could fit the text) reflected the views on relationships that we held at that time. We had projected ourselves into the text.

Consequently, if you are trying to understand how audiences read texts, you can use the idea of projection and argue that any one person's reading of a text is a reflection of themselves: that is, they project their own ideas and feelings on to the text. Our conscious and our unconscious feelings and beliefs will be reflected in the way we interpret a text. This is a simple but also quite startling idea.

This approach takes us into analysis of how the mechanisms of cinematic identification work for individuals rather than groups, and begins to tap into our unconscious readings, which are notoriously difficult to ascertain.

Two common student questions about textual analysis

Students analysing texts often raise two related and significant issues, as expressed in the following questions.

> Did the producers consciously intend to create the meanings we see in texts?
> Aren't we reading too much into the text?

Finding out the intentions of the producers of media texts is of some use, particularly because the intention to sell, persuade, or entertain is usually profit driven and guided by vested interests on the part of the media producers. It is a good idea to be mindful of who might benefit from a text being interpreted and responded to in a particular manner. However, the following points suggest it doesn't matter that many audience members don't know the specific intentions of media producers because the meanings audiences draw from texts are not necessarily derived from or even related to understandings of the intentions of the texts' producers.

1 Textual analysis focuses mainly on the practices of representation evident in media texts, and on the content of the media images and words. Meaning is inseparable from interpretation, that is, meaning is not activated until it is extracted from a text because meaning is essentially about understanding. The best intentions in the world and the most careful and explicit encoding of meaning will literally mean nothing unless someone reads, views, or hears the text and attributes some significance to it. It is the act of interpretation that brings the text to life.

2 A central argument in this book is that much of what motivates people ideologically and aesthetically exists at an unconscious level (see p. 175). Sexist and racist stereotypes are so deeply embedded in the culture in which we live that they may become part of our unconscious, thus influencing the texts that we produce and our understanding of the texts we consume.

3 Media studies does not just look at the intentions of authors but also takes a wider view. It is concerned with how people read and make sense of the texts in their overall social context, and because of this it looks at audiences and explores the relationships between production, mediation, consumption, and meaning, rather than focusing on the intentions of the producers of media texts alone.

4 Many media texts are the product not of a single person, but of large groups of people working within the constraints of the media industry. Individual intention can sometimes be lost in this collective form of production.

In relation to the common student question, 'Aren't we reading too much into texts?', there is a useful distinction between reading things into a text (projection) and reading things out of a text (exegesis). If the reading comes purely from the reader, then that particular reading may be of little value in determining the meaning, although it tells you interesting things about the reader. You can ensure that a particular reading is coming out of a text by paying close attention to the codes and conventions, structure, and composition of the piece, by acquiring knowledge of its cultural context, and by checking to see if the meaning you derive from the text resonates for other readers.

Conclusion

Text, context, and audience need to be taken account of when trying to analyse the meanings of texts. Media meanings are dependent on the text itself, on its context, and its audience. As we take more and more aspects into account, we aim to get closer to seeing the potential and actual meanings of a text. There won't be one simple answer to what a text means, but we argue here that some readings and meanings are more complete than others.

This book offers a variety of approaches for reading texts: semiological analysis, analysis of narrative structure, mythological analysis, socio-cultural analysis, political economy approaches, and ideological and discourse analysis. In your work you will gradually be able to use all these approaches in the study of any one text. As long as you make clear what aspects of the text you are focusing on—whether it be background information, textual codes, social and historical context, or actual audience research—then you will be able to support the readings of texts you make and the meanings you see in them.

This chapter has

- explored the potential meanings of texts
- considered the importance of text, contexts, and audiences in these meanings
- looked at various theories of media audiences, including direct effects, reinforcement, uses-and-gratifications, ethnographic research, and projection.

Discussion points

1   How can the contexts of space and time affect readings of media texts?
2   Do you ever see situations in which you or other people appear to be behaving by following a media script (for example imitating characters from *The Simpsons*, *South Park*, or *The Big Bang Theory*, or saying in an American accent 'd'oh!' or 'Like, oh my God!')? What affects are these behavioural scripts having on social interaction?
3   Which of all the approaches to audience studies discussed in the chapter do you find most useful and why?
4   What are the strengths and weaknesses of these different approaches?

Summary

You should now be able to

- explain the difference between a text and its context
- explain what different factors need to be taken into account when reading a media text
- explain, with examples, why these factors are important
- explain the difference between the inscribed reader and the actual reader
- explain the terms 'dominant/preferred reading', 'negotiated reading', and 'alternative/oppositional reading'
- explain what the differences between quantitative and qualitative audience research are and show what is valuable for each kind of research
- give an overview and explanation of different audience theories and research methods
- explain the terms 'textual analysis', 'auteur theory', 'reinforcement', 'uses-and-gratification', 'cultivation', and 'desensitisation'
- explain and illustrate how the theory of projection relates to audiences.

CHAPTER 7

New Media and Technological Development

We've entered a new era of virtuality, where the interpenetration of a plethora of communications media, from CCTV and mobile phones to webcams and cable channels, has created an environment in which never before have so many watched so many others, doing so very little.

Will Self, quoted in *The Media*

This chapter will

▶ identify the characteristics of new media

▶ consider the implications of technological development and its relationship to social change

▶ define technological determinism and the digital divide

▶ consider positive and negative aspects of technological change.

Technological development is nothing new: it has been happening since sticks and stones were first fashioned into rudimentary tools. It is the accelerated rate of change in recent years and its powerful impact on the role of the media in society that interests us here. This chapter explores technological developments in the media, and considers some positive and negative aspects of these developments.

At the end of the nineteenth century the technologies of film, photography, recording, telegraphy, and telephony were radically changing practices and patterns of human communication and behaviour. At the time people didn't know how these technologies would affect business, social relationships, and political communication. We are in a similar situation at the beginning of the twenty-first century with the latest media technologies. We don't know exactly what will happen but we can suggest some significant issues and note some of the contradictory possibilities of new media.

Characteristics of new media

digital media
Media such as digital videogames, the internet, and other forms of computerised media that mathematically process and convert whatever information needs to be represented into numerical form. The information can then be manipulated, reproduced, converted, shared, and transmitted in versatile, swift, immaterial ways.

analogue media
Analogue media such as photography, print, and radio use material processes and mechanical modes of representation to transcribe and transmit content in forms such as physical data or electrical signals.

The term 'new media' is often used very loosely, but it is worth pausing to consider what it means. Generally, new media refers to **digital media** as opposed to **analogue media**. Analogue media encodes information such as sounds or appearances into an 'analogous' form, such as printed words or painted pictures, transcribing the original into a physical representation. Analogue media can be tactile objects, such as books, photographs, and magazines, or the information can be further converted into a signal, such as light and soundwaves, which can be projected or broadcast to many recipients, as is the case with cinema, television, and radio. Without getting too technical, digitisation encodes information in numerical form (such as the binary system of zeros and ones used in computers). This mathematical information is a symbolic representation of the original data, just as paintings and typed words are symbolic representations; however, digital data can be stored, processed, compressed, manipulated, and multiplied far more readily as it is not bound to any physical artefact. Digitisation has revolutionised the ways information is mediated, modified, organised, produced, reproduced, distributed, and consumed. Wireless technologies such as satellite signals, cellular telephony, Bluetooth, and infrared further liberate the transmission of information from material and mechanical constraints such as telephone lines and electric cables.

Digitisation has been described by new media analyst Manuel Castells (2000, p. 2) as a 'universal language' that is able to unite different communities around the globe and that can customise and integrate the production of words, sounds, and images. New media or digital media are characterised by interactivity, immateriality (or virtuality), non-linearity and hypertextual networks, convergence, and decentralisation.

Interactivity

All media texts and technologies are interactive to a certain extent, in that people take an active role in textual production and interpretation; however, the term is usually used to refer to forms of communication in which the audience is able to use technology to manipulate the structure, sound, or image of the text itself. In this sense, interactivity is a property of the medium of communication that empowers the user.

Where conventional media allow media consumers agency in the way they receive and interpret media messages, digital technologies enable reciprocal, two-way communication, with a very fast feedback loop that promises to change the asymmetrical power relations of mass communication by giving citizens more choice and control. Interactivity can take different forms, offering different degrees of participation. Navigation through, say, a website or a series of sites involves choosing an individual pathway by clicking on hyperlinks to different sections of information according to the media user's needs and interests. Interactivity may also involve contributing to media texts, such as blogging (**blog** is short for 'web log'), chatting online, vodcasting, podcasting, editing a collaboratively authored webpage such as Wikipedia, or shopping online and uploading consumer reviews on sites such as Amazon or the Internet Movie Database (IMDB). In virtual environments, such as digital game worlds, users may experience a more immersive, participatory form of interaction (see below) in relation to virtual reality and immateriality.

blog
A blog (web log) is a website where people can record their diaries or other personal commentaries; often used as an alternative journalistic media outlet.

Immateriality and virtual reality

Digital media texts are 'dematerialised', as Lister et al. (2003, p. 16) put it, meaning that they are liberated from their physical form: for example, in semiotic terms the signified content of a photograph or book is separated from the signifier (the film negative or the paper) that carries the content. Immateriality (or virtuality) affects the way media users experience the media in that we no longer necessarily come into contact with a physical object, such as a book, a video, or a vinyl record, but it also affects virtual experiences of space, time, motion, and our own identities. We navigate the virtual 'desktop' on our computer screen to access 'cyberspace', which is a virtual space entered through a virtual 'window' on our computer screen. Via the mouse we use tools such as scissors, pencils, paperclips, and paste analogous to tools on our actual desk, and we open portals similar to actual windows in our offices or homes to access external spaces and places that hold information we want. Each of these virtual spaces or objects has a material counterpart or reference point. In this sense everyday life is lived to a large extent in immaterial screen space, which can be understood as a form of virtual reality.

Once in cyberspace we might 'visit sites' such as YouTube and 'open' other windows to view video clips, or we might immerse ourselves in a virtual reality construct, such as *Habbo Hotel*, *Blue Mars*, or *Second Life*, which is furnished with interactive avatars, a graphic interface, and even its own economy. In 2009 the *Second Life* virtual goods economy reportedly grew to US$567 million. A virtual world such as *Second Life* or its offline cousin, *Sims*, involves another level of immersion in virtual reality—a simulated reality in which fantasy identities can be constructed without the need for the user's physical body to bear a close relationship to the identity projected to others. This liberating aspect of new media has been lauded as a harbinger of equality because in the virtual environment of cyberspace it is not possible to discriminate against people on the basis of corporeal stigma such as age, skin colour, weight, gender, appearance, or physical ability. Race, sex, and disabilities, for instance, are rendered invisible so racism, sexism, and discrimination on the basis of physical disability are, theoretically, eliminated and online communities are organised according to the shared interests of disembodied participants. Despite the initial popularity of *Second Life*, the rise of Twitter and Facebook has overshadowed involvement in virtual worlds. Sometimes people forget that screen media space is not just a virtual world—it has an interface with reality. For instance, champion swimmer Stephanie Rice lost sponsorship support from Jaguar after she made an offensive tweet that many considered to promote homophobia in response to the Wallabies' rugby win against South Africa in a 2010 Tri-Nations game.

As the technology becomes more sophisticated, the differences between the real world and the virtual world are gradually blurring. Virtual real estate developers have made an actual fortune building and selling virtual properties for real money, often to new participants who don't want to start from scratch and gradually build up their online capital. This blurring of the boundaries between the real and the virtual is increasing as more convincing simulations of reality are made possible, and as media use penetrates ever more aspects of everyday life, thereby enabling a seamless interface between mediated and actual spaces, experiences, and modes of communication.

Non-linearity and networks

New media functions on the principle of networks rather than linear or hierarchical structures. Conventional media are often organised in such a way as to encourage audiences to follow a linear, one-way path through information. We are, for example, meant to listen to a radio interview from start to finish. The broadcast medium does not make it possible to start at the end and backtrack to the beginning of the interview, or to listen to all the questions first, followed by all the answers in reverse order. To do so would destroy the meaning of the interview. Some conventional media, such as books, offer more ways of manipulating the order of information by using the index to skip to the page that is of interest. New media are characterised by a much higher degree of non-linearity and indexicality, and are often structured as networks. Thus, once it is digitised, a radio interview transcript or a film can be organised into chunks of information that users can navigate through in much the same way they navigate through a book index or they might use an internet navigation bar to locate information and jump directly to a point of interest.

hypertext
Chunks of text or data connected by electronic links in a networked database. Hyperlinks enable the user to navigate through information along multiple, non-linear pathways.

The non-sequential way of organising and accessing digitally encoded information in new media is termed '**hypertext**'. The prefix 'hyper' refers to something that exceeds or extends over or beyond given limits, just as hyperlinks take a user outside or beyond a given web page. In *New Media*, Lister et al. define hypertext as

> a work which is made up from discrete units of material in which each one carries a number of pathways to other units. The work is a web of connection which the user explores using the navigational aids of the interface design. Each discrete 'node' in the web has a number of entrances and exits or links (2003, p. 24).

This principle of networked information originated with the development of the internet in the 1960s because the US Defense Department wanted to establish a computer system that could withstand a nuclear attack, re-routing packets of information through independent pathways to avoid losing data if the centralised computer system was destroyed. Not only is the internet itself and the individual websites that comprise it organised according to this non-linear network principle, but hypertextuality is also increasingly coming to characterise contemporary forms of storytelling (see media convergence below).

Convergence

Media convergence is a trend in which different media sources, such as newspapers, telephones, stereos, radios, and televisions merge or converge so that they can be accessed together by the one multipurpose machine. A personal computer can be used to read a newspaper and watch television episodes online, and a cell phone, such as Apple's iPhone, can be used to access email and use internet applications, navigate, take digital photos and videos, and listen to music. Convergence affects media consumption as is evident in the examples above. It also affects media distribution, ownership, and production. **Multiplatforming** refers to the same media content (for instance, a news story) being distributed across several different media forms or platforms: the same news story can be accessed in a newspaper, on the radio, on television, and online in print, audio, or audiovisual form. Multiplatforming itself is possible not only because of technological convergence and the flexibility enabled by digitisation, but also because of the conglomeration or convergence of ownership whereby one media corporation owns websites, newspapers and magazines, radio stations, game divisions, and television networks. This form of convergence of media ownership and control is described as **vertical integration**. The media giant News Corporation, for example, owns websites such as TeamXbox and Foxsports.com, the Fox broadcast network, and the Twentieth Century Fox movie and television studio, as well as many newspapers,

multiplatforming
A process of media convergence that involves distributing branded content across multiple outlets, for instance, the narrative and characters of a film or television franchise can be distributed as films, novels, games, soundtrack CDs, and as other merchandise, including clothes.

vertical integration
This term describes a concentration of power when a media company owns various parts of the production, distribution, and exhibition chain, for example printing presses, magazine companies, content providers such as photographic databases, the distribution vehicles, and retail outlets.

including *The Wall Street Journal* and *The Australian*, magazines such as *Vogue Living*, and sports teams such as the Melbourne Storm national rugby league team. Former holdings included the disgraced UK tabloid *News of the World*, which was closed down after a phone hacking journalistic ethics scandal in 2011. Vertical integration differs from **horizontal integration** whereby a media company owns several different types of the same part of the production process, such as a number of games development companies being owned by the same parent company. Disney, for example, also owns Miramax, and in December 2007 Vivendi combined its video games unit with Activision to form Activision Blizzard. In order to avoid creating corporate monopolies that limit fair competition and diverse outputs, regulations have been put in place to control convergence of ownership, as when Hollywood studios were prevented from owning the theatres that exhibited their films.

horizontal integration
This is a form of convergence of media ownership in which a corporation owns several companies involved in the same aspect of media production.

In terms of media production, convergence is having a noticeable effect on storytelling and communication strategies. The advent of blogs has shifted conceptions of news from an authoritative, 'objective', or balanced account of issues and events to more subjective commentary that blends journalism with journal writing; the popularity of home cinemas with surround sound and widescreen high-definition digital television (HDTV) is narrowing the distinction between film and television. Furthermore, the ways multiplayer online games such as *World of Warcraft* and game consoles such as Xbox, PlayStation, and the 3D, remote-control features of Nintendo's Wii can explore space and narrative in digital games has also influenced the way scriptwriters have developed narratives in films such as *Inception* and *Scott Pilgrim vs the World*, and in the disjunctive chronologies and interwoven storylines of television programs such as *Ringer* and *Dexter*. This last example, *Dexter*, demonstrates clearly how pervasive media convergence and trans-media storytelling are becoming. The television series is not only *influenced* by online media, comics, and graphic novels (as evident in the 'Dark Defender' comic book superhero storyline and the animated 'Early Cuts' webisodes), it is also partly *dependent* on web-based clues and an active online cult fan base, to the extent that internet activity surrounding the series has *been channelled into* an online game.

Dexter Game On, also known as the 'Infinity Killer' game, is an alternate reality game (ARG) and an example of trans-media storytelling that combines techniques of television narration with interactive, immersive gaming conventions, demonstrating multiplatforming and media convergence, and the formation of a collaborative online community that uses its collective intelligence to solve the puzzle of the game. According to screen theorist Jason Mittell

> ARGs are an interesting cult phenomenon taking advantage of the ubiquitous role media play in our daily lives. Typically ARGs are launched subtly with a few well-placed clues (or 'rabbit holes'), leading players into a trail of websites, phone numbers, newspaper ads, and physical

events that posit an alternate immersive reality with embedded mysteries and puzzles. An ARG by its definition must operate in secret, as the goal is to obscure the boundaries between an emerging storyline and real life (<http://flowtv.org/?p=165>).

Mittell (2006) points out the contradiction of asking audiences to believe in and participate in an alternate reality that they have already conceptualised as fictional on television. While this creates a tension between the two media, ARGs can also be symbiotic as they feed back into the television series and provide new story threads when producers tap into the ideas and theories users discuss online.

As these news and entertainment examples suggest, convergence of media technologies can lead to a standardisation of content that can decrease the substance and efficiency of communication, but it can also enrich communication by providing more options for senders and receivers of messages and by enabling the creation of multimodal texts that combine a variety of media forms.

Decentralisation

Decentralisation refers to the dispersal and personalisation of new media in contrast with conventional media, and to the higher degree of market segmentation and fragmentation that characterises new media. There has been a shift from a central one-to-many mass communication or broadcast system in which one source or input signal is transmitted simultaneously to many recipients, to a networked, many-to-many model of media production, transmission, and consumption in which there are multiple inputs, outputs, and connections. The media have been integrated into and dispersed throughout many aspects of everyday life and, as Lister et al. write, 'Consumption of media texts has been marked by a shift from a limited number of standardised texts to a very large number of highly differentiated texts. The media audience has fragmented and differentiated' (2003, p. 30). These changes to texts and audiences mean that for some media, such as subscription television, the business model and industry goals have shifted considerably: subscription television is not reliant on audience ratings to secure advertisers in the same way as broadcast television. The goal of cable stations such as HBO and Showtime is to achieve high levels of audience loyalty to at least one quality television series so that people will continue their monthly subscriptions.

In addition to the dispersal of audiences and corresponding changes in the industry, media production has become decentralised in that ordinary citizens have become producers of blogs, digital videos, and other media. Formerly, media production required expensive capital, such as a printing press or a broadcast licence, whereas now it only requires access to a computer with an internet connection or a modern cell phone to record and disseminate text, images, and sounds. Such digital media are called 'prosumer' technologies because they equalise the power balance between media producers and consumers, in some cases eliminating the distinction between them altogether so that people using such technologies are termed 'produsers' (producer-consumers). As discussed below, the participatory and democratic freedoms that such media technologies offer are counterbalanced by the potential for technological development to be used for surveillance and other mechanisms that limit the freedoms of citizens.

The most radical recent advance in the decentralisation and dispersal of new media involves ongoing developments in multimodal wireless communication technologies that are 'diffusing around the world faster than any other communication technology to date' (Castells et al. 2007, p. 1). To give an example of the blinding speed at which new media is spreading, the number of cellular phone subscribers in Africa recently rose about 2000 per cent in a five-year period (Castells et al. 2007, p. 23). As mobile phones become more sophisticated, and the cost of wirelessly accessing the internet decreases, and download speed increases, high levels of cell phone penetration may enable developing nations to leapfrog ahead without having to invest in costly fixed line infrastructure and personal computer hardware and software, particularly if Wi-Fi systems are also set up to provide the possibility of free access to digital information in public places. Other colourfully named wireless technologies and devices, such as Bluetooth, Infrared, and Blackberry then enable that digital information to be shared very easily, leading to further levels of dispersal and interconnectivity.

Case study: Television convergence, digitisation, and interactivity

In Australia the analogue television signal began to be switched off in 2010. By the end of 2013 all television will be broadcast in digital form, as is already happening to varying degrees worldwide. Because of differences between film and television (such as image resolution, the size and shape of television screens compared to those of cinema, distractions of the domestic environment of television reception, and the constraints of shooting schedules, budgets, and the studio environment), television has traditionally had a more limited audiovisual style. Most television productions emphasise close-ups and use less mobile framing and less sophisticated layers of sound than feature films. The introduction of HDTV, which compresses more data into an audiovisual image, is making the style and quality of television productions more cinematic. Indeed, the period TV series *Mad Men* is actually shot on 35mm film for the retro look, which suggests that celluloid may be destined for a niche aesthetic in productions aiming for a nostalgic look and feel. At the same time, more television shows and feature films are being shot in 3D or on high-definition digital video instead of celluloid (*The Curious Case of Benjamin Button* and *Avatar*, for example), and are using serialised narratives to capitalise on allegiance to characters in a way similar to television (as has the *Pirates of the Caribbean* quadrilogy, and superhero film franchises). HDTV can be filmed and watched in wide screen format, and LCD and PLASMA screens and home entertainment systems with surround sound and a digital game interface are very popular. These developments demonstrate the convergence of film and television, but television is also converging with the internet.

Increasingly, subscription to multiple-channel cable and satellite television, the streaming of television episodes online via sites such as YouTube, AOL, MSN, and MySpace, and the use of BitTorrent to globalise the release dates of popular television series means that people are able to access programs they want whenever they want. This shifts power away from the linear, centralised scheduling timetables of the television networks. Whereas television used to **broadcast** material designed to appeal to a broad, nationwide audience, now producers can operate on **narrowcast** principles, targeting specialist markets and niche audiences.

broadcast
A means of media transmission that makes information available to a broad spectrum of the population.

narrowcast
Narrowcast media transmission caters for small groups of people.

Interactivity is also transforming television. TiVo (see <www.tivo.com>), for example, offers home networking features such as podcasts, Yahoo! Weather & Traffic, local movie schedules, and online shopping for entertainment tickets — all accessed through the television via a keyboard connected to the TiVo set top box. This kind of interactive television has arisen from digitisation and the empowerment of media consumers. Increased consumer choice relates to increasing personalised control over scheduling, the ability to bypass advertisements, and the ability to access the internet via the television.

Digital video recorders (DVRs), also known as personal video recorders (PVRs), and services such as TiVo and Foxtel's IQ demonstrate how technological developments are accelerating media convergence and changing relationships between media producers, consumers, and technologies. DVRs function in the same way as standard VCRs, with the added advantage of having a hard drive on which digital media programming can be stored. This offers users greater agency as they can skip commercials, or program personal details and preferences into the hard drive so it will automatically record favourite shows. TiVo offers a season pass (recording every episode of a series automatically), and is capable of scanning available program selections to search for programs featuring actors on a user's wish list, or using its own initiative to record new programs its user may enjoy, based on previous viewing preferences.

The ability of this technology to collect information about its user and create a consumer profile is similar to the way Facebook's facial recognition software allows automated identification and tagging of photographs and Amazon gives customers personalised notification of new releases, based on their searches and sales history. However, consumer profiling raises concerns about privacy because media producers can use such details as ammunition for aggressive marketing strategies and government agencies or other groups can coopt facial recognition software for purposes such as surveillance. Since websites and DVRs can hold information such as credit card details to facilitate online commerce, and since interactive media are designed for two-way information flows, concerns about confidentiality are very real results of technological convergence. Indeed, services such as TiVo collect and sell information about consumer preferences to television networks so that they can target the audience more effectively.

Implications of new media

Technological determinism is the belief that technological innovation reshapes social life and drives social change. Marshall McLuhan, who is famous for saying that 'The medium is the message', could be described as a technological determinist. In other words, the technological medium itself is of paramount importance because the means used to communicate a message has a social logic that informs the way we think, the way we represent things, and the way we perceive and extend ourselves into the world, which implies that new forms of cultural interaction come into being as a result of technological change. We are beginning to see ourselves as global citizens in part because new communication technologies have enabled us to network and relate to each other in this way. Two examples are how the internet facilitates instantaneous global communication and Slingbox technology enables US cable television subscribers to access and view their cable service anywhere in the world that a satellite uplink is available. The concept of technological determinism also suggests that different media also lead to different ways of organising knowledge and power. Communications theorist Neil Postman claims that all technology has an 'embedded ideology' that comes encoded with a value system or 'an ideological bias, a predisposition to construct the world as one thing rather than another, to value one thing over another' (1993, p. 13). Print media, for example, privileges sight, literacy, education, and the print media producer, correlating with a fairly impersonal, linear, rational way of thinking and relating to others. Newer media forms, such as wireless mobile communication and computer-mediated communication, offer increasing interactivity, autonomy, and choice on the part of the user, as well as unprecedented personal control over the production, manipulation, and distribution of content.

Figure 7.1 Weapon of mass distraction

Source: Courtesy of Laugh it Off

The weapon of mass distraction image (Figure 7.1) illustrates different possible positions in relation to technological determinism and the reciprocal influence of media technology on society. It shows a human brain literally plugged in to a television set, suggesting that humans are the power source and creative input that fuels the development of media texts and technologies, but also that the media distracts us from real life concerns and determines, to a certain extent, what we think about.

With regard to technological determinism, Castells' position is that there is a two-way or dialectical interaction between technology and society: 'Technology does not determine society: it embodies it. But nor does technology determine technological innovation: it uses it' (2000, p. 5), which suggests that technology and society are mutually constitutive, rather than that one is driven by the other. Without necessarily taking a technological determinist stance, it is clear that media digitisation does have a number of social, political, legal, and economic implications that are worth considering. These include the digital divide, democratisation, issues to do with media piracy, copyright law, and corporate monopolies, and changes in social behaviour related to new ways in which the media are involved in everyday life.

The digital divide

At present there exists a digital divide, an economic division between people who have access to the new media and those who do not, and a skill division between those who are comfortable with the new media and those who are not (see p. 5). As Castells writes, 'While technology per se does not determine technological evolution and social change, technology (or the lack of it) embodies the capacity of societies to transform themselves' (2000, p. 7).

The economic division can be seen in terms of those who have technology and those who do not. Globally, there is a broad split between north and south global hemispheres, between developed and developing nations, and between rich and poor nations. Access to computer technologies, the internet, and mobile-phone technology is predominantly available to the better-off. This is not just experienced internationally, but also within countries where some people have access to new technologies but many don't (such as people of colour, elderly people, and those living in isolated rural areas). As Castells writes:

> Differential timing in access to the power of technology for people, countries and regions is a critical source of inequality in our society. The switched-off areas are culturally and spatially discontinuous: they are in the American inner cities or in the French *banlieues*, as much as in the shanty towns of Africa or in the deprived rural areas of China or India (2000, p. 33).

The danger is that the digital divide can increase the ever-widening gap between the haves and the have-nots, but as the technology develops and its prices drop, it becomes more readily available; there is evidence that the new technologies are being eagerly taken up across the globe. People with low incomes, say, may find purchasing a computer prohibitively expensive, but they can budget for a mobile phone with prepaid billing: 'The availability of prepaid systems has made it possible for the global telephone divide to be narrowed more rapidly than the internet divide' (Castells et al. 2007, p. 32). At the same time as this is happening wireless technology is facilitating the interchange of ideas and goods, and therefore technological developments have the potential for increasing global equality.

The skill division is predominantly generational. Author Marc Prensky has described 'two tribes' of digital users: the 'digital immigrants' and the 'digital natives' (Prensky 2004). The digital natives, anyone under 25 and a lot of people between 25 and 40, have grown up with computers, video games, and the internet; they have no fear of these technologies and turn to them first as sources of entertainment, information, and communication. The new technologies are not second nature to digital immigrants, who include older people, even if they do manage to use such technologies. (There is a third group who simply avoid, fear, and don't know how to use the technologies—but these technophobes will soon die out!)

ICTs
Information and communication technologies, such as computers.

A potential impact of projects that aim to bolster the use of information and communication technologies (**ICTs**) among older people, poor people, and those who live in the developing world is that they make the developing world a more substantial target for marketing and for the dispersion of Western ideologies; however, when marginalised groups are neither represented in nor adequately served by the media and afforded equal access to it, the resulting inequity constitutes a danger to democracy:

> The ability to communicate is a basic human right that is denied to some according to their ability to gain access to technology. Without basic telecommunications services, groups are not able to fully participate in the global economy, participate meaningfully in political discourse, or even socially interact with the global village (Snow 2001, p. 21).

Democratisation

Despite these digital divides and the concentration of media ownership in the hands of a few multinational corporations, there is an overall media trend towards democratisation—increased access to information and participation in communication—that continues the trends of the media developed since the advent of printing. The internet is the major element here. Its ability to cross national boundaries, to enable two-way interactivity, to sort information at incredibly high speeds, and to make massive amounts of information available is simply phenomenal.

Democratisation is not just seen in terms of receiving information. It is now possible for anyone to become a media practitioner and publicise their point of view, which takes the democratic right of freedom of speech to new levels. Anyone with fairly basic technical skills can set up their own website or make their own movies; in developed nations these skills are now taught in primary schools. The digital technologies of audiovisual recording and editing also make it possible for people to make and distribute their own films or music CDs to a standard never before achieved. In addition, the use of blogs, whereby individuals can set up their own world wide web personal communication commentaries, has challenged the standard journalistic outlets of press, radio, and television. As Henry Jenkins writes:

> Bloggers are turning the hunting and gathering, sampling and critiquing the rest of us do online into an extreme sport. We surf the Web; these guys snowboard it. Bloggers are the minutemen of the digital revolution ... Blogs are thus more dynamic than older-style home pages, more permanent than posts to a net discussion list. They are more private and personal than traditional journalism, more public than diaries (Jenkins 2006, p. 179).

People turn to blogs as sources of information that may not feature the news values and conventions of balance that characterise conventional journalism, but that can instead offer diverse perspectives and a richness of context, commentary, depth, and detail in reportage. By extension, blogging is often referred to as 'citizen journalism' as it bypasses the media gatekeepers (examples of this are numerous in relation to unauthorised photographs of and documents regarding the Iraq war being leaked and discussed on the internet via WikiLeaks and other sites). Wikis and blogs are particularly important self-publishing tools in contexts where the media is controlled by the state, such as China; however, as discussed below, the WikiLeaks phenomenon demonstrates it is also important for citizens to be able to access and publish information independently, even in democratic countries that enjoy freedom of the press.

An obvious and direct aspect of the democratisation attributed to new media is that interactive media restructure the power relations of political communication. In addition, networks, according to media analyst Terry Flew, 'facilitate a politics beyond the formal political sphere' (Flew 2005, p. 57). The internet is increasingly used as a tool for political communication that extends beyond and often undermines traditional sources of political authority, rendering politics more participatory. One of the big benefits of new media in the political sphere is that voters can use it to speak to politicians directly. For example, in 2007, YouTube users posted videos with questions to US presidential candidates, who were asked to respond live on CNN. In one of these videos a snowman and his little snow child ask candidates how they will combat global warming (see Figure 7.2).

Figure 7.2   Billiam the Snowman, YouTube video image

Source: Nathan Hamel and Greg Hamel of Kotas

The advantages of using interactive and personalised modes of address to actively engage voters in political communication are now well understood by politicians, and voters use social media to subscribe to political campaigns and follow their progress. Julia Gillard and Tony Abbott used YouTube channels, Twitter, and Facebook during the lead-up to the 2010 Australian federal election to address young voters, hone image management strategies, and disseminate political advertising, with varying degrees of success.

Although politicians can effectively use new media to establish greater public profiles, it can also be used to undermine politicians and political parties. Before the 2010 election a number of anti-Abbott and anti-Gillard Facebook pages were set up, and many satirical political advertisements were made and posted online. There was a large selection of these easily available on YouTube, which were also shared on Facebook. These included the Liberals' ads (which also ran on TV) that showed Gillard's and Rudd's faces on lemons as a voiceover made puns about Labor politicians being 'lemons', the Rudd lemon getting 'the chop', and the Gillard lemon having 'leaks'. Even Swedish furniture company IKEA got in on the action, releasing an advertisement with the tag line 'Kevin, here's a cabinet that won't let you down' (see Figure 7.3). There were also a number of anti-Liberal ads that were popular on YouTube, such as a parody of *The Addams Family* theme song about 'The Abbott Family' that claimed 'they're tricky and they're sneaky', and a 'Time Warp' parody cartoon that presented an animated Abbott exclaiming 'let's go backwards'. People also weighed in on other political issues using video-sharing technology around this time. The political organisation GetUp! created an advertisement encouraging people to enrol to vote that played like a blockbuster movie trailer, using action movie footage and superimposing politicians faces onto those of action heroes to convey their message in a humorous yet exciting way.

GetUp! is not a political party, but it is a youth media organisation that has been a significant force and has used the media in powerful ways to communicate

Figure 7.3   IKEA Hemnes Cabinet advertisement

Source: Courtesy of HOST creative agency, Sydney

information about the policies of each of the major parties in Australian politics. The democratic aspects of social media largely stem from users generating their own content (rather than only receiving content from established media organisations). Sites such as YouTube, Facebook, and Twitter enable ordinary people to broadcast their opinions and connect with like-minded people throughout the world. While some political clips on YouTube are humorous and slick, like the ones mentioned above, other YouTube postings simply show video documenting politicians making promises, contradicting themselves, or making discriminatory comments; the YouTube community then engages with and comments on the footage. Such online ads demonstrate the democratisation of new media because their content makes a statement about the importance of free speech and two-way political communication. The form in which such political communication is disseminated shows the power of 'prosumer' technology and its impact on national politics (Wood 2007).

The negative side of this democratisation is put forward by author Andrew Keen in his book *The Cult of the Amateur: How the Internet is Killing Our Culture* (2007). The publicity for this book points out economic, cultural, and legal problems of the internet:

> Keen warns our professional newspapers, magazines, music, and movies are being overtaken by an avalanche of amateur, user-generated free content. Advertising revenue is being siphoned off by free classified ads on sites like Craigslist; television networks are under attack from free user-generated programming on YouTube and the like; file-sharing and digital piracy have devastated the multibillion-dollar music business and threaten to undermine our movie industry. Worse, Keen claims, our cut-and-paste online culture in which intellectual property is freely swapped, downloaded, remashed, and aggregated threatens over 200 years of copyright protection and intellectual property rights, robbing artists, authors, journalists, musicians, editors, and producers of the fruits of their creative labors.
>
> In today's self-broadcasting culture, where amateurism is celebrated and anyone with an opinion, however ill-informed, can publish a blog, post a video on YouTube, or change an entry on Wikipedia, the distinction between trained expert and uninformed amateur becomes dangerously blurred. When anonymous bloggers and videographers, unconstrained by professional standards or editorial filters, can alter the public debate and manipulate public opinion, 'truth' becomes a commodity to be bought, sold, packaged, and reinvented.
>
> The very anonymity that the Web 2.0 offers calls into question the reliability of the information we receive and creates an environment in which sexual predators and identity thieves can roam free.
>
> Source: <http://www.randomhouse.com/book/90898/the-cult-of-the-amateur-by-andrew-keen/9780385520812/?view=print>

Once again, some commentators view new media with fear.

Economic and legal consequences: piracy, copyright, and copyleft

The ease of producing, transforming, and sharing knowledge on the internet has prompted debates about authorship, piracy, and the rights of content creators, versus the responsibility to protect the freedoms of user communities and the public interest in maintaining the internet as a shared resource or an 'information commons', a term coined by Stanford law professor Lawrence Lessig.

Some argue that software developers have intellectual property rights as well as the rights to protect and profit from their own ideas by means of copyright licences. There is also the argument that copyright protection helps maintain industry standards. Microsoft dominates the market, which means it has become the standard, and the majority of consumers are obliged to use Microsoft compatible software. Because of the large amount of Microsoft users, Microsoft products make money, and therefore more are developed, continuing a cycle that keeps Microsoft on top. Apple Macintosh also holds an increasing share of the market, and the same principles apply in relation to Apple products. One criticism of these types of monopolies is that they limit innovation, yet they are also seen to offer users the advantage of uniformity among the choice of available products, which prevents the potential confusions and incompatibilities that might arise from multiple competing software architectures.

Comparatively, proponents of open source media, also known as the 'freeware' movement, argue that the advantages of an industry standard can be achieved by freely sharing software code rather than using copyright laws to protect it. The open source movement draws on a global pool of talent to exchange and build on ideas based on what is called the 'copyleft' system which permits users to copy, modify, change, and sell open source programs as long as they pass on the same rights to others and publicise their own code too (Hassan 2004, p. 119). Nobody owns or authors open source code such as that of the Linux operating system; instead, a number of users add to and improve on it incrementally, continually sharing the code that they use to modify it so issues of incompatibility do not arise. Flew observes that the open source movement has practical and philosophical advantages:

> In contrast to the rationalistic, individualistic, and materialistic subject of liberal economics and those who participate in commodity production in order to promote their personal economic wealth, open source taps into the strong wellsprings of giving, reciprocity, status acquisition through giving without material reward, and creative altruism that have been a part of internet culture long before it was discovered by business (Flew 2005, p. 220).

It is interesting to speculate about how the characteristics of the internet and the patterns of interaction it has fostered may ultimately influence law, social relations, and business.

As discussed above, the global, networked, information sharing characteristics of the internet make it difficult to regulate and protect intellectual property, and relatively easy for users to copy and disseminate media content and evade national territorial jurisdictions and legislation. These economic and legal consequences of new media also impact on the music industry, most famously in the meteoric rise and fall of the file-sharing site Napster and subsequent commercialisation of MP3 technology through Apple iTunes pay-per-song online music store. The music industry has had to reinvent itself a number of times to stay relevant and profitable as new recording technologies develop, such as when audiocassette recorders became widely available and then later CD burners. Today, peer-to-peer (P2P) file sharing, MP3s and iPods pose a significant challenge. The ability to upload, download, exchange, store, and create your own music and music libraries is threatening to make the CD industry and radio music stations redundant. The term for this process is '**disintermediation**'. Disintermediation is jargon for eliminating the intermediary, which translates as cutting out the middle man, namely, in the case of music, the record company. If people are getting access to music straight from the musician, bypassing the need for a producer, a manager, and a commercial distributor, the question is how the music industry will survive and how musicians themselves will be able to make a living. Some artists, such as Pearl

> **disintermediation**
> To bypass intermediaries, such as publishers and distributors, in order to transmit media directly from the creator to the consumer via self-publishing tools and techniques.

Jam, sell tickets to live concerts and uplink those concerts to the web as a response to widespread bootleg recordings (Flew 2005, p. 97). On the other hand, new media occasionally create marketable musicians, such as teenager Justin Bieber, who became an international pop sensation (injecting millions of dollars into the music industry) after a talent-scout discovered videos of him performing on YouTube.

In addition to challenges faced in the music industry, the strike by the Writers' Guild of America in Hollywood that began in 2007 and continued into 2008 hinged on screenwriters' rights to and payment for the dissemination of their material online. Similar copyright and intellectual property issues are being confronted in relation to video piracy as digitisation makes it increasingly easy to copy and share film and television content. In 2007 the communications giant Viacom Inc. sued Google, the owner of YouTube, 'in a US$1 billion (AUD$1.23 billion) lawsuit accusing the website of massive international copyright infringement' (Balogh 2007, p. 18). The Digital Millennium Copyright Act (DMCA) offers legal safe harbour that protects web hosts as long as they remove copyright infringing material when asked to do so. YouTube follows this protocol, and used the DMCA as its main line of defence in the lawsuit. In 2010, the court ruled in favour of YouTube, stating that it was indeed protected by the DMCA, though Viacom indicated it intends to appeal the decision. YouTube and similar sites represent a popular and important function of the internet, and YouTube winning this court case will surely have a significant impact on the future of the internet and the rights and freedoms of its users. Legal uncertainty around what it is acceptable to publish on the internet is still a major concern, and in 2011 these issues were brought to the fore, and made international headlines in relation to WikiLeaks.

WikiLeaks is an organisation that releases private and classified information online—particularly information about governments and their actions. Such information is acquired through anonymous sources, ostensibly in the democratic interests of freedom of information. After WikiLeaks made secret US diplomatic cables public, the US Justice Department opened a criminal investigation into the organisation and its director, Julian Assange. Nevertheless, Assange has not been prosecuted in any country for WikiLeaks publications, and it is difficult to find criminal charges that apply to the re-publishing of material that others obtained. Assange and WikiLeaks have many supporters, as well as detractors, around the world, and the international debate WikiLeaks has incited highlights the many issues regarding online information sharing that will need to be resolved in the coming decades.

Social behaviour changes

It is important to consider the ways in which the new technologies may be changing social behaviour. Some people have criticised digital games as forms of technology that discourage children from developing their physiques through exercise, or that are morally dangerous because of their emphasis on sex and violence. Others, such as Marc Prensky, argue that in fact these technologies are developing a whole set of new and valuable skills, including advanced motor-coordination skills that enable young children to develop the reaction responses and skills needed by jet pilots, and the ability to multitask, which enables children to receive and act on many different information sources at the same time. All these new technologies and the possibility of online shopping will also affect how retailers operate; overall, more people will be able to find their work and their entertainment in the private space of the home. Certainly, the introduction of the iPad is having a far-reaching impact on the print media publishing industry and on the ways in which people read and consume traditional media such as music, magazines, books, and television.

The technologies are also influencing how we relate to and communicate with each other, most obviously through mobile phones, Blackberries, iPhones, the internet, and the increasing popularity of moving through public space to the music of a personal soundtrack playing on any one of a number of portable devices. These personal media technologies can create a sense of virtual companionship when people are alone, and a sense of insulated personal space when in a crowd. Not only does wireless digital networking technology provide opportunities for meeting people from all over the globe, but some people also suggest it allows for a freer form of communication. The fact that people are meeting through virtual worlds and virtual chat spaces, which are in some senses anonymous, enables people to experiment, to be bolder in the things they say, thereby creating a virtual public sphere. Internet chat rooms and virtual worlds enable people to experiment and play with their identities and to indulge in their fantasy lives in a way that previous communication forms did not.

But there are also negative aspects to all this. While some internet relationships reportedly are successful others suggest that there is a huge discrepancy between meeting someone in cyberspace and meeting face to face. Worse than this are the practices of internet predators in stalking or the luring of children or teenagers into sexual situations. Blogging, SMS, cell phone videos, online video publication, and emailing enable playful communication but they have also enabled anonymous and painful sexual harassment and bullying, as well as providing ways to publicise serious issues. While interactive media have many positive uses, misuse can have devastating outcomes including suicide by teenagers who are persecuted by peers that bully and humiliate them online, such as when 18-year-old Tyler Clementi leapt to his death from a New York bridge in 2010 after his classmates posted a YouTube video of him kissing another man. In Australia, cadets in the Defence Force were involved in a high profile case in 2011 when they secretly used Skype to broadcast fellow cadets having sex. After bragging about the incident on Facebook, the cadets concerned were dismissed but their misconduct fed widespread fears about the misuse of interactive media services.

Research into the social differentiation of wireless uses and users suggests that women largely use mobile media such as cell phones for remote parenting and social connectivity, men use such media for business and status, and adolescents use it for social networking and entertainment (Castells et al. 2007, p. 46). Each demographic has its own goals and codes of etiquette: adults switch their phones to silent during meetings and consider it rude when someone accepts a call during a business or social engagement and annoying when their own phone rings repeatedly, whereas young people who are not yet fully in the workforce consider it rude to switch off phones and reject calls, and consider that the number and frequency of communication exchanges signal popularity and status. Preferences for different styles of communication also follow interesting social patterns across age, gender, and nationality. Young people who have grown up with the internet and mobile phones report suffering withdrawal symptoms when their phones are lost, stolen, or broken, and experiencing internet addiction affliction disorder (IAAD) when denied internet access. Furthermore, research also suggests that 'Americans prefer asynchronous communication methods such as email and voice-mail, because they are considered more efficient, keeping things brief, leaving users in greater control', and they use hands free sets rather than SMS because they usually drive instead of using public transport (Castells et al. 2007, p. 37). It is interesting to test such research by thinking critically about how and why you and the people you know use new media.

Conclusion

This chapter has examined defining characteristics of new media such as digitisation, interactivity, virtuality, non-linearity, decentralisation, and convergence, and has developed a framework for thinking critically about technological developments by considering the positive and negative impacts they can have on society. While there has been considerable negative publicity about, for example, violent digital games and their links to aggressive behaviour, many games involve exciting interaction through the internet with other players, thus helping to develop cooperative social relations. Many games also encourage participants to develop technical skills, manual dexterity, and conceptual agility. The technology therefore has the potential for positive human development but, inevitably, it also involves a commercial dimension: gaming is a multibillion-dollar facet of the media entertainment industry that generated US$100 billion dollars in 2010. Increasingly, merchandise, sponsorships, and product placement also play a part. One example of this is the use of enhanced product placement in film and television programs and in their spin-off online alternate reality games. *The Lost Experience*, an ARG that promoted the *Lost* television show and a spinoff novel *Bad Twin* remains a classic example of product placement that incorporated clues in sponsored sites advertising Sprite and Jeep. When critiquing the role of the media in society, it is important not to lose sight of who benefits from new media technologies and contents.

Understanding the implications of technological developments in the media has also necessitated coming to grips with concepts such as democratisation and the digital divide. It is important to remember that the benefits of new media are unequally distributed around the globe. Some countries with low levels of PC penetration have astoundingly high levels of wireless internet technology uptake (Japan, for example). Elsewhere, high laptop ownership and readily available wireless connection inhibits interest in mobile phones and mobile internet access; furthermore, in some regions people don't have access to new media at all (Castells et al. 2007, p. 36). In summary, then, we need to draw together different aspects of studying new media technologies, texts, and modes of production, distribution, and consumption in order to consider how new media might affect social behaviour now, in the future, in our own communities, and around the world.

This chapter has

- examined the key characteristics of new media
- introduced the concept of technological determinism
- discussed the implications of new media technologies such as the digital divide, copyright and piracy concerns, and social behaviour changes.

Discussion points

1   In what ways are new media more democratic than conventional media?
2   Who, if anyone, might benefit from, and who might be responsible for, the digital divide?
3   Consider why fan communities form around particular digital games and game consoles such as Xbox, Wii, or PlayStation. What advantages and pleasures do these games offer in terms of virtuality and interactivity?
4   What impact do you think massive mergers, such as Vivendi combining its video games unit with Activision to form Activision Blizzard, might have on gameplay and innovation now that the *Guitar Hero* and *World of Warcraft* franchises reside under one roof? Would mobile phone technology have developed and dispersed so swiftly if Nokia had merged with Eriksson, Motorola, and Siemens?

Summary

You should now be able to

- give examples of the impact of digitisation on media production, consumption, and distribution
- list and explain five important characteristics of new media
- analyse new communication technologies, and assess their relationship to social change and democratisation
- evaluate how the digital divide impacts on your community and the communities of others.

PART 2

Pictures: Semiotic Analysis ▶

Whoever controls the media—the images—controls the culture.

Allen Ginsberg

OVERVIEW OF PART 2

Part 2 begins to look at media texts in detail. The focus in the first chapter is on still images, mainly advertising photographs, and the methodology used is semiology or semiotics. After an explanation of semiology, we will illustrate its use as a method of textual analysis by working through a number of examples, and we will then broaden out the discussion to consider representational strategies in television and internet advertising.

CHAPTER 8

Semiology

Let's refer to the US marines we see in the foreground as 'sharpshooters', not 'snipers'
which carries a negative connotation.

Fox News internal memo, quoted in *Outfoxed*

This chapter will

▶ explain how to use the semiotic method to analyse media texts

▶ define key terms and techniques used in semiotic analysis

▶ offer examples using semiology to analyse the signs, codes, and conventions with which
media texts communicate

▶ outline how the modality or truth status of a text influences meaning and interpretation.

Semiology, also known as semiotics, began as a method for analysing language. It is
now used for analysing how all sign systems work. It explores the logic and
methodology behind communication, and shows how we can understand
systematically, through the semiotic method, what communications mean. It is
concerned with meaning and with the ways in which meanings are produced and
transmitted.

Semiology suggests that all communication is based on sign
systems that work through certain rules and structures. Language
(words) is the most important and dominant sign system for humans,
but the world is full of other sign systems—traffic lights, road signs,
navigation bars in a website, editing and photographic conventions

semiology
Semiology (also called semiotics) is
the science of signs, or the study of
signs and sign systems.

in film and television, mathematical symbols, clothes, hairstyles, hand signals, Morse
code, and so on. All forms of the media are sign systems. All systems can be analysed
using semiology.

Semiology originated as a means of understanding language. One of its founders
was linguist Ferdinand de Saussure who taught semiotic analysis in a course in

general linguistics in 1906 (Saussure 1974; Culler 1976; Gordon 1996). Another pioneer of the study of signs and sign systems was Charles Saunders Peirce, who sought to understand non-language sign systems (Peirce 1958). C S Peirce founded the American tradition of semiotics when he developed an early account of 'sign theory' and various categories of signs in the 1860s. The methodologies of Saussure, Peirce, and others have been used as a means of analysing media products (Fiske 1990; Hall 1997; Hawkes 1977, 1996). Roland Barthes' book *Mythologies* (Barthes 1973) was one of the most significant applications of semiology in media studies, and despite its age, it is still a readable and relevant text.

How do signs communicate?

The communication model of signs can be understood according to Figure 8.1.

SENDER ⟶ MESSAGE/SIGN SYSTEM ⟶ RECEIVER

Figure 8.1 Communication model of signs

sign
Communicates meaning by standing in for or representing a thing or an idea.

signifier
The visible, tangible, or audible aspect of a sign that carries the meaning.

signified
The thing or idea that a sign refers to.

Any message, any meaning, can only be communicated through signs and a sign system. The sign is the central aspect of semiology. A **sign** is any signal that communicates something to us. The nature of the sign can be understood in two similar ways:

1   Signs work on the basis that the sign stands in for, or represents, something else—the meaning, concept, or idea to which it refers.
2   Every sign consists of a signifier and a signified, as Figure 8.2 illustrates. The **signifier** is whatever material form is used to convey meaning: letters, images, sounds, and so forth. The **signified** is the concept that the images, sounds, or letters communicate.

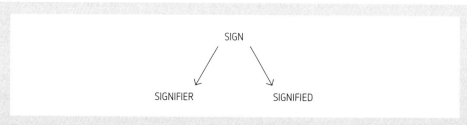

Figure 8.2 Relationship between sign, signifier, and signified

Using the first way of understanding the nature of signs (point 1, above), we can see that the letters 'd-o-g' make up the word 'dog'. This formation of letters constitutes the sign that stands in for or represents the idea of a four-footed canine mammal.

Using the second way of understanding signs (point 2), we can illustrate the distinction between signifiers and signifieds by once again thinking of the sign 'dog'. The signifier is the letters 'd-o-g' arranged into the word 'dog' (or the signifier could be a picture of a dog). The signified is the idea or concept of a dog (see Figure 8.3).

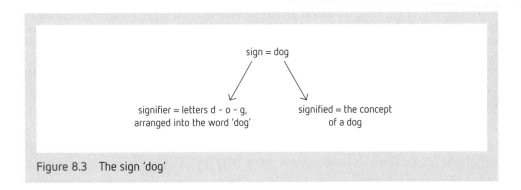

Figure 8.3 The sign 'dog'

An example that shows the distinction between signifier and signified is a picture of a man offering a woman a rose, as in the reality TV program *The Bachelor*. The gesture can be understood as a sign. The rose here is the signifier, and what is signified is the man's love for or attraction to the woman. Roses do not necessarily signify love, which means that the gesture (sign) is based on a shared code, or convention, that roses can stand in for, or represent, love.

This may seem a slightly complicated way of understanding messages but it is useful for media study because it draws our attention to the processes of representation or signification involved in the actions of the media: all media messages, all their signs, work on the basis of something standing in for something else; all signs include a signifier and a signified. This helps us see the construction involved in media messages, and reminds us that what we are seeing is not 'reality' (although it may resemble it) but signs and signifiers that aim to represent the real world.

There are numerous aspects to semiological analysis. In exploring how signs communicate, how semiology works, we will focus on the following key points, which are explored in more detail below.

- Signs communicate through codes and conventions.
- These signs and conventions are culturally shared—they depend on cultural knowledge.
- Signs communicate through systems of difference.
- Signs communicate through denotations and connotations.

Signs communicate through codes and conventions

code

Codes are standardised formulae for communicating meaning.

convention

Conventions are methods of organising signs to communicate meaning in ways that become habituated and widely shared over time.

All sign systems have a set of elements that are combined according to certain rules, codes, and conventions. The English language is based on twenty-six letters, which can combine into words and grammatical patterns. We have to learn and understand the correct codes in order to communicate: the letters 'd-o-g', for example, are the code for describing a certain group of four-legged, furry creatures. Sentences are put together according to the conventions of grammar. The words '**code**' and '**convention**' are key words in media study.

All media messages use codes and communicate through conventions. These codes and conventions are sometimes difficult to spot because we become so used to them that we decode them automatically, without noticing. For instance, it seems perfectly obvious that the most important part of a print media text should be written in the largest and boldest font, with less important information in smaller, finer print. The typeface is chosen according to a code of priority and prominence. It is also conventional to organise this information with the most salient points displayed at the top and centre of the text. The fact that such codes and conventions are used to determine font styles and sizes becomes unnoticeable: we decode the underlying message about the text's relative importance without realising it and tend to skim over small print, assuming it is unimportant (sometimes to our own detriment).

Email and SMS messages communicate using a special code that is more informal and abbreviated than commonly used written language usually is, making use of emoticons and acronyms. Emoticons are graphic representations of emotions, used in communication that is not face to face. For instance, ':-)' is the emoticon code for smiling. Acronyms and abbreviations are a concession to the small screens of mobile phones, and the quick style of communication that is being used. Thus, in SMS conventions, vowels are sometimes omitted, so 'text message' becomes 'txt msg'. The sounds of certain letters and numbers can also be used to substitute for longer spellings, for instance, the use of brevity conventions of SMS or email, the phrase 'Great, see you later!' can be translated into the code 'gr8, c u L8R!' This code is sometimes referred to as 'digital literacy' or 'net-speak' and was incorporated into mainstream language use and media advertising in the early 2000s. Towards the end of the decade it lost its freshness and popularity as mobile phone users increasingly adopted predictive text, a quick, automated way of writing messages without having to manually spell out words letter by letter. The informal, abbreviated net-speak code is still used in online chat and email where predictive text is unavailable. Mobile phones have affected communication in many ways, especially by encouraging brevity and informality.

Codes and conventions depend on cultural knowledge

Sign systems will only work successfully with people who know and share the same codes. For example, a retired person who used to work as a secretary and has never used a mobile phone is not likely to understand the 'gr8, c u L8R!' message, but they might be able to use and understand shorthand, another code that involves brevity conventions for quick communication. Different languages are a good example of different sets of codes and conventions used to represent or stand in for the world. The letters 'd–o–g' are signs in the English language code. French uses the letters 'c–h–i–e–n' to refer to canines. All languages have different words. To understand these different signs you have to have learnt the code (the language); however, cultural knowledge is something more than simply knowing what the code means. It is being aware of all the things that might be suggested by the code. The following points elaborate on this.

Signs communicate through systems of difference

One of Saussure's central points in analysing language was the understanding that words don't mean anything on their own. Their meanings depend on the fact that words are part of a system of difference: they only take on meaning in relation to other words. 'Up', for example, means nothing unless we can relate it to the word and concept 'down'. We can only understand what dogs are in relation to our knowledge of other animals—cats, wolves, horses, and so on—from which we know they are different. The red of a traffic light means nothing in itself; it is only in relation to the context and code of red as opposed to green as opposed to amber that we make sense of it through a system of difference.

Signs communicate through denotations and connotations

Signs work on two levels of meaning: denotation and connotation.

Denotation

denotation

Denotation is what Barthes calls 'the first order of signification'. It is the most obvious level on which a sign communicates and it refers to the commonsense meaning of the sign. The denotative meaning can be expressed by describing the sign as simply as possible.

To consider what a text denotes is to analyse it on a purely descriptive level without delving into what it might imply. It is simply to ask 'What is there?' **Denotation** attempts to describe without comment, evaluation, or judgment, the contents of an image. At this level, signs are as close to value-free as possible. On a denotative level the American flag, say, is a rectangular shape consisting of horizontal stripes of red, alternating with stripes of white, with a smaller rectangle of blue in the upper left-hand corner. The blue rectangle contains white star shapes, also arranged in horizontal rows.

Connotation

connotation

Operating on the second order of signification, connotation refers to the emotions, values, and associations that a sign gives rise to in the reader, viewer, or listener. The connotative meaning of a sign can be expressed by quickly jotting down what it reminds you of or makes you feel or imagine.

Semiology suggests that all signs carry with them a set of **connotations** or associations, that is, they will remind the viewer of certain feelings, beliefs, or ideas that are attached to the signifier. It is our task, when analysing images semiologically, to ask what are all the possible connotations associated with any particular sign or element in the image. Objects, colours, clothes, words, print styles, lighting, camera angles, body language, and so on can all carry connotations.

To return to our example of the American flag, we might note that the flag is associated with (has symbolic connotations of) patriotism, liberty, and justice, at least for most Americans. We would also note that stars are associated with excellence, celebrities, heaven, dreams, and so on. The blue rectangle represents the sky, which, through phrases such as 'free as a bird in the sky', has connotations of freedom (liberty). Each star also represents an individual state in America, and the fact that they are grouped together, instead of being dispersed at random all over the flag, has connotations of unity.

A similar way of describing this mode of analysis, and an approach you may have come across elsewhere, is symbolism, which suggests that particular objects or images carry symbolic meaning. The colour red symbolises passion, danger, and sexuality in Western culture. (Note that in China red signifies good luck and prosperity; it also signifies communism, a further illustration that symbols are culturally specific.) Peirce also gives the term 'symbolic' a more specific meaning, which we will discuss when we elaborate on different types of signs.

Connotations are associative meanings that the viewer or audience perceives in an image and they work on two levels: individual and cultural. For the purposes of this book, we are only interested in the cultural level and the way connotations help us see the interaction between the sign and the values of a culture, but we do need to understand both levels.

- *Individual connotations* The experiences we have in life as individuals shape our ways of seeing the world and our responses. This works in all aspects of our lives, including our responses to images. If, for example, the first time a young girl smells a rose is also a time that she has an upsetting experience (perhaps at a funeral), the smell or sight of roses may subsequently serve to remind her of, or suggest to her, sadness. Seeing roses may continue to carry this individual connotation for this girl, so that seeing roses in a media text would produce distress rather than connotations of love or romance. While it is important to acknowledge the presence of these individual connotations and look out for them when we analyse the meaning of images, they are not useful for a semiotic analysis because they are not connotations normally shared by other people.

- *Cultural connotations* This second level of connotations points to the way that different objects carry associations and connotations that are shared collectively by many people in a culture. So, for example, a gift of roses is culturally acknowledged as carrying romantic connotations. Fiske's analysis of the meanings attached to jeans points to the different connotations—such as freedom, youthfulness, and equality—associated with jeans by groups of people (Fiske 1989b, pp. 1–21). Being aware of these connotations will make us aware of the cultural meanings in images.

Connotations will not be the same for all cultures, which is why it is important for us always to think about an image's context and the cultural knowledge that different audiences will have. Neither will connotations always be shared by all people in a culture, but as long as we can see that they are shared by a significant number of people they will be important in analysing the possible meanings of any texts.

Commentary

Lady Gaga made headlines when she wore a dress, hat, purse, and shoes fashioned from raw red meat to accept an award at MTV's Video Music Awards in 2010 (Plate 5). This was obviously an outfit meant to make a statement, and it did so largely through connotations that *meat* has in Western society. Gaga said she wore the dress as a form of protest against the US military's 'Don't ask, don't tell' policy, which barred openly gay people from the US army and upheld that people could be discharged from military service if they were discovered to be gay. According to Gaga, she wore the meat dress to promote the idea that if 'we don't fight for our rights, pretty soon we're gonna have as much rights as the meat on our bones'. This intended meaning may not be obvious and Gaga herself noted that there are many possible ways the dress can be understood; that is, it has a number of connotative meanings.

One powerful interpretation connects the outfit with animal rights activism. In our culture, cow meat is a substance that is usually cooked and consumed, and a beautiful woman clothed in raw meat seems bizarre and even disgusting. Using meat as clothing in this way creates an association between raw meat and the other parts of animals that people wear regularly, such as leather and fur. Those viewing the dress might question whether wearing raw meat is really that different from, or any less inappropriate than wearing other parts of an animal. From this point of view, the meat dress signifies animals being murdered for fashion, and communicates the associative meaning (the connotation) that this is wrong.

It is worth noting that real meat was used to create Lady Gaga's outfit, and the animal rights group People for the Ethical Treatment of Animals (PETA) criticised Gaga for dressing in animal body parts. This response indicates they understood the dress to signify that it is okay for animals to be killed for fashion. Nevertheless, PETA also reported that Gaga's meat outfit encouraged lots of people to download a copy of a vegetarianism manual from their website, which suggests that many people did decipher the message to be that humans should not exploit animals.

Other interpretations of Gaga's meaty attire relate to the representation of women. On one hand, the outfit could be understood to reference the unrefined, animalistic nature of carnal desires, and to therefore make a statement about the female wearer's 'raw' sexuality. On the other hand, it could be seen to have connotations regarding women being treated as 'pieces of meat'. When people looked at Gaga at the awards show, they saw a famous female body in a slinky, revealing dress. However, it was a body literally covered in meat. Potentially, this suggests that when women are ogled and evaluated for attractiveness, they become like a piece of meat—graded for 'quality' in contexts such as nightclubs, which are often referred to as 'meat markets'.

All these interpretations are affected by the context of who made these garments, where they were worn, and by whom. Lady Gaga's outfit was created by a famous fashion designer, Franc Fernandez, and it was worn at an A-list red carpet event by Gaga, who is widely known for her unconventional, statement-making fashion. Such a context allowed for someone wearing an outfit made of raw meat to be understood as an artistic display. Think about what a meat suit or meat dress would signify if you made it and wore it to the supermarket. What connotations would a meat outfit have then? What other connotations might Gaga's meat dress carry in various contexts?

Iconic, indexical, and symbolic signs

iconic sign
The relationship between the signified and the signifier is based on likeness or resemblance.

indexical sign
The relationship between the signifier is one of indication, direction or measurement, sequence or causation.

symbolic sign
The relationship between the signifier and the signified is arbitrary (there is no natural link) and is based on culture, context, and convention.

Peirce's analysis of signs introduces further categories into the analysis of signs by splitting signs into three types: **iconic**, **indexical**, and **symbolic**.

Iconic signs are signs that resemble that which they signify. All photographs or film signs are iconic in that the image literally looks like what it refers to. Similarly, paintings or diagrams that look like what they signify are iconic. The sounds of the wind whistling and wolves howling in a horror film are also iconic signs, because the recorded sounds resemble noises that the wind or real wolves actually make.

Indexical signs are signs that indicate or point to something else. (The index finger is the one we use for pointing, and a book index points us back to a page reference.) So a knock on the door, for example, is a sign that indicates someone wants to come in, smoke indicates fire, indicator lights on a car flicker to signal that the car is going to turn. Thermometers, speedometers, analogue clocks, and graphs are all examples of indexes because they indicate, point to, or measure temperature, speed, time, and so forth. The relationship between an indexical sign and its signified has been termed an 'existential', or physical, connection.

Symbolic signs are signs that stand in for, but have no resemblance to, their signified. The most obvious example is language, which uses symbols, letters, and words to stand in for what is being described. Similarly, road signs and mathematical signs are usually symbolic. The important point here is that there is no necessary connection between sign and symbol; the signs are, in Saussure's words, **arbitrary signifiers**.

arbitrary signifiers
Arbitrary signifiers have no logical connection to their signified. The signifier does not look or sound like the signified, nor does it point to the signified in a causal or indexical fashion.

An easy way to remember these different kinds of signs is to think of your computer screen. The image of the printer on your tool bar is called an icon because it looks like a printer. The arrow-shaped cursor that appears when you use the mouse to pull down a menu and select a file, tool, or function is literally pointing you to further information, so it is an indexical sign. Website addresses are indexes that point you to a webpage's location on the internet. The sound that indicates that you have new email, or the beep that computers make when you hit the wrong key, are also indexes, because they prompt you to check your inbox or point out that you have made an error. Nearly every key on your computer keyboard has a symbol on it. The $ sign doesn't resemble money; it is simply a symbol that stands for money.

Look around you and identify examples of iconic, indexical, and symbolic signs. It is most likely that you will be able to see examples of iconic and symbolic signs in most social situations. Note that a sign can belong to more than one category.

Clothes as sign systems

As a way of applying semiological analysis, try the following exercise. You may find it useful to read Fiske's analysis of the meaning of jeans as preparation for this (Fiske 1989b, pp. 1–21).

As we have seen with Lady Gaga's meat dress (Plate 5), an item of clothing can be a powerful signifier. The clothes we wear everyday also act as sign systems to tell other people and ourselves who we think we are. They don't just keep us warm or comfortable, they give messages about ourselves. Arrange with a friend to semiologically analyse each other's appearance, that is, look at the clothes each of you are wearing as signs and signifiers. What do they signify? What do they connote? You can include hairstyles, make-up, and any jewellery in this analysis—they are all sign systems. Try to apply all the relevant concepts: look for iconic, indexical, and symbolic signs in your clothes, understand how systems of difference work by imagining different kinds of clothing, different colours, and each of you wearing the other's clothes. Consider how all these things would change the meaning of the clothes.

You might also consider dress codes and conventions, and how they relate to context, social class, and to the economics of the fashion industry. Consider each item of apparel as a sign and break it down into signifier and signified (for instance, jeans are a signifier, and the idea or meaning that is signified by wearing jeans may be youth or freedom).

The language, or codes, of visual images

When analysing how meaning is constructed in photographs and still images, we must consider the codes of technical representation and the codes of content.

Codes of technical representation

In different media there are different codes and conventions at work, as we indicated above in our discussion of text messages and the use of particular font sizes in print media. Other codes and conventions are used in images and screen media, including conventions such as continuity editing (see p. 250), which govern how different shots should be combined in film and television. When a dialogue scene is being edited, the shot-reverse-shot convention is an editing pattern used to show the speaker, then the reaction of the other person. When there is a significant transition in time or space in a film or television text, such as a flashback sequence, it is conventional to use a dissolve or a fade instead of a straight cut. Camera angles are also used according to conventions, such as when a low angle shot (looking upwards) is used to make a figure seem powerful or dominant.

We can analyse the significance of the photographic codes in any image by asking the question: *How* has it been photographed? The answer may include any of the following elements: camera angle, framing and cropping, focus, film stock (black and white or colour), and lighting. All these contribute to the meaning of the image. We can look at each of them and ask what is denoted and what is connoted: for example, the use of soft backlighting to produce a halo effect around a person's head will have certain connotations, and the use of top or side light to create a heavy shadow over their eyes, or to cast half of their face in shadow, will have different connotations. These lighting codes can make a person seem angelic, brooding and inscrutable, or sinister and deceitful, as though they have a shadow side or something to hide. Similarly, grainy images and hand-held footage are part of a technical code of realism that is often used in documentary style programs or photojournalism to give a sense of immediacy and authenticity.

Codes of content

We can also analyse any image by asking the question: *What* has been photographed? The answer may include any of the following elements: objects, settings, clothing or costumes, body language, body position, and colours. All these elements contribute to the meaning of the image, as they denote and connote something. Fashion photography relies on long-standing conventions of composition to show off the clothing and the model's body to best advantage, and this in turn often draws on body language, poses, and photographic codes of representation that are common in soft porn. Thus advertising can borrow pornographic codes of representation to help create a feeling of desire surrounding the fashion item on display.

You are already familiar with many of these codes of technical representation and codes of content, probably without realising it. Semiotic analysis slows down the process of automatically decoding or interpreting these codes and asks how the meaning was constructed. Codes of technical representation and codes of content both need to be considered when analysing any image. We need to ask how each of these elements contribute, as signs and signifiers, to the meaning of the text. This will be explored, with detailed examples, in the next chapter.

Modality

The final semiotic term we want to introduce is the concept of **modality**. Modality is a term originally used by linguists to refer to words that qualify the degree of certainty expressed in a statement (words such as 'maybe' or 'might' are called modal auxiliaries). In language, modality markers are the utterances that tell a reader or

> **modality**
> A measure of the degree of certainty or realism associated with an instance of communication.

listener how sure the writer or speaker is that what they are saying is true. If I say, 'Umm, I think it might rain tomorrow, don't you?', I am making a low modality statement. The modality markers 'umm', 'think', 'might', and the question mark indicate that I am not certain whether it will really rain. In contrast, the following statement is high modality: 'It is definitely going to rain tomorrow.' Modality is an important concept in semiotic analysis because it indicates what the dominant view of reality is, and it indicates who we are most likely to believe or trust. In the example above, we are likely to believe the person who sounds most certain. Note how high modality language is used in news reports: statements are not qualified, they are asserted as fact, which leads us to believe that the journalists have carefully researched the story and thoroughly checked the facts.

The concept of modality can also be applied to visual texts: 'In a commonsense view, "realism" in the visual code corresponds to "truth" in the verbal code: a realistic visual representation is also likely to be seen as true' (Hodge & Kress 1991, p. 130). Cartoons and animated films are low modality texts, whereas live action is more realistic and therefore has a higher truth status. The grainy or informal image of a snapshot or a home video, the hand-held footage in a documentary, and the black and white pictures in a newspaper are all high modality texts. Modal markers and codes of technical representation, such as composition, lighting, camera technique, and film stock, tell us that we should believe these images represent real people and events. The airbrushed, Photoshopped, posed, and professionally lit images in a fashion magazine have a weaker relationship to reality than the snapshot or news photo, but they are higher modality than a cartoon sketch or a computer animated image of a talking animal such as Mickey Mouse or Nemo.

Modality works to position media consumers in relation to media texts by inviting us to agree with and believe in the views represented in the media message to a greater or lesser degree. According to social semioticians Bob Hodge and Gunter Kress, 'Social control rests on control over the representation of reality … Whoever controls modality can control which version of reality will be selected out as the valid version' (Hodge & Kress 1991, p. 147).

Conclusion

In this chapter we have investigated how signs can be broken down into signifiers (images, words, or another medium carrying a message) and signifieds (the meaning or concept that is referred to), and we have introduced different types of signs: icons (signs that resemble), indexes (signs that indicate), and symbols (arbitrary signs). We have established that signs communicate through systems of difference and through denotation (the descriptive or literal level of meaning) and connotation (the associative level of meaning), as well as through accepted codes, conventions, and modality markers.

There is more to semiology and you can explore the topic through further reading, but the outline above will give you enough to start engaging critically in some close textual analysis of images.

This chapter has

- explained what semiology is and how to use it to analyse media texts
- defined key semiotic terms and techniques related to the types and components of signs and codes of communication
- offered examples of semiotic analysis to show how signs make meanings
- introduced the concept of modality or truth status.

Discussion points

1   What are C S Peirce's three categories of signs? What examples of each can you see around you right now?
2   How do codes of content differ from codes of technical representation on cell phones?
3   Consider how modality influences who you believe or trust in a television show, news broadcast, or magazine article.
4   If the very next person you see were to ask you on a date, what would the exact words of your response be? Which parts of your reply might be termed 'modality markers'?

Summary

You should now be able to

- explain what semiology is
- outline the steps or techniques employed to analyse media images using the semiotic method
- define the following terms: 'signified', 'signifier', 'denotation', 'connotation', 'index', 'icon', 'symbol', 'code', 'convention', and 'modality'
- apply these terms in an analysis of a media image of your choice.

CHAPTER 9

Reading Images and Advertisements

There are no just images, there are just images.

Jean-Luc Godard

This chapter will

▶ demonstrate the semiological approach by analysing a number of case study images

▶ explore the interplay of words and images, and consider how audience, context, and intertextuality can affect meaning and interpretation

▶ analyse the relationship between signs, social contexts, and ideology

▶ evaluate the strengths and limitations of semiology.

What follows is a series of examples, exercises, and case studies that use semiology to analyse different images (Figures 9.1 and 9.2). Each analysis raises questions for you to answer, and is followed by a detailed commentary on the image in question. The examples at the beginning of this chapter use photographs, particularly advertisements. Later in the chapter we move on to consider television and internet advertising, looking at how these media forms address the audience differently and use varied strategies of representation to catch and hold attention, and to persuade people to purchase products and buy into the particular lifestyles and values promoted in the commercials.

Advertisements are a rich source for semiotic analysis: they usually combine images with written text, are very carefully put together so as to have maximum effect on an audience, they are a form of propaganda, but will only work if they give audiences some form of pleasure, they are ubiquitous in Western culture, they often reveal important ideological attitudes, and because they are static, they are often easier for media students to analyse than moving images. Do not, though, assume that advertisers themselves know or care about semiology. Although some might (particularly advertisers who have studied communication or media studies), they do not need to know the theory of semiology in order to design advertisements. Semiology is primarily a tool of analysis, not of media construction.

Meaning and interpretation

Print media images represent a moment frozen in time, and often invite us to imagine a larger story of which the single moment is a part, a story in which we might be able to imagine ourselves participating in some way. A particularly useful question to ask about any image in order to reveal something of its intended meaning is: What is the **implied narrative** of the image? This involves asking what you think has just happened in the image and what is going to happen next: in other words, what story is the image telling? We can also ask where the viewer or interpreter of the text is positioned within the implied narrative. Are we one of the characters? Are we being asked to enter into the story world in a particular role? Many advertisements invite us to take an imaginary role in the implied narrative of the text, and to play out a version of that role in real life by purchasing the product.

implied narrative
The story that a picture suggests, including the events that may have happened immediately prior to the moment in the image, and immediately afterwards.

Media texts and images can imply different things to different people in different contexts. Texts are open to many interpretations due to the polysemic nature of images and the ways in which differing contexts, audiences, and connotations can influence meaning. 'Polysemic' thus means many meanings. In addition, the meanings of signs and texts depend on cultural knowledge of other texts circulating in popular culture. In this sense meaning is constructed **intertextually**, in connection with the meanings of related texts. Intertextuality means that some signs extend beyond themselves, incorporating references to other texts on which their meaning in some ways depends. Shows such as *Community* rely heavily on intertextuality as they constantly refer to other media texts. From its very first episode, *Community*

intertextuality
The process of knowingly borrowing and referring to other texts, or interpreting one text in the light of other related texts.

playfully invokes knowledge of other television series and famous films such as John Hughes' teenpic *The Breakfast Club*. Without knowledge of the intertexts, one would have no idea why the character Abed suddenly says things that seem out of character, weaving in lines of dialogue from popular films. The 'Modern Warfare' episode references just about every action movie from *Aliens* to *The Matrix*, and Abed throws in a line about the sitcom *Friends* for good measure: 'To be blunt, Jeff and Britta is no Ross and Rachel. Your sexual tension and lack of chemistry is putting us all on edge, which is why, ironically, and hear this on every level, you're keeping us from being friends'. *Community*, in turn, is mentioned by characters in other television shows such as *30 Rock* and *Cougar Town*. Due to the polysemic nature of media texts, audiences would come up with different meanings for Abed's words (and perhaps be very confused) if they didn't recognise the intertextual references that form part of a pop-cultural role-playing game.

In print media we often don't have the benefit of as much narrative context as television series or movies contain, so there need to be other ways of narrowing the possible meanings of images. Image captions work as a form of what Barthes calls '**anchorage**' (Barthes 1977; O'Sullivan et al. 1994, p. 13): this ties down or anchors the image to a certain meaning for us, thereby reducing the polysemic possibilities; it also shows us how to view it. News presenters on television are often referred to as 'news anchors' for the same reason: they introduce, interpret, and explain the images we see. Thinking about how words, captions, and titles anchor the meaning of images to one particular interpretation is an important step in semiotic analysis, focusing on the relationship between words and images. Words often crystallise the more nebulous meanings or connotations that images convey.

anchorage
Anchorage limits polysemy by articulating the preferred meaning of a text, as a caption labels an image.

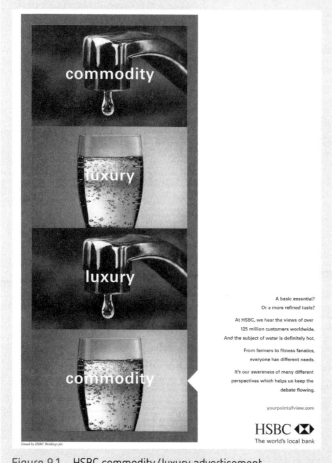

Figure 9.1   HSBC commodity/luxury advertisement

Source: HSBC Bank Australia Limited

Notice how, for example, the captions change the meaning of the pictures of water in Figure 9.1, even though the pictures themselves remain exactly the same.

Without any accompanying captions, the top images of the dripping tap and the glass of sparkling water could be interpreted in many ways: as a symbol or implied narrative of slow and steady progress in which a glass is filled drop by drop, or as promoting mineral water, or advertising the services of a plumber who fixes dripping faucets. The first image of the tap is labelled 'commodity' and the first image of the glass of water is labelled 'luxury', and then the captions are reversed when the images are repeated. These words anchor the meaning by telling us how to think about the water in the images. The text to the right shows the HSBC logo, which restricts the meanings of the images further and indicates it is an advertisement for a bank, not a plumber or a soft drink. These captions, together with the claim that 'It's our awareness of many different perspectives that keeps the debate flowing', show that the images are part of an advertising campaign for a bank, and that the advertisement is deliberately playing with the ideas of polysemy and anchorage to make us think carefully about our views and assumptions. In the global context of pollution, climate change, and pervasive commercialisation, water can be a luxury and a commodity, a basic essential and, in the case of brands such as San Pellegrino sparkling mineral water, a luxury commodity for people of 'refined taste', as the small print suggests.

We can now use the techniques of semiology and the concepts of implied narrative, polysemy, intertextuality, and anchorage to analyse how words and images work together to construct meaning in media texts. The object of such analysis is to raise awareness of the possible meanings that can be produced through analysis of signs and signifiers, photographic codes, and cultural codes of understanding. This will equip you with the skills to decode what the different signifiers represent, and will enable you to give a detailed argument to support your findings. It is also important to consider who the audience is, and how the cultural and social position of the reader affects meaning.

Case study: Analysis of the surgeon image and its caption

We will analyse a photograph (Figure 9.2) of a surgeon operating by posing a number of questions about the image and thinking through the three different elements of text, audience, and context. We will consider who is being addressed and what kind of a text this looks like. We don't know what the context of production or reception is, or what the photographer intended the text to mean, so we will have to make an educated guess by paying careful attention to the text's signifiers, codes, and conventions. To begin the analysis, do the following.

Figure 9.2   Doctor operating

Source: British Film Institute

1   Write down your immediate reaction to this image. How does it make you feel?
2   Write down what type of photograph you think this is, where it might be found, and who might have taken it.
3   Write a brief caption to go with the image of the surgeon.

As media analysts, we need to unpack the signifiers and assumptions that prompt such interpretations, ask what semiological codes and conventions lead to these readings, and what cultural knowledge is required to read the image in this way.

Common responses suggest that people feel uneasy, threatened, or disturbed by the image of the surgeon. People also tend to think that the image may be a news image, or a still from a low-budget horror or science-fiction film.

Text

The image is read through its signs and signifiers, content, codes, and conventions. We have focused on four key aspects of the image in order to tease out the factors that influence interpretation.

1   *Photographic composition and conventions* The most important factors here are the lighting, the camera angle, and the camera lens. The low angle puts us, as viewers, into a subordinate position because we are looking up at the doctor who therefore seems dominant. The camera lens is a wide-angle lens, which has the effect of distorting our vision so that the hand is made to appear unnaturally large in relation to the rest of the body. The size of this signifier emphasises its threat to the viewer. Furthermore, the lighting is harsh, and it shows part of the hospital in shadow. This plays on the way in which darkness is associated with fear, the unknown, and other negative connotations.

2   *The type of photograph* Is this photograph coded as a family snapshot, an art portrait, a news photo, or an advertisement? There are conflicting signifiers here, which complicates our analysis. Some signifiers connote reality, and some suggest that the image does not represent a real surgeon performing an operation. The fact that it is in black and white, and the stark lighting, connote documentary realism, but the photographer has framed the subject artfully (rather than snapping the photo spontaneously). The photographic code of black and white can signify reality, or it can locate the photo in an era prior to the availability of colour photography. We often associate black and white photos with evidence or facts. They have a high modality (a close connection with reality and authenticity) because newspapers have traditionally contained black and white photos, and because they are often used in documentaries (to show evidence of a bygone era); however, as colour printing processes become less expensive, and more prevalent in newspapers, black and white photography is more often understood as serious art photography. Because the composition of the photograph suggests that it has been staged instead of snapped, we might assume that it is art or a professional publicity still, rather than a photo documenting a real operation.

3   *The photographic content* The signs and signifiers of the surgeon, the mask, and gloves. We recognise that the costume denotes a doctor, a surgeon. Doctors connote, among other attributes, illness, healing, medicine, and science. Surgeons have threatening connotations

for many people because surgery is generally undertaken when something is perceived to be seriously wrong with a patient. Signifiers such as the surgical mask and latex gloves carry a number of connotations. The mask, as well as making the doctor anonymous, hidden, and impersonal, connotes danger and warfare through its similarity to gas masks and to the mask worn by Darth Vader in *Star Wars*. The latex gloves connote the need for protection against germs; they also make the doctor seem even more impersonal. Doctors put on gloves when they are going to do something to the bodies of patients, so the gloves also signify the threat of invasion of the body.

4   *The setting* As a sign, the hospital operating theatre is a place that connotes sickness and life and death situations—consequently, it is a place of anxiety. The setting can be thought of with more favourable connotations—the hospital is, after all, potentially a place offering health and care. But in relation to this image we tend to foreground the unsettling connotations because of the photographic codes—the way the image has been photographed.

This analysis aims to develop your semiological analytic skills and to demonstrate the importance of considering who the audience is. Interpretations will depend on the cultural and social position of the readers, and on the assumptions about the audience that are embedded in the text.

Audience

Consider who the implied reader is and how the audience is positioned or addressed by the image by constructing a story about the image of the surgeon and suggesting what may have happened immediately before and after the photograph was taken.

In addition to drawing on understandings of textual conventions and thinking through how the audience is being addressed, we can supplement our interpretation by imagining the story, context, and relationships in which an image is located. Question how the viewer is situated in the image and its implied narrative.

The low camera angle from which the photograph of the surgeon is taken puts us in the position, the point of view, of the patient, and we are thereby invited to identify with the patient. The audience members are positioned as vulnerable to and in need of medical intervention, so the inscribed reader is someone who might need to have surgery themselves. With a different camera angle and point of view, such as an over-the-shoulder shot, the inscribed reader would alter, perhaps addressing medical students and showing how to perform a surgical procedure.

The image shows the surgeon's hand reaching towards the camera, suggesting that he is in the middle of an operation. The lighting is stark and the lens makes the hand unnaturally large and overwhelming, suggesting that the surgery is serious and life threatening. Perhaps the patient has just been rushed into the emergency room and the doctor is fighting to save the patient's life. This is not the only story that can be associated with the photograph—you may have come up with different implied narratives. The implied narrative that we have constructed draws on the codes, conventions, and culturally specific connotations discussed above and it assumes that the text is addressing a particular audience. We could make further inferences about the inscribed reader if we had additional information about the context of the image, how and why it was produced, and how and where it is intended to be received.

Images are often polysemic, thus, the surgeon might be performing an autopsy in a morgue, delivering a baby, demonstrating a procedure for medical students, performing a minor, elective surgical procedure such as rhinoplasty, or even acting in a film about a mad scientist. But the capacity of images to carry a number of meanings does not suggest images can mean anything at all. Images and texts are open to an infinite number of possible interpretations, but they have a more limited number of plausible interpretations. The figure in this photograph is clearly meant to be a doctor, not a lawyer. He is wearing hospital garb, not a tie and a pin-striped suit and is in an operating theatre rather than a courtroom. These things are denoted, hence, there are limitations to polysemy.

Context

Consider how the context of the image and its relationship to other similar images influences its meaning. We have been working with the assumption that the photo exists in the context of a newspaper feature article or a science fiction film based on a number of signifiers that suggest this. In different contexts of reception, our understanding of the inscribed reader and the meaning of the photograph would shift substantially. The way we interpret the meaning of the photograph would alter radically if, for example, the context of reception was a medical textbook, an advertisement for latex gloves, or a religious anti-abortion publication. Notice how information about context affects our understanding of the inscribed reader and the meaning of the text.

Intertextuality

We read the image of the surgeon in relation to other images with which we are familiar. Thus our readings are dependent on our cultural knowledge and are constructed intertextually (in conjunction with the meanings produced in related texts).

The image of the surgeon takes on disturbing connotations through cinematic conventions. It is similar to the kind of images we see in black and white science fiction films. A recurrent conventional figure, or sign, in such films is the mad scientist or doctor. This figure has featured in movies and popular literature since the days of Mary Shelley's *Frankenstein*, and more recently films such as *Event Horizon* and *Sunshine*. The photographic codes complement this: horror and science fiction films use similar conventions of harsh shadows and distorted camera views to create disturbance.

Captions

Captions anchor the image to a particular meaning, narrowing the polysemic possibilities. Refer back to the caption you gave this image and reflect on how it expresses your initial interpretation.

The photo is actually of Dr Christiaan Barnard, who performed the world's first heart transplant operations in the late 1960s, and the original newspaper caption was 'Hands that save'. This draws our attention to the way captions and context can give a particular meaning to an image, as well as to the way a photograph can convey an attitude to its subject matter. In this case, in contrast to the caption's words of hope, the photograph seems to reflect the unease that some people felt about heart transplants at the time (1967). Heart transplant operations were new and unsafe, and some people questioned the morality of performing them. Thus we can see connections between the image and the fictional figure of the mad scientist who is understood to be mad because they usurp the powers of God and nature.

When analysing the relationship between words and images, think back to what you have learnt about connotations and paradigms (see p. 87). Remember that the author of the text could have chosen many different words from a paradigm or set of possibilities. A technique that semioticians sometimes employ to decode the meaning of a text makes use of paradigms and connotations to consider what the text leaves out, and why. Think of different terms that could have been used in the caption for this photo, and suggest why they were not. The caption could have read, for instance, 'Doctors who save', or 'Scientists who save', or 'Hands that heal'. This last caption has a similar denotation to 'Hands that save', but it would have changed the connotative meaning because healing implies a natural process in which the body gradually restores itself to health. The term 'healer' and the phrase 'healing hands' can also be used to refer to New Age or mystical techniques rather than scientific or medical treatments. Such connotations would detract from the intended emphasis on the skill of the surgeon and the technological advancement signified by the new heart transplant procedure. 'Saving' as opposed to 'healing' implies an active agent intervening in a life or death situation. It also includes a spiritual connotation but a more Christian one since God or Jesus are often referred to as 'saviours'. Thus the caption 'Hands that save' works effectively to link the medical discourse to the discourse of heroism and the ideology of a god-like individualism (instead of associating Dr Barnard with mad scientists or mystical healers). The words in the caption reinforce the photographic code of the low camera angle to enhance the sense of power associated with the surgeon.

Advertisements and ideology

We will now take semiotic analysis a stage further. The concept of ideology will be discussed fully in Part 3, but it is important to introduce it here. What is the ideological meaning of the images you are looking at? Ideology (see p. 34) means a set of values, beliefs, and feelings that, together, offer a view of the world. Each image contains an implied view of society, of the world, and of our roles in it. You can analyse advertisements with this in mind. Barthes demonstrates this in his essay 'Myth Today' (Barthes 1973, pp. 109–59). Other theorists, such as Hodge and Kress, suggest that sign systems are the ways in which social groups can communicate ideas about how society is structured, what values are preferred. The dominant social groups can use sign systems to give messages that support their values and their domination. In their book *Social Semiotics*, Hodge and Kress write: 'In order to sustain these structures of domination the dominant groups attempt to represent the world in forms that reflect their own interests, the interests of their power' (Hodge & Kress 1991, p. 3). By this the authors mean that it is in the best interests of the dominant group (the wealthiest, most privileged, and most powerful people, such as those who own the media and have political influence) to represent the world in a way that legitimates and reinforces their own position or ideology. In a capitalist society where money is power and success is measured by the accumulation of material objects, the media function to create desires for products that are associated with the trappings of success. Advertising and other media texts that represent the lifestyles of the well to do invite us to agree that it is desirable to buy into a materialist, consumerist lifestyle and the value system that goes with it. The ideology of affluence that is often communicated in commercial media suggests that owning products that make you look and feel more like the wealthiest members of society is a way to link your own identity to this concept of success. When we buy into this belief system, we implicitly agree that material wealth is an appropriate measure of success, therefore we consent to the ideological values of economic growth and consumerism.

If this seems to be a complicated way of understanding how ideology is communicated in media images, it may help to think back to the SEARCH acronym introduced in Chapter 3 (pp. 38–40). Remember that beliefs related to class, race, age, sexuality, and so forth are represented in media texts, and that such representations communicate ideological values about what is natural, good, normal, and desirable. We will consider the ideology presented in the following advertisements.

Case study: Colorbond fencing advertisement

Consider the advertisement for Colorbond fencing (Plate 1). It includes a wealth of semiological detail for analysis, but we want to go to the heart of the ideology that it presents. Advertisements often work by showing ideal characters in ideal situations. When you are considering this image, ask yourself what is ideal about the situation depicted.

This Colorbond advertisement idealises family life and property ownership and, through that, marriage and heterosexuality. 'What is unusual about that?' you might ask, for surely these are perfectly normal and healthy ideals. They certainly are 'normal', and this is what we want to explore—the way this image conjures up a whole story, implies and supports a whole lifestyle, and thereby presents an ideological construct. We will demonstrate how this is implicit in the image, which is supposedly concerned with selling fencing.

The Colorbond advertisement offers us two images, a past and a present, which together construct an implied narrative. This narrative is about the positive rewards of following a traditional suburban family lifestyle, a normal or ideal pattern of life. The top image implies the new suburban home of a young family: the fence, lawn, and tree signify a suburban backyard, and this is consolidated by the puppy (the family pet), clothes on the washing line, and what seems to be a child's sneaker in the puppy's mouth. The tree is a sapling, newly planted, which, together with the general emptiness of the rest of the back yard, implies a new garden and, by implication, a new house. The contrast between the established trees over the fence in the bottom picture and the absence of anything over the fence in the top picture suggests that the first picture is depicting a new housing estate where nothing has grown very tall yet—an estate from which the vegetation has been removed for a fresh start. This suggests two complementary stories of what has happened in the past. The first is a romance: a young couple met, fell in love, got married, had a child, and bought a house. The second is a story of enterprise and solid financial investment in property: a housing estate in an expanding suburb is being sold and occupied by property owners, who are contributing to the prosperity and development of Australia.

The second picture in the Colorbond advertisement expands on these narratives. The passage of time—ten years—brings things to fruition. The garden has grown (witness the tree) and industrious gardening by the owners of the property has produced a much more picturesque setting (although we don't see the labour, just the finished product). Beyond the fence, we see signs that this same process is happening all around, as the gardens of neighbours are also blooming. Humans are out of sight in both images, but the implied stories of marriage and children and of domestic success and modest prosperity allude to the absent characters in these stories. There is also a suggested narrative of the future: a story of continuing prosperity and growth.

These scenes imply that progress and happiness can be found in the domestic lifestyle of the suburban quarter-acre block, in a country that is still young but is growing ever more beautiful and prosperous. The Australian ideological dream of domestic bliss is thus encapsulated in these images. The advertisement offers its audience the pleasure of putting these connotations together, in the same way as a jigsaw puzzle offers entertainment. It shows us parts of the implied whole, a common way for signs to work; a sign suggests something more. In semiology this is described as **metonymy** (O'Sullivan et al. 1994, pp. 181–2). If someone says 'I'll take the wheel' they mean that they will drive the car, and in this context one part of the car (the steering wheel) is a metonym for the entire vehicle and the act of driving it. Similarly, in the 'Hands that save' caption of Figure 9.2 above, 'hands' is a metonym. Part of the body, the hands, stands in for the whole person (Dr Barnard) and for his actions (performing surgery).

> **metonymy**
> Metonyms are signs in which one part or element stands in for or represents something larger.

Behind the metonym of the fenced garden standing in for a larger ideal or ideology of family values, heterosexuality, and home ownership is the assumption that this is the desirable lifestyle. Here, the aspect of private property is crucial. The central sign is the fence and the accompanying caption: 'Only a Colorbond fence will look as good in ten years' time as the day it was put up'. The fence confirms ownership of property, which is the confirmation of success in white, Western, Australian culture. The fence divides up the land, apportioning it out to those who have the money to purchase land. In doing so, the whole capitalist ideology of Western culture is encapsulated. It is not problematised or questioned; it is normalised. We can see this normalisation process at work by thinking about how else land could be treated. Think about Aboriginal culture's view of the land: it is not to be owned; we are simply the caretakers of what is there for everyone to communally use. White and Aboriginal views about land and ownership are two quite different ideologies. The image in the Colorbond advertisement supports the white view of land as something to be divided up and privately owned. While it could be said that caretaking is going on in relation to this land, it is caretaking within a European garden tradition—the flowers and plants, planted in such an orderly way, are not native to Australia, and they are watered with reticulated water, yet this artificially created culture is shown as normal. Note also the biblical connotations carried by gardens in the Western tradition: the association with the Garden of Eden enables a reading of the domestic garden as an idealised paradise, a place of rest and recreation, an escape from the demands of work.

While the fence recedes in terms of visual prominence in the second image, being more covered up and masked by the new growth, it is still there as the marker of boundaries. It continues to confirm property ownership, which is the confirmation of success in white, Western, Australian culture.

Yet there is, in this advertisement, a hint of something that might disturb its domestic paradise. The caption 'Only a Colorbond fence will look as good in ten years' time as the day it was put up' draws our attention to the other side of the passage of time—decay. While the garden grows, the owners are growing old. The Colorbond fence does not age. Ageing and decay are the shadow side of the garden's growth. We call it a shadow side because of our culture's refusal to accept decay and ageing as part of the processes of nature. Ageing is rarely celebrated in Western culture. People seek to hold on to youth and, in an ageist culture, the elderly are often held up for ridicule. This advertisement raises the spectre of decay and old age but instead of drawing our attention to the problem of an ageist culture, it affirms the ideology of finding ways of avoiding age and decay. It attempts to show ageing and decay can be defeated in the process of raising a family and owning private property.

The advertisement makes sense to us as an audience because we understand how its signs and signifiers relate to myths of the ideal nuclear family. At the same time, it also confirms these ideological values through its narrative. We are so imbued with these ideals that on seeing this advertisement in our day-to-day lives, we probably would not consciously see all that we have discussed (any more than the advertisers deliberately intended the ideology). Ideology is sometimes difficult to see because it is so obvious to us, which means that you will need to look carefully to discover what ideological assumptions are being confirmed in any advertisement you analyse. You will see many images that link together elements of property owning, marriage, and, by implication, families, in similar ideological constructions.

Analysing television and internet advertisements

In addition to considering ideology in advertising, it is also crucial to consider how media technologies and media audiences factor into the meanings of texts. Reading images depends on more than a nuanced knowledge of semiotics; it also depends on a contextual awareness of how audiences use the media and how media producers and advertisers target audiences. In addition, as discussed in Chapter 7, some theorists have argued that the medium itself sends a message. It is important to question how different advertising mediums invite different representational techniques and give different messages to media consumers. In the examples discussed below we argue that the message sent to consumers in interactive online automotive advertising is 'This is *your* car: you customised it, added personal touches, and discovered its special features during a virtual test drive. Now it has your name on it, so you might as well buy it.'

The luxury car industry has invested extensively in innovative ways to reach its market, moving beyond print, radio, and television advertising and sponsorship initiatives to pioneer new forms of internet advertising that foster a sense of personal investment in the product. To date, internet advertising has impacted on print advertising revenue more than on television advertising, but as technology advances and the target demographic for television and print advertising moves online, this will change.

Online advertising was initially characterised by pop-ups and sponsored sites, in which a small window would appear when a visitor accessed a web page, or a host site such as Google or Amazon would priority list certain links at the top of the screen or down the side bar. With the increasing efficiency of pop-up blockers, banners have become more popular. Banners are animated or graphic advertisements that cannot be blocked or deleted by visitors to a website. Online advertising is advantageous in that it accesses an international market in a relatively inexpensive manner, and it is possible to plant ads on sites that are likely to attract interested clientele in the target market.

For instance, Toyota Prius ran online banner advertisements displayed across the top of *The New Yorker* website in 2011 to attract the attention of cosmopolitan, educated, affluent clientele who presumably read about news, culture, and current affairs online and are likely to desire a quality hybrid automobile. The advertisement featured mouse-rollover and moving images and an interactive 'Click to expand' button (accessed at <www.newyorker.com>, 11 October 2011). The link takes you to the Toyota Prius site <www.toyota.com/upcoming-vehicles/prius-family>, which showcases the car's features, details finance options, and provides an interactive gallery of images.

Both internet pop-ups and banners have subsequently influenced television advertising strategies. The station and program logos that appear in the corner of the television screen, and the ads for upcoming programs or goods and services that pop up or scroll along the bottom of the screen are called bugs in the USA and **digital onscreen graphics (dogs)** in the UK and Australia (Copeland 2007, p. 273). These branding and advertising mechanisms and the terminology associated with them are derived from internet advertising. Pop-up and banner style advertising techniques are used on television to ensure that viewers do not change the channel when an advertisement appears, because it appears on screen while the main program is still showing. Ironically, new media advertising techniques that were originally designed to give users more interactive choices developed into strategies to force us to view ads.

> digital onscreen graphics (dogs)
> Dogs or bugs often take the form of station logos or other information added at the bottom of the frame during post production. Such graphics can brand television programs and the networks on which they screen, they can prevent piracy, advertise the next program, or offer viewers extra information.

Film and television have in turn had an impact on online advertisements as audio-visual technology, file compression, faster download times, and enhanced interactivity make digital video a viable option for internet advertising. Between 1998 and 2003 BMW, for instance, used the marketing strategy of branded content (a more sophisticated version of product placement) and commissioned *The Hire*, a series of short films from internationally renowned film directors such as Guy Ritchie,

John Woo, Wong Kar Wai, Tony Scott, Ang Lee, and Alejandro Gonzáles Iñárritu. Each six-minute film had a $1 million budget and a narrative featuring a new BMW car, expertly driven by actor Clive Owen through scenes of danger, passion, and intrigue. The films were only available online at <www.bmwfilms.com>, where they could be viewed, or they could be downloaded for free. As a large percentage of BMW's target market (wealthy, middle-aged males) can afford and is connected to broadband, the advertisements not only reached their target market, but also created an aura of stylish sophistication and exclusivity that circulated around the films and the product they advertised. DVD copies of *The Hire* are now prized as collector's editions, but you can also view the films on YouTube <www.youtube.com>.

MINI, a division of BMW of North America, also created a series of films in February 2007 to launch a newly designed model. In conjunction with a newly enhanced model launch of the MINI Cooper in 2007, MINI launched the Hammer and Coop online series of webisodes (see Plate 2 and Figure 9.3), along with an internet music video featuring a fun, retro theme aimed at a younger, masculine demographic. Hammer is an asphalt kicking, kung-fu fighting pseudo hero and Coop is a talking MINI Cooper S with lightning bolt racing graphics and a cheeky British attitude. The series of webisodes as well as an action name generator were available on a specific Hammer and Coop website separate from the regular brand website. In 2007 you could watch the series and generate your own Hammer and Coop alias, such as Mad Dog, at <www. hammerandcoop.com/#>.

By the mid 2000s internet technology had become even

Figure 9.3 MINI's Hammer and Coop movie poster

Source: Poster © 2008 MINI, a division of BMW of North America, LLC. All rights reserved. The MINI and BMW trademark, model names and logo are registered trademarks. Poster provided by MINI USA. Illustrations © 2006 Boris Vallego and Julie Bell.

more accessible, so that more affordable cars such as Chevrolet could successfully target a broader demographic in yet more inventive and interactive ways. Chevy's 2006 advertising campaign was an online competition that invited visitors to the website to select and sequence pre-shot video footage of Chevy trucks driving through ruggedly beautiful off-road environments such as sand dunes, mountains, and rivers, and then to write advertising text and taglines, then play the whole advertisement set to music. What better way to get cheap creative input? In a similar appeal to interactivity, the Volkswagen 'Unpimp Your Ride' online campaign not only allowed prospective buyers to use an online 'GTI Configurator' to customise their dream car's colour and features, it invited them to take it on a virtual joyride in a dynamically generated video featuring the beautiful, blonde German engineer, Helga. VW brought Helga to life by creating a social networking page and ring tones for her. Best of all, a series of web ads with Helga and another German engineer who fancied himself a rap artist received over 20 million YouTube views and went viral in the course of the month-long campaign. Viral advertising relies on audiences actively engaging with ads and spreading them through their social networks (see Chapter 14 on culture jamming).

These innovative advertising strategies demonstrate that as media technology changes, it leads to different patterns of media consumption and to changing strategies in the advertising industry; however, many of the semiotic strategies used by advertisers and many of the underlying ideological messages remain the same.

Why use semiology?

What are the advantages, strengths, and weaknesses of using semiology as a methodology for text analysis?

Advantages of semiological analysis of media texts

1   The first advantage is practicality. Semiology is a helpful method for taking images apart. It gives a set of guidelines, checkpoints of things to do when we face an image, and serves as a guide through the maze of meanings. When we get stuck we can go back to check connotations, or codes, or ask what is being signified. It can also be usefully applied beyond media texts to any cultural sign system, such as the wearing of clothes or the organisation of social space in buildings and architecture.

2   Semiology is a method that stresses the relation of one text to others and to society as a whole. Its insistence on cultural codes and conventions encourages us to make links and comparisons with other texts and other genres, and leads us to see meaning as socially produced. Semiology's insistence on connotations draws attention to the way texts relate to wider social meanings and to the role that readers and audiences play in constructing meanings. In doing so, semiology draws attention away from individual

authors and their creative 'genius' and intentions. One of Barthes' famous essays is entitled 'The Death of the Author' (Barthes 1977, pp. 142–8). This movement away from the emphasis on authorial intent and ownership of a text can be seen as a strength or weakness, depending on one's point of view. This is one of the distinctive features of the methodology of semiology: it does not focus on the intentions of individual creators. At times, we find it useful to return to individual authors, but whatever your viewpoint this is one of the distinctive features of the methodology of semiology: it is not interested in the intentions of message creators.

3   Semiology's insistence on breaking the sign into signifiers and signifieds, showing how something always stands in for something else, prises texts away from the notion that they are unproblematic reflections of reality. By continually asking what is being signified by a particular sign, we realise that texts are constructions of meaning rather than transparent reflections of reality. Stuart Hall puts it this way:

> Saussure's great achievement was to force us to focus on ... how language actually works and the role it plays in the production of meaning. In doing so he saved language from the status of a mere transparent medium between things and meanings. He showed instead that representation was a practice (Hall 1997, p. 34).

This is particularly important in relation to photography, film, and digital cameras, because they can so easily appear real, unmediated, and unconstructed. Semiology helps remind us that they are not, that they are constructions.

4   The way Barthes used semiology—seeing signs as wider systems of social myths— enables us to analyse ideology in media texts.

The limitations of semiological analysis of media texts

1   Semiology is just one approach to texts and the media. It does not cover everything and therefore we need other approaches alongside it.

2   The project or dream of semiology as a science of signs has been productive, but it has also led to the main fallibility of semiology. In the end, semiology's acknowledgment of polysemy and its awareness that cultural knowledges, contexts, and audiences are elements that need to be taken into account in understanding meanings, actually leads to the realisation that there are too many variables. We can point to significant probabilities and preferred meanings of texts, but other possible readings also have to be acknowledged. Philosopher Jacques Derrida adds to the semiotic method by introducing the concept of *différance*, an ongoing process of signification in which each sign or signifier refers to something else with which it is associated, and so on, so that the meaning will always be incomplete. Thus the term '*différance*' indicates that a sign is meaningful because it differs from other signs (black gets its meaning in relation to other colours because it is distinct from other colours), and because meaning is indefinitely deferred through the process of

différance
Refers to an endless chain of signification in which each sign or signifier is linked to or associated with something else, so that the complete or final meaning is infinitely deferred.

association (black is associated with darkness, which is associated with mystery, which is associated with suspicion and crime, and so on). Ironically, the science of signs has proven that we can't find the absolute meaning. So we have to go beyond semiology as a way of understanding media.

3   Saussure focuses on the rules of language and sign systems (he calls the abstract, formal system of rules and conventions **langue**). While this is useful, it does not take into account the concrete processes of language that Saussure calls **parole**, a term that refers to actual instances of speech and language use that is necessarily dynamic, contextual, and transient rather than predictable or rule-bound. Even the sign systems themselves can change over time so it is best to be wary of a cogs-in-the-machine view of communication, wherein language and its rules, and signs and their meanings, are fixed in time. The rules of language do not control language users; rather, it is the other way around. The reality is that people can break and change codes, struggle over meanings, and exert some autonomy over and through the systems: we can speak language. Because languages change meanings over time, there is more flexibility than is allowed for in Saussure's approach.

langue
Langue is the fundamental structure that underlies and governs language and expression.

parole
Parole is a particular instance of language use or expression, when the underlying rules (*langue*) are put into practice.

Conclusion

This chapter has explained techniques for reading images and advertisements by working through a series of examples, analysing their implied narratives and intertextual meanings, and examining the influence of text, audience, and context on meaning and interpretation. We have considered the advantages and limitations of using semiology to decode the ideological meanings of images and to examine how broadcast media and internet advertising campaigns address and engage their target audiences. As long as we are aware of these limitations and of other possible approaches, semiology should still be a helpful and ultimately useful means to an end, that end being understanding media texts and, by extension, understanding the place of media in society.

This chapter has

- showed how to use semiology to analyse media images
- discussed the relationship between words and images in media texts
- considered how the medium of representation (print, television, or internet, for example) affects meaning and how the audience, the context, and intertextuality affect meaning and interpretation
- analysed the ideological meanings of signs
- weighed up the strengths and limitations of semiology.

Discussion points

1   Do you think we contribute to stereotyping when we interpret social signs and form assumptions about people based on the connotations that their appearance and possessions carry?

2   Choose an image from any magazine and work out who the inscribed reader is and how the spectator is positioned or addressed.

3   Find an advertisement that is available in several media, such as a movie trailer and a poster for the same film. In what sense can these types of publicity material be considered metonyms? Analyse whether the two versions address the audience differently and use different codes of representation.

Summary

You should now be able to

- discuss the relationship between words and images in media texts
- use semiology for decoding the ideological meanings in media texts
- explain and apply the following terms: 'polysemy', 'metonymy', 'anchorage', and 'implied narrative'
- employ these terms and techniques in an analysis of an advertisement, discussing how the reader is positioned in relation to the text
- evaluate the strengths and weaknesses of semiotics as an analytic tool.

CHAPTER 10

Model Essay: Semiotic Analysis of an Advertisement

▶

Historians and archaeologists will one day discover that the ads of our time are the richest and most faithful reflections that any society ever made of its entire range of activities.

Marshall McLuhan

This chapter will

▶ use semiotic terms and techniques to analyse an advertisement

▶ analyse the relationship between image, text, intertext, and context

▶ consider how the reader is interpellated

▶ interpret possible ideological meanings in the text

▶ demonstrate the development of an argument and the use of quotations to substantiate or clarify points in an essay.

What follows is an example of how to write an essay using semiotic techniques to analyse an advertisement. It includes in-text references and a bibliography. The bracketed references in this essay refer to books listed in the essay's bibliography, rather than the bibliography of this book. In academic essays it is important to give evidence of reading and research. Always include references to and terminology from the course material in the unit you are studying, and define key terms and concepts with care. It is also advisable to include and discuss quotes from other academic books and articles to support, clarify, and substantiate your ideas. Academic essays should also feature a clear **introduction**, a **thesis statement**, a **conclusion**, and an alphabetised bibliography or references list.

introduction
The introduction of an essay should include an outline of what you aim to achieve (state essay topic, objectives, and the text you are analysing) and how you intend to achieve it (your methodology and structure).

thesis statement
The part of an essay that outlines the central argument is called the thesis; it should be briefly stated in the introduction, and developed throughout the essay. Writers should also consider possible objections and counterarguments (the antithesis) in order to weigh up different points of view and defend their ideas.

conclusion
The conclusion of an essay should summarise the key points and briefly discuss their significance, with reference to the objectives stated in the introduction.

Essay topic

Undertake a semiotic textual analysis of an advertisement, showing how meaning is constructed. Consider signs, signifiers, connotations, codes, and anchorage, as well as the possible ideological meanings of the advertisement.

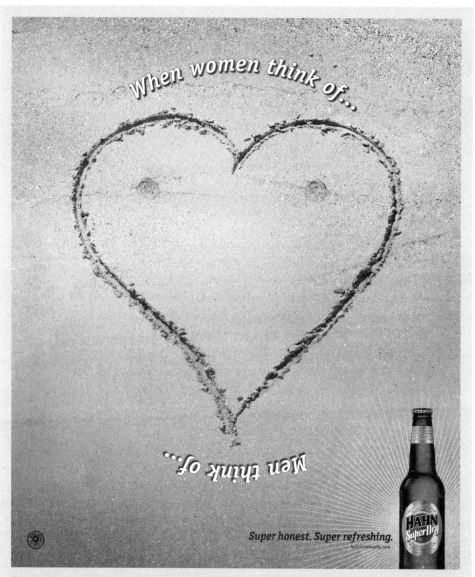

Figure 10.1 Hahn Loveboobs advertisement

Source: Hahn Loveboobs advertisement courtesy of Andrew Disley at Lion Nathan

Advertisements exist as a means of selling products (see Figure 10.1) by creating an association between a brand and a desirable lifestyle or identity. Within media images of and messages about products, lifestyles, and identities, many ideological messages are encoded. Here, 'ideology' can be understood as 'the practice of reproducing social relations of inequality within the sphere of signification and discourse' (O'Sullivan et al. 1986, p. 107). O'Sullivan et al. claim that ideology is communicated through signs, including advertisements, and that ideology serves the interests of the wealthiest, most powerful groups in society. More generally, ideology can refer to any world view or set of assumptions and beliefs that are taken for granted as being natural and normal, but that are actually socially constructed. Ideology is not neutral; it is always implicated within power relations that privilege certain people over others; however, texts can contain resistant ideologies that challenge the dominant ideology. Feminist ideology, for instance, challenges the privileged position of men within the dominant patriarchal ideology.

Using semiotic analysis to decode its meaning this essay aims to denaturalise the ideological messages in a Hahn beer advertisement. The Hahn advertisement appeared in the *Weekend Australian Magazine* in *The Australian* national newspaper in March 2007; it was also screened simultaneously as a television advertisement and publicised on the Hahn website. Following the semiotic method I will work through denotations, connotations, context, intertextuality, and the way the text addresses its audience to support the argument that the image reinforces patriarchal ideology, but it also communicates more subtle ideological messages about gender, class, consumerism, and age.

Bob Hodge and Gunter Kress, authors of *Social Semiotics*, write that

> Semiotics has been defined as 'the science of the life of signs in society' … In its terms everything in a culture can be seen as a form of communication, organised in ways akin to verbal language, to be understood in terms of a common set of fundamental rules or principles (1991, p. 1).

Semiotic analysis was originally developed by Ferdinand de Saussure to analyse language. As Hodge and Kress suggest, semiotic analysis can also be used as a means of understanding communication such as media texts.

The first level of signification considered in semiotic analysis is denotation, which means 'the commonsense, obvious meaning of the sign' (Fiske 1990, p. 91). On a denotative or descriptive level, the advertisement depicts a heart-shaped figure with two dots drawn in the sand, captioned with text above and below the image and accompanied by a picture of a Hahn Super Dry beer bottle on the lower right. Even if it isn't noticed at first, the sand drawing also denotes breasts, or 'boobs'. The beer bottle is surrounded by pale lines that radiate outwards. The caption above the heart shape reads 'When women think of …', and the caption below it, written in text that is upside down, reads 'Men think of …' Beside the picture of the beer bottle are the words 'Super honest. Super refreshing'. The Hahn web address <hahnloveboobs.com> is visible in small print in the lower corner beside the beer. There is also a small image of a bottle top at the bottom left of the advertisement containing a message to drink responsibly in the form of another web address <www.drinkaware.com.au>.

In addition to denotative meanings, elements in the advertisement also communicate connotations or associations. Connotations operate at the second level of signification and depend on cultural knowledge. For example, the heart has connotations of sweethearts, romance, and love due to cultural knowledge of St Valentine's Day gifts and cards. Additionally, the lines that radiate outwards from the Hahn logo have connotations of rays of light, suggesting that the beer itself is an energy source, or that it has super powers. This reading is reinforced by the repetition of the word 'super' in the text on and near the bottle, and by association with the visual style of superhero comic books, in which similar radiating lines often suggest power. The halo effect of the rays also has religious connotations, and the golden colour of the bottle and its silver label carry connotations of something precious.

The advertisement contains what semiotician C S Peirce described as iconic, indexical, and symbolic signs (1958). The photograph is an iconic sign because the images resemble sand and beer. Iconic signs such as pictorial images have a 'likeness' to the 'thing, person or place being represented' (G Dyer 1982, p. 124). The internet address is indexical, because it points or directs us to a location in cyberspace. Symbols are signs that 'have no logical connection between the sign and what it means' (Crow 2003, p. 33). The letters 'H-A-H-N' are symbols that are understood to refer to the brand name of the beer through linguistic conventions.

The meanings of different components of the advertisement can be decoded when we consider the target audience of the image, the context in which the image is located, and the intertextual relationship the image has with the simultaneous television and internet advertisements for the product.

We can determine who the intended reader of the advertisement is by considering who it is implicitly addressing. According to Fiske

> One of the most ubiquitous and insidious ideological practices is what Althusser calls 'interpellation' or 'hailing'. All communication addresses someone, and in addressing them it places them in a social relationship. In recognising ourselves as the addressee and in responding to the communication we participate in our own social, and therefore ideological, construction (1990, pp. 174–5).

Following Fiske's claim that all communication addresses someone, the beer ad addresses Hahn's target market which seems to be men aged 18–38. Although it acknowledges what women think and feel, the advertisement primarily invites viewers to link the male desire for a voluptuous woman with the desire to buy Hahn. It is designed to be easy for male viewers to put themselves into the picture. By interpellating viewers into a youthful, masculine, heterosexual identity, it is implied that this subject position is normal and natural. People from all demographics were exposed to the advertisement on Australia television and magazines, and it was publicised globally online. But a wealthy female connoisseur of fine wine, a gay man with little interest in women's breasts, or a Muslim who abstains from alcohol would probably not feel the advertisement addressed them, hence they wouldn't necessarily accept the social position or internalise the ideology that the text assumes.

Advertisements use established conventions of signification such as metaphors, metonyms, and symbolism to construct meaning. The 'boobs' and the sand are metonyms because, 'metonymy works by associating meanings within the same plane. Its basic definition is making a part stand for the whole' (Fiske 1990, p. 95). Sand is a metonym because it is just one part of the surf, sand, and sun that beaches entail and that, in the context of both the advertisement and Australian culture, connotes the outdoor lifestyle, fun times, and holiday romance or summer fling that might be enjoyed on the beach. Similarly, 'boobs' is a metonymic signifier for a sexually desirable woman. Boobs are a part of female anatomy that stands for the whole woman, literally reducing her to a body part: boobs are an object of desire, just as beer is. Interpreted in this light, the advertisement provides an example of sexual objectification and commodification in which the woman is 'constructed as an object for the "look" of the male spectator' (Walters 1995, p. 51).

An implied narrative underlies the advertisement and helps make sense of the text, just as interpellation positions us in relation to the text. The composition of the advertisement places the viewer close so we look straight down on the heart and see the grainy texture of sand and droplets of condensation on the beer bottle. The implied narrative is that the viewer is the person on the beach who has just drawn in the sand and who is within reach of the bottle of beer. That person is not pictured in the print advertisement, which invites everyone who sees it to insert themselves into the narrative. Those who visit the website or see the television advertisement know there is a larger intertextual implied narrative suggested by the image. In the screen versions of the advertisement a young, attractive, white couple are on the beach together. The curvaceous, bikini-clad woman draws a heart in the sand and gazes adoringly at her partner, indicating that she loves him. Her love interest is standing opposite her where the camera (and therefore the audience) is positioned. As he looks down at her message he sees an inverted heart; he also sees her cleavage, so he places two dots representing nipples in the heart. This suggests that instead of loving *her*, he loves boobs. This implies conventional ideologies of femininity and masculinity in which women are interested in love and romance, whereas men are interested in having sex.

The meanings of the heart in the sand and the beer bottle are anchored by the words written on the advertisement. According to Fiske, the term 'anchorage' describes the 'function of words used as captions for photographs' (1990, p. 110). Fiske points out that visual images are polysemic (they have many possible meanings), so words can be used to anchor the meaning of an image by reducing the range of plausible meanings. On a denotative level, the word 'boobs' ensures that the audience knows the symbol in the sand is meant to represent breasts rather than a heart or a 'beach bum', which are other meanings that viewers might form in the absence of any caption to anchor the image. The word 'refreshing' has connotations of something new and revitalising, which is consistent with a surfie youth culture lifestyle devoid of worries about serious things such as responsibilities or commitment.

The playful, youthful associations with surfie boys and beach babes links with other ideological messages related to age and class. The humour of the wordplay about 'love' and 'boobs' and Hahn being a 'refreshing' drink for 'refreshingly honest' young people is directed at those who might see political correctness as a false or dishonest veneer that politely covers over what people really think and feel. It also targets people who use the word 'boobs' to describe breasts. Signifiers in the advertisement suggest that sexism is permissible within the context of a young, male, lower-middle-class subculture. Beach sand, boobs, and beer are not generally used to advertise expensive beverages, or venues in which wealthy, mature, professional people might nibble seafood salads and sip chardonnay. Hahn is not a costly boutique beer so it is affordable for young consumers who do not have much money. Hence, although the images may be desirable to individuals from a range of social circumstances, the connotations operate predominantly within a class-specific context that primarily targets readers of a certain age and gender. The process of interpellation is, however, also more complex as the ad addresses a secondary audience of young, postfeminist women who accept contemporary sexuality and gender roles and are neither offended nor threatened by ironic, playful forms of sexism.

The fact that the advertisement is primarily directed at a young, male audience is precisely what invites a tolerant, humorous reading or response. In Australia, if not elsewhere, there is a cultural stereotype of young men being playful, harmless, larrikins and easygoing pranksters. Youth makes their actions and attitudes seem more excusable. There is a permissiveness associated with late adolescence (even if such behaviour persists into middle age) that is best summed up by the phrase 'Boys will be boys'. Within this ideology or view of masculinity, it seems acceptable and natural for 'boys' to make fun of political correctness. This ideological perspective turns the serious issue of sexism into a good lark, or something they'll grow out of, a natural and playful rebellion against adult relationships and responsibilities.

The reading that patriarchal ideology is endorsed and privileged is supported by textual evidence, such as codes of representation that suggest some messages in the text are dominant, some subordinate. Hodge and Kress claim conventions organise signs and help us to interpret them 'via codes which organise signifieds and signifiers' (Hodge & Kress 1991, p. 262). One common way of organising signifiers is by placing them in a hierarchy. In the Hahn advertisement the text is arranged so the most important messages are the largest, and nearest the top of the page. The instruction to drink responsibly is written in the smallest font at the bottom of the page and is literally marginalised (printed near the margin), so as not to discourage consumption. The woman's viewpoint is written the right way up at the top of the page (which initially implies the female perspective is 'right', or important), whereas the man's viewpoint is upside down. This means viewers of the advertisement have to turn the page around and literally see the world in a new way, from a masculine perspective, to be able to get the joke about the inverted heart's resemblance to breasts. The phrase 'Men think of … [boobs]' ultimately has priority because when we turn the page around it is upright at the top of the page and it makes a lasting impression, reinforcing a heterosexual patriarchal ideology.

The advertisement makes a mild sexist joke, but in doing so it invites viewers to see the situation from the woman's point of view as well as the man's, and it depicts women as being subjects with thoughts and feelings as well as being sexualised objects. The advertisement explicitly states, 'Women *think* …', and it is clear in the television advertisement that the woman also *feels* miffed when her boyfriend responds to her romantic gesture with a crude joke. The 'Super honest. Super refreshing.' tagline suggests that she ultimately accepts his masculine perspective on sexual relationships is different from hers, and sees it as refreshingly honest.

In conclusion, I have shown the Hahn advertisement has connotations of youth, sexiness, and fun in the sun that, by association, makes the product desirable. It is important to stress that the advertisement only works for those who have the relevant cultural knowledge and share the belief that such things are desirable. The advertisement is open to oppositional readings, especially by those outside the target market. A reading is 'oppositional' when 'the audience disagrees with dominant values expressed within the preferred reading of the text' (Bell et al. 1999, p. 21). Feminists, for instance, may interpret the advertisement as gender discrimination, not harmless fun. Deeply religious or conservative people may view sexual references and alcohol consumption as problematic.

The Hahn advertisement shows dominant patriarchal, consumerist ideologies maintaining their privileged place, but these ideologies are not entirely accepted as natural and normal. They are represented as being in dialogue with other ways of seeing the world, such as feminism and messages about responsible alcohol consumption. Indeed, the advertisement literally interpellates viewers into different subject positions, encouraging us to see the world from different points of view and acknowledge diverse perspectives and interpretations.

Bibliography

Bell, A, Joyce, M & Rivers, D 1999, *Advanced Media Studies*, Hodder & Stoughton, London.

Crow, D 2003, *Visible Signs*, AVA Publishing SA, Crans-près-Céligny, Switzerland.

Dyer, G 1982, *Advertising as Communication*, Methuen, London.

Fiske, J 1990, *An Introduction to Communication Studies*, 2nd edn, Routledge, London.

Hodge, R & Kress, G 1991, *Social Semiotics*, Polity Press, New York.

O'Sullivan, T, Hartley, J, Saunders, D & Fiske, J 1986, *Key Concepts in Communication*, Methuen, New York.

Peirce, C S 1958, *Collected Papers, 1931–58*, vols 7–8 (ed. Arthur Burke), Harvard University Press, Cambridge, MA.

Walters, S D 1995, *Material Girls: Making Sense of Feminist Cultural Theory*, University of California Press, Berkeley.

Conclusion

This model essay has demonstrated how to analyse an advertisement's components, consider the intended market, the context, and the signifiers, connotations, codes, and conventions that create meaning. It exemplifies how to define key terms and concepts, incorporate quotations to support ideas, and construct an argument about the ideological messages in a text. These techniques can also be applied to other texts, such as magazine covers, DVD covers, and websites.

This chapter has

- shown how to set out an essay using semiotics to analyse an advertisement.

Discussion points

1   Can you find any elements of the Hahn advertisement that have not been discussed in the essay, or aspects that you would interpret differently?

2   How might your own experiences and ideas influence your interpretation of the advertisement and affect the argument about its meaning?

3   Consider how the elements in the SEARCH acronym (sex and sexuality, environment, age, race and religion, class, and handicap) relate to signifiers in the Hahn advertisement and to your own reading of the ad.

Summary

You should now be able to

- write your own essay, using semiotics to analyse a media text.

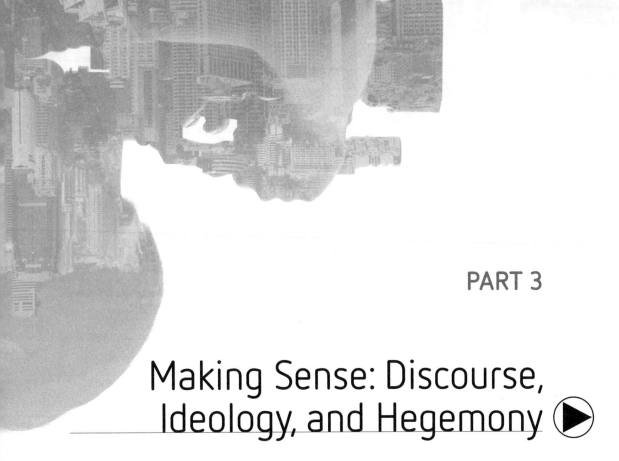

Making Sense: Discourse, Ideology, and Hegemony ▶

It's all around us, here even in this room. You can see it out your window, or on your television. You feel it when you go to work or go to church or pay your taxes. It is the world that has been pulled over your eyes.

Morpheus, *The Matrix*

OVERVIEW OF PART 3

Part 3 extends the process of semiological analysis by exploring the concepts of discourse, ideology, and hegemony. After reading this part, you should be able to use all three concepts in your analysis of the media, media texts, and the relationship between the media and society.

CHAPTER 11

Defining Discourse and Ideology

To me what makes the world tolerable is that it's going insane—that's what keeps me going.

Errol Morris, director, *The Thin Blue Line*

This chapter will

▶ give definitions of discourse and ideology

▶ illustrate how these terms describe all human communication and are also concerned with social power

▶ consider Western discourses of criminality

▶ discuss the importance of beliefs, feelings, actions, and common sense in relation to ideology

▶ explain and illustrate the concept of 'unconscious consciousness'

▶ consider whether it is possible to have no ideology.

The terms 'discourse', 'ideology', and 'hegemony' relate to the work of three important theorists: Michel Foucault, Louis Althusser, and Antonio Gramsci. These terms are first, concerned with the way any ideas and values are felt and expressed in a society, and second, concerned with issues of social power.

The work of these theorists argues that power is unequally distributed in society—there are dominant and subordinate groups—and that this power is partly maintained and reproduced by the circulation of ideas and beliefs. These ideas and beliefs are circulated through language and texts via the media and social institutions such as the family and the education system. These terms have been enormously influential in the development of media and cultural studies. They are complex: they contain various possible meanings and can be interpreted in many ways. Alongside their use in the work of Foucault, Althusser, and Gramsci, they have been the subject matter of numerous essays, articles, and books and have formed the theoretical basis for much media analysis.

We use the terms 'ideology' and 'discourse' first as terms for discussing how ideas and values are presented in the media. Then we use 'ideology' as the main way of discussing issues of social power and the media, whereas the term 'discourse' refers to the ways in which these ideologies are *communicated*, and 'hegemony' (which will be discussed in Chapters 12 and 13) refers to the ways in which ideologies are *negotiated*, maintained, and disputed.

Discourse

We have already used the terms 'discourse' and 'discursive frame' in relation to language as demonstrated by John Fiske (p. 69).

Discourse comes from the French word *discours*, which means dialogue, speech, or conversation. Its simplest meaning is the articulation, voicing, or putting forward of a point of view. This act of articulation is usually part of an exchange of ideas among several speakers or social groups. Each group develops its own jargon and methods of encoding and communicating knowledge. This knowledge is shared among members of the group, hence discourse relies on collective understanding. Thus discourse is a social process of constructing meaning within a mutually understood set of rules. In this sense discourse is quite a neutral, descriptive, or innocent term: as humans we need discourses to communicate with each other.

Note that discourses find expression in texts and other communicative practices as well as in speech. The term 'discourse' typically refers to the collective discussion or interplay of meanings and ideas circulating around a particular subject, incorporating these different modes of expression and instances of communication.

discourse analysis
Explores the ways in which power and knowledge are communicated through texts, language use, and systems of thought.

Foucault's theory of discourse is that societies tend to bring together a range of voices, ideas, and beliefs into overall discourses that offer ways of understanding the world (Fiske 1987, pp. 14–15). Any society has a number of discourses by which it makes sense of the world and which we can study by means of Foucault's techniques of **discourse analysis**.

| What are the main Western discourses of criminality? | |

Foucault has used the notion of discourse to examine how societies understand and make sense of sexuality, madness, and criminality (Foucault 1981; Rabinow 1984; Fillingham 1995). He argues that a range of ways of thinking (discourses) are brought together to make sense of these areas, and that these discourses can and do change over time. In relation to crime and criminality, for instance, he sees how medical, legal, religious, and moral discourses define criminality and criminals and suggest ways of dealing with them. Medical discourses define criminals in terms of being sick or healthy, and if they are deemed sick then they need curing and rehabilitation; religious and moral discourses define criminals in terms of being good or evil, deserving rewards or punishment; and legal discourses define criminals as a danger to other people and, being concerned with the preservation of other people's safety and property, decide what courses of action to take to prevent further crimes. Thus we can see three kinds of possible treatment for criminals, based on three discourses for understanding their actions: *rehabilitation* or cure for their sickness, *punishment* (which could take various forms) for their evil deeds, and some form of *restriction* (for example, the removal of limbs or imprisonment) to prevent future crimes.

You are probably aware that elements of all three of these discourses—medical, religious, and legal—are present in the way societies construct prisons and use imprisonment today. Prisons are simultaneously supposed to be instruments of rehabilitation, punishment, and crime prevention. Which of these predominates in practice?

For Foucault, discourses are always linked to what he calls 'disciplinary power' in that they are 'concerned with the regulation, surveillance, and government of, first, the human species or whole populations, and second, the individual and the body' (Hall 1994, p. 123). They are, in other words, the means of organising and transmitting social control. In this sense discourse is a less neutral, innocent term as it is involved in maintaining social power.

Foucault suggests that at different historical moments these discourses cohere in different ways: religious and moral discourses used to be the dominant ways of understanding criminality (see Foucault 1979). Now legal and medical discourses carry more weight. There is a continuous struggle between competing discourses, each of which attempts to instate itself as the overall discourse for making sense of a particular aspect of the world. Because this model understands that the dominant discourse changes over time, it incorporates the possibility of social change. New discourses can emerge that challenge existing power relations. This is the major difference between discourse theories and theories of ideology, which seem to suggest a much more fixed view of how society works.

The second major difference between discourse and ideology is that discourses tend to be modes of thought, speech, or expression whereas ideologies can be these things as well as being material in the sense that they can be found in buildings or activities. Rosary beads and crucifixes, for example, are part of the ideology of Catholicism, but not part of the discourse of Catholicism, whereas Scorsese's films, in which these material objects frequently appear, are part of that discourse because film is a mode of expression. Discourses do, of course, result in material practices—the kind of prison that a society builds will depend on its discourse of crime and criminality—but discourses remain modes of thinking and speaking, modes of expression.

Discourses of criminality in *Dead Man Walking*

In the film *Dead Man Walking*, Sean Penn plays a convicted criminal sentenced to death by lethal injection as a punishment for rape and murder. Susan Sarandon is cast as a nun who acts as his spiritual adviser and seeks to rehabilitate him and redeem his soul. In this film the religious discourse is linked to rehabilitation, the medical discourse is linked with administering the punishment, and the legal discourse is bound up with the restrictive aspects of prison policy and politics. Each of these discourses can be conceptualised as a set of discussions in which ideas linking medicine, law, and religion to prison are articulated and circulate in society. These ideas find expression in interpersonal conversations (such as those between Sarandon and Penn's characters, and between audience members after they see the film), in mediated communication such as the film text itself, and in the written laws that condone or prohibit capital punishment.

Within contemporary Australian media many news reports focus on the length or severity of sentences imposed on criminals, how appropriate these are, and what the effects are on the victims of crime. Embedded within these reports and discussions you will again find various discursive positions in relation to crime.

Ideology

Ideology is a complex term (see p. 34). Within media studies it is defined as follows. Ideologies are sets of social values, ideas, beliefs, feelings, and representations by which people collectively make sense of the world they live in, thus constituting a world view. This world view is naturalised, a taken for granted, commonsense view about the way the world works. It is important to note that this definition is linked to, but somewhat different from, one that you may already have come across; within politics, the term 'ideology' is often used to refer to a set of deliberately formulated, coherent, rational ideas that are used as ways of defining how society can be organised, such as a conservative, or socialist, or eco-friendly, or fascist ideology, which can be personalised into a Cameron ideology, an Obama ideology, a Gillard ideology, and so on. When used in this way the term ideology usually suggests that the ideas are in some way unrealistic, rigid, and dogmatic. Our definition of ideology extends its meaning beyond the rational to include feelings, and beyond a narrow political view to consider all aspects of the world.

Every person has a set of values, beliefs, and feelings that make sense to them and enable them to function in the world (see Errol Morris' quotation at the beginning of this chapter). Whatever we do—whether it is donating money to a charity, angling for a promotion at work, inviting someone to go to a concert, or watching television—it not only has to make sense to us in some way but it also enacts the way that we make sense of our world. Our actions arise from our view of the world and they act out our values, beliefs, and feelings, flesh out the fact that, say, we believe it makes sense to help those less fortunate than ourselves, or to compete with others in order to become successful, or to initiate a relationship by going on a date rather than by means of arranged marriage. Since the way we conduct our lives is an interconnected social practice, this stresses that people make sense of the world collectively. In all societies there are shared values, beliefs, and feelings that govern how people act and live together, a shared common sense. Institutions such as schools and television contribute to this interconnectedness, since they provide forums for a wide range of individuals to receive the same message. If an ideology is to have a significant social impact, it must be shared and agreed upon by a large group of people, which is why the mass media are so important in communicating and reinforcing ideologies.

Beliefs and feelings in ideologies: 'unconscious consciousness'

Our definition stresses that beliefs and feelings are important to any ideology. This takes us out of the realm of the purely rational and conscious; people's ideologies are connected to their hearts as well as their heads, and ideologies are not consciously thought out. They operate at the level of what Althusser called 'unconscious consciousness'.

This is a very useful concept. We perform many human actions without being conscious of our motives. We do not always think carefully about what we are doing; many of our social actions are imbued with beliefs, feelings, and values, and are performed with unconscious motives.

A simple example illustrates this. What happens when you and a person of the opposite sex approach a door together? Who goes through first? Does either of you hold the door for the other or invite the other to go first? Does either of you immediately go in front of the other? Watch other people and yourself in this situation. Normally, you would do whatever you do without much conscious thought, but behind the choices you make lies an ideology of gender relations (and/or age).

There are a number of different possibilities:

- the man holds the door open for the woman, who goes through
- the man opens the door for the woman, who then invites the man to go through
- the woman maintains or quickens her pace, while the man slows his, allowing the woman to arrive at and go through the door first
- the woman holds the door open for the man; and so on.

Tradition has women going first. How can we understand the ideology of this?

The following are different interpretations of what this means in terms of gender relations:

- it shows male respect for and deference towards women and constitutes a recognition that women are superior
- it shows women as powerful
- it shows men treating women as inferior and weak, as needing male help for this activity
- it suggests that although women go first, men control the action by opening the door, thus demonstrating male power
- it demonstrates male fears since men who open doors for women are sending women into environments first so that the women will ease the way socially for them, thus allaying male fears about their own social skills
- it relates to a medieval ideology and code of chivalrous behaviour
- it is a way of showing that men and women are different.

Most of these views suggest that men control what happens. While these explanations allow for the possibility that women might take positive action in advancing towards the door first and might even enjoy being shown respect, they can still be seen as accepting the notion of male power. People wanting to challenge such behaviour might deliberately break the convention by having women wait for men to pass through first, or by taking turns in going first. This may seem a trivial incident, yet it is an aspect of day-to-day gender relations. Now that you have read this, the next time you come to a door with someone of the opposite sex you will be conscious of what is happening, which will encourage you to reflect on what gender ideologies and relations are implicit in such actions. It may also make you wonder what to do next!

The point is that in many areas of life, people act at the level of unconscious consciousness; they do and say things without thinking about their motives or their unconscious assumptions and ideological world views.

The consequence of our living and behaving through unconscious consciousness is that certain patterns of behaviour become naturalised, defined as part of human nature, regarded as common sense or the way things are. These behaviour patterns are not seen as ideological by those who practise them. Indeed, they are not even thought about much, which relates back to our ideas about language and the social construction of reality (pp. 61–2): neither language nor social organisations are natural; both are constructed even though both are often regarded by people as natural and normal. We have already suggested that you should think carefully whenever anyone suggests that the way humans act is normal or natural. If someone says to you that something is just human nature, look for the ideological implications in the action they are describing. Remember that the consequence of naturalising behaviour is to naturalise and thereby hide ideology. In this way ideology is capable of reinforcing existing power relations and social structures in a manner that inevitably works to the advantage of one group (the dominant group in that context), and disadvantages others by making them seem abnormal, different, or deviant.

Conclusion

We can never fully escape the framework of our own perceptions of the world. Ideology is constituted by and concealed in our world view, and in language. Trying to see ideology and step outside it or look around it is like trying to see contact lenses when we are looking through them. In *The Matrix*, when Morpheus offers Neo the choice to understand what the Matrix is or remain in a world of dreams and illusions, and when he later shows Neo 'the construct', the way he describes the Matrix also works as a good description of ideology: 'The Matrix [ideology] is everywhere, it's all around us … it is the world that has been pulled over your eyes.' As Levinas says, we see the world as we are, not as it is. It is possible for us to become aware of our ideologies, to become conscious of our unconscious consciousness and sometimes to make changes to our world view and how we live in the world but we will still always have a set of values, beliefs, and feelings that guide our behaviour, determining how we think, feel, and act, even if they are new. Our ideologies may change over time, and you will probably be aware of changes you have gone through in your own life. But in losing one ideology or world view, we replace it with another. This is not a bad or a good thing; it is just the way things are. Ideology as a world view simply describes the state we live in.

In this sense ideology is a neutral term, a description of how people will always function on the basis of their world view. We should also note that in any society different groups may have quite different ideologies that may be contradictory. So there is room for a variety of ideologies, different world views that we expect to find in the media. It is useful as a critical term as a way of picking out the naturalised world view, the commonsense assumptions that lie behind any media text.

This chapter has

- defined the terms 'discourse' and 'ideology'
- examined discourses of criminality
- explained and illustrated unconscious consciousness.

Discussion points

1   Think of film and television shows that explore criminality and punishment, such as *Breaking Bad*, *Underbelly*, *Lie to Me*, *Law and Order*, *Sons of Anarchy*, *Misfits*, *Dead Man Walking*, *The Town*, *The Departed*, *The Shawshank Redemption*, *Public Enemies*, or *The Silence of the Lambs*. What discourses surround the issues of crime and imprisonment in each of these?

2   Apply your understanding of the term 'discourse' by identifying and discussing the different discourses used to communicate about and make sense of drug use in television series such as *Weeds, Breaking Bad, Sons of Anarchy,* and *Misfits,* and films such as *Pineapple Express, Fear and Loathing in Las Vegas, Trainspotting,* and *Scarface.*

3   Can you find any examples of *unconscious consciousness* operating in your daily life? What ideological implications underpin these examples?

Summary

You should now be able to

- explain what the terms 'discourse' and 'ideology' mean
- discuss different and changing discourses of criminality
- explain unconscious consciousness
- show how natural, commonsense ideas and actions are ideological
- consider the ideologies of gendered behaviour.

CHAPTER 12

Where Are Discourses and Ideologies Found?

> *Surely one of the most visible lessons taught by the twentieth century has been the existence, not so much of a number of different realities, but of a number of different lenses with which to see the same reality.*
>
> Michael Arlen

This chapter will

▶ show how discourses and ideologies are embedded in language, texts, institutions, and identities

▶ introduce the key terms interpellation, identity, and subjectivity

▶ analyse media texts that demonstrate ideology and interpellation at work

▶ consider how our identities and subjectivities are constructed.

The previous chapter defined discourse and ideology and suggested that it is difficult to see these clearly because they are naturalised, commonsense ways of understanding the world. To try to make the concepts easier to understand and identify we can ask: Where are discourses and ideologies embedded? Can we see them? What examples will illustrate them?

There are three places to look for and find ideologies:

1   in language, texts, and representations
2   in material institutions
3   in our heads and hearts (our subjectivities and our identities).

Discourses and ideologies in language, texts, and representations

Language, texts, and representations are the most significant sites for media studies. In our analysis of language (p. 69) and advertisements (p. 151), discourse frameworks and ideological meanings have already been mentioned. To see these in media texts simply ask the following question of any text you analyse: What are the values, beliefs, and feelings that inform the way this text makes sense of the world?

Case study: Children's early readers—ideology at work

Look at children's early readers as an example. The books children are given to learn to read are a fascinating repository of ideological meanings and discursive frameworks and are particularly interesting because they are one of the early media sources that socialise children. *The Key Words Reading Scheme* (Murray 1964, 1990), first published in 1964 and better known as the Ladybird *Peter and Jane* books, is a readily accessible example. Try to locate copies of these books to look at. The early editions are obviously out of date and have been superseded by a new series (*Learn to Play: Tom and Kate*, first published 1990), but the *Peter and Jane* series was still being published in 1990 and may well be familiar to you. Because they are from a past era it is easier for us to see the ideologies they present. All countries and all school systems have some equivalent to these books, such as the *Dick and Dora Happy Venture Readers* in Australia and the *Dick and Jane* series in America.

A close look at the illustrations and text from these books reveals a number of significant ideological, discursive aspects.

The first point to make is that they present one family—Peter and Jane and their parents—as the ideal, natural, normal family. This family discourse is imbued with a particular set of ideologies, the most obvious being its ideologies of class, ethnicity, and gender. Peter and Jane's family is the nuclear family: mum, dad, two children, and pet dog. The home is middle-class and suburban. The illustrations show a detached home (which signifies middle-class in the United Kingdom) and a sizeable garden, and combined with the storylines, the series depicts a family with enough money to buy good toys and go on regular holidays. The family members are white, though later editions of the series included some people of colour as background characters.

The values of the children are conformist in relation to two institutions: the police and schools. In *Boys and Girls* (a title that seems interested in setting up difference and delineating acceptable behaviour for the two genders) the text reads: 'Peter and Jane like the school'. In *Things We Like* the text reads:

> 'Look, Jane, that is a Police car. It says POLICE on it. That is the Police Station. I like the Police,' says Peter. 'They help you.'
>
> 'Yes,' says Jane. 'The Police help you.'

Without wishing to denigrate the institutions of the police and education, it is clear from the perspectives of class and ethnicity that the police and schools may have very different meanings for, say, Aboriginal children, black South Africans, African Americans, or black Britons living in inner-city areas, where the police, for example, may not be seen so simply as 'good' but as agents supporting the dominant white middle class.

It is in the gender area that the stereotyped ideology is most apparent in these books. The boy is always older than the girl, thus validating male power through age. Jane also looks up to Peter. This is literally so in a number of illustrations that depict Jane in physically lower positions, often sitting rather than standing. This age hierarchy continues in the narrative, in which Peter is the main character. He is given more actions to do whereas Jane is often given a supportive role, praising and validating Peter's behaviour. She acts as cheerleader for his football exploits: 'Peter has the red ball. He plays with the boys with the red ball.' Jane looks on. '"That was good, Peter," says Jane. "That was good."' Jane also tends to serve Peter: 'I want a cake, please,' says Peter. 'A cake for me, please,' he says. 'Here you are,' says Jane. 'Here are some cakes.'

Both children are socialised into helping with domestic chores, which encourages ideals of pride in property and reinforces the notion that good behaviour is rewarded. But these chores are clearly divided on the basis of gender: boys work outside the house, girls work inside. '"Here we are at home," says Daddy. Peter helps Daddy with the car, and Jane helps Mummy get the tea. "Good girl," says Mummy to Jane. "You are a good girl to help me like this."' Mother is depicted in the home more than Father, who goes out more: 'Peter and Jane are in the car with Daddy. They like it in the car. Mummy is at home.'

All of these gendered differences are presented as normal, and thus ideologies of gender, class, and ethnicity are naturalised. Children do not necessarily internalise these values when they read the books, but if they do not they will not find themselves reflected in these stories. And children whose families are different from this normal, ideal family may perceive themselves as different, as not fitting within the norm. Children who are not white, middle-class, and living with happily married parents are not being addressed. Either you take on these values as normal, or there is no space for you in the narrative.

You can do a similar ideological analysis by looking at the children's reading books you had when you were growing up or at children's television programs. Educational programs such as *Sesame Street* and *Playschool* present a more modern world than the world of Peter and Jane but they still carry ideological meanings. Entertainment cartoons such as *The Simpsons*, *South Park*, and *Angela Anaconda* also present various ideological views of the family and children.

We have used childhood in relation to readers to show how people from a young age are ideologically socialised and to encourage you to reflect on your childhood experiences. But the point is that all media texts, all forms of language and representation, carry ideological meanings; many of our examples throughout this book aim to show how they work.

In relation to how children grow up within ideological frameworks Barthes went beyond texts when he analysed children's toys. He saw that toys were also instruments of socialisation, determining how children would see and understand the world. Toys, like media texts, are socialising agents. They help children to learn what their role in society might entail, and they enable them to practise playing that role. Dolls, trucks, tea sets, and toy medical instruments enable children to imitate adult behaviour and practise adult roles, while children's media texts model adult roles and enable children to explore these possibilities via the mechanisms of identification and fantasy. As Barthes says, 'The fact that French toys *literally* prefigure the world of adult functions obviously cannot but prepare the child to accept them, constituting for him, even before he can think about it the alibi of a Nature which has at all times created soldiers, postmen and Vespas' (Barthes 1973, p. 53). This leads us directly into more material areas of ideology, which are explored next.

Ideologies in material institutions

So far in this chapter, we have spoken of ideology in terms of representations; however, ideology can also be see in actual material institutions and human activities. Most obviously, this can be seen in the buildings that structure our lives, marking out our territory, determining how we can behave and act in the world. In Australia the idealised quarter-acre suburban block is a space for families to grow up and socialise in; in the United Kingdom, flats or terraced houses do the same. These architectural arrangements confirm that we live in family-based spaces. Our houses structure some space as communal and social, for the whole family; other spaces in houses (bedrooms, toilets, bathrooms, and so on) are defined as more personal and private. Many Western cultures structure their buildings around the culture and ideology of the family, so that it seems perfectly normal and natural to live in these separate spaces rather than in more communal forms. Visit any new housing estate and you will see how the structure of rooms is built around adults' and children's spaces. Familial ideology is embodied and naturalised through architecture.

These architectures do change. Feminists have noted how, with the gradual emancipation of women since the nineteenth century, kitchen and cooking areas, which were once separated and placed in inferior positions at the back of houses, have become bigger, more central, more comfortable, and more communal, showing the increased status of the activities conducted in them and the sharing of domestic activities with men.

Case study: Educational buildings as an example of ideology in material institutions

As a more extended example, it is interesting to look at educational buildings to see how the organisation of interior spaces has a built-in ideology of education.

Write down your thoughts on what ideology of education is built into lecture theatres and then read the following commentary.

Lecture theatres are built for one-way transmission: knowledge is given out from one person, one source, to many people. Those seated are invited to look at and interact with the lecturer, not each other. They are invited, by the desks attached to the seats, to take notes, thus validating what the lecturer is saying. Apart from the taking of notes, the theatre is essentially a passive learning place—the student remains seated and doesn't talk—and one in which students absorb information and knowledge from the lecturer, the overheads, the screen, and the whiteboard. Education is focused on the mind and rationality rather than the body and feelings.

First, this suggests that knowledge is not to be gained experientially but by accepting views from authority. It sees knowledge as rational rather than emotional. It suggests that knowledge is there to be transmitted to students, rather like pouring knowledge from a jug into the students' upturned mouths. In this process, the lecturer is given power and a voice: the lecturer speaks, students listen; the lecturer may stand and move about, students remain in their seats; the lecturer can survey all of the students at once.

Second, lecture theatre education is like mass production in factories. Many students are dealt with at one sitting and are regulated through the timing of lectures. No attention is paid to whether the time of the lecture is a good time for learning—education is controlled by the demands of time-and-space management, as in a factory, only here the product is students' minds, not cars or televisions.

You could argue that what education and the lecture theatre teach, what the ideology of education is, is that students have nothing worth saying. Education teaches you to be silent, to respect your elders, to keep still, and to ignore your body, your emotions, and your experiences.

Imagine for a moment a round building in which students sit on cushions arranged in a circle, all on one level, where before students start learning they enhance their concentration through meditation. You can see how such a building and its organisation of space would embody a different ideology of what knowledge, learning, and education are.

We have painted a somewhat one-sided view of the lecture theatre here. It does have an element of performance and pleasure built into it: like a theatre for plays, it is an auditorium (literally, 'a place for hearing'), with fairly comfortable seats and a stage for the lecturer to perform on. In addition, music, videos, and films can be transmitted. There are ways of using the space that challenge some of the aspects described here; however, inviting student response and interaction, while possible within the space, is not what this building has been constructed for. It does not reflect the ideology of education that has informed its architecture.

The material institutions we live in organise us in terms of space and time and this reflects the ideology of our culture. This is not to suggest that there is a conspiracy to socialise us; rather, these architectural patterns have evolved as a way of fitting in with the dominant trends of a society. They become so much part of our everyday landscape that they seem quite normal to us. We lose sight of the process of social construction—until we see another way of doing things and realise that our own way is not the only or the natural way.

Ideologies in our heads, hearts, subjectivities, and identities

Are our identities ideological?

While texts and discourses exist outside us, ideology is internalised by us. If we accept values such as those represented in the *Peter and Jane* books, then we carry those ideologies as part of who we are. The idea here is that our identities (our concepts of who we are) are, like language and ideologies, constructed, which was discussed in Chapter 4 when looking at our individual names (pp. 65–6). This is quite a challenging belief because it causes us to question ourselves. What this suggests is that our personality, our individual identity, and our subjectivity have been produced by a number of external factors. Our ethnicity, class, religion, and gender are, once again, the most obvious. Ask yourself: Would you be a different person if you were of a different nationality, or if you were from a different class, or if you were of the opposite sex? Would you be different if you had been born in a different century? How would you be different? By asking these questions, you may begin to get a sense of the constructedness of your own identity. Identity can also be formed by things such as height, weight, attractiveness, and so on. All these factors go towards who we are and how we think of ourselves. Would being fatter, thinner, or more attractive or having a name such as Sunny or Mohamed change how you feel about yourself and how you are perceived by other people? So, in our identity we internalise particular ways of thinking, feeling, and believing, we take on particular ideologies. One of the most interesting aspects of the new media technologies is in relation to identity. The cartoon joke that says, 'On the internet nobody knows you're a dog' that comes with a picture of a dog working on a computer, expresses this. Many people who play internet games or indulge in internet chat construct for themselves a new personality, an avatar, that expresses new parts of themselves. The possibility of playing with identity is seen as one of the most exciting aspects of the new technologies.

Interpellation

We can understand this process by using the term interpellate or **interpellation** (see also the advertisement analysis, p. 164). For example my teachers 'hailed' or 'interpellated' me, Michael, as 'the wild Irishman' and I accepted this, recognised myself, and internalised the ideological values of the wild Irishman as my identity (see p. 65). Althusser used the term, arguing that 'the process of internalising ideologies', which we have been discussing above, 'is facilitated through interpellation' (Althusser 1977, pp. 162–70; O'Sullivan et al. 1994, pp. 155–6). This 'hailing' has the effect of putting us in our place or positioning the addressee in relation to the addresser.

> **interpellation**
> A process in which we internalise ideologies as a response to being hailed or addressed.

The Nintendo game *Joanna Dark*, for instance, released to rival *Lara Croft: Tomb Raider*, was advertised with the tag line: 'Are you man enough for Joanna Dark?' This question is hailing—addressing—the audience as male, as though only men would play the computer game. The audience is also positioned within the discourse of sexuality and is assumed to be not just male, but also heterosexual. There is a good reason for this: the game *Joanna Dark* is in '3D first person shooter' format, which means that those who play the game have to *be* Joanna Dark. In other words, male players have to transvest themselves, in a virtual sense, and occupy a female body in order to participate in the game. So as to overcome any discomfort that this act of virtual transvestism might cause, the marketing strategy interpellates audience members into a position of sexual conquest. Joanna Dark's character is code named Perfect Dark, thus the fantasy of conquering the perfect woman fuses with the fantasy of inhabiting a body that is a perfect combat machine. Instead of threatening the player's masculinity by asking him to pretend to be a woman, the text interpellates audience members into a subject position in which they willingly take on Joanna Dark as a challenge. This communicative strategy works because competitiveness and a sexually predatory attitude is an accepted (though not necessarily acceptable) part of the dominant discourse of masculinity.

Gender is central to identity, and gender socialisation is one of the earliest processes of interpellation. Try to remember, or imagine, how people talked to you when you were young and how much they encouraged you to see yourself as either a boy or a girl. ('It's a boy' or 'It's a girl' may have been the very first words spoken in your presence.) To confirm this gender identity you probably adopted certain kinds of appropriate male or female behaviour. Simply being labelled as 'boy' or 'girl' may determine your behaviour to some extent. Note how you yourself might talk differently to boys or girls, thus interpellating them in different ways. Think of the following popular nursery rhyme that contrasts 'typical' good or bad gender characteristics:

Sugar and spice and all things nice, that's what little girls are made of.

Slugs and snails and puppy dogs' tails, that's what little boys are made of.

The rhyme interpellates us at an early age with male or female characteristics; if we want to prove by our behaviour that we are typical boys and girls we behave accordingly.

Pick up a copy of any newspaper and note how it interpellates its readership into particular subject positions. Do you notice that different sections of the newspaper seem to be addressing different social subjects? The sports section hails the reader as male, the social pages hail the reader as female, the finance section positions readers as anonymous but tends to locate them within a privileged, well-educated class. What are the specific differences in these modes of address? Do journalists speak to the public differently, depending on whether they assume that they are addressing a male or a female, a professional, or a tradesperson? You might also notice that the local news section and the world news section locate the reader within a particular national identity, assuming allegiance to and interest in that nation's celebrities, issues, and events. For world news, the same event will be reported differently in different countries, in a manner that is geared to position the audience to respond in certain ways, depending on whose interests are at stake.

Nationality and interpellation

National identity is also crucial in our understanding of who we are. In South Africa new ways of describing citizenship and the nation emerged after the first democratic elections in 1994 in the form of slogans such as 'the new South Africa' and 'the rainbow nation'. These phrases assume that all South Africans share a desire to distance themselves from the divisive past of apartheid, and they address and interpellate citizens as members of a unified but diverse and colourful group with a hopeful future.

In Australia, because the history of white settlement is relatively short, many Australians feel that establishing a national identity is a crucial task. Phrases such as 'un-Australian' (used to describe certain activities, such as snobbishness, being pretentious, cheating, or betraying the code of mateship) and 'a fair go' are typically Australian. They mark out the territory of what 'we', as Australians, understand as acceptable behaviour; when we are spoken to using these terms, we are interpellated as Australians.

mode of address
Refers to the way a text speaks to or addresses its audience.

The media work as a hailing, interpellating system. The way they address us (their **modes of address**), constantly interpellates us—as family, as citizens, as children, and so on. This is particularly true of television and radio, where there is often a 'direct address' by announcers to 'you', the listener. Such modes of address give us our identities and subjectivities.

Case study: Interpellation in sports coverage

It is useful to examine how the pronouns 'us' and 'we' and the possessive 'our' are used in the media as forms of interpellation. During the Sydney Olympics the *Sydney Morning Herald* headline on the day of Catherine Freeman's 400 metre final was 'Race of *Our* Lives' (emphasis added); when Australia recorded an amazing Test cricket win over Pakistan in 1999 the *West Australian* headline was '*WE* DID IT' (Figure 12.1; emphasis added). Who is being interpellated in these headlines? Who is being included within 'our' and 'we'? Are you included? Who is being excluded (since any notion of an inclusive we/us always implies an excluded them/other)? And what ideologies and discourses of identity are being constructed and circulated here?

The Freeman caption occurs in the context of the Olympic Games. As this competition is held between nations, Freeman's race is Australia's race and the 'our' of the caption assumes all readers to be Australians (although many non-Australians would have been in Sydney at the time). What is significant here in the construction of Australian national identity is that an Aboriginal woman becomes the leading symbol and representative of Australia. It thus includes and unites Aborigines and non-Aborigines, men and women, together as 'us', as Australian. It could be argued that the reverence and adulation shown by the Australian media and people to Catherine Freeman goes against the norms of discrimination against Aboriginal people and was part of a public-relations campaign attempting to show the rest of the world that

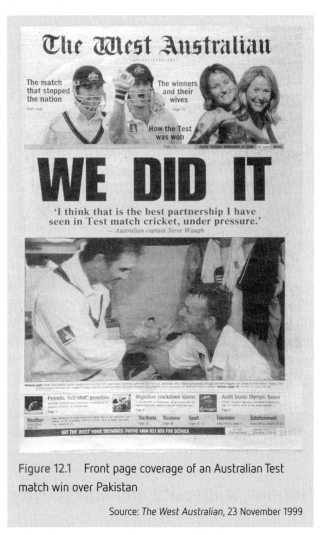

Figure 12.1   Front page coverage of an Australian Test match win over Pakistan

Source: *The West Australian*, 23 November 1999

Australia was a well-integrated, non-discriminatory, multicultural society. Alternatively, it may be seen as a powerful symbol and example of reconciliation and a challenge to discrimination.

The cricket headline example, in the context of the other words and photographs of the front page, has further complexities. The 'we' here could again be seen as referring to all Australians, but as it is a picture of two white men it could be seen as interpellating just white, male Australians or even just white, male, cricket-loving Australians. There is a further complexity in that the 'we' may refer only to Adam Gilchrist and Justin Langer, and since these men both played for Western Australia the 'we' comes to mean Western Australians in opposition to other Australians; the headline can thus be read within a context and history of interstate rivalry within Australia. The implied and excluded 'them' is most obviously the Pakistani cricket team, but this could be widened to be all Pakistanis, all non-Australians, or all non-Western Australians. The headline is thus not as inclusive of all Australians in its interpellation as the Freeman headline. The other words and images are interesting in the way they provide further narrative threads and interpellated positions.

- The reference to the players' wives seeks to interpellate and include female readers (though within a heterosexual and competitive discourse).
- The image of mateship and teamwork draws on earlier digger ideologies of Australian warriors (the two sporting heroes may be viewed as similar to the young male heroes of the film *Gallipoli*) that naturalises the idea of inter-nation conflicts between 'us' and 'them'. This is supported by the caption 'How the Test was Won', which is a wordplay on 'How the West was Won', a celebration of the subjugation of the indigenous native peoples of the USA.
- Finally, the caption, 'The Match that Stopped the Nation', refers us to the Melbourne Cup horse race, thereby making this event equally significant and nationally inclusive. The words 'we', 'us', and 'our' thus become rich interpellative mechanisms worthy of detailed analysis.

We hope you can come to an understanding of this process of interpellation and can see how it may relate to your own identity in terms of nationality, gender, ethnicity, and so on. If you have never been in a situation in which your identity has been challenged, for example by moving to a new society or by changing your name (or even by going to the gym, which tends to change body image), the process of interpellation may be difficult to see. While your national identity, your personal name, and your body shape may seem to be a natural part of you, try to see these as parts of your constructed subjectivity and be aware of how the media will address messages to specific aspects of your identity for marketing purposes or to serve other vested interests. Also, please note that throughout this book we use our own structures of interpellation in the way that 'we' address 'you'.

Notions of identity and subjectivity

Are we cogs in the machine, or do we have free will?

'Identity' and '**subjectivity**' are terms often used in media studies. They are partly interchangeable: both refer to the way we understand who we are—our identity—and the position from which we look at and understand the world—our subjectivity. A key question for both is: Are these natural or are they socially constructed? And this raises another question: Are we defined and determined by forces outside of us—like cogs in a machine—or are we self-determining, autonomous individuals with free will? We live in a culture that stresses individuality, encourages us to believe that every person has unique qualities, and puts forward the view that we have control over who we are, what we do, and how others see us, but this view is questionable.

subjectivity

Pertains to an individual's personal thoughts and experiences, their own—subjective—way of seeing the world as distinct from general or universal experience, and objectivity.

On the one hand Western culture glorifies the individual and understands much of what happens to the world in terms of individual actions (see Chapter 23). News stories and political events are presented to us as the stories of individuals—politicians, businesspeople, criminals, and so on—and what they do. Entertainment, sports coverage, films, and television programs focus on individual stars and personalities. These media products are often also packaged in terms of the individual stars they feature. Magazines gossip about the private lives of individuals. History is often presented and taught in terms of key individuals. Even media studies sometimes stresses the individual role of media moguls, such as Bill Gates, and influential film directors, such as James Cameron or Tim Burton. These characteristics of the media relate to the ideology of individualism that permeates Western culture.

On the other hand, the nineteenth and twentieth centuries produced numerous academic and theoretical perspectives that show the opposite—that individuals are not in control of their own destinies, that we are subject to forces beyond our individual, conscious control. Challenges to the view that individuals have control over their own destiny have come from several major sources.

1 Darwinian theories of evolution and survival of the fittest suggest that we are determined by our genetic and biological evolution, which determines what we do and who will survive.

2 Marxist theory sees class struggle and economics as the motor and determinant of history (it holds that we act in accordance with these impersonal forces). According to **Marxism**, it is the actions of whole groups or classes, not the actions of individuals, which change the world. The following passage paraphrases Marx's view that humans have only a limited degree of autonomy: People make history, but only on the basis of conditions which are not of their own making (see Marx [1852], 1948).

Marxism

The theories developed by Karl Marx, including that the struggle between different groups in society (classes) brings about historical change, that economic needs are the most important factor in determining people's behaviour, and what people think and believe is controlled, often unconsciously, by the dominant social groups.

3 Freud, the father of psychoanalysis, and his followers have argued that we are determined by our unconscious, driven by our basic drives towards survival and pleasure. We act on the basis of these unconscious desires and the fears associated with them, rather than on our conscious choices.

4   B F Skinner and other behaviourist psychologists have suggested that all human activities are simply determined responses to external stimuli: in other words, we do not act, we react (see Skinner 1976).

5   Saussure and other linguists have suggested that language determines who we are, what we think, and how we understand the world; rather than saying 'we speak language', we could say 'language speaks us'.

6   More recently, feminists have put forward the view that gender is the key factor determining who we are and how we behave.

7   Those working on the problem of racism have proposed that ethnic origins are the most important factor dictating behaviour and identity.

8   The theory of memes, developed by scientists such as Richard Dawkins and Susan Blackmore, argues that humans evolve through imitating others, that successful memes—patterns of behaviour—are passed on from one person to another and thus become part of who we are, our identity.

So we have two polarised positions. The first sees humans as possessing individual autonomy and free will—the ability to make our own choices and determine our own destiny. The second sees humans as cogs in the machinery of biology, psychology, history, and culture.

The term 'subjectivity' draws attention to our autonomy and to the fact that our actions are predetermined or subject to influences beyond our conscious control (Fiske 1987, pp. 48–61). The word 'subject' (derived from a Latin word that means 'thrown under') is about us having power: in grammatical terms, sentences are built around the structure subject–verb–object: someone or something (subject) does something (verb) to someone or something (object). Similarly, to 'subject someone to something' is to have power over them. On the other hand, we talk of people being subjects of kings and queens: as subjects we are under the power of other people and other forces. When we think of our own subjectivities it is helpful to see both the autonomous power we have (the fact that we have our own way of seeing and operating in the world) and the determined quality of our identity or subjectivity (the way it has been shaped by outside forces).

Conclusion

We do not have a final answer to the question 'Do humans have free will or is their behaviour determined?' (although we hope you noticed that we presented most of the nineteenth- and twentieth-century theories that challenged human autonomy in terms of the individuals who pioneered them). However, we do question the notion that individual identity is something existing outside culture. It is useful to see the ways in which individual identity is actually a social construct. Discussing this, cultural theorist Kathryn Woodward states:

> Identity can be seen as the interface between subjective positions and social and cultural situations ... Identity gives us an idea of who we are and of how we relate to others and to the world in which we live. Identity marks the ways in which we are the same as others who share that position, and the ways in which we are different from those who do not (Woodward 1997, pp. 1–2).

Woodward stresses the role of 'symbolic systems'—the media, images, and language—in contributing to our identities: 'Representation as a cultural process establishes individual and collective identities, and symbolic systems provide possible answers to the questions: Who am I? What could I be? Who do I want to be?' (Woodward 1997, p. 14).

We argue that ideologies are found within these symbolic systems (and in material systems such as buildings), and that these are therefore an important aspect contributing to the construction of our identities and subjectivities. Understanding this is a form of consciousness raising (raising awareness of social and political issues) that can give us more power and awareness in terms of understanding ourselves and others, and can help us to decide how we would like to act in future. Seeing how we are determined by the ideology we were born into, seeing how our behaviour has been shaped since birth (when people first start telling us who we are and how we should act) can give us a broader set of social choices about who we want to be and what we can do in the future. We can break out of earlier ideological constrictions.

This chapter has

- shown that discourses and ideologies can be found in language and representations, material institutions, and in individual identities and subjectivities
- defined and illustrated 'interpellation'
- examined issues of individual identity.

Discussion points

1   Look back at children's readers and books you grew up with and see what ideologies and discourses of class, ethnicity, gender, and the family are embedded in them.
2   Look at children's television programs to see what ideologies they construct.
3   Look at the architectural plans for new public buildings or houses. What ideology or ideologies are they constructing?
4   Consider how many different names you are known by. What are the ideological implications of these different names and how do they contribute to your own identity and subjectivity?

5   Look for examples of interpellation in the press, magazines, and television and discuss how these work.

6   Examine ways in which the media interpellate people as Australian.

7   Discuss the validity of theories that suggest individuals do not have autonomy.

Summary

You should now be able to

- discuss where you can find discourses and ideology
- find examples of ideology in symbolic systems—language and media representations—and in material institutions
- define interpellation and show how media texts interpellate audiences
- find examples of media interpellations
- reflect and comment on how these concepts relate to your own sense of identity and your social position
- explain briefly how and why individual identity can be understood as a social construction
- denaturalise ideology by identifying areas in your everyday life and surroundings where assumptions about social values are present.

CHAPTER 13

Dominant Ideology and Hegemony

The ideas of the ruling class are in every epoch the ruling ideas.

Karl Marx

This chapter will

▶   introduce dominant ideology theory

▶   explain how repressive and ideological state apparatuses work

▶   explain and illustrate the terms 'ideological work' and 'incorporation'

▶   show the limitations of dominant ideology theory

▶   suggest that the media are sites of contradictory ideologies

▶   introduce the liberal pluralist model of society

▶   introduce and illustrate the concept of hegemony

▶   examine the discourses and ideology of Christmas.

The focus of this chapter is specifically on issues of social power in relation to ideology and the media. It will look first at Althusser's dominant ideology model, then question and modify it, and then introduce Gramsci's hegemony model.

Dominant ideology

Is there just one ideology or are there many ideologies?

So far we have talked about ideology and ideologies, which may have prompted you to ask if there is just one ideology or are there many? We argue here that there are numerous ideologies. Each social group has its own way of thinking, feeling, believing, and making sense of the world. It is possible to talk about ideologies (or discourses) of masculinity and femininity, of Australianness, Britishness, or Asianness, of blackness or whiteness, of teenagers or senior citizens, of middle and working class, and so on. In this sense we have used the term simply as a description of how people always think and feel through ideology and in recognition of the existence of different ideologies.

We now want to introduce and consider the idea of a 'dominant' or 'ruling' ideology, as suggested by the French Marxist philosopher Louis Althusser (Althusser 1977, pp. 147–8).

This use of the term was Althusser's way of understanding how social power is maintained in society by the dominant social groups. Althusser, following on from Marx, suggested that each society has a **dominant ideology**. Marx, in an earlier version of this idea, talked of the 'ruling ideas' of a culture, suggesting that when the proletariat or the subordinate group internalised and accepted the ideas of the ruling class they formed a kind of 'false consciousness'.

dominant ideology
A world view that supports the ruling class as dominant, the status quo, yet is shared by the majority of people.

The dominant ideology—comprising a set of shared feelings, values, beliefs, and so on—is shared by the majority of people in a society, thus making it dominant in two senses. First, it is dominant in numerical terms. Second, it is dominant in the sense that it tends to support the interests of the dominant, ruling groups. We are interested in the way dominant ideas, beliefs, and values, which support particular groups in society (whites, the middle class, men), come to be accepted and believed by many people in society. We are also interested in the way the media contribute to this acceptance.

Below are some relevant extracts from the works of Marx and Althusser. They are complex and densely packed with concepts and ideas, but this density means they are rich with meaning and import.

First, here is Marx discussing ruling ideas.

The ideas of the ruling class are in every epoch the ruling ideas: in other words, the class that is the ruling material force in society is at the same time its ruling *intellectual* force. The class that has the means of material production at its disposal has control at the same time over the means of mental production, so that in consequence the ideas of those who lack the means of mental production are, in general, subject to it. The dominant ideas are nothing more than the ideal expression of the dominant material relationships grasped as ideas and thus of the relationships which make one class the ruling one; they are consequently the ideas of its dominance. The individuals composing the ruling class possess, among other things, consciousness, and therefore think. In so far, therefore, as they rule as a class and determine the whole extent of an epoch, it is self-evident that they do this in their whole range and thus, among other things, rule also as thinkers, as producers of ideas, and regulate the production and distribution of the ideas of their age: thus their ideas are the ruling ideas of the epoch (Marx [1846], 1974, p. 64).

Marx, as you can see, stresses ideas, but sees these as determined by material forces, that is, the forces of economic ownership and production.

Althusser's wider concept of ideology takes us a stage further in the argument about how societies adhere to values and ideas supporting the dominant groups and how ideology is not worked out consciously or conspiratorially.

> It is customary to suggest that ideology belongs to the region of 'consciousness' ... In truth ideology has very little to do with 'consciousness', even supposing this term to have an unambiguous meaning. It is profoundly unconscious ... Ideology is indeed a system of representations, but in the majority of cases these representations have nothing to do with consciousness ... they are perceived/accepted/suffered cultural objects and they act functionally on men via a process that escapes them. Men 'live' their ideologies ... *not as a form of consciousness, but as an object of their 'world'*—as their 'world' itself ... The ruling ideology is then the ideology of the ruling class. But the ruling class does not maintain with the ruling ideology, which is its own ideology, an external and lucid relation of pure utility and cunning ... the bourgeoisie has to believe its own myth before it can convince others (Althusser 1977, pp. 233–4).

Althusser's concept of ideology thus goes beyond pure ideas and consciousness to the way in which people believe in ideology. He sees ideology as an unconscious force that people live rather than see: it is lived 'as their "world" itself'. Both these extracts argue that ruling ideas or ideology are so deeply embedded in our society that they are shared by almost everyone and seem totally normal.

We can see similar ideas in the film *The Matrix* when Morpheus suggests that the constructed world of the Matrix has been used to blind Neo to the truth (see p. 177). When Neo asks 'What truth?', Morpheus replies, 'That you are a slave, Neo. That you, like everyone else was born into bondage, kept inside a prison that you cannot smell, taste or touch. A prison for your mind'. The Matrix, like the dominant ideology, has been accepted as good and natural even though it may not benefit the majority of people. The force of the dominant ideology, or the illusion of the Matrix, prevents individuals or groups from questioning or challenging those in power or overthrowing the system that exploits them.

As another example, think how unproblematically people accept the basic notion of private property, the notion that individuals can claim exclusive ownership over all kinds of goods and land. Private property is so taken for granted in Western society that it may seem ludicrous to challenge it, and indeed, it may seem as though everyone benefits from it because everyone owns something. We certainly do not want our precious possessions taken away from us. But private property has evolved in societies where ownership of property is predominantly in the hands of a minority. According to a study by the World Institute for Development Economics Research of the United Nations University, the richest 2 per cent of adults in the world own more than half the world's wealth (Davies et al. 2008, p. 7). Who really benefits from the system of private property, a system well maintained by laws and law-enforcement bodies? (Some offences against private property in Western cultures are traditionally subject to punishments greater than those meted out for some assault offences; for example, fraud can attract a harsher penalty than rape.)

What happens to this commonsense ideology when we say 'All property is theft'? This saying, attributed to the French philosopher Pierre-Joseph Proudhon and taken up by Marx, asks us to rethink and re-evaluate the social conditions of property. To say I own something is to deny others the right to share it: it is to steal it from them. How much of our own property have we actually made ourselves? Have we really stolen it from someone else? Compare this ideology with Aboriginal ways of relating to material things or to the African concept of *ubuntu* (which refers to community and shared responsibility in terms of child rearing, social welfare, and so on). Ideas of community, sharing, land guardianship, and communal ownership offer a very different possibility, a different way of organising how we live in the world and use its resources.

This is not to say that private property is wrong. Rather, it is suggested here that this ideology, which is shared by most people in the West, may actually be most beneficial to those who traditionally have owned the most. This dominant ideology (dominant because it is supported by most people) supports the dominant (socially powerful) groups. What we want to do here is to shake up your common sense, your accepted values, just to show that there are other points of view.

In these times, as the world's resources are depleted, questions relating to the desirability of our system of private property may be particularly urgent. The ultimate aim of our consumerist society is for everyone to possess their own car, fridge, electrical goods, and so on. The economic growth of our society is built on this attainment of an ideal and comfortable style of living. If this were achievable it would be wonderful, but the possibility of planetary survival, given the continuing explosion of private ownership of consumer goods, is questionable. The Latin word from which the term 'consume' derives—*consumo*—means to destroy, the implication being that consumers are destroyers. The ecological crisis may reach a point at which society will have to find some new way of living, some new ideology, in order to survive.

RSAs and ISAs

Why do subordinate groups accept the power of the dominant groups?

Althusser wanted to understand how ideology was transmitted socially, how it was that people took and accepted the values of the dominant groups even if these views might not be in everyone's interests. He suggested two sets of mechanisms that achieved this: repressive state apparatuses (RSAs) and ideological state apparatuses (ISAs) (Althusser 1977, pp. 133–48).

RSAs

RSAs are mechanisms that are called into play to force people to conform to the dominant ideology. They are used deliberately, to control, punish, and coerce people who attempt to challenge the system. They are primarily the institutions of the law, the law courts, the police, the prison system, and the army, all of which are used to deal with people who trouble and disrupt society. RSAs do not work ideologically on people's feelings and beliefs; they work directly through force (including force of law) and, when necessary, through punishment. They are only deployed for extreme forms of social disorder, such as crime or mass protest. In the media, censorship laws and policy restrictions on media ownership provide this form of control.

RSAs
Repressive state apparatuses—the institutions of force that societies use to control people, for example the army, police, law courts, and prisons.

ISAs

ISAs, of much more interest to media studies, are the institutions through which people are socialised into accepting the dominant ideology. ISAs do not force people; they work more like hypnosis, convincing people or winning their consent to the dominant ideology. Althusser identified key institutions that carry out this socialisation process: religion, the family, the education system, and the media.

ISAs
Ideological state apparatuses—the institutions of socialisation and persuasion that societies use to control people, for example religion, family, education, and media.

The media are now very important; in many ways they have taken over the central role once occupied by the church, which has declined considerably since the nineteenth century in many countries (although fundamentalist churches still have significant influence on small groups of people). Together with the family and the education system, the media offer ways of understanding and making sense of the world and of ourselves. They explain how people should think, act, and feel. It is important to note that these institutions may not always agree: religion, education, and family ideologies may at times conflict with each other and with the ideologies presented in the media.

The media as an ISA

How do the media work ideologically? What values and beliefs do they construct as normal, natural, and desirable? How do the media work in relation to the dominant ideology? These are major questions in media studies and there are no simple answers, indeed, they are the subject of much debate in media studies. We will outline some of the main positions below.

Althusser's basic argument is that the media tend to support the dominant ideology. They do this by producing programs and products that support the values of white, patriarchal, capitalist culture; however, to do this successfully the media have to overcome two problems.

1 In order to win support for the dominant ideology the media must also win the support of subordinate and minority groups in society (women, indigenous people, the working class, and so on). They must come up with products that give these groups pleasure, since these groups comprise the bulk of the audience.

2 The media are often drawn to addressing social tensions, focusing on social conflict and problems. News and current affairs, for example, focus on moments of social disruption and conflict, 'bad' news. Drama, fiction, and films are nearly always based on conflicts between characters and between value systems. Police dramas, for instance, one of the major prime-time genres of popular television, always focus on moments of, and places associated with, social breakdown. They choose to explore crime, and consequently, at some level, consider the social causes of crime, touching on poverty, inequality, unemployment, drugs, and so on—major social issues that threaten to disrupt society. Situation comedies focus on the family and gender relations and thus draw attention to the battle of the sexes and the breakdown of the family unit.

Thus the media often draw our attention to social problems. But this does not mean that they call into question the ultimate desirability of the current social system. What is of interest here is how these programs deal with and resolve the social issues raised while still supporting the dominant ideology. Television news, by providing a forum and mouthpiece for dominant institutional voices, ultimately reassures and normalises every disruptive act, thereby allaying our fears about the stability of our world. Police dramas, while they depict poverty and crime and raise them as potential social problems, tend to turn criminals into psychopaths, sick individuals, not like us (thereby reassuring us that we are not like criminals) and the police into figures that we identify with. Situation comedies, while they do raise issues relating to the family and gender relations, relieve our tension through the safety valve of humour. In all these examples, we can say that the ways the media deal with the problems constitute ideological work: ultimately, their resolution will not disturb society. Rather, they allow the predominant ideology to be maintained.

How do the media do ideological work?

We will now explore three ways in which the media do this ideological work.

1 By 'masking and displacing' social issues and problems

As discussed above, the media can hide or avoid social problems. This happens in a number of ways.

• Some issues are simply avoided or rendered invisible. These are the issues that do not get media coverage at all. Some social groups are notably absent from certain types of media representations: popular drama rarely features Aboriginal culture, handicapped and differently abled groups, gay culture, and so on. Such groups are often marginalised through their exclusion.

- Social difference is masked or displaced by interpellations that address all social groups under a unifying label. The three most common interpellations or forms of address used by the media are to address the audience as 'family members', 'citizens of a nation' (for example Australians, South Africans), and as 'members of the public'. Sometimes we are addressed as all three at the same time. These labels and interpellations are not false. We are all family members, citizens of a nation, and members of the public. But these labels—which are used to unite us, to bring us together as equals, and to suggest that we share the same aims, needs, and desires, and the same views about the ideal family and national goals—also mask and displace differences: differences between white and indigenous Australians, between rich and poor, between two- and one-parent families, between men and women, among others. These interpellations focus on some parts of our identity rather than others: 'family member' focuses on our family and domestic identities rather than on our working identities as trade unionists, factory workers, office cleaners, company managers, and so on. Social differences, particularly those relating to class and ethnicity, are dissolved into the unities of domestic and national identity. The media thus favour interpellations that unite us rather than those that highlight social difference. The common family address heard on television—'You and your family'—assumes all viewers watch as parts of families, thereby excluding viewers who are not 'family viewers'.

- Social problems and contradictions are often masked or displaced by being understood in personal or psychological terms or within a moral framework of good and evil, rather than in social terms. Police dramas are a good example of this. A criminal's behaviour is often understood as the result of individual personality disorders: the criminal has a psychological problem. The social causes of crime, such as unemployment and drug trafficking, which have the potential to portray this criminal as typical of a social group, are displaced in favour of personal, psychological explanations. When you next watch television, listen to the radio, or read a newspaper article, see how the social problems being raised are addressed. Are they explained as the result of social causes or are they personalised in terms of individuals with particular personal problems? Consider how contemporary television series represent drugs and drug-taking: *Breaking Bad* is a good example of a series that focuses on individuals caught up in the problems of drugs and drug trafficking. The series aligns viewers with Walt, a high school chemistry teacher with a disabled son who finds he has terminal cancer, a new baby on the way, and no means to provide for his family. The audience becomes so enmeshed with Walt's personal problems that his decision to use his knowledge of chemistry to cook and deal crystal meth in a desperate bid to avoid leaving his family destitute almost seems like a reasonable choice. It is only in subsequent seasons that Walt's successful dealership is seen to have devastating effects on innocent people, and that drug trafficking is placed in a wider social context that draws attention to social problems such as addiction, border control, and gang warfare. Mainstream police procedural dramas such as *Law and Order* or reality programs such as *Border Patrol*, on the other hand, align the audience with the law enforcers and remain focused primarily on the regulatory and judicial context.

2 By incorporating or containing other ideological positions

Rather than attempting to disallow or even censor dissident ideological voices the media sometimes neutralise these voices by allowing them space but containing them within the overall system. Since the end of the Second World War, youth cultures in Western societies have threatened to disrupt ideologies of how youths should behave. Popular artists such as rappers Eminem and P Diddy and the comedian Ali G have managed to amass a huge fan base because they actively resist the dominant order. These prominent figures in youth culture undermine what they see as political correctness and set out to alienate members of 'nice', 'responsible', 'mature' social groups. As Nick Hornby, author of the novel *High Fidelity*, argues, by contrast with the violent misogyny of Eminem's rap collective D12, whose bestselling album *Devils Night* contains lyrics such as 'Independent women in the house/show us your tits and shut your mother f—ing mouth', the 'sonic ferocity', obscenity, and nihilism of groups such as the Sex Pistols and Nirvana seem 'thoughtful and politically engaged' (*Weekend Australian*, 3–4 November 2001, pp. 4–6). But all these figures are allowed some space in the media and are thus made acceptable.

incorporation or recuperation
The processes by which dangerous, rebellious, radical ideas and movements are made acceptable, not by banning or criminalising them but by partially accepting them; 'incorporated' means, literally, 'taken into the main body'.

Some attempts are made to curtail youth movements through legal and police action focused on drugs and youth gatherings (the RSAs at work), but the movements are often better contained by allowing them to continue within the confines of the society: in other words they are accommodated, or **incorporated**, or **recuperated**, or contained within society in such a way as to defuse their radical potential.

The challenges thrown out by youth cultures are incorporated into an ideology that recognises teenage years as a natural time of rebellion—this is what it means to be a teenager, so it is acceptable. Popular music is incorporated into the music industry, television shows such as *Rage*, and radio station playlists (radio announcers provide the music with a context and accompanying commentary that gives it a safe, socially acceptable interpretation). The new technologies of popular music—iPods, MP3 players, mobile phone ring tones, and peer-to-peer file sharing (P2P)—construct music in terms of fashion and technological sophistication rather than a voice of social challenge. Significantly, the 'noise pollution' associated with youths playing music on large, portable 'boom boxes' in public in the 1980s has been effectively neutralised by the introduction of personalised musical devices with discrete headphones.

These days, owning certain portable technologies and using them to consume music in public can function as a generational marker. For example, Apple products such as iPods, iPads, and iPhones are now seen as fashionable accessories, a trend reinforced by slick advertising and clever product placement in films—30 per cent of the top movies in 2010 featured Apple products.[1] While music technologies also have business applications and are being taken up by older people too, part of the appeal of Apple products is their strong association with youth culture and members of Generation Y, or the 'Millennial Generation'. The commercialisation and popularisation of elements of youth culture defuse them of their radical challenge.

In relation to who has the right to speak on the media, democratic societies have actually encouraged 'other' voices: for example, television channels such as Australia's SBS and the United Kingdom's Channel 4 are understood to be forums for the articulation of marginalised positions. But it can be argued that these forums again function to incorporate these different voices (rather than allowing them to fulfil their radical potential) by including them as a minority part of the mainstream, thereby preventing the social groups represented from feeling left out and causing social disruption. Similarly, while mainstream television channels occasionally present challenging programs that question the dominant ideology, their very positioning within normal television schedules—surrounded by advertisements, trailers, and other non-challenging programs—functions so as to neutralise their messages, which get lost by being incorporated into the overall output of television and by the way in which audiences have been encouraged to be passive spectators.

We can even see incorporation at work in narrative structures—the way stories are put together (see p. 260). Many popular fictions are drawn to social problems. Initially, a narrative may give support to a radical point of view, but then the way that the narrative is structured and resolved neutralises this point of view. Thus, as a whole, the narrative incorporates or contains radical positions, which is why we stress the importance of narrative structure in relation to ideological meanings.

residual discourse
Set of ideas and beliefs from the past that are still accepted by some people.

Residual, dominant, and emergent discourses

In his analysis of media, society, and ideology, *Marxism and Literature*, cultural theorist Raymond Williams has described three different kinds of discourse: **residual discourses**, **dominant discourses**, and **emergent discourses** (Williams 1977b). These are very useful terms for media analysis. Today many texts explore the ways in which men and women relate. For women this is often presented as a question of

dominant discourse
Contemporary ideas and beliefs shared by a majority of people.

emergent discourse
New ideas and beliefs held by a few people at first, and then gradually becoming accepted by more people.

---

[1] Dilger, D E 2011 'Apple products appeared in 30% of all top movies in 2010' <http://www.appleinsider.com/articles/11/02/22/apple_products_appeared_in_30_of_all_top_movies_in_2010.html>. Published 22 February 2011; [Accessed 1 August 2011]

how to balance desires for relationship, children, work, freedom, and independence; for men it is a question of how to balance their traditional masculine qualities of assertion and aggression with a more caring, emotional masculinity, and to balance their desire for relationship and independence. Williams would see this in terms of residual, dominant, and emergent discourses of femininity and masculinity. Residual discourses might relate to women's desires to be swept of their feet by a knight in shining armour, a man who would save and look after them, or to men's patriarchal beliefs in their right to treat women as property. Dominant discourses relate to the ideas and beliefs about masculinity and femininity that are currently shared by most people in Western societies—beliefs that women and men are equal, but different, and that this equality should be reflected in equal opportunities, equal wages, and shared domestic responsibilities. These discourses emerged from the 1960s onwards influenced by what was then the new and emergent discourse of feminism. Current emergent discourses of femininity and masculinity might suggest that women and men can live separately, or that children can be brought up perfectly well by same-sex couples.

In relation to media texts Williams argues that it is possible for all three discourses to be present in a text at the same time, which brings us back to incorporation. You can probably find films and media stories in which women say that they want to have their independence but also want to get married and have children—*No Strings Attached, Switch, Knocked Up, He's Just Not That Into You, The Proposal,* and many other films and television programs are good examples of this. It quite often happens that the emergent discourses—for example the desire for independence or to explore different sexual experiences—end up being subsumed into the more traditional, residual, and dominant discourses of monogamous marriage, children, and family. The narratives thus include the three kinds of discourse, but although they allow the women to explore new possibilities at first, they end up by placing them back in traditional roles and in this sense they once again incorporate and contain these new aspects of femininity.

3 By giving audiences texts that are pleasurable

There is one more crucial aspect of the media to be noted here: pleasure. Most people use the media for pleasure and relaxation, so the media work hard to give us pleasures. As audience members and consumers, our feelings of pleasure (our emotional responses) may be more important than our ideological understandings of the media—if we enjoy a program, who cares what its ideology is? Ultimately, this attitude is crucial for the media to win our support. Fiction stories offer the pleasures of suspense, excitement, spectacle, chases, emotional involvement and identification with characters, humour, and so on (see Chapter 19). Most advertisements, films, and television programs offer us the pleasure of looking at and identifying with the beautiful people and objects that are portrayed. Such texts subtly seduce us into conceding that they represent ideal types and desirable commodities, and believing that if we purchase the products or emulate the people represented, we will be more like the models or actors and will find pleasure, happiness, and desirability. If a media text such as an advertisement for fast food offers us pleasure, it is hard to resist. Try telling a child with a sweet tooth and a desire for a cute toy that comes with a Happy Meal that hamburgers and milkshakes are unhealthy and ideologically unsound. In consuming the product we may also consume the ideologies it presents.

The limitations of dominant ideology theory

This description of how the media work ideologically contains many useful insights. Using the terms and methods given above to unpack the ideological work of the media will reveal a lot, but there are problems associated with this model too.

Throughout this book we have stressed the contradictory nature of the media, its good and bad possibilities (see pp. 12–13). The dominant ideology model, while useful, ultimately runs the danger of seeing the media purely in a bad light and allowing no possibility for alternative positions.

First, the model is too simple in the way it suggests ideology is just administered by the dominant groups and accepted by the masses. It paints ideology as too much of a one-way system. It suggests that the dominant ideology is always imposed from above and accepted unproblematically by people. This does not account for people who refuse to accept these values or for the two-way struggle that goes on between dominant and subordinate groups in establishing social values. Ideology can easily be thought of as an all-powerful force that the media wield to induce conformity and that the ruling members of society use to brainwash and subordinate the rest of us, but this is not strictly the case. People are not sheep who are helplessly herded about by ideological forces. Just as media audiences do not passively accept and absorb the intended meaning of media texts (see pp. 101–02), individuals and groups do not always accept or conform to the dominant ideology. More importantly, it is possible to have many different ideologies, many different world views, any of which can challenge the dominant ideology.

Second, the argument about incorporation given above is too rigid: you can argue that democratic societies are able to neutralise any dissident voices through incorporation but it can also be argued that rather than being neutralised, radical ideas are actually being popularised and are thus beginning to shift the overall ideology of society. The dominant ideology model doesn't allow for the fact that there are people working in the media who challenge the dominant ideologies. It is important to remember that the media and their producers and consumers are capable of representing and engaging with alternative ideas: ideological assumptions and norms can be challenged and changed. Films such as *An Inconvenient Truth* or *The Eleventh Hour*, for example, have been able to challenge the dominant ideology in relation to issues of climate change. As John Hartley has argued in analysing media representations of ethnicity and Aboriginality:

> [I]f we accept that the media ... encourage racism in certain of their ways of reporting the world, then we have also to believe that they can influence ... for positive change as well as negatively ... that the media are forces for progressive social change as well as for negative social stereotyping (Hartley & McKee 1996, p. 73).

The theory of dominant ideology is thus too rigid and simplistic. It does not allow for contradictions and variations within the development and establishment of ideology.

Third, because media technologies are now more accessible, so people can write their own blogs, produce their own videos, CDs, and so forth, means that the media are no longer so controlled by elite groups.

We want you to be aware of situations in which the media are an expression of the dominant ideology but also to see them as a site for competing and contradictory ideologies as well as a place where you as journalists, filmmakers, or scriptwriters can do positive and creative work. Taking account of these criticisms, there are two other models of society for thinking about how the media work ideologically.

Liberal pluralism

liberal pluralism
A liberalist pluralist society is one that includes many different social groups with different viewpoints; they all have the liberty and opportunity to speak out.

The models of society discussed so far suggest an imbalance and struggle between dominant and subordinate groups. The **liberal pluralist** model of society, probably the viewpoint of most Western democratic countries, offers a different perspective. A pluralist society has many different social groups, and therefore exhibits a plurality of many different voices that may have different social perspectives and positions, but within a democracy all are allowed to speak and will have some access to the media. This suggests that different social positions simply coexist alongside others, in the same way that, say, people of different ethnic backgrounds coexist. According to this view of society, everyone has a chance to produce media products within the free marketplace of the media and audiences are free to accept whatever views they wish to. This pluralist position argues that we all have the right and opportunity to speak and that within the society we are all equal.

We value the opportunities of democracy and see the possibilities for the media to present many different voices and a whole range of sometimes contradictory ideological viewpoints (including our own) but we still return to an overall view that society and the world as a whole are unequally positioned. Gramsci's model of hegemony is a way of acknowledging these imbalances and understanding how the media can be a site of competing ideologies and discourses.

Hegemony

The word '**hegemony**' comes from *hegemonia*, the Greek word for leader. Theories of hegemony were developed by Antonio Gramsci, a leader of the Italian Communist Party in the 1920s and 1930s who was imprisoned by the fascist Mussolini regime.

hegemony
Power and leadership maintained through processes of struggle and negotiation, especially through winning the consent of the majority of people to accept the ideas or ideologies of the dominant group as common sense.

Hegemony is a way of understanding how one social group maintains its ultimate power over subordinate groups. This power and control is exercised through influence, persuasion, and struggle. The concept of hegemony explains why oppressed groups don't revolt: their ideas, needs, or interests are being represented or recognised by the system to a certain extent, enough that they consent to their place in society. So when we speak of the maintenance of hegemony we are referring to a way of maintaining power, but we also acknowledge resistance to the exercise of that power. The major point about hegemony is that it suggests that maintaining power over others is always a process in struggle: it is never stable, it involves participation and negotiation on both sides, and it is a two-way process (in contrast to ideology, which tends to be conceived of as a one-way process, imposed from the top down). It is in this two-way process that people can use the media in ways that can challenge the dominant ideas and ideology.

| How is hegemony maintained? | |

Just as Althusser recognised the power of RSAs to maintain social control, Gramsci acknowledged that coercion—force—was one method that could be used to maintain power and leadership. This was particularly the way that authoritarian states, such as the Soviet Union, fascist countries including Second World War Italy and postwar Spain and Portugal, and the South African apartheid regime, maintained power by using institutions such as the police, the law, and the army, all of which have the capacity to enforce compliance and punish dissidents (see p. 197). But Gramsci was most interested in how hegemony is maintained through consent.

Consent as a method of maintaining hegemony parallels the way in which ISAs are maintained. Gramsci saw consent as the basis of the social organisation of the democratic societies that predominate in Western culture. The notion of hegemony as maintained by consent brings us back to a question posed at the beginning of this book: How do the media win support for their representations?

It can be seen how hegemony works by imagining an example of it at a micro social level: the interactions of a parent and child. The parent holds the main power (in the same way as the dominant groups in society hold power) over the child, yet cannot always make the child do what the parent wants. Children have wills of their own, and parents constantly have to resort to bribery or blackmail ('You can watch television if you do your homework') or to the granting of concessions ('You can have half of the sweets now and half later') in order to get their way. (They could use force as well, but this would not win consent.) Parent and child are involved in a process of negotiation and struggle.

At a macro social level, similar negotiations and struggles go on between bosses and trade unions, political parties and lobby groups, men and women, whites and Aborigines, and so on.

Gramsci's theory of the continual negotiation and struggle between dominant and subordinate social groups suggests that there must be some positive reward for the subordinate groups in order for them to accept their social conditions: Western democracies, for example, must offer enough freedoms, pleasures, comfortable lifestyles, and media entertainments for members of subordinate groups to accept the status quo.

The big question is whether these rewards and concessions will result in only small and gradual changes that actually leave the dominant powers still in control or whether they can lead to fundamental social change. In relation to gender ask yourself whether, despite all the changes and concessions won by women and feminism, the hegemony of men, of patriarchy, is still maintained. In relation to halting climate change, will gradual changes that allow us still to operate within a culture of economic growth and consumerism work or will we need to adopt fundamentally different ways of living? We cannot give a definite answer to these questions but there is one other aspect of Gramsci's theory that is useful for understanding how the media work: the idea of **counter-hegemony**. People working within the media (and elsewhere) can attempt to challenge the dominant ideology, as Hartley suggested above, by working to produce a counter-hegemonic world view (see Chapter 14).

counter-hegemony
A world view or activity that is in opposition to and challenges the dominant world view.

The aim is to get popular support for a new discourse or ideology that will challenge the status quo. It is this possibility for change and contradiction that takes us out of the impasse of a dominant ideology imposed from above. Such counter-hegemonic activities are explored in the next chapter. Once again, it is important to note that the new media technologies of the internet and digital communication have opened up many new channels of communication that provide an increased means for people to engage in communication struggles.

Case study: Christmas ideologies, discourses, and hegemonic struggle

By now you should be beginning to see the complexity of ideology and hegemony and their potential richness as ways of understanding how societies work. What follows is one last example: Christmas. By analysing the contradictory ideologies and competing discourses of Christmas we will illustrate how ideology is rarely simple, and how hegemonic forces win our consent by incorporating conflicting ideologies and offering us various pleasures associated with media consumption.

Most societies are based on a set of contrasting and competing ideologies or discourses. Some of these will be very old, others more recent; some will be current, others will relate to the emerging values of new groups in society (as Williams suggests with his categorisation of residual, dominant, or emergent discourses; see p. 201).

Christmas is used as an example of this complexity. While Christmas is not actually a media text, within Western cultures it can be considered a media event and it is certainly a social and cultural phenomenon that creates a great deal of media attention—including advertising blitzes, Christmas songs and carols on the radio and in the shops, and special cinema releases and television programming. More recent Christmas films include *A Christmas Carol* starring Jim Carrey, *A Very Harold and Kumar Christmas*, and *Once Upon a Christmas Dream*. Older Christmas-themed movies get played on television at this time of year too, such as *It's a Wonderful Life*, *Love Actually*, *The Polar Express*, *Home Alone*, and even *The Grinch* and *The Nightmare Before Christmas*. Many television series have Christmas specials, even the residents on Ramsay Street in *Neighbours* encourage Christmas festivities, and news programs follow stories about Christmas celebrations and Santa sightings. All together, Christmas becomes a media event; a media event is something that, like the Olympics or an election, overshadows and

Figure 13.1   Christmas cartoon

Source: Bestie, The Ink Group, 1994

disrupts normal programming and involves a bevy of special features and interviews across a number of media forms.

It is useful to consider Christmas, which derives from Western cultural traditions, in relation to other religious traditions. Holy days and the texts, rituals, and celebrations through which they are communicated are elements of religious discourse. In this respect Christmas coexists with holy days that are relevant to other religions: Hindus and Jews celebrate different versions of the festival of lights, called Diwali (for Hindus) and Hanukkah (for Jews); Muslims celebrate Ramadan and Eid-ul Fitr. Each religion can be understood as a value system, a way of making sense of the world: an ideology. Depending on where you live, Christianity may not be the dominant religious ideology, but you will still almost certainly be exposed to the media hype surrounding Christmas. You might think holy days would not be easily commercialised. Ramadan involves regular intervals of prayer and a strict period of fasting from dawn until sunset, followed by Eid-ul Fitr (feasting and celebration at the end of the month of fasting). Fasting is accompanied by other forms of voluntary deprivation (donating money to the poor and giving up pleasures and luxuries such as going to the cinema).

This custom is intended to make people value and give thanks for what is normally taken for granted, and to foster compassion and understanding for those who are less fortunate. However, Christmas has been almost totally commercialised and is gradually being exported throughout the world. Although there are some underlying similarities, Ramadan is in many ways the complete opposite of the excess consumption that characterises Christmas. Shopping centres may raise banners saying, 'We wish our Muslim customers well during the holy month of Ramadan', but they rarely advertise a 'Ramadan Sale' and Disney does not produce animated films teaching children about 'the spirit of Ramadan'.

Christmas was established as a major festival in the West in the nineteenth century, particularly in the USA and Victorian England. Many of the traditions and rituals of Christmas were formulated then and have persisted and developed since. Five distinct ideological strands or discourses that converge in Christmas as a cultural experience are identified below.

1   *Christianity* Christmas is of course a religious celebration of the Christian faith. The word derives from a church service (Mass) that celebrates the birth of the central figure of the Christian religion, Jesus (Christ), and it honours a more minor figure, Saint Nicholas (Santa Claus). As such, it emphasises love, spirituality, new birth, and the giving of presents to express our love and care for one another.

2   *Magic and myth* Father Christmas, or Santa Claus, is part of the magical discourse of childhood in which fantasies of generous elves and flying reindeer are played out against the fairytale backdrop of the North Pole. Children are persuaded to be good by being told that Santa needs little helpers, and that Santa won't bring gifts to naughty children. For many children, Santa is the central figure of Christmas and opening presents is the main event. Bible stories, baby Jesus, and attendance at church are becoming, for children, a subsidiary or residual discourse.

3   *Saturnalia and pagan festivals* Christmas is founded on and related to older religious festivals, for example, Greek and Roman festivals of Saturnalia (a winter celebration for Saturn,

the Roman god of agriculture, a time for wild revelry prior to the deprivation, frugality, and the cold of winter) and pagan celebrations that celebrate death and rebirth in the depth of winter and the move towards spring. The natural symbols of these festivals—trees, holly, mistletoe, and so on—connect with the fact that the religions associated with these older festivals involved worship of the earth and nature. Historically, Christianity incorporated these symbols partly to help establish itself as a successor to pagan religions. ('Festival' derives from the Latin words 'vale', which means farewell, and 'fest', from the Latin word for feasting, so it literally means 'farewell to feasting'; similarly, 'carnival' derives from the Latin words for farewell (vale) and the flesh (carne), thus meaning 'farewell to the flesh', because there will be little meat to eat until new animals are born in spring.)

Saturnalia allowed great indulgence, as do many holidays that today are seen as pleasurable breaks from work rather than as times of religious contemplation (holy days). Saturnalia also involved a social topsy-turviness—the turning upside down of normal cultural values and conventions. This occurred in such practices as role-reversal games (such as the rich serving and feeding the poor). Christianity won its audience over to the Christian story partly through maintaining and incorporating these other traditions and their pleasures. Saturnalia and other pagan traditions are still fundamental to Christmas. They have been blended with the religious story, even though they conflict with the religious meaning of Christmas in some ways. The holiday period allows for excessive partying, drinking, and merry-making, alongside observance of Christian religious ceremonies and the notion of giving to others and to the poor. While the contradictory nature of these elements may involve clashes between religious observance and general celebration, they tend to coexist reasonably well.

4   *Family* Christmas has become a time for celebrating and honouring the family, one of the cornerstones of modern society. The ideal is for everyone to spend Christmas Day with their families, an ideal that is lived out by many, but of course it breaks down for those people who do not have a family or do not live near their family. In reality it also often provokes major stress among families. Christmas is a time when there is a rise in marital and family breakdowns as well as a rise in suicides. Thus, as the holiday attempts to cement the ideology of the family, it also makes the cracks in the structure all too visible.

5   *Consumerism* While all four aspects—Christianity, magic and myth, Saturnalia, and the ideal of the family—are still central to Christmas, it has now become primarily a celebration of capitalism and materialism. Christmas is the time for a mass celebration and frenzy of consumerism, a mass spending of money. Christmas has become progressively more commercialised, such that the spending of money and the selling of goods is now the predominant feature of Christmas. It is often said that Christmas begins earlier each year, which is a reflection of the fact that the success of Christmas is measured, to a large extent, by shop sales. In 2011 Christmas goods, decorations, and music were being displayed in shops in September.

These five ideological aspects blend. It is difficult to take any one position on how to judge Christmas because all five contradictory aspects are in play at once. Presents, for example, are inscribed into all the discourses: they can be seen as an expression of our Christian love and charity to one another, they magically appear, they offer great pleasure, indulgence, and enjoyment, and the biggest presents are usually given to family members at present-giving rituals focused on family gatherings. And presents cost money—the more expensive the present the better it is deemed to be. Nearly everyone can find something positive in the present-giving aspect of Christmas, which accounts for its popularity. Those who decry Christmas—because it is too commercial, or because they are disgusted by the waste of money involved, or because they are atheists and disagree with the promotion of religion, or because they are Christian and disapprove of the orgy of indulgence that occurs—risk being labelled scrooges and being seen as outsiders.

Many Australians still hold on to old traditions that are linked to their British heritage, some of which, particularly the tradition of roast turkey and Christmas pudding, and the emphasis on winter, are clearly out of place in the Australian climate. But there is increasingly a move towards champagne breakfasts on the beach, picnics with cold meats, salads, and summer puddings, which is an attempt to construct new traditions and new ways of celebrating that take Christmas into another dimension. Some clever entrepreneurs are encouraging the celebration of Christmas in July as a way of connecting Christmas with winter and getting people to spend even more money on celebrations. It will be interesting to see how multicultural Australia develops Christmas rituals.

In this example of Christmas as a repository of different ideologies and discourses (residual, dominant, and emergent), contradictory aspects are at work, but they can exist relatively comfortably side-by-side. Similar contradictions can be found in media texts. The idea of contradictory ideological aspects and the attempt to understand how they work together is central to this book. You may well find traces of new and old ideological positions, and traces of progressive and conservative discourses, within the same media text. You will begin to see how different ideological elements interact, how they are linked, and how they are often cemented over (or sugar-coated, as is Christmas) with the promise of pleasure.

The discursive struggles and contradictions can also be seen in terms of hegemony. Different people find different ways of negotiating the Christmas event but most people consent to imprudent financial and dietary splurging during the festive season as the media constantly foregrounds the pleasures of giving and receiving, good will, and togetherness. Those who resist Christmas and refuse to buy into the consumerist ideology that has become so central to media representations of Christmas become outsiders, Grinches who must be persuaded of the value of Christmas and reincorporated into the dominant order.

The movie *The Grinch* (based on the book *How the Grinch Stole Christmas* by Dr Seuss) is a good example of hegemony at work because it gives space to and incorporates resistance to the ideology of Christmas, particularly the materialistic aspect. In the end the Grinch is won over, he accepts Christmas but rejects its materialism: 'Maybe Christmas,' he thought, '*doesn't* come from a store. Maybe Christmas … perhaps … means a little bit more!' He is then rewarded by love and acceptance: 'The Grinch's small heart grew three sizes that day!' But this acceptance of the spirit of Christmas barely masks the materialism that is still the predominant discourse of Christmas.

Conclusion

In this chapter significant similarities between dominant ideology and hegemony have been noticed in that both operate through a mixture of coercion and consent; the limitations of dominant ideology and how hegemony introduces a more flexible system of struggle and negotiation than the rigidity of dominant ideology have also been noted. It is useful to relate the processes of hegemonic negotiation back to the idea of ideological work (pp. 198–203), and to see ideological work—masking, displacing, incorporation—as similar to the hegemonic processes of winning consent.

We have noted how media texts can include contradictory discourses, radical and conservative aspects, residual and emergent discourses at the same time, and the importance of pleasure within media texts as another way of winning audience consent.

You should now be able to use theories of discourse, ideology, and hegemony as a way to unpack the complexities of media texts and their often contradictory messages and meanings. Instead of seeing texts as having total control over audiences, the concept of hegemony fits in with media theory that understands that audiences can do things to texts in the readings they make of them and the pleasures they derive from them, and that media practitioners can also challenge the dominant ideology.

This chapter has

- defined dominant ideology, ISAs, and RSAs
- explained and illustrated ideological work and incorporation
- defined the terms 'residual', 'dominant', and 'emergent discourses'
- considered liberal pluralism
- defined and illustrated hegemony.

Discussion points

1   How often do you notice the media addressing or interpellating its audience—you—as Australian or as a family member? Collect examples of these interpellations.

2   What are the similarities and differences between dominant ideology and hegemony theories?

3   Consider *The Simpsons, South Park, The Biggest Loser, The X-Factor*, and *RuPaul's Drag Race*. Are these programs products of the dominant ideology, examples of programs presenting counter-hegemonic values, or products that demonstrate that we live in a liberal pluralist society?

4   Find examples of residual, dominant, and emergent discourses within the way Christmas is represented in the media.

Summary

You should now be able to

- explain and critically comment on Althusser's theory of dominant ideology
- explain what ISAs and RSAs are and how they operate
- explain the concept of ideological work in the media and give examples
- define and illustrate 'incorporation'
- explain briefly the theory of hegemony and compare it to dominant ideology
- explain the concept of a liberal pluralist society
- explain the concepts of residual, dominant, and emergent discourses and find examples of these in relation to discourses of gender in media texts
- analyse how media texts reinforce, challenge, or negotiate the dominant ideology
- analyse the discourses of Christmas within Australian society.

CHAPTER 14

Culture Jamming and Counter-hegemony

'Culture Jamming' sticks where rational discourse slides off. It is, simply, the viral introduction of radical ideas. It is viral in that it uses the enemy's own resources to replicate itself—corporate logos, marketing psychology, clean typography, 'adspeak'. It is radical because—ideally—the message, once deciphered, causes damage to blind belief. Fake ads, fake newspaper articles, parodies, pastiche. The best CJ is totally unexpected, surprising, shocking in its implications.

Source: <www.abrupt.org/CJ/CJ.html>

This chapter will

▶ discuss ways in which media consumers can actively and creatively engage with the media, considering issues such as technology, humour, and legality

▶ outline some objectives of media activism

▶ offer a working definition of culture jamming

▶ analyse several examples of culture jamming

▶ explore the strengths and limitations of culture jamming as a counter-hegemonic discourse.

This chapter considers ways in which media audiences and media consumers can actively and creatively engage with the media and challenge dominant ideologies with a counter-hegemonic discourse.

Culture jamming is understood as a mode of resistance to the norms and conventions of mass culture that exposes and opposes the media's underlying power structures and ideological messages (Klein 2000). The term 'jamming' can refer to an obstruction, that is, the equivalent of a traffic jam for the media; it can also reference a more playful, spontaneous form of improvising and engaging with the media, as when musicians jam together. Culture jammers use their

culture jamming
A form of media activism that subverts and reworks the intended meaning of existing media texts, or parodies major corporations, public figures, and their media images.

familiarity with the codes and conventions of advertising and other forms of communication to throw a spanner in the production of meaning by creating spoofs, defacing texts, and subverting the intended meanings of the media texts that they choose to rework. Often they actively try to denaturalise the media images that we see every day by making us notice and question their underlying messages.

The objectives of culture jamming often include consciousness raising (raising awareness of social and political issues) as well as using the media to criticise the media and dominant culture. Culture jamming techniques can also be used simply to be clever or funny, without a political or critical motive. While purely comedic reworking of brands and ads may or may not be classified as culture jamming, the use of the communication techniques and styles associated with the movement for the purposes of product promotion is definitely not culture jamming, as our discussion of the Sprite examples below demonstrates (see p. 225). An actual ad cannot be an instance of culture jamming. The co-option of jamming strategies such as satire and graffiti into commercial branding is discussed later in this chapter, but bear in mind that culture jamming is a form of communication that can come only from outside commercial culture, not from inside the media industry.

What follows is several examples of culture jamming and a discussion of the issues that they raise.

- Graffiti campaigns conducted by feminists and anti-smoking activists.
- An email exchange that developed into an online campaign against Nike's employment policy regarding the manufacture of merchandise in free-trade zones.
- Recent innovations involving YouTube remixes, contagious media, and social networking.
- Posters designed by media students to jam a government public information campaign.
- Legal issues arising from culture jamming initiatives such as the Black Labour jam by Laugh it Off.
- The co-option or recuperation of communication strategies used in culture jamming back into mainstream advertising as a strategy to sell soft drinks and fashion merchandise.

media activism
Activities involving individuals or lobby groups that attempt to change the way in which the media works, or that use the media to make a social or political statement.

Culture jamming emerges out of a tradition of **media activism**, dating back to the 1970s, that addresses images in billboards and outdoor advertisements. In the 1970s, feminists, unhappy about the sexual objectification of women, started to paint slogans and captions on images of women used in outdoor advertisements. Such political graffiti drew attention to the sexism in these images and in so doing challenged patriarchy. To point out the harmful effects of smoking, anti-smoking campaigners adopted similar tactics, painting captions on cigarette advertisements. Both campaigns, in conjunction with political lobbying, appear to have had some effect in terms of bringing about changes to representations of women in advertising, limitations on cigarette advertising, and harsher regulation around smoking. This form of communication uses existing media texts (which normally reinforce the dominant ideology) to make an ideological critique. One Australian campaign promoting the value of people learning emergency first aid featured billboards showing a picture of a man who had collapsed. The caption read: 'Your husband's collapsed, what do you do?' The image implied an ideology of family support between husband and wife. Graffiti on one of the billboards read, 'Take his wallet', humorously undercutting the family ideal and exposing the possible economic inequalities experienced in marriage.

The Diesel spoof (Figure 14.1) shows how culture jammers have exposed the way that advertising offers tantalising images of unattainable perfection that serve to fuel consumption.

Figure 14.1   Inadequacy is fuelled by Desire

Source: Courtesy of Laugh it Off

Diesel's famously ironic and cryptic advertising campaigns frequently appear to criticise media messages, social norms, and the process of advertising itself. While the original Diesel 'Successful Living' and 'Happiness: Sponsored by Diesel' campaigns make fun of the notion that a corporation can brand anything, even an emotion, the 'Inadequacy is fuelled by Desire' jam playfully points out how Diesel is complicit in the same cycle of consumption that it critiques. The image shows an ordinary young couple frolicking in an artificial paradise, literally burning with desire for Diesel clothes. The text of the Diesel jam reads: 'Inadequate is how the media make you feel so that you desire what they are selling.'

Typically, the advertising industry relies on the fact that most people compensate for the feeling that they can't measure up to the ideals of beauty and wealth embodied by models in ads by buying products that are supposed to make them look and feel better. Laugh it Off, the authors of the culture jam, seem to be urging media audiences to 'slit desire in the throat and break capitalism's kneecaps' by refusing to consume such products, even by doing 'textual violence' to brands by defacing advertisements. Because the majority of culture jamming opposes aspects of the dominant culture it is sometimes referred to as a counter-cultural activity, or as a counter-hegemonic discourse. If capitalism and consumerism are part of the dominant culture, as expressed and promoted through the mass media, and if our consent for these ideologies is won by offering us the pleasures of consumption and the illusion of enhanced desirability, then it is clear why texts such as the Diesel jam can be considered to be counter-hegemonic. The discourse of mass culture speaks to us about consumption and appearance, and the counter-cultural discourse of culture jamming speaks about refusing to consume, and refusing to be seduced by images that offer unattainable, unhealthy, or unethical ideals. It is the form of communication (appropriating mass media texts and technologies), as well as the content of individual messages, that makes culture jamming subversive.

Technology

The content or message of media texts can communicate ideological values. In what sense can media technologies also be influential in challenging or reinforcing social norms and power dynamics?

Email and other forms of computer mediated communication (CMC) have been celebrated as being both democratic and empowering mediums of mass communication because they enable individuals and small groups to get their message out to large numbers of people without having to contend with restrictive policies and regulations or prohibitively expensive equipment and production costs. The world-famous 'McLibel' case, in which a handful of media activists used the internet to publicise a legal battle against McDonald's, was run on a second-hand computer in a rented room. CMC is also characterised by a direct feedback loop in which the senders and receivers of messages can exchange views and negotiate meanings.

While there are feedback mechanisms with traditional media such as newspapers, radio, and television, CMC is structured to facilitate a two-way flow of information, rather than the asymmetrical transmission of information in which the sender and receiver are separated by space, time, and an imbalance of communicative resources. In traditional media, audience members lack control over the means of transmitting messages, a gap that can only be bridged by initiatives such as phone calls or letters to the editor, or formal processes such as media research, ratings, and opinion polls. Mass media producers have an impersonal relationship with those who receive their messages and media consumers have less power and agency in the communicative exchange: consumers control the interpretation of the message, but they don't have access to the means of constructing their own media products and sending responses straight back to the producers. In online communication, the sender and receiver are connected by wireless technology or the network of phone and cable lines that link their computers to one another, so it is possible for the communicative exchange to retain some interpersonal characteristics. This in itself can be empowering for media consumers because they can make their point of view known and communicate it to other individuals with whom they have some personal connection.

For example, fans and critics of the popular vampire romance franchise, The Twilight Saga, interact with each other using digital media including online fan fiction and video spoofs to express not just their opinions about the narrative, but their views on its gender politics. In particular, the YouTube video *Buffy vs Edward* intercuts footage from the TV series *Buffy the Vampire Slayer* and the movie *Twilight*, showing Buffy mocking Edward's obsessive and inappropriate stalking behaviour and sneering at the suggestion that young women yearn for romance and need men to protect them. The vid culminates with Buffy unceremoniously trumping Edward in a clever cut to Robert Pattinson's death scene as Cedric Diggory in *Harry Potter and the Goblet of Fire*.

Case study: Use of email as a subversive technology

While he was a student at the Massachusetts Institute of Technology, Jonah Peretti made a statement against Nike's employment policies by putting in a routine request to have his sneakers customised. For a fee of $50 Nike offers to personalise their products by stitching a word or phrase under the Nike swoosh logo. This service, called 'iD', is part of a branding exercise that relates Nike to freedom of choice and freedom of expression by encouraging customers to build their own shoes. Noting the irony of this slogan in light of the conditions that employees who actually do build Nike shoes reportedly endure in free-trade zones, Peretti chose the word 'sweatshop'. In the email exchange that followed, Nike cancelled Peretti's order on the grounds that 'sweatshop' was 'inappropriate slang'. The ensuing email exchange spread spontaneously after Peretti forwarded it to friends who were interested in the subject, and they passed it on to their friends. Initially, everyone received the email exchange from someone they knew. Eventually, the exchange circulated around the globe and became part of a broader media campaign against the negative aspects of globalisation in general and Nike's alleged labour practices in particular.

In the following correspondence between Peretti and Nike you will note that none of Nike's messages address the issue of whether the company engages in unethical labour practices. For Peretti, Nike's refusal to engage with the issues he was raising was worse than an admission of guilt because it meant that no headway could be made.

Dear NIKE iD,

Thank you for your quick response to my inquiry about my custom ZOOM XC USA running shoes. Although I commend you for your prompt customer service, I disagree with the claim that my personal iD was inappropriate slang. After consulting Webster's Dictionary, I discovered that 'sweatshop' is in fact part of standard English, and not slang. The word means: 'a shop or factory in which workers are employed for long hours at low wages and under unhealthy conditions' and its origin dates from 1892. So my personal iD does meet the criteria detailed in your first email.

Your web site advertises that the NIKE iD program is 'about freedom to choose and freedom to express who you are'. I share Nike's love of freedom and personal expression. The site also says that 'If you want it done right ... build it yourself'. I was thrilled to be able to build my own shoes, and my personal iD was offered as a small token of appreciation for the sweatshop workers poised to help me realize my vision. I hope that you will value my freedom of expression and reconsider your decision to reject my order.

Thank you, Jonah Peretti

From: 'Personalize, NIKE iD' <nikeid_personalize@nike.com>

To: "Jonah H. Peretti" <peretti@ ....>

Subject: RE: Your NIKE iD order o16468000

Dear NIKE iD Customer

Regarding the rules for personalization it also states on the NIKE iD website that 'Nike reserves the right to cancel any personal iD up to 24 hours after it has been submitted'. In addition, it further explains: 'While we honor most personal iDs, we cannot honor every one. Some may be (or contain) others' trademarks, or the names of certain professional sports teams, athletes or celebrities that Nike does not have the right to use. Others may contain material that we consider inappropriate or simply do not want to place on our products. Unfortunately, at times this obliges us to decline personal iDs that may otherwise seem unobjectionable. In any event, we will let you know if we decline your personal iD, and we will offer you the chance to submit another.' With these rules in mind, we cannot accept your order as submitted. If you wish to reorder your NIKE iD product with a new personalization please visit us again at www.nike.com

Thank you, NIKE iD

Dear NIKE iD

Thank you for the time and energy you have spent on my request. I have decided to order the shoes with a different iD, but I would like to make one small request. Could you please send me a color snapshot of the ten-year-old Vietnamese girl who makes my shoes?

Thanks

Jonah Peretti

<no response>

Peretti has since gone on to co-found the *The Huffington Post* and he is CEO of BuzzFeed, an online media business that tracks internet trends and internet memes, which are images, videos, or phrases that catch on and spread like wildfire online. Read about Peretti's five tips to make content go viral at <http://techcrunch.com/2010/08/13/five-viral-rules-video>.

Culture jamming exercises

Print media

- Select an ad, a brand, a slogan, a magazine cover, or some other form of print media text that sends a message you disagree with or promotes a product, ideology, or ethic you object to, find hypocritical, or find humorous.
- Write down the intended meaning of the text, where you found it, its intended effect, and its inscribed reader and target audience.
- Use marking pens, collage, or software such as Photoshop to manipulate the image and rework or challenge its meaning (for example, add or delete text or images, write speech bubbles, or captions).
- Write down what your new intended meaning is, what effects you hope your jam might have, where you would like to publicise it, and who you would like to see it. (Sending it to friends via Facebook is one of the easiest ways to self-publish.)
- Show your jam to someone in the original target audience and ask them what it means to them.

Broadcast media

Take a television or radio advertisement and make up your own alternative or subversive soundtrack to replace the original.

Wireless communication, vidding, and social networking

How might you use your mobile phone, YouTube, or Facebook as culture jamming technologies for the purpose of media activism or political communication?

Around the world, many media students and media consumers have put the steps in the culture jamming exercise above into practice. One example is two media and journalism students, jammers Holly Zwalf and Shannon Huber, who wrote for a campus magazine, *Heretical/Philosophia*, a joint University of Queensland and Queensland University of Technology student publication (in which Figure 14.2 was originally published in 2006). These students noticed that a Queensland Transport media campaign aimed at improving security might actually be making the public feel insecure in the context of frightening media messages related to the war on terror and television shows such as *Border Security*. The campaign featured a series of posters in buses and train stations that targeted public transport users in much the same way that announcements in airports the world over tell passengers to report unattended baggage. The official posters state that 'Terrorism is no longer a world away' and urge citizens to become actively involved in 'Keeping our public transport system safe'. The intended meaning is that unclaimed baggage may contain a bomb planted by terrorists, and the public should all help contribute to counterterrorism initiatives. A perhaps unintended result of such messages is that they can create a culture of fear and mistrust (in the words of the culture jammers, 'keeping our public scared out of their wits') as citizens become de facto surveillance agents for the government, watching out for unusual behaviour or appearances, and reporting suspicious activity or abandoned baggage.

The jammers wanted to reveal the sub-texts and potential side effects of fear campaigns because they felt that such messages could contribute to anti-Muslim sentiment and racial divisiveness in the Australian community. They changed some of the text accompanying the campaign posters, keeping the 'What's wrong with this picture?' slogan which cleverly interpellates audience members into the position of looking for something anomalous. They also retained the official answer to the question: 'Bags without people don't make sense' and the injunction to report suspicious baggage or behaviour to the national security hotline. The text they changed and added articulates the implications of the implied narrative when taken to the extreme. It reveals possible negative effects of the campaign along with assumptions about the race and culture of the inscribed reader: 'normal' Australians (pronounced 'Stra-yins' with a broad Aussie accent).

The small print reads:

> This picture is part of a national campaign to instil fear into the hearts of every member of the public 'cos hey, if everyone is really, really scared then our country will be really, really safe! Safe from people who are not real Stra-yins. People who act suspicious. People who have bags or are standing near abandoned bags. People who have different coloured skin to normal Stra-yins. If you see a bag, report it. If you see a Muslim, report it. If you see a bag and a Muslim at the same time, definitely report it. They are most likely about to execute a well-thought-out plan to exterminate our noble Anglo-Saxon culture and fuck our economy in the process. Report anything suspicious (bags, Muslims and people with opinions) to transport staff or call the National Security Hotline.

Figure 14.2   What's wrong with this picture?

Source: Zwalf & Huber, *Heretical/Philosophia*, 2006

Case study: Laugh it Off—media, law, and humour

Accessible, affordable, interactive media technologies have enabled culture jamming in its different forms to spread through youth culture across the globe, informing far-flung groups of people about common concerns. While the Nike activists involved in the examples discussed above were challenging corporate culture in the USA and Australia, South African students at Rhodes University were also learning about the media and taking media technologies into their own hands. In 1999 Justin Nurse and his friend Chris Verrijdt played around with ideas in the journalism design studio at Rhodes and began printing brand satires on T-shirts. They used the logo of a popular beer to make a political statement about labour exploitation (Figure 14.3).

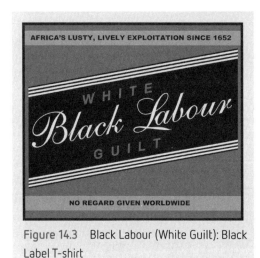

Figure 14.3 Black Labour (White Guilt): Black Label T-shirt

Source: Courtesy of Laugh it Off

Black Label advertising campaigns target a black, working-class market with a beer that is produced by South African Breweries (SAB is one of the world's largest brewery companies). Laugh it Off made a T-shirt using the same fonts and colours that appear on Black Label beer bottles and in its ads, but the text reads 'Black Labour, White Guilt'. This ambiguous, polysemic slogan touched a nerve for several reasons. It refers to exploitative employment practices under apartheid, and to complex feelings about affirmative action employment policies and black economic empowerment strategies in the 'new' democratic South Africa. Laugh it Off was making the point that 'while the political landscape of the new South Africa has changed, the economic impoverishment of the black majority has remained the same—but now whites feel guilty about it' (Nurse 2003, p. 10). The T-shirt also acknowledges the fact that many apartheid-era employers in vineyards, mines, and breweries commonly gave black labourers part of their salary in alcohol, thus exacerbating social problems and economic inequity:

> With no job prospects, nor any real chance of a better life, alcohol further entrenched alcoholism as the working-class escape mechanism. It is this self-same dynamic that SAB are profiting from and therefore perpetuating as a result—to this day ... By targeting this market, and associating themselves so closely with this black working class in their marketing campaigns (for example, mine workers drinking Black Label together at the end of a hard day's work), Black Label must accept the consequences of their association. We believe that in a democratic arena, someone making a comment about, and on behalf of, the black working class is perfectly justified in using a symbol that has been heavily associated with them. All that Laugh it Off did was to use the vocabulary of our media-rich environment: the brand (Nurse 2003, p. 11).

Unfortunately, South African Breweries did not feel that the use of its brand as a form of 'empowered social vocabulary' was justified at all, and promptly sued Laugh it Off. The resulting court cases attracted significant media coverage and foregrounded a range of issues that are pertinent to culture jamming.

One cartoonist, Zapiro, caricatured a lawyer making a statement to a judge saying, 'SA Breweries will not tolerate anyone taking the piss out of their beers!', while Justin Nurse (clad in the offending T-shirt) quips, 'I never knew that was one of their ingredients'. Another news article showed images of Nurse and his colleagues leaving the court with Black Label beer cans clattering a trail behind their car beneath a banner that read, 'Just Sued'. They even had hip-hop songs, protest marches, and pep rallies devoted to supporting their cause. This playful and comical approach to serious issues is characteristic of Laugh it Off, and of much culture jamming. As we note in Chapter 19 (pp. 324–6), comedy can be subversive as it attracts attention in memorable ways and allows jesters to challenge authority. The use of humour might suggest to audiences, though, that the issues themselves shouldn't be taken seriously. Paradoxically, culture jams that are intended to be humorous run the risk of attracting legal consequences if the messages are taken *too* seriously.

While progressive, socially conscious lawyers agreed to take on Laugh it Off's case on a pro bono basis, SAB had access to enormous resources to fund its legal team. Rather than laughing it off and accepting that the Black Labour T-shirt was effectively giving SAB free advertising and establishing a strong link between Black Label and youth culture, SAB lawyers argued that international legal precedent prevented brand parody on the basis of copyright infringement and brand tarnishment. SAB did not have any direct evidence that sales had suffered as a result of the T-shirt, but trademark violation and brand tarnishment can be said to occur if people may come to form negative associations with a brand because of culture jamming activity. In some cases culture jamming could also attract charges of **defamation** if untrue allegations are made or implied and if an individual or corporation's reputation and livelihood are damaged by the jam. Laugh it Off used **freedom of speech** as a defence against the charges of trademark and copyright violation, defending their right to create T-shirts that 'make people stop to think, and start to talk'. If they themselves were not making money from the sale of T-shirts that parodied the Black Label brand (for instance, if they just published the image on the internet) they might not have attracted a lawsuit.

defamation
Defamation involves publicising information that is untrue and so injures someone's reputation, or if it is deemed to be not in the public interest for that information to be published.

freedom of speech
The right to express opinions publicly without interference from government or other sectors. This right is subject to legal limitations that restrict the publication of material that incites hatred or violence, or is defamatory.

Laugh it Off did not win their first court case. Shortly thereafter an image of a battered, bruised Justin Nurse wearing his now famous T-shirt and boxing gloves appeared on the cover of youth culture magazine *SL* (*Student Life*), with the caption, 'I fought the Law (and the law won)'. Laugh it Off then went back for round two of the legal sparring match, appealing to the Supreme Court. Again, they came off somewhat the worse for wear and were asked to pay SAB legal costs and fines reputed to be in the vicinity of half a million rand. Undaunted, they took their case to the Constitutional Court, arguing for the right to freedom of speech and trusting in the fact that South Africa has a liberal constitution designed to protect democracy, equity, and human rights and freedoms. Laugh it Off won the final round.

Limitations of culture jamming

adbusting

Adbusting involves modifying advertisements to undermine their intended meaning (for more information see <www.adbusters.org>).

Adbusting is a particular type of culture jamming. There are a number of criticisms of adbusting and related forms of culture jamming.

1 First and foremost, adbusting works within the system that it is attempting to critique. It is still a form of advertising, and it runs the risk of reinforcing brand recognition for the companies it is trying to undermine. In other words, the more clever the graffiti, the more negative publicity that it generates, the more likely people are to remember the brand in question when they walk into a shop—and that is one of the major goals of advertising.

2 The controversy that surrounds a brand or corporation as a result of media activism can end up making the product seem more desirable, particularly to members of the youth market who wish to be identified with controversial and radical positions.

3 There can be serious legal implications. Culture jammers can be sued for brand tarnishment, brand infringement, copyright violation, and even defamation.

4 The use of controversy and humour can serve to focus attention on the ad, not the issue, or it can trivialise the issue.

5 Developments in media technology can be considered a strength and a weakness of culture jamming. The Nike email example (see pp. 217–19) raises questions about the subversive potential of digital image manipulation and online media activism. Access to online communication is still only available to a cultural elite—despite rapid growth in internet use the sweatshop workers themselves are not likely to have the facilities to participate in this form of media activism given that by 2011 only 24 per cent of the population of Asia use the internet (<www.internetworldstats .com>). The internet is largely dominated by the English language and it requires computer literacy which, in turn, requires training and technology. So, despite being a more democratic medium in which more people are able to become media producers, CMC is still exclusive to some degree.

6 Organisations such as Adbusters and Laugh it Off have been called hypocritical for jamming ads and printing the jams on calendars, stickers, clothing, and other commodities that they then proceed to sell. Even culture jamming has been incorporated as an advertising strategy. Once marketing strategists realised that it was perceived as cool, they began to construct ad campaigns that appealed to the consumer's awareness of the very process of advertising. In Australia a brand of beer called Piss developed cult status when it launched the no-frills ad campaign 'Buy Piss, Drink Piss, Get Pissed'. This was successful (irrespective of the taste of the beverage itself) because it did not involve inflating the price of the product with expensive advertisements and pricey graphics on the labels and packaging. This campaign is not a *bona fide* jam, but it made its mark precisely because, like culture jamming, it was

perceived to be honest and upfront about marketing mechanisms instead of trying to seduce the consumer with desirable but unattainable images.

The irreverent, humorous, and critical tone of culture jamming has also been co-opted by Sprite in a series of television ads that parody the persuasion strategies and trends that feature in mainstream media. In 2000, Sprite created a television advertisement that told the viewer that they didn't need sports stars like Grant Hill to tell them to buy a soft drink because it was cool. The ad used celebrity endorsement as a selling point but it simultaneously undermined the practice of celebrity endorsement, laughed at the advertising industry's ploys, and acknowledged that audience members and Sprite consumers are media savvy, cynical, and acutely aware that they are being manipulated.

In 2004, having established a brand identity closely aligned with the hip-hop scene, Sprite produced another television ad, this one making fun of 'wiggas'. A wigga is a white negro, a wannabe, who appropriates the trappings of black culture. The ad shows young black people looking on knowingly and laughing derisively as a group of white youths cruise by listening to rap music and wearing gold chains and blue jeans so low-slung that they fall right down off their hips and end up around their ankles. The tag line of the advertisement playfully disses cola soft-drink ads, trend followers, and consumerism with the slogan 'Sprite: see through it'. The ad is acknowledging that you can't acquire identity, culture, or cool by purchasing style or buying into a subculture. At the same time it is making the claim that Sprite is an authentic and legitimate part of the hip-hop subculture, thus elevating Sprite from a commodity or a brand to an integral part of identity and culture. Cleverly, the advertisers are harnessing the subversive, counter-cultural modes of communication that characterise both hip-hop and culture jamming in order to actively promote consumption while apparently critiquing consumerism. Note that we might call Sprite's parodic and self-reflexive advertisements or Diesel's use of irony examples of postmodern media culture, but it would not be accurate to call them culture jamming since they originate within the media industry and motivate consumption.

A further example of the impact that counter-hegemonic movements have had on advertising can be found in the way that political activism has been exploited to market fashion merchandise to young consumers. The anti-corporate, anti-globalisation movement, for example, has been co-opted to boost the sales of American Apparel, a company whose advertisements claim that the brand is 'sweatshop free' and 'environmentally friendly'. In this way advertising and culture jamming can be understood as forms of political communication, but we can also see how social and political issues are themselves becoming commodified. Of course people do have to make a living and if they are doing so in environmentally friendly ways it is a positive step.

As journalist Meg Carter points out, the communication styles and methods of counter-culture and mainstream culture are rapidly converging: 'Sony, Diesel and

Puma have appropriated the communication tactics of political activists by taking their advertising onto the streets, emulating the look of flyposting in their legitimate ads, and using typography or imagery inspired by graffiti' (Carter 2004, p. 24). The examples above illustrate recuperation or incorporation as discussed above (see p. 200).

Recuperation involves the conversion of subcultural signifiers such as fashion garments, accessories, hairstyles, slang, music, etc., into mass-produced commodities (see Hebdige 1979, p. 94). Body piercing and tattooing stopped being a challenge to social norms when it became possible to buy do-it-yourself removable Celtic armband tattoos and adhesive pseudo navel rings from any novelty store. Something so common and commercially available no longer signifies anything remotely cool, angst-ridden, or rebellious: it now signifies conformity. The homogeneity of mass production undermines any possibility that such objects could articulate a unique identity or a radical lifestyle statement. The other part of the process of recuperation involves the 'labelling' and redefinition of 'deviant' practices (Hebdige 1979, p. 94). This second mode of recuperation is exemplified when the police or the media refer to graffiti as 'aerosol art' instead of 'vandalism', or when a commercially successful film such as *8 Mile* repositions Eminem as a misunderstood poet attempting to transcend his socio-economic background instead of a gutter-mouthed misogynistic trailer-trash worthy of censorship. In the process of recuperation we see mass culture incorporating and repackaging the less threatening aspects of subculture.

The most extreme instance of this is the appropriation of culture jamming itself by government agencies. In 2011 the British intelligence agency MI6 hacked a terrorist website (the Jihad magazine *Inspire*) that instructed people how to build pipe bombs by redirecting those who attempted to download the instructions to a site that gave lessons on baking cupcakes ('Terror Trap Takes the Cake'). Who would have thought government counter-terrorism agencies would co-opt counter-cultural media strategies to fight subversive acts of terrorism with a sense of humour?

Despite the limitations of culture jamming as noted above, it has been a very significant form of challenge to dominant ideology and the power of the media. If it has been recuperated there may be some new form of media resistance that will emerge in the future as subversive uses for new technologies continue to be discovered.

Conclusion

This chapter has examined the use of conventional and new media technologies for media activism and counter-hegemonic purposes, and it has discussed issues related to copyright law and the use of humour that arise in culture jamming. Part 3 has focused more broadly on the ideologies and discourses of the media, looking at the media as an instrument of dominant ideology and as a hegemonic instrument of contradictory and alternative ideologies. These issues are explored further in Part 4, where many of the aesthetic practices of media storytelling are also considered.

This chapter has

- defined the term 'culture jamming' and explained some of its objectives and techniques
- analysed the intended meaning, inscribed reader, and potential effects of some culture-jamming initiatives
- investigated the subversive potential of media technologies and discussed how they might be influential in challenging social norms and power dynamics
- evaluated the strengths and limitations of culture jamming.

Discussion points

1   Do you think the use of humour trivialises serious issues, or makes them more memorable?
2   Counter-cultural communication strategies can be used for exploitative purposes as well as to initiate positive social, political, and environmental changes. Is it possible for media texts such as advertisements to promote progressive ideas and ideals as well as selling goods and services?
3   Are there any circumstances in which you think that culture jamming should be illegal?

Summary

You should now be able to

- discuss the objectives of media activism
- define the term 'culture jamming'
- analyse the strengths and limitations of culture jamming
- evaluate the effectiveness of culture jamming as a counter-hegemonic discourse that challenges dominant ideology
- using culture jamming as a tool, apply what you have learnt to respond to the mass media and create your own media jam.

PART 4

Stories: Approaches for
Narrative Analysis ▶

The truth about stories is that that's all we are.

Thomas King, *The Truth About Stories*

OVERVIEW OF PART 4

Part 4 builds on the concepts of semiology that were discussed in Part 2 and the critical terms 'discourse', 'ideology', and 'hegemony' that were introduced in Part 3.

Here we will look into stories, one of the oldest and most common forms of communication and entertainment. Stories engage audiences through their exciting and involving narratives. A number of different ways to approach and understand how stories communicate to us will be offered. Fictional stories found in feature films, television series, and serials will be analysed, as will stories and narratives constructed in factual programs, documentaries, reality TV, and video and internet games.

CHAPTER 15

Genres, Codes, and Conventions

Sex, money, and violence. That's all we ever see.

Anon.

This chapter will

▶ consider the meaning of the term 'genre'

▶ examine the western genre

▶ consider the way media codes and conventions can evolve.

Genres

What are genres? How and why have they evolved? What is genre theory?

The quotation opening this chapter is a comment by an elderly Eastern European man who was discussing cinema at an evening class that Michael once ran. The man's words point to the fact that cinema and television have a tendency to tell the same stories over and over again. This repetition and familiarity is found in terms of content—the subject matter of sex, money, and violence, for example—and in terms of the way this content is put into different types of familiar stories, or different genres. It is probably obvious to you that whenever you go to the cinema or switch on the television you can easily and quickly identify what type of film or television story you are watching, which demonstrates the skills you have developed as a viewer to recognise the codes and conventions of a particular genre and their predominance within the media. Let's start our examination of storytelling by examining the term '**genre**'.

genre
Groups of texts that share a set of conventional characteristics such as content, narrative structure, and visual style, are classified as textual types or genres.

Within media studies the term 'genre' was first used as a means of critical analysis in relation to film, and then television. It has been and can be used in relation to literature and other arts, and also in relation to video games, magazines, and other media forms. It is a term that was first used by media analysts but is now also used by audiences in everyday conversation about the media. An explanation of how it was first developed in relation to film and television will be given, in which the way the study of genre is relevant to media texts, industries, and audiences will be discussed.

People can often quickly classify any film or program as belonging to a particular genre—horror, musical, sitcom, crime, soap opera, and so on—by recognising similarities, familiar codes, and conventions. Genres are useful for

- producers who make and sell their product by identifying it as part of an already successful, and therefore marketable, generic formula
- film and television makers who can communicate easily and quickly through these formulas and can also work creatively within the form
- audiences who use genre as a basis for their choice of films or television programs and as a key to understanding them.

The constituencies represented in the diagram below (Figure 15.1) (the film and television industry, filmmakers, and audiences) can all use genres and generic formulas beneficially.

Figure 15.1 Uses of genres

Genres evolved initially through the film industry. Producers wanting to make money realised they could capitalise on a successful film by offering viewers something similar, more of the same. Of course it had to be different in some ways, but featuring the same actors, stars, and/or the same kind of story with some new developments—a crucial pattern of repetition and variation—were the main methods adopted by the industry. This practice developed with the very beginnings of silent cinema and it can already be seen to be successfully operating by the 1920s.

It continues today, as successful films and characters return time and again to the screen—James Bond, Shrek, Bat Man, and Johnny Depp's character Captain Jack Sparrow in *Pirates of the Caribbean*, to name a few. Genre study began in the 1960s as a way of studying and understanding Hollywood films. It showed several things.

- Most genres are immediately identifiable through their familiar **iconography**, that is, their recurrent use of visual images: the western genre features the iconography of cowboys, hats, guns, horses, cattle, wagon trains, saloons, frontier settings, and so on. Some genres will also have their own visual style, such as the extreme camera angles and harsh lighting style of *film noir*.

- Genre stories work through repetition of familiar plot lines.

- Genres were economically beneficial for the film studios as a way of organising the production, distribution, and exhibition of films.

- Genres were initially critically regarded as cheap and valueless, a cinematic form of pulp fiction, the name given to trashy dime novels and magazines that would be literally pulped if not sold. Quentin Tarantino deliberately used the term in his film *Pulp Fiction*, his celebration of cheap generic elements. Later, though, critics began to see value and complexity in these generic stories.

- Many directors—in the western genre, John Ford, Howard Hawks, and Sam Peckinpah, among others—worked within these generic plots to produce their own deeply crafted and often complex visions of American society; later, critics of genre began to celebrate and validate these.

- Genres continually evolve. Alongside the repetition of familiar codes and conventions, variations on the genre are introduced that give a new inflection, and often a new direction, to the genre (see discussion of the western below). *Film noir*—those complex and dark thrillers made in black and white in the 1940s and 1950s—returned in the 1970s, 1980s, and 1990s, having evolved into colour films; they still influence many films today. Thus a genre can continually develop to encompass new elements and produce new meanings.

- Genre theorist Steven Neale suggests that genres focus on a '**core problematic**', an issue of social importance that the genre explores (Neale 1980). This problem is often structured as a dramatic conflict with two sets of competing values in opposition. In the family melodrama genre, for instance, there is a central opposition between the main character's desire for individual freedom versus the need to fulfil expected social and familial role and duties. This is particularly the case for women but can also be experienced by men, as in *American Beauty*. This simple, but effective, device of oppositional values (binary oppositions) is discussed in more detail below (pp. 235–7), but it's useful to mention now as part of the conventions of genre.

iconography
Visual images (icons) associated with a particular genre that are repeatedly used.

film noir
French for 'black film'; black and white thrillers or detective stories made in the 1940s and 1950s conventionally featuring low-key lighting, retrospective voice-over narration, flashbacks, suspicion, intrigue, crime, urban settings, and *femmes fatales*.

core problematic
Central problem or opposition that a genre explores.

The Eastern European man who complained about the constant diet of 'sex, money, and violence' saw commercial cinema as cheap and trashy, as promoting American capitalist ideals, and, most importantly, as formulaic, repetitive, and obvious. We may well ask why people watch genre films when the nature of the formulaic plot means that it is generally fairly easy to predict how the story will end. At one level this sense of obvious knowingness provides its own pleasures. Those who watch genre films often find a sense of satisfaction in being able to predict what will happen next, and they take pleasure in having these expectations subverted, manipulated, or confirmed. The horror-spoof film series *Scream* is an ongoing success because it makes the characteristics of the genre explicit and reworks them playfully. Avid consumers of certain genres such as horror and science fiction also become adept at spotting intertextual references to other films and recognising the familiar iconography and conventions that characterise the genre, and they enjoy this sense of expertise.

But more importantly, the way Hollywood keeps returning to the same issues is actually a potential way of talking about and confronting some of the major human concerns, conflicts, and problems that society faces. The constant diet of sex, money, and violence provides the opportunity for exploring these fundamentally important concerns. Genres such as the western and the gangster film have been understood as a way for American society to reflect upon itself, its history, and its development, a way of America talking to itself.

How has genre theory developed?

Genre theory for popular cinema was established at a time when most films were easily placed in a few key genres: western, gangster, and musical. Since then, a number of things have happened.

1   The advent of television has widened the scope of film culture and has established a whole new set of television forms or genres—game shows, current-affairs programs, situation comedies, soap operas, reality TV, and so on.

2   Cinema has helped to nurture a generation of media watchers who are incredibly knowledgeable and sophisticated as viewers. Television, VCRs, and DVDs have enhanced media literacy by recycling older films that would, prior to television, have disappeared from general public viewing after their initial release. This generation of media watchers has seen an enormous amount of popular film and television that spans a considerable historical time period. While they may not have studied the media, they know a good deal about media texts, techniques, and technologies, and in particular, they know about genres. Program makers need to be aware of the skills of their audience: they must provide novel material that continues to enthral and entertain them, but they can also rely on the audience being able to appreciate, if not actually analyse, quite complicated variations on genres.

3   The consequence of this has been what is called '**generic hybridisation**'. This hybridisation can have a number of effects: it can broaden the market appeal by attracting audiences who like different genres, it can unsettle audience expectations and provide fresh pleasures and surprises, and it can challenge cultural norms and ideas by reworking the conventions and characters that are usually

generic hybridisation
Generic hybrids are texts that blend the codes and conventions of two or more genres to produce a new combination.

used to convey the dominant ideology. Quentin Tarantino's generic hybrid *Kill Bill* attracted fans of westerns, martial arts films, anime, and comedies (postmodern style is discussed in Chapter 24). *Kick-Ass* blends elements of action, comedy, comic book, and martial arts genres, as well as buddy movies and coming of age films to tell the story of a teenage superhero. *American Beauty* (which will be discussed more fully in Chapter 16) combines elements of thriller, *film noir*, melodrama, and comedy. Some examples of hybridity on television include *Border Security*, a high-rating series about Australian customs officials that combines a documentary style with the interwoven storyline structure of soap opera and content similar to a crime drama, *South Park* and *Drawn Together*, which are both animated genre hybrids, and *Firefly*, which blended the western genre with science fiction and fantasy. These are all groundbreaking series in terms of the way they play across genres, but generic hybridity happens on more subtle levels too. In a medical drama such as *House*, a hybrid that incorporates the narrative structure of an investigative crime series, the doctors work as detectives to solve the illness rather than solve a crime. In addition to following false leads and breaking into patients' homes without search warrants to find evidence that may help them to find the pathogen, Dr House's team also gathers to do a differential diagnosis in much the same way that Detective Goren and his team on *Law & Order* scrutinise a line-up of the usual suspects, eliminating them one by one.

To show how you can start thinking about genres in more depth, comment is made below on one popular genre: the western.

The western

The western is probably the most well known of all genres to come out of Hollywood. While the western is partly an attempt to look at, explore, and understand America's own past, that exploration has a mythic quality, that is, it tells us more about America's ideas about itself than the actual realities of American history. Many critics argue that although set in the past, the stories are often related to contemporary events. The myth of the western and the heroic cowboy also speaks to people from many different cultures; in this sense it has had a universal appeal. The popularity of the genre has inspired many interesting books and articles about the western.

Jim Kitses has argued that there are several key oppositions that mark out the central themes and core problematic of the western: the wilderness versus civilisation, the individual versus the community, nature versus culture, the west versus the east

(Kitses 2004). These oppositions are played out through violent conflict that is enacted across the frontier, the boundary that separates civilised society and law and order, from the freedom of the wilderness or paradise that lies beyond the frontier. Stories are often about either the hero's establishment of law and order in this wilderness (the bringing of civilisation to the west) or the hero's escape from the constraints of civilisation to live life more fully outside the law and society (often also a journey of self-discovery for the hero). The idea of crossing the frontier, of going west to a 'manifest destiny' is central to American culture. This goes back to the very formation of America by European colonists, who sought freedom from the political and religious constraints of Europe. The ideal of the USA as a land of freedom and opportunity is encapsulated in the continual search for new frontiers, new freedoms. (Science-fiction films, which portray space or cyberspace as the final frontier, continue this tradition and the connection between the two genres is evident in hybrid films such as *Cowboys & Aliens*.) The western traditionally explores the historical period when America established its new civilisation beyond the frontier, roughly from 1860–90.

Table 15.1 gives examples of Kitses' binary oppositions.

Table 15.1 **Kitses' oppositions**

THE WILDERNESS	CIVILISATION
The Individual	**The Community**
freedom	restriction
honour	institutions
self-knowledge	illusion
integrity	compromise
self-interest	social responsibility
solipsism	democracy
Nature	**Culture**
purity	corruption
experience	knowledge
empiricism	legalism
pragmatism	idealism
brutalisation	refinement
savagery	humanity
The West	**The East**
the west	the east
America	Europe

THE WILDERNESS	CIVILISATION
The West	**The East**
the frontier	America
equality	class
agrarianism	industrialism
tradition	change
the past	the future

Source: Adapted from Kitses 2004

The beauty of this schema is that it can be interpreted in many different ways, which makes it a rich framework for storytelling. The wilderness, for example, can be seen positively as a paradise of freedom and beauty as opposed to the restrictive and corrupt world of civilisation, or can be seen as a savage and brutal world in need of the restraining control of civilisation. The history of the western shows significant changes in its representations over time, one example being the way Native Americans were portrayed initially as savage redskins or Indians (opposed to the cowboys), but gradually came to be represented more positively as humane, intelligent carers of the land, as seen in *Dances with Wolves*. Other critics have regarded the western as a blank canvas on which a whole multitude of stories can be presented, giving it great diversity.

All of the above description shows how the western worked through patterns of repetition and variation and established codes and conventions that enabled filmmakers an opportunity to develop their own concerns and provided a formula that was easily followed by audiences and easily produced by film studios. Its popularity at the box office made it a money maker.

The western was extremely popular from the earliest days of silent film with films that included *The Great Train Robbery*. It developed its own iconography (as mentioned above), familiar plots, and stars such as Roy Rogers, and reached a high point in the 1940s and 1950s through the films of John Ford that featured, among other stars, John Wayne and Henry Fonda. Films in this period explored new psychological aspects, but after this period the genre lost some of its popularity. In the late 1960s, when US film censorship regulations were relaxed, the western was reinvented by filmmakers such as Italian Sergio Leone, who made what came to be called 'spaghetti westerns' (often shot in Spain) and Sam Peckinpah. Leone used Clint Eastwood as an antihero and he and Peckinpah introduced much bleaker, more extreme representations of violence and moral ambiguity that challenged many of the earlier ideals and reworked the western conventions. Their films were also seen as commentaries on the political events and culture of the 1960s and 1970s, such as the Vietnam War.

Westerns then declined in popularity, apart from occasional films such as *Dances with Wolves*, *The Unforgiven*, or *Dead Man*, but many films continued to reference western themes, such as *Thelma and Louise*, *Natural Born Killers*, and *City Slickers*, each of which took aspects of the western and reworked them in a contemporary setting, illustrating genre hybridisation: *Thelma and Louise* drew heavily on western iconography, particularly the scenes shot in Monument Valley, but radically altered the traditionally male genre by making women the heroes, by letting women occupy male spaces and situations. *City Slickers* explored the myth of the male hero and western masculinity in a different way, by putting contemporary New York non-macho men into the western situation. *Natural Born Killers* intentionally used elements of the western to problematise ideas about right and wrong or heroism and villainy via characters such as the outlaw and the lawman, the cowboy and the Indian.

In 2005 *Brokeback Mountain* broke new ground by presenting an explicitly gay cowboy story (many earlier westerns had homoerotic elements, as did the recent Jesse James film; see below). Television series such as *McLeod's Daughters* and *Deadwood* heralded a potential revival of the genre. The extreme language of *Deadwood* meant that it was not broadcast on free-to-air television stations in Australia but it nevertheless established a popular following through cable and DVD rentals. *Deadwood* mixes aspects of soap opera with western themes and goes further than Leone and Peckinpah in highlighting the grim brutality of frontier life. Its success may have prompted big film productions that brought films such as *The Assassination of Jesse James by the Coward Robert Ford* into cinemas in 2007 and, more recently, westerns such as the Coen brothers' remake of *True Grit* (2010). The Jesse James film was a big-budget film starring Brad Pitt. It was a long film that was very much a psychological character study rather than an action-packed adventure but it featured familiar western imagery and plot lines—hats, guns, horses, the wide open landscape, train robberies, gunfights. It also reworked the Jesse James story, which had already been the subject of over thirty feature films. Critics noted that the film could be interpreted as a study on the theme of celebrities and their fans, which linked it to contemporary twenty-first century culture and another example of how a western can be used to deal with contemporary concerns (see Chapter 23).

The film poster (Figure 15.2) contains significant western elements: the gun, holster, and belt, the clothes, particularly Ford's hat, the landscape, and the print font of the film's title, which is similar to old 'wanted' posters. Yet the poses of the characters suggest contemplation and introspection rather than action and thus point to the main themes of the film and suggest a difference from more typical action westerns. The advertising caption, 'A Masterwork', also seeks to elevate the western to the status of art, beyond the pulp fiction aesthetic of many westerns.

While these new westerns have been moderately successful it seems unlikely that there will be a return to mass production of the genre. For contemporary audiences it is perfectly possible to watch and enjoy new westerns without extensive knowledge of the genre, but insight into the genre's familiar codes and conventions can heighten appreciation and understanding.

Figure 15.2   *The Assassination of Jesse James by the Coward Robert Ford*

Codes and conventions

Can the meanings of media conventions change over time?

Genres work on the basis of codes and conventions that are easily recognised by the audience, mainly because of their familiarity. This is evident in our earlier discussions of semiology (pp. 134–5) and media images of smoking (p. 55). Can the meanings of film codes and conventions change through time? Can they be reworked so that they are not necessarily fixed to one meaning? James Dean and Judy Garland are now widely recognised as gay icons, though they would not have been understood as such by mainstream audiences when their films were first released. In this case the cultural context has changed radically, and this has resulted in a rereading of classic texts in light of discoveries about the private lives of the stars, and public perceptions of what forms of sexuality are deemed acceptable or even cool.

The history of art and cultural production is a history of people finding new styles, new aesthetic conventions, and new means of representation and expression. It is also replete with examples of people rediscovering and reworking old styles into something new—neoclassicism, neorealism, postmodernism, and so on. Each new style is seen initially as an aesthetic breakthrough, as unconventional and challenging. Such innovations supplant more traditional, conservative styles and are often rejected by some people because they are too radical. In time, the new style becomes familiar and conventional, so that eventually, it does not have the same impact and its meaning changes. It becomes traditional and clichéd, and in time more new styles and conventions emerge that offer further breakthroughs.

montage

Montage (the French word for editing) refers to two specific ways of joining together shots from different spaces and times—MTV-style collage of images set to music, and/or Soviet montage or political montage using Sergei Eisenstein's technique of juxtaposition.

A good example of the way conventions can change in the way they are used is found in the evolution of the filmmaking style known as **montage**. In the 1920s, Russian filmmakers such as Sergei Eisenstein and Dziga Vertov developed a stylistic form of editing known as Soviet montage. Montage is the practice of joining or editing short pieces of film together as the basis for telling stories. First used in the 1920s, it was designed to complement the revolutionary ideals of the communist revolution, and was theorised as a film style that was radically different from the conventional techniques of the capitalist Hollywood filmmaking system. Today the aesthetic techniques of Soviet montage continue to thrive, but they are no longer the exclusive province of radical filmmaking. On the contrary, montage has been taken over by mainstream filmmakers, and the best place to see it in action today is in advertising or on MTV (which is really an extended advertisement for the music industry)—the most potent forms of capitalist screen production.

What we can see from this is that a particular film style or convention does not guarantee particular kinds of political or social use or meaning. Forms and conventions can be used in different contexts to give them different meanings. This is very important in film and video because many new techniques are often developed for radical and innovative purposes. Like Soviet montage, they may be used originally to challenge the dominant system but they can then be appropriated by the dominant system, which uses the same technique in a non-challenging way. This can be seen as another instance of hegemonic recuperation (see p. 200). The most innovative television advertisements often borrow techniques, styles, and conventions from experimental, radical filmmakers. The surrealist films of Czech animator Jan Svankmajer challenged the conventions of his society, but his techniques—and, indeed, he himself—have been used by advertisers to sell commodities.

Koyaanisqatsi

Filmmaker Godfrey Reggio is an interesting case of someone who was very aware of conventions and how to use them. He was the director of the films *Koyaanisqatsi* and *Powasqaatsi* (similar to *Baraka*). In his previous work, which aimed to raise public awareness about the abuse of young people, he used advertising billboards, where he employed 'conventional techniques in an unconventional way' (Reggio 1990). In other words, he took the apparatus of capitalist advertising to promote radical, socialist ideas.

Reggio (1990) has stated that in *Koyaanisqatsi* and *Powasqaatsi* he was 'trying to let people see from another point of view things that we see every day—looking for things people have seen zillions of times to see them afresh, from another point of view'. He hoped that his images would shock and disturb viewers, making them question where modern society is going. He wanted to do this as spectacularly as possible, partly to attract the audience, but also to draw attention to the way our society is becoming increasingly fascinated by spectacle and images. He used the techniques of time-lapse photography to critique modern-day industrial societies. By speeding up the action, the humans who are portrayed appear as insects or robots, functioning unthinkingly, automatically. This technique also shows the city as an animated, live creature, whose arteries pulsate with the red and white corpuscles of speeding car lights replayed in fast motion. When it was first released *Koyaanisqatsi* was an unusual film to watch. It gave audiences pleasure but challenged the dominant ideology. Since then the techniques that Reggio used to critique society have once again been appropriated by advertisers to celebrate modern societies: accelerated images of urban societies are constantly used as trailers to promote commercial television stations and programs such as *Las Vegas*, or advertisements to sell gas and electricity.

Paradoxically, it has now become somewhat conventional to use unconventional images to try to create audience interest. In the 1990s, some of the advertising campaigns for the Benetton clothing company were similar to Reggio's work in that they used unusual, shocking images such as portraits of convicted murderers and serial rapists on death row.

This form of campaign aims to raise awareness of issues such as the death penalty at the same time as heightening consumer recognition and awareness of the Benetton brand. The tension between these two objectives (one humanitarian, the other profit driven) has led to accusations that Benetton is guilty of the commodification of social issues. *Juice* magazine caused a stir when it featured photos of supposedly murdered corpses (as if taken by police photographers) in clothes advertisements with the words 'Fashion to die for' (Figures 15.3 and 15.4). These styles and the images associated with them were attempts to break taboos of what is acceptable.

The development of cartoons over the past fifteen years shows a similar tendency to challenge conventions. When *The Simpsons* was first produced (in 1990) it was considered too shocking to be broadcast on British television. The 'Itchy and Scratchy' cartoons within the show were considered particularly gruesome. Gradually, *The Simpsons* has become more and more accepted and popular and less shocking, but newer cartoon shows, such as *South Park*, and *The Family Guy* have each pushed the boundaries further in terms of what is conventionally acceptable and funny.

Dogma 95 (spelt 'Dogme' in Europe) is a recent film movement that deliberately defines itself in opposition to mainstream filmmaking practices, by attempting to challenge the dominant ideology. Members of the Dogma collective sign a vow of chastity that is a set of realist rules or conventions based on the Dogma manifesto, among them that Dogma filmmakers vow to avoid the high-budget illusions of

Figures 15.3 and 15.4   These fashion spreads in *Juice* are examples of heroin chic

Source: *Juice*, June 1996, pp. 62–3, 66

commercial Hollywood cinema by shooting on location using hand-held digital video, natural light, and available props. They don't use special effects, non-diegetic music, fancy editing, or genre formulas. They aim to get back to the essence of filmmaking as compelling storytelling, rather than focusing on filmmaking as a commercial venture. Those who make Dogma-style films feel that mainstream filmmakers have their artistic integrity compromised by commercial constraints. Directors, for instance, are sometimes compelled to use a certain star in order to obtain financial backing for a film, or are asked to change an ending or cut a scene to get a broader age rating so more people will see the film. Another Dogma rule states that, in recognition that film production is a collaborative process, film directors don't get credited as the author of the film. In a sense, Dogma filmmakers are making an ideological statement resisting capitalism and individualism through their aesthetic choices, conventions, and filmmaking practices.

Television genres

While the concept of genre works for film and television texts, there are important differences, and some genres are medium specific. Reality-based programming such as news, documentary, lifestyle shows, game shows, and reality television typically don't translate well to film. There are exceptions, such as feature length documentaries, the *Jackass* movies, and films about reality television (*The Truman Show*, *American Dreamz*) or news broadcasting (*Morning Glory*), but film lacks the sense of immediacy and 'liveness' that these television genres rely on. Imagine going to the cinema once every few weeks to watch the news, or spending nine or ten hours in the cinema watching a fortnight's worth of *MasterChef*. Television also operates on the basis of a predictable schedule organised around the assumption of a general audience that may include people of all ages, hence the restrictions of scheduling family-friendly content also impact on what genres are developed for television, and how audiences use genre as a concept that guides viewing choices.

The different schedules and time scales of film and television production and the size and nature of the stories told relate to a key difference determining the genres found in each medium: narrative structures. Film genres tend to feature closed storylines that are resolved by the end of the film, whereas television genres tend to be open narratives developed in episodic instalments each night or each week, which means that certain genres, such as romantic comedy, that lead inevitably towards a closed ending, aren't well suited to television: as soon as the couple forms, the incentive to keep watching the series would evaporate. Furthermore, serial television genres, medical dramas such as *Grey's Anatomy* and *House*, that lack a strong central storyline and that are constantly introducing new characters and dilemmas, have few corollaries on the big screen.

The closest examples of an ongoing narrative in genre film are film franchises and sequels such as the James Bond films or the *Pirates of the Caribbean* series. The enormous popularity of such series suggests a degree of convergence between film and television, and changes in audience and industry practices that impact on genre. Film sequelisation capitalises on the addictive desire to know what happens next when a story ends with a cliff-hanger; it also harnesses audience allegiance to characters such as Captain Jack Sparrow or James Bond. The film industry uses these attributes, which are associated with the serialised narratives of television genres, to enhance the appeal of the action blockbuster genre—a genre that is exclusive to the cinema due to its massive budget and the need for big stars, location shooting, and special effects.

Because television is consumed mostly in private homes equipped with devices such as DVD recorders and remote controls, television audiences need to be able to recognise genres much more swiftly as they station surf and search for something to watch. Neale describes this as the 'rapid deployment of genre-recognition skills' (Neale 2001, p. 4). This need for clear branding of genres has led to the increasing use of sonic branding, with theme songs and canned laughter frequently used to signal genre and visual branding using digital onscreen graphics such as program and channel logos popping up at the bottom of the screen. Changes in the media industry and audience practices since the 1980s have also seen the growing popularity of cable and satellite television, and with this the emergence of genre-specific channels such as the Sci-Fi Channel or Animal Planet to cater to true genre enthusiasts.

Conclusion

Most films and most television programs fit into a specific genre and operate under similar principles to those outlined above, such as the use of repetition and variation, and of familiar plot lines or structures. Genre theory can also be applied to computer games, distinguishing particular types of game and the codes and conventions within which they operate, and noticing how they themselves often draw on the pre-existing imagery of popular cinema genres. Knowledge about genre should give you greater insight into cinema, television, and all the uses of the language of the moving image that are discussed in the next chapters.

This chapter has

- defined genre and its main characteristics
- noted the importance of repetition and variation within genres
- discussed the western as an example of genre
- examined how codes and conventions can change their meanings
- distinguished how genre functions differently for film and television industries and audiences.

Discussion points

1 How much is your own media consumption based on genre?
2 Apply Kitses' oppositional table (Table 15.1, p. 236) to any western.
3 Watch a Dogma film such as *The Idiots*, *Celebration*, or *Italian for Beginners*. Consider how a mainstream Hollywood director such as Steven Spielberg would have filmed the same story, and how the experience of spectatorship differs. Why might Dogma filmmakers want to challenge Hollywood norms?

Summary

You should now be able to

- define genre
- explain why genres are so popular
- identify the iconographic characteristics of specific genres
- show how genres operate on the principles of repetition and variation
- discuss generic features of the western
- use Kitses' oppositional table (Table 15.1, p. 236) to analyse a western
- define and illustrate the term 'generic hybridisation'
- use genre theory for analysing films and television programs
- comment on how filmic codes and conventions change over time.

ONLY A COLORBOND FENCE WILL LOOK AS GOOD IN TEN YEARS' TIME AS THE DAY IT WAS PUT UP.

A COLORBOND® steel fence won't rot, warp, flake, peel or be eaten by termites. Which makes it reassuredly maintenance free: a simple hose-down will do. And because it's easy to install, you can do-it-yourself if you like. For more information and the name of your local contractor, call 008 022 999. **BHP** Colorbond

Plate 1   Advertisement for Colorbond fencing

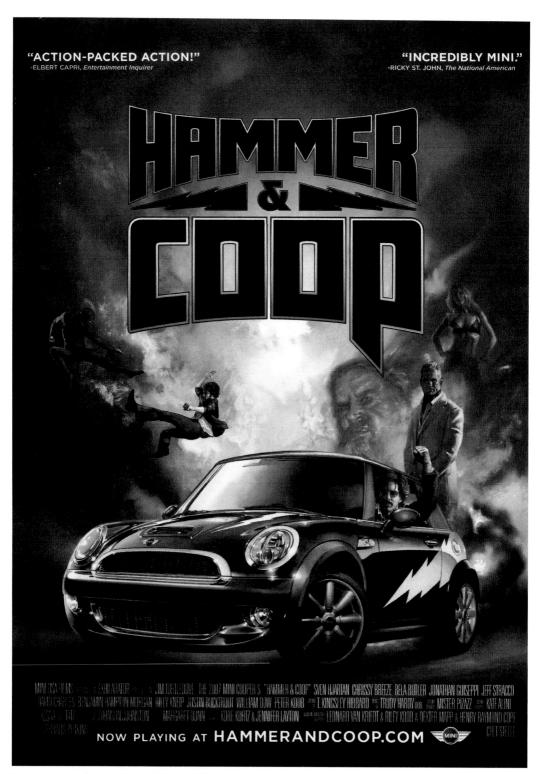

Plate 2   Hammer and Coop MINI publicity image

Plate 3   Young Designers Emporium advertisement

Plate 4   Lynx/Axe 'Rise Up' still from viral video advertisement

Plate 5   Lady Gaga's meat dress

Plates 6 and 7   Ella Baché sunscreen advertisements

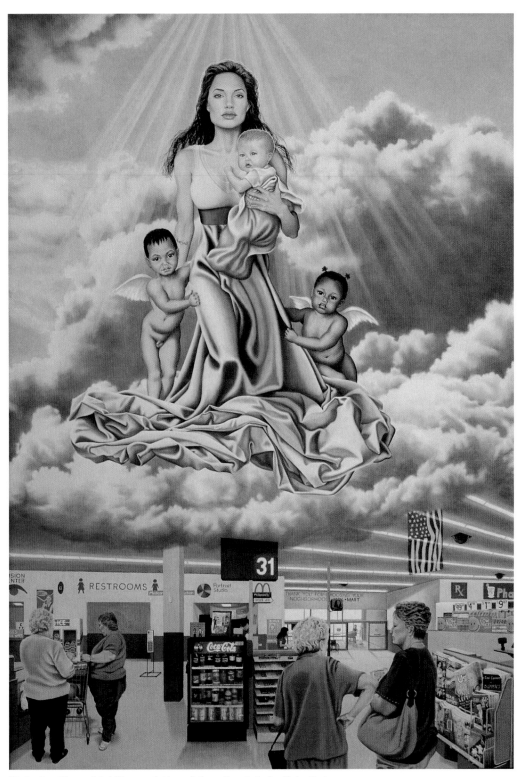

Plate 8 *Blessed Art Thou* painting of Angelina Jolie by Kate Kretz

Plate 9   Gordon Bennett's *Altered Body Print*
(Shadow Figure Howling at the Moon)

Plate 11   Cover of the Benetton magazine,
Colors

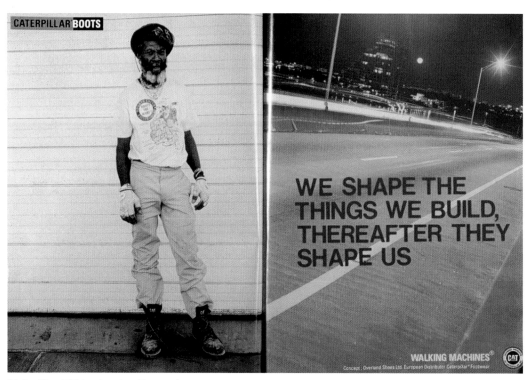

Plate 10   CAT boots advertisement

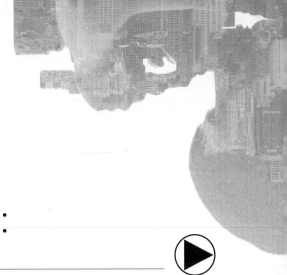

CHAPTER 16

The Language of Film:
American Beauty

*I'm trying to find a way of making every frame, every shot in the movie, tell the
same story.*

Sam Mendes, director, *American Beauty*

This chapter will

▶ give a detailed analysis of a short sequence from the film *American Beauty*

▶ explore the conventions and language of film narrative

▶ focus specifically on the use of *mise-en-scène*, cinematography, editing,
and sound

▶ help you with your own film or television textual analysis assignments.

Before reading this chapter, watch the opening two minutes of the
film *American Beauty* and if possible view the whole film. It will be
useful if you can refer back to this sequence using a DVD as you read
the analysis below.

    Having explored aspects of genre, the aim of this chapter is to
show you how to go about a detailed textual analysis of a short
sequence of film, video, or television by exploring the four elements
of the 'language of film' (Bordwell & Thompson 2004): ***mise-en-scène***,
cinematography, **editing**, and **sound**. Each of these aspects needs
to be looked at closely. While this chapter focuses specifically on
a feature film, the analytic techniques presented will be useful for
analysing any media moving-image form.

    The way film language is analysed here should be helpful in
showing how you could approach an assignment or essay in which
you are required to undertake a close analysis of cinematic style.

mise-en-scène
A French theatrical term meaning
literally 'placed in the scene'.
Mise-en-scène refers to *what*
has been filmed: settings, objects,
costumes, actors, and the way these
are visually arranged and lit.

cinematography
The processes of filming the *mise-
en-scène*—*how* things are filmed.
This includes the angles (for example
high or low) and positioning of the
camera (for example long-shot or
close-up); focus and framing, any
camera movements (for example
pan, track, zoom, or tilt), any special
camera effects (for example slow
motion or time lapse), the film stock
used, and processing methods.

editing
The process of joining or splicing
together separate pieces of film,
separate shots. Edits may cut directly,
dissolve, mix, fade, wipe, etc.

soundtrack
The recorded combination of human voices, sound effects, and music.

For this kind of detailed sequence analysis you should transcribe what happens in every shot within the sequence, as demonstrated in the shot list at the end of this chapter. To transcribe a sequence you will need to watch the sequence several times over, pausing repeatedly to take notes. It is helpful to watch once with the sound muted so that you can focus closely on the *mise-en-scène* (content of the shot), cinematography (how content is filmed), and editing. Then listen to the soundtrack without looking at the image so as to focus on sound. Next, watch the vision with the sound up and note the relationship between sound and image. Later, add in extra details such as shot duration and make notes about lighting, performance, and your responses to each shot. Finally, reflect on the significance and meaning of the different aspects that you have transcribed and the relationships between them. Try to consider the impact that the different techniques have as well as thinking about what the director's intentions might have been.

American Beauty

The film *American Beauty*, directed by Sam Mendes, scripted by Alan Ball, with cinematography by Conrad Hall, was made and released in the USA in 1999. The film stars Kevin Spacey as Lester Burnham, a middle-aged family man re-evaluating his life. Annette Bening plays Carolyn, his ambitious wife and Thora Birch is Jane, his sullen teenage daughter. Mena Suvari plays Jane's beautiful friend, a cheerleader called Angela. This chapter will consider in detail how the film's *mise-en-scène*, cinematography, editing, and soundtrack contribute to the construction of meaning and emotional impact, by analysing a two-minute sequence starting immediately after the film's title. We will consider this with reference to typical film and narrative conventions. According to Quentin Tarantino, 'In the first ten minutes of nine out of ten movies the movie tells you what kind of movie it's gonna be. It tells you everything that you basically need to know' (cited in Smith 1994, p. 42). Like many other films, the opening of *American Beauty* is very important because it is designed to establish the narrative world, introduce the characters and issues, and capture the audience's attention so that they want to keep watching. The film actually begins with a short sequence in which Jane, Lester's daughter, is talking and being videoed by her boyfriend Ricky. Our analysis starts after this as the title for the film appears.

The film's title

American Beauty was successful at the box office and with critics, winning five Oscars. 'American Beauty' is the name of a particular rose, and roses and rose petals are significant images in the film, but the film's title can be read as being about contemporary American society and values in general and about the nature of beauty. There are many films exploring such issues, supporting or questioning the ideals of America and the American dream; these often focus on single individuals or families as a way of personalising the issues. However, a title such as 'Meet The Burnhams' or 'Lester's Life' would lose this general social aspect. Such explorations of family relationships and human desires can also be relevant to many non-American audiences. Note that the film was directed by Sam Mendes, an Englishman who felt it was relevant to his own life and he has stated in the director's commentary on the DVD that the theme of the film is that 'Beauty is found in the places you least expect it'.

Mendes regarded the film as a satire but also as 'something far more haunting and poetic' (Mendes 2004). He saw it as a film in which all the main characters are 'trapped in prisons of their own making at the beginning and then gradually escape … It becomes a rites-of-passage story for all of them' (Mendes 2004). Mendes also commented that he tends to read scripts in visual terms, that is, he finds visual means to interpret the script: 'I'm trying to find a way of making every frame, every shot in this movie tell the same story' (Mendes 2004). This draws our attention to the visual combination of cinematography and *mise-en-scène* and we aim to explore how he uses these to tell the story.

Shot 1, the first shot after the film's title—*American Beauty*—is important visually and for its soundtrack; it lasts a long time, 22 seconds, and acts as a conventional '**establishing shot**' to show us Lester's neighbourhood. It is an aerial shot: the camera slowly moves down from the sky to focus on Lester's street. It allows us to see the whole of Lester's community, suggesting that the film is about an individual—Lester and his family—and a neighbourhood, typical of many American suburbs. From the trees we can see it is autumn or winter, a time of death. Note also that this shot is repeated but in reverse at the end of the film (see also narrative structure on pp. 276–9). To make the introduction of this shot smooth it fades in so the scene gradually appears before us rather than plunging us straight into the action. In contrast, at the end of the film there is a direct cut to a black screen and silence, which Mendes hoped would be conventionally jarring for the audience, his 'final attempt to keep the audience on the wrong foot'. This, and all quotes from Mendes used in our analysis, can be found on the director's commentary of the *American Beauty* DVD.

establishing shot
A wide or long shot conventionally used to show the whole of a location or set so that we can see and understand the space the action is taking place in. Normally followed by shots that are closer to the action.

This aerial, overview, bird's-eye view is typical of many films but it is particularly apt for this film: its view from the heavens is linked with Lester's voice-over, which is speaking after his death—maybe from heaven. The camera is positioned at a high angle, looking down on the action in many instances throughout the film, reinforcing the sense that Lester is a disembodied spirit looking back on his life. In terms of *mise-en-scène* it is worth noting that the suburb is full of houses that look very similar and the colour is somewhat muted. These aspects of *mise-en-scène* suggest a community of dull conformity and order.

Music and sound

The soundtrack combines two main elements: music and Lester's voice-over. The music starts just before the image appears. This is a conventional narrative device. We are used to seeing images and hearing music together and, though the music is often **non-diegetic sound** (that is, sound that is added from a source outside the story world as opposed to **diegetic sound**), audiences are happy to hear the music as emotionally appropriate to the visuals.

non-diegetic sound
Sound that comes from somewhere outside the story world, such as the musical score, which the screen characters cannot hear.

diegetic sound
Sound that comes directly from the fictional world (the diegesis) of a screen text.

The music is very carefully woven into this opening sequence to give us a sense of rhythm and to highlight key points in the script. It combines subtly with Lester's voice-over and the cutting between shots, as if punctuating the sequence, alerting us to what is most significant. There is one central musical phrase that is repeated forty times, in ten cycles (or verses) of four. There are several pauses and variations so that it retains audience interest, but once we have heard the first cycle we can anticipate the music quite predictably.

Repetition is a common device in music, particularly in the increasingly popular minimalist music of the late twentieth and early twenty-first centuries. Constant repetition can produce a sense of timelessness, finding beauty in something very simple. This might be linked to the neighbour Ricky's ideas of beauty in the film, shown in the sequence where he has filmed a bag blown by the wind repeatedly going round in circles (like this music). Alternatively, the musical repetition might be equivalent to the repetitious vicious circle and dullness of Lester's suburban life.

The first musical pause comes straight after Lester says, 'This is my neighbourhood'. There is a single high note played as the cycle ends as if to give a musical full stop, while we take in what we are hearing and seeing. The second pause coincides with Lester's own dramatic pause after his comment, 'In less than a year I'll be dead.' This is a striking statement and it sets up one of the major narrative questions and audience hooks: How, when, and why will Lester die? To give more emphasis to this statement the audience also has the first cut in this sequence, to shot 2 (the overhead view of Lester in bed) with the sound of the ringing alarm clock. Cutting in this way doesn't just move the narrative forward: it highlights the drama. The jarring clock counterpoints Lester's alarming statement and is a symbolic wake-up call.

After he stops the alarm there is a wonderful addition to the music soundtrack. A brief descending, coming down sound that is finished with a single low thudding bass note, on the first beat of the next cycle. This coming-down sound complements the visually descending camera movement and angles. It also parallels Lester's own spiritual and emotional state as he is coming down to earth and realising the inadequacies of his life. Shot 3 is a dog's-eye view of Lester's feet and his slippers from under his bed. The low level camera works with the music to show that Lester is, at this point in his life, feeling as low as he can go. Because the shot size has moved from the first extreme long shot, through tighter framing to a close-up, this sequence draws the audience into increasing intimacy with the character as Lester's voice-over invites us into his suburb, his home, and now into his emotional life.

The musical phrase begins its third cycle and Lester resumes his monologue. As this cycle is coming to an end Lester makes another dramatic comment: 'In a way I'm dead already.' This time the music doesn't pause, but to highlight the drama the next cycle is played an octave higher to lift the drama and intensity (a quick drumbeat is added to the music) and played with no voice-over; we are simply able to observe Lester (shots 4–6) and enjoy the music. As the cycle ends Lester says, 'Look at me', and this leads directly and powerfully into the next, the fifth cycle, which is highlighted by the bass note on the first beat, but also a brief rising sequence leading into the first beat.

The beginning of the sixth cycle coincides with a shift from Lester, inside the house, to Carolyn his wife, outside the house. There is no pause in the music but to parallel this shift in location and character the music changes by adding another descending sound, by using a string instrument rather than marimba, and by lowering the volume. The change and development in the music helps us follow the change and development of narrative.

Film music is rarely analysed in great depth but can be hugely important in creating atmosphere and in highlighting, complementing, and developing the drama and the narrative.

Lester's voice-over

Lester's voice-over introduction provides important narrative information and gives us a particular viewpoint, or sound-point, from which to understand this story. It also draws on the *film noir* convention in which the main character tells events through voice-over, relating events in flashback form, constructing a circular narrative that ends where it started. *American Beauty* is thus linked to the noir themes of mystery, murder, darkness, and circularity. The specific idea of a character giving their life story after their death is found in *Sunset Boulevard*, the *film-noir* that Ball and Mendes were both conscious of; cine-literate audiences would also note this reference.

The use of voice-over encourages audiences to form a specific affinity with the character who is speaking. By hearing how Lester sees the world we too begin to see and hear things from his point of view (this is also visually encouraged in shots 13, 15, and 16, which show Lester watching and listening to the other characters). Thus an identification and sympathy is established with Lester right from the start, but through *film-noir* conventions we are used to such characters being doomed and/ or flawed. If we just saw him being a loser at the beginning of the film we might not value him; if we heard about him from his wife's point of view we might see him differently, but because we hear his point of view (and clearly he has some self-awareness about his own limitations) we are invited to be on his side. Mendes comments that there is 'something so wonderfully lonely about the voice that hovers over the film ... a loneliness that is present in much of the movie'. The voice-over sets up this mood, working with the bird's-eye view of the camera to create a sense that Lester is somehow alienated from his own life. This loneliness is also established in the way that Lester is isolated in screen space. In the opening sequence he is not interacting with anyone and he is often alone throughout the film.

Cinematography, *mise-en-scène*, and editing

Shot 2 is an overhead shot of Lester in bed. It is significant both cinematographically and in terms of *mise-en-scène*. Overhead shots are not used often. They do not represent a normal, human point of view or perspective. The view relates to the previous shot, which was also high up, so it is a continuation of this god-like, aerial perspective and gradually moving to earth. But conventionally, this viewpoint, particularly within the home, is disturbing and disorienting. It signifies that this domestic home is out of balance, something is wrong, dysfunctional. In terms of *mise-en-scène* it shows a man alone in a double bed. This also says something about his relationship with his absent partner—he is alone. The distorted shadow of the lampshade on the left also expresses the disturbance of his domestic life. Colour is important here: Mendes has remarked that 'the story is told in terms of colour'; the film has a 'muted palette' and is 'very monochromatic, blues and greys, probably the most colour you see for the first half hour, apart from the red of the roses' (Mendes 2004). In this opening sequence there seems to be a contrast between the outside of the house and inside. From the outside Lester's life appears to be shiny bright and picture perfect, as represented by the bold colours, particularly green, red, white, and blue in the exterior shots, but from the inside his house looks and feels gloomier, more shadowy. This shot shows the monochromatic muted palette with the blue sheets, paralleling the depressing tone of his interior monologue; both suggest the dullness and shadow quality of Lester's suburban life.

At the end of shot 2 Lester starts to roll over and we cut to a close-up of him completing this movement, and then facing the camera, still placed above him, and with considerable shadows cast across his face, again emphasising the darkness of Lester's life. This camera position is not so strange as we are now close to Lester's face. The editing sequence has thus moved us in three successive shots from extreme long establishing shot, to long shot, to close-up. This is a typical and conventional method of camera storytelling. Film theorists David Bordwell and Kristin Thompson (2004, p. 310) note how standard editing techniques, known as **continuity editing**, developed as a way of making stories unfold seamlessly, a way of smoothing out the potential disruption of editing from one space to another.

continuity editing
A system of editing, established in Hollywood by about 1920, for telling stories smoothly. It uses particular techniques and conventions for filming within a scene such as the use of establishing shot, use of shot-reverse shot, eyeline match, match on action, observance of 180 degree rule, and continuity of action, sound, and lighting.

The use of 'match-on-action' (see Bordwell & Thompson 2004, p. 315), wherein a movement or action is started in one shot and completed in the next, is one such technique: here, Lester's rolling movement is the action that is matched between the two shots to provide continuity and smoothness between shots. Because we are watching Lester move we aren't disturbed by the cut, indeed, we may not even be consciously aware of it. Meanwhile, the look on Lester's face, which we can now study closely, confirms the midlife crisis and dysfunctionality already indicated by his comments on his own deadness, and by the cinematography and *mise-en-scène*.

Shots 4–6 continue to focus on Lester; they show him putting on slippers and in the shower. The slippers connote dullness and lack of glamour, while the dog's-eye view from under the bed might signify a sense of unease, of something watching and lurking unseen in suburbia, as well as showing the final coming down to earth of this sequence. In terms of colour the shower shots use dull blues and greys though the camera movement gives some dynamism to the shots. 'Moving pictures', as cinema has been called, are about movement that provides spectator interest. Filmmakers create movement either by having something move within the scene—Lester rolling over—or by moving the camera, as in shots 1, 5, 6, 7, 10, 12, and 15. The shower shot also has a certain shock value in showing Lester jerking off, masturbating, confirming his anti-hero status. The *mise-en-scène* places Lester behind the glass door and the frames of the shower, contributing to Mendes' aim to find a visual way of showing Lester's imprisonment, the first of a visual 'series of jail cells'. We see this again in shots 13, 15, and 16, which show Lester behind the prison bars of the window. This is a great way of visually signifying that the often idealised domestic home is actually a prison, trapping Lester, while the glass barriers illustrate the way he is separated from other people.

Shot duration often decreases and the pace of editing will increase in order to heighten suspense around the climactic moments in a scene, sequence, or story, a form of **rhythmic editing** or **rhythmic montage**. In this sequence the first and last shots are quite long (22 and 20 seconds), which gives a sense of balance and time to take in these important shots. The overall pace, with several of the shots lasting about 5 seconds, is typical of contemporary commercial cinema editing. As cinema has developed, the speed of editing has increased. Audiences are stimulated by constant change and are also quick readers of visual images. Commercial cinema and television, with the need to please audiences, have increased the pace of their editing, which is one reason why older films seem slower to us: in terms of editing pace they usually are.

rhythmic editing or rhythmic montage
Rhythmic editing means the pace of editing—how long each shot lasts.

Cutting the rose

Shot 7, the extreme close-up of the red rose, is very significant. It is the rose of the title and red (in complete contrast to the dull blues and greys) is the most important colour in the film. Red was a major element in the advertising posters, which showed the image of the rose petals that are also central to Lester's sexual fantasy. It is the colour of blood, which is shown dramatically at the end. Throughout the film, sexuality, passion, beauty, anger, and death are all linked by the colour red. The camera tilts down until the rose is cut. This downward movement is again linked to Lester's description of his own life and all the camera movement that has gone before, paralleling Lester's comment: 'It's all downhill from here.' The next shot reveals that it is Carolyn, Lester's wife, who has cut the rose, so the rose leads us into the next sequence of the narrative. The red rose thus acts in terms of developing the narrative, what comes immediately before and after, and in setting up an important **motif** that will be developed later in the film.

> **motif**
> Any significant element (an object, colour, place, sound, camera movement, or angle) that recurs or is developed throughout a film.

But it has further meanings. To emphasise its power the shot is an extreme close-up that fills the screen in sharp contrast to all the earlier colours: no words are spoken over it and there is no background distraction: we are totally focused on the rose. This technique of blurring out the background is used again in the cheerleaders' sequence when Lester fantasises about Angela: as we go into extreme close-up of Lester's face the background of other spectators has just become black; similarly, when the camera focuses on Angela the other girls have disappeared and the gym background has been darkened. Since she is heavily associated with the rose petals it is worth noting the similarity of technique in these two sequences that are connected to the American Beauty rose. Note also that the focus used in this close-up is very sensitive to any change in focal distance so that as the camera tilts down it has to pull focus: this takes the petals out of focus but brings the stem, which we are now looking at, into focus. This could represent a movement in our attention from petals (seductive beauty) to thorns (the dangerous power of the femme fatale), or from the beautiful façade of Lester's life to the fact that his life is about to be nipped in the bud, or it could simply be a way of directing our attention to the act of cutting that takes place next.

The cutting of the rose is particularly important when we consider it in relation to editing or montage. The Russian filmmakers and theorists of the early twentieth century argued that when any two images are shown one after another, viewers will link them, seeing a relationship and producing a reading or meaning based on this relationship. Sergei Eisenstein claimed that the editing process is central to the composition of meaning in a film because spectators form 'associative links' between shots (Eisenstein 1992, p. 147). 'Montage,' he writes, 'is an idea that arises from the collision of independent shots' (Eisenstein 1992, p. 140). Eisenstein described one kind of editing process as '**intellectual editing** or **intellectual montage**' whereby two linked images would produce a concept or idea.

> **intellectual editing or intellectual montage**
> Two images linked together produce an idea or concept.

The first image here is of Lester masturbating, the second of Carolyn cutting the rose; thus a link is created between Lester's upstanding penis and the full-bloom red rose (even though Lester's penis is not actually visible, is purely imagined). In terms of intellectual montage, Carolyn's action, cutting the rose in this next shot, can then be understood as a form of symbolic castration, and, as we quickly come to realise, this is a good description of the current marital relationship between Lester and Carolyn in which he has been emasculated within the domestic setting and Carolyn has become the dominant partner. This is a good visual illustration of how filmmakers can convey a huge amount of information about characters in a single image or action. In the briefest of moments, Carolyn's castrating character and her relationship with Lester are encapsulated.

Shots 7–9

In the three shots (7–9) that introduce Carolyn, we have another typical narrative film convention. Whereas the first three shots of the film moved from establishing long shot to close-up, here we have the reverse: close-up, where we are unsure exactly where we are but interest is created by the close-up itself, and by the questions: Where are we? Who is cutting the rose?, leading to mid shot and then establishing shot, which places Carolyn in the garden, in front of her house.

There are several other points of interest in these shots. In relation to editing, note the technique of smoothly linking two shots by placing the main focus of visual interest in these different shots in the same area of the screen or frame; this is a form of **graphic editing** or **graphic montage**: in shot 7 the rose and its stem are placed just to the right of the centre of the frame so that is the area we are focusing our attention on; the next shot (8) has Carolyn standing in exactly the same area of the frame or screen so we are immediately focused on her. You can find other examples of this technique, most notably the cut from the aerial shot 1, where the main visual focus is on a small part of Lester's street, between the two rows of houses; this is exactly the same space on the screen that Lester's face is in for shot 2, so our eye is already focused on this spot, making the transition and narrative easy to follow.

> **graphic editing or graphic montage**
> The linking of two separate shots through visual similarity or contrast.

In relation to framing (cinematography) and *mise-en-scène* note how the establishing shot 9 places the camera directly at right angles to the street and garden fence in front of us. This position can be described as theatrical in that it replicates a front-on position in relation to the action, a position similar to the best seat in the house of a theatre, from where one looks at right angles to the stage. Some commentators have noted Mendes' main work as a theatre director and how at times he treats scenes almost as though they would be played on a theatre stage. One obvious example is the dinner-table sequence between Lester, Carolyn, and Jane. Once again the camera and audience are positioned at right angles, this time to the table. The resulting images are quite two-dimensional, quite flat, lacking any depth, which could be part of Mendes' satirical technique at this stage in the film to make Lester's home life seem flat.

Two other aspects of *mise-en-scène* worth noting are Carolyn's costume and the white picket fencing around the houses. Carolyn's costume is a grey business-like suit. It immediately tells us something about her character—she is a businesswoman rather than a housewife. White picket fences are standard and stereotypical signifiers of idealised American dream homes, seen in countless films and television programs. Their appearance may be read satirically or ironically—that is, rather than seeing this as perfect home and community, it is all too good to be true, so much so that we wonder about the problems lying beneath the surface.

At the end of shot 9 we hear the sound of a dog barking. This is an example of a **sound bridge**, which smoothly leads us to the next shot, where we see the dog. It also shows how off-screen sound works to extend the boundaries of screen space, helping the spectator to imagine an entire world that exists beyond the borders of the frame. Camera movement is motivated by the movement of the dog, so it is subordinated to narrative. This again is conventional in mainstream feature films and one way in which the 'cinematic apparatus', defined by Jean-Louis Baudry as 'the ensemble of equipment and operations necessary for the production of a film and its projection' (Baudry 1992, p. 693), is often made invisible for the spectator. This means that all the processes of filmmaking—cameras and their movements, lighting, editing, sound booms, microphones, and so on (the cinematic apparatus)—are used to tell the story, but we as audience are encouraged to focus on the story and not consciously notice any of the camera and sound recording technology. The apparatus operates virtually invisibly; the skill of the filmmakers is in maintaining this invisibility. When this apparatus is accidentally revealed—seeing the sound boom or a continuity error, for example—the cinematic illusion is destroyed, often provoking laughter.

> **sound bridge**
> Sound is used to link two separate shots.

End of the sequence

The appearance of the dog Fitzy leads to the introduction of Lester's gay neighbours. There is satirical humour here: first, in their stereotypically camp concern with the dog's behaviour, second, in the fact that this conventional and normal neighbourhood can include gay men as part of that normality (their costume, too, is a very conformist style and colour), and third, in the clone-like naming of both of them as Jim, which draws attention to stereotyping since it represents gay men as a type rather than as individuals. Such stereotyping is foregrounded and denaturalised throughout *American Beauty*, but it is also reinforced in problematic ways. Homosexuality and the dangers of its denial and repression will be a major theme in the film as represented by the neighbours just about to move in on the other side of Lester's house; indeed, the film might be seen as an exploration of aspects of masculinity since the male characters are the major figures in the film. (As a screenwriter on the TV series *Six Feet Under*, Alan Ball also explored issues around homosexuality.)

The final shots (13–16) further demonstrate Lester's imprisonment and his estrangement from Carolyn and the rest of the world. Shots 13 and 16 both show Lester framed/imprisoned by the window. This sequence encourages us to observe Lester as well as, through editing, to see the world through his eyes. In shot 13 he is seen watching and so we assume that the next shot will be his point of view. We are thus being stitched, by the editing and cinematography, into seeing the world through Lester's eyes, which we do in shot 16 as he looks out of the window.

Shot 16 is the most cinematographically complex shot in the sequence; it combines with sound manipulation to further draw us into Lester's world. The shot begins with the camera tracking from left to right as Jim and Carolyn meet. This movement allows it to frame Lester in the background between Jim and Carolyn. Initially, Jim and Carolyn's trivial conversation dominates the shot—they are in the foreground, Lester is in the background and out of focus, and at first we probably don't notice him. Gradually, this situation is reversed using three separate techniques. First, the camera slowly zooms in on Lester until Carolyn and Jim are excluded from the frame. Second, at the same time it does a literal change of focus, so that Carolyn and Jim go out of focus while Lester becomes clearly defined. And third, to complement this visual change there is an equivalent pulling focus in the soundtrack as the sound of Carolyn and Jim's conversation fades away while Lester's voice comes back into prominence. Thus we have come back into Lester's point of view, which is where we started with his voice-over. This short sequence has introduced major aspects of Lester's life and now the story can begin.

Table 16.1   Shot list

1	22 sec.	Music: Fade-in of extreme long shot (ELS): Aerial view of Lester's neighbourhood; camera slowly descends; voice-over and music.
2	10 sec.	High angle long shot (LS): Lester in bed, alarm clock ringing; switches off alarm and begins to roll over; coming down sound effect; music and voice-over.
3	7 sec.	High angle close-up Lester; match on action as he rolls over; music starts with higher pitch.
4	3 sec.	Close-up (CU) slippers. Low level 'dog's-eye view' shot from under the bed.
5	4 sec.	CU shower and Lester's face, camera pans left to right; shower sounds.
6	13 sec.	Medium shot (MS) Lester showering; camera continues to pan left to right and creep zooms in slightly; music develops; shower sounds.
7	4 sec.	CU rose tilt down; rose goes out of focus; focus on stem being cut, background out of focus.

(continued)

Table 16.1 Shot list (*continued*)

8	6 sec.	Medium close-up (MCU) Carolyn (wife): lifts up rose (she is in same place on screen as rose was in previous shot).
9	5 sec.	LS (establishing) Carolyn in left corner; 180 degrees — white picket fence — dog barks at end of shot, sound bridge.
10	2 sec.	CU rapid pan right to left; picket fence and dog.
11	4 sec.	LS Jim 1 at gate of fence with dog.
12	7 sec.	LS Jim 2 at door: camera pans right to left to two Jims and dog.
13	3 sec.	MCU Lester framed behind window.
14	3 sec.	LS of Jim approaching Carolyn.
15	20 sec.	MS Carolyn and Jim meeting; camera tracks forward and pans right to left to CU of Jim and Carolyn. Between them, in the background, Lester watches from the window and the camera slowly zooms towards him as his voice-over (V/O) begins, pulling focus from Carolyn and Jim to Lester.
16	6 sec.	CU behind Lester out of window to Carolyn and Jim.

Conclusion

In this analysis we have aimed to show how carefully a film sequence can be crafted. We have deconstructed the sequence examining all the aspects of film language that communicate to us. This is a skilful example of film narrative and storytelling, producing a sequence that will engage its audience and which will then give an interesting view of contemporary American and Western families and society. We can learn a lot about how to make films and how they communicate to us through such detailed analysis. Further features of the film's narrative will be explored in subsequent chapters.

This chapter has

- demonstrated how to analyse a short film extract
- explored the language of film.

Discussion points

1 What view of the American family does *American Beauty* present?
2 What is beautiful in *American Beauty*?
3 What other examples can you find of significant uses of *mise-en-scène* or cinematography in *American Beauty*?

Summary

You should now be able to

- define and use the terms '*mise-en-scène*' and 'cinematography'
- explain the terms 'continuity editing', 'rhythmic', 'graphic', and 'intellectual editing'
- show how all of the above can contribute to a film's meanings and emotional effects
- be aware of how sound and music communicate in screen texts
- notice conventional techniques of narrative filmmaking
- do your own detailed analysis of any film, television, or DVD sequence.

CHAPTER 17

Narrative Structure and Binary Oppositions

We mostly understand ourselves through an endless series of stories told to ourselves by ourselves and others. The so-called facts of our individual worlds are arbitrary, facts that fit whatever fiction we have chosen to believe in.

Jeanette Winterson, *Art Objects: Essays on Ecstasy and Effrontery*

This chapter will
- ▶ define narrative
- ▶ explain and examine how narratives are structured
- ▶ examine the importance of the structural position of characters in narratives
- ▶ look closely at the significance of narrative endings
- ▶ explain and examine the term 'binary oppositions' in relation to narrative
- ▶ look at the way couples are represented in narratives
- ▶ consider the key distinctions between film and television narratives
- ▶ discuss pornography in the media
- ▶ examine how narratives are structured in computer and internet games.

This chapter will explore the narrative structures of fiction films, television texts, and narratives found in other media forms.

The importance of narrative

What are narratives and why do we like them?

Narratives, or stories, are a basic way of making sense of our experience. This is a cultural process shared by all societies; humans understand and relate experiences through stories. When people talk about things that happen, both in fiction and in real life, they put these experiences into a story or **narrative** structure with a beginning, a middle, and an end. We have fictional stories but we also have feature stories about current affairs in the newspaper, documentary stories, and sports stories. When we relate our own daily experiences—'How was your day at work?'— our accounts often come out as stories.

narrative

A sequence of events taking place over a given period of time that are linked, mainly through cause and effect.

But stories and narratives are something more than this sequence of events. It is very normal to ask: What's the point of the story? or What's the moral of the story? This idea of stories having a moral, a point, or a lesson to teach goes back to stories such as Aesop's fables, biblical stories, myths, and legends, and is just as relevant today in media narratives. All these stories can be considered as means by which societies talk to themselves. They look at certain human issues and questions and by the end of the narrative, a solution, resolution, or overall message about the problem has been presented. Family sitcoms, for example, show us how to relate to teenage siblings or deal with parents; programs such as *Glee*, *Teen Wolf*, and *Gossip Girl* show us how to live out young adult sexuality and explore relationship issues. The point is that stories have a point to make—they are trying to communicate something, to send a message to audiences. The message is often not fully realised until the end of the story—in comedy it is with the delivery of the punch line. We wait in anticipation for this final delivery, which usually resolves not only the preceding conflicts and questions that have been set up but also provides us with a position to make some kind of judgment or evaluation of all that has gone before: thus we get the message. The logic of storytelling is to communicate some message, some point, and any good analysis or reading of that story will aim to try and understand what those messages are.

The aim of this chapter is to analyse how stories work by looking at their structure. The first stage will be to identify the components of any story's structure. The second, more significant, stage is to see how the narrative structure relates to and affects the meaning of the story. The argument being made here is that the way a story is told or structured will affect how it is understood. When analysing the relationship between narrative structure and meaning, a detailed transcript, as was done for *American Beauty* in the previous chapter, would not be useful. It would be more helpful to make a rough map of the whole film, break it down into scenes, and note the function of each scene and character in the overall story. This technique, known as a 'plot segmentation' (Bordwell & Thompson 2004, p. 93), gives a film analyst an overview of how the story is organised in time, space, and causation. A plot segmentation of *American Beauty* would foreground the circular nature of the narrative and would establish the relationships between the different storylines and characters.

Narrative structure and structuralism

structuralism
A method of analysis that involves looking for and examining the underlying structures of meaning in language, social relationships, narratives, and so forth.

The approach offered here is based on **structuralism**. Structuralism was developed in the field of anthropology, particularly by Claude Lévi-Strauss (1978), for analysing many aspects of human society, such as kinship patterns and cooking practices. It has also been used to study myths, and has been applied in many other academic areas. In media studies, structuralism is used to analyse narrative. Its broad aim is to go beneath the surface of any media text to see how the story structure contributes to meaning.

> Can we find specific structures in stories and are these structures important?

The importance of narrative structure is made clearer if we distinguish structure from content. A useful example is to look at how gay characters have been represented in films. This is well documented in Vito Russo's book *The Celluloid Closet* (1981), which has provided the basis for an excellent documentary film. He argues that most early representations of gay characters were negative in that they laughed at and demeaned homosexuality or showed gay characters as deviant and criminal. Russo argues that from the 1970s on, films sympathetic to or supportive of gay characters began to appear, but he draws attention to the way these characters are positioned or structured in the narrative. He finds that however sympathetically the gay characters may be portrayed, more often than not the story provides an unhappy ending for them. At the end of his book, Russo includes, alongside a bibliography and filmography, a necrology that charts the various endings assigned to gay characters, drawing attention to the predominance of unhappy endings for them: suicides, madness, solitude, imprisonment, death. The crucial point is that the narrative structure shows that gay characters will end up unhappy no matter how sympathetically they are portrayed. This is a damning conclusion. We can still see this tendency in films such as *Brokeback Mountain* and *The Adventures of Priscilla, Queen of the Desert*, which, while being very affirmative gay films, do not have classically happy endings.

Popular television series such as *Modern Family*, *Glee*, *Gossip Girl*, *Greek*, *Brothers and Sisters*, and *RuPaul's Drag Race* are making homosexuality an accepted part of mainstream popular culture by making fun of it, celebrating it, and exploring (or exploiting) its dramatic potential with a range of ongoing stories, both sad and happy. The extended narratives of television mean that there isn't closure or resolution to the stories of many of these characters until the entire program is axed. This means that television has the potential to depict a wide range of possibilities, to open issues for ongoing discussion rather than closing the subject with a definitive ending. In some ways the ongoing storylines of television are closer to real life than the neat resolutions offered in many films because television always leaves us with new dilemmas, challenges, and questions.

The successful queer-themed television series *The L Word* featured lesbian, bisexual, and transgender characters, focusing on their lives and relationships. Like *The Sopranos* series finale, this progressive show ended its sixth and final season with an episode much the same as any other; in the final episode the characters continued on in the same manner as usual—breaking up, drinking, talking, and hosting a party— and none of the season's overarching questions, including a murder mystery, were resolved. Many of the show's fans were disappointed that there wasn't a dramatic, satisfying conclusion that tied up all the loose ends. However, in refusing to give viewers definite resolutions, happy or sad, the show indicated that for these characters, as in the real world, life goes on and that not everything can be easily resolved. *The L Word's* finale also hinted that there are fresh challenges and new experiences ahead for its characters, even if we won't be there to watch.

How does narrative structure determine meanings?

Narrative pattern

There is a basic structural pattern to narratives. According to cultural theorist Tzvetan Todorov, all narrative is a movement between two equilibriums:

> At the start of the narrative there is always a stable situation … something occurs which introduces a disequilibrium, a disturbance to this situation … At the end of the story, the equilibrium is then re-established but is no longer that of the beginning (Todorov 1975, p. 163).

The equilibrium established at the end is a form of resolution of the questions, enigmas, and desires that have been introduced by the disturbance. This can be expressed diagrammatically (see Figure 17.1).

Figure 17.1   Basic structural pattern of narratives

The disturbing incident at the beginning of the story catalyses changes for the main characters and often also sets up a goal or objective that the protagonist strives to attain. This creates a narrative question in the reader's or audience's mind that draws us through the story: we continually wonder how the protagonists will deal with the trials and tribulations they face. Of course, the central narrative question is only answered at the end of the story when the major crisis is finally resolved, but before that point we are seduced further into the narrative world as the main characters encounter obstacles, turning points, complications, and conflicts that threaten to prevent them from attaining their objectives. These dramas need to be overcome before a new equilibrium can be attained, and before the audience can feel a sense of narrative closure.

Consider how this works in the film *Legally Blonde*. The opening credits sequence shows Elle (Reese Witherspoon) in a stable and very positive situation. She is highly successful, adored by her women friends, and seemingly adored by her boyfriend. We see all this and hear the song 'Perfect Day', which confirms her happiness and stability. The stage is set for her prospective engagement. The disruption comes quickly (as in most films and stories so as to immediately engage the viewer/reader) when she is dumped by her boyfriend and this then sets up a twofold goal, or enigma: her goal to get into Harvard and her goal to win her boyfriend back. Audience members want to know whether she will succeed in these goals. As the narrative proceeds these questions begin to be answered—we learn fairly soon that she does get into Harvard so the question then becomes will she succeed there, and then later she gets involved in a particular court case and we want to know the outcome of that. New characters are introduced and new disruptions and questions are set up.

All these questions reach a resolution at the end. The ending finishes off the story, provides a new stability, and an answer to the central narrative questions.

There are several important consequences of the basic narrative structure. First, it suggests that all problems and disruptions must have a resolution, an answer, which means that narrative as a formal structure is a reassuring and comforting structure: even if the ending is potentially unhappy (in films that end with the death of the main characters, for example, such as *The Assassination of Jesse James* or *American Beauty*), at least it is resolved. This does not fit with our experience of real life: we know that the resolution to a problem often raises new problems, choices, or questions, and that there is rarely a definitive ending to situations or disruptions. Narratives, however, serve to put a reassuring frame on the way we see and structure life.

Second, because there is closure to the story, audiences are invited to do nothing more than feel an emotional response. The closure suggests finality, which means that the audience is not invited to act, to do something in response, even if it is a confronting story. This is an issue that some storytellers have wanted to challenge by creating stories that do not have closed narrative structures (see Brecht, pp. 327–8).

Third, the way stories are told suggests the inevitability of the outcome—there are no other possible solutions, it had to end that way. But it is possible to produce narratives that suggest a range of different outcomes and narrative possibilities. Films such as *The Butterfly Effect* or *Sliding Doors* do this, while *Bill and Ted's Excellent Adventure* provides a humorous example with three possible endings. While such narratives are rare in film and television, a branching narrative structure that invites audience interaction and participation by offering choices among multiple pathways, settings, and character traits is increasingly common in computer games, interactive television, and other variants of computer-mediated communication. DVD releases of films often include as a special feature scenes that were not included in the final version, or an alternative ending that was shot but not used. This draws our attention to the fact that narratives are constructed, not inevitable outcomes.

Q&A—What importance do questions have in narrative structure?

Narratives are essentially driven by questions and answers that hook the audience into the narrative—we want to know what happens next. All narratives set up key puzzles or questions. There tend to be one or two major questions and a host of smaller ones, and each one is answered at some stage. This is what Barthes (1974) has called the 'hermeneutic code' because the word 'hermeneutic' refers to enquiry and interpretation. The British Film Institute has described the way audiences are involved in film narrative as follows:

a   The viewer is prompted to ask questions—for example, Who dunnit?, Who is this mysterious stranger?, Will they fall in love?

b   He/she watches on, confident of getting an answer eventually.

c   The film, meanwhile, lays down in the viewer's path a series of false trails, dead ends, and delays, keeping us from the answer—just yet.

d   The film introduces smaller questions that get answered quicker.

e   The film also leaves 'lying around' certain clues, hints, and tantalising revelations about the original 'big' question. These lure the viewer onwards.

f   The viewer predicts, from time to time, answers to questions and then adjusts these predictions according to new evidence and re-predicts until he/she reaches the conclusion with a start of surprise or satisfaction of expectations fulfilled.

British Film Institute, *Teaching Notes on Narrative*, unpublished

Q&A in *American Beauty*

The big question, as discussed previously (see p. 248), is how and why will Lester die? As the narrative progresses it becomes clear that someone will kill him and the question then becomes a 'who-will-dunnit'? Can we pick the killer? We are given some very obvious suspects, particularly his wife and his daughter's boyfriend, so we keep trying to decide between these different characters and their motives.

We change our prediction that Carolyn will kill him when she herself hears the shot. There is also a major question about whether Lester can find a happier way to live. These two questions persist throughout the film. Alongside this are the numerous, other, smaller questions, such as: Is Ricky, the neighbour, a dangerous psychopath? Will Lester's daughter Jane get together with Ricky? Will Lester and Angela get together? Will Carolyn sell a house?

The narrative sets up a suspenseful question—for example, 'Will Lester lose his job?'—that it then answers quickly, in this case 'Yes', but this sets up new questions: 'How will Lester survive? What will he do now?'

This ongoing process of asking and answering questions leaves us both satisfied and wanting more: we become involved viewers, emotionally, imaginatively, and intellectually engaged with the story world rather than distanced from it as we might be while watching an **avant-garde** film that encourages us to question the institution of cinema and the dream-like stories it offers. We can see here that film audiences are active participants in the process of making meaning. Our imaginations, intellect, and other faculties are constantly stretching to find answers to the questions raised over the course of the narrative, and to relate what is happening in the story to our own experiences and knowledge of the world. We must also consider the possibility that media audiences are passive to the extent that they tend to become immersed in the narrative world and are not encouraged to question the capitalist, consumerist values that underlie many mainstream cinema texts and the versions of reality they construct.

> **avant-garde**
> Literally means 'advance guard'; refers to cultural products that are seen as unconventionally new and different from mainstream culture but which will supposedly lead cultural developments forward.

The structural position of characters

How are characters structurally positioned in narratives, and how does this positioning contribute to meaning?

There are six useful questions to ask about any narrative.

1 Who and/or what makes things happen in the narrative (social and psychological determination)?
2 Whose point of view do we see and hear things from and in what sequential order are events presented to us?
3 What structural roles do people have in the narrative?
4 What is the dominant discourse or the hierarchy of discourses?
5 Are women positioned differently from men in the narrative?
6 What does the ending tell you about the ideology of the film?

The answers to these questions carry consequences in terms of the text's meanings.

1 Who and/or what makes things happen?

Events may be driven by the actions of impersonal forces such as tornadoes and earthquakes, by social forces such as poverty and war, or by humans, either in groups or as individuals. Whichever of these determines events, most mainstream narratives focus on individual humans and how they respond to these events.

The Day After Tomorrow: concern with global warming or human relationships?

When viewing *The Day After Tomorrow*, are audiences more interested in how the main characters deal with the new ice age and how it is affecting their interpersonal relationships or are they concerned with how this is affecting the global population? Audiences are normally encouraged, by the way events are filmed and the way the story is presented, to take up a position of identification with the main characters, or to empathise with them. Furthermore, audiences are usually invited to understand these characters psychologically rather than socially, that is, audience members are encouraged to ask what makes the characters tick as individuals. Instead of being given a larger social, political, and economic context from which to make sense of their lives, we are given psychological reasons from their past and present lives for the way characters feel and act.

Popular narratives tend to privilege, or at least show more interest in, the psychological over the social, which relates to the whole ideology of individualism that permeates Western society. We can see this at work in the type of history that we are taught. Traditionally, history has been presented in terms of key historical figures, personalities who made history (the kings and queens version of history). We have learnt about individuals—Queen Elizabeth, Christopher Columbus, Joan of Arc, Nelson Mandela, Yagan (the nineteenth-century Aboriginal leader of the Nyungar people of Western Australia), Captain Cook, Hitler, and so on—rather than about major economic shifts and changes.

Film and television narratives have this same interest in individuals, maybe because it is easier to represent and understand individuals—they can be made memorable by being endowed with interesting characteristics—than it is to represent and understand social forces, which are more complex and abstract. In the case of film, it became clear early on that audiences were interested in individual actors (stars). This may be related to the size of the screen and the use of close-ups that enlarged the human face to huge proportions. The interest in individuals crosses most areas of media and the industry has actively constructed and encouraged this fascination with individual stars, directors, and media personalities as a marketing device. News stories, for example, are often structured around key individuals, and sports coverage focuses on stars and personalities (see Chapter 23) and it is often easy to think of film history in terms of individual directors rather than in terms of movements in film.

Most film narratives focus on one or two major characters. Our attention is held by them being made into interesting characters—attractive, witty, cruel, loving, and so on—and by having stars, who are themselves often charismatic, fascinating, and well-known people, play these parts. But more important than this is the general pattern of narrative that shows main characters going through an individual process of change, growth, and development: paralleling the narrative pattern of stable situation–disruption–new stable situation, there is usually a pattern of character change (see Figure 17.2).

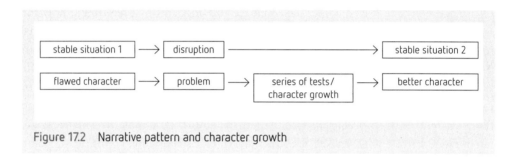

Figure 17.2   Narrative pattern and character growth

What happens to main characters in the course of a narrative?

Major characters are initially presented in narratives as having some kind of flaw in their character or an emotional problem. The film then provides a situation that tests them out: they have to work through a series of problems and in so doing resolve their own character flaw—they go through a process of moral development and character growth. Characters do not always get better; some remain flawed and end up unhappy—Citizen Kane, for one, never learns from his situation, though we as audience can learn something from observing his failure to change.

Television protagonists present a different kind of narrative development in relation to character and character flaws. In television series and serials characters may follow extended character arcs, developing and changing over a long period of time. In a long-running soap opera such as *The Bold and the Beautiful* a character may move from evil to good and back again, and develop many relationships and goals along the way. In such cases a particular character's learning curve and a particular narrative question may be extended over several episodes or even several series rather than being resolved in a single episode or text. Alternatively, television characters might just go on exhibiting the same flawed character throughout a series. This is particularly true for situation comedies, or shows such as *The Simpsons*, but such characteristics are also found in many dramas; basically, the main characters exhibit the same flaws week after week. Homer Simpson's selfish and irresponsible gluttony, and Dr House's blunt rudeness to all his staff and patients in *House* are but a few. The witnessing and playing out of these flaws is central to audience pleasure without any need for them to be resolved.

In *American Beauty*, Lester is seriously flawed, but by the end of the film he has transformed himself and his whole way of being. In *The Day After Tomorrow*, one of the main characters is a father who neglects his son. The onset of an ice age makes him realise this, testing him to change his behaviour, to become a good father, and thus a better person. The drama of global warming and ice age disaster becomes a backdrop for a feel-good story about family relationships. The narrative focuses more on the characters' growth than on the social problems that provoke it. This is the danger of narratives that focus on these individual psychological stories: wider social and political issues become background, one example being the trivialisation of global warming. Some people argue that the narrative hook of individuals and their psychological stories gives the opportunity to examine the serious issue of global warming discussed in the popular media that we might otherwise ignore. Yet another argument is that the family concerns of *American Beauty* and *The Day After Tomorrow* relate to wider social concerns felt in Western society about masculinity (*American Beauty*) or father–son relationships (*The Day After Tomorrow*), that these in themselves are important social issues.

The question posed here is this: does the stress on individual growth and resolution relegate social issues to second place in mainstream narratives? Most films and television programs privilege the psychological over the social. They may include both, but they focus mainly on individual characters.

Narratives do not have to work like this. The Soviet montage film movement of the 1920s–1930s concentrated on social groups and issues, rather than heroic individuals with whom audience members could identify on a personal level. These films often used untrained actors to play nameless characters who embodied or typified a particular social class or identity.

In terms of gender, *Thelma and Louise* provides an interesting example of the balance between social and psychological issues. The film raises social issues that are significant for women, such as rape, domestic drudgery, male oppression, and the law's unequal treatment of women. But does it raise awareness about the position of women in society or does it just focus on the desires, problems, and motivations of two individuals? Feminist film critic Angela Martin (1979) asks the following question of feminist film studies: 'Are we looking for images of real women or films which are really about women?' She is distinguishing between films that show individual women understood in psychological terms and films about the social conditions that women in general endure. The latter puts more stress on the social problems experienced by women and the need for these to be changed if women's lives are to be improved.

The final point to make is that if you stress social causes and problems in a narrative, then the narrative's answer to these will be in terms of social issues and contexts; if you stress psychological causes and problems, then the narrative's answers will be to work on people's individual characters, and the social problems will thus become a background to the psychological problems. This is particularly significant in relation to how we are invited to understand texts that represent crime and criminality. If the narrative presents criminals as produced by social forces, and if the narrative focuses primarily on these forces, then the logic of the story is that we must change society to solve the crime problem. If, however, crimes are committed by psychologically deviant individuals who need to change their characters, then the solution suggested by the narrative is that we must change the individuals. The social issues again recede into the background as the individual issues are foregrounded. Perhaps the best film narratives combine individual psychological issues with social concerns as equally important and interlinked, as do *Crash* and *Babel*.

2 From whose point of view do we see and hear things? What is the order of events?

point of view
The positions cameras take and whose viewpoint they show the viewer.

'**Point of view**' is an important cinematic term that raises questions about where the viewer is positioned in relation to the screen characters and the narrative world, and about how the text addresses its audience. It stresses the way we, as audiences, are invited to view and hear events. Often films encourage identification with a main character, particularly through the device of first-person, voice-over narration, as in *American Beauty*, or by point-of-view shots that encourage us to see things from the perspective of the main character, as in *Legally Blonde*. Close-ups are another technique that literally bring us into intimate proximity with screen characters and can invite a sense of identification. (Note how rare it is for minor characters to be filmed in close-up, and how rarely the camera will position the audience in line with their audiovisual or subjective point of view.) In these ways we may be invited to sympathise with characters even if they are murderers or criminals. Alfred Hitchcock's famous film *Psycho* uses certain techniques to encourage the audience to sympathise with the character of Marion Crane, who has stolen $40 000, and to see events from her point of view. Her murder in the film shocks audiences because a strong identification has been established with her, but the film then goes on to establish sympathy with her murderer by showing many events from his point of view. Our identification with Lester in *American Beauty* makes the scene where he violently throws his dinner at the wall and abuses his wife much more acceptable than if we had been positioned to identify with his wife Carolyn's point of view.

Most narratives invite viewers to identify with characters and to be emotionally involved with the events shown. Emotional involvement comes about because audiences are encouraged to enjoy being close to (simulated) exciting events. In the cinema we can almost feel what it is like to go on a rollercoaster ride, to fly in an aeroplane, to be part of a bank robbery, to make love, to be in a fight, or a car crash, and so on. These virtual experiences are dependent on camera work, editing choices, and sound techniques, all of which draw us into the action, making us feel part of the events being portrayed. This encourages a viewing experience based on strong emotional responsiveness; such emotional viewing experiences are often more stimulating than a detached, intellectual appraisal of the same issues and events.

It is, however, possible to present events in different ways. Some narratives invite detachment rather than identification. In order to facilitate detachment, these films may use long shots (to encourage the audience to distance themselves from the action) and slower editing. They may also avoid presenting events from the point of view of any particular character. All these techniques are designed to encourage the audience to be critical and detached in their viewing, and to make them aware of the construction of the film itself, unlike the techniques of traditional Hollywood cinema, which try to convince the audience of the realism of the story. In *Dogville* Lars von Trier deliberately challenges Hollywood's conventions of realism by setting his whole film on a virtually empty set in which he puts written signs stating whose house is which but not actually building the houses. He is challenging the illusion of reality that most films try to create. While this may be less conventionally exciting, in the sense that the emotions are not so immediately engaged, it has the advantage of encouraging critical thought about what is being portrayed. You can find excellent examples of this detached style of viewing in several of Peter Greenaway's films, including *Drowning By Numbers* and *The Cook, The Thief, His Wife and Her Lover*, or in the documentaries of Peter Watkins (*Edvard Munch* and *The Freethinker*). Can you think of other examples?

Case study: Analysis of the narrative structure of *Elephant*

In the film *Elephant*, Gus Van Sant was responding to the Columbine High School massacre. As Van Sant says in the Production Notes Press Release Kit for *Elephant*: 'American school shootings had reached an all-time high. I wanted to make something that tried to capture the atmosphere of kids going to school in that time.' He uses several structural techniques that are significant in the way we view the film and that make it different from many mainstream films.

- In terms of cinematography Van Sant uses long tracking shots, in which the camera follows students walking around the school. There are very few cuts and often little action other than the students walking through hallways. Occasionally, the film goes into slow motion for a few seconds and then resumes normal speed. All this creates the following possible effects for audiences: the lack of action and continual tracking shots encourage us to become fascinated with simply observing the school environment (which Van Sant wanted to communicate) and builds a sense of suspense as we wait for something to happen. The camera technique adopts a similar camera style or convention used in many contemporary documentary films (see p. 310) and thus gives an added sense of realism. The lack of editing, shot-reverse-shot, and point of view shots encourages audiences to watch with more distance rather than become emotionally identified with any characters.

- The film has no main characters; rather, it introduces and weaves its narrative around a number of different school students, giving no one predominant point of view, which allows us to observe a group, a general social situation. This is a technique found in other films, particularly those of Robert Altman, such as *Short Cuts* or *Gosford Park*, Paul Haggis' film *Crash*, or the more mainstream *Love, Actually* (directed by Richard Curtis), but it is still not the normal film narrative convention.

- The consequence of the previous two points is that we are given no strong point of identification — we begin to see the world through multiple points of view.

- In terms of narrative structure the events are not presented in a simple sequential series of events. Although the film focuses on the events of one particular day, starts at the beginning of the day, and finishes with the shooting, it includes several flashback elements and also shows us some events more than once but from different perspectives. Consequently, we see the boys who will do the shooting entering the school early on but we have to wait to see what will happen. This waiting to find out what will happen is complicated because most audiences, aware of the real events of Columbine and elsewhere, will know what is going to happen. Therefore there is not a sense of suspense and uncertainty about what will happen; there is foreknowledge. We watch the events and the characters knowing what fate is in store for them.

- These structural cinematic and narrative techniques are used for a purpose: Van Sant has no simple answer to explain the Columbine and other high school shootings. Whereas most mainstream films want to give us a clear point of view from which to understand events Van Sant wanted to make a film that raises questions, provokes discussion, and points out the problems and contradictions of contemporary students' experiences. He used the title *Elephant* believing it referred to the parable in which a group of blind men try to identify what an elephant is by just feeling one part: each man — after feeling just an ear, or leg, or tail, or tusk, or trunk — thinks he knows what he is feeling, but he doesn't. *Elephant* is 'about a problem that was hard to identify, because of different ways of looking at it', according to Van Sant's production notes and press kit. Whereas most narratives work in terms of explaining events in terms of cause and effect, this film refuses to do this. As Van Sant says, 'We didn't want to explain anything'. He didn't want to find 'an explanation for something that doesn't necessarily have an explanation', which is particularly challenging in this film because so many people in the audience are looking for some explanation, some simple way of making sense of such terrible events.

The narrative order of events

The most straightforward narrative sequence presents events in a strict chronological order. But this sequential narrative doesn't show everything—it cuts out time to leave out the boring bits, and only focuses on certain people and events. Only occasional narratives, like the television series *24* (in which an entire 24-episode series covers just one day in the life of a counterterrorist operative) or the experimental film *Timecode*, show events in real time, but these examples also only show scenes from particular points of view.

Many films—*Elephant* is one—break up the chronological sequence of the narrative, flashing back, or forward, or retelling events. This can have important consequences for how we interpret the film. The script for *American Beauty* provides a good example. The original script started with a courtroom scene in which Jane and Ricky are being tried for the murder of Lester. It then goes back to the beginning of the film, Lester having a dream, and then waking up. Sam Mendes discarded the dream sequence because it did not fit the tone of his 'lonely' film; he and writer Alan Ball also decided in the last week of editing to discard the courtroom scene, 'and it changed the whole nature of the film' (Mendes DVD commentary). He doesn't say how it did this but we can speculate that the initial emphasis on Jane and Ricky in court would have made them more significant in the story and would have made the story more of a courtroom thriller in which we would have been overly concerned with Jane and Ricky's possible prosecution. This would take our attention away from Lester's personal story, which is what the film in its final version and sequence is focused on. We discuss some of the effects of flashback structures more in the section about narrative endings (pp. 276–9). These kinds of structural positionings are crucial in constructing our responses to any narrative, and it is important to be aware of this process of construction.

3 What structural roles do people have in the narrative?

The way characters are positioned in the narrative tells us something about how audiences are expected to understand them. Consider, for instance, how many mainstream films and television programs consistently portray people of colour in minor roles, or cast characters with English accents as villains or petty criminals. Later in this chapter the different kinds of structural roles assigned to men and women in narratives are discussed. Many films invite us to be, for example, interested in the male hero's search for knowledge by providing us with information about what he thinks and feels: we are invited to identify with him. In contrast, we are often invited to watch female characters without knowing their personalities: they tend to be more objects of visual pleasure whose structural role might be to sing songs or perform strip routines: the audience is encouraged to objectify them. Similarly, male characters are often set at the centre of a film while women serve secondary support functions, such as wife, mother, or mistress, as in *American Beauty*. In this way women are structured as supports or appendages of men. In this chapter we also examine the way characters are structurally positioned at the end of narratives. This positioning encourages us to understand the character in a particular way (as discussed above in relation to gay characters; see p. 260). Analysing the structural position of characters requires us to think not so much about what characters do as about their positions in the narrative.

4 What is the dominant discourse or the hierarchy of discourses?

To develop the idea that characters' structural positions in narratives contribute to meaning let us consider the terms 'dominant discourse' and 'hierarchy of discourses', as used by cultural theorist Colin MacCabe (1974). In a film or television narrative we are presented with a number of different discourses that explain or comment on the situation. Most obviously, there are characters' voices. Thus in *American Beauty* we have the voices of Lester, Carolyn his wife, Jane his daughter, Angela, both Jims, Ricky, Ricky's father, Ricky's mother, and so on. Each of these characters have quite different ways of making sense of the world and speaking about it—different discourses, coexisting alongside each other. MacCabe argues that a narrative will organise these voices into a particular hierarchy, so that one voice is heard as more important, more truthful than another. For example we hear both Ricky's and his father's competing discourses about homosexuality and drugs and we also hear Carolyn's and Lester's perspectives on the same subjects.

Whose voice do we most believe in and trust?	

Our job as film analysts or audience members is to work out whose voice, whose discourse, the film presents as most truthful: the hierarchy of voices must be determined. In this case Ricky's view of the world is clearly seen as superior to that of his repressed and violent father. In general the film uses our allegiance with particular characters to discredit negative discourses in which homosexuality is viewed as sinful or abnormal and it makes a mockery of the legal, medical, and moral discourses that condemn recreational drug use.

Minor characters or discourses can be important in directing us how to think about people and events: when Lester catches out Carolyn and her lover at the burger store it is the manager of the store who comments, 'You are *so* busted!' Though the store manager appears in only a couple of scenes in the whole film and has little to do with the ongoing narrative, her comment carries great weight and directs the audience to look down on Carolyn, who has been caught out. Such minor characters can act the role traditionally played in Greek dramas by the chorus: ordinary figures who play no real part in the narrative but comment on the action and explain to the audience what is going on and how to understand and interpret events. Their choric voice is always high up on the hierarchy of discourses.

MacCabe suggests that in addition to the discourses of the characters we must pay attention to the discourse of film language. By this he means that the things that comprise film discourse—camera style, lighting, editing, music, and so on—invite us to see and hear things in a particular way and contribute to the way we position people in the discourse hierarchy. Thus, in *American Beauty*:

- the camera and lighting show Angela as sexy in the way they frame and light her body
- some of the lighting on Ricky's father portrays him as potentially sinister while the way he and his wife are positioned in terms of *mise-en-scène* shows us how dysfunctional their marriage is
- music and sound plays a crucial role in the moment when Ricky first videos Jane, an act that could be presented as voyeuristic, intrusive, and perverted but the music soundtrack is gentle and mystical and it is this that tells us that what Ricky is doing is fine and romantic.

MacCabe's argument is that viewers make sense of all these competing voices, linking and comparing them until they are arranged into a hierarchy that finally produces a dominant discourse, the discourse that will ultimately give us the truth about events. Of course different audiences may make different readings, but we argue that it is possible to look at the film's arrangement of the different discourses and, from that, deduce what audiences are being invited to think and feel. Viewed in this manner, it makes sense to ask: 'What does the film think about what it is showing us?', or 'What is its project?' (what does it project to us on the screen?). Looking at the film's hierarchy of discourses and seeking out its dominant discourse becomes a way of understanding what the overall film is presenting and how this is inscribed into its narrative structure. These are useful questions that will shift our attention away from our own personal reactions. Asking these questions is similar to looking for a film's preferred reading (see p. 102). You can investigate the dominant discourse of any text by asking

1   What or whose different voices or discourses are presented?
2   How would you order them in a hierarchy (which is most persuasive)?
3   What is the dominant discourse?

At this point it would be easy to fall into the intentionalist position and argue that the dominant discourse is that held by the director (what the film thinks is what the director thinks). While the view of the director is significant, there is a dominant discourse in the text that is the product of not only the director's intention, but also of a host of factors beyond this.

5 Are women positioned differently from men in the narrative?

Many critics have suggested that recurrent patterns are apparent in the structural roles usually given to men and women. Table 17.1, below, suggests some of the main roles, characteristics, and functions that men and women tend to have or fulfil in narratives, as well as some of the gender lines that transect different genres.

Table 17.1 **Structural roles of men and women in film—oppositions**

Male hero	Female heroine
identification	objectification
narrative movement and control	narrative stasis and spectacle
primary characters	secondary characters
active	passive
feelings expressed by external actions	feelings expressed by displays of emotion
strong	weak
work or other public world	home or other private world
investigators	investigated
known	unknown
westerns, thrillers	melodramas, musicals

These are generalisations and do not apply to all narratives but they show interesting tendencies in the representation of men and women. We briefly mentioned above the difference between identification with men and objectification of women (see p. 271). This is a useful distinction that draws our attention to how we watch films. We sometimes ask students to list their favourite male and female stars. We then suggest that for heterosexuals their favourite same-sex stars represent the kinds of women or men they themselves would like to be, the kinds of women or men they identify with; favourite opposite-sex stars represent the kinds of women or men they desire, the kinds of women or men they objectify. This points to two major viewing pleasures we are offered and experience as film viewers—the opportunity to imagine oneself as an all-powerful fantasy figure (the character we most identify with) and the opportunity to gaze erotically on a beautiful fantasy figure whom we desire and objectify.

Film theorist and filmmaker Laura Mulvey notes these two different kinds of viewing pleasure, and in one of the most influential pieces of feminist criticism describes the way women and men are presented in films:

> Woman as Image, Man as Bearer of the Look: In a world ordered by sexual imbalance, pleasure in looking has been split between active/male and passive/female. The determining male gaze projects its phantasy on to the female figure, which is styled accordingly. In their traditional

exhibitionist role women are simultaneously looked at and displayed, with their appearance coded for strong visual and erotic impact so that they can be said to connote *to-be-looked-at-ness*. Woman displayed as sexual object is the *leit-motif* of erotic spectacle: from pin-ups to striptease, from Ziegfeld to Busby Berkeley, she holds the look, plays to and signifies male desire (Mulvey 1985, p. 304).

She continues, arguing that in many mainstream films audiences are invited to identify with men and objectify women, regardless of whether they are male or female. Thus female audiences are asked to look through a male perspective, to see things through men's eyes. Mulvey demonstrates that identification with male heroes is produced primarily through narrative position and editing techniques: in the narrative men are often the major characters—they are introduced at the beginning of the story, we know the most about them, and they are involved in unravelling the enigma in the story. Through editing and camera position we are often encouraged to see the things they see and thus we are stitched into their point of view. All these elements create a position of identification.

Women, on the other hand, are often seen from the outside: we rarely know their thoughts or hear their voices as narrative voice-overs, they are part of the enigma to be investigated, and we don't see things from their point of view. Furthermore, in the kinds of narratives Mulvey critiques, women often play disempowered characters who are punished, persecuted, or endangered within the narrative world. Such character positions do not invite identification. They become the object of the look (or gaze) of both the male characters in the movie, who we see looking, and of us, the audience. The camera delights in shots of women that use lighting, soft focus, framing, music, and erotic costuming to create an erotic spectacle. Often these techniques will be employed to full effect while female characters perform actions— dancing, singing, and so on—that invite the camera, the male characters, and the audience to take pleasure in looking at them. Author and critic John Berger sums up the differences between the portrayal of men and women:

One might simplify this by saying *men act* and *women appear*. Men look at women. Women watch themselves being looked at. This determines not only most relations between men and women but also the relation of women to themselves. The surveyor of woman in herself is male: the surveyed female. Thus she turns herself into an object—and most particularly an object of vision: a sight (Berger 1972, p. 47).

This explains the uncomfortable relationship between female subjectivity and personal appearance, and it foregrounds the point that being looked at is a passive subject position. This relates to the idea of narrative stasis: the narrative pausing to enable spectators to dwell on the spectacle of the female form. While female characters may function to provide visual pleasure and create desire in film narratives, the male actor's deeds and actions are usually what drive the plot forward. We can see all this in the relationship between Lester and Angela in *American Beauty*, the way he gazes at her, the way she 'stops' the narrative in the cheerleading scene, the way we are much more involved in Lester's thoughts and actions. In *Legally Blonde*, the situation is more complex: in this film female appearance is still very important, and Elle is very much a figure of attraction, but this is presented from the woman's point of view. We see and experience the world from a female perspective, Elle has the dominant discourse, she is not simply an object of spectacle. Her role in the courtroom is as investigator and it is she who explains events, a normal male role.

Mulvey's work, along with the work of other feminists, draws attention to the politics of looking and the emphasis on visual appearance that is associated with women in film.

Table 17.1 (p. 274) also suggests that women are often secondary or subordinate characters in films, that men are more important. This is normally the case for genres such as westerns, thrillers, science-fiction films, and crime movies. Content analysis reveals that, on the whole, there are more major roles in film narratives for men than for women. However, there are genres where women often take the primary roles— notably musicals, melodramas, and soap operas—but as the table suggests, these roles tend to operate differently from male roles. Often the women playing such roles are being reactive (they respond to events rather than initiate actions), the focus is on feelings rather than action, and the settings tend to be the private, domestic world of home rather than the professional, public world of work. These are not necessarily negative aspects, but they tend to portray women as less powerful and by suggesting almost mutually exclusive male and female spheres, they can be seen to be excluding women from meaningful public life.

You may think that these observations refer to the kinds of media texts produced in the past, and that the situation is now different because there are many films and television shows—*Weeds*, *Desperate Housewives*, *The Good Wife*, *True Blood*, *Kill Bill*, *Salt*, and *True Grit*, to name some—that have women as central and strong characters. Even so, it is still worth considering how our attitudes (and the attitudes of established media producers who are currently in positions of power and making decisions about media content) have been and are still being influenced by the cumulative impressions of masculinity and femininity that we have acquired throughout our viewing histories. Many films in which women take a prominent role, such as *The Proposal* starring Sandra Bullock as an assertive boss, are still romantic comedies, in which the ultimate goal of the main character is to find a love interest. Most of the changes in the way race and gender are represented are very recent and figure in only a small proportion of media texts produced globally. The emergent trend to include strong female characters is a marketing device that still frequently positions the value of these characters in relation to their physical appearance. Even in texts such as the *Charlie's Angels* franchise, the women are not the most powerful characters in the narrative: they all defer to their boss Charlie, and their appearances are still of central importance.

6 What does the ending tell you about the ideology of the film?

Consider the importance of narrative endings and resolutions, which are an essential part of the narrative pattern. Endings are significant in determining a narrative's ideological meaning. There are different ways of ending stories. Let's explore this further.

Note three different possible types of ending: closed/circular, closed/progress, and open or unresolved (Figures 17.3–17.5).

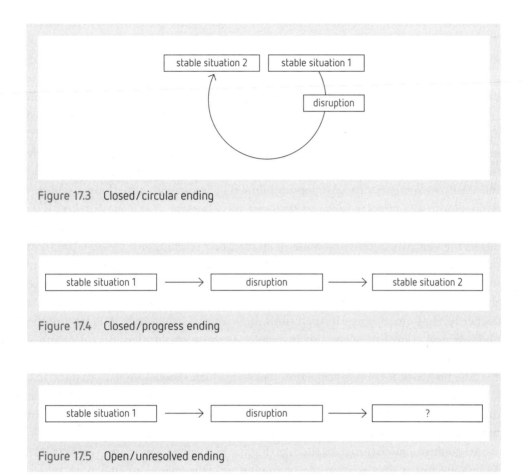

Figure 17.3   Closed/circular ending

Figure 17.4   Closed/progress ending

Figure 17.5   Open/unresolved ending

Most narratives are closed in that they answer all the questions set up in the narrative and they resolve any problems that the film sets up. The closed/circular ending (Figure 17.3) is one that ends where it started. This seems to be a very common cinematic device (much more so than in novels), where shots at or near the end echo or directly repeat the opening shots. *Fight Club* is a good example of a film in which the opening shots are seen again near the ending of the film. Seeing these same shots signals to the audience that the end is coming. It may have some connection with the way in the past cinema-goers would pay a single entry fee that would allow them to stay in the cinema and watch the movie being screened again. Audiences could enter at any time and stay for as long as they wanted. The normal point of exit would be when you reached the 'this is where we came in' moment, indicated by the repetition of images that occurred at the moment of arrival.

The circular characteristic is found particularly in flashback films, which start at one point in time, go into the past, and then return to the original point for the ending—*Citizen Kane* and *The Notebook* are good examples. The ideological point about such narratives is that, in a sense, they don't go anywhere, they don't progress, and they just bring you back to where you started. This suggests that progress is impossible, that it is impossible to change things. The status quo is thereby reinforced. This view of society is fatalistic and conservative. However, the cyclical, flashback narrative structure can also indicate other things. The structure of a film can make a statement that the issue at the heart of the film is unresolvable, or that it is a problem that tends to resurface; a pattern that repeats itself over and over again in families, in individuals, or in society. *Nil by Mouth* and *The War Zone* are examples of narratives that deal with the cycle of domestic violence and family abuse, and both are structured to avoid closure and progress. An open or unresolved ending can leave the audience with the responsibility for defining their own ideas and positions, and can even encourage us to take action. Films that work with time loop paradoxes frequently have a circular narrative structure too (*Inception*, *The Time Traveller's Wife*, *Terminator*, and *Donnie Darko*). Few films have a truly cyclical narrative structure that denies the audience a satisfying sense of closure. *Lost Highway* and *Memento* are films that leave the audience at the beginning of the narrative, freshly engaged with exactly the same questions that they began with. But in each case we have more knowledge about the characters and their situations, and as a consequence we move on to a deeper level of questioning. In such films the narrative structure is indicative of the philosophical enormity of the unanswerable questions about identity and memory with which they grapple.

The flashback form was popular in *film noir*, which showed humans trapped in a hostile universe. These films suggest that whatever humans do, they are doomed to their preordained ending. Similar circular patterns can be seen in many cartoons or situation comedies today.

In contrast, closed/progress endings (Figure 17.4) allow for progress and change. Things are not as they were at the beginning (whether happy or unhappy), which suggests that humans can change their life situations. This relates to the process of moral change and growth that main characters go through. It is a pattern that is usually positive—characters learn and become better people during the narrative— and it suggests that we can move on from the status quo.

When watching a film or television program, try to determine whether, and how, it reproduces these closed or circular and closed or progress patterns.

Comparison of *American Beauty* and *Legally Blonde* narratives

Both films illustrate the closed/progress model: the progress is demonstrated by the main characters, particularly Lester in *American Beauty* and Elle in *Legally Blonde*. They have gone through their trials and tribulations, progressed, and emerged as better people. Closure is indicated in the resolution of all the major questions. There is an interesting and obvious difference though: Lester is dead; Elle is alive. There is also a slight element of circularity in *Legally Blonde* and definite circularity in *American Beauty*. In *Legally Blonde* the film started with Elle's desire to get engaged. At the end this desire is satisfactorily resolved (though with a different man) and the film has thus come full circle. This is further emphasised by the reprise of the title song, 'Perfect Day'. *American Beauty* started with the information that Lester would be dead in less than a year. This voice speaks from the future, and it means Lester's death is a foregone conclusion. The ending brings the circle to a close and the final shot of the film is an exact reverse of the opening shot.

Mainstream and non-mainstream cinema

Mainstream Hollywood cinema tends towards closed endings; however, films can be open or unresolved, which is sometimes the case in relation to mainstream cinema. The horror genre—films such as *Let Me In*, and those in the *Ring*, *Saw*, and *Final Destination* franchises—has traditionally had open endings. This is not only so that there will be room for a sequel (though this is commercially sensible) but more because the horror genre is meant to disturb us. Part of the power and the pleasure of horror films is that they allow us to experience, in a safe cinematic setting, fear and to confront things that frighten and fascinate us. But the nature of fear is about being unsafe, and it is important for the success of the genre that the endings of the stories leave open the possibility for the horror to return. Thus we leave the cinema with the beginnings of the sequel already taking root in the shadowy corners of our minds, waiting to haunt our nightmares and surface in our thoughts when we are alone and the lights are out. Refusing the comfort of a closed ending allows the narrative structure to create disturbance. Critics have suggested that at times of moral and social uncertainty, commercial films may not offer clearly resolved endings (Wood 1986), but non-mainstream narratives are the usual place to find more open endings.

Non-mainstream narratives with open or unresolved endings are often found in so-called arthouse films, a type of film that is more intellectually oriented than commercial cinema. Arthouse films frequently present a challenge to the audience and to the dominant order and accepted norms of society. They often aim to say something meaningful and many have a slower editing pace and a more consciously artistic approach. Endings can be deliberately ambiguous, inviting spectators to think reflectively about what they have seen, to puzzle out the meanings, and to explore the moral and social dilemmas raised. Art films may thus reflect more of the uncertainties of real life; they certainly don't offer us easy answers and are not so comfortable and reassuring, as discussed above with *Elephant*. *Hurt Locker*, *Black Swan*, *Antichrist*, *Caché* (*Hidden*), and *Irreversible* are good examples of films that unsettle and challenge the audience because they deal with disturbing subject matter in complex ways without presenting characters to whom the audience can easily relate.

Open or unresolved endings are also found in avant-garde, experimental, and independent films, films not discussed in this book, but it is important to recognise that they exist as alternatives to mainstream cinema. Such films work with different narrative patterns, even with no narrative at all.

In relation to endings, think about how characters are positioned at the end of narratives. Most obviously, consider whether they receive rewards or punishments, happy or unhappy endings. This gives a good indication as to whether their actions and behaviour are legitimated. For example ask about a character: is that character dead or alive, married or single, alone or with someone, rewarded or punished, and so on? These structural positions show us what to think about a character, as demonstrated earlier in relation to gay characters in films (p. 260).

As films come to a close the filmmakers need to try to answer all the unresolved questions but also decide at exactly what point to end the film. You can do an interesting exercise by stopping a film a few minutes before it ends and asking people to predict what is going to happen. The actual ending usually tells you something about the ideology of the film.

Case study: The ending of *Legally Blonde*

What are the ideological meanings of the ending of *Legally Blonde*?

Many films could finish at a number of different points. Each place would give a slightly different inflection to the story we have seen. Remember that the key questions the film had set up earlier were: Can Elle win her boyfriend back? Can she get into Harvard? Can she be a successful lawyer? These personal questions relate to wider ideological questions about femininity and whether blonde women can succeed in previously male-dominated areas. The film is essentially a battle of the sexes struggle between femininity and masculinity, and a debate about how women should act and appear. By the end of *Legally Blonde* Elle has won her court case, thus solving that issue and proving herself a successful lawyer. As she leaves the court in triumph this could be the end of the film. But it continues as we see Elle graduating from Harvard. We have identified several possible ending moments; each ending moment answers some of the narrative questions posed earlier and constructs a slightly different view on the wider gender questions. First watch the ending and decide for yourself what possible moments it could end at, how each ending would carry a different ideological meaning, and why the ending is sequenced in this order. Then read our analysis.

1   If *Legally Blonde* were to end as Elle walks out of the courtroom, triumphant and alone, it would signify that she is a successful, individual lawyer. The ending shows her focus on work, career, professional success, self-sufficiency, and independence. The film supports an ideology of successful professional independence for women. But wait ...

2   The film could end at the graduation ceremony after she has looked at Vivian, her female friend, and at Emmet, her male friend, and Warner, her ex-lover, and as she exhorts people to 'Have faith in yourself—we did it'. This ending celebrates Elle in top position at Harvard but in a position where she speaks for the community and acknowledges her connection with her friends. This ending would endorse an ideology of community but a community based on hierarchy and professional success. But wait ...

3   If the film ends just after she smiles at her female friend and we see the caption about them being 'best friends', then the triumph of sisterhood and the ideology of female solidarity are placed above the values of community, romance, or family. But wait …

4   If the film ends after we see the unsuccessful Warner and the caption about his failure, then the ending stresses the failure of masculinity, the value of femininity and its triumph over masculinity—a pro-female, anti-male ideology. But wait …

5   If the film ends as we see that Paulette and her UPS boyfriend are happily married and naming their daughter Elle, this signals the triumph of femininity: the woman gets her man. It also celebrates the family and the reproduction of the dominant social order with the new generation. This ending unites femininity and masculinity; however, in this unification the male figure is subordinate and the triumph of the feminine matriarchal line is indicated in the passing on of Elle's name to the next generation. But wait …

6   The film could end when we see everyone throwing their hats in the air, which emphasises once again the value of the community. There is success for everyone. Romance is maintained within the broader scope of a whole community, and is thus a less individualistic ideology. But wait …

7   The film could end as we cut to Emmett and read that he is proposing to Elle tonight. This ending suggests that marriage is the most important thing for a woman, an ideology of romance and heterosexuality is once again valued. In this ideology the man appears initially to be the active, dominant partner but we realise that this is where we came in. Elle is finally getting what she wanted at the beginning of the film—a proposal—and the implication is that she has actually made all this happen, she is calling the shots. So, ultimately, the film endorses a traditional, stereotypical, heterosexual, romance ideology but one in which the woman has a certain amount of power. But wait …

8   The film goes back to a final close-up of Elle (this is the actual ending the filmmakers used). Who is she looking at? This time she is not looking at Emmett. She looks away from him up to the heavens. Her final triumph is transcendent; she is separate and above all the relationships of community, friends, family, lover: she has discovered herself. This final ending suggests an individualistic ideology, a film of individuation in which the hero, Elle, has journeyed to enlightenment beyond the collective, beyond friendship, beyond marriage.

You can do this kind of narrative ending analysis with any film and it should produce some interesting insights and debates. Individual interpretations of the significance of an ending can vary considerably. Some viewers may argue that *Legally Blonde* reinforces dominant ideologies—not just individualism—as well as elements of patriarchal ideology. As *Legally Blonde 2: Red, White and Blonde* demonstrates, beauty, marriage, and family relationships are still ranked highest on the feminine agenda (even if gay rights, animal rights, and the rights of gay animals are important too). And while endings are important in constructing meaning we need to remember that actual audiences will not always accept what the ending offers. They may well focus on other moments in the story as more significant.

Binary oppositions

binary oppositions
A means of cultural classification that splits the world into sets of dualistic opposing categories, such as male and female, black and white.

We can develop narrative analysis further through the application of **binary oppositions**. These are used by many critics (Kitses 2004; Turner 2006, p. 104). You can see them at work in Table 17.1 (p. 274), in Kitses' western oppositions (Table 15.1, pp. 236–7), and in our analysis of language (p. 88). You may well have encountered them elsewhere. The concept of opposition or duality is fundamental in the organisation of language, as it is in Western philosophical thinking as a whole. Aristotle expressed this when he stated that 'Everything is either A or not A'. He used opposition or negation as a means of definition, a use that is apparent in language; as discussed in relation to semiology, words don't mean anything on their own— they have meaning in relation to other words (through systems of difference). Each word or concept is defined by its opposite and only makes sense if we understand its opposite as well. 'Yes', for example, is understood in relation to 'no', 'right' in relation to 'left' or 'wrong', 'up' to 'down', 'light' to 'dark', 'good' to 'bad', 'black' to 'white', 'masculine' to 'feminine', and so on. We make sense of the world through oppositions. As Hartley puts it, 'Such binaries are a feature of *culture* not *nature*; they are products of signifying systems, and function to structure our perceptions of the natural and social world into order and meaning' (O'Sullivan et al. 1994, p. 30).

So we, as humans, create these categories. 'Binary' is derived from the Greek word *bio*, meaning 'two'. It is about splitting or pairing things into twos: positive and negative, yes and no, and so on. It is the basic numerical system used in computers. All computer decisions are based on asking and answering yes or no questions. Whichever answer is chosen will lead automatically to the next stage of computation.

This system of duality has been challenged by those who argue that it creates separation and does not adequately represent reality. While, for instance, male–female is one of the central binaries that we use today (and also that we use throughout the book) the fact is that biologically, this opposition may not adequately describe reality. First, there is no absolutely clear dividing line, since it is possible to be hermaphrodite (male and female). There are also numerous gradations or variations of what is male and what is female. The chromosomal and hormonal differences used to biologically define male and female difference show that nearly all men have some female chromosomal or hormonal elements, while nearly all women similarly have male elements. Few people are 100 per cent male or female in these terms. Thus, biologically, the categories of male and female are more fluid than Western culture has traditionally recognised; the lines of difference are not so clear-cut.

Note that binary oppositions such as male and female and right and wrong are hierarchical: one term is often privileged over the other and the devalued or negative term tends to be defined in relation to the dominant category. The male–female opposition has been objected to because male is taken as the primary category against which female is defined. As Turner puts it:

Assuming male and female are opposites means that, automatically, women *are* what men are *not*; if the male is strong, then the female must be weak, and on it goes ... we can see the accretion of negatives on the female side as a necessary product of the assumption that male and female are opposites. To continue the chain is to end up with good (male) versus bad (female) (Turner 2006, p. 104).

The binary system and way of categorising the world also implicitly condones adversarial or oppositional ways of thinking in which there are rigid, mutually exclusive discursive positions and winners and losers of debates, instead of negotiated compromises and flexible positions that entail mutual incorporation of different perspectives. We can see how our political systems often work in this way or how the media, in its ways of reporting events, nearly always frames things in terms of opposition and conflict. These may be very limited and limiting ways of seeing the world.

Chinese culture offers a way of thinking about oppositions in the ancient yin and yang symbol (Figure 17.6), which again splits male and female but has some differences.

The symbol is an image of opposites: the yin stands for the passive principle of the universe, characterised as female, dark, passive, yielding, negative, and absorbing; yang stands for the active principle of the universe, characterised as masculine, light, active, firm, positive, and expansionary. This is not unlike Western oppositions around gender, which similarly link a whole set of attributes to each position (male or female). These sets of oppositions around gender have come under attack from feminists who argue that women should not be positioned as one set of characteristics, particularly if these are

Figure 17.6   Yin and yang symbol

negative and less powerful than the set assigned to men. The major point to make here is that while yin and yang is a system of opposites, it is also a system and symbol of equality and complementarity. The two sides take up equal space in the overall circle, which represents the world and the universe, so the feminine, yin, is of equal importance to the masculine, yang (incidentally, circles are often seen as a feminine symbol, because they are linked to ovulation cycles, seasonal cycles, and the shape of eggs—thus the feminine is the overall defining structure here). Moreover, yin and yang are complementary since each includes an aspect of the other, an internal feminine in the masculine and vice versa (the black and white dots), as an essential part of them. Even the separation between the two principles is not a rigid straight line but a flowing curved line that allows a blending of the two: they depend on each other to form a complete whole. So this Chinese system of difference is not about two elements opposing each other in conflict, but about working together.

How binary oppositions function in narratives

Let's return to the use of binary oppositions in narrative analysis. Narratives are organised around conflict and opposition, which are fundamental to narrative interest. There has to be some kind of struggle, some disruption that sets up conflict. The conflict is most obviously between individual characters, but this will also indicate conflict between different value systems. Indeed, the overall structure of all narratives can be seen as involving the resolution of conflict between two opposing forces. The term '**dialectical synthesis**' refers to a discussion or argument between two competing or opposing sides. In a philosophical argument or an academic essay, these two sides are called the thesis (what is being argued for) and the antithesis (the counterclaims, or alternative points, perspectives, views, and voices that are being argued against the thesis). In a narrative, the thesis and the antithesis relate to whatever binary opposition structures the story contains and, just as in an argument or essay, each side must engage with the other and be able to explain or understand the opposing point or perspective in order to be able to refute or incorporate it. When the two sides come to terms with each other, the dialectical synthesis or narrative resolution is reached.

dialectical synthesis
Two opposing forces (such as good and evil, or thesis and antithesis) generate conflict or debate that is resolved when the two sides come together in a form of synthesis.

We can discern many different oppositions within the structure of a single narrative.

Jim Kitses was one of the first media critics to use oppositions in his illuminating analysis of the western (see Table 15.1, pp. 236–7). He suggests that the western is replete with general oppositions such as wilderness versus civilisation and antagonistic characters such as cowboys and Indians, outlaws and lawmen.

In specific films these general categories would be linked to the personal and individual stories of particular characters, for example John Wayne or Clint Eastwood as the heroes would be aligned with either nature or culture, or with values such as self-interest and individualism or social responsibility and community. In different films they may be on different sides, for example they might play an outlaw in one film, the sheriff in another. Kitses' list of binary oppositions is enormously helpful in relation to the western genre, as already discussed. It is also useful as an example of this structured system of oppositions; we can apply it to other genres and narratives.

Note, first, that in the system of binary oppositions when we make a list it is important to see vertical connections between all the categories listed on either the right or left side of the table; in the above example 'the west', 'wilderness', 'individual', 'freedom', and so on are all linked in some way, they are literally on the same side of this opposing equation, which shows how the dramatic conflict contains a whole series of elements on each side.

Second, oppositions can be observed between particular characters, between different human characteristics, between different settings or even colours, and so on. These then cohere to provide a central opposition between two different value systems. Analysis of this opposition leads us to a deeper understanding of what the film is essentially concerned with.

Third, ultimately the film must find some resolution between these oppositions, and fourth, the richness of this system is that while there is usually some sense of right versus wrong, good versus evil (so that one side of the oppositions is preferred), it is not absolutely clear-cut good and bad. In the simplest of dramas—films such as *Star Wars* or *The Lord of the Rings* trilogy—this might be the case, but even in these films there are complications. 'Evil' Darth Vader turns out to be 'good' Luke Skywalker's father; Gollum in his split personality shows aspects of good and evil, and the power of the ring brings out the dark side of good Bilbo and Frodo. Other narratives show more complex ambiguities between good and evil, between the two oppositional sides, and the resolution often shows the need to combine elements or to have some crossovers between the two sides. Over time, value systems change so that in the opposition cowboys versus Indians, for example, there has been a gradual change from seeing the cowboys as good, the Indians as bad, to the reverse. The same basic binary opposition is used but with different inflections.

Once again, the idea of dialectical synthesis can help us to understand how resolution is reached. Just as the thesis and the antithesis must be brought together into a synthesis, the protagonist and the antagonist in a story typically need to take on aspects of each other's value systems and character traits in order for the conflict between them to be resolved. Western cowboy heroes, for example, often bring civilisation and community to the wild west frontier, but paradoxically, their ability to enforce law and order is dependent on the strength of their individualism, and they themselves remain free (outside or beyond the law) in the wilderness. In order for a cowboy hero to defeat the Indians, he frequently needs to acquire traditional Indian skills, such as tracking and hunting, and often he understands Indian culture and language better than characters such as the settler or the merchant, who are totally aligned with civilisation and the east.

You should find a clear set of oppositions in almost every mainstream narrative you analyse and finding it will provide a key to understanding and interpreting the story and its structure.

Some films, such as Darren Aronofsky's Academy Award winning feature *Black Swan*, are explicitly structured around binary oppositions to the extent that the theme of the narrative *is* duality. Even a brief narrative extract such as the film trailer shows that the oppositions between the black swan's power and the white swan's purity; sexual experimentation and sexual repression; insanity and sanity are structuring themes. The film's ending makes a powerful, if heavy-handed, statement about the negative consequences of failing to achieve dialectical synthesis or a harmonious balance of opposing traits within the self.

Look at Gordon Bennett's *Altered Body Print (Shadow Figure Howling at the Moon)* (Plate 9, discussed on pp. 442–3) and consider how he is using binary oppositions.

Coupling endings

> How many film and television narratives end with coupling?

We will extend this analysis of the resolution of binary oppositions to looking at how film and television narratives often work by focusing on couples, one particular binary, and using these as a central part of the narrative. It has been suggested that cinema is a machine for making couples. This is because many film endings lead to romance and actual or potential marriage. The final result of all the narrative drama, tests, tension, and suspense is for a man and woman to get together as a heterosexual pair. While this is obviously not true of all films it is common. The end of *Cinema Paradiso* is a fascinating example that self-consciously draws attention to this convention at the same time as challenging it: the climax of the film shows numerous clips from famous films of couples falling into each other's arms and kissing passionately. While this demonstrates cinema's love of coupling at the end of a narrative, the hero of *Cinema Paradiso* is actually left on his own at the end of the film. He has left behind his childhood sweetheart and, as he watches the kissing couples on the screen, his only coupling is with cinema itself. The predominance of successful coupling as the desirable end-product of narratives reproduces an ideology of heterosexual, monogamous romance and marriage, which goes back before cinema to other storytelling traditions, and to plays and novels. It is encapsulated in fairy tales, which invariably begin with the introduction, 'Once upon time there was a …' and end with the phrase 'and they lived happily ever after' (suggesting a heterosexual couple who have just married).

While the statement that cinema is a machine for making couples was initially directed at film texts, it also says something useful about the cinema as an institution, as a place that audiences visit. The cinema is a place that once had a special significance for (hetero)sexual couples. When sexual expression was more repressed in real life, the cinema traditionally offered couples a space of darkness, privacy, and eroticism, a place where they could experiment with physical intimacy at the same time as watching it. Eroticism and romance, the focus on sexuality and love, have always been a major part of the cinematic output, complementing or encouraging the feelings of couples in the audience. Cinema has traditionally been a space to which you invite a partner. Today you can still see many couples attending the cinema as part of their romantic connection. Many of the advertisements screened in the cinema before the main film are addressed to couples; they focus on such activities as eating out together and buying furniture for the family home. There is an interesting contrast between advertisements in local cinemas, which tend to portray a normal, family-oriented, routine lifestyle, and the actual stories of drama, fantasy, and excitement that audiences come to see.

Happy endings with successful coupling were the norm for Hollywood films from the 1930s to the 1950s. Movies with happy endings are still being made and they are now often referred to as feel-good movies, but since the 1960s there have also been more unhappy, unresolved endings. The earlier films can be seen as a reflection of the optimism of American society and the durability of the family unit from the 1930s to the 1950s; films from the 1960s and after reflect the increasing instability of and uncertainty about social values and of the fact that the family unit has been under considerable pressure in the past four decades.

Couple endings can have many variations: examples include tragic endings in which the couples separate or the failure of the couple to come together. Many westerns end with the male hero walking away alone into the sunset, continuing on his journey or quest and remaining outside society and marriage. Non-heterosexual couples are another possibility: male buddies, female buddies, gay and lesbian couples, or family couples such as estranged mother and son, or father and daughter.

Case study: Coupling endings: *My Best Friend's Wedding* and *Knocked Up*

The now classic romantic comedy *My Best Friend's Wedding*, directed by PJ Hogan, offers an interesting variation on the couple ending, especially because its title leads us to expect that a wedding will be the happy conclusion. The film is based around four characters. Julianne Potter (Julia Roberts) has a best friend, Michael O'Neal (Dermot Mulroney), who is engaged to be married to Kimmy Wallace (Cameron Diaz). Julianne has another friend, George Downey (Rupert Everett), who is gay. Julianne, having learnt of the impending marriage, realises that she really loves Michael and wants him herself. By the end of the film she has failed to win him; Kimmy and Michael are happily married and Julianne is left on her own, although she still has her career and her gay friend George (her new best friend?). The film concludes with a shot of Julianne and George dancing happily together at the wedding.

In traditional storytelling, getting married is a happy ending. The ending of this film may suggest that strong-willed career women who take an active role in determining their own destiny don't get rewarded by the conventional pleasures of marriage (whereas the ditzy, devoted girl does). Nevertheless, a number of elements demonstrate that non-marriage and strong friendship are as good as, if not preferable to, heterosexual marriage, and that the outsiders (an unmarried career-oriented woman and a gay man) are actually the ones who find the happier ending.

The film is a comedy and the characters played by Roberts and Everett are funnier, more knowing, and more attractive than those played by Diaz and Mulroney (the ones who end up 'happily married'). The comic tone of the film is satirical of American manners, particularly in relation to marriage and the family. We are invited to like Roberts' and Everett's characters, and to laugh at the other couple. Although the lead women are fighting over him for most of the film, Mulroney's character, Michael, is something of a nonentity. In the end it seems that marriage to him would be far less fun and fulfilling than freedom and friendship with her gay best friend, who—unlike Michael—will never leave her to marry another woman. (It's notable here that a partner for the gay character is never an option; although George does not necessarily end up unhappy, he is never granted the possibility of forming romantic bonds. George is a sympathetic gay character, and the friendship he shares with Julianne is genuine and significant. Nevertheless, like many sidelined gay characters in mainstream film, his main function in the narrative is to prop up a heterosexual tale.)

The topics of heterosexual bonding, marriage, and family are the central issues of many films and television shows, particularly romantic comedies, melodramas, soap operas, and sit-coms. The conclusions of mainstream films used to almost always point to happiness through the establishment of the heterosexual couple and the family. However, an increasing ambivalence about 'the happy couple' can be seen as a reflection of the changing state of marriage, sexuality, and the family in the West over the past thirty years. There is a crisis in these institutions, an ever-increasing uncertainty about how to live out sexual desire and relationships. Media narratives can be seen to suggest different solutions to these issues. Even as a romantic comedy (a genre built around heterosexual coupling), *My Best Friend's Wedding* shows up the expectation of a 'happily ever after' as problematic. This film posits a contented 'buddy' ending outside the norms of marriage and heterosexuality as one possibility and recent films such as *The Kids are All Right* go even further by exploring the difficulties of married life for a lesbian couple who reunite with the sperm donor father of their teenage children. A number of contemporary films explore differing formations of love and family, yet a large percentage of them still ultimately reinforce coupling and having children as the path to fulfilment and happiness.

Ten years after *My Best Friend's Wedding* came the romantic comedy *Knocked Up*, directed by Judd Apatow. This is a story about Alison Scott (Katherine Heigl), a single, successful, career-driven woman who is not just unmarried when she becomes pregnant, but is not even in a relationship. Despite this unconventional premise, however, the film guides us towards quite a traditional ending in terms of romantic heterosexual coupling and co-parenting. In the film, Alison's career as a TV presenter is going well, and while out celebrating a promotion one night she meets Ben (Seth Rogen), a sweet-natured, unemployed marijuana-smoker. After drinking too much they end up having a one-night stand, and don't see each other again until eight weeks later when Alison discovers that she is pregnant. For the sake of the unborn baby, the mismatched pair attempt to form a relationship, but it quickly turns sour and they break up. At the same time, Alison's sister, Debbie (Leslie Mann), and her husband, Pete (Paul Rudd), are having marriage problems. By the time Alison goes into labour Ben has proved himself a worthy father by having read pregnancy books, found a stable job, and secured an apartment with a nursery. Meanwhile, Ben also helps Pete see how grateful he is for Debbie and their children, and Debbie and Pete reconcile. As the credits role, a montage of the joyful trio, Alison, Ben and their child, reinforces their happy ending. Despite the roundabout ways both couples in the film reach contentment through committed heterosexual partnering and children, such an ending undermines the possibility of alternatives to the heterosexual nuclear family and reinforces dominant social norms. The examples of *My Best Friend's Wedding* and *Knocked Up* show how film narratives tackle the central concerns of romantic love and family, and offer suggestions as to how problems around these issues can be resolved—some more conservative than others.

Television narratives

Television is a narrative form that originally had close ties to both radio and cinema, but it has evolved in the context of rapid economic and technological transformation. The evolution of television can be traced through three distinct eras. TVI lasted from approximately 1948–1975; TVII ran from about 1975–1995; and we are now in the era of TVIII. In the early years of television (TVI), audiences were restricted to fixed schedules on a limited range of local or national broadcast channels. The second period (TVII) was characterised by greater consumer choice due to industry deregulation, the possibility of recording programs on VCRs and watching them later, and the proliferation of cable and satellite channels that catered to niche audiences (see Nelson 2007). TVIII is the digital era, which television scholars Glen Creeber and Matt Hills describe as 'television's present state and beyond; a time of increased fragmentation, consumer interactivity and global market economies' (2007, p. 1). This era is characterised by user-generated content, the streaming, downloading, and multiplatforming of content, and binge-viewing of DVD box sets.

> In what ways are television programs different from films that we watch in the cinema?

Most of what we have said about narrative applies to film and cinema but only partially to television dramas, which are equally important media texts. It is possible to apply all the above concepts to television but there are some major differences.

The first major difference is the context of reception. In contrast to the private, darkened space of cinema, suitable for couples, the television, a much smaller screen, was initially introduced for domestic and family viewing. Its original location was usually in the collective family space, the living room, to be viewed by all members of the family, often together, and quite possibly engaged in other activities at the same time. This togetherness is now fragmented, partly by programming schedules, which mean that different family members can watch at different times of the day, but also by the increased manufacture of televisions and their correspondingly cheaper prices: we now find television sets in rooms other than communal family rooms, such as bedrooms, where television can be watched more privately. Recently though, the establishment of home theatre rooms has brought in a viewing experience closer to cinema—darkened rooms with big screens and surround sound.

The second major difference is that television tends to be more dialogue-driven and is divided into short, self-contained segments so that the storylines can be followed by someone who is not giving the screen their undivided attention. The structure of televisual narratives invites a different kind of engagement, and different interpretive practices arise from the context of reception. Often, instead of *gazing* intently at the screen as we do in the cinema, television audience members *glance* at the set while they are going about other everyday activities such as studying, ironing clothes, making lunch, or talking on the phone. These different viewing patterns also relate to the differing content and styles of the two media. Television texts often focus on everyday life and family concerns and they are watched routinely in private or domestic circumstances. Because it is situated in the home, television also has a tone or mode of address that is more conversational than film (figures on television tend to address or acknowledge the viewer as a participant, sometimes implicitly including them as part of a live studio audience). In contrast, film maintains a sense of voyeurism and generally does not acknowledge the audience explicitly (for example, screen characters rarely look directly at the camera or acknowledge that they are performing a role or being watched).

There are also major differences between television and film in relation to narrative structure. Television's predominant form is episodic or serial in structure. Whereas cinema offers films that are complete narratives in themselves—one-offs, usually with closed endings—television offers programs in which the narrative continues week after week, either as serials, in which the story carries on and develops from one episode to the next, as in the *Underbelly* television series, or as series in which there is some development from one week to the next but each episode has its own particular story. Situation comedies, such as *The Simpsons* and *Modern Family*, operate in this way. Many series today combine complete stories in a single episode alongside a continual developing narrative, such as *Sea Patrol* and *Burn Notice*.

Television's most extreme form of the continuous series is the soap opera. Programs such as *Neighbours* and *Eastenders* go on for years due to soap opera's serialised, open-ended, never-ending narrative structure.

Media convergence and other changes to the television industry, particularly the fact that audiences can now use their televisions as a portal to go online and access the internet instead of relying on local broadcast channels, mean that television narratives now also continue on multiple platforms and even in entirely different media forms. For instance, the storyline of *Jericho* extended well beyond the television screen: even after the series was cancelled, the characters lived on in print and web-based tie-ins including comic books, alternative reality games, webisodes, and a planned movie. There are obvious practical and economic reasons that these serialised, multiplatform narratives are developing in the television industry. The need to win regular audiences was met by regular broadcast programming—same program, same time each week. Now television creators continue to capitalise on the established familiarity with characters and settings that brings audiences back to programs they like, even when viewers stream, download, or record the program, or when the narrative extends across different storytelling platforms. Economically, it makes for much cheaper production costs when you can use the same sets, costumes, and so on each week or reuse the designs developed by the original art director in subsequent iterations of the narrative in different media. The formulaic format predominates in television schedules for non-fiction programs as well: game shows, travel programs, sports and cooking shows, even the news and weather reports are all programmed in regular weekly or daily episodes, often running for a season of many episodes, and now frequently being accompanied by companion websites that offer supplementary material. The aim is to build up a loyal audience.

Fragmentation and flow

According to television scholar Nicholas Abercrombie (1996), television narration is characterised by fragmentation and flow. **Flow** relates to the carefully constructed schedule, a sequence of events designed to keep viewers sitting in front of the television as they move from news through family viewing to late-night movies, and so on. The experience of watching television is not an experience of consuming discrete products (commercials, news, fiction of various genres), but of one unified act of media consumption: 'We are watching television, not watching a specific programme' (Abercrombie 1996, p. 12). In addition, because television features ongoing storylines, each episode and each series is designed to flow into the next, without answering all of the narrative questions or achieving closure at the end of any single episode.

flow
The continual sequence of television programs, trailers, and advertisements that blend together.

Fragmentation refers to the segmentation and discontinuity that characterises television texts and television as a media form. Each program is fragmented by commercials, and, as stated above, their narratives tend to lack closure (they take serial or episodic form and play out over a number of nights or weeks). The fact that television is, paradoxically, both continuous and fragmented produces a 'decentred' experience of viewing and is characteristic of the postmodern condition (according to Kaplan, cited in Abercrombie 1996, pp. 16–17). The fragmented experience of television consumption also relates to disruptions characteristic of the domestic context of reception.

fragmentation
The way television often features stories that are broken up over a number of episodes, are full of short separate scenes, and are interrupted by commercials.

Some commentators have noted that television tends to be character driven, whereas the majority of films are plot-driven and include more action. Film narratives tend to focus on one or two characters at the centre of the story and a plot line that involves one or two major questions such as 'Will Bella end up with Edward or Jacob?' Television fictions are often organised around multiple stories and groups of characters in a community. The multiple story was originally the province of soap operas, which keep a group of stories going over many episodes. This approach has been adopted in many television series. Consider, for example, the way in which the television series *Grey's Anatomy* and *Brothers and Sisters* feature separate but interrelated stories in each episode. These self-contained stories usually relate to the ongoing narrative concerns of the series. Multistorylines are suited to representing communities and groups of characters.

Are these narrative structures of television also geared towards couple-making? Many television series are built around couples or individuals who would like to be in a couple. In some series the constant unresolved sexual tension or attraction between a couple is a major narrative element; this is true of series such as *The Mentalist*, *Bones*, *Californication*, and *Castle*. Other series, such as *Glee*, *Gossip Girl*, and *One Tree Hill*, focus on the constant making and breaking of couples, shown most explicitly in the series *How I Met Your Mother*. Given the contemporary fragmentation of the family and marriage (see case study, pp. 287–8), television series—*Community*, *It's Always Sunny in Philadelphia*, and *The Big Bang Theory*, for example—now often focus on groups of friends, and on the fact that people don't get into successful, happily ever after couples. Other shows—*Desperate Housewives* and *United States of Tara*, for example—feature stable couples but explore their problems, while some programs—*30 Rock*, *NCIS*, *Breaking Bad*, *Supernatural*, *Hawaii Five-O*—feature non-romantic couples.

Internet narratives

People are now making narrative entertainments to go directly onto the internet that can be viewed on computers or mobile phones, entertainments that are increasingly popular with young people. The nature of this form, as discussed by writer and producer Chris Corbett, is different yet again from film and television as internet narratives are compressed into very short sequences, ideally no more than five minutes. In conversation with ABC broadcaster Antony Funnell, Corbett, who has produced a series of children's narratives on YouTube called *Tiny Town*, describes it thus:

Antony Funnell	I'm interested in the length of each episode. How did you determine the length, and is there conventional wisdom about the ideal duration for such productions?
Chris Corbett	There is … It seems to me it couldn't go over five minutes. There's something about five minutes for these 'webisodes' that just seems a bit long, and it's interesting when I'm watching one myself, you know, your hand hovers on the mouse if it starts to lose you at any point; and there's a new American show called *Quarter Life* that's done very professionally … they're 8-minute episodes, and I found myself drifting off during that. I thought 8 minutes is too long. So I'd say ideally the length of an episode would be between 4 and 5 minutes.
Antony Funnell	And as a professional writer who's used to writing episodes that are much longer, was that a challenge?
Chris Corbett	Well it was, because you would think that writing 4 minutes or 5 minutes of something would be easier, but in fact you need to be much more concise. If you lose people—if you're writing an episode of television, you can afford

to lose people for a few minutes. They might go, 'Oh, that scene didn't work', they're not necessarily going to switch off. There's a general feeling on the internet that if you lose people for 10 or 15 seconds ... they'll just click that button and they're off to something else, or they'll jump ahead. So you really can't afford to lose people at all at any point. Everything has to have a drive and a momentum to it.

Media Report, ABC Radio National, 20 December 2007

Not only are these internet productions changing narrative form but they also demonstrate the increased democratisation of the new media. Corbett and his team are able to produce their products very cheaply and can bypass the conventional media television channels; previously, trying to get a television pilot episode for a new show up and running would cost a lot of money and also have to be approved by the television station, which could be a difficult, involved, and time-consuming process. Now, people such as Corbett can simply go ahead, make a product, and put it online. If it is successful it will begin to make some money.

Pornography

We want to include a brief analysis of pornography. We realise that pornography is not often used as a topic for analysis in formal academic studies (though there is some significant research by leading scholars such as Linda Williams, author of *Hard Core* (1999), Catharine Lumby, Kath Albury, and Alan McKee (2002), who conducted the 'Understanding Pornography in Australia' research project). However, pornography is important for a number of reasons: because of its ubiquity, because of its importance in driving media technological change, because of its significance for sexuality and in relation to censorship, and in relation to issues discussed above—genre, narrative structure, binaries, and coupling endings.

1   Within the media industries pornography is a very significant player. Although it does not figure on free to air television stations (though explicit sex-service adverts appear on late-night television) or screen in mainstream cinemas it has its own outlets through satellite and cable television channels, sex cinemas, so-called men's entertainment magazines, DVD hire and purchase, and, most importantly, the internet. Pornography has significantly influenced mainstream media productions, which themselves have included more and more sexually explicit material and often use visual imagery that seems to derive from the porn genre. Economically, porn is very big business and it is being widely distributed and consumed. While it does not receive the media attention that popular cinema does and it is difficult to obtain accurate figures, the annual revenue of the adult entertainment industry (including internet porn), estimated to be worth over $10 billion, rivals the Hollywood film industry's annual US box office revenue (Johnston 2007).

2   Pornography has always been an important player in the development of media technologies. No sooner was photography developed in the mid-nineteenth century than thousands of pornographic photos of women were being distributed; the potential economic profits from such photos drove the improvements in photographic techniques and processes. The economic profit motive is the essential driving force behind pornography, which has also been influential in determining how media technologies develop and prosper. In the early 1970s there were two formats being marketed for video recording and playback: VHS and Betamax. Betamax tried to prevent the copying, distribution, and playing of pornography on their machines; consequently, people went out and bought the VHS system, which did allow the playing and copying of pornography and, as a result, Betamax became history. In recent years internet, telephone, and text technologies have been the pornography and sex industry sites, again making huge profits and driving the development of these technologies. The advances in computer graphics and animation, using techniques such as human capture in films such as *Beowulf*, are also being exploited by pornography. Feminist author and screen theorist Barbara Creed (2003) points out that there is enormous potential to use digital stars in the porn industry because little talent is required, and physical perfection and contortion are easier to create than convincing performances. It is increasingly possible to simulate sexual representations without using actual humans. The more this occurs, the more it will raise interesting questions as to what is acceptable and legal: while the use of real humans for pornography may in some cases be exploitative, abusive, and illegal, how, for example, will we deal with exploitative and abusive representations that don't use real people?

3   Regulation of the media industries is another area in which pornography raises interesting debates. Representations of sexuality are one of the two major concerns about censorship (violence is the other). Different countries have different legislation about sexual representations and about actual sexual behaviour. In Canada it is legal for teenagers to have sexual contact from the age of fourteen but it is not legal to make and show explicitly sexual media programs for people under the age of 18. Consequently, there can be little explicit sexual education provided through the media for young people. Yet despite pornography's legal prohibition to people under the age of 18, the reality is that young people can and do get access to pornography, which becomes one of the main arenas for them to learn about sexuality. Some campaigners in Canada are anxious that, while the teenagers are taking in the messages of pornography, they cannot legally provide teenagers with positive and helpful media messages about sexuality.

     In terms of censorship, the history of pornography over the last forty years has been one of continual struggle and debate; it appears that increasingly explicit material keeps breaking the barriers of what is acceptable and what can be portrayed.

Some people argue that for men and women and for different sexual orientations, pornography has allowed significant freedom and explorations offering liberation from sexual repression; others see it as exploitative and abusive to women and young people, and others see it as corrupt for everyone. Around the world media regulations generally prohibit showing genital arousal on television or in mainstream cinemas. This means that erect penises are not shown, but because female genital arousal is less visible, it is acceptable to show naked women. This leads to systematic inequity in terms of the sexualised objectification of women and men.

4   Pornography offers an interesting case study for many of the areas that have been raised so far in Part 4. Pornography is one of the sites where men and women learn about sexuality so it is important to ask what kinds of messages and information are being presented. Textual analysis is one of the means by which this can be done; genre studies, narratology, and structuralism are others.

It is clear that pornography can be seen as a genre in its own right, one that can be analysed like the western or other genres in terms of its iconography, visual style, patterns of repetition and variation, and developments. Regulatory bodies, academic researchers, industry, and audience members divide pornography itself into subgenres such as soft porn (for example, *Playboy* magazine), hard porn (extremely explicit material that may include degrading and dangerous content such as violent sexualised content), child pornography, and erotica (artistic treatments of sexuality, such as that found in *Pillow Book*). Pornography also crosses over a variety of media: film, DVD, photography, literature, phone and text lines, magazines, interactive internet connections. In this way it broadens genre study out as we consider what the links are across these different media.

In terms of narrative structure there are obvious links and parallels. Narrative structure can be described in sexual terms: like striptease and sexual behaviour it provides a structure of enticement, excitement, tease, questions and answers, which is linked to the final goal of narrative resolution, or sexual satisfaction. This is most often represented in terms of male climax, or orgasm. Such climax can be said to parallel the narrative climax of films. Some feminist scholars have argued that while most mainstream narratives are based on a climactic structure that parallels the stereotypical understanding of male sexual excitement and orgasm, they argue that other narrative forms, such as soap opera, operate on a basis of a series of climactic moments that go on and on in the same way that female sexual pleasure and orgasm can be experienced. Another parallel in sexual and narrative structures is the desire for delay and progression—people enjoy moments of delay in both situations—for example the delay of gazing at a beautiful erotic image and holding on to this for some time but then desiring progress, getting to the next stage or phase.

In terms of binary oppositions the most obvious opposition is the relationship between men and women, masculine and feminine. There is of course homosexual pornography but much of this can also be analysed in terms of oppositional roles: subservient and dominant, for example. It would be interesting to analyse pornographic representations from the point of view of binaries. Given that most pornography is geared towards moments of sexual resolution, how are these resolutions presented in terms of the male–female opposition? Is there, for example, an equality of male–female relations in terms of power, pleasure, and how they are visually presented or are there significant differences? All this demonstrates how the genre clearly relates to the issue of coupling and coupling endings that we outlined above. Overall analysis of the genre, its structure and oppositions can provide insight into the ideologies of masculinity and femininity, into gender relationships and into ideologies of sexuality and sexual behaviour.

Computer and internet games

Cinema was the predominant media entertainment in the first half of the twentieth century; television was for the second half. While both media are still very important in the twenty-first century they are gradually being superseded by the media attraction of digital games and internet interactions. Young people are now spending more time in front of computer screens than television or cinema screens; the new kinds of media entertainment offered by computer games and the internet share some similarities with cinema and television but also introduce some differences, so it is interesting to consider the extent to which games draw on the characteristics of Hollywood productions and vice versa. Can the narrative analytic frameworks set up in this chapter be applied to the new media? Do they operate as narratives and follow the conventions of genre? Do they position audiences in certain ways? Do they work through binary oppositional frameworks? What new elements do they introduce?

Narratives

A key difference between films and games is 'the relative importance of narrative structure or narrative development' (King & Krzywinska 2002, p. 21). The most obvious use of narrative in many games involves

> cut-scenes [that are] short, pre-rendered audio-visual sequences in which the player usually performs the role of a more detached observer than is the case in the more active periods of gameplay. Many games use cut-scenes to establish the initial setting and background storyline ... Cut-scenes are also used at varying intervals throughout many games, to forward the storyline (King & Krzywinska 2002, pp. 11–12).

The cut-scene narrative component of games often looks more cinematic than the rest of the game, but lacks the distinctive quality of interactivity and functions more like gift wrapping to lure the player into the interactive game activity. Once players are immersed in the game, the story tends to unfold in real time. Unlike film narratives, which routinely skip over slow-moving or non-essential action, games seldom use ellipses and they tend to involve extended periods of gameplay, often using a repetitive and episodic structure. This generates a sense of immediacy that differentiates game narratives from film narratives and perhaps brings them closer to the narrative structures typical of some television genres that present events in real time.

The narrative structure of digital games operates on at least three levels and is partly based on the same principle as genre: repetition and variation within a three act structure organised around a beginning, middle, and end. On one level, the expository cut-scene storyline elements of game narratives are predetermined and repetitive. On another, in the extended second act that involves active gameplay, the player controls variables in the narrative and becomes the author of their own storyline each time they play. As King and Krzywinska put it, digital games often invoke the cause/effect structure of narrative, even if it is not linear:

> moments of the most heightened and intensively interactive gameplay often entail features such as cause/effect relationships and linear progression (although the latter, in particular, is far from always guaranteed: it is quite possible to regress, to lose ground, during activities such as combat or the negotiation of difficult terrain) (2002, p. 24).

On a third level players can also become creators or authors of the games they play by substantially contributing to the text as they create mods and skins. Mods are game modifications that involve creating new spaces and scenarios; skins are customised character appearances.

Most computer games do have an end in sight, which means there is some kind of goal involved for the participant, often a competitive one that involves playing against either the computer or against other participants. This also makes the games close to the narratives of sports. But there are significant differences between the narratives of computer games and film or television narratives.

First, the narrative of each game is likely to be slightly different every time you play (a form of generic variation), whereas an individual film story, for example *American Beauty*, is the same every time you watch it. An interactive game called *American Beauty* might feature the same characters as the film but the narrative route and process would be different each time: there is in general more fluidity to outcomes within the game world.

Second, endings can happen in very different places. A game where you are fighting against some killer opposition, for example, can result in you being killed—game over—very quickly. One of the narrative pleasures of games is that you can get better and go further, kill more opponents, score more points, last longer in the game. Thus, as the narrative lasts longer and its resolution changes, it can progressively get better.

Third, for some games this can mean an almost infinite regression: once you can win at one level, then you can go to the next, and so on. With some games you will finally be able to win every time at every level; when you do, it's time for a new one. With others you might be in a system where you are always trying to beat your best score and thus you could go on playing forever—there is no ultimate narrative resolution.

Another set of games, such as the *Dr Who* Nintendo and Wii games, or the *Iron Man 2* computer games based on popular films and television series, rely on players' intertextual knowledge of backstory, an established fictional universe, and familiar characters. In the multiplayer X-Box game, *South Park Let's Go Tower Defense Play*, irreverent in-jokes and controversial narrative lines are directed at fans of the *South Park* TV series. Despite these similarities between film, television, and digital games on the levels of narrative and genre, there are also significant differences. In film the conventions of the action genre dictate that Robert Downey Jr's character Tony Stark will overcome insurmountable obstacles and live through to the end of the *Iron Man* films. By contrast, the digital games based on the *Iron Man* film franchise work within the same genre and, though they are modelled closely on sequences from the films, operate according to different conventions and expectations. Players expect to die many times before ever completing the game, or even to play as a War Machine fighting against Stark, which leads to a higher degree of uncertainty and suspense.

> The fact that the experience of games can entail large measures of anxiety and uncertainty— to an extent not usually found in the cinema, because of its particular narrative regime—has been linked by some commentators to the role they might perform in the socialization process for adolescent males. Playing a game ... to achieve mastery in the face of the stresses and anxieties it creates, is seen as one way of practicing the 'performance' of dominant versions of masculinity (King & Krzywinska 2002, p. 53).

In addition to similarities and differences in the social functions and narrative structures of film, television, and digital games, games can also be understood in relation to genre. Games can easily be based on the settings, characters, motives, and contexts of popular genres since action, fantasy, and science-fiction genres come with their own established sets of rules, conventions, and expectations that fill in a lot of the backstory and 'offer instantly recognisable frames of reference that allow gameplay to proceed with only minimal elaboration of the specific scenario' (King & Krzywinska 2006, p. 55). *The Sims* draws on conventions of the soap opera genre, and the *Who Wants to be a Millionaire* games are directly based on the television game show. Further, as King and Krzywinska point out, teleportation is an accepted convention of the science-fiction and fantasy genres, hence while it is not out of place in the futuristic military first-person shooter *Doom* and the massively multiplayer online role-playing game (MMORPG) *EverQuest*, it would be incongruous in the badass gangster underworld of *Grand Theft Auto*.

Most of the games discussed so far are goal-directed and thus have similarities to narratives requiring resolution. But many other games, such as the virtual worlds of *The Sims*, or internet chat rooms, provide worlds where people can visit and play in a virtual space that isn't so goal oriented or geared towards narrative resolution. The choices and variety of possibilities are more like those we face in daily life—Where do I want to go today? Who do I want to visit? and so on—but done in a virtual world. The narrative resolutions here are simply dependent on how long you want to play. It's more like having a telephone conversation with someone: the narrative will depend on your interactions, your mood, time constraints, and so on. But whereas in a telephone conversation you just speak to one person, with multiple user domains (MUDs) and internet games and chat you have many more people. Part of the excitement here is meeting new people (perhaps a parallel to the idea of variation described here as one of the pleasures of genre narratives). Your participation will have a narrative closure that occurs when you decide to leave the game or online environment. Even though your departure may be triggered by you feeling some kind of resolution, some satisfaction in what you have done, it is not really the same as the ordered narrative resolutions of film and television fictions.

Binary oppositions in games

Many games are based on oppositional structures: you play against the game itself or against other players. The structure is most obviously one of goodies versus baddies, heroes versus villains, so binary structures are central to how the games are presented. There are two things to point out. The first is that while there is a similarity to film and television narratives in this structure, the big difference is that the games tend to construct a much more black and white world. The games do not have the oppositional subtleties or complexities that can be found in the best film narratives, which allow for more crossovers and interconnections between the two sets of oppositions. But the games certainly encourage participants to see the world in quite simplistic, binary, oppositional terms.

The second point is that these oppositional structures carry ideological positions. In the USA, when, early this century, army recruitment was falling, the army decided to offer a free computer game that simulated army action. The game was widely distributed and proved highly popular (mainly with boys and young men) and army recruitment figures substantially improved. The excitement of simulated war games, in which no one was really injured or killed, led to an increase in those volunteering for armed service. This simulated game also depicted an enemy who could be seen as related to the USA's wars in Iraq and Afghanistan, and on terrorism. In contrast to this, Arab countries in the same period recognised that most computer war games presented Arab figures as the baddies, so they started to produce games that featured

Jewish figures as the baddies and Arab figures as heroes. The problem with any of these oppositional war games is that they can easily demonise particular social or racial groups.

Interactivity and first person—alternative narratives

Computer and internet games offer other significant differences from film and television narratives. They introduce a high degree of interactivity and they do so from a first-person perspective. Interactivity means that you, as participant, are involved in the game, its narrative, and how it unfolds. This makes two differences from film narratives: first, some games allow the possibility for different narrative developments since you can choose at various stages what direction the narrative can go in. Thus there are numerous possible narrative developments and different possible resolutions, unlike in film narratives, which move towards a single, fixed ending. So, once again, game narratives are more fluid, more open.

Second, because you as participant are involved in making choices and decisions about what should happen you become an active author of the game rather than just a receiving reader, as you are in film narratives, which means you are much more directly involved. Digital games require intervention, not just interpretation, and this shifts the emphasis away from narrative. Players must

> respond to events in a manner that affects what happens on screen, something not usually demanded of readers of books or viewers of films. Success often depends on rapid responses, effective hand-eye coordination and learned moves or skills effected through devices such as joypads and keyboards, or puzzle-solving skills (King & Krzywinska 2002, pp. 22–3).

This involvement is also from a first-person perspective, again a major difference from film and television narratives, which you watch from the outside, from a third-person, observer perspective. One of the major pleasures of computer and internet games is that you get to enter the drama, the game, the narrative itself, in a much more involved and active position. The impression of aliveness and presence in the game world arises from the experience of inhabiting and exploring a digital landscape, acting as a central figure in the narrative. As King and Krzywinska write:

> The possibility of seeming to move 'inside' the fictional world on screen is sometimes seen as a defining characteristic of games, especially those based recognizably on individual films, franchises or film genres. The player can, at one remove, 'become' the central figure in a cinematic environment, following and extending the kinds of experiences offered in film (King & Krzywinska 2002, p. 4).

The *District 9* online game, for example, can be played as either human or alien. The world of the film is extended in terms of both interactivity and variation of perspective/allegiance. This first-person perspective is linked to the possibility of exploring different aspects of your own personality as you can construct new identities for yourself, particularly in the form of avatars, the form and identity that you decide to present yourself as in the game. While films and stories have traditionally offered readers or viewers the chance to identify with different characters—to imagine yourself as Johnny Depp being Captain Jack Sparrow or Keira Knightley being Elizabeth Swann in the *Pirates of the Caribbean*—computer and internet games offer you even more freedoms to explore and discover different parts of yourself in active participation.

Film, television, and computer crossovers

Digital games form a multibillion dollar aspect of the entertainment media industry and tie-in games are valued highly in Hollywood as a way of capitalising on existing film audiences and attracting new audiences, particularly in the lucrative youth market. The opening sequence in which Daniel Craig in his role as James Bond pursues his target across vertiginous rooftops in *Casino Royale* is clearly designed with the game tie-in in mind; in fact the series of 007 games released since 1995 helped broaden the audience to include a whole new generation of Bond fans, according to new media analysts Geoff King and Tanya Krzywinska in *Cinema/Videogames/Interfaces* (2002, p. 8). The tie-ins between cinema, the internet, and games are perfectly illustrated by the websites of popular films such as the one for *Pirates of the Caribbean*, which invites you to navigate through a variety of windows of information, consumer purchases, and gaming interactivity.

In addition to this, computer games, television, and cinema are all mutually influencing each other: computer games have been influenced by cinema and television visual and narrative styles. In order to make computer games more and more attractive they aimed to improve their graphics and sound quality and the complexity of their narratives. The result is that games can now offer visual and aural pleasures that are coming closer to those offered by cinema and television. While computer games are often spinoffs from films or television programs, cinematic styles are now changing in response to the technologies of the computer games. Animation techniques, which form the basis of most computer games, have developed and become increasingly popular in the cinema, as can be seen in *Avatar*. Films such as *Beowulf* and *300* adopt motion capture animation techniques or visual manipulations that make them look more like computer games graphics than traditional realist cinema. Narrative sequences in cinema now sometimes resemble sequences from games in the way the camera can move through space, turn corners, and negotiate movement through buildings. A film such as *TRON: Legacy* plays on this in the way many of its action sequences involve protagonists moving with impossible dexterity and speed in the virtual world of the computer game on which the film itself is based.

Overall then, it could be argued that, to a large extent, the interactive and immersive experiences of gameplay offer alternative and complementary pleasures to those offered in film and television narratives. There are links and similarities in the narrative structures and actions of the computer games world and the cinematic and television worlds, as well as significant differences. Perhaps narrative theory can never fully encompass the differences between identification with characters and active participation as a protagonist, nor can it account for the kinaesthetic, experiential, and technological dimensions of gameplay. There are also crossovers between games, cinema, and television and we expect that these crossovers will continue, with the three media all influencing each other.

Conclusion

We have described narrative as a pattern of dialectical synthesis structured around the resolution of binary oppositions and shown that this pattern affects meanings. Understanding these structures is another way of seeing how texts work and of interpreting them. Close examination of how characters in texts are positioned, how they are presented to audiences, and where characters are at the ends of texts, can reveal the ideological meanings and social values of a text. The focus here has been on fiction but the same analytic methods can be applied to non-fiction texts such as documentaries, news, sports, and quiz and chat shows, as the following chapter on non-fiction texts demonstrates. We have also considered whether and how these approaches can be applied to computer and internet games.

This chapter has

- defined narrative and narrative structure
- argued that narrative structure can determine meaning
- examined the structural positioning of characters in narratives
- considered the importance of narrative endings and resolutions
- defined and illustrated the term 'binary oppositions' in narrative
- compared television and film narratives
- considered narrative in computer and internet games.

Discussion points

1   How are crime, criminals, and policing usually presented and resolved in film and television narratives? In social or psychological terms? From the point of view of criminal or law officers? What are the ideological implications of different narrative structures?

2   How many different kinds of narrative structure can you find?

3   Find a film that breaks up the chronological narrative sequence, such as *Elephant*. First, rearrange the plot segments into their chronological order. Then compare these two different ways of presenting the narrative and consider how the non-chronological sequence changes the way we understand and respond to the narrative.

4   Examine the endings of films or television programs of your own choice in relation to the idea of coupling.

5   Television has been described as a domestic medium. Does this claim still have currency in the era of TVIII? How do changing television technologies, exhibition formats, and reception modes affect audience responses?

Summary

You should now be able to

- explain the importance and prevalence of narrative
- define and illustrate the terms 'narrative structure' and 'binary oppositions'
- show how narratives work through a structure of disruption, narrative questions, and resolution
- discuss the ways in which characters are structurally positioned in narratives and the consequences of this
- explain and illustrate the use in a narrative of flaws in major characters
- explain and illustrate the ideological implications of narrative endings
- give examples of non-mainstream narrative techniques
- explain and illustrate the term 'hierarchy of discourse'
- compare the different ways men and women are positioned in narratives
- draw up a list of binary oppositions for any film or television text and consider how these are worked through and resolved
- comment on the way contemporary film and television fictions represent couples
- discuss some of the key similarities and differences between film and television narratives
- define and illustrate the terms 'flow' and 'fragmentation' in relation to television
- consider how narrative structural analysis can be used for analysis of computer and internet games.

CHAPTER 18

Documentary and Reality TV

Reality television is not the end of civilisation as we know it; it is civilisation as we know it.

Germaine Greer, *Media Studies: The Essential Resource*

This chapter will

▶ apply narrative structure and binary opposition analysis to non-fiction television
▶ consider the development of documentaries and reality TV
▶ problematise issues related to truth and realism
▶ demonstrate how concepts such as discourse and generic hybridity relate to reality-based media
▶ discuss responses to reality TV.

While previous chapters focused on fictional entertainment media, this chapter looks at a variety of reality-based programming ranging from television news through documentaries to examples of reality TV. It will demonstrate how structuralist narrative approaches can be applied to non-fiction texts and examine how the concepts of modality and generic hybridity relate to reality-based media. We will question why reality TV became so popular and why it has given rise to social controversy and panic about moral degeneration.

Non-fiction television: news

Since television began it has produced many non-fiction programs; the most prevalent have been news, current affairs, documentaries, sports, quiz shows, and chat shows. In recent years television has been inundated with reality TV programs. The analytic tools used in the previous chapter—narrative structure and binary oppositions—can be applied to all these programs. To exemplify this we will look at news and sports programs.

The news is broadcast several times a day. In narrative terms it is not a 'sequence of events taking place over a given period of time that are linked, mainly through cause and effect' (see p. 259); rather, it is the putting together of a whole series of different events and stories. But these different events are contained and positioned within a narrative format. The overall nature of this format is to take the disturbances of world events and present them in a way that is ultimately reassuring and/or entertaining (see Chapter 2 for discussion of gatekeeping and agenda setting).

The news is presented by newsreaders whose familiar faces and voices are the channels or discourses through which all news is filtered to us. They represent the dominant discourse and deliver the news with clarity and certainty. News presenters are usually authoritative, attractive, and well spoken. No matter how disturbing the events are, the studio presence of the newsreaders creates a distance between us and the raw reality and gives a sense of familiar comfort. The news is structured with a beginning, a middle, and an end. The structure is normally a series of headlines that act as the disruption of our stable situation, as in fictional narratives. The lead stories are then elaborated on in more detail and presented in order of importance, followed by other non-headline stories. The sequence conventionally ends with sports stories and sometimes a feel-good story about animals, celebrities, or children, thus moving us from disturbing political and social events, often heralded by some stirring music, to pleasurable and positive, reassuring events. Finally, the newsreaders sign off and wish us a good evening or say goodbye. Often headlines are repeated but by this stage they have been made familiar and acceptable; they are thus contained within the format of the news. All of which leads us in the end to reassurance, closure, and acceptance (stable situation 2), a state that requires us to do nothing.

Watkins draws attention to the similar structure of news presentations, what he calls their 'monoform', that treats all stories in the same way:

> This same method of story-telling is used night after night, year after year, no matter what the emotional demand of the theme or subject being presented. The repetitive, split-second similarity in the way that it organises sounds and images blurs the distinctions between different themes and subjects, and between what might otherwise be entirely different emotional responses to them. There is no allowance for differentiation of information, whether about a terrible air-crash, or a man who has painted his pet elephant pink. Both stories are presented via the same grid-lock and narrative structure … This repetitive story-telling pattern, linked with the fact that it is closed (has no space for the audience to reflect or intervene), and that it usually consists of a dense, non-stop bombardment of violent juxtapositions of image, sound and conflicting themes, has had a devastating effect on society (Watkins 1997, p. 6).

Watkins sees this sameness in the manner of representation as extending beyond news coverage to all areas of the audiovisual media (see <www.mnsi.net/~pwatkins> for information about Watkins' films and his extremely critical views on the media).

Documentary theorist Bill Nichols, looking at the form and structure of news coverage, suggests that the point of view constructed for audiences is a position of 'viewer–observer', a position that means people are detached from the news coverage. Consequently,

> News reportage urges us to look but not care, see but not act, know but not change. The news exists less to orient us towards action than to perpetuate itself as commodity, something to be fetishised and consumed (Nichols 1991, p. 194).

The entertainment factor of news is present in the way that the headlines can also act as narrative teasers—a glimpse of some exciting images, or a few words that set up a story with 'More of that later'. In the world of ratings and audiences television news has to sell itself to win its audience through a discourse of entertainment and pleasurable viewing. To do so, news stories invariably use a binary discourse to construct and explain events. This 'exciting' conflict between opposing parties or individuals is the overriding structure for nearly all stories.

Sports and quiz shows

direct address
Direct address to camera is when the person on screen looks straight into the camera as though they are looking at and addressing the audience directly. This breaks the conventions of cinematic realism by acknowledging the process of filming; it also substitutes a different sense of realism, intimacy, and immediacy.

One of the dominant features of television discourse is the use of **direct address**, a person speaking to and facing the camera: they bid us good morning or good night and wish us a safe weekend on Fridays. These voices are more intimate and directly connected to us than other voices. They are allowed to look at the camera and hence directly at us; they are the mediators for other people whom they introduce, frame, and question, and they comment on what we have just seen or heard. The faceless voice-overs that announce programs are also privileged discourses. Like the voice of God, they emerge out of nowhere and speak with authority.

There is a structural similarity in the format of a whole range of non-fiction programs that are introduced and fronted by professional television presenters. These programs also work in terms of narrative structures, as seen in sports programs and quiz shows, two of the most popular areas of television programming. Sports events themselves are clearly based on a narrative format setting up a conflict–opposition, usually between two individuals (boxing, tennis) or two teams (netball, football), sometimes between groups of individuals (running, swimming). The final whistle, or the end of the match or race, determines the narrative closure, by which time the question of who will win will be satisfactorily answered. The actual sport is mediated and developed by commentary, pre- and post-match discussion and analysis, and interviews with and stories about individual players, programs that build up and prepare us for coming events. All these extra-event elements can be analysed to see how they construct events and narratives in particular ways. You may notice some particular features, for example the partisan, nationalist nature of commentary so that an event such as the Olympics is mediated by whichever country is broadcasting: Australian coverage is obsessed by Australian participants and how many medals Australia has won. The commentary also expresses the value systems endorsed by the sport: strength, physicality, and determination in many 'masculine' sports, grace, beauty, and dexterity in more 'feminine' sports, and cooperation in team sports. Analysis of the history of sports coverage shows that more and more entertainment factors have been introduced into sports coverage such as the music and dance opening extravaganzas of the Olympic Games and the World Cup, the use of classical music theme tunes to go with those events, the use of increasingly fashionable sports clothing, personal and emotional stories about the competitors, the ever-developing use of new camera technologies, slow motion, new camera angles, and instant replays, comedic commentators such as Roy and HG, and the creation of sports stars and celebrities. The marketing of David Beckham is an exemplary case (see p. 426) and the importance of his personality was demonstrated when he played an exhibition football match in Australia in 2007 drawing a crowd of 80 000. The highlights were Beckham scoring a goal and later taking off his shirt. All these aspects have widened the appeal of sports, particularly to women and family audiences, so now there is something of interest for all spectators. The narrative strategy of waiting for the final result of a sports competition is the perfect audience hook.

A similar narrative hook is found in quiz shows. Here there is an added element in that audiences can be surrogate participants, can try to answer the questions themselves, and then wait to see if they are right. Quiz shows build up suspense and excitement through the use of music and delaying the revelation of the right answer; they create emotional interest by finding out competitors' personal stories. Sports and quiz shows work because the final outcome is always unknown: our desire for narrative resolution and closure is central to our involvement and we won't get it unless we watch until the show ends. Quiz and sports programs present a world view of competition, success, and failure. The added ingredient in quiz shows is often the possibility of winning huge sums of money, luxury travel, or expensive consumer goods. In this way the shows support a materialist, consumer-driven, capitalist view of the world: money equals happiness. Both these types of programs are mediated by professional commentators or quiz show hosts who guide us through the events.

Documentary

Documentaries have always been an important part of film and television. When film was invented at the end of the nineteenth century two distinct strands of filmmaking evolved. One used film to tell spectacular fictional stories about individual characters; these developed into Hollywood feature films. The other used film to

documentaries
Films and television programs about real-life situations.

record or document reality, as seen in the first short films by the Lumière brothers (1895) such as *Workers Leaving a Factory* and *Train Arriving at a Station*. Both strands continued, but fiction and spectacle were and remain commercially dominant.

The term 'documentary' is used because film is a kind of document, a record of reality; but also because it derives from the Latin word *doceo*, which means to warn or advise. Documentaries are often a kind of warning or advice about important world issues. The compelling low-budget documentary *Catfish* is a good example of this: it warns of the potential for deception, delusion, and misrepresentation when people form relationships via social networking media such as Facebook. In flagging the dangers of online relationships, the film also exposes the lies of a small-town housewife living a life she would like to escape. Because the filmmakers apparently reconstruct and stage some scenes, bait and emotionally manipulate an insecure and mentally unwell woman into a very public admission of her deceit, and in doing so reveal damaging personal information about her and her family, *Catfish* also raises issues about the ethics of documentary filmmaking.

Documentary ethics: Do documentaries exploit their subjects?

We identify two major issues about documentary. The first is the question of documentary ethics and whether documentary makers exploit and victimise their subjects. This is an important issue that you might consider if you are making documentaries yourself: How are you treating your subjects and what will happen to them as a result of being filmed? Who has power in the filming situation? Craig Gilbert, producer of *An American Family*, commented: 'We are using human beings to make a point … we are "exploiting" them to make our films … and the fact is that our incomes and our careers often depend on our ability to conceal the truth of this exploitation from our subjects' (Gilbert 1988, p. 293). Is the very act of pointing a camera at someone and shooting them a form of exploitation or intrusion? In Australia the family who was filmed in the documentary series *Sylvania Waters* ended up publicly burning the videotapes of the series and condemning the producers for exploiting them. In the documentary *Crumb*, an account of cartoon artist Robert Crumb, his brother is filmed discussing and exposing his own private life. Did he realise what he was letting himself reveal when he was interviewed? The intimate and rather pathetic details of his life were then broadcast in cinemas in a sequence that was presented in such a way as to make audiences laugh at him. Shortly after viewing the film he committed suicide. The whole issue of victimisation and exploitation by the media is very important in texts dealing with real people rather than paid actors.

Do documentaries capture reality and tell the truth?

The second issue is focused on the perennial questions of the truth status of documentaries: Can they actually tell the truth, the whole truth and nothing but the truth? Do they capture reality? Can they offer an unbiased, objective view of the world or just a partial truth? Do they show or construct reality? From all that was said in Part 1 about the media's construction of reality it will be clear that we don't think documentaries can be simple, unbiased windows on the world; even though visual and sound recording techniques offer the possibility of recording and capturing reality unlike any previous aesthetic techniques, there is always a process of construction (selection and framing of events, editing, point of view, commentary, and so on), and these constructions will always come from a particular position (see pp. 75–81). Documentary maker and producer John Grierson's comment on the problem of documentary and how it 'captured reality' was that filmmakers engage in 'the creative construction of actuality'. Grierson acknowledged and embraced the fact that filmmakers would interpret and construct events—'actuality'—in particular ways. Documentarists have developed various approaches, styles, and conventions in their work and all of them have to deal with the issue and problem of how to capture reality.

Documentary history: Flaherty and Dziga Vertov

Robert Flaherty made films from the 1920s onwards and is sometimes regarded as the father of documentary filmmaking. He used his movie camera as an anthropological tool to document his studies of Inuit (Eskimo) communities while he lived in their midst. *Nanook of the North* (1922) is his most renowned film. Flaherty faced issues about documentary ethics and truthfulness. Sometimes he would stage aspects of the situation that he was filming, such as asking hunters to use traditional weapons to harpoon seals instead of using their guns. Sometimes he would ask his subjects to undergo dangerous tasks for the benefit of his films. This technique documented traditional practices and made the films appear more authentic, but it was not an accurate representation of Inuit hunting practices in the 1920s. Flaherty's aim was to record the experiences, cultural practices, and living conditions of these remote communities in an honest manner that represented the essence of real life, even if it didn't mirror it exactly as it happened.

In contrast, Russian filmmaker Dziga Vertov, who was working around the same time as Flaherty, firmly believed that filmmakers should not manipulate events for the camera. He was opposed to the nostalgic and theatrical illusions presented in fiction film and wanted to use film to expose social reality, even to expose the reality of the filmmaking process itself. His most famous film is *The Man with a Movie Camera* (1929), which incorporates newsreel footage and shots of the process of filming and editing. Vertov saw the movie camera as a mechanical eye that was capable of looking at reality in a way that human beings cannot. He celebrated the camera as a new machine: 'I am eye. I am a mechanical eye. I, a machine, am showing you a world the likes of which only I can see … My road is towards the creation of a fresh perception of the world … more perfect than the human eye' (Edwards 1985, p. 45).

Dziga Vertov felt it was important that the film audience was made aware of the filmmakers' interventions in the production process as decisions were made about selecting and editing footage.

Cinéma vérité and observational documentary

expository documentary
A voice-over commentary explains what we see, thereby controlling our viewpoint.

cinéma vérité
French for 'cinema truth'. A documentary style developed in France in the 1950s and 1960s, *cinéma vérité* is similar to direct cinema, fly-on-the-wall documentary, and observational documentary, but the filmmakers participate more directly and self-reflexively in the narrative.

direct cinema
The North American corollary of *cinéma vérité*, direct cinema has an observational style, but does not involve interviews or intervention by the filmmakers.

The earliest documentaries were what Nichols calls '**expository**, voice of God' documentaries. In them a commentator explains everything that is happening for the viewer. During the 1950s film equipment technologies developed that made camera and sound equipment lighter and more user-friendly; consequently, filmmakers could more easily and unobtrusively follow people around and record their actions and words. This gave rise to a radical change in documentary and catalysed movements in the USA and Europe, known variously as *cinéma vérité*, **direct cinema**, fly on the wall, or observational documentary. Documentarists such as Richard Leacock, Don Pennebaker, the Mayles brothers, Frederick Wiseman, Jean Rouch, and Roger Graef believed that with the new technology documentaries really could capture what was happening. Once it had, then the results could be shown to the world.

Cinéma vérité literally means 'film truth', though ethnographic filmmaker Jean Rouch prefers to translate it as 'cinema sincerity'. He is said to have invented *cinéma vérité* when he was on location, filming in a remote area and accidentally knocked his camera tripod into the river. From that point on he had to hold the camera when filming, creating the unsteady footage and mobile framing that we now associate with documentary realism. Rouch found that this mode of filming gave him a more spontaneous, intimate relationship with the people and events he was filming (Rouch 1995). It also allowed the footage to be less staged or controlled because the camera could be situated amid the action and respond dynamically to changes. Up to this point cameras had always been placed on tripods, largely because they were too heavy and bulky to carry. The development of lightweight 16 mm cameras and portable sound recording equipment, such as the Nagra tape recorder, and later super 8 and inexpensive home video cameras personalised movie making, rendering it accessible to more people and changing the conventions and aesthetic outcomes of filmmaking. Technological advances in filmmaking were swiftly transferred to television, with the emergence of British televérité current affairs shows such as *World in Action* (1962), which capitalised on the introduction of 16 mm cameras (Sexton 2003).

In *cinéma vérité* films the camera is imagined to be an eye that views and records life itself with as little contrivance, intervention, illusion, or manipulation as possible. The conventions of *cinéma vérité* include hand-held footage, minimal editing (long takes in chronological sequence), and the absence of non-diegetic music or voice-over narration. The films of *cinéma vérité* are not staged and scripted fictions—they contain actual people in actual settings rather than actors in studios. Rouch sees *cinéma vérité* as a form of expression in which the filmmaker says to the audience, 'This is what I saw. I didn't fake it, this is what happened. I didn't pay anyone … I didn't change anyone's behaviour. I looked at what happened with my subjective eye and this is what I believe took place' (cited in MacDonald & Cousins 1996, p. 265). The main difference between *cinéma vérité* and its US counterpart, direct cinema, is that the latter assumes the camera can capture an objective record of events. Rouch acknowledges that the camera can't capture objective truth because the filmmaker is always making decisions about what to focus on and what to ignore, and because only one particular version or perspective on reality can be recorded. In addition, knowing you are being observed or filmed changes behaviour, resulting in what Rouch calls 'provoked reality'. As such, this filmmaking was more like a fly in the soup (affecting reality) than a fly on the wall (watching but unnoticed). To add a self-reflexive, participatory element and another level of realism, Rouch would often ask the people he filmed to watch the footage and comment on it. He then used their own commentary to explain the images, instead of using the 'voice of God' expository narration.

Despite the continued popularity of this observational style its limitations are recognised and today we have a fascinating contradiction around documentary. Documentary's realist premise—that it can innocently, impartially, and objectively record the world—has been challenged: it is accepted by many that documentaries can't capture unmediated reality. Therefore, if all representations are constructions, documentary filmmaking should be discredited. But this realisation can free up documentary filmmaking from its link with realism: in its documentation of the real world it can use many techniques and include all manner of representational modes. Consequently, we have a flowering of documentary practices that are not restricted by the need to capture pure truth; instead, documentarists can experiment with numerous ways of presenting reality and capturing different truths.

'Some form of truth is the always receding goal of documentary film'

Taking this contradiction further Linda Williams has asserted that 'some form of truth is the always receding goal of documentary film' (Williams 1993, p. 20).

In saying this she seems to recognise that documentary can never capture pure truth or objective reality since it is always relative and getting away from us; nevertheless, documentarists still seek a truth. She thus recognises the impossibility of finding absolute truth but insists on the importance of attempting to find partial truths about the world. This perhaps explains how many viewers are caught between their own sophistication and cynicism about the media whereby they can dismiss television and films as constructions, hype, biased, and so on, but at the same time still be fascinated by the possibility of seeing reality captured by film or video and are thus drawn to documentaries and reality TV.

Given this fascination with reality, the availability of increasingly sophisticated film and video technology, and a range of exciting stylistic possibilities, there has been, since 1990, an amazing increase in documentary production, exhibition, and popularity. Today documentaries are often screened in mainstream and arthouse cinemas, and there are many documentaries on television that are gaining big audiences.

Documentary styles and conventions

You can use your knowledge of semiotics to analyse the codes and conventions of reality-based screen texts. It is easy to identify documentaries because they use familiar signs and conventions, such as the jerky, hand-held camera, low resolution or poorly lit images, interviews where people speak directly to the camera, interviews that hide the identity of the speaker, subtitles used over poor quality sound recording, surveillance cameras, voice-over commentators giving matter of fact observations, use of archival footage, re-enactments, and so on.

Over time these signs and conventions have developed different connotations of authenticity. Often when a technique is used for the first time—such as hand-held cameras—its originality gives it an added reality quotient, a greater degree of authenticity and we don't see it as a convention; however, the more it is used the more familiar and conventional it becomes so that gradually it loses its strong realistic authenticity and we are more aware of processes of construction.

As documentary analysts Jane Roscoe and Craig Hight point out in their book *Faking It: Mock-Documentary and the Subversion of Factuality* (2001), the distrust of special effects and cinematic illusions arises from technological advances that allow digital image manipulation and computer-generated imagery to produce fakes that look astonishingly real. This threatens the truth status of images that we would previously have accepted as documentary evidence, hence technological developments have led us to question the concepts of truth and reality. Perhaps the popularity of reality TV is both a symptom and a cause of this escalating distrust of the media and the uncertainty about what we can count on, what we know, and what counts as knowledge.

Generic hybridity

Generic hybrids (p. 235) are texts that blend the codes and conventions of two or more genres to produce a new combination. If we think of documentary and news as genres, then we can see that these core types of non-fiction texts have spawned many new crossbreeds. The sheer diversity of generic hybrids emerging from the documentary tradition is made possible because documentary filmmaking itself has always encompassed a wide range of styles, techniques, and topics.

The boundaries that once separated documentary from feature film, information from entertainment, fact from fiction are now much more blurred or fluid. Documentaries such as *Touching the Void* have moved closer to traditional forms of entertainment: they tell narrative stories, they often focus on key individuals and personalities, and they use humour, suspense, exciting pictures, catchy soundtracks, and all the standard techniques of dramatic storytelling (all of which is partly driven by ratings and getting production money). Fictional film and television often use documentary techniques in relation to camera work and visual style. You may have noticed that contemporary films will often move into black and white footage or use unsteady hand-held camera in sequences that aim to convey a sense of immediacy or authenticity. Documentary filmmaking techniques, associated with factual representation rather than with fiction, are used extensively in films such as *District 9*, *Quarantine*, *Cloverfield*, and *Monsters*. The hugely successful but very low-budget horror films *Paranormal Activity*, *Paranormal Activity 2*, and *The Blair Witch Project* employ documentary-style footage and subject matter especially effectively. Each of these horror films is supposedly filmed by the characters themselves as they document their experiences of creepy phenomena, and each is shot almost entirely using hand-held cameras. This technique places viewers right in the middle of the action when, for example, the terrified students in *The Blair Witch Project* run through the dark forest and the camera jerks and shakes along with them. Or, as the couple in *Paranormal Activity* set up their camera with night vision, then go to bed, and we watch as they sleep unaware of what's creeping into their bedroom. It also makes these events seem much more realistic (and therefore more frightening), because we are used to shaky home videos recording things that really happen to us and our friends and family.

This documentary style is also evident in the streetwise look of recent films dramatising real events (*Snowtown* and *The Hurt Locker*) and in many advertisements and programs, such as *Jersey Shore* and *Frontline*, which use documentary styles and technologies to create a realistic effect. The producers of *Frontline* felt that recording continuous action as if documenting a real-life situation, and using the Hi-8 cameras that are conventionally used in documentary filmmaking, would give the program power and realism. Other films actually mix fiction and documentary. *True Stories*, a brilliant play on the blurred line between fact and fiction, is one such film. The most significant mixes of fiction and documentary are mockumentaries, which form a whole genre on their own.

Mockumentaries

This Is Spinal Tap is one of the most well-known early mockumentaries. It imitated the style and conventions of music documentary but was actually about a fictional rock music group. (So successful was the film that the group did actually get asked to play concerts and thus developed a real music career.) The main pleasure for audiences is the humour of the film, based on send-up—mocking—of the genre, which is dependent on the audience's knowledge of rockumentary conventions. Casey Affleck's film about Joaquin Phoenix's faux rap career *I'm Still Here* involved an elaborate, long-running hoax in which Phoenix publically announced his change of career from film actor to rapper, cultivated dishevelled hair and clothing, and, to all appearances, descended into a life of undisciplined drug use and debauchery for the year during which Affleck filmed him. Phoenix remained in character during public appearances as audiences laughed at his attempts to rap. Humour is a major factor in many mockumentary films, such as *Kenny*, *Borat*, and *Brüno*. It is also apparent in mockumentary television series such as *Modern Family*, *Parks and Recreation*, *Summer Heights High*, and *The Office*. Additionally, as these titles suggest, there is pleasure in seeing people who could be like us, the audience, on screen. But humour is not the only factor behind mockumentaries. Some of the earliest examples of fictions using a documentary, realistic format were not comic at all. Orson Welles' famous 1930s radio broadcast of *War of the Worlds* was presented as a real live-news story. So convinced were some people by the realism of the broadcast that they started to flee New York in the belief that aliens were invading. Watkins developed the form most powerfully in *Culloden* (1964) and *The War Game* (1966). *Culloden* was a documentary about an eighteenth-century battle between Scotland and England that re-enacted the battle as if a television reporting crew was on hand to film the events and interview the participants. No viewer would actually have thought this possible but it gave the historical events a contemporary immediacy and invited viewers to be aware of the conventions of documentary reporting. *The War Game*, shot in documentary format, was an imaginary look at what might happen in the event of a nuclear war in Britain. The realism of the events was deeply disturbing, so much so that the BBC banned the film, arguing that people would be confused by the documentary format and believe it was real.

Roscoe and Hight have argued that while there is humour in the mockumentary form it also has a serious function in that it challenges viewers about the boundaries between fact and fiction. By making the documentary conventions visible it encourages viewers to realise that all documentaries are constructions, 'thus questioning and challenging documentary's authority' (Roscoe and Hight 1997, p. 78) that otherwise tends to be accepted at face value. Another kind of pleasure for audiences may come from their attempt to sort out documentary from mockumentary, testing their ability to interpret signs and signifiers. Have you ever seen programs where you are not clear at first if it is a real documentary?

Self-reflexive documentaries

Many filmmakers are themselves aware of the limitations of the media and its ability to capture truth. Rather than making mockumentaries they continue to make documentaries but within what Nichols has called a 'self-reflexive' mode (Nichols 2001, p. 125). This **self-reflexivity** invites audiences to be aware of the processes of construction and to question what is being presented. Our attention may be drawn to the filmmaker's presence and involvement in the project, encouraging the viewer to question the film's truth, as do the films of Michael Moore and Nick Broomfield who are active participants in their own films; or attention may be drawn to the filmmaking process itself (as Dziga Vertov and Rouch did) as a way of exploring the whole issue of film truth and reality.

> **self-reflexivity**
> The process whereby media texts self-consciously refer back to themselves, often drawing our attention to their construction.

The 2007 Australian documentary *Forbidden Lie$*, about Norma Khouri, who authored a novel purporting to document the honour killing of a Muslim woman, uses highly self-reflexive techniques to problematise the constructed nature of truth and fiction, revealing that the filmmaker herself was seduced by Khouri's lies. Near the end of the film, the actress playing the part of the woman who was allegedly killed opens her eyes and looks directly at the camera, shattering the illusion of the re-enactment, and the false backdrop depicting a home environment in which Khouri is being interviewed is abruptly moved away and revealed to be a studio set.

Errol Morris' film *The Thin Blue Line* is another excellent example of the reflexive documentary style. This mystery enquiry is focused on interviews with two men involved in a murder. In its search for truth and reality, the film reveals that all we have are ways of representing, re-enacting, and reconstructing events. It shows how our lives are so imbued with media realities that it has become difficult to tell if we are living life or watching a movie. Crossing the boundaries of *film noir* and documentary, *The Thin Blue Line* combines a mixture of elements into a tense and pleasurable narrative that includes stylised interviews, reconstructions, clips from fiction films, slow motion footage, an absorbing music soundtrack, and a plethora of different voices, or discourses, that cannot be placed into a simple hierarchy. There is no overall dominant discourse, no expository voice of God, or commentary that makes the subject of the documentary clear. In this way meanings are more open, and are dependent on readers. The film challenges the certainties of realist texts, making it difficult to discern preferred readings. One of the main insights is that ultimately we may not be able to know the world, that we may not be able to find 'the truth' (Williams 1993).

In addition to labels such as 'self-reflexivity', terms such as 'raw' and 'cooked' are sometimes used to describe different styles of documentary filmmaking. Raw documentaries—*Video Nation* and *Race Around the World*—are those in which cameras are given to ordinary people to record stories with minimal manipulation or artistry (it is this type of documentary that *Paranormal Activity* and *Paranormal Activity 2* mimic). The presentation of unrefined live action footage is increasingly apparent online with the growing popularity of video-sharing and video blogging (or 'vlogging'). Many people now own portable digital recording devices or mobile phones that can record good quality videos so they are easily able to shoot an event or blog entry and publish it on social networking sites such as YouTube without much editing. In contrast, cooked documentaries are those that employ elaborate techniques and have high production values, such as the spectacular cinematography in *Touching the Void*, which uses actors to simulate and reconstruct the experiences of the protagonists some twenty years after the events.

Documentary is a rich form that has evolved through various stages in its attempts to record reality and offers a perfect area for you to consider all the questions about media truth, objectivity, bias, and construction that were raised in Chapter 5. Additionally, documentaries have often relied on narrative and have been based around conflicts so you can fruitfully apply binary oppositions and narrative structure as tools for analysis in the same way as can be done for fictional stories.

Reality TV

reality TV
The general premise is that reality-based programs portray people who are not actors saying lines that are not scripted in situations that are drawn from real life but often are constructed and filmed in a manner designed to capture a sense of authenticity, immediacy, and realism.

While documentaries have become ever more popular, the most significant development in television production of the past few years has been the growth of so-called **reality TV**. Following on from the phenomenal success of *Big Brother* and *Survivor* around the turn of the century, there was an amazing expansion of programs.

There are various forms of eliminatory competition (*Australia's Got Talent, Britain's Got Talent, Dancing with the Stars, The Biggest Loser, America's Next Top Model*) and makeover programs (*Extreme Makeover, Ladette to Lady, Trinny and Susannah Undress …* , *Pimp My Ride*). The competition game show formats are distinctive because of the level of audience participation and interactivity they invite via the internet, telephone, and merchandising.

Drama has also been harnessed to documentary to produce generic hybrids such as docudrama and docusoaps and shows documenting danger and crime. These forms of reality television have capitalised on the successful formula of soap opera by focusing on emotional dramas played out between characters that the audience can identify with. To hook the audience, they often draw on the cliff-hanger format of ongoing storylines and a kind of voyeuristic fascination with other people's crisis situations.

There have also been programs that have documented the humour and spectacle of the world, often using amateur or surveillance footage. The strain of reality TV that blends comedy and documentary strategies has a long history. It was originally called comedy *vérité* (Mills 2004) and it evolved out of candid moments caught on experimental film and funny responses in vox pop news surveys to include programs such as *Candid Camera* and *Funniest Home Videos*.

Reality TV is characterised by the following:

1   *Originality and unpredictability* This appears to be a new form of television, both in its use of ordinary, non-actor people, but more so in its presentation of a staged, yet still documentary, reality. Initially, *Big Brother* and *Survivor* were so absorbing, partly because audiences had seen nothing quite like them before. Part of the appeal of reality TV is its unpredictability and spontaneity. While we don't know what will happen in traditional fictions, we do know that there are some controlling forces— writers, producers, and directors—who will shape the material. With the reality TV shows, control is there in the format of the program—one person eliminated each week, for example—but who that is can be quite unpredictable.

2   *Authenticity* Reality TV programs have developed out of the technological possibilities that make it possible to, for example, record the activities of *Big Brother* housemates from many different angles for 24 hours a day. In terms of the aesthetic style of reality TV and the way in which it cues an audience response, media analyst Morwenna Crago notes that '*Big Brother*'s unself-reflexive unveiling of the "workings" of the documentary process is specifically designed to produce authenticity, just as the proponents of *cinéma vérité* thought it would be possible to display the "truth" of their own observation, guaranteed in some way because we, the audience, could observe them apparently in the act of observing' (Crago 2002, p. 113). Most other reality TV shows also rely on certain characteristics to give the impression that what we are viewing is genuine and unplanned. Crago (2002) refers to these characteristics as 'the aesthetics of authenticity', which include:

   • display of the televisual apparatus on screen (visible microphones, etc.)
   • liveness and immediacy of the action
   • surveillance-style footage
   • shaky hand-held camera when contestants are asked to make video diaries
   • metadiscourse surrounding the show constructs it as a lab experiment, a nature study, a confessional, and a competition—all established material for documentaries, talk shows, and news reports
   • subtitles and voice-over tell us what really happened if the sound or lighting quality isn't great or an action is obscured
   • action and dialogue are unscripted and the contestants or guests are not trained actors.

The authentic is fascinating (even when people aren't doing anything much) because it is real. As with gossip, we are intrigued by the ordinary and the private. Some webcam sites that simply document people doing totally mundane, everyday but private activities have achieved similar popularity. There is a fascination with human emotions and the psychology of private life and these shows seem to offer the possibility of really seeing inside people as we look in on human experiments in a laboratory situation.

3   *Economics* The production costs of reality TV programs are much smaller than those of fiction or costume dramas. The main costs are recording technologies and limited set construction; there are few actor costs (presenters do still play a significant role), no scriptwriting costs, no costume costs, and so on. Furthermore, some significant costs will be met by commercial companies in return for product placement. *MasterChef* ensures that its sponsors' kitchen products are visible and that the contestants use them while cooking, and *Project Runway* requires contestants to create their designs with the help of certain computer products, highlighting their advantages and capabilities. In other reality TV shows, people working for particular companies are the feature of the program, which serves the commercial interests of these companies as well as the shows' producers. For example, shows such as *Undercover Boss* and *Jerseylicious* are an effective form of advertising for the companies on which they focus. When the US version of *Undercover Boss* featured 1-800-FLOWERS, the florist franchise went to number one on Google Trends within a few hours of the episode airing. *Jerseylicious*, on the other hand, focuses on the owners of the renovated Gatsby Salon in New Jersey, and the show has proved to be a very successful advertisement for the now extremely popular salon. Built-in product placement such as this bypasses the threat of audiences who use their remote controls to skip over commercial breaks. Finally, there is considerable money to be made by the telephone networks when shows depend on audience participation by phoning or texting in to the programs. Given the ratings success of reality TV all this has meant a big challenge to the continuation of expensive drama productions.

4   *Democratisation* Just as media technology has increasingly given people the chance to produce their own media products, reality TV has increasingly offered spaces for non-actors to appear on screen and become famous as television personalities or celebrities (see Chapter 23). Quiz shows were one of the first television formats that did this, but reality TV has taken it to new levels: it suggests a revaluing of the ordinary, everyday working class in relation to the privileged, fantasy space occupied by the middle- and upper-class characters that populate many fictional film and television texts. Furthermore, reality TV invites a high degree of participation and interactivity through gossip, phone and internet voting, and official show websites that feature updates, discussion boards, quizzes, games, contestants' blogs, as well as tie-ins such as *The Biggest Loser*'s online 'Diet Club', which people can join to lose weight along with the show's contestants. This means that reality TV offers media audiences

more control and input than do carefully scripted, preshot programs. There is also a possibility of identification with and celebration of the participants who show that almost anyone can break into the media world. In a sense we could say that reality television is celebrating a more democratic ideology than fictional texts.

5   *Escapism* Reality TV is in fact an extraordinary escape from reality. Rather than use the current media technology to really investigate the realities of our contemporary world, most reality TV offers us an escape from reality that is far too mundane or grim to be considered.

6   *Cultural dumbing down* The fact that many programs feature ordinary people (as opposed to skilled actors) just 'being themselves' (as opposed to acting in a complex fictional narrative), has made some commentators deride the programs and the audiences who watch them. They see both as evidence of the dumbing down of television. These programs have attracted controversy and criticism for their celebration of low culture and the grimier aspects of humanity. Prominent authors, such as Salman Rushdie, have launched scathing critiques of reality TV on the grounds that its popularity reflects the moral degeneration of society:

> Add the contestants' exhibitionism to the viewers' voyeurism and you get a picture of a society sickly in thrall to what Saul Bellow called 'event glamour'. Such is the glamour of these banal but brilliantly spotlit events that anything resembling a real value — modesty, decency, intelligence, humour, selflessness; you can write your own list — is rendered redundant. In this inverted ethical universe, worse is better. The show presents 'reality' as a prize fight and suggests that in life as on TV, anything goes (cited in Rayner et al. 2004, pp. 127–8).

Nevertheless, others have argued that reality TV entices audiences with drama, passion, and intrigue, and presents us with an understanding of contemporary cultural issues in much the same way that Shakespeare's (high culture) plays did in the sixteenth century. From this perspective, reality TV is both popular and socially useful.

7   *Ideology of competition* Rushdie and other critics see reality TV as promoting a ruthless kind of social Darwinism, an ethic of survival of the fittest, in which back-stabbing competitiveness gets rewarded on screen while invasiveness and gossip is indulged in by off-screen viewers for whom television provides a distraction from important and valuable concerns or pursuits. While the programs give us a chance to see, explore, and understand human emotions, these are often presented within situations and structures of competition, hierarchy, rewards, failure, and success. Rather than have a program just watching a group of people interacting, the programs usually ask people to compete against each other. It is as if this is the natural order of the world, and that competition, not cooperation is human nature.

The makeover programs stress the value of image and appearance for social success. These programs don't have to work in these ways: the reality series *Worlds*

Apart took average American families and got them to live for a short time with families in remote, 'primitive' communities in Africa or Papua-New Guinea. The results, directly confronting the extreme opposites of wealth and lifestyles, were fascinating, particularly as the American families dealt with some of their own prejudices, weaknesses, and inadequacies, inviting audiences to see their everyday life and values in a new light.

Conclusion

Reality TV and documentaries continue to thrive. It will be fascinating to see how they develop in future. They share several characteristics with fictional films and television and thus can be analysed in similar ways. While they present us with views of reality it is important to be able to see and show the various ways in which they are constructions of reality, to be able to deconstruct them, and to ask what values and ideologies they represent.

This chapter has

- considered the structure of non-fiction television—news, sports, and quiz shows
- given a brief history of documentary
- considered problems of ethics and truth in relation to documentary
- discussed mockumentaries
- discussed reality TV.

Discussion points

1   Compare and contrast television news broadcasts from different channels on the same day. How similar or different are the structure and order of stories? How different are their presentation? What elements of entertainment and what binaries of conflict can you find in the stories?

2   Watch any sports and/or quiz program and analyse the verbal discourse of commentators and/or quiz show hosts. What discourses of nationalism, gender, and the family do they construct?

3   Go through a week's television program and identify how much programming can be classified as reality TV. Write down a list of reality-based TV programs, and then divide them into different groups or categories. Briefly note your responses to these programs. What do you like or dislike about them? Can you write a definition of reality TV that encompasses all of your examples?

4   Why are reality TV programs so popular?

5   Do you agree with Rushdie's criticisms of reality TV?

Summary

You should now be able to

- apply narrative structure and binary oppositions to non-fiction film and television
- analyse the verbal discourse of sports commentators and quiz show hosts
- define the term 'documentary'
- discuss documentary ethics and documentary truth
- give a brief history of the development of documentary
- comment on the generic developments of documentary and reality TV
- discuss the ways in which these programs are authentic and/or constructions
- apply concepts such as discourse, modality, and generic hybridity to reality-based media
- debate the pros and cons of reality TV and suggest reasons for its escalating popularity.

CHAPTER 19

Why Stories?

Oh blessed art, how often in dark hours when the savage ring of life tightens around
me have you kindled warm love in my heart and transported me to a better world.

Franz von Schober, *The Music Show*, ABC Radio National, 2004

This chapter will

▶ examine the pleasures readers get from stories

▶ look at some specific theoretical approaches to stories and fictions

▶ consider the relationship between real life and stories.

The pleasures of stories

Franz von Schober's words are addressed to music but could be applied to many
artistic forms, including literature, film, and television fictions. They lead into
consideration of the questions: Why do people watch film and television narratives
or read stories? What do they get out of these experiences?

These are big questions that have produced volumes of theoretical work. The
simplest answer is that people get various pleasures from watching and reading
narratives. But how do we define and explain these pleasures? We will consider a
number of possible viewpoints on this, drawing on various writers and critics.

Fictions and reality

Do fictions have any connection to our everyday lives?

Von Schober's words suggest a split between reality—'the savage ring of life', and fictions (art)—'a better world'. We can understand the connection between reality and fictions in two different ways. The first suggests that fictions occupy a completely different space: the space of imagination, fantasy, and unreality; places of escape, where we find consolation from everyday problems. The second argues that while fiction might offer a particular kind of experience there are always connections between fiction and reality. They allow us to see a wide range of human characters and experiences from across the globe. Even though they might be about imaginary characters (Harry Potter, Buzz Lightyear, Carrie Bradshaw), fantasy creatures (dragons in *The Hobbit*, the kraken in *Pirates of the Caribbean*), and constructed stories (the television series *Dr Who* or the film *Inception*), and even though they can be set in the future (*Moon*, *Star Trek*) or in invented places (Pandora, Gotham City), they are always connected to and have something to say about our world and ourselves. Like fables they have a human, moral, point to make. Every fiction deals with real concerns as diverse as relationships, history, social conditions, or emotional states. They are ways of exploring real-life issues at the same time as they allow us to exercise our imaginations; they also enrich our experiences.

This has already been demonstrated in the discussion of genres, such as the western, that explore American culture, allowing the USA to talk to itself about itself (see genres, pp. 235–8). We have shown this in the discussion of representations of coupling, the family, and sexual expression (see pp. 286–8), subjects that feature in many narratives.

It has been argued that narratives are always related to the historical and social moment of their production. *Ten Canoes*, a film that is set in a timeless past, can be understood in relation to contemporary Aboriginal culture and concerns; Australian films made in the 1970s that look back at Australia's past actually reflect and deal with concerns of the 1970s. *My Brilliant Career*, a film ostensibly about feminist issues in 1900, arose out of and reflects the concerns of Australian feminists in the 1970s. *Sunshine*, set in the future, is a reflection of current concerns and anxieties about climate change and technological change. Furthermore, when we turn to stories that are in some sense fantastic and unreal—myths, legends, fairy tales, science fiction—we can connect these to an internal or psychic reality. Jungian author Robert Johnson reports on a schoolboy giving a definition of myths as 'Something that is true on the inside, but not true on the outside' (Johnson 1987, p. 2). A myth is true: it is not true in the outer, physical sense, but it is an accurate expression of a psychological situation, of the inner condition of the psyche. Similarly, Bettelheim argues that children know that fairy tales are not real but recognise on some level that these stories have internal, human truths they need to learn to help them grow up happily: 'The child intuitively comprehends that although these stories are *unreal*, they are not *untrue*; that while what these stories tell about does not happen in fact, it must happen as inner experience and personal development' (Bettelheim 1978, p. 73).

Fictions can be compared to dreams. According to Freud and other psychoanalytic thinkers (Freud 1976a; Ullman & Zimmerman 1979), dreams are messages about our real-life selves. Fictions are also messages about our world (or about the world of the authors of the fiction). Creators use fiction as a way of talking about issues that concern them in real life. In this way, fictional texts and the real world are inextricably linked. This link is part of the media-world connection. Our pleasure in fictions derives partly from the fact that we learn something from them, that we gain insight and understanding into how people, society, and ourselves as individuals, work. There is thus an important relationship between the fictional and the real, between texts and society.

We will further explore how fictions work by looking at a number of theories that aim to understand what happens in the viewing, reading, and listening process.

Aristotle, catharsis, tragedy, and comedy

catharsis
The expression and release, or purging, of emotions by audiences at the climax of a tragedy or drama.

The classic model of what happens when someone consumes a fictional text is found in Aristotle's analysis of Greek tragedy. He suggested that the experience enables people to feel extreme emotions, particularly fear and terror, provoked by the story, and then at the end to experience a purging of these emotions in a moment of **catharsis** or emotional release (Wellek & Warren 1976, p. 36; Benjamin 1977, p. 38). More recently, the catharsis hypothesis has been used by media effects theorists to suggest that sometimes watching violent films is a good outlet for our aggressive impulses, allowing them to be safely explored and contained in the fantasy space of the cinema instead of being played out in real life.

Audiences experience the feelings and dilemmas of characters through identification with them. They can understand extreme situations that they might never experience in their own lives. As audience members experience and therefore begin to understand the world inhabited by the characters, they empathise with them, and this empathy makes them develop as people. 'The function of literature … is to relieve us … from the pressure of emotions' (Wellek & Warren 1976, p. 36). Notions that texts serve to release pent-up emotions have also been applied to comedy. Some theorists argue that in letting out air, laughter acts as a release valve, and is therefore a form of relaxation. Laughter is increasingly being seen as therapeutic (Koestler 1975; Powell & Paton 1988), an activity that makes us healthier. Generating laughter is a common aim of media comedy fictions, which are very popular.

There are other ways in which comedy is a release or safety valve. Freud suggested that comedy allows us to speak about social taboos and repressed topics, particularly sexuality. It is a way of speaking the unspeakable (Freud 1976b).

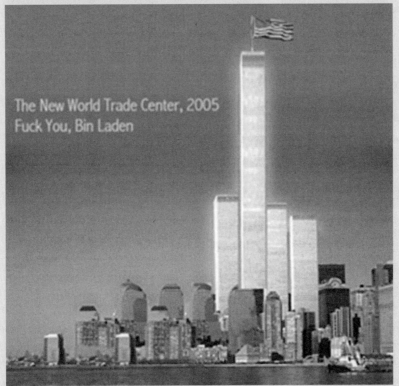

Figures 19.1 and 19.2   Joke images circulated by email after the September 11 attacks on the World Trade Center and the Pentagon

Source: Anonymous

There is debate over whether the function of comedy as a safety valve is socially progressive or reactionary. It can be progressive (that is, it can contribute to social change and development) by raising issues that would otherwise not be dealt with. But it can also be reactionary (that is, it can help to maintain the social status quo) because once there has been a release of tension, there is no need to deal with the social problem that produced the tension. Some comedy shows extend the boundaries of what is socially acceptable and break social taboos: when shows such as *Californication*, *Little Britain*, and *South Park* first appeared audiences were divided on whether they were funny or unacceptable. Author and philosopher Umberto Eco saw the potentially anarchic quality of comedy when he described it as 'the ultimate subversion of authority' in his novel *The Name of the Rose*.

A key question is: Does humour contribute to social change, or do people continue to accept the things that they laugh about and enjoy the release of tension rather than take social action? At its best, comedy can raise our awareness of social ills and can thereby contribute to social change. Laughter can make serious material seem harmless; it can be a subversive agent of social change, or a mechanism for trivialising significant issues.

While comedy, which invariably laughs at someone, can satirise those in power and authority, it has often been turned on minority or oppressed social groups—Irish, Poles, Aborigines, Jews, non-whites, women—in a racist and sexist fashion. A useful question to ask about comedy and jokes is: Who is the joke against? Answering this will begin to reveal its progressive or reactionary tendencies.

How soon after a serious event is it acceptable to make jokes about it? Can you remember when you first heard a joke about the September 11 attacks and what your reaction to this comedy was (see Figures 19.1 and 19.2.)?

Marxism and Brecht

Thinking about comedy and catharsis as emotional release leads to the question of whether media texts should provoke audiences to social action. Marxist ideas are relevant here (see pp. 189, 194).

Marxist interpretations of literature and film endeavour to show how narratives reveal the struggle between social groups and classes, and how the stories of individual characters are part of these struggles and of the changing economic forces that determine our actions. It is possible to carry out Marxist analyses of films and literature produced by non-Marxists or writers who lived before Marx: Marxist interpretations exist of the works of Shakespeare, the Brontë sisters, Balzac, and other writers. There are also Marxist analyses of films, cultural theorist Frederic Jameson's examination of *Dog Day Afternoon* (Jameson 1977), for example.

Marxism's answer to the question 'Why do we need stories?' is that they show us what is wrong with our society and they point to a better world. Viewed in this light, they are part of a revolutionary movement in that they contribute to social understanding and social change. According to Marxists, in a classless society people might actually no longer need stories or art, because life would be perfect. There would be no more fictions. Austrian author Ernst Fischer writes of the Dutch artist Mondrian, who held Marxist views: 'Reality would, he believed, increasingly displace the work of art, which was essentially a substitute for an equilibrium that reality lacked at present. "Art will disappear as life gains more equilibrium"' (Fischer 1963, p. 7). According to Marxism then, stories are signs that things are not perfect.

One of the most influential Marxist practitioners and theorists was the playwright and poet Bertolt Brecht. He challenged the worth of theatre as catharsis, arguing that this form of emotional involvement and release

- encourages acceptance of life as it is
- privileges emotional response over intellectual insight and understanding
- contributes to maintaining the status quo rather than provoking social change (Willett 1964; Benjamin 1977).

In Brecht's view, a narrative might explore social problems, but if it works through emotionally involving its audience the final result is the banality of a good cry, or a comment such as: How terrible, how terrible things are, but that's life. According to Brecht, theatre that works through emotions fails to provoke audiences to action: the only thing such texts might prompt audiences to do is go for a drink after the show.

Brecht argued that it is the way stories are told, their form and structure (the final narrative closure, the level of suspense, and so on), that produces these effects, and therefore viewing pleasure. He wanted to challenge narrative inevitability and reassurance (see p. 262). He argued for a different kind of storytelling, **epic theatre**, that would produce 'pleasurable learning' (Willett 1964, pp. 72–3), learning that would allow audiences to see the world in a new way, revealing new truths. I (Michael) first came across this kind of learning when I saw the 7.84 Theatre Company in the United Kingdom. Its name referred to the statistical distribution of wealth in Britain in the 1970s, a time when 7 per cent of the population owned 84 per cent of the country's wealth. My view of the United Kingdom as a basically egalitarian, democratic society (which is how it was then and still is often presented in the media) was shaken by this wider social truth. In Australia, which is often referred to as a classless society, the current figures for wealth ownership are virtually the same. Learning the following facts was a similarly shocking revelation for many: 'In some states in Australia, between 50 and 60 per cent of all children in custody are aboriginal, although they represent less than 4 per cent of the juvenile population', and 'The United States consumes 33% of the world's resources' (*New Internationalist* 1997, p. 6).

What would be important to Brecht about these statistics would be that rather than focusing on individual, psychological concerns, they reveal certain deep-seated political truths about society: they uncover the inequality of social structures. He sought a theatrical form that could encompass such teachings while still involving

epic theatre
A form of storytelling or theatre developed by German playwright Bertolt Brecht that challenged conventional storytelling forms by encouraging audience detachment and understanding rather than emotional identification.

the audience and in doing so broke away from the emphasis on psychological concerns that, as we have seen, is the dominant form of mainstream media (pp. 265–8).

Brecht's most famous technique for achieving this aim was the use of *Verfremdung*, which has been translated as 'alienation' or 'distanciation'. *Verfremdung* techniques are theatrical devices, now sometimes called Brechtian devices, that interrupt the realistic flow of the narrative in such a way that audience members are jolted out of their emotional involvement with the exciting narrative, or out of their identification with the main characters. Such techniques aim to make audiences think critically about what is happening by putting them in a distant or alienated position.

Verfremdung (distanciation, alienation)
Aesthetic techniques that make the audience step back from their emotional narrative involvement to a more critical position, which often enables them to see familiar things in a surprising new way.

Advocates of this technique argue that such reflection leads to insight, understanding, and ultimately to acceptance of the need to act. Moreover, it is argued that this learning process is pleasurable for oppressed audiences since it contributes to their liberation. Whereas catharsis produces a pleasurable emotional release that occurs while the audience is watching the play, the release that is provoked by a Brecht play comes afterwards, from doing something about problems raised in the text. An example of the stress on social factors and *Verfremdung* is found in the film *Kuhle Wampe*, scripted by Brecht (1932). A man commits suicide because of his poverty and unemployment. The camera doesn't show him jumping or falling to his death so as to shock and excite us. It just shows him leaving his watch behind (saving what is still valuable for his family) and then gives the grimly ironic caption: 'One less Unemployed'. Clearly, a good way of dealing with unemployment figures! The man thus represents a social group rather than a psychological type and the audience is encouraged to view the event with critical distance rather than emotional excitement. *Dogville* is an interesting contemporary film that also adopts some of these Brechtian techniques.

These revolutionary ideas were very influential on a group of film and television makers in the 1960s and 1970s. The most famous of these was the French film director Jean-Luc Godard. Godard tried to incorporate Brechtian devices into his films in order to make spectators think critically, come to new understandings of society, and be provoked into social action. Filmmaking and film going became an actively political pastime rather than a purely pleasurable recreation.

myths
Stories that often feature ancient gods or fantasy creatures, that recount how a society evolved. At a rational, scientific level they are fantastic, impossible, and unreal, but they may contain social and psychological truths and insights that offer symbolic resolutions to real issues or questions.

Lévi-Strauss and the purpose of myths

Another approach to narrative is found in the structuralist work of French anthropologist Claude Lévi-Strauss, who examined the role of **myths** (one of the earliest forms of stories) in 'primitive' cultures

(Lévi-Strauss 1978; Turner 2006, p. 103). He argued that myths served an important function for these societies. In his book *Mythologies*, Barthes also uses the term 'myth' to refer to the ideologies that lie behind cultural signs (Barthes 1973). Myths dealt with the central problems and contradictions felt by a culture; in story form (often stories about gods or heroes) they played these conflicts out to a resolution that gave societies some sort of framework for how to live. Media analyst Graeme Turner explains myth as follows:

> Within myths, contradictions and inequities which could not be resolved in the real world were resolved symbolically. The function of myth was to place those contradictions—between humans and the natural environment, for instance, or between life and death—as part of natural existence. Myths negotiated a peace between men and women and their environment so that they could live in it without agonizing over its frustrations and cruelties (Turner 2006, p. 103).

Lévi-Strauss' theory stressed the play of binary oppositions as structures that set up and resolve contradictions. The result is not social action, but social peace and acceptance of the status quo. Our discussion of contemporary media narratives and their resolution of oppositions relating to contemporary social concerns—the desire for marriage and family versus friendship and multiple partners, for example—suggests that media narratives can be seen, using Lévi-Strauss' terms, as forms of contemporary myths.

The idea of rites of passage is worth mentioning here. Rites of passage are traditional points or periods of significant change in a person's life—birth, marriage, and death are the most obvious, but most societies also have traditional rites that help mark the transition of young adults from childhood to adulthood. They are often described as death and rebirth rituals or as initiation ceremonies—a symbolic death is experienced that allows new life to come forward at the same time as another stage of life is left behind. Modern and postmodern Western culture has lost many of these traditions, although remnants of them can be seen in many of the adolescent activities of teenagers involving sex and drugs; for example, the schoolies' week celebrations that Australian school leavers indulge in—traditionally, a week of relatively excessive holidaying and partying—are a kind of initiation into, as well as a challenge to, adult life.

While there may be an absence of formal rituals in real life, film, television, and fiction narratives fill some of this gap by providing numerous examples of rites of passage and initiation stories. *Kick-Ass*, *Easy A*, *Juno*, *Samson and Delilah*, and *An Education* are all examples of coming of age films. Historian Mircea Eliade expresses this well when he writes about the appeal of fairy tales:

> It is impossible to deny that the ordeals and adventures of the heroes and heroines of fairy tales are almost always translated into initiatory terms ... initiatory scenarios ... are the expression of a psychodrama that answers a deep need in the human being. Every man [sic]

wants to experience certain perilous situations, to confront exceptional ordeals, to make his way into the Other World—and he experiences all this, on the level of his imaginative life, by hearing or reading fairy tales (Eliade 1963, as quoted in Bettelheim 1978, p. 35).

This holds true for many other film, television, and written narratives.

Entertainment, escapism, and utopia: musicals and soap operas

The pleasures we get from media products are often described as escapist, while the texts themselves are belittled as just entertainment. Saying something is escapist or just entertainment is a way of dismissing it. These disparaging terms are presented as self-evident—it is assumed that they don't need explanation, that we know what they mean. This does not do justice to the terms. Film studies professor Richard Dyer has written most illuminatingly about the term 'entertainment', analysing its history, development, and meanings (Dyer 1992). He has also written about popular genres that are often dismissed as escapist, particularly musicals and soap operas (Dyer 1981; Dyer et al. 1981).

To describe a media text as escapist is to suggest that people watching it are avoiding reality, that they are not facing up to the real world. It suggests that the text is unrealistic, that it promotes irresponsible avoidance of social problems. Escapist entertainment is often contrasted with realistic stories that explore the grim realities of life and so are deemed to be more worthy and valuable. We don't agree with this characterisation of popular entertainment as simply escapist. Dyer has suggested that many cultural products have a utopian element to them: they point to the possibilities of a better world (as suggested by the Marxist analysis of media texts; see pp. 326–7).

There is a long and respectable tradition of utopian writing and visions. The utopian vision of a perfect world can inspire readers with hope and optimism and can give a blueprint for how they would like to live. It is something to work towards; it suggests the possibility of social change (in contrast to many realist stories that simply confirm how terrible life is rather than positing an alternative). These escapist visions involve an escape to something as well as an escape from something.

Dyer suggests that the musical and soap opera can present ideal values and ideal ways of living (what we escape to) that are in direct contrast to the realities of everyday life (what we escape from). The musical offers the following ideal qualities as a response to their mundane, everyday opposites:

- abundance *vs* scarcity
- energy *vs* tiredness and exhaustion
- community *vs* isolation and alienation

- transparency in human relations *vs* human deviousness
- intensity of experience *vs* lacklustre lives and boredom (Dyer 1981).

In classic films such as *Singin' in the Rain*, and modern versions of the musical such as the films *Burlesque*, *Nine*, and *Bran Nue Dae*, as well as the musical TV series *Glee*, the musical provides all five elements of contrast between the ideal world that we escape into and the everyday world. Particularly in spontaneous song and dance numbers, musicals offer the open and simple expression of intense and exciting feeling (often love, joy, and friendship), and there is a great outpouring of energy and movement. Even in the musical biopics *The Runaways* and *Control*, bleak films that undermine the conventions of the musical genre, these contrasts between social realism and the transcendent, uplifting possibilities of music are apparent. Typical musicals show people brought together in a sharing, caring community where there is plenty of material and emotional sustenance for everyone (in fact there is often an abundance of it). *Glee* encapsulates this function of the musical, as the show revolves around a group of high school outcasts who are brought together by their Glee Club, where they find solidarity and friendship, and can sing their troubles away. This contrasts with the dull grind of daily life, where people work hard for a living but often don't have enough, materially or emotionally, where human relations may be unclear and conducted with ulterior motives, where people are stressed, tired, or bored, and where many live isolated and alienated lives.

The documentary *Amandla* gives an account of how popular music and song were major factors in developing and supporting the revolutionary struggle of the African National Congress against apartheid in South Africa. *Amandla* is not a musical but it shows how the utopian aspects of music, far from being escapist, were directed specifically into commenting on and changing social realities for the better. Perhaps it is important that this popular culture musical form and expression was not broadcast by the media but sung and participated in by people in the streets—an example of popular culture created by the people, not for the people (see p. 38). The grass roots nature of the *toyi toyi* dance and protest songs shown in *Amandla*, rather than being broadcast to the entire nation, enabled it to operate under the radar and thereby avoid possible banning. This meant that music could be used to communicate political messages from township to township across the country. In some ways the use of music as a form of political expression and social commentary continues in South Africa today through the subcultures of hip-hop and *kwaito* music.

All this is to illustrate that so-called escapist entertainments have a connection to our real lives and can offer something positive. There can of course be a negative side to entertainment. Some game shows and gambling (especially as presented in lottery advertisements) offer magical fixes to our scarcity problems, but these fixes promote the same consumerist values on which much of our culture is built. (Interestingly, research has shown that many lottery winners actually end up losing friends and most of their money and fighting with their families, ending up little better off than before.) Game shows and lotteries operate like the circuses provided by Roman emperors, as devices to keep people happy and distracted from social and political problems. You may want to question these forms of entertainment but entertainment that is simple and easy to watch, and accessible to many people, should not be denigrated as a whole for these reasons. Examine each example to see what is being presented. In so doing, you may find valuable elements, as Dyer has pointed out.

The utopian visions provided by the media give us pleasure and are sources of aspiration and inspiration. The flipside to this is the media's presentation of dystopias or dystopic views of the world, stories of social breakdown, decay, and apocalypse (*The Road*, *Mad Max: Fury Road*, *Blade Runner*, *The Matrix*, *The Day After Tomorrow*, and *Children of Men*, for example). These dystopic texts also relate to our present world. They provide us with warnings of what could happen to us.

In *The Pleasure of the Text* (1975) Barthes adds another dimension to thinking about audiences and our responses to fictions when he discusses the pleasures of reading fictions. He uses the French word ***jouissance*** (bliss), which he distinguishes from ***plaisir*** (pleasure).

Barthes is aiming to convey a difference between *plaisir*, which is straightforward enjoyment of fictions that don't really have a deep impact on us, and *jouissance*, a disturbing, yet blissful experience that produces an extremely heightened response. This may be experienced with fictions that have a potentially life-changing impact on us, making us see the world anew.

To clarify this try to make a list of fictions that you have simply enjoyed and fictions that have thrilled you with *jouissance*. Compare your list with a friend's list and try to explain to each other what the nature of the *jouissance* impact was on you.

jouissance
A French word, one meaning of which is bliss or ecstasy; much more powerful, and sometimes more disturbing, than *plaisir* (pleasure).

plaisir
French for pleasure; the kind of enjoyment derived from fictions that do not have a strong or enduring impact.

Realisms

The aesthetic tradition that seems closest to real life is the mimetic tradition of **realism**. In contrast with escapist entertainment, mimetic cultural productions aim to imitate reality, to produce narratives and stories that are recognised as realistic.

This mimetic tradition started with Greek culture and the history of mimetic art is a history of continually evolving styles and methods used to reproduce reality. The styles evolve partly because people's perceptions of reality are always changing so reality is impossible to capture. 'Realism' is an important critical term in relation to nineteenth-century painting and literature, and twentieth-century

realism
Objects in art—paintings, sculpture, literature—that appear true to real life and the aesthetic methods or styles used to create them. Realism, the dominant aesthetic in painting and literature in the nineteenth century, aimed for verisimilitude and focused on the lives of ordinary people.

film and television. Raymond Williams has explained the different elements that make up realist texts:

- ordinary people, particularly the working classes, as subject matter
- serious treatment of their lives
- contemporary social contexts (Williams 1977a, pp. 61–74).

The fact that working-class people were finally being represented in these ways was itself a major factor in audience pleasure: the pleasure of people seeing themselves seriously represented, recognising their own lives and society. Film theorist Roy Armes makes the important distinction between realism as an aim or attitude (aiming to tell the truth, to show things with verisimilitude so that they look very similar to what we see in our daily lives) and realism as a method or style (a set of artistic or stylistic conventions that try to achieve this aim) (Armes 1971). Because there are numerous, changing ways of seeing the world there are also many realist styles or sets of conventions (realisms). Neorealism, Soviet realism, Dogma 95, *cinéma vérité*, direct cinema, naturalism, kitchen-sink realism, social realism, magic realism, and dirty realism are all used to describe styles or tendencies in literature and in film and television products. As each new style appears it wins an audience because of its freshness and stylistic innovations.

Films with a high degree of verisimilitude—for example the films of Mike Leigh—are perceived to be more accurate representations of society, and so are therefore often interpreted as offering productive, instructive social commentary. The connections these styles forge with real-life issues and their seriousness mean that they have tended to be given more cultural weight than escapist entertainment. Because they appear realistic it is sometimes easy to forget the construction involved in their representations.

Fantasy

In contrast with an understanding of fictions that sees them as imitations of real life, the use of the term 'fantasy' to describe and analyse fictions draws attention to dreams, imagination, the subconscious, and story worlds that differ significantly from everyday experience. Links have traditionally been made between films and dreams. The description of Hollywood as a dream factory points to the desirable aspects of Hollywood films (they provide wish fulfilment, as do dreams) and their unrealistic nature, living in a dream world.

Fantasies are essentially unreal, the product of our dreams and imaginations, but this is one of the most exciting things about film and television stories: they give filmmakers and audiences a chance to live out their wildest and most extreme fantasies. This has been the source of some controversy, particularly in relation to representations of sex and violence. Some people argue that these representations are dangerous and have the potential to corrupt us or lead us to commit violent acts (see pp. 48–9). Others reject this, saying that

1   we are capable of recognising that we are not seeing real events
2   these stories allow us to safely work through difficult aspects of ourselves, and our society.

The second point is an argument that it is important to allow violent representations because they give us a chance to explore and understand our own violent tendencies. Very few people are murderers, but many of us, at some point in our lives, dream of or feel like killing or attacking someone. Looking at and understanding these dark and repressed sides of ourselves enables us to cope with them. Denying us the opportunity to explore them will repress them further, and that could be harmful. Stories allow us to play out, in our imaginations, a whole set of possible actions, to test them out, to see what happens if …

Literary theorist Rosemary Jackson describes fantasy as 'the literature of subversion'. According to Jackson, this literature of subversion 'attempts to compensate for a lack resulting from cultural constraints; it is a literature of desire, which seeks that which is experienced as absence or loss' (Jackson 1981, p. 3). This is similar, in some ways, to Dyer's view of the utopian musical. Jackson sees media texts that portray extreme human behaviour as explorations of areas and desires that society normally represses.

Illuminating what happens when our fantasies are played out on screen, film theorist Victor Perkins describes audiences as 'participant observers' (Perkins 1990, ch. 7). He notes that the language of film, the way stories are told, enables audiences to feel as if they are participating in the events on screen, thus involving them in extreme actions and intense emotions—killing, being killed, making love, chariot racing, and so on. At the same time, we still know we are in the cinema; part of us remains detached and observes what is happening on the screen and in ourselves as we experience these situations. We are simultaneously participants and observers. The cinema becomes a playground where we experience all sorts of emotions and actions and at the same time reflect critically and rationally on how it feels and on what the consequences are for ourselves and others. This testing ground provides a significant arena of pleasure and learning.

We have already referred to Bettelheim's argument that violent fairy tales are actually good for children as a way of letting them face and explore their own violent capacities (see p. 50). On ABC Radio National's *Media Report*, Robert Kee, a noted Hollywood scriptwriter, discussed the social role of dark media fantasies with interviewer Donna McLachlan.

McLachlan   What is your feeling about the kind of depth and strength of some of these monsters that are appearing on screen, *American Psycho*, and Hannibal Lecter and so on? Is it disturbing, do you think, that there is that portrayal of the monster, or is it healthy?

Kee   Oh, it's very healthy. Human beings are angel and devil, and a perfect balance of the two. And the fascinating thing about human beings is you never know from one day to the next which you're going to get. I mean, on Monday they build Notre Dame Cathedral and on Tuesday, Auschwitz, and which is it going to be? And you only need to pick up a newspaper from one day to the next, and you see this constant manifestation of the deep evil in human beings. And what all of us try to do, of course, is deny it exists in us. It's that backpack serial killer over there, it's not me. But every time you cut somebody off in traffic, every time you slam a door in somebody's face, every time you're rude to a clerk, every time you take advantage of somebody, there's a little bit of evil seeping out of you, and you enjoyed cutting that guy off in traffic, and don't deny it. And so if we turn our backs on the dark side of our nature, if we just try to avoid it and insist it doesn't exist, it's going to sneak up from behind us and swallow us whole.

And art, which has the power to illuminate these dark corners of human nature, can make us understand that it's us, and it's in our nature. It doesn't mean that we're evil ourselves, that we're going to be overcome by our own evil nature, but it's always there, and the power is there, and as long as we understand that and are aware of it, then we can keep ourselves in balance and go round being a decent human being (Kee 2001).

Stories that go beyond everyday realism—horror movies, the surreal explorations of film directors such as David Lynch, and films that show unrealistic possibilities—allow us an even wider testing-out of human feelings and experiences. Films such as *Black Swan*, *Fight Club*, *TRON: Legacy*, *The Matrix*, *Crouching Tiger, Hidden Dragon*, and *Source Code* can be understood (like myths discussed above, pp. 329–30) as allowing audiences to explore their inner world, their psychic processes, or as symbolic of external social situations. The fantasies they portray—having a real-life double (*Black Swan*, *Fight Club*), living in a computer-generated reality (*TRON: Legacy*, *The Matrix*),

"One does not become enlightened by imagining figures of light, but by making the darkness conscious." C.G. JUNG.

Figure 19.3   Cartoon illustrating consequences of denial of our shadow selves

Source: Ron Pyatt, 1990

being able to fly (*Crouching Tiger*), living the same day over and over (*Source Code*)—enable the main characters to explore internal psychological states and allow the audience a space to consider what it is to be human.

It is worth noting that these kinds of fantasy explorations seem to be one of the pleasures offered within the virtual world of computer games and the internet. The opportunity to construct your own avatar and to enter a virtual world that is not subject to the natural laws of physics or the real world gives participants the opportunity to explore their fantasy worlds.

The hero's journey: Joseph Campbell

Joseph Campbell, who was a professor of mythology and theorist, described general, recurring patterns in all forms of storytelling. Campbell is not the only one to have sought out such general patterns. The structuralist work of folklorist Vladimir Propp, who analysed the common characteristics of fairy tales, is most well known in media studies (Propp 1975; Turner 2006, pp. 98–102). He looked at fairy tales and concluded that a recurrent pattern involving set characters and plot actions forms the basis of all fairy tales. According to Propp, these characters are the villain, the donor (the provider), the helper, the princess (or the person who is being sought), the princess' father, the dispatcher, the hero (or the victim), and the false hero. Film narratives have been subjected to Propp's analysis and have revealed similar set characters. The main characters in *Star Wars* fit Propp's character types neatly.

Table 19.1 **Propp's spheres of action and *Star Wars* character types**

the villain	Darth Vader
the donor	Obi-wan Kenobi
the helper	Han Solo
the princess	Princess Leia
the dispatcher	R2-D2
the hero	Luke Skywalker
the false hero	Darth Vader

Source: Turner 2006, p. 102

Propp's structure comprises six stages:

1 preparation
2 complication
3 transference

4   struggle

5   return

6   recognition.

Propp's work can be understood as an elaboration of Todorov's narrative structure (p. 261) and can be fruitfully applied to many film texts. A humorous email (Figure 19.4) circulated across the globe was claimed to have been found in the dustbin of *Harry Potter* author J K Rowling. It draws attention to the structural similarities of many stories.

Harry Potter and the Philosopher's Stone
~~Star Wars A New Hope~~: synopsis

~~Luke Skywalker~~ *Harry Potter* is an orphan living with his uncle and aunt
on the remote wilderness of ~~Tatooine~~ *suburbia*. *Muggles*
He is rescued from ~~aliens~~ *Muggles* by wise, bearded ~~Ben Kenobi~~ *Hagrid*, who turns
out to be a ~~Jedi Knight~~ *wizard*.
~~Ben~~ *Hagrid* reveals to ~~Luke~~ *Harry* that ~~Luke's~~ *Harry's* father was also a ~~Jedi Knight~~ *wizard*, and
was the best ~~pilot~~ *Quidditch player* he had ever seen.
~~Luke~~ *Harry* is also instructed in how to use ~~the Jedi light sabre~~ *a magic wand* as he too
trains to become a ~~Jedi~~ *wizard*.
~~Luke~~ *Harry* has many adventures in ~~the galaxy~~ *Hogwarts* and makes new friends
such as ~~Han Solo~~ *Ron* and ~~Princess Leia~~ *Hermione*.
In the course of these adventures he distinguishes himself as a top
~~X-wing pilot~~ *Quidditch seeker* in the ~~battle of the Death Star~~ *Quidditch match*, making the ~~direct hit~~ *catch* that
secures ~~the Rebels~~ *Gryffindor* victory against the forces of evil, *Slytherin*.
~~Luke~~ *Harry* also sees off the threat of ~~Darth Vader~~ *Lord Voldemort*, who we know
murdered his ~~uncle and aunt~~ *parents*.
In the finale, ~~Luke~~ *Harry* and his new friends ~~receive medals of valour~~ *win the House Cup*.

All of this will be set to an orchestral score composed by John Williams.

Figure 19.4   Humorous Harry Potter email

Source: Anonymous

Propp's work does not go much beyond discovering and describing these patterns. Joseph Campbell's approach is similar in that he too looks for structural patterns in myths, fairy tales, and stories from all over the world, but Campbell progresses beyond this to explain what this structure means for human beings. In this way, his work has a similar aim to the work of Lévi-Strauss in understanding the role and meanings of myths and stories in human society.

Campbell gives a very different view of the media to the approaches that we have presented in this book. Much of our analysis has stressed the social construction of representations. We have presented methods for deconstructing texts, a process that makes us aware of the ideological and social meanings inscribed in them and reveals that the media are produced by dominant social groups in such a way as to reproduce the dominant values of society.

Campbell draws on a quite different theoretical framework. His theories are greatly influenced by the work of Jung, and his aim is much more a celebration of media texts than a warning critique. Campbell stresses the universal aspects of human nature and societies. He suggests that there are similar universal human patterns and truths found in the myths, legends, and religious beliefs of all cultures and argues that the stories in them present a blueprint that shows us how to act in the world to find enlightenment, fulfilment, and achieve our human potential. He argues that they have a dominant pattern or structure, which he calls 'the hero's journey'. Campbell's work is accessible in his books and in video interviews (Campbell 1972, 1988a, 1988b, 1991; Golden 1992).

The hero's journey involves a hero who goes through tests, struggles, and problems on the way to achieving their goal. Campbell suggests that this structure provides a framework that shows us how to act as humans if we are to realise our heroic potential. According to Campbell, we are all (men and women) heroes with the potential to find our heroic fulfilment. To do this, we have to undertake a hero's journey by 'following our bliss'. This idea of following your bliss is crucial to Campbell's work. He suggests that each of us can find something that truly moves and touches us. Only by following our bliss can we realise our potential, our happiness. He notes though that many pressures of contemporary society, such as trying to survive economically and to conform socially, do not encourage this. We are thus faced with the challenge of deciding whether to do what society pressures us to do or following our own spirit. Earlier, Campbell argues, so-called primitive societies were more able to encourage people to do this than modern industrial, secular, capitalist societies, which have lost this capacity.

The stages of the hero's journey outlined by Campbell in his book *The Hero with a Thousand Faces* (Campbell 1972, pp. ix–x) are

1   departure
    • the call to adventure
    • refusal of the call

- supernatural aid
- the crossing of the first threshold
- the belly of the whale

2   initiation
- the road of trials
- the meeting with the goddess
- woman as the temptress
- atonement with the father
- apotheosis
- the ultimate boon

3   return
- refusal of the return
- the magic flight
- rescue from without
- the crossing of the return threshold
- master of the two worlds
- freedom to live.

Campbell elaborates on each of these stages, finding examples of them in a multitude of stories. He suggests that, like ancient myths and stories, film and television narratives are our modern myths in that they include and illustrate these same heroic structures. This is graphically illustrated in many films and stories, such as *Beowulf*, *Star Wars*, and *The Matrix*. In fact, *Star Wars* and George Miller's *Mad Max* films are directly based on and inspired by Campbell's theories. The popular success of these films suggests that they resonate deeply with the beliefs and feelings of audiences.

Originally, Campbell built his theories on analysis of pre-existing myths and stories. Now there has been an interesting reversal. George Lucas and Miller know about Campbell's work and used it in constructing their stories. In Hollywood today many scriptwriters learn about Campbell and use his ideas and narrative formula as a basis for writing their stories (Vogler 1992).

Campbell has been criticised for his Jungian position and the way that his theories can be aligned with an ideology of individualism. The universalist aspects of his theories are seen by some as deriving from a Western perspective that fails to see and acknowledge the differences between cultures. The focus on the hero supports a typical American ideology of individual power rather than acknowledging the importance of society as a whole. We can see how some of his ideas have been taken up, appropriated, by big business in their advertising campaigns with slogans such as Nike's 'Just do it', advertisements that present and celebrate ordinary people as heroes, or encourage us to follow our bliss.

Australian playwright David Williamson offered this Australian critique on Campbell's ideas when asked if he thought American film producers relied on Campbell's notion of the hero's journey:

> I think that they do very much have that story structure firmly in their heads, that the hero must start out, must go through a series of challenges, each of which he or she overcomes, and becomes a better and stronger person at every turning point, and finally ends up the film a true hero. Now I think Australia and Australian writers tend to believe that this is a falsified picture of life, that life proceeds more often according to the neuroses theory where people keep making the same mistakes over and over again—which is more conducive to a comedic approach than a heroic, dramatic approach …
>
> Many of us, it's my observation, don't conform to the hero's journey in our lives, we battle on, we get through our lives and we do tend to make the same mistakes time and time again, however well-meaning. Yes, so I, if anything, would tend to satirise the hero's journey rather than take it seriously (Radio National, *Big Ideas*, February 2004).

Whether you like Campbell's theory or agree with Williamson it is clear that Campbell's ideas have been very influential in film and television production over the past thirty years.

Psychoanalysis

psychoanalysis
Psychoanalysis, as developed by Sigmund Freud, argued that people are motivated by their unconscious, that there are several developmental stages people go through as they grow up, and that psychoanalysis can make people aware of their unconscious conflicts, fantasies, and desires (which are attributed chiefly to the development of the sexual instinct) through the free association of ideas, analysis, and interpretation of their dreams.

Sigmund Freud and Carl Jung developed psychoanalytic theory in the early twentieth century. Within media and film studies **psychoanalysis** has been used in two ways: first, to explain the psychological pleasures of the viewing experience, and second, as a method for interpreting stories to show how stories often illustrate psychoanalytic truths.

The pleasures of viewing and looking at images on screens

scopophilia
From the Greek; love of looking, a basic human drive.

Freud argued that one of the key human drives or desires is the desire to look (Mulvey 1989). This desire, called **scopophilia**, is a source of great pleasure and satisfaction. One aspect of scopophilia is voyeurism, the desire to look secretly at events, to spy on people, which can be seen as one of the pleasures offered by film and television texts. Audiences indulge in the fantasy that the actors on screen are real people acting out their lives before cameras, seemingly without realising those cameras are there. Audiences watch these events unfold, often from a darkened auditorium. We choose to believe that we are being permitted to see the most intimate aspects of these lives, beyond what we experience in relation to most people we actually know. Films such as *Rear Window*, *Blue Velvet*, *Disturbia*, and *American Beauty* consciously explore these pleasures. Voyeuristic vision is characterised by distance (the observer is separated or concealed from the observed in some manner) and secrecy (the observed is not aware that they are being watched, and does not consent to it). The combination of distance and deception leads to a sense of control and objectification. In *American Beauty*, Ricky films Lester or Jane without them knowing he is playing the role of a peeping Tom, a voyeur. The use of point-of-view shots and long shots conveys the distant, controlling nature of voyeurism. The pleasures of identification and objectification (see pp. 274–5) can also be said to be built on scopophilia, as we either psychologically identify with characters on screen or turn them into visual objects of desire. Fetishistic scopophilia develops this look of desire. It is more to do with being absorbed in the pleasures of looking, rather than controlling or objectifying what the viewer is looking at. The huge size of the cinema screen is tailor-made for objective and fetishistic looking. Often the object that is being fetishised (frequently a part of the body) takes on huge proportions and is fragmented, so it fills the screen in close-up and overwhelms the viewer with its desirability. This is a different experience from the scopophilic pleasure derived from voyeurism. In *American Beauty*, when Lester watches Angela dance and perform her cheer-leading routine at the sports stadium his gaze is fetishistic and scopophilic. Angela is filmed in slow motion; the camera fragments her body and moves into close-up, even though Lester is actually seated some distance from her. The use of close-ups and slow motion conveys the overwhelming and obsessive nature of fetishism.

Freud argued that men desired women but also feared them because their lack of a penis posed the 'threat of castration'. The fetish object results in the 'disavowal of castration': it is a substitute for the missing penis, it fills the gap in a reassuring way, but it then becomes the focus of sexual excitement. It can take on disproportionate importance because it is taking the place of something that is deeply desired. A fetish for silk, velvet, or fur, for instance, may be a reassuring substitute for the feeling of skin or hair. The film *There's Something About Mary* depicts the villain as having a fetish for the shoes worn by Cameron Diaz's character. A shoe fetish is often explained as an analogy between the action of a foot slipping into a shoe and sexual intercourse.

Freud and Jung both make interesting comments on the psychological value of phantasies (the dreams people have and daydreams they indulge in). Freud suggests, rather negatively, that 'A happy person never phantasies, only an unsatisfied one', which perhaps suggests that only neurotic people would want to watch films or read stories. Jung argues, much more positively, that phantasy is 'the creative activity whence issue the solutions to all answerable questions; it is the mother of all possibilities' (Jung 1923, p. 573).

Psychoanalysis as an interpretive method

Psychoanalytic interpretations of stories suggest that the way characters behave can be understood in psychoanalytic terms. Psychoanalysis argues that humans go through patterns and stages of development as they grow up, develop, and mature. Negotiating these stages is crucial to our health and emotional and psychological growth. We can see a direct parallel in this process of negotiating struggles and growth with our previous discussion of how characters in narratives go through a process of moral growth (pp. 266–7). Oedipus is the most famous specific example. Oedipus, in the Greek play *Oedipus the King* by Sophocles, killed his father and married his mother. Freud used Oedipus' name for his discovery of the Oedipus complex: the unconscious desire that male children have to kill their father so they can replace him and have sex with their mother. The play, Freud thought, was about the struggle of the Oedipus complex. It is possible to interpret many texts in a Freudian way: to understand some male rivalries as symbolic struggles with the father; some male attractions as symbolic desire for the mother.

Filmmaker Alfred Hitchcock consciously used Freud's ideas in *Psycho*, in which Norman Bates cannot come to terms with his own sexuality because of his connection to his (dead) mother; it is this that leads him to become a murderer. Such films demonstrate the failure to successfully overcome psychological problems, whereas films such as *Analyse This* or *The Day After Tomorrow* show characters successfully negotiating psychological struggles. David Lynch explores aspects of the unconscious and Freudian desire very explicitly in *Blue Velvet* and *Lost Highway*. Freud theorised that everyone represses many of their desires but no matter how hard they try these **repressed desires** will come back in some disturbed form to trouble them.

repressed desire
The act of repression forms the unconscious. Forbidden material (Oedipal desire, for example) is rejected from conscious thought, but not destroyed. It is stored in the unconscious from where it continues to produce effects.

Critics, including Robin Wood, have interpreted horror films as illustrating this mechanism of repression where the monstrous characters represent the return of the repressed (Wood 1986). Freud also theorised all people as having three layers of personality—the id, the ego, and the super ego. Individuals in real life struggle to find a balance between their id (the force that seeks to satisfy all of their desires without concern for anyone else) and their super ego (the parental, moralistic controlling force that won't permit pleasure)—a balance in which the aim is for the ego to achieve progressive conquest of the id. Similarly, we can interpret film narratives as representing this struggle where different characters represent the different forces. The pleasure we have as audience is in seeing these psychological dramas being acted out. Many cartoons can be easily interpreted in this way: Bart and Homer in *The Simpsons* seem to represent the id, while Marge and Lisa are much more like the super ego. Homer, because he is an adult, has to try to hold down his id instincts. In *South Park* the children mainly represent the id, while several of the adults (though not all) are more the super ego. One of the pleasures in cartoons for children is the amount of space given to id characters. Bettelheim argued that fairy tales work in this way too, telling stories about these struggles so that 'as stories unfold they give conscious credence to id pressures and show ways to satisfy these that are in line with ego and superego requirements' (Bettelheim 1978). You don't need to consciously understand Freudian theory to understand what the story is presenting.

Filmmaker and playwright David Mamet has written: 'I would suggest that those who are interested [in filmmaking] might want to do some reading in psychoanalysis, which is a great storehouse of information about movies' (Mamet 1991, p. 7). Mamet sees psychoanalysis as a tool for understanding human character that can then be used by writers or filmmakers, even by readers of texts. Freud once wrote that he had discovered nothing about human personality that writers and artists hadn't already known about and demonstrated. Whether or not Freud's ideas are right they have become part of popular common sense so that today psychoanalytic ideas inform many media products. Most people know something about his ideas of the unconscious, the Oedipus complex, Freudian slips, and so on. *Analyse This* is a good example of a film that explains some aspects of psychoanalysis but wouldn't be so popular if audiences didn't already understand the basics.

The application of psychoanalytic theory, mainly deriving from Freud and the subsequent work of psychoanalyst Jacques Lacan, to media studies is too complex to pursue here, but there is a body of reading and other research you can follow up (Lapsley & Westlake 1989, Chapter 3; Kaplan 1990; Leader & Groves 1995).

Reading as a transformative experience

We have given a brief summary of some approaches for understanding what happens when people view or read fiction and have argued that there is always some connection between real-life events and fiction. But the difference in our experience of these two realities has also been acknowledged. We want to reflect now on what the viewing experience is like and how this compares to real, everyday experiences. My brother has asked me, Michael, why I watch so many films, and he suggests that part of me is missing out on real life. His comments suggest that I am having surrogate experiences through these films rather than actually doing the things myself, as though reading about or watching real life is not the same as actually living it. Similarly, I am surprised at how many people watch sports events rather than participating in the sports themselves—it seems to make sense to say that participation is more pleasurable than observation. Part of me agrees with my brother, and as I get older it seems more important to experience many things for myself rather than read about or watch them.

But the experience of viewing fictions is not just surrogate experience. It is an intense form of human experience, a part of real life that yields profound pleasures. These pleasures can be compared to those found in meditation, ritual, and mysticism. The origins of fiction and stories lie in myths and religious rites; stories serve direct spiritual ends. The fiction experience invites us into an altered state of consciousness, a different way of being, that can be more intense than many real-life experiences. It may be deeply spiritual, filling us with wonder and revelation, thereby helping us in our everyday lives, it gives space and time for contemplation, allowing us to put our lives in perspective, and it may help to recreate us, as suggested by the word 'recreation'. Just as our dreams are sometimes more intense than our daily experiences, so too, being immersed in fictions can stimulate our hearts, minds, and emotions in extraordinarily fulfilling ways. While the fiction experience seems to be about external events—it comprises stories happening to other people—it actually allows us to go on an inward journey. As we consume fictions, we leave behind the mundane practicalities of everyday life to travel deep into the heart of ourselves, discovering our core beliefs, feelings, and desires.

The ideological values of stories

This mystical view of stories and fictions sounds very positive, but stories still carry values or ideologies. Indigenous Canadian writer and scholar Thomas King illustrates this well: he argues that stories are fundamental in explaining how people and cultures operate—people learn about themselves and their culture through stories. He examines two different creation myths, the Christian myth of Genesis—Adam and Eve, and a Native American creation myth. King argues that these kinds of stories form the basis for people's understanding of humanity, the earth, and the universe. He compares the two myths and finds some fundamental differences:

> The elements in Genesis create a particular universe governed by a series of hierarchies—God, man, animals, plants—that celebrate law, order, and good government, while in our Native story, the universe is governed by series of co-operations … that celebrate equality and balance (King 2003, pp. 23–4).

He concludes from these differences

> So here are our choices: a world in which creation is a solitary, individual act or a world in which creation is a shared activity; a world that begins in harmony and slides towards chaos or a world that begins in chaos and moves towards harmony; a world marked by competition or a world determined by co-operation (King 2003, pp. 23–4).

We can express this through another binary table.

Table 19.2 **Differences in Christian and Native American genesis stories**

Christianity	Native American
hierarchies	equality
law and order	cooperation

Christianity	Native American
individual god	many gods
harmony to chaos	chaos to harmony
competition	cooperation

King suggests that both these stories construct reality but notes that one story—the Christian myth—has become dominant so that its reality (hierarchical, competitive) has become dominant, while the indigenous world view of equal cooperation is subordinated. He asks whether Western culture in general 'has fostered stories that encourage egotism and self-interest' (King 2003, p. 26). The point King is making is that stories construct human value systems, ideologies, so people need to look closely at what those are. And if, as he says, you are unhappy with your value systems and 'want to change society, then change the stories you tell'.

Conclusion

This chapter has explored the question of why people read and watch stories, what pleasures they take from them, and what values and meanings stories can carry. It has done this by offering a number of theoretical and critical perspectives that suggest some answers to these questions. The chapter has also looked at

- the connections between fiction and stories and the real world
- tragedy, comedy, and the theory of catharsis
- Marxist approaches, with Brecht as an example
- entertainment as escape or utopia, with musicals and soap operas as examples
- the role of myths, first from Lévi-Strauss' perspective, and then through the ideas of Joseph Campbell and the hero's journey
- the different approaches of realism and fantasy
- psychoanalysis as a method for analysing stories and the pleasure derived from them
- stories as a mystically transforming experience
- the ideological values of stories.

Discussion points

1 Why do you read or watch stories? What kinds of stories do you like? Why?
2 Look at one or more of the following comedies: *South Park*, *Little Britain*, *The Simpsons*, *Fahrenheit 9/11*, *Supersize Me*, *Bridesmaids*, or *Legally Blonde*. Consider what, if any, social ills they are dealing with, whether they are contributing to social change, and who or what is being laughed at.

3 Think of examples of film or television narratives that have had a major impact on you in some way. Why and how did they do this? Describe the different reactions they produced in you.
4 Discuss the pros and cons of realism and fantasy as storytelling forms.
5 How valid and useful do you find the theory of the hero's journey?
6 How valid and useful do you find psychoanalysis as an approach for understanding stories?

Summary

You should now be able to

- comment on and discuss the relationship between fictional texts and the real world
- explain and apply all the approaches listed in the conclusion in relation to understanding how stories work
- define and illustrate the terms 'catharsis', 'Verfremdung', 'myth', and 'realism'
- comment on the ideological values of stories.

Part 4 has given you a whole series of ways for analysing and interpreting texts and stories. These are presented in summary form in Figure 19.5. This should be a useful guide and checklist for any text analysis you are doing.

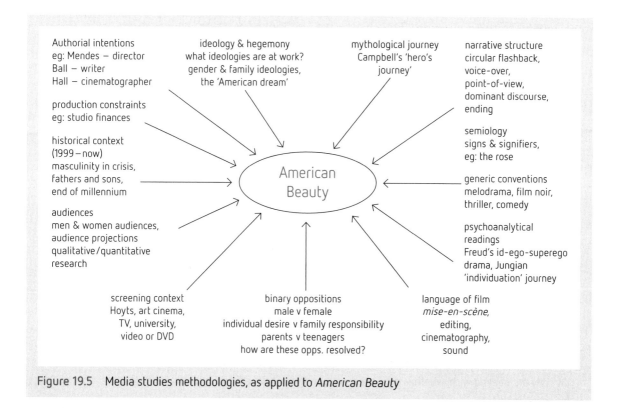

Figure 19.5   Media studies methodologies, as applied to *American Beauty*

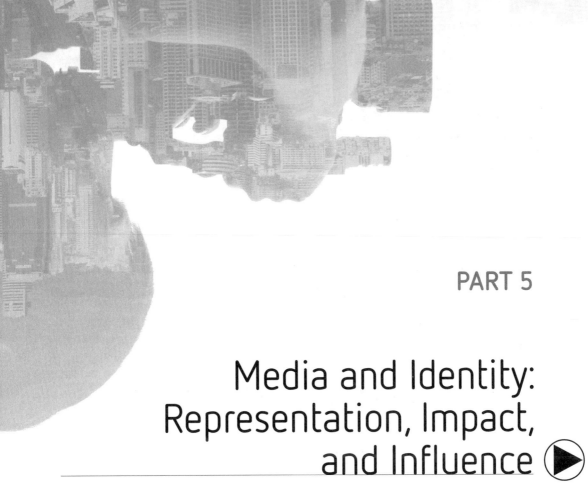

Media and Identity: Representation, Impact, and Influence

Representation as a cultural process establishes individual and collective identities, and symbolic systems provide possible answers to the questions: Who am I? What could I be? Who do I want to be?

Kathryn Woodward, *Identity and Difference*

OVERVIEW OF PART 5

In Part 5, the concepts of ideology and discourse will be used to examine media representations of gendered and ethnic identities. Stars and celebrities will be used as examples, and consideration will also be given to how gender and ethnicity are experienced in the real world. Hopefully, these chapters will have some personal relevance to you in understanding your own identity as female or male, your ethnic identity, and your own personal interest in stars and celebrities.

CHAPTER 20

Feminism, Postfeminism, and Ideologies of Femininity

Feminism has fought no wars. It has killed no opponents. It has set up no concentration camps, starved no enemies, practised no cruelties. Its battles have been for education, for the vote, for better working conditions, for safety on the streets, for child care, for social welfare, for rape crisis centres, women's refuges, reforms in the law. If someone says 'Oh, I'm not a feminist', I ask 'Why? What's your problem?'

Dale Spender, Man Made Language

This chapter will

▶ differentiate between sex and gender

▶ outline the nature/nurture debate

▶ discuss patriarchy and feminism

▶ consider the development of feminism and postfeminism

▶ analyse textual representations of women to show how femininity is constructed in the media.

The role of the media in identity formation is complex and contested. Rather than claiming that particular media texts have direct effects on the way we see ourselves and others, this chapter and the chapters that follow will consider the media as agents of socialisation, carriers of culture, and ways of communicating ideology. After introducing some key terms related to identity and gender studies, feminism and ideologies of femininity will be discussed, and a range of texts that illustrate how women are constructed and represented in the media will be analysed. The analyses focus on the contradictory ideologies and discourses of femininity found in advertising imagery since the 1990s. The aim is to see how certain ideological shifts have occurred in response to feminism and how these have both progressive and regressive potential. As such, this is a good example of ideological work, of the struggle over the maintenance of male hegemony, and of the simultaneous appearance of different ideological positions in the media. These points extend the discussion of ideology, discourse, and hegemony found in Part 3.

Sex and gender: What's the difference?

In thinking about the categories of male and female, masculinity and femininity, it is useful to make a distinction between two defining terms: 'sex' and 'gender'. Sexual difference is a biological distinction based on male and female genitalia and chromosomal and hormonal differences. Gender is about social and cultural roles, personality traits, and behaviours that are deemed socially acceptable for men and women in relation to concepts of masculinity and femininity. Gender study arises from concerns about the relative social positions of men and women, and about the social inequalities and the social struggles between them. Our interest in the question of gender comes from the fact that sex and gender are two of the most important ways that humans classify themselves and other people.

Gender issues also intersect with sexual desire and sexual expression. Sexuality, in Western culture, is often connected with heterosexuality, love, marriage, and the family. The social institutions of marriage and the family are ideally meant to include, and be the natural outlet for, sexual feelings and sexual expression. The dominant ideology has been that people find love and sexual satisfaction in monogamous relationships and in families, although the reality is that these social institutions coexist with other forms of sexual and emotional relationships. An explanation of gender identity, sexuality, and social experience enhances our understandings of ourselves, our families, and our roles in the communities and social structures in which we live.

Biological essentialism *vs* the social construction of gender

The nature/nurture debate asks: Which factor has the strongest influence on the development of gender identity—nature (biological and genetic factors) or nurture (social expectations)?

One of the major arguments about gender is between essentialist definitions of gender and the view that gender is a social construction. The **biological essentialist** position sees gender as being based on genetic, biological, and psychological differences. It holds that men and women are essentially (inevitably) different in their biological and emotional make-up, and that this determines how they feel and act. An essentialist would argue that due to hormones and physiology, women are naturally more nurturing and gentle because they are built to breed and care for children. Men are naturally more competitive, aggressive, smart, and powerful because of testosterone and a stronger musculature that enables them to protect their mate and young. Essentialism naturalises dominant ideologies of gender, heterosexuality, and patriarchy. It reduces everything to inescapable binary oppositions with no possibility of change, deviation, or development.

The **social constructionist** position sees gender characteristics as a consequence of how people are socialised. Even as children males and females are treated differently and encounter attitudes and beliefs (some present in media texts and narratives, some directly experienced through social interaction) that shape our expectations of how we should behave and what we might achieve. A constructivist would argue that it is these social pressures, not the particular physiology or aptitudes that we are born with, that primarily influence the formation of adult identity. A cultural studies approach to media analysis aims to deconstruct identity and subjectivity. It shows that who we think we are is a result of a series of interpellations, discourses, and social structures into which we are born: ethnicity, class, and gender position, alongside nationality and language, structure people's identities and subjectivities. Through analysis these identities are questioned, destabilised, and undermined, challenging 'commonsense' assumptions about what is normal or natural. You might ask yourself to what extent you think that your own sexuality and your identity as a woman or a man are biologically determined or influenced by your family, culture, and education.

Essentialist and constructivist perspectives can also be extended to include race and sexuality and to support or undermine stereotypes and generalisations associated with these aspects of identity. This complex debate about biological essentialism and social construction cannot be resolved here. Our approach is to accept elements of both, but to stress the influence of socialisation.

> **biological essentialist**
> The belief that the physical body—the hormones, inherent instincts, and genetic predispositions etc.—defines the essence of identity and determines personality characteristics, behaviour, and abilities.

> **social constructionist**
> Sees identity as constructed by external social forces such as the media, family, education, religion, and expectations of community members.

Gender, queer theory, and the fluidity of identity

Judith Butler is a theorist who was influential in extending feminist analysis into a new field called 'queer theory'. Butler argues that all gender behaviour is 'performative' (Butler 1998). Men and women learn to embody gender roles through 'the structure of impersonation by which any gender is assumed … Gender is a kind of imitation for which there is no original' (Butler 1998, p. 722). However, this does not mean that we are always performing gender as though we are actors in a play, nor does it mean that we consciously enact femininity or masculinity. Instead, Butler is arguing that the requirements of our role as a girl or boy, then later as a woman or man, are ingrained in us since birth. One of the first things said when a baby is born is 'It's a boy!' or 'It's a girl!', and from that moment on we are conditioned to behave in a manner that 'matches' our sex—females are expected to be feminine, and males are expected to be masculine. For Butler, this conditioning means we are constantly repeating the behaviour and actions that society tells us 'belong' to the body we inhabit (female or male). We are all *doing* a gender rather than *being* a gender. For Butler, 'doing gender' in this way is actually what creates our identity and sense of self, and there is no essential reality behind these roles. Women and men are socialised into a compulsory performance of normal gender roles that they must perform on pain of ostracism, violence, punishment, and repression. Two questions are crucial here: first, what range of roles and identities are available for women and men? and second, are these roles performative or is there something that makes women essentially feminine and men essentially masculine?

Deborah Cameron (2007) cites the contemporary popular idea that 'men are from Mars and women are from Venus' as an idea that supports the myth of gender difference—that men and women are different beings from alien planets and therefore speak different kinds of language. Cameron points out that the reality is that we live in a society and time in Western cultures where differences between men and women have actually become less and less marked over the past forty to fifty years; consequently, no group of women and men in history has ever been so similar as affluent Western men and women are, sharing the same educational opportunities, career opportunities, aspirations, and values. She believes that the myth of profound difference is being used to reassure people that gender difference does still matter. She argues that in people's minds gender does still make a difference and is very important to our sense of identity, our social relations, and our sexual relations; people don't want to think it's just a trivial difference, such as being left or right handed. But Cameron doesn't accept that there is a profound difference. The debate surrounding biological essentialism and social construction also relates to questions about sexuality: are people born heterosexual, homosexual, or bisexual, or do they acquire a sexual orientation during the course of their life, and how does sexuality relate to gender behaviour?

These questions affect everyone in a very personal way because our gender identity and our sexual identity are fundamental to how we understand ourselves. Many people are very passionate about their stance on the matter, which is reflected in public debate about these issues. For example, when Lady Gaga's song 'Born This Way' was released it was widely interpreted to be promoting the notion that people are 'born' gay or straight, in the same way people are born blue-eyed, black-skinned,

Chinese, or Italian. The popularity of the song prompted a number of people to weigh in on the essentialist versus constructionist debate in public forums such as blog sites and newspaper columns. The tensions between essentialism and constructionism became apparent in these discussions, which represented the differing positions on the topic. Some argued that people are indeed born gay or straight, and many of them held this idea up as another reason why gay people should not be persecuted for their sexual orientation—these people took the stance that you can't help who you are if you are born that way, and people should not be discriminated against for things out of their control. Others asserted that nobody is 'born' gay or straight, because all sexuality categories, including heterosexuality, are socially constructed. (Importantly, this is a different position from one that maintains heterosexuality is the norm and homosexuality is an aberrant 'choice'.) Still others upheld that there are both essential and constructed elements of gender and sexuality.

You, as readers, might note that we, as authors, have stressed gender differences throughout this book. Do you think this means we are supporting the myth of difference, the oppositional duality of men and women, or are we drawing your attention to the way the media and culture construct these differences for us?

Patriarchy

Society is based not just on different genders but also on unequally positioned genders: masculinity and femininity are differently valued. **Patriarchy** is a system based on the law of the father. This is so in two ways: first, through lineage (children are given their father's family name rather than their mother's); and second, through the legal and political institutions that, although no longer given over into the exclusive power of men, have developed as male institutions. In the past women could not hold political office, they were excluded from voting rights (women won the right to vote only after protracted struggle), they had lesser legal rights, and married women were regarded as the property of their husbands. Religion is one of the last major institutions still divided over the issue of whether women have the right to hold positions of power, as evident in the news article about gender equity and Islam ('Saudis Acknowledge Women Exist' discussed on pp. 86–9), and the struggle of women to be ordained in the Anglican and Catholic Churches.

Historically, most cultures have privileged men with greater rights than women, and most continue to give them greater benefits in terms of power and wages. This denigration of femininity, alongside the inequality in power between the sexes, can lead to a sexist, **misogynist** society as well as to a rejection of men's own gentler characteristics.

patriarchy
A social structure in which the father or a male figure is the leader and descent is reckoned on the male line. Masculine power and authority dominate social, political, and economic institutions, thereby oppressing women.

misogyny
Hatred of women and femininity (literally, hatred of the womb).

Feminism

feminism
The movement for women's
equality and liberation.

Feminism has had an enormous impact on society. Initially, feminists fought for women's social, legal, political, and economic rights, and attempted to understand how the construction of femininity was related to the status of women. This altered understandings of gender roles and identities and led to important social changes that had far-reaching impacts on women and men.

Feminism should be understood in the context of a long history of patriarchy and the oppression of women that stretches back through the centuries. The history of feminism has many stages, sometimes described as first-wave feminism, second-wave feminism, and third-wave feminism. First-wave feminism can be traced back to the late eighteenth century but was at its peak between 1880 and the 1920s, during which time the focus was on legal advances in the public sphere. The emphasis of the first wave of feminism was on attaining full citizenship, legal equity, and recognition that women should have the same rights and opportunities enjoyed by other citizens, including the right to vote. The efforts of early feminists such as Mary Wollstonecraft, author of *A Vindication of the Rights of Woman* (written in 1792), included the struggle for emancipation and suffrage (the right to vote). In the nineteenth century and the early twentieth century, first-wave feminism involved novelists such as George Eliot (a woman) and Virginia Woolf, and political theorists such as John Stuart Mill and his wife Harriet Taylor Mill, all of whom raised questions about women's rights, duties, and responsibilities.

The most well-known strand of feminism, now known as second-wave feminism, emerged in the late 1960s and it has had enormous influence on Western society. Where the earlier feminist movement had concentrated on gaining equity for women in the public sphere, the second wave of feminism acknowledged that the oppression of women in a patriarchal system also extends to the private sphere, including personal relationships. This insight is expressed in the slogan 'The personal is political', marking a shift to include concerns such as domestic violence, women's reproductive rights (abortion and contraception), childcare, relationships, the body, emotions, and sexuality. The second-wave feminist struggle against sexual oppression and harassment focused on the exploitation of women through sex and on how women's bodies and appearances are controlled and valued. Consciousness raising groups raised an awareness of the ways in which women (as well as men) have internalised patriarchal expectations, and sought to liberate women from pre-conceptions of how they ought to behave. Feminist analyses of the media also critiqued the way women tend to be visually represented as sexual objects, developing a body of theory to analyse and understand this practice (see, for example, Mulvey's work in the field of feminist psychoanalysis and film studies, pp. 274–6).

Since that time, and particularly since the 1980s, there have been many new developments and debates in relation to the social roles of women and men, and the construction of gender and sexual identities. Different strands of feminism have developed, and there have also been reactions against feminism. *Backlash: The Undeclared War Against American Women* is the title of a book by feminist author Susan Faludi. This book looks at developments, particularly in the USA, that suggest that patriarchy has been fighting the advances that women have made over the last few decades (Faludi 1992). Faludi cites the men's movement and commentators such as Robert Bly as part of this backlash, and points to the misogyny in films such as *Fatal Attraction* and *Basic Instinct* as further examples. The backlash has been successful insofar as feminism has taken on negative connotations, including, ironically, that feminists are unfeminine (hairy, power-hungry, butch lesbian separatists who aim to oppress men). This perception has led some women (and men) to reject feminism.

The advertisement shown in Figure 20.1, which is aimed at men, is deliberately politically incorrect and as such can be seen as part of the backlash against feminism. The caption 'What's wrong with this picture?' implies that there is nothing wrong with the fantasy that women should look sexy while devoting themselves to domestic labour for men who ogle their bodies and laze about on the couch. The punch line, 'You never mix your whites with your coloureds', jokingly suggests that the only thing wrong is that the woman hasn't sorted the laundry properly. It combines a knowingness about feminist debates around the unequal division of domestic labour and the sexual objectification of women with the suggestion that men have certain instinctive, essential, sexual drives that can only be satisfied by treating women as objects of visual, and ultimately sexual, pleasure. Note that the context of reception also influences interpretation of the image in significant ways. In South Africa, for

Figure 20.1   Advertisement for *RALPH* magazine

Source: *RALPH* magazine, 1997

instance, a country sensitive to racial discrimination, the advertisement would be read within the discourse of gender politics and political incorrectness, but the punch line takes on added significance.

'Third-wave feminism' tends to be used as an umbrella term to describe an era of feminist thinking that has developed since the 1980s. While first- and second-wave feminism stressed the construction of femininity and fought for equality with men, some third-wave feminists argue that there might be important differences between men and women (and between women) and that traditional feminine qualities and characteristics need to be revalidated and endorsed. The intersection of contemporary feminist theory with a body of theory by and about lesbians has been particularly productive in this respect, in that it recognises that women's desires do not necessarily revolve around men, marriage, and family. Many third-wave feminists have also acknowledged that although patriarchy privileges men, men also seem to suffer from it in various ways. Many men have come to feel the privilege of paid employment (being, or having to be, the breadwinner) and the exemption from parenting duties as a burden in the first instance and a sacrifice in the second.

Third-wave feminism has explored the fact that much first- and second-wave feminist theory was the product of the white, middle-class elite that did not understand or include the experiences of women of colour. The African American feminist theorist bell hooks spells her name with lower-case letters to signify the fact that she is a member of a doubly marginalised group and that being a woman of colour differentiates her experiences from those of white women. Feminism, hooks claims, should be opposed to all systems of domination (including oppression on the basis of race, class, sexuality, and gender; see hooks 2000). This careful attention to difference, diversity, and the historical or contextual specificity of women's experiences is a core characteristic of third-wave feminism, and it arose from feminist critiques of homogeneity that date back to civil rights movements in the 1960s and 1970s. The third wave of feminism is also characterised by a focus on youth movements and issues, and a critical resistance to earlier codes of feminist behaviour or appearance (for example, body hair as a symbol of resistance to patriarchal norms).

Postfeminism

postfeminism
The term can be used to suggest that feminism is in the past, is outdated, no longer relevant to contemporary gender dynamics. Alternatively, postfeminism can refer to a postmodern approach to feminism, and/or contemporary critiques of earlier feminisms.

The term '**postfeminism**' is often used in relation to theories and ideas that reject much of earlier feminist orthodoxy and/or that embrace a postmodern approach to feminism (see Chapter 24 for a discussion of postmodernism). There is a tension between two different understandings of postfeminism. On the one hand, postfeminism is associated with antifeminist discourse and with the sense that we have entered an era after feminism, in which resistance to patriarchal oppression is no longer necessary. On the other hand, postfeminist theory is a sophisticated postmodern or poststructural critique of earlier approaches to feminism that were seen as being extreme, essentialist, caught up in dualisms, or flawed and misguided in other ways. Interestingly, feminism has had such an impact on both the media and society that its fundamental insights and goals have, in many ways, been internalised and affirmed in both these strands of postfeminist discourse. Some postfeminists take the benefits of first- and second-wave feminism for granted: it is from a position of increased equity and changed attitudes that they are able to critique earlier feminist positions. Postfeminism is thus distinct from feminism in the 1960s and 1970s and challenges this feminism, but at the same time it is still built on and linked to earlier feminist movements. There is an extensive body of research and writing related to this field that you may well want to pursue further yourself.

The limitations of second-wave feminism

Postfeminist theory articulates the limitations in earlier feminisms, which can be broadly categorised as follows.

Second-wave feminism and sex

Recent feminist theory suggests that earlier perspectives on sexuality were restricted and restrictive. In the struggle to shift definitions and representations of women away from the purely sexual, second-wave feminism objected strongly to media texts in which the female body was sexualised. These feminists argued that such representations interpellated the audience into a masculine subject position, encouraging viewers to take pleasure in the controlling, possessive gaze and participate in the process of sexual objectification. These critiques of objectification still have force and we may still rightly object to women being reduced to images that sell commodities by making men think about sex. The danger in this is that the attempt to control objectification also censors women's efforts to represent and express their own sexuality, or to enjoy media representations of female sexuality. While this aspect of second-wave feminism can be seen as repressive of women's sexuality, it should be noted that women's magazines today do not display any such aversion to sex or sexuality. They are full of articles, information, stories, and pictures that explicitly explore issues of female sexuality.

There is currently a host of new possibilities for women in terms of the expression of sexuality (Tasker & Negra 2007; McRobbie 2009; Taylor 2012). The opening up of these possibilities is partly related to the reappropriation or reclaiming of particular signifiers of femininity. Wearing make-up, for example, may at first seem to undermine the feminist position that a woman's worth is not located in her appearance, or in her status as an object that is sexually appealing to men, but postfeminists may wear make-up in a way that draws attention to the artifice involved in beautification, inviting the viewer to recognise that a mask is being worn. It can thus be worn with irony, humour, and playfulness, and thereby become part of a game that involves playing with identity and celebrating femininity. This play with identity challenges essential notions of the self, and makes it acceptable, in feminist terms, for women to create different identities for themselves through make-up, hairstyles, and clothes. Apart from giving women the freedom to be ironic and knowing about their assumption of feminine identities, make-up can also be used as an instrument of power in relation to men, allowing women to assert their sexual attractiveness as power over men. Some recent advertising campaigns for make-up (see, for example, Figure 20.2) show it being worn aggressively rather than enticingly.

Another form of asserting a postfeminist position, or 'girl power', was evident in a clothing brand called Bad Girl, marketed using a logo with a halo over it (subverting the good girl–bad girl division by celebrating the deviance of the bad girl). In her influential book *Bad Girls: The Media, Sex and Feminism in the 90s* (Lumby 1997), postfeminist theorist Catharine Lumby explores the positions of a new generation of feminists in debates about pornography, censorship, and the media. Signs of oppression (such as the label 'bad girl', or even images of sexism and objectification) can thus be reclaimed and reused by the oppressed group, in this case women, as a sign of power and agency. For more recent developments in this area of scholarship, see Angela McRobbie's critique of postfeminist culture and promiscuity in *The Aftermath of Feminism* (2009) or Anthea Taylor's *Single Women in Popular Culture: The Limits of Postfeminism* (2011).

Figure 20.2　Advertisement for 17 Cosmetics. The caption reads: It's not make-up, it's ammunition. 'I'm the last bird you'll peck on the cheek, mate.'

Source: *17 Cosmetics*, 1998; photograph by Mosche Brakha

Valuing differences between women and men

The second general limitation of second-wave feminism has been seen as its approach to questions of differences between men and women. Over time feminist theorists have attempted to understand what constitutes women's identities, and to explore the issue of whether gender identity is essential or constructed (Butler 1990). Postfeminists and third-wave feminists develop the point about the construction of femininity further, suggesting that all gender roles for men and women are socially constructed and that gender categories are themselves subject to question.

Class and ethnicity in feminism

Postfeminism challenges the perceived dominance of white, middle-class voices in second-wave feminism by taking care to include a range of women's voices and positions. The experiences and concerns of a black, or so-called coloured, South African woman will have similarities with, but not be identical to, the experiences and concerns of a Maori woman, a well-off Singaporean business woman, or a white female academic from California or London. Each of these women will experience patriarchy in distinct ways, and no woman can speak for all of them.

Feminism today

Earlier feminism was not a simple, unified set of ideas. It was a variety of evolving positions that, despite sharing the overall objective of developing women's lives for the better, differed on how this was to be achieved. Many current female students are members of third-wave feminist and postfeminist generations; they were born into a world where they are treated differently from the way their mothers were treated, and they have opportunities that their mothers never had (male students have also been affected by these new ways of living). It is interesting that many people take these 'new' rights for women—the ones that first- and second-wave feminism fought for—as given and many do not want to label themselves as feminists. While they are the product of feminism and support many of its ideals, they also challenge it. These contested ideas about femininity and feminism emerge in a variety of media texts.

Lady Gaga is one example of a contemporary female icon who adheres to social expectations regarding sexualised femininity but also pushes the boundaries of how a female can and should be understood. Gaga is slim and attractive, and is widely known to have had plastic surgery to make her face more traditionally appealing. Like many other female pop stars, most of her songs are about romantic relationships, sex, and nightclub culture; and she often reveals a lot of skin in her video clips. In these ways, Gaga can be seen to have moved away from the older ideals of feminism to prioritise beauty and sexual relationships with men. However, this does not mean that Gaga is antifeminist, but rather third-wave or postfeminist. She extends the perimeters of what is acceptable regarding female representation, and therefore opens up new possibilities for how women might be valued and how they might express themselves.

First, she is known for her eccentric, artistic fashion, which is frequently 'unsexy' (for example, see the discussion of Gaga's meat dress on pp. 137–8, Plate 5). Second, her film clips include the energetic group dances and provocative posing that are now commonplace in this medium, yet Gaga's film clips also feature elements that are confronting and subversive. For example: glasses frames made from smoking cigarettes, lurching dancing, coffin pods for 'monsters', swallowing rosary beads, and simulated birth scenes complete with goo. The third point relates to the persona she has built up. Gaga has labelled herself 'Mother Monster' and calls her millions of fans her 'little monsters'. In this way, she is a self-proclaimed 'Lady' and 'Mother', but she merges this with ideas about monstrosity. Hence, Gaga can be seen to embody accepted forms of sexualised femininity but she also exaggerates and subverts these, creating a spectacle and asking us to reflect on her as an artist. It is interesting to think about the different reactions people have had to Lady Gaga; to what extent are their responses influenced by older notions of femininity and womanhood?

Earlier feminist concerns and struggles produced many social changes that are now part of the media landscape and that feature in contemporary life for women:

- equal rights in terms of pay and job opportunities
- challenges to sexual discrimination and sexual harassment
- acceptance that women can enter any field of work
- acceptance that having children does not preclude full participation in the paid workforce and in public life generally, because caring for children should not be just women's work but a shared parental and social responsibility
- increased maternity benefits
- more freedom in terms of marriage and divorce
- a greater understanding and privileging of women's feelings, skills, and sexualities.

This rosy picture should not disguise the fact that women are still discriminated against in numerous ways: women's political power, in terms of parliamentary representation, is low, and struggles around equal pay, childcare facilities, violence against women, and general misogynist tendencies continue.

Case study: Women and advertisements

Advertisements featuring and addressed to women are a good place to look at media ideologies and discourses of femininity. The following examples (Figures 20.3–20.5, and Plates 3 and 4) show some contradictory aspects of the construction of femininity in the contemporary, postfeminist era. Take a few minutes to look at each and consider what in them is significant in relation to constructions of femininity.

Some of the advertisements appear to offer women some pleasure and some power, and thus appear to have progressive aspects, while at the same time being traditional and patriarchal; others present a postfeminist perspective.

Advertisement 1

The Wedgwood advertisement (Figure 20.3) is interesting in the way it wins a female audience over to very traditional aspects of marriage. It is the most conservative of the four images. It wins women through its mode of address, the pleasures it offers, and by masking or displacing potentially problematic issues to do with marriage. Initially, it is useful to consider what the implied narrative underpinning the image might be (you may wish to refer back to the section on implied narrative, p. 145). Ask yourself what has just happened in the scene depicted in the advertisement, and what is going to happen next? It looks as though the wedding ceremony (the service) has finished, and the couple appear to be relaxing after the reception, at the beginning of their honeymoon. Honeymoons traditionally feature three things: ordering room service from the honeymoon suite in a hotel, the ritual of unwrapping wedding gifts, and, of course, consummating the relationship.

Figure 20.3   Advertisement for Wedgwood dinner service

Source: 'Happy Wedding Day' advertisement 1994, reproduced with permission of Wedgwood, Barlaston, Stoke-on-Trent, England

Mode of address

Mode of address (see p. 186) refers to the different ways in which a text speaks to or addresses its audience. In this advertisement, who is speaking to whom? We read it as though it is a woman speaker addressing other women for four reasons.

1   The woman in the photograph is looking more directly at the camera (and therefore, at us, the audience) than is the man.
2   The caption talks about 'service' being received, and because it is the woman who is being served by the man holding the bottle, it is therefore her speaking.
3   Weddings are traditionally a feminine topic—men would not normally be represented in the media as discussing marriage in this way.
4   The advertisement appears in *Mode Brides*, a magazine aimed at, and bought and read by, women.

The advertisement thus foregrounds a woman's voice and women's discourses, and consequently gives women power, even if it is within the traditional context of marriage, historically a bulwark of patriarchy. She is the person commenting on, describing, and consequently owning this event, which is appropriate, since the bride and her family traditionally organise (and pay for) the wedding.

Pleasure

One of the ways in which hegemony works is by winning the consent of subordinate groups and persuading them to accept their position by offering certain pleasures. Numerous pleasures for women are made available in this advertisement.

- *Humour* There are three puns in the caption to this advertisement. In addition to the simple meaning of 'wedding service', the word 'service' can mean dinner service (crockery and cutlery), room service, and sexual services.
- *Sexual pleasure* Narratively, the picture suggests that the wedding has just happened and the honeymoon is about to commence. In the context, the bottle and the champagne are phallic, as they suggest the sexual activity that lies ahead for the bride and groom. In the context of the pun on sexual services, the advertisement is also suggesting that the woman will be pleasured by the groom (that he will service her).
- *Wealth* The setting is beautiful and the scene is pleasingly photographed, suggesting wealth through the furnishings, the clothing, the garden in the background, and, most importantly, through the expensive and tasteful dinner service.
- *The traditionally feminine pleasures of marriage* The traditionally feminine dreams of, and excitement over, marriage are referenced here, as is the common perception that a woman's wedding day is the most exciting day of her life.

Masking and displacing

This is a wonderful example of ideological work. In this picture, women's domestic work is subtly acknowledged, but is then masked behind other pleasures. The advertisement wants us to answer the question 'What will happen next?' with 'She will receive ecstatic sexual pleasure'. But there is an alternative answer: over the years of her marriage, she will do lots of cooking, serving of meals, and washing up. While this labour is alluded to by the dinner service, which is designed for these domestic routines, it is masked by the way the dinner service becomes an aesthetic object of beauty and pleasure, a gift.

Women's domestic labour is also displaced by the fact that the advertisement depicts the woman being served (and suggests that she will later be serviced sexually)—by her husband—thereby drawing attention away from the fact that women in marriages tend to be the servers rather than those who are served. A feminist saying of the 1970s states 'It starts when you sink in his arms and ends with your arms in his sink'. This nicely points out the way that, for women, the discourse of romance and pleasure can often turn into the reality of domestic drudgery in traditional gender relations. In this advertisement the discourse of romance and pleasure is used to outweigh the realities of what marriage is for most women. While the wedding gifts are potentially a reminder of this housework, their beauty distracts the audience from this unsavoury allusion.

This advertisement shows how the foregrounding of interests and pleasures may win women over to traditional feminine roles.

Advertisement 2

Ideological contradictions and ideological work are demonstrated well in the Continental Slim-a-Soup advertisement (Figure 20.4). Like the Wedgwood advertisement, this one plays with the theme of women's sexuality and their relatively new sexual freedom. But it goes on to place severe limitations on it and finally channels women's desire into more traditional avenues.

Women's desire

Women's desire is foregrounded through the sexually appealing image of the man. The female audience is invited to take sexual pleasure in objectifying the man, thus acknowledging active female sexuality.

Restrictions on women's desires

Having invited women to take sexual pleasure in viewing the man, the advertisement then negates this through a focus on health discourses and by playing on the guilt associated with contravening social norms related to body shape and passive sexuality. Safe sex is a major issue confronting us today. This advertisement advocates safe sex as no sex. Instead of tackling safe sex in terms of safe sexual practices, women are encouraged to displace their desire back into the safer arena of food. This displacement is reinforced by making viewers feel guilty. Guilt has traditionally been used by Christianity (and other religions) to suppress sexuality for men and women. The West represses sexuality in many ways, but at the same time, through advertising and other popular media products, consistently foregrounds sexual desire. This is one of the fascinating contradictions of Western culture. Sexual advertising may work because people are sexually repressed, since desire works on the basis of absence or lack. If people were sexually happy, these advertisements, which seem to be offering us sexual satisfaction through the purchase of goods, would not work. People would not need to buy the goods because they would already be sexually satisfied. Consequently, advertisers need people to be sexually repressed. This advertisement suggests that if the narrator followed her sexual desire, she would feel guilty.

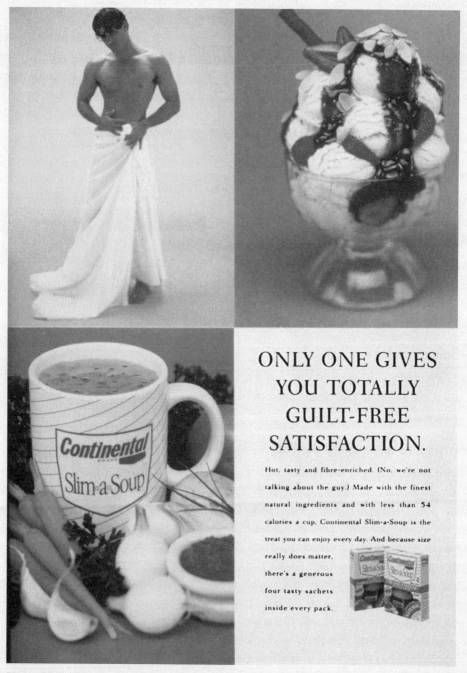

ONLY ONE GIVES YOU TOTALLY GUILT-FREE SATISFACTION.

Hot, tasty and fibre-enriched. (No, we're not talking about the guy.) Made with the finest natural ingredients and with less than 54 calories a cup, Continental Slim-a-Soup is the treat you can enjoy every day. And because size really does matter, there's a generous four tasty sachets inside every pack.

Figure 20.4 Continental Soup advertisement

Source: Continental Brand Foods

Food

This advertisement proposes that the substitute for sex is food. The ice cream is presented as desirable (including the phallic chocolate wafer) but while female desire is acknowledged, it is simultaneously dismissed. Ice cream, like sex, will not be good for the female reader (even though she might want them both). Vegetable soup, however, will be. Again this draws on a health discourse (of nutrition). While it is undoubtedly true that vegetables are healthier than sweets, the real reason women are being asked to reject ice cream is because of physical appearance. The suggestion is that consuming ice cream will make women fat and as a result they will not conform to (male) ideals of femininity. There is indeed an interesting reference to size in the advertising copy ('and because size really does matter'), which, while it is partly a joke about how women may enjoy sex with well-endowed men, it is also a subtle reminder to women to be conscious of their own size, weight, and appearance. Consequently, the narrative resolution and structure of this advertisement is to present various forbidden pleasures for women that are then finally denied, in the guise of a health discourse, in favour of traditional values.

The advertisement offers aspects of a progressive discourse about women's sexuality but then incorporates them back into a traditional view of feminine roles and ideal femininity.

Advertisement 3

This advertisement (Plate 3) was intended to show that fashion is something that is in your blood, or under your skin—a sense of style that is innate and distinctive, like the fashionable clothing produced by the Young Designers Emporium; however, a number of key signifiers in the ad work to convey a more unsettling message about women, vanity, and physical appearance. The Jupiter Drawing Room, the advertising agency that created the image, noted that they were playing on an awareness that the youth market tends to be attracted to things that shock their parents' generation. Another advertisement in this series depicts a young woman drawing a red ribbon out of her wrist, with the caption 'In your blood'. The configuration of the initials 'Y D E' on the page reads 'DYE' or, phonetically, 'die', thus connoting death and creating an association between death and the fashion industry in which fabric and coloured dyes are so important. Presumably, Young Designers' clothes are desirable enough to die for, if you are the kind of person who has an innate sense of style, a person who has fashion 'in your blood'. The resemblance between the red fabric or ribbon and blood reinforces the connotations of death, leading critics to interpret the advertisements as images of suicide. These oppositional readings are extreme, but a semiotic analysis does reveal links between the image and the phrase 'fashion victim', and between that phrase and many other media representations of women as victims (victims of violence and crime and sexual abuse, victims in slasher films, and so on).

The phrase 'fashion victim' and the advertising image itself are particularly powerful because the woman is deliberately cutting herself, and it connects to social realities in disturbing ways. For many women, being a fashion victim and obsessing over appearances hurts only the bank balance, but it can also lead to plastic surgery, eating disorders, and other forms of self-wounding. This is related to the actual site of the cut on the body of the woman in the image, and to the tape over her breasts (which is similar to the kind of tape models use in fashion shoots). The 'wound' is over her uterus, a part of the body associated with uniquely female forms of power and creativity. While it is true that many young women channel their creativity into designing their own clothing or style, and into many areas other than family and children, the image looks like an attack on the heart of femininity itself, in the form of abdominal surgery (like a caesarean or hysterectomy).

The Young Designers Emporium advertisement makes a radical statement asserting the importance of the traditionally feminine preoccupation with fashion and style by suggesting that such interests are not superficial but actually run deep under the skin and in the blood as a creative force. While validating fashion as a serious interest, the image is simultaneously sending a negative message to and about women, and thus it communicates contradictory ideologies of femininity.

Advertisement 4

Axe (also known as Lynx in the UK, Ireland, New Zealand, Australia, and China) 'Rise' is a shower gel whose target market is young, heterosexual men, and whose main selling point is that the smell is supposed to be irresistible to women. This image (Plate 4) is a still from an online digital video advertising campaign that shows a man wake up, shower, get ready, and leave his apartment without paying any attention to the beautiful women who surround him, blending into the background of his life. The text for the ad reads 'Look at this guy. He just missed out on 10 hot girls. But so did you. Rise up and stay alert'. The women are artfully camouflaged with body paint to blend in with the rug, the walls, and the furniture. This clever strategy makes the audience want to forward the ad to friends and watch it more than once until they have spotted all the hidden women. On one hand, the advertisement is just another example in which women are literally objectified in order to sell a product with the promise of sex (why else would the man need to 'rise up'?). On the other hand, the advertisement is criticising men who are perhaps blinded by unrealistic expectations and gender fantasies promoted in the mass media. It encourages men to notice the beauty of women who are already in their lives, women who come in all different colours, shapes, and sizes, but who blend into the background because they don't flaunt themselves.

Advertisement 5

Nobody Denim (Figure 20.5) offers a good example of postfeminist advertising strategies. The label itself is playfully reworking the idea that most media images of women feature models so thin that they have practically 'no body', and are 'nobodies' lacking in individuality because they all have the same stereotypical kind of beauty. The caption 'Do u measure up?' (using the SMS abbreviation of 'you') is a self-conscious reference to the famous Levi's campaign, 'Do you fit the legend?', implying that Nobody Denim is in the same league as Levi's and that the customer has to be good enough to fit the clothes, rather than the other way around. The advertisement is part of a series that features models tied up with tape measures, with another tape measure visible in the background linking the images. This could all be interpreted as yet another media message that young people have to be thin and wear designer labels in order to measure up to media ideals of beauty; however, the advertisement's playful appropriation of stereotypes and its incorporation of gender ambiguity situates it firmly in postmodern terrain and reveals an awareness of feminist critiques of the beauty myth (see Wolf 1990). One panel of the advertisement shows a young woman in heavy make-up wearing a T-shirt with the word 'Foxy' across the breast, and another shows three figures from the waist down, their backs to the camera, posing as though they are at a urinal. These three models wear jeans, and nothing else. At least one of the models has a clearly defined waist, signifying femininity. At least one could be either male or female, so the advertisement makes us laugh by manipulating our expectations about gender and making fun of the feminist slogan 'Anything a man can do, a woman can do better'. The implicit critique of media images that exploit female sexuality and promote unhealthy ideals though is subtle and can readily be overlooked, in which case the advertisement may reinforce the norms of which it is making fun.

Figure 20.5   Advertisement for the clothing label Nobody Denim: 'Do u Measure Up?'

Source: Courtesy of Avant Card

The danger with postfeminism's devil-may-care attitude about gender and sexuality, evident in some postfeminist media texts, is that it assumes that gender relations and the power dynamics they entail are issues that have been resolved, rather than being ongoing concerns linked to race, class, and other forms of identity and oppression. Many depict assertive female characters who don't give a damn about issues such as sexism because they already have the benefits of equal opportunity; the models in the Nobody Denim advertisement are all slender, young, fair-skinned, and beautiful, and they look as though they come from privileged, middle-class backgrounds.

Conclusion

These are complex advertisements in their mixture of discourses and the way they present different aspects of ideologies about femininity. Many contemporary advertisements offer something positive to women but ultimately reassert aspects of traditional femininity. In this way we can see a hegemonic struggle taking place: women win something, but the traditional roles and power relations are not ultimately shifted. Others are more obviously challenging. Significantly, in modern advertising we can see evidence of a heightened degree of awareness about the problems inherent in the objectification of women, the denigration of traditionally female spheres

368 Part 5 Media and Identity: Representation, Impact, and Influence

of interest, and the representation of women in passive or stereotypical roles. Feminist critiques of the media and society have caused us to question the commodification and objectification of the female body, denaturalising patriarchal ideology. Even though sexist representations are still present in the media, media producers and media audiences now recognise that they are problematic and audiences are more likely to view such images with humour, irony, or a critical eye rather than accepting them unquestioningly. These images enable us to use the critical tools of ideology, hegemony, and discourse as a way of understanding what they are doing.

In relation to the wider social hegemonic struggle between men and women Cameron (2007) voices an interesting perspective. Over the past fifty years in Western culture, women have won more and more power and equality and are now present in more aspects of the public sphere than ever before, including in the media where many women have important jobs. Consequently, it could be argued that, as women achieve power and bring their feminine values into the public arena, society is gradually being feminised. But Cameron suggests that actually the opportunities that have opened up for middle-class educated women, which in many ways make their lives more like men's, depend on a focus on individual achievement and individual freedom, whereas women's lives in every social class used to revolve around their domestic, reproductive, and caring responsibilities, carried out in the community as well as home. So in order for women to take up positions of power they have to become more like men and therefore society has been masculinised because the values that people are living by are symbolically or traditionally masculine values such as being focused on the individual, or on getting ahead.

This chapter has

- outlined major terms and concepts for understanding gender
- considered the issue of biological essentialism versus social construction
- traced the history and developments of feminism
- examined in detail how women are represented in advertisements
- considered the social role of women from a hegemonic perspective.

Discussion points

1   Discuss the pros and cons of the nature versus nature debate in relation to the construction of femininity and masculinity.
2   All gender behaviour is performance. Discuss.
3   How valid do you find third-wave feminism's criticisms of earlier feminism?
4   What's wrong or right with contemporary representations of women in advertising? Discuss, with examples.

Summary

You should now be able to

- articulate your own position in the nature versus nurture debate
- explain the arguments about gender between biological essentialism and social construction
- explain the difference between sex and gender
- define the terms 'patriarchy', 'feminism', 'misogyny', and 'postfeminism'
- outline the main concerns of the three waves of feminism and explain how and why feminist concerns have changed over time
- analyse how the different discourses of femininity present in media texts relate to patriarchal or feminist ideologies and to changing perceptions of gender roles.

CHAPTER 21

Ideologies and Discourses of Masculinity

Homo sapiens—male n. once dominant species on planet Earth, entered into swift decline in latter half of 20th century due to social, environmental and economic factors. Now confined almost exclusively to research-based sanctuaries around the world.

Encyclopaedia Britannica, 2090

This chapter will

▶ examine dominant masculinity and other variations

▶ consider the crisis of masculinity

▶ analyse media representations of men.

Representations and ideologies of masculinity have already been discussed a number of times (seeing *American Beauty*, and *The Day After Tomorrow*, as films that explore contemporary masculinity, p. 267). In the last chapter we examined feminism and ideologies of femininity and now we look at discourses and ideologies of masculinity in media representations and in real life. Our interest is in how these relate and how they contribute to masculine identity. It will also be useful for you to think about your own views about men and masculinity. What do you like best and what do you like least about men and masculinity (in the real world)? What male film stars, pop stars, and television personalities do you like most, and what characteristics do they have that you like? Think about how your answers relate to the rest of this chapter.

Introductory points

Patriarchy and masculinity

The previous chapter argued that we live in a patriarchal society. The dominant values of patriarchal society are linked to values encouraged in men and masculinity. Western society encourages competitiveness and individuality. It also encourages aggression and violence as ways of solving problems. All these values are central in the way we work, in the economic sphere, in terms of our education system, the way we interact socially, and in the ways boys are socialised into becoming men. You could say that warfare is the ultimate problem-solving device of patriarchy. Our culture still tends to validate such male characteristics while at the same time denigrating female characteristics and femininity.

Dominant and alternative ideals of masculinity

Just as with ideologies and femininities, we should remember that there is not only one version of masculinity but many possible variations of male behaviour: there are many masculinities. A short list of male stars demonstrates some different styles of masculinity: Johnny Depp, Seth Rogan, Brad Pitt, Jay Chou, Tiger Woods, Sam Worthington, Michael Cera, 50 Cent, Kanye West, Leonardo DiCaprio, and Charlie Sheen all offer something different. Different ethnic groups may have different masculinities: African American masculinities, for example, may be different from white masculinities.

However, as with ideology and femininity, there is a dominant ideal of masculinity. In the 1980s this ideal was epitomised by stars such as Arnold Schwarzenegger and Clint Eastwood, both of whom represented strength, toughness, attractiveness, heterosexuality, and whiteness. These ideals are still found at the beginning of the twenty-first century—but there are many other possibilities and the ideals are being questioned. The ideal version of dominant masculinity presents a problem for real men because it is so difficult to attain. Many comic actors draw attention to the impossibility of achieving perfect masculinity and point to its ridiculousness, but heroic film texts still predominate.

Alongside the media ideals there are also dominant versions of masculinity and femininity lived out in the real world, which is less clear-cut, but we argue that as a consequence of our socialisation and upbringing men and women are likely to develop certain patterns of typical behaviour. While the behaviour of some women and men will not conform to these patterns, it is still possible to see general tendencies in masculine and feminine behaviour and identity in how men and women act and feel.

Masculinity in crisis

Since the 1970s masculinity has become an issue in Western culture; people speak of masculinity being in crisis, which suggests that the old masculine ideals are no longer universally accepted and that people have begun to question what it means to be a man. Bookshops have sections on men's health and men's issues, universities have courses in men's studies, and there is an extensive research related to masculinity.

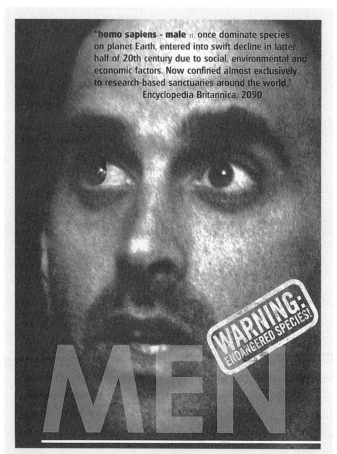

Figure 21.1 Extract from an article in *Cleo* magazine

Source: Text from *Cleo*, May 1998; photograph by Jasmine Martin

Jokes are made about and against men in the way they used to be made against women. Essentialist notions of identity are being challenged and people are beginning to realise that if gender roles are socially constructed they do not necessarily have to accept or respect the roles, values, and expectations that have been associated with masculinity. This crisis was prompted by two movements: feminism and the gay rights movement. Feminists, having first looked at and questioned the construction of femininity, then began to problematise masculinity, seeing it too as a social construction and also challenging some of the values associated with masculinity. Consequently, some men began to question and look at their own masculine identities.

Figure 21.1 is the opening text from an article published in *Cleo*. The article imagines a world in which men have become redundant. The text is a mock encyclopaedia entry on *Homo sapiens*. This article is typical of media products that comment on or make reference to a crisis in masculinity.

Three waves of critical masculinity studies

In parallel with the growth of feminism, the gay rights movement challenged the oppression of lesbians and gay men by heterosexist society. The gay movement offered many insights into both homosexual and heterosexual masculinity and challenged some of the stereotypes of so-called normal masculinity. Most recently, a body of work called queer theory (see p. 351) is continuing this task in different ways.

Feminism and the gay rights movement challenged normal masculinity and suggested new possibilities for masculine identity. Researchers such as Tim Edwards identify three waves of masculinity studies, similar to the three waves of feminism. In *Cultures of Masculinity* (2006) Edwards states that the first wave studied the social construction of sex roles; since the 1980s second-wave masculinity studies or the so-called 'men's movement' has been exploring masculinity further and critiquing the limitations of the sex role paradigm. The second wave was characterised by the work of Robert Bly (*Iron John*, 1990), Steve Biddulph (*Manhood*, 1994; *Raising Boys*, 1997), and Raewyn (previously known as Robert) Connell (*Gender and Power* 1987; *Masculinities* 1995). This wave looked to find ways of changing and revalidating masculinity. The third wave of critical masculinity studies is influenced by concepts drawn from queer theory such as performativity and by poststructuralist ideas about normativity. As a result, by the start of the twenty-first century, masculinity was in question. It is now seen as more fluid than ever before, in the sense that there are more options available for men as to how to be masculine. The damaging nature of patriarchy to women and men has been acknowledged, and attempts have been made to find new versions of masculinity that challenge the oppression and sexism of patriarchal masculinity. And as Cameron argues (see p. 368), the social gap and differences between women and men in Western culture have become much smaller.

With awareness of the crisis of masculinity, many popular films, television programs, newspaper and magazine articles, and advertisements address the question of what it means to be a man today. Gay culture has become much more acceptable and has influenced ideals of masculinity.

The points above suggest that masculinity is not only in crisis but is also a problem for our society. Critiques of patriarchy have in some cases implied a vilification of masculinity. As a man, how do I, Michael, feel and write about this? In many ways I am critical of masculinity and patriarchy, and I recognise ways in which men are sexist and oppress women. I would like to see social changes. But I am also sympathetic towards men's position in our society. I think it is important to see that men too have suffered under patriarchy, in trying to live up to its limiting and impossible ideals. Men's failings hurt themselves as well as others, and they are predominantly the result of society, not biology. But criticism alone won't always help matters; we need to understand the processes that have produced patriarchy and we need to make changes in masculinity. At the same time, I want to validate the positive aspects of masculinity alongside the positive aspects of femininity; I see them as complementary.

Media representations of masculinity

To develop all these issues we will now look at various media representations of masculinity. Comments will refer to media representations and to masculinity as lived in the actual world.

What kinds of masculinity does the media offer?

Masculine characteristics

Power is the major attribute that is seen as the key signifier and definer of masculinity, in the media and in the real world. Masculinity is achieved by having physical (see, for example, Figure 21.2) and/or social power.

The valuation of physical power can be seen in sports, in stars such as Sylvester Stallone and Arnold Schwarzenegger, and in films such as *The Expendables* and *Beowulf*, a valuation that is confirmed in countless media narratives in which the hero proves himself and wins the day through physical contest. The message—'might equals right'—still predominates in texts that conclude with fighting. Male body attractiveness is also often linked to developed muscularity.

The ideal male also has social power, meaning wealth and influence in the world of business. Richard Gere's character in *Pretty Woman*, Michael Douglas' character Gordon Gekko in the *Wall Street* films, and Daniel Craig as James Bond are typical. Their desirability is linked to social power—in this way power functions as an aphrodisiac. Like Brosnan, Gere's beauty is expressed through his clothes, which are, significantly, professional clothes (he wears business suits and ties), thereby linking male identity to the professional world. Men are often defined by their jobs: a successful man is a man who does well professionally. This locates masculine identity in the public world of work rather than the private world of domesticity (the feminine world). Men who are purely domestic are not considered real men.

Figure 21.3 is an advertisement for men's shirts. The caption of the advertisement (not shown)—'There's a decision-maker inside all our shirts'—draws attention to the rational qualities of the well-dressed man depicted, whose professional skills confirm his successful male identity.

Male power inevitably involves power over something or someone, or both. This includes not only male power over women, but also over other men, over the environment, and over themselves, which is linked to the fact that male relationships are often competitive or controlling. Masculinity is consequently not just a problem for women but also for men and the environment as a whole. The ability to control (controlling others and self-control) is linked to power and rational abilities. Thus control is a defining feature of ideal masculinity.

Women, in contrast, are conventionally given power in representations in just one way: they have sexual power that they can use over men, as demonstrated by Jennifer Aniston's *femme fatale* character in *Derailed*. This has positive aspects in that it acknowledges female sexuality and in the simple fact that women are shown as having a measure of power. But it also has negative aspects: it reduces women to their sexuality (we cannot see them as separate from it), it encourages us to see women primarily as sex objects, and it denies women other forms of power. The logic is that the only way women have power is through their sexuality, which encourages women

Figure 21.2   Advertisement for Levi's jeans

Source: Levi's Jeans, 1993

Figure 21.3   Advertisement for Van Heusen shirts. The caption reads: 'There's a decision-maker in all our shirts.'

Source: Van Heusen Company, 1985

who want power to learn to use this attribute in a manipulating way rather than attempting other ways of gaining power. In addition, this trend devalues women who are not stereotypically sexy, and it diminishes the worth of attributes such as intelligence, eloquence, practicality, agility, humour, and kindness.

Men and women together

Since masculinity and femininity partly define themselves in relation to each other—masculinity defines itself in relation to femininity, and vice versa—it is useful to look at images of men and women together and to consider the limitations of oppositional thought. Such representations tend to highlight the binary opposition that makes discourses of masculinity and femininity work. Men and women are often represented together in a context of heterosexual coupling (see pp. 286–8). Consider the way men and women are coupled in Figures 21.4–21.6. What power relationships are established? Who looks or is looked at? Who has the dominant discourse? What different, complementary, opposite, and desirable characteristics are depicted for women and men?

Figure 21.4   Advertisement for Creda heaters, c. 1980

Source: General Domestic Appliances Ltd

Figure 21.5   Biff cartoon, 1989

Source: Mick Kidd

Figure 21.6   Advertisement for Pino aftershave

Source: Vidal, 1995

Men together

Many media representations present stories about men relating to other men. Two themes predominate: struggle and friendship between male buddies. Many stories show both: male rivalry turns to male friendship when the protagonists find themselves fighting alongside one another or against each other. Depicting male characters fighting alongside one another allows them to be physically close and provides a situation in which each can earn or win the respect of the other, which leads to friendship. Other narratives involving fighting encourage men to distrust each other, to see men as rivals, or present the playing out of father–son relationships.

These hero stories can be seen as dramas of masculinity. The stories are about men finding their true masculinity, their masculine identity, as in the film *300*. The process of testing they go through initiates them into masculinity. Traditionally, westerns and gangster movies have validated typical masculine characteristics (in stars such as John Wayne and Clint Eastwood), but many stories today carry an interesting tension as to whether they are celebrating or critiquing masculinity. Films such as *The Departed*, *Gangs of New York*, *Reservoir Dogs*, *Fight Club*, *The Fighter*, and *The Assassination of Jesse James* seem to revel in moments of male aggression and male power, and at the same time show how futile and destructive—to self and others—such masculinity is. These films can be read as celebrations and critiques of masculinity.

Homophobia is fear of same-sex intimacy. Men's fear of intimacy with other men is often a fear of homosexuality, and it is often expressed in an aggressive manner. The medium only depicts intimacy between men in certain situations: war films when a buddy is dying, sports, after goal-scoring exploits, and in other dramas in which men fight, drink, or joke together. Buddy films contain an interesting tension: they validate male friendship but reject any homosexual possibilities. Male bonding has also been interpreted as a rejection of femininity and hence as part of misogyny. Yet some critics argue that these buddy movies unconsciously suggest strong love and homoerotic attraction between men. They argue that the male stars are filmed in such a way as to make them visually attractive not only to female characters in the film and women in the film audience, but also to male characters in the film and men in the audience. The actual narrative structure may deny or disavow male attraction, but the way it is filmed suggests **homoeroticism**.

homophobia
Fear of same-sex intimacy, though most commonly used to refer to men's fear of homosexuality and emotional closeness between men.

homoeroticism
Sexual desire between same-sex couples, though most commonly used to refer to men; also often refers to the pleasure received in gazing at an attractive member of the same sex in sport, film, etc.

The central relationship in the Australian film *Chopper*, directed by Andrew Dominik, is between Mark 'Chopper' Read (Eric Bana) and his best mate Jimmy, played by Simon Lyndon. In one scene the depth of emotion between these two men erupts into physicality and Chopper is stabbed by his friend—the two are gripped in what looks like a dying embrace as Jimmy plunges the knife into Chopper's torso again and again. 'If you keep stabbing me I'm gonna die, mate', Chopper says without any evidence of anger. The two characters lock eyes and it looks for a moment as though they are about to kiss. It is an ambiguous cinematic moment, charged with a twisted kind of homoeroticism. This theme is repeated in the relationship between Jesse James (Brad Pitt) and Robert Ford (Casey Affleck) in *The Assassination of Jesse James by the Outlaw Robert Ford*, Dominik's next film.

Look at the images of male bonding in the Ella Baché sunscreen advertisements in Plates 6 and 7. Is this bonding depicted as powerful, ridiculous, or homoerotic?

Men and feelings

It has been suggested that men learn to hide their feelings (or that they don't have many feelings) and that they learn to value rationality over emotion. In reality, men's feelings are repressed in many ways as they grow up. The most obvious example is the way that men have been taught not to cry; however, this does not mean they do not feel. It just makes the realisation and expression of feeling more difficult. While women are encouraged to show their tears but not their anger, men are encouraged to hide their tears but show their anger. The socialisation of boys teaches them that anger and aggression are legitimate feelings for men: it is OK to be angry; indeed, it can confirm masculinity. This is shown repeatedly in media representations. Traditionally, men have not been encouraged to discuss their feelings and traditionally they are not represented as doing so. Instead, their feelings are expressed through violent action.

Male violence

Male violence has two aspects: destruction of others and self-destruction.

Destruction of others

Male violence towards women, children, and other men is prevalent throughout the world. It occurs in private and domestic spheres and in public spheres (including large-scale armed conflict). Anger may sometimes be a useful and appropriate response for men and women, but how that anger can be appropriately expressed is a vexed question. The male solution—fighting—permeates all media, which may help to endorse this behaviour for individual men and promote it as the best way of solving social problems. The ubiquity of violence as a problem-solving strategy endorses warfare as a legitimate problem-solving strategy, which is not to argue a direct-effects response mechanism: the argument here is not that men see violence on television and imitate it; nor is it an argument for repressive censorship of media violence. Both these views are too simplistic. Rather, we want to draw your attention to the issue of male violence and to media representations of male fighting and anger towards others. Hopefully, this will make you think about what model of masculinity the media offers us and how this might relate to the way men act in the real world. We think the question of how to work with male anger and violence is one of the major social issues the world faces at present.

Self-destruction

Violent actions are not always towards other people. Many male feelings of anger are, masochistically, turned inwards (there is an ironic similarity between the words 'machismo' and 'masochism'). The culture of pain and **masochism** is found in everyday images of masculinity, such as the King of Shaves advertisement (see Figure 21.7), which implies that men suffer self-inflicted pain and discomfort every day as part of the price they pay to embody an acceptable (clean-shaven) image of masculinity.

masochism
Pleasure (or perverse sexual gratification) felt when experiencing pain, humiliation, or deprivation. The term is derived from the name of erotic novelist Leopold von Sacher-Masoch.

The discourse of masochism is prevalent in sport, one of the defining arenas of traditional masculinity. Sport is often presented as an arena of endurance: 'No pain, no gain', 'When the going gets tough, the tough get going', and so on. (It doesn't have to be this way, but typically, male sport is understood in terms of power, strength, and competition—winning and losing—rather than grace, elegance, transcendence of time, beauty of the human form, and so on.)

The following comments by professional sportsmen show sport as a regime of endurance and punishment for the body.

> Your thigh muscles swell up as if you were going to burst. You zig-zag along. The whole body is under terrible pressure (P Trentin, cyclist).

> The feeling of lack of air is terrible. You think you're going to pass out—that you're not far from dying. It's true you say to yourself maybe that's what dying feels like (B Thevenet, cyclist).

> Up to the middle of the race the fatigue increases. You're practically dead but you have to carry on. To reduce the pain you think about how much the others are suffering. Your thighs swell up, your

Figure 21.7 King of Shaves advertisement

'Bloody Murder' advertisement for King of Shaves, courtesy of Paul Irwin, Director of Creative Partners (Aust) Ltd

> arms hardly make it and your back stops responding. When you get to 1,500 metres you tell yourself that if you had any sense you'd stop there and then.

> But you have to keep going. Right up to the end the burning sensation gets worse—you feel as if your whole body is on fire from head to toe ... rowing involves 100% effort and that means 100% pain (Y Fraysse, oarsman) (Brohm 1978, p. 25).

What these quotations demonstrate is that the body is being disciplined and controlled. Pleasure is not involved or, if it is, it is the pleasure of pain—masochism.

Boxing is a sport in which the competitors deliberately inflict and suffer pain and serious physical injury. The image of Vitali Klitschko's battered face (Figure 21.8) shows these wounds being borne with stoic resolve. The implied narrative suggested by the low angle shot, the boxer's proud expression, and the caption is that Klitschko has been rejected by his girlfriend because he lost the fight; it also reinforces the idea that real men don't cry or require sympathy when disappointed or hurt in any way. This illustrates how the media can function to reinforce the dominant discourse of masculinity, and how women are or can be complicit in supporting notions of ideal masculinity.

Images of masochism and brutal physicality feature prominently in films directed by Martin Scorsese such as *The Departed* and *Raging Bull*. In *Raging Bull* Robert de Niro plays the part of boxer Jake La Motta. He typically invites people to attack and hurt him, which reaches its climax when de Niro beats his own head and fists against a brick wall. This self-destructive violence is directed specifically against the head, the source of rationality and control. Film theorists such as Yvonne Tasker have noticed how many male film heroes undergo testing rituals that involve extreme pain and often body wounding (Tasker 1993). This certainly relates to male initiation ceremonies of many traditional cultures. Such ceremonies test young men by inflicting pain on them. It also resonates with Robert Bly's (Bly 1990) idea that masculinity is about wounding. Clearly, masculinity and pain are strongly linked. Pain is a way in which men can express their feelings.

Fight Club explores similar themes. Here the pleasure, emotional release, and bonding found in fighting with other men is initially shown as beneficial and health restoring (despite the physical injuries involved) for Edward Norton's spirit and for many other men. It is contrasted with the self-help support groups shown earlier in the film. It is noticeable that the character played by Meatloaf, who has lost his testicles to cancer (the threat of castration is a recurrent theme in the film) and grown breasts, thereby becoming emasculated or feminised, finds more benefit in this ultramale brotherhood than in the support groups. The film seems to be suggesting that fighting is better than hugging! It seemed to resonate with male audiences, and it may be that this reassertion of the value of traditional male expression and aggression is part of a reaction against the influences of feminism and the emergence of the sensitive New Age man. As film critic Amy Taubin has argued, in dealing with issues of masculinity, the film is another example of homoeroticism:

> Shot in a wet-dream half light that gilds the men's bodies as they pound each other's heads into the cement, the Fight Club sequences are a perfect balance of aesthetics and adrenaline; they feel like a solution to the mind/body split (Taubin 1999, pp. 16–18).

Men in frocks

A number of comedy films feature men cross-dressing—men wearing women's clothes—to disguise themselves as females for a period of time, tricking all the other characters around them but making audiences laugh at the 'absurdity' of a man

PUCKER UP, SWEETIE
Vitali Klitschko, after being pummelled by Lennox Lewis, can't understand why his beloved Olga won't give him a sympathy peck on the cheek.

zone two **allsport**

AUGUST 2003   SA SPORTS ILLUSTRATED   • **69**

Figure 21.8   The boxer Vitali Klitschko. The caption reads: 'Pucker up, sweetie. Vitali Klitschko after being pummelled by Lennox Lewis can't understand why his beloved Olga won't give him a sympathy peck on the cheek.'

Source: Courtesy of Getty/ImageTouchline Photo in *South African Sports Illustrated*, August 2003 trying to be a woman. Films that follow this pattern include *Some Like it Hot*, *Tootsie*, *Mrs Doubtfire*, *Sorority Boys*, *White Chicks*, and the three *Big Momma* films. In the *Big Momma* franchise, Martin Lawrence plays an FBI agent who disguises himself as the large, elderly matriarch 'Big Momma' to go undercover. These films have been critically ridiculed, but have made millions at the box office. Like Robin Williams' character in *Mrs Doubtfire*, Lawrence's character crosses boundaries of age as well as gender when he transforms into 'Big Momma'. A significant percentage of the films' humour derives from the visual comedy of what appears to be an old lady with the physical capabilities of a young, fit man. Nevertheless, the main source of comedy the films rely on is a man, with 'manly' interests and urges, presenting as a woman—a masquerade which inevitably leads to comical mix-ups and misrecognitions. Such texts are interesting because they present a transgression of dominant masculinity. Note the following points.

1   This transgression is threatening to the establishment because it blurs the normal gender definitions that give people their identity and are used in the support of patriarchy.

2   Men in drag are often represented humorously, thus making the situation less threatening. The male figures are made to appear ridiculous. Some argue that the laughter generated by such representations is directed against femininity, in that femininity is being parodied. If this is so, then this would make these texts misogynist. Others argue that the humour arises from the fact that these texts reveal that gender identity is a construction or a mask, and as such, they challenge patriarchy.

3   In these films the male characters find that assuming a female persona means they can express their feelings better and be more emotional, and their time spent as a woman gives them insight into the challenges women face (such as sexism in the workplace). In films such as *Tootsie* and *Mrs Doubtfire* where the cross-dressing character is also a trained actor, the 'skill' it takes for these male characters to impersonate women is emphasised; therefore it is masculine skills that are being applauded rather than feminine attributes.

4   The transgression of gender norms in these films is temporary. With rare exception— *Some Like it Hot*—the cross-dressing characters revert to their original gender by the end of the film. In having the main characters reassume their masculine identity, they *ultimately* reassert normal gender positions in their narrative structure, thus avoiding any possibility of gender uncertainty.

It is also important to note that these types of cross-dressing comedies are distinct from those films that explore the lives of transgender characters—those who identify with a gender other than the one they were assigned at birth—including *The Crying Game*, *The Adventures of Priscilla, Queen of the Desert*, *Kinky Boots*, and *Transamerica*. Rather than presenting gender-crossing as funny, these films address the struggles faced by those who do not fit the restrictive male-masculine, female-feminine mould. When a male in women's attire can *pass* for a biological female, this is more disturbing than when ineffective cross-dressing leaves no doubt as to their biological sex. In such situations there is uncertainty about the stability of gender categories (see Figure 21.9). Cross-dressing is usually considered more transgressive when men dress as women than when women dress as men. There are some examples of film comedies in which a girl disguises herself as a boy, including *Victor Victoria, Just One of the Guys*, and *She's the Man*, but the gender-crossing they feature is not deemed to trouble gender categories to the same extent as that in male cross-dressing films. You may wonder why this is the case. One suggestion is that because masculinity is valued more highly than femininity in patriarchy, women dressing in men's clothes is seen as a positive thing, whereas men dressing as women are seen to be losing power and authority. Men dressing as women are seen to be devaluing themselves and, more importantly, masculinity (and consequently patriarchy). This makes cross-dressing a subversive act that can be a powerful attack on patriarchy.

How do you read the cross-dressing images shown in Figures 21.9–21.11? Are they humorous or serious? If humorous, then who or what are we being asked to laugh at?

Figure 21.9   Image from *Men in Frocks*

Source: Photograph by Ed Heath, published in C Kirk, *Men in Frocks*, GMP Publishers, Norfolk, 1984

Figure 21.10   Advertisement for 17 Cosmetics

Source: 17 Cosmetics, 1998; photograph by Mosche Brakha

Figure 21.11   Advertisement for Ursa computers

Source: Videolab, 1995

Gay representations

There have always been underground films, stories, and magazines made by and about gay men, including the films of Kenneth Anger and the novels and plays of Jean Genet. There have also been many gay filmmakers and stars working in apparently heterosexual films. Their work in mainstream film has often been read from a gay perspective by gay audiences, as exemplified in Vito Russo's book *The Celluloid Closet* (Russo 1981) and in the documentary it inspired. Mainstream films overtly about gay issues tended to pathologise gay characters as sick or criminal, as Russo argues (see p. 260), but since the growth of the gay rights movement there have been more films celebrating gay men (and lesbian women) and providing much more optimistic resolutions, such as the films of Pedro Almodovar. And now there are several instances of gay representations on popular television (see p. 261).

Men advertising hygiene products, cosmetics, and fragrances

The cosmetics market, traditionally aimed at women, has realised it has a huge potential male market. In order to win this market, it has to overcome the perception that the purchase and use of cosmetics are feminine activities. Focusing on men looking and smelling desirable may risk making them seem effeminate so advertisers also need to focus on more traditional male qualities. Shaving advertisements are a rich source to examine. At the same time as stressing how attractive shaving can make men, the advertisements manage to maintain the ideal of masculine strength and proximity to physical danger by showing razors as instruments of technological power, capable of providing dangerously close shaves. Many are framed in terms of competition (beating rival products), and many link shavers to sports activities and achievements in sport.

Advertisements for perfumes marketed at men are similarly linked to physical activities. Such advertising strategies ensure that men wearing male perfumes are not challenging traditional masculinity and the virility with which it is associated; rather, these advertisements suggest that by wearing male perfumes, men are strengthening their traditional masculinity. The imagery of the advertisement for XS (Figure 21.12), a perfume produced by the house of Paco Rabanne, emphasises phallic strength. One of the most successful advertising campaigns in recent years has been for Old Spice shower gel for men, starring Isaiah Mustafa as 'the man your man could smell like', if only he used Old Spice. The Old Spice ad (Figure 21.13) appealed to both men and women with its knowing, humorous representation of gender ideals and it went viral on YouTube, becoming one of the most viewed commercials in history. Interestingly, 'The man your man could smell like' doesn't have to do much in these advertisements to assert his masculinity: all he does is wear Old Spice in a shower, on a yacht, on a beach, on a horse without his shirt on … This ad presents a fresh take on the long-standing strategy of Old Spice's rival company, Axe, which specialises in advertisements that show 'the Axe effect', which involves women tearing off their clothes when they catch the scent of Axe on a man. Figure 21.14 uses the caption 'Liberation! Happy Women's Day, guys' and an image of women throwing their bras in the air. It recuperates the concept of women's liberation and its association with 'bra burning', defusing its threat to men by playfully turning it into yet another opportunity for men to think about naked women and sex. Even though women take on a more traditional masculine quality in the way they respond sexually to the

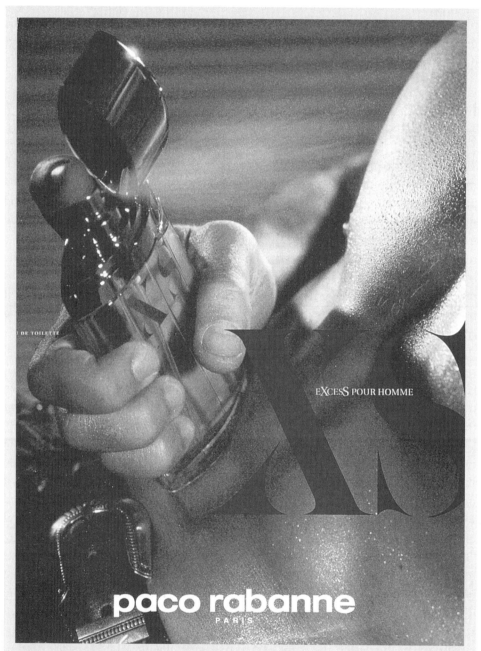

Figure 21.12   Advertisement for Paco Rabanne XS perfume

Source: Paco Rabanne; published in *Cleo*, September 1994

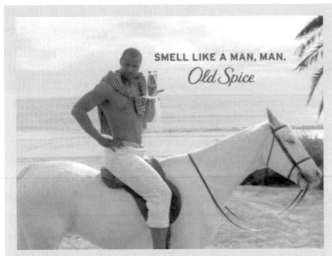

Figure 21.13 Advertisement for Old Spice: The man your man could smell like

Source: Courtesy of The Advertising Archives

Figure 21.14 Advertisement for Lynx/ Axe: Happy Women's Day!

Source: Courtesy of Lowe Bull advertising agency, Johannesburg

scent and rush out to purchase Old Spice or Axe for their partners, men still have the overall power. In the past few years it has become much more acceptable for men to care about their appearance as shown in **metrosexuality**.

Metrosexuality doesn't designate a different kind of sexuality so much as it refers to a market consisting of urban, open-minded men who pay attention to fashion and appearance and look just gay enough to attract the attention of men as well as women. David Beckham is the most well-known metrosexual example as he blends traditional masculine sporting prowess with concern for fashion, appearance, and occasional cross-dressing—a good example of the blending of residual and emergent discourses (see pp. 205, 426).

metrosexuals
Young, stylish, urban men who care about and spend considerable money on their appearance and are attractive to women (and, often, to other men).

Male pin-ups

Since the mid-1970s, representations of the naked male body as an object of desire have become more frequent (this may be partially linked to the increased visibility of gay culture). Richard Dyer (1982) was one of the first critics to explore this phenomenon. Representations of naked men have often been a source of humour (in contrast to representations of naked women). It is as though humour is being

Figure 21.15   Advertisement for Wolf shoes

Source: *Intransit International*, 1988

used as a way of defusing feelings of unease about the portrayal of naked men, a tendency still evident in films such as *The Full Monty*, which ultimately refuses to show 'the full monty' (full frontal male nudity). But while humour still persists in some representations of male nudity, many are now explicit about showing the male body as an object of desire; these representations aim to provoke not laughter but desire. Such images have become very common, and demonstrate that there is a trend towards men being seen as objects of the sexual gaze. In this context, it is interesting to note that the advertisement for Wolf shoes (Figure 21.15) combines humour and sexual desirability.

Many critics have argued against the portrayal of women as sexual objects in the media. How do you assess the fact that men are now being portrayed in similar ways? Is this an example of equality? Does it validate the active sexual desire of women and gay men? Does it denigrate men by making them sexual objects? Does it threaten men who can't live up to these visual ideals? In what ways are male pin-ups and male exhibitionism different from the portrayal of females as sexual objects? Do male pin-ups work? Are they amusing or sexual?

Explore these questions by collecting and examining media images of men as sexual objects. How do you and your friends feel about these images? Is there a difference between male and female attitudes towards them? Note particularly how imagery of strength, work, and sport, as well as the fact that male models tend not to look at the camera, may help to maintain masculine identity. Note, too, the considerable emphasis on the body and skin, including the taut muscularity and smooth hairlessness of the bodies depicted (simultaneously suggesting masculinity and femininity). Keeping these questions in mind, look at Figure 21.15 and Plates 6 and 7 in terms of how they represent male power and desirability.

Look at Figures 21.16 and 21.17, which are images from a campaign for Kolotex hosiery that promote Voodoo pantihose. The image in Figure 21.16 was the first image to appear on billboards. How do you read this image, in which there is a combination of humour and sexual desirability? After a couple of weeks, the second image (Figure 21.17) was revealed to show the couple. How do you read Figure 21.16 in terms of issues of the relative power of men and women, and in relation to Figure 21.17?

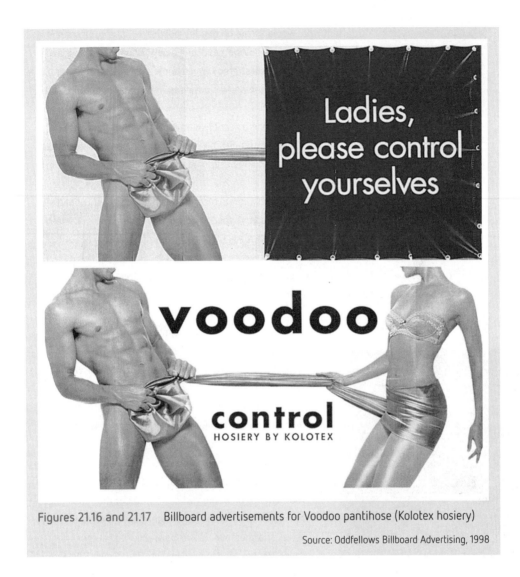

Figures 21.16 and 21.17   Billboard advertisements for Voodoo pantihose (Kolotex hosiery)

Source: Oddfellows Billboard Advertising, 1998

Voodoo pantihose

The following quote is from Janet Hogan, the managing director of Oddfellows Billboard Advertising, the advertising agency behind the campaign for Voodoo Control pantihose. It is a good example of how authors' intentions can be important in the construction of meaning, how images are produced in relation to contemporary ideas about sexual representations, the changing roles of men and women, and how audiences can read texts.

> In keeping with past Voodoo advertising, the billboard for Voodoo Control pantihose was designed to reinforce Voodoo's positioning as the pantihose for women in control; women who believe that promoting their sexuality does not in any way compromise their liberated status.
>
> The campaign has been so hugely successful ... because it deliberately challenges political correctness and recognises that the vast majority of women aren't hung up over

gender stereotyping. Most think the whole issue of gender politics is boring, academic, counterproductive and out of touch with everyday women. They enjoy risqué advertising and the irony and humour implicit in the role reversal strategy which underpins Voodoo marketing.

To create maximum impact and intrigue, the ad was designed in two stages: a teaser ad followed by a reveal of the product.

The first stage shows on the left hand side a scantily clad male trying to cover himself with a piece of cloth. The message on the right: 'Ladies please control yourselves' leaves the audience to assume that the fellow is struggling against some over zealous females trying in vain to disrobe him.

With the reveal, Stage 2, it becomes clear that it is in fact him pulling on the cloth, engaged in a sort of sexual tug of war with a woman wearing Voodoo Control pantihose. The gold cloth pulled tightly around her waist and thighs emphasises the firming, flattering quality of Control top pantihose.

It is up to the reader to read as much or as little as she/he likes into the ad.

Most consumers would undoubtedly read very little. They simply respond to the cultural cues present.

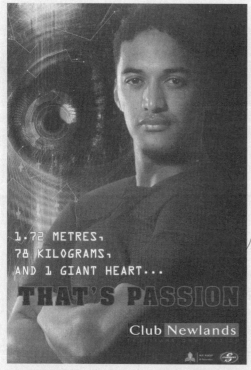

Figure 21.18 Rugby player Breyton Paulse: '1.72 metres, 78 kilograms, and 1 giant heart … THAT'S PASSION'

Source: Courtesy of Club Newlands

On one level the ad is simply a sexy demonstration of the product being advertised. On another, the struggle between the sexes; a (vulnerable?) male trying to dominate the female, but unable to.

If she epitomises the role model most modern women aspire to: feminine, strong, and ultimately in control, the ads epitomise the complexity of contemporary sexual mores, where really anything goes. Indeed, Voodoo is being rewarded with massive sales by the majority of women who are grateful that someone has dared to take on the thought police and do it with style and humour (correspondence to author from Janet Hogan, Managing Director, Oddfellows Billboard Advertising, July, 1998).

Images of masculinity in sports stars

Sporting heroes provide important role models, particularly for young men, therefore the kinds of cultural values, ideologies, attributes, and practices that sport promotes have considerable social significance for the construction of a dominant masculinity. In the poster of Breyton Paulse (Figure 21.18), a key player in South African rugby (he played right wing for the Springboks, the Stormers, and the Western Province), we see a rare instance in which the passionate expression of emotion is legitimated for men and between men. Paulse is well known for his fearlessness and expertise on the rugby field, and for his genuine warmth and dedication to community organisations and to his fans. Despite his relative lack of stature, his courage and endurance earn him the reputation for having a 'giant heart', and his commitment to the game warrants the tag 'THAT'S PASSION'. This emotive aspect is framed within the discourses of science, technology, and military strategy that reassert the masculinity of sports stars and sports fans and distance them from the feminised connotations of words such as 'heart' and 'passion'. The picture features numbers quantifying Paulse's vital statistics, distinctive blue lighting often found in science-fiction films or emanating from computer screens, and a background image of an eye-like vortex lined with a spiral of vectors. These aesthetic elements of the picture signify that sport involves a passionate dedication that is measured, strategic, and calculated.

The fact that the sportsmen in Figures 21.18 and 21.19 are pictured wearing a kind of body armour that offers a degree of protection in the dangerous contact sport links sport to warfare. This association is not uncommon. Some theorists have argued that sport is a ritualised form of warfare that promotes and naturalises an adversarial ideology, framing masculinity within an overarching discourse of calculated capitalist competitiveness:

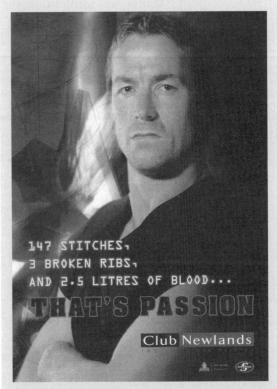

Figure 21.19   Rugby player Corne Krige: '147 stitches, 3 broken ribs, and 2.5 litres of blood ... THAT'S PASSION'

Source: Courtesy of Club Newlands

> Sport makes competition appear natural and thoroughly human ... The increasing importance of the media as the carrier of this sporting discourse makes the two institutions mutually convergent with capitalist ideology (Cunningham & Miller 1994, p. 66).

The combative aspect of sport is most evident in the poster of the team captain, Corne Krige (Figure 21.19), a sports star of international standing. Now retired, Krige featured in Nike product endorsements (thereby embodying the ideologies of freedom, individualism, and capitalism that the Nike brand stands for), and he literally came to represent South Africa on the many occasions he played for his country. Fans who identify with Krige may therefore value and internalise aspects of these identities and ideologies. In addition, Krige represents a particular form of masculinity that sports fans may also admire or seek to emulate. In the Club Newlands image (Figure 21.19) his passion for the game is literally measured in blood, sweat, and pain. While the background of Krige's image is marked with a pattern like a scientific diagram, it also features the crosshairs of a rifle sight. The colour red and the flames can be interpreted as signifiers of ferocity and rage—a form of passion closely linked to conflict.

Within this formulation, the team's captain equates to a chief or a general, and the sportsmen are equated with warriors, fighting for their country and embodying physical perfection, strength, and speed. If we think through the different aspects involved in sport, we can see that a range of values and seemingly oppositional ideologies are brought together in this discourse of masculinity.

Table 21.1   **Sporting discourse of masculinity**

competitiveness	AND	cooperation
individualism	AND	team spirit
brawn	AND	brain
discipline	AND	heroism

All of these values are harnessed to masculinity and are often framed in terms of heroism and service to one's country.

Because sports stars represent their countries in international competitions, their bodies are inscribed with the discourse of nationalism and the ideology of patriotism. The figure of the sports star provides a symbolic synthesis for the ideological tensions between these different value systems. In being a fan of Krige or of any individual sports star, boys and men can admire, participate in, internalise, and then propagate the masculine values they represent. Emulating his physique and behaviour is facilitated and encouraged by the media systems through which you can buy and wear the Nike sportswear that Krige endorses or simply watch television or buy tickets to see each game he plays.

Conclusion

This chapter has defined the main characteristics of dominant masculinity but argued that there are other models of masculinity to be found in media representations and the real world. It has been argued that masculinity is in crisis, and has been going through significant changes over the past thirty years. Correspondingly, so have media representations of men. Look out for traditional representations of dominant masculinity as well as for new and changing representations, such as the image of the sensitive new-age guy (SNAG), the metrosexual, and representations that reflect the crisis of masculinity.

In the last decade or so films and television programs have tended to deal more sensitively with male issues, with relationships between fathers and sons, and with men's emotions and vulnerabilities; advertisements play with role reversals and documentaries focus on male issues. The influence of gay culture has affected many areas of mainstream masculinity through areas such as clothing styles and popular music. All these factors have affected our ideas about sexuality and gender. Many young people are now much more fluid in their understandings of and feelings about gender and sexual identity.

The changes in masculinity dovetail with changes in femininity: both areas are going through processes of exploration and development. Women may be more conscious of this through feminism's direct impact on their lives, while men's awareness of how these issues impinge on them is more recent. In discussions among students, there has been a broad trend towards women saying that while they feel oppressed in many ways and are critical of media representations, they actually enjoy being women. In contrast, men, who tend not to have the same complaints about their place in society and the way they are represented in the media, often feel confused about being men. It is as though contemporary male roles are more uncertain than current female roles. Whereas women feel they have something to gain from these changes, men may sometimes feel threatened. We should strive to create a climate in which women and men feel they have much to gain from such changes.

This chapter has

- outlined the main characteristics of dominant masculinity
- noted that there are alternative ideologies of masculinity
- considered the crisis of masculinity
- noted the significance of feminism and the gay rights movement in relation to masculinity
- analysed media representations of masculinity
- considered the representation of male sports stars.

Discussion points

1   Do contemporary media representations reflect a crisis of masculinity?
2   Consider how the media represent men together. How many times are men subjected to tests that prove their masculinity? Pay special attention to father and son relationships. Are these representations celebrating or critiquing traditional masculinity? Look for any homophobic and homoerotic tendencies.
3   What ideologies of masculinity do sports stars encapsulate?

Summary

You should now be able to

- discuss traditional and contemporary ideologies and characteristics of masculinity
- discuss the crisis of masculinity
- explain how social forces, such as patriarchy, feminism, and the gay rights movement, have influenced masculinity
- comment on and illustrate the importance of power in relation to masculinity
- discuss media representations of male violence and male feelings
- find examples in the media of different ideologies of masculinity
- comment on media representations of male cross-dressing
- define and use the terms 'homophobic', 'homoerotic', 'masochism', and 'metrosexual'
- find media examples to illustrate these terms
- analyse media representations of male sport
- use the theory of residual, dominant, and emergent discourses to analyse media representations of masculinity.

CHAPTER 22

Ethnicity, Ideology, and the Media

Why aren't there no brothers on the wall?

Do The Right Thing, Spike Lee

This chapter will

▶ examine media representations of ethnicity

▶ consider the significance of absence of representation

▶ give an overview of European or majority world historical relationships

▶ explore the terms 'Eurocentrism' and 'Orientalism'

▶ examine discourses of ethnicity using binary oppositions and stereotypes.

Let us start with three points about ethnicity.

1 Like gender, ethnicity and nationality are major ways humans classify their own and other people's identity: 'I'm Australian', 'I'm Aboriginal', 'I'm Asian', 'I'm Indian', 'I'm Zulu', and so on.

2 The world is divided into different and unequally positioned ethnic groups and cultures; there are many inequalities of power and wealth between these groups, who are, consequently, often in conflict internally and with other ethnic groups.

3 The media are important in giving us constructions, images, and representations—discourses—of ethnic difference. As such, they offer us ways to understand ethnicity and ethnic issues.

In this chapter, we refer to images and ideologies of ethnicity in the media, as well as to how ethnicity is lived and experienced in the real world. While we use the terms 'ethnicity' and 'race', it is important to point out that there is a major problem with the term 'race'. Not only is it without scientific basis, but because it suggests biological differences, using it is also tantamount to accepting the proposition that these essential differences exist. To speak of ethnic groups and ethnicity, on the other hand, is to refer to cultural differences between social groups. While we do not accept the baggage associated with the term 'race', it is used occasionally because it is so much a part of common-sense understandings and definitions.

Representation of ethnic groups and ethnicity

How important is ethnic invisibility—absence of representation?

Consider the significance of the following scene from the film *Crash*, directed by Paul Haggis. This film is set in multiracial Los Angeles. It explores tensions between a number of ethnic groups, focusing mainly on the struggle between African Americans, Iranians, and Latin Americans.

We follow the story of two African American youths who share a meal in a diner and banter about the racial politics of tipping the waitress; then they squabble about whether an uptight, wealthy white woman played by Sandra Bullock is racist because she exhibits fear and aversion when she sees them approach. Then they draw a gun and hijack her car. This film puts issues of representation and biased perception right at its centre. Representation is an important political issue. It is important for ethnic groups to be represented in the media in ways that honour diversity instead of stereotyping groups of people. African Americans, like Australian Aborigines, have consistently been denied their own images, stories, representations, histories, social customs, and rituals, and until this matter is redressed the lack will continue to contribute to ethnic and racial inequality. It is necessary to fight for these representations.

As film analysts Robert Stam and Louise Spence have argued, a structuring absence is when the lack of images of people of colour defines white people as the central, natural identity category (Stam & Spence 1983, p. 7). Absence of representation 'is as bad as distorting stereotypes' (Stam & Spence 1983, p. 7) and can be even more problematic than negative representations. The absence of diverse representations of African Americans in the media affects the way African Americans see and understand themselves (remember Ngugi's argument that indigenous Africans have been deprived of their own language and thus their cultural identity; see p. 71). *Crash* is itself a representation that gives a voice and a face to African American points of view, and Haggis' film is one of a number that have emerged from Hollywood since 1990, suggesting that African Americans are beginning to gain a foothold in Hollywood from which to represent themselves (Bogle 1973; Diawara 1993; Reid 1997). This shift is also evident in the acknowledgment of African American film stars at the Academy Awards in recent years.

The other major concern is the misrepresentation of ethnic groups. It is important to see who is accorded the right and the ability to make representations, who has access to the media. The tendency within Western culture has been for media representations to be produced by whites and thus most epitomise a white view of the world and of other ethnic groups. This is explored further after consideration of the black–white opposition and the historical realities on which relationships between people of colour and whites have been built.

Black–white oppositions

Ethnic conflicts have existed throughout history. Many wars that have complex economic and social causes are also cultural conflicts between ethnic groups. Ethnic conflict is involved in many of the armed conflicts around the world today. Central to the argument about representations of ethnicity is the idea that whites and people of colour have fundamentally opposed natures. This apparently simple opposition is actually complex. The descriptions 'black' and 'white' do not do justice to the multiplicity and range of different ethnic groups. But because they are popular labels they are useful for understanding the discourses surrounding ethnicity.

Issues of ethnicity and their representation are further complicated by other factors, including education, age, gender, attitude, location, and circumstance. Class, too, can significantly influence relations between different ethnicities, though it does not determine them or how films portray these matters. For example, in both *Crash* and *The Blind Side* Sandra Bullock plays an upper-class white woman who encounters lower-class black men, yet these interactions play out very differently in each film. In *Crash*, as described above, her character anxiously clutches her husband's arm when they pass two black men while walking at night, and her fears are confirmed when the men steal her car. In contrast, Bullock's character in *The Blind Side* comes across a young black man with nowhere warm to sleep and her first response is to invite him to stay with her and her family. This film explores the tensions that arise as the poor black man becomes a member of the wealthy white family.

The opposition black–white carries within it notions of inequality, subordinate and dominant groups, and of groups who are different and opposed to each other, which points to the idea that ethnic groups are in conflict over power. The white–black opposition can be expressed in various ways, all of which point to its historical origins.

Table 22.1 **Black–white opposition**

white	black
White	people of colour
European descent	non-European descent
West	East

The last two sets of oppositions—European descent–non-European descent, and West–East—draw attention to the history behind these oppositions: the realities of global European expansion since the fifteenth century. Note that once again this oppositional form of thought polarises groups in extreme ways that make it seem as though there is no middle ground, and they have nothing in common. In actuality, each of these pairs of terms is situated on a continuum with subtle gradations of difference linking the extremes at each end.

The history of the West and 'the rest'

The historical relationship between Europe and the rest of the world has a number of elements, all of which demonstrate European domination of other cultures.

Exploration and discovery

These were, and still often are, the terms used to describe the invasion of other lands and cultures by Europeans. The Americas, Africa, and Australasia were said to be discovered, despite the fact that they had indigenous populations at the time of the so-called discovery.

Extermination

In colonised lands, the colonisers employed repressive policies against the indigenous peoples, and in many cases virtually exterminated them.

Colonisation

Europeans started to settle and live in these 'new' lands, setting up a number of European colonies, such as the Americas and Australia.

Colonialism

Colonialism refers to the acquisition and maintenance of colonies. Colonialism involved control and domination of the indigenous population, who were subjected to laws originating in Europe. Colonialism was established in, among other places, Africa, the Middle East, India, Pakistan, and parts of the Asia–Pacific region.

Exploitation

The prime motives behind colonisation were the exploitation of the natural resources of colonised lands (through mining and agriculture, for example), the exploitation of the labour of indigenous peoples (particularly through slavery), and the opening up of new markets for European goods. In more recent history, the USA's economic domination of some countries, particularly in Latin America, has been called neocolonialism (new colonialism). One instance of this domination is cigarettes and tobacco, which are being subjected to increasing regulation in the West but aggressively promoted in the majority world (also called the Third World), thereby providing new markets for tobacco and cigarette companies. The wealth and dominance of Europe and the USA (also called the First World, developed nations, the minority world, and the Western world) are largely built on the exploitation of the wealth, labour, and resources of these other countries.

The relationship between the majority world and the minority world has been described in ways that make the exploitation involved in this relationship invisible. First, the term that the United Kingdom used in relation to its empire was 'the Commonwealth' (meaning the wealth held in common by all the nations). The idea as it was expressed is one of sharing, equality, and mutual interests, whereas the reality was that its aims were to siphon wealth to the United Kingdom from the other countries of the Commonwealth. Second, the advantages of imperial exploitation have become culturally naturalised in relation to products such as tea and coffee. Tea drinking is seen as a quintessential British activity, and coffee has become a marker of European sophistication, the essence of café culture. Both drinks are available in these countries thanks to the plantations, cheap labour, and imperial trading companies established by Europeans in South America and Asia.

Imperialism

Out of colonialism grew a number of European empires—predominantly the Dutch, French, German, and British empires—and subsequently America's neocolonial empire. These empires were initially about control over lands and peoples. Nowadays we think of empires in terms of financial power and control such that even if countries have regained their independence, as in most of Africa, they are in many ways still subject to the power and control of the World Bank, the International Monetary Fund, and multinational corporations owned by the minority world. Cultural imperialism, which refers to the extension of empire through the control and dissemination of cultural products (largely through the media), is discussed in the globalisation section (see Chapter 25).

Integration

Integration and assimilation indicate the absorption or incorporation of ethnic groups or minorities into the dominant or colonising culture in a manner that eradicates difference and renders it invisible once the language and culture of the dominant group are adopted. Multiculturalism champions the idea of unity in diversity, a kind of cultural pluralism, in a positive way (see pp. 403–4); however, multiculturalism is still a form of integration that serves the interests of the dominant group by uniting the nation within a common or shared identity in order to reduce dissent.

Postcolonialism

This term describes the situation in existence since majority world countries achieved their political independence. It is an important critical term (see Chapter 24).

The advertisement for the Drop the Debt campaign (Figure 22.1) is a wonderful example of the media's capacity to be an agent of positive social change. Created with the intention of shocking people into awareness and action, its purpose is to represent the fact that Westerners and developed nations are literally sucking Africa dry. A Drop the Debt press release from 2004 states that 'African nations currently spend approximately $13.5 billion per year repaying debts—more than double the amount they spend on healthcare, and roughly equal to the amount needed to combat HIV/AIDS each year'. The image of the healthy white baby sucking much-needed nutrients from an emaciated African woman encourages viewers from developed nations to examine their personal consumption habits. It is part of a global campaign that aimed to put pressure on governments to change foreign aid policy, and on the World Bank and International Monetary Fund to waive loan repayments owed to them by poor nations. The scale of the figures in the image reminds us that the First World consumes far more than its fair share of the earth's resources. When we consume more than we need, we are using money and resources that could help save lives and thus we inadvertently deprive others of what they need to live. The caption, 'Haven't we taken enough?', anchors the meaning of the image, and prompts us to remember that we are all consumers, and thus we are all implicated in the global economic relations that widen the gap between the rich and the poor.

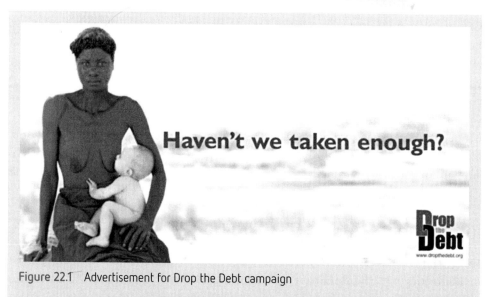

Figure 22.1   Advertisement for Drop the Debt campaign

Source: Photo courtesy of Red Cell, Drop the Debt, and photographer Tif Hunter

Homi Bhabha and the shadow history of the West

The eight elements discussed above are useful for understanding the relationship that has existed between Europe and the rest of the world from the fifteenth to the twenty-first century. What follows is an excerpt from an interview with the cultural theorist Homi Bhabha, in which Bhabha notes that the major twentieth-century ideas of Western culture have their basis in the eighteenth and nineteenth centuries, the time of colonialism, which he describes as 'the founding moment of modernity'. Thus, according to Bhabha, the West's ideas about itself are linked to the moment and realities of colonialism.

Interviewer	I'd like to refer to your comment that the founding moment of modernity was the moment of colonialism ... You said 'the colonial moment is the history of the West'. Can you elaborate on this remark?
Homi Bhabha	I think we need to draw attention to the fact that the advent of Western modernity, located as it generally is in the eighteenth and nineteenth centuries, was the moment when certain master narratives of the state, the citizen, cultural value, art, science, the novel, when these major cultural discourses and identities came to define the 'Enlightenment' of Western society and the critical rationality of Western personhood. The time at which these things were happening was the same time at which the West was producing another history of itself through its colonial possessions and relations. That ideological tension, visible in the history of the West as a despotic power, at the very moment of the birth of democracy and modernity, has not been adequately written in a contradictory and contrapuntal discourse of tradition. Unable to resolve that contradiction perhaps, the history of the West as a despotic power, a colonial power, has not been adequately written side by side with its claims to democracy and solidarity. The material legacy of this repressed history is inscribed in the return of post-colonial peoples to the metropolis. Their very presence there changes the politics of the metropolis, its cultural ideologies and its intellectual traditions, because they—as a people who have been recipients of a colonial cultural experience—displace some of the great metropolitan narratives of progress and law and order, and question the authority and authenticity of those narratives. The other point I'm trying to make is not only that the history of colonialism is the history of the West but also that the history of colonialism is a counter-history to the normative, traditional history of the West (Rutherford 1990, p. 218).

This is a complex and important statement. What is the difference between the two 'histories of the West' that Bhabha discusses? How does he understand the current relationship between Western peoples and postcolonial peoples? It might help to consider what the key characteristics of democracy are and what the term 'Enlightenment' means.

Bhabha suggests that there are two histories of the West, dating from the eighteenth and nineteenth centuries. The first is full of the positive ideals expressed in the French Revolution (liberty, fraternity, equality) and *The Rights of Man*, a document central to the American Revolution. These democratic and liberal ideals are the basis of the commonly accepted view of the development of the West until the present. They have had, and continue to have, an enormous impact on the development of democracy, democratic ideals, and human rights across the world. Bhabha does not deny these and, indeed, values them as positive and progressive. But his view is that at exactly the same time as the struggle for the rights of man was being conducted, the West was also involved in instituting and perpetuating slavery, racial extermination, religious persecution, and exploitation in the colonies. This second, shadow, and thus often hidden history is the other side of democratic, enlightened ideals. Bhabha exposes the obvious contradiction between these and argues that globally we have to acknowledge the historical consequences of these two histories and begin to try and reconcile them.

Bhabha also points to the fact that since the 1950s, from which time many former colonies began to achieve independence, many people from Asia, Africa, and the West Indies emigrated to what had become, through colonialism, their 'mother' countries. Consequently, the processes of immigration have forced minority world countries to face the consequences of their colonial exploitation.

Returning to the discussion of the history of the West and the non-West it is important to note the following three points about our contemporary situation.

1 The twentieth century saw a gradual fightback by the majority world. Many countries, African, Asian, and Middle Eastern states in particular, have achieved various forms of political independence since 1945. Economic independence, though, has been more difficult to achieve: multinational conglomerates are still able to dominate in majority world markets, even those that don't have Western political rule.

2 Japan and China, two non-Western powers, have maintained their independence, and have established their own economic empires that penetrate the Western world.

3 Economically, other Asian countries are now coming to the fore in the world, raising the possibility of a new world order for the twenty-first century, in which the countries of the Asia–Pacific region may have considerable economic power.

In relation to the media, it is important to understand that racial attitudes and beliefs have been built on the official history and the shadow history of the minority and majority worlds, and that these histories provide a framework for understanding the European–non-European opposition.

'The Other'

Another way of characterising the oppositions referred to above (black–white, East–West, and so on) is significant in media studies and cultural studies. These oppositions characterise everything that is not Western or European, or basically everything that is foreign, as 'the Other'. It should be noted that this term is used to highlight the political nature of such oppositions. It is not a straightforward description. The term 'Other' highlights the fact that that which falls into the category of Other has historically been seen as deviant, unnatural, and strange because it exists outside the boundaries of what the West deems normal and considers to be part of itself, or the same as itself. The use of the term 'the Other' draws attention to the way this judgmental stance supports the notion that Europeans are superior to their 'others'.

Eurocentrism

Another significant opposition is core–periphery. This opposition draws attention to **Eurocentrism**, which privileges European values and views. A Eurocentric approach takes European values, judgments, beliefs, and cultures as normal, natural, and ideal. It makes European values central, relegating others to the outside, the margins, the periphery. Many ethnic groups, their values and beliefs pushed to the edges of society, feel marginalised by this tendency on the part of dominant groups.

> **Eurocentrism**
> Places European values in a privileged, central position, and sees the world from a European perspective.

The core–periphery opposition has immediate resonance for a white Australian audience. Populated predominantly by people of European descent, Australia can be said to be part of the core. At the same time, it is geographically located almost as far east of Europe as you can go (c. 113–153° latitude east; only New Zealand, at c. 168–178°, is further east). Also, Australia is part of the southern hemisphere, which is made up predominantly of the majority world, and as a colony, it has a history of cultural cringe in that it has perceived its culture and achievements as being inferior to those of Europe. For all these reasons, Australia can also be said to be located on the periphery. It may be that Australia is in a unique position to appreciate the benefits of being part of the core and the disadvantages of the marginalisation that stems from being part of the periphery.

Multiculturalism

Multiculturalism aims to celebrate, integrate, and include all the different ethnic cultures that are part of one whole national culture, such as in Australia or South

multiculturalism
As a policy or a critical concept, multiculturalism celebrates unity in diversity by bringing together a range of cultural groups within a larger identity or community without privileging one culture over another.

Africa. One of the major issues in relation to multiculturalism has been the notion of integration of cultures and what this means. Some argue that integration means the outsider group taking on the values and identities of the host culture or the dominant culture: the danger here is that a monoculture would result. Others suggest that both cultures can change by drawing from each other. The dominant tendency in terms of white relationships with people of colour has been for white cultures to expect people of colour to take on white values and thus lose much of their cultural identities. Consequently, some groups have refused this option. They have sought out their own cultural heritage as an important source of their identity and have tried to sustain a separate cultural identity. This process of maintaining cultural distinctiveness has been reinforced when immigrant groups attempting to integrate have met with continued racial discrimination by the host population. Films such as *The Kings of Mykonos* and *Looking for Alibrandi* consider the cultural distinctiveness of ethnic groups who are labelled 'wogs' in Australia, and the musical *Bran Nue Dae* celebrates the lives and talents of its Aboriginal characters. These sorts of films explore the complex issues of discrimination and identity formation in a warm and humorous way.

Scripted mainstream television has been criticised for its lack of ethnic diversity, though there are some popular shows with multiethnic casts, such as *Grey's Anatomy* and *Glee*, which feature Asian, African American, Jewish as well as white characters. Even *Desperate Housewives* has introduced an African American central character in its seventh season. Nevertheless, while including characters from a range of ethnic backgrounds better reflects the multicultural world we live in, these primetime shows don't typically deal with racial or ethnic issues in a deep way.

Many outsider groups integrate through adopting markers of mainstream identity: clothing styles, hairstyles, particular sports, and other cultural pursuits, to name but a few. Many do this at the same time as searching for and preserving their own cultural roots and histories. In Australia this dual pursuit applies to Aborigines, who have faced the problems of invasion and colonialism, as well as to non-British immigrants who have made Australia multicultural. The issue of what integration means for these groups and for white Australians, as we all struggle over multiculturalism and land rights, is critical. As we enter the twenty-first century, we must continue to investigate issues relating to our cultural and national identity.

All the oppositions discussed above are central to questions about representation of ethnicity in the media. We have located these oppositions within a historical context: the real relations existing between whites and people of colour. It is important to understand that real relations of ethnicity are always represented and understood within the discourses of race and ethnicity that use these oppositions. These discourses need to be examined in order to understand current media representations of ethnicity.

Discourses of race and ethnicity

Media studies is interested in looking at the various voices or discourses of ethnicity and race, both in the past and in contemporary culture. It aims to see if and how these voices are linked, to see what overall discourse of ethnicity and race they produce. Different discourses, or ways of thinking, come from a range of fields—medical, philosophical, anthropological, and aesthetic. Put together, these constitute and organise our discourses of ethnicity and race. When we say 'organise', we don't mean that these ideas are deliberately put together; rather we mean that, through the culture's common sense, they shape the way we see particular issues.

One example of nineteenth-century Western discourse is the European belief in European racial superiority. This principle was supported by the combined discourses of Christianity, the scientific rationality of the Enlightenment, and (later) Darwinian philosophies of evolution, all of which argued that Europeans were more advanced, civilised, and moral than the peoples whom they were colonising. This discourse of superiority was thus used to justify their colonialist and imperialist exploits. Despite the fact that contact with colonised cultures and peoples was beneficial to European culture and detrimental to other cultures, many Europeans thought they were actually helping these indigenous peoples. European philosophers held that Europeans were more fully evolved, more civilised than other races, hence, other races needed civilising, and Europeans felt they had been charged with this task. The notion of white superiority and moral responsibility meant that whites felt that they carried the burden of maintaining order and control, establishing right and wrong. The phrase 'the white man's burden' was used to refer to this duty to civilise the colonies. Ironically, this belief was self-perpetuating because when Western structures, rules, regulations, political systems, literacy standards, and languages were imposed, of course the Westerners themselves were more accomplished in all fields because their background knowledge and experience gave them that advantage. Any mistakes or disputes that occurred as the colonised group adapted to or resisted the new system were taken as proof of inferiority. Colonial exploits, which included mass murder, rape, and wide-scale plunder, were partly carried out on the basis of this religious, missionary, do-gooding.

Thus discourses of white superiority, which are discourses of race, justified exploitation of the colonies and the colonised peoples.

Orientalism

One of the key texts relating to discourses of race is *Orientalism* by Edward Said (1980). Said examines the way in which Western countries have understood cultures of the 'Far East' and 'Middle East', countries beyond the 'Oriental line' (which divides the globe geographically between East and West). He suggests that there was

Orientalism
The way Europe has perceived, understood, and attempted to control cultures beyond the Oriental line.

a set of discourses about race that together constituted a discourse of **Orientalism**.

Said defines Orientalism in various ways. First, he sees it as a European method for understanding unfamiliar cultures:

> Orientalism is the generic term ... to describe the Western approach to the Orient; Orientalism is the discipline by which the Orient was (and is) approached systematically as a topic of learning, discovery, and practice (Said 1980, p. 73).

This definition does not refer to the exploitation inherent in Orientalism, but his second broader definition draws attention to the relations of power involved in Orientalism:

> Orientalism can be discussed and analysed as the corporate institution for dealing with the Orient—by making statements about it, authorising views of it, describing it, by teaching it, settling it, ruling over it: in short, Orientalism as a Western style for dominating, restructuring and having authority over the Orient (Said 1980, p. 3).

This definition shows that Orientalism contributes to maintaining European cultural hegemony over the Orient. Said's work focuses on Europe's relation to Eastern countries, but his approach has also been used to think about Europe's understanding of other non-European cultures, particularly African cultures, as well as Aboriginal culture and the culture of Native Americans.

Binary oppositions and stereotypes

Discourses of ethnicity circulating in the media will be examined by looking at

1 the use of binary oppositions as a way of depicting the differences between Europe and its Others
2 the use of stereotypical representations of non-Europeans and Europeans.

Binary oppositions

White, Orientalist definitions work by defining people of colour in terms of their differences from whites. A series of categories, or oppositions, is used by white culture to define and delineate cultures of the Other and, by implication, white culture (see Table 22.2).

Table 22.2 **White culture, Other culture—oppositions**

Other	White
Oriental	occidental
primitive	civilised

Other	White
savage	sophisticated
body	mind
irrational	rational
natural	cultural
eternal	historical
ancient	modern
mysterious	known
magical	scientific
heathen	Christian
underprivileged	privileged
evil	good
innocent	knowing
exotic	ordinary
erotic	repressed
free	controlled

You will probably be able to find many of these oppositions at play in media texts that include white and Other characters. Several elements of the left-hand column of the table above are signified in the advertisement for Persian carpets (see Figure 22.2; Table 22.2).

This advertisement draws on the Oriental characteristics of the left-hand column. It explicitly states that it offers exoticism and also treasures. The word 'treasures' connotes a world of piracy and fairy tales, the world of *1001 Nights*. It takes us to fictional worlds and the past. The advertisement contains sexual promise by means of the signifier of the alluring woman who is made mysterious through costume, through the veil that hides her from us. (In its original context, in 1993, the veil would connote something of the harem, and the colour of the veil, which in the original advertisement is red, connotes passion. In the post 9/11 climate of invasion of Iraq and conflict between Muslims and Christians the costume may have more threatening connotations.) The landscape places the woman outside time in a natural environment

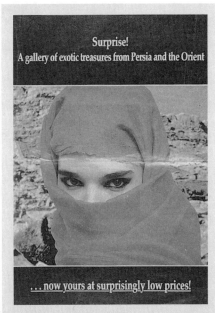

Figure 22.2   Advertisement for Persian carpets

Source: *Claremont/Nedlands Post*, 1993

that is outside or beyond the modern, civilised world, stretching back timelessly so that the image and the costume could come from the past. This advertisement thus offers escape from the modern world. It also clearly positions the woman—the Other—as an exotic treasure, an object that can be bought or possessed.

While the Diesel advertisement (Figure 22.3) does not depict perceptions of the Orient, it does depict the racial other and works within a similar set of binary oppositions to those listed above. In keeping with Diesel's playful, ironic mode of expression, however, the hierarchy of oppositions is inverted, Eurocentrism is undermined, and it raises a number of questions: Does it promote a critical awareness of stereotypical assumptions about race and culture? Does it invert stereotypes? Does it legitimate hierarchies or adversarial thought? Does Diesel's use of humour trivialise racism? Does the advertisement promote racial integration and assimilation into the materialistic value system of consumer culture?

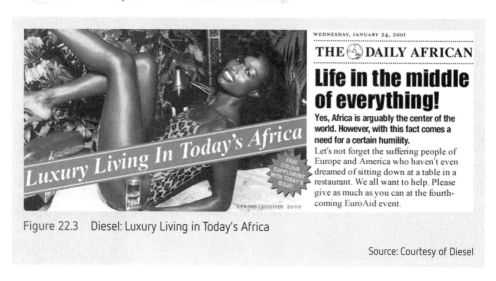

Figure 22.3   Diesel: Luxury Living in Today's Africa

Source: Courtesy of Diesel

The Orient as a projection of the white psyche

shadow
Parts of our personality that we have hidden, denied, and repressed, also known as the alter-ego.

As discussed above (pp. 103–4) projection suggests that what we see in the world and other people are aspects—projections—of repressed features of our own personalities, our own psyches, aspects of our desires that we normally disown or repress. Jung suggested that we all have a **shadow** side that incorporates these rejected parts of ourselves (see p. 335); that is, the side we project on to other people. Looking at the binary oppositions it could be argued that the Oriental, Other qualities represent what is repressed by white culture, so, if white culture officially denies and rejects aspects of bodily nature in favour of rationality, if it represses sexuality, if it denies savage wildness in favour of civilised behaviour, if it limits its thoughts and beliefs to Christianity, then all its negative or denied aspects may well be projected elsewhere, such as onto the Orient or the Other. In the caption to the 1939 illustration for a British boy's adventure story set in East Africa (Figure 22.4), the reference to imagination gives the game away. This illustration is from the white imagination; the Other figures play out the repressed white side.

The consequence of this understanding is that Orientalist discourse can be seen as an incredibly rich source of information, not about the Orient, but about the West itself. A study of Orientalist discourse as a projection of the repressed side of the white psyche reveals a great deal about the West. Such a notion is obvious if we consider the concept of exoticism. For something to be exotic it has to be strange, foreign, and exciting. To anyone born in a so-called exotic culture everything there will seem quite normal—far from exotic. Things can only seem exotic to the foreign eye. Thus a description of a culture or a person as exotic tells us about the beholder rather than the beheld. This view can also illuminate how whites have used stereotypes of people of colour.

As fine a state of frenzy as can well be imagined.

Figure 22.4   Illustration from *Top-All Book for Boys*, 1939

Source: Frederick Warne

Stereotypes

Stereotypes act as a shorthand for delineating character. Though they may involve some truth about the social realities of people's lives (Dyer 1993), they are limiting because

- they suggest that particular characteristics are shared by many people
- they suggest that these characteristics are part of the essential nature of these people (that is, that they are genetic, or biological) rather than connected to any social realities
- in many instances stereotypes are used pejoratively by dominant groups to describe subordinate groups.

Looking back at films, comics, and popular literature of the twentieth century you will find that the history of white representations of Other cultures and peoples is dominated by stereotyping. These stereotypes may now seem outdated, but they are still apparent in films such as *The Mummy* and the *Indiana Jones* films, and they

Figure 22.5 Cover of *Top-All Book for Boys*, 1939

Source: Frederick Warne

Figure 22.6 Poster for the film *The Battle of Elderbush Gulch*, c. 1920

Source: British Film Industry

were historically important in reflecting and maintaining dominant racist discourses through the twentieth century. They also include interesting representations of white characters so we can ask what kinds of stereotypes of whiteness are being presented.

Dyer was one of the first critics to suggest that whites can also be seen as a specific ethnic group. As analysts, we can begin to think about how whites and whiteness are being represented, what particular characteristics and stereotypes are involved. Many people believe that only media texts depicting people of colour and racial conflict are about race, but it is also the case that texts that have an all-white cast are also making implicit ideological statements about race by naturalising whiteness and portraying it as the norm.

Consider the 1930s representation and celebration of white masculinity in Figure 22.5. This cover of the British boys' annual, *The Top-All Book for Boys*, 1939, shows how children are introduced to stereotypes at an early age. *The Top-All Book* was awarded as a Methodist Sunday School prize, legitimating it within an official religious discourse. The title of the book, *Top-All*, and the illustration—one boy elevated over others on a cricket field—demonstrate the stereotypical ideology of masculinity that involves, in this instance, male sporting competitiveness and hierarchy. Such a cover might appeal equally to young white boys in England or Australia. This book included stories set in India and Africa (then parts of the British empire) and thus provided images of people of colour and whites, and a way of understanding the relationship between the two races. One of the stories has many similarities to the film *Indiana Jones and the Temple of Doom*, thus demonstrating how racist discourses from the 1930s were still prevalent in the 1980s.

The dangerous savage and the civilised white

When white and Other characters are depicted together we see how the stereotypes connect. Early twentieth-century representations differentiated between the civilised white and savage other. This stereotype portrays people of colour as dangerous and animal-like. It suggests that they are uncivilised and want to attack and harm whites, they are savages who threaten innocent women and children (Figure 22.6).

The perceived threat to women is understood as a sexual threat. This perception relates to the fear of miscegenation—sexual mixing of races—understood as a potential for the contamination of the white race. Mixed-race sexual relations have been a taboo area for official white culture, although throughout the history of race relations, white men have sexually used women of colour.

In the past, representations of attacks by indigenous peoples on whites have depicted such attacks as the result of the savage, evil nature of indigenous peoples. They are rarely presented as the last resort of peoples whose lands are being stolen and whose lifestyles are being destroyed by white invaders. The representation of these attacks as savage and animal justifies white violence as a defence against savagery and as an attempt to impose restraint on animal-like savages (see Figure 22.7). The stereotype of the black savage is thus very useful in justifying white oppression of indigenous populations.

Such stereotypes have been popularised by westerns that show Native Americans as savages, by Tarzan stories that show Africans as savages, and by numerous other stories, set in Africa, Asia, and Australia, that deal with relations between people of colour and whites. When the two groups are portrayed together it is invariably to demonstrate a fundamental opposition in their natures and ways of being that then justifies white violence—coded as a form of honourable retribution against savages—and suggests that whites need to exercise control over native populations in order to tame them. The whites are thus shown to be heroic, more intelligent, and more in control of their emotions, more rational.

"Down, dogs!" he stormed. "Do you dare snarl at me?"

Figure 22.7   Illustration from *Top-All Book for Boys*, 1939

Source: Frederick Warne

This stereotype has been used negatively in white representations. Some texts have, though, reclaimed the stereotype, reworking it to positive ends. Some US films made in the early 1970s began to capitalise on African American cinema audiences: African American heroes were introduced in films such as *Slaughter*, *Shaft* (remade in 2000 with Samuel L Jackson in the lead role and the actor who played Shaft in the original film playing his uncle), *Foxy Brown*, and Tarantino's *Jackie Brown* (with Pam Grier, star of the 1975 film *Sheba Baby*). These films redefine perceptions of race and gender.

The African American heroes in these movies are strong, powerful, and sexually potent figures who elicit positive identification from young African American audiences and envious admiration from white audiences. But while this genre, known as blaxploitation, was a move forward in some ways, as D Leab (1975) puts it, the shift 'from Sambo to Superspade' is still, in some ways, a reconfirmation of the stereotype of the black savage. Many fictional characters in films, comics, television programs, and pornographic movies still draw on this stereotype (Hernton 1970; Baker & Boyd 1997).

The noble savage

The noble savage is a variation on the dangerous savage stereotype. It too sees people of colour as uncivilised, but puts this in a positive light. The noble savage draws on European ideas established by the eighteenth-century philosopher Jean-Jacques Rousseau (see Rousseau 1974) and developed in the nineteenth century by American philosophers, including Henry David Thoreau (see Thoreau 1973). These authors regarded civilisation as corrupted and unnatural, and thought that people living outside European civilisation were pure and noble because of their relationship with nature, their distance from the decadence of European civilisation. Non-Europeans were thus thought to have a higher morality than whites. This stereotype draws on Christian traditions in that it sees the savage state as similar to the state of Adam and Eve in the Garden of Eden—a before-the-fall state. This is a great example of Eurocentrism, whereby Other cultures are understood in terms of white beliefs, religions, and mythologies, which shows the way white culture projects its own beliefs and values onto other cultures.

While this stereotype portrays people of colour as morally superior to whites, it is still limiting in that it locks them into a predetermined mould, denying them their own histories, glossing over the specificity of their own different cultures, and portraying them as incapable of change. The stereotype of the noble savage can be found in films such as *Avatar*, *Walkabout* (Figure 22.8), *Geronimo*, and *Dances with Wolves*, in which native cultures are portrayed as morally superior but essentially static and without internal diversity or a history of cultural development. *Avatar*, a film widely understood to dramatise the impact of colonialism on Indigenous people generally, and to allude to America's recent military campaigns in particular, shows the tall, blue-skinned Na'vi as a simple, peaceful species that have a spiritual, respectful attitude to the environment, in stark contrast with the destructive humans who seek to invade their home.

Figure 22.8 Image from the film *Walkabout*, 1971

Source: Scott Murray, *Cinema Papers*

There are a number of other stereotypes that are pervasive in the media: seeing people of colour as childlike in comparison to the responsible, adult white; seeing them as figures of fun and entertainment; seeing them as deviously clever and evil; seeing women of colour as sexually exotic and alluring, and so on. Traces of these discourses are still apparent in current media representations. What is interesting is that they are able to take a number of different characteristics and make them all negative. So whether people of colour are portrayed as savage or childlike, poor or rich, stupid or clever, they are always presented as being in need of white control and authority, thus justifying white power.

Recent representations

These stereotypical representations have been challenged, changed, or developed in recent years. Sometimes this results in further issues being raised. Black rap artists, representing a streetwise, powerful masculinity may offer strong role models but these positive qualities are often offset by their sexism, and their association with criminality and violence. The cultural theorist Matthew Henry critiques media images of contemporary black masculinity, suggesting that

> A particular type of black masculinity—one defined mainly by an urban aesthetic, a nihilistic attitude, and an aggressive posturing—has made its way into the cultural mainstream ... This image of masculinity has developed mainly as a result of the commodification of hip-hop culture and the ubiquity of rap music ... More specifically, it is the result of the popularity of the urban 'gangsta' (Henry 2002, p. 114).

Henry makes the point that race, class, and gender are inseparable aspects of identity, and claims that men of colour are affected by the power dynamics that inform each of these positions. According to Henry, as blacks within a racist social and political hierarchy, men of colour have neither power nor privilege, yet, as males within a patriarchal power structure, they have both (Henry 2002, p. 115). In an analysis of the film *Shaft*, Henry argues that contemporary media representations of black male violence arise from a need to compensate for being disempowered:

> One way of compensating for a perceived loss of power, potency or manhood is to adopt the 'tough guise': black male identity is increasingly defined within popular culture by rampant materialism, physical strength, and the acquisition of respect through violence (Henry 2002, p. 116).

While Henry has focused on one particular trend in representations of race in the media, there have also been many other developments. The films *Bran Nue Dae*, *Samson and Delilah*, *Jindabyne*, *Mad Bastards*, and *Rabbit Proof Fence* are among a number of Australian films that explore Aboriginal and white Australian history and relationships. *Rabbit Proof Fence* presents an Aboriginal point of view, challenges

Aboriginal stereotypes, and indeed, shows up white stereotypes of power and control. *Ten Canoes* goes one step further: it presents a story of Aboriginal culture in which there is no white, no European, presence at all and is the first film ever to use entirely Aboriginal language (though director Rolf de Heer and cinematographer Ian Jones are white Australians). The films *Crash*, *The Blind Side*, *Babel*, *Breaking and Entering*, and *A Mighty Heart* all explore the complexities of modern global and ethnic tensions and relationships.

Further work

You can develop your analysis of media representations of ethnicity by using various methods outlined in this book:

- *Verisimilitude*—consider the accuracy of representations and be aware of stereotypes and the sociohistorical contexts of production and reception.
- *Structuralism*—consider story, structure, values, binary oppositions, and endings.
- *Content analysis*—consider the frequency and proportion with which people of colour are (or are not) represented and link this to *media effects research*.
- *Political economy*—consider the context of production, money, and power relations.
- *Spectatorship and identification*—consider which characters we are invited to identify with and relate to.
- *Character analysis*—consider identity politics in light of the roles, relationships, and power dynamics that exist between characters in media texts.

Conclusion

People of colour are producing their own representations, and there is increased visibility for them in film and television fictions and in the media generally. Legislation regarding representation of minorities in American media has led to increased roles and recognition for performers and media personalities including Oprah Winfrey, Eddie Murphy, Beyoncé Knowles, Will Smith, and Halle Berry. Within the music industry and the sports world many black performers have for a long time achieved huge success and a space for black voices and images. Many advertisements aimed at a youth market include positive representations of sexy, streetwise people of colour. A number of African American and Asian writers and directors have produced hit films in America, most notably Spike Lee, Ang Lee, and M Night Shayamalan. Indigenous African cinemas have emerged, such as that led by the director Ousmane Sembene. There are a number of Aboriginal filmmakers—Tracey Moffat, Richard Franklin, and Rachel Perkins—working in Australia. A tradition of black British filmmaking has also developed. We should of course remember that the biggest film industry in the world is the Indian cinema, famous for its Bollywood productions.

This chapter has

- considered ways for understanding ethnicity and black–white oppositions
- examined the history of black–white relations
- defined and examined Eurocentrism, multiculturalism, Orientalism
- applied binary oppositions to media representations of ethnicity
- examined stereotypes of ethnicity.

Discussion points

1 Choose a film made by a director or writer from a race or background different from your own and examine its representations of race and ethnic issues.

2 Compare how Aboriginal–white relationships are represented in *Rabbit Proof Fence* and *Jindabyne*.

Summary

You should now be able to

- comment on the history of race relationships
- discuss the issue of ethnic invisibility in the media
- comment on the historical relationship between Europe and the rest of the world
- define and explain the terms 'Eurocentrism' and 'Orientalism' and use them in your analysis of media texts
- demonstrate how binary oppositions and stereotypes can be used to analyse media representations of ethnicity
- discuss contemporary representations of ethnicity.

CHAPTER 23

Stars and Celebrities

We are all voyeurs to one degree or another, including me, but with fame comes the predatory prowl of a carrion press that has an insatiable appetite for salaciousness and abhors being denied access to anyone, from pimps to presidents (a journey that becomes shorter every year), and, confused and resentful because it can't get what it wants, resorts to inventing stories about you because it is part of a culture whose most pressing moral imperative is that anything is acceptable if it makes money.

Marlon Brando, *Brando: Songs My Mother Taught Me*

This chapter will

▶   examine the phenomenon of stars and celebrities

▶   explore how the star system works as a marketing device

▶   explain star image

▶   analyse stars as texts that embody cultural meanings, values, and ideologies

▶   relate stardom to the mechanisms of identification and fandom

▶   present a case study on stardom, media, and identity.

Contemporary media are obsessed with stories about individuals, which reflects the dominance of the ideology of individualism (see pp. 34, 189, 265) that has permeated Western culture and media since the early twentieth century. In the early days of cinema, 'motion pictures did not include cast lists and actors were not promoted as identities independent of the roles they played on film' (Boorstin 2006, p. 80). Theorist Daniel Boorstin's research shows that in the early twentieth century almost three-quarters of the people who received media coverage were figures from business, politics, and the professions, whereas by the 1920s over half were from entertainment: fan magazines had begun to popularise the private lives of movie stars. A significant moment in this shift of media attention from business to entertainment and in the corresponding shift of fan attention from screen characters to actors came in 1910 when the film producer Carl Laemmle sought to brand his films by associating them with the lead actress contracted to his studio, the Independent Motion Picture company:

> Laemmle announced in the press that [...] the anonymous actress who had appeared in many of his films, had died. However, when she miraculously made an appearance to disprove this fact, Laemmle reported to the newspapers that the crowds were so hysterical that they tore off her clothes. This was equally untrue, but the ensuing furore burned her name, Florence Lawrence, into the public's consciousness. Lawrence became a huge star, earning $80 000 in 1912 (Cousins 2004, p. 42).

Today the media and the public are fascinated with stories about prominent individuals from the entertainment industries. Following cinema's successful use of the star system as a central method in filmmaking and marketing, television established its own familiar faces, actors, and personalities who encouraged audiences to return week after week, and launched shows such as *Famous*, *Gossip Girl*, and *TMZ* to foster even more interest in these dazzling people. *TMZ* began as a celebrity website that has migrated across to network television. It features user-generated content such as mobile phone footage of celebrities spotted within a thirty mile zone (TMZ) of Hollywood. Other entertainment industries, particularly music and sport, also use well-known performers to attract fans to games and concerts and to sell merchandise such as football jerseys and music CDs and DVDs. In addition, newspapers increasingly report on individual stars and celebrities and frame more and more stories in terms of individuals rather than issues. Magazines devoted to gossip about stars' and celebrities' private and personal lives divert the attention of shoppers at the supermarket checkout, who idly glance at the glossy images and sensational headlines while they wait in line. In contemporary popular culture practically everyone knows the trials and tribulations of A-list celebrities and the names of their nearest and dearest as well as, or better than, they know the members of parliament or the names of world leaders.

To understand the cult of celebrity and its place in our culture, two related issues need to be considered. The first concerns how stars operate as a financial and ideological system within the film and entertainment industries. The second is to ask why the media are becoming more and more obsessed with celebrities, and how this affects popular culture and society. We note a number of starting points.

- It's useful to note some distinctions between the terms '**star**', '**celebrity**', and 'media personality'. Stars originated as a term in relation to the entertainment industries, particularly the cinema, but

star
Stardom is an elite type of celebrity based, at least initially, on a person's outstanding professional achievement. Stars play well-publicised leading roles in popular culture and entertainment media. They consistently outshine colleagues and competitors, and their personal and professional lives attract significant attention.

celebrity
A celebrity is a well-known, highly visible public figure whose private life and public appearances frequently attract the media spotlight, often for reasons other than their professional standing or abilities.

also popular music and sport. They are people who excel in their chosen field but also, and more importantly, attract a large popular following. They appear literally as larger than life in the cinema or they are separated from the audience on a stage or a sports field where the audience tries to get as close to them as possible. Celebrity is based largely on biographical information. Celebrity, Paul Watson argues, is 'a mode of stardom relatively unconnected to the sphere of professional work. In other words, celebrity is sustained not by someone's excellence or ability in their chosen profession' (2003, p. 173). Instead of focusing on professional performance, celebrity relies almost entirely on an individual's charisma and the ability to attract sustained media interest in their private life and public appearances at high profile events. Celebrity doesn't happen because someone has extraordinary qualities—it is discursively constructed by the way in which the person is publicised and meanings about them circulate, 'a consequence of the way individuals are treated by the media' (Turner 2004, p. 7). It is possible to be a celebrity who is famous for being famous, or famous for being rich, or notorious, or a socialite, but such people, for example Paris Hilton or contestants on reality television shows, would not be described as stars. Personalities are more a product of television and are more familiar and everyday—appearing regularly in homes via the television, seeming smaller than in the cinema and more accessible. Either they are being themselves (newsreaders, chat show hosts, television chefs, and so on) or they are associated with long-standing roles they play (for example, James Van der Beek is famous just for his one role as Dawson in *Dawson's Creek*).

- Media image is important. While stars in the cinema have always been sold through their image, this has now permeated many fields, including, in politics, John F Kennedy, who is reckoned to have won the 1960 American presidential election because on television he looked nicer than the five-o'clock-shadowed, sweaty Richard Nixon. Since then political parties depend more and more on the media image of their leader—how they look, how convincing they sound, whether they can communicate easily with citizens, how acceptable their private lives are—rather than on their political abilities or their party's policies. Image, spectacle, presentation, and private lives are all-important. The rise of celebrity culture and the disproportionate interest constructed around the superficial relevance of public figures and their actions is indicative of a shift 'towards a culture that privileges the momentary, the visual and the sensational over the enduring, the written and the rational' (Turner 2004, p. 4). This focus on image relates to contemporary postmodern culture's emphasis on spectacle and surface reality (see p. 448).

- There has been an increased focus on stars' and celebrities' private lives. The desire to know what stars are really like and to know about their private and personal lives is escalating. In the 1950s it was easy for publicists to present Rock Hudson (in America) and Dirk Bogarde (in Britain) as two of the most popular, heterosexually desirable film stars who played in numerous romantic films.

Their gay sexuality, while known about by people close to them and within the industry, was easily kept secret from the female fans who adored them and male fans who might emulate them. Such a situation is unimaginable today. Change has come about partly through the huge increase in media product and the advance in technologies for recording and capturing private lives and the acceptance of the right of the media to invade people's privacy. This focus on private life relates to a desire to find out the real truth about people—as discussed in relation to reality TV. It gives rise to contentious issues about what rights the media have to follow people around and publicise their private lives, and illustrates the way that publicity combines a discourse of celebration and adulation of stars with a discourse of scurrilous gossip and scandal mongering—stars seem to be loved and hated by the media and media consumers.

- Contemporary culture is 'addicted to celebrity' (see Schultz 2004), gossip, and personality in which, today, virtually all events are presented in terms of stars, celebrities, and personalities, a phenomenon driven by market forces. The tabloid press (the cheaper, popular newspapers) gained higher circulation by running stories about well-known people, focusing on sports and entertainment. To be competitive, magazines and serious newspapers increasingly had to follow suit; they now give more coverage to leisure and lifestyle and present events in terms of personalities more than they once did. In his 2007 interview with Larry King, Al Gore lamented how serious news has given way to a greater concentration on news about celebrities (such as Paris Hilton's brief stint in jail), rather than about real news such as politics and the environment. Even politicians actively court celebrity status using popular media (consider Gore's own documentary *An Inconvenient Truth*, and Hillary Clinton's use of *The Sopranos* in her 2007 election campaign. The media also use celebrities to engage with social, political, and environmental issues (for instance James Cameron used his film *Avatar* to promote environmental conservation—and not just on Pandora—he helped Earth Day Network plant a million trees on planet Earth. Natalie Portman designed a range of leather-free shoes to promote veganism and protest cruelty to animals; she also appeared in the documentary *Saving a Species: Gorillas on the Brink*). Another trend uses celebrity endorsement to encourage the consumption of branded causes, such as cyclist Lance Armstrong's ubiquitous rubber armband and Angelina Jolie becoming known as the face of the United Nations. What these examples suggest is that Gore's claim has broader implications, not all of them negative, and that the tension between real news, serious issues, and celebrity discourse exists on a continuum rather than as mutually exclusive, oppositional categories.

- Democratisation and short turnaround time are issues. The success of reality programs such as *MasterChef* and *The Farmer Wants a Wife* points to two other factors: the way that ordinary people can now become famous and the way that they are quickly found, celebrated, and then forgotten.

Having looked at the wider discourse of stardom and celebrity, consider now how stars operate in the media industry by focusing on the following three interconnected aspects:

bankability
The stars' potential to guarantee a film's financial box-office success.

1 stars as financial and industrial commodities: **bankability**
2 celebrities as texts: star image
3 stars as the embodiment of social and ideological values.

These aspects of stardom are linked because stars are images, manufactured out of a range of materials, that are sold as commodities and consumed on the strength of their meanings (see Dyer 1998).

Stars as financial and industrial commodities: bankability

How much are stars worth and what makes a star bankable?

When film researcher Christine Gledhill describes stars as 'cogs in the mass entertainment industry selling desires and ideologies' (1991, prologue), she is expressing the view that the media industry and stardom are entirely reliant on marketability. Stars are the basis on which media texts get financed, labour that helps produce the texts, a selling point for the texts and their associated merchandise. Put quite simply the star system is a marketing device for entertainment products that stars appear in, the newspapers, magazines, television programs, and so on that feature photographs and stories about stars, and for the commodities that the stars endorse. Later in this chapter it will also be argued that stars are used to sell (or at least to get fans to buy into) values, ideals, and lifestyles, which is an ideological approach to analysing celebrity culture. Here we will focus on a political economy approach (see Chapter 2, p. 22) to stardom that considers stars as marketable commodities in the media industry and examines the implications of the economic foundations of the star system. In this sense the media industry regards stars as bankable commodities (rather than people or texts). Below is a list of the ten best-paid actors in 2011.

Table 23.1 **Highest-paid actors**

Actor	2010/11 income (in US dollars)
1 Leonardo DiCaprio	$77 million
2 Johnny Depp	$50 million

Actor	2010/11 income (in US dollars)
3 Adam Sandler	$40 million
4 Will Smith	$36 million
5 Tom Hanks	$35 million
6 Ben Stiller	$34 million
7 Robert Downey Jr	$31 million
8 Sarah Jessica Parker	$30 million
9 Angelina Jolie	$30 million
10 Mark Wahlberg	$28 million

Source: <www.forbes.com/wealth/celebrities/list?&ascend=true&sort=rank>, 2011,

Accessed 7 September 2011

These stars are not so highly paid because they are twenty-eight to seventy-seven times better than actors who only earn $1 million per year, or exponentially better at their jobs than school teachers or journalists who may earn in the vicinity of $50 000 per year. They earn this much because within the economy of stardom they are bankable. If they feature prominently in publicity material for a film, that film will earn at least $100 million at the US box office alone, so from the financier's point of view the star's salary is a secure investment. The reason for this is because people often base their selection of films on their favourite stars in much the same way that they choose films based on a preference for a particular genre. Stars, like genres, generate expectations and guarantee the satisfaction of certain pleasures. Fame and fortune are virtually inseparable because popularity generates profit. In other words, the economics of the media industry and the bankability of a star (the guarantee that their popularity will ensure massive profits from the sale of products, media texts, and tickets to see the stars perform) are central to attaining and maintaining star status.

A political economy approach to studying celebrity reveals that the bankability of stars is not just a matter of financial calculations: it is itself subject to cultural value systems. Consider what this list of the highest paid actors in 2011 indicates about whom and what we value. You might notice that all but one of the highest-paid performers are white, and that 80 per cent are male. Furthermore, the top ten male actors earn on average $37.1 million dollars per year while the top ten female actors earn on average $21.6 million dollars, which is about 40 per cent less than their male counterparts. Indeed, Angelina Jolie was paid $10 million for *Mr & Mrs Smith* whereas her co-star Brad Pitt earned double that: $20 million. This suggests that social inequities are reproduced and represented in the economy of stardom. If we see stars' salaries and marketability as a measure of the degree to which they are valued (or what they represent is valued), we can note some broad trends. Just as film is accorded higher cultural status than television, males and white people still tend to be accorded higher monetary and cultural value than females and people of colour. As Dyer puts it,

> If you are not white, middle-class, heterosexual and male you are not going to fit 'the cultural world' too well—women only fit uneasily, whilst blacks, gays and even the working-class hardly fit at all (Dyer 2006, p. 162).

In October 2007 Warner Bros. president of production Jeff Robinov announced that 'We are no longer doing movies with women in the lead'. The reason given was the failure of three woman-centred action movies produced for Warner Bros. by Joel Silver—Jodie Foster's *The Brave One*, *The Reaping*, with Hilary Swank, and *The Invasion*, starring Nicole Kidman. On the surface, Robinov seemed to be making a logical business decision, but his calculation of the bankability of female stars neglected to account for the roles of the men who wrote, directed, and produced these films. Commentator Nikki Finke (2007), among others, asked why Robinov would blacklist female stars when the men responsible for equally expensive flops such as *Superman Returns*, *Alexander*, *Grindhouse*, and *A Good Year* remain in good standing <www.deadlinehollywooddaily.com/>.

While the popularity (and hence the perceived bankability) of film stars may be influenced by cultural value systems, other arenas of celebrity are judged more by achievement. Discourses of celebrity vary in different media. In sports a star's value is measured by their success in competitions rather than just by popularity or appearance. Prominent figures in music, sports, and public life perform as themselves and gain attention on the basis of merit, achievements, and expertise. *Forbes* magazine's 2011 'Celebrity 100' issue ranked the world's most powerful celebrities across all sectors of the entertainment industry. Singer Justin Bieber made the list, along with Taylor Swift and golfer Tiger Woods, but Lady Gaga and Oprah Winfrey, a woman of colour, eclipsed them all and took the top two places. Indeed, Oprah earned $290 million in 2011 and has maintained her place as highest-earning celebrity for over a decade. Contrary to the move away from female-centred films at WB, there has been a strong trend towards casting women in leading roles in new television drama and comedy series in the USA, which suggests that women and people of colour are more successful in television, sport, and publishing—areas where familiarity, business acumen, and merit are valued highly and enable members of otherwise disadvantaged groups the chance to succeed, despite ideological values that may work against them.

Forbes also devised a way of evaluating the bankability of film stars, a method based on the profit earned for each dollar spent on the star's salary, rather than on the star's income alone. By this valuation system, many of the most bankable stars turned out to be women.

Table 23.2   Bankability: profit earned for each dollar spent on a star's salary in 2010

Star	Profit in US dollars
Shia LeBeouf	$81
Anne Hathaway	$64
Daniel Radcliffe	$61
Robert Downey Jr.	$33
Cate Blanchett	$27
Jennifer Aniston	$21
Meryl Streep	$21
Johnny Depp	$18
Nicholas Cage	$17
Sarah Jessica Parker	$17

Source: <www.forbes.com/2007/08/03/celebrities-hollywood-movies-biz-cz_dp_0806starpayback.html>

Accessed 3 August 2011

Of the ten most bankable actors, half are women and the most expensive stars don't necessarily give the best return to studios. This may mean Shia LeBeouf and Anne Hathaway are underpaid, but it may equally mean that some big name Hollywood actors earn unreasonably inflated salaries. The biggest disappointers were Hollywood's top-earning funnymen. Adam Sandler and Ben Stiller are in the list of Hollywood's top ten highest-earning actors but they didn't make it into the top ten bankable stars.

The importance of the popularity and marketability of stars as media commodities is also evident in sports, even though sport is primarily a merit-based form of celebrity. Sports stars now often earn more money through their endorsements than through their salaries. In 2010 golf king Tiger Woods earned more than any athlete in history in a single year. Of his $105 million income, more came from lucrative sponsorship and endorsement contracts with companies such as Nike, Tag Heuer, and Gillette than did from the competition prize money he won. Following his highly publicised infidelities, Woods has been dropped by several sponsors and his 2011 income fell to $75 million. In the process of selling or selling out, some sports stars have gone so far as to legally change their names to the brand name of the product they endorse. Gary Hocking, a footballer who played for the Geelong Cats in Australia, was paid to temporarily change his name to Whiskas (a brand of cat food) so that the sports commentators would have to say the product name every time they commented on the star's performance.

Because the figures examined above indicate that within the economy of stardom, image trumps expertise, it is now necessary to examine the concept of stars as images in more detail.

Star image

What is a star image and how is this sold?

The media are not selling us the stars themselves (much as we might like to buy Matt Damon or Katherine Heigl and take them home), they are selling the **star's image**. A star's image is constructed out of what we see or read about them, their media visibility. The star image is based on the social values they embody (see p. 425). Each individual star has their own image and appeal, which is what audiences are drawn to. The images are sold first through what Richard Dyer and others called 'primary circulation', that is, the films, DVDs, television programs, concerts, and sports events that they perform in. Stars are then sold and supported by the images of 'secondary circulation', that is, all the media outlets that give further information about and publicity for the star: interviews, publicity photos, reviews, Academy Award ceremonies, fanzines, websites, ads, gossip, and so on, that focus on the star's performance and their offscreen, 'real' life. It is important to note first, that this image can and will change over time, as the star grows older, plays different roles, and goes through personal life changes. These changes and developments themselves become a source of fascination. Consider how Britney Spears' media image has changed over time. Having been portrayed as everything from a sexy schoolgirl to a caring wife and mother, the singer struggled to freshen up her tarnished image with her own signature perfume and overcame rumours of mental illness and substance abuse, and legal battles regarding child custody to make a comeback with her successful 2011 album *Femme Fatale*.

> **star image**
> The qualities, ideals, and values that a star represents, based on their films and other performances, and on media information circulated about them.

Second, while stars must have some level of professional competence—that is, be relatively good actors, singers, or players—some theorists have questioned whether performance is really central to the star phenomenon. Gledhill suggests that 'actors become stars when their off-screen lifestyles and personalities equal or surpass acting ability in importance' (Gledhill 1991, p. xiv). Gledhill's point can be extended to include other forms of ability or prowess besides acting. David Beckham's popularity is based on his image as much as on his excellence as a sportsman. Other equally proficient soccer players have not attracted the same degree of attention or adulation.

For actors their star image is based on a combination of their actual screen roles, the stories that circulate about them, and their personal lives. Nicole Kidman's star image is based partly on the roles she plays in films and partly on what we see and hear about her private life, particularly her marriage to and subsequent divorce from Tom Cruise, her remarriage to singer Keith Urban, and her identity as an Australian within an American industry. Her film roles and image have developed from comedy and thrillers into musicals and serious films as she extends her performance range, but audiences will understand this image in relation to the image of her personal life: when we see her with Cruise acting as the troubled wife in *Eyes Wide Shut*, then as single mother in *The Others*, as a woman faithfully waiting for Mr Right in *Cold Mountain*, and later a beleaguered feminist who outshines her husband in *The Stepford Wives*, we interpret her performances partly in the light of our wider knowledge of her personal life.

Whenever we see stars who are familiar from other roles or publicity about them we bring this information into how we construct their image and read the film. This means audiences read films and stars on the basis of **intertextual** and **extratextual** knowledge. For example, Jennifer Aniston has starred in a number of films since playing the good-hearted, fashion savvy character Rachel in the long-running sitcom *Friends*. Nevertheless, our perception of each new film character she plays is affected by our understanding of Rachel, as well as Aniston's previous film roles. This intertextuality means that Rachel's drawn-out quest for a stable romantic partner and her on-again, off-again relationship with Ross (played by David Schwimmer) informs how we construe her roles in romantic comedies like *The Switch*, *Love Happens*, *Along Came Polly*, *He's Just Not That Into You*, *The Bounty Hunter*, and *Bruce Almighty*. We are led to believe that in some ways she plays herself in these films: an attractive woman struggling to find love or commitment, or both, someone who is a little neurotic but always well-meaning and fun. Existing opinions about Aniston and the characters she plays also lead us to make predictions about how these films will end. Extratextual knowledge reinforces these expectations, as information gained through external sources such as gossip, magazines, online blogs and celebrity websites feeds into our view of stars. In Aniston's case, her widely publicised break-ups with high-profile men such as Brad Pitt, Vince Vaughn, and John Mayer reinforce the public perception that she is unlucky in love—but that her fairy tale isn't over just yet.

> **intertextual knowledge**
> Knowledge and information gained from other related media texts.
>
> **extratextual knowledge**
> Knowledge and information taken from sources external to the text.

Stars as the embodiment of social and ideological values

Why are some people elevated to stardom rather than others?

Star images are ideological insofar as they represent social values. Richard Dyer argues that stars embody social values that need, or are felt to need, assertion or reassertion. Dyer claims that 'The general image of stardom can be seen as a version of the American dream, organised around the themes of consumption, success and ordinariness' (Dyer 2006, p. 154). This begins to explain why certain stars are successful: what they represent through their star image connects with audience desires, beliefs, and values.

The success of any star and their image is built on a threefold combination: the work of the media industries plus the actual contributions of the star plus the audiences who pay to see the star. Marilyn Monroe was originally just one of a number of starlets being groomed and marketed by the film studios. Why did she succeed when others did not? It was a combination of her individual talents, marketed by the industry, that connected with audiences.

In a sense stars offer audiences symbolic resolution to cultural concerns. Dyer (1987) has argued that it was Monroe's complex image of female sexuality and her ability to embody contradictions that connected with the cultural concerns of 1950s and 1960s audiences (for example, their contradictory views of sexuality). She could connect to many people in different ways: she could be seen as victim or heroine, appeal to men as sex object or as comedienne, and to women as someone actively exploring her own sexuality or struggling to survive in a male-dominated world.

David Beckham's image is similarly successful because he embodies cultural complexity and contradictions. His image is linked to all the products he endorses, such as Police shades and Adidas sportswear: his identity and reputation are mapped onto the brand and consumed along with the products. When buying the products, consumers are also buying into the fashionable, athletic, handsome image, sexuality, and affluent lifestyle Beckham embodies. Beckham's popularity can be explained by the incredible scope and flexibility of his image: he can be many things to many people. His sporting prowess coupled with his well-publicised sexual prowess gives him a masculine appeal that is hard to match. Despite having succumbed to the charms of several of his admirers, he is known as a loving husband and devoted father, yet at the same time his edgy tattoos and transgressions give him street cred and associate him with freedom and rebellion. In this way his contradictory image legitimates the fantasy of sexual availability while he is simultaneously being a responsible family man. Beckham's flair for fashion and his ability to wear nothing but Armani briefs, or everything from diamond earrings and a ponytail to a tuxedo, ripped jeans, and cornrow braids have also extended his appeal into the pink market. He has even been credited with embodying a new type of identity: the metrosexual (see p. 387). Here, the star is representative of and embodies changing social norms, discourses, and shifting boundaries around gender and sexuality. Beckham's image has many ideological slants so a broad demographic can identify with him on some level and he can be used to sell practically anything.

Stars 'personalise social meanings and ideologies' (Gledhill 1991, p. xiv), and can be seen to embody cultural archetypes. For many people, the iconic figures of Marilyn Monroe and John Wayne give an identifiable, personal form to the social meanings and ideologies surrounding femininity and masculinity, in particularly Western ways. Stars such as Katharine Hepburn, Jodie Foster, Sigourney Weaver, and Angelina Jolie come to be seen as the embodiment of aspects of feminism. In a similar way, Judy Garland, Liza Minnelli, James Dean, and the contemporary actors Ellen Degeneres and Rupert Everett personify meanings associated with gay culture. This close association between a star and the ideas they embody rubs off on those who engage with the media texts circulating around the star, thus implicating stars in the production of personal and cultural identity: 'Celebrity becomes a key site of media attention and personal aspiration, as well as one of the key places where cultural meanings are negotiated and organised' (Turner 2004, p. 6). As theorist Steven Cohan puts it, 'It is a truth almost universally acknowledged that a single man in possession of a Judy Garland CD must *not* be in want of a wife' (Cohan 2001, p. 119). The connection between stars and audiences can be further explored via an analysis of identification and fandom.

Identification and fandom

How are fandom and stardom related?

With the decline of the nuclear and extended families, and localised community networks, para-social interaction (interactions and relations with people we do not know) is growing in importance, 'constructing a new dimension of community through the media' (Turner 2004, p. 6). The media actively encourage a sense of familiarity and friendship with stars and celebrities (see how magazine covers often refer to stars by their first names—Nicole, Julia, Brad). There is a range of possible connections between stars and their fans. At one extreme there is the danger of stars being stalked by fans: 'the obsessive fan appears to have been "taken over" by the text in a way that "we" have not, or has wilfully submitted to a zealousness that, in the extreme, can manifest itself in the pathological behaviour of a stalker' (Casey et al. 2002, p. 93). At the other extreme there can be simple indifference, dislike, or disregard. In between there is a range of identificatory practices, all of which are linked to the fan's sense of the star as someone extraordinary, beyond the realm of the everyday, different from us, and as a real and ordinary person, just like us.

Stardom, as film studies academic Linda Mizejewski points out, is reliant on culturally defined concepts of authenticity, privacy, and individuality in relation to publicity, performance, and the personae that stars enact and project (Mizejewski 2001, p. 166). Mizejewski goes on to say:

> Fans are incited to peel away public and textual images in order to discover the 'real' or private person underneath ... While star appeal depends on connection and identification, for example, it also depends on adulation and glamour; fans simultaneously need to imagine the star is fully human and ordinary, but also larger than life and extraordinary (Mizejewski 2001, p. 166).

Working together, fan identification and media publicity function to mask or bridge the gap between the star and the audience, which also serves an ideological purpose. As tabloid television theorist John Langer puts it, 'By appearing to reduce the distance through intimacy, the personality system operates to mask the gap between the powerful and the powerless, ensuring that the real unities of power, class, prestige, and interest can continue relatively intact and unexamined' (Langer 2006, p. 194).

As the quote by Marlon Brando at the beginning of this chapter suggests, the discourse of stardom and celebrity involves journalistic coverage of celebrities' private lives in order to invite a sense of intimacy and identification among fans. This coverage, which is an occupational hazard of stardom, is sometimes excessively invasive. Extreme instances of the invasion of privacy by the media include the hounding of Princess Diana and unauthorised, well-publicised photographs of stars' private parts and private moments.

How do media technologies facilitate fandom, and to what effect?

Fandom extends beyond the avid consumption of media products to include the production and circulation of meanings about celebrities and the texts they star in. It also offers an opportunity for social connection as fans group together, sharing and communicating with each other. Henry Jenkins describes how interactive media technologies such as the internet have reshaped the cultural practices of fandom to create online communities:

> As the community enlarges and as reaction time shortens, fandom becomes much more effective as a platform for consumer activism. Fans can quickly mobilize grassroots efforts to save programs or protest unpopular developments. New fandoms emerge rapidly on the web — in some cases before media products actually reach the market. As early participants spread news about emergent fandoms, supporters quickly develop the infrastructure for supporting critical dialogue, producing annotated program guides, providing regular production updates, and creating original fan stories and artwork (Jenkins 2002).

In this sense media technologies provide a feedback loop to media producers, and enable fans to produce their own texts featuring stars. For the majority of people, however, engagement with stars and celebrities plays out in less fanatical forms of identification. However it is expressed, fandom represents participation in the discourse of celebrity and a kind of ownership or appropriation of the star, which leads to an incorporation of the star's identity into the fan's identity.

identification
A feeling of connectedness to another person. It involves seeing aspects of oneself in that person, experiencing a sense of relatedness or overlapping of identity.

Identification with stars involves the 'negotiation between self and other' via 'the recognition of similarities and differences' (Stacey 2006, p. 253). It is also a negotiation between the actual self and an imaginary self: 'It is this gap between the film star and everyday people that produces the self-transformation to be more like the star. Thus the difference provides the space for the production of a fantasy self more like the ideal' (Stacey 2006, p. 254). As film theorist Jackie Stacey's research suggests, there are two main forms of identification: identificatory fantasies and identificatory practices. The fantasy aspect is usually played out in the cinema or in celebrity interviews when we enjoy being inside an actor's life or a character's world. Often this means aspiring to the power, privilege, and beauty of the star, and feeling empathy for and identifying with the star or their screen persona. In this sense we can see ourselves in the star or the character they play, imagine ourselves in their position. We may also indulge in objectifying fantasies in which we see the star as erotic object of desire (see pp. 274–5).

Identificatory practices occur in everyday life when we buy the Police sunglasses David Beckham endorses or the Sarah Jessica Parker marketed Garnier hair dye, Bitten clothing, and Covet perfume. In this sense we could say that desire and identification drive consumption. The star is a public persona, but modes of identification are mostly related to the private, personal, domestic sphere, so the star bridges the public and private spheres via practices of identification.

Academic writing is also part of the discourse of stardom and celebrity. Different theoretical paradigms—psychoanalysis, Marxism, feminism—have tried to explain the process of identification with stars. In the 1920s Freud defined identification as 'the earliest expression of an emotional tie with another person' (cited in Brown & Fraser 2004, p. 101). The sense of identification as an interpersonal, emotional bond persists in film and media studies literature today. Psychoanalysts also discuss narcissistic identification. Narcissus, a figure in Greek mythology, fell in love with his own reflection, so narcissistic identification refers to the sense in which a fan perceives or imagines that the star's image reflects some aspect of their own identity. We like to feel that the star is like us in some way, that we share a common quality, and that is why we relate to them and admire them. In contrast, Marxist theorists foreground the economic relations of stardom and refer to identification as interpellation: the star text positions consumers in alignment with a certain kind of social identity. Texts that feature stars often interpellate the viewer into a position of desire, and the hegemonic force of the media encourages consumerism and persuades us to consent to the idea that the ideological values a star stands for are natural and good. Indeed, some feminists have suggested that 'Identification itself has been seen as a cultural process complicit with the reproduction of dominant culture by reinforcing patriarchal forms of identity' (Stacey 1991, p. 147).

Stars are, by definition, extraordinary and ideal, yet through the process of identification with the characters they play and through access to the ordinary, human dramas of their personal lives they become more accessible to the public. In this way public fascination with stars can be based on difference and aspiration or similarity and identification. The extensive publicity surrounding, for example, Reese Witherspoon and Jake Gyllenhaal's relationship breakdown offered the public a chance to fantasise about two attractive, unattainable stars who suddenly became 'available', while it simultaneously made the 'perfect couple' seem more human (many people can empathise with the difficulties of ending a relationship amicably amid jealousy and gossip, and this generates sympathy and attention for the stars). In many cases when stars reveal their personal trials and tribulations to the press, ordinariness is used as an image management strategy to facilitate identification between fans and stars.

This desire to know the star can of course never be fully realised, just as we cannot actually become the star. For one thing, as Dyer writes, whatever information we consume about the stars' private lives is actually media-constructed: 'We never know them as real people, only as they are found in media texts' (Dyer 1998). It is this unattainable desire to know someone and to identify with them that drives us on as fans, and maintains the whole star system. The stars' ultimate unknowability and inaccessibility keep us coming back for more.

It is interesting to think back to how the ideas, science, and philosophies of the twentieth century have challenged the myth of individual autonomy (see the discussion on subjectivity, pp. 188–90). Perhaps the West's obsession with stars is an attempt to hold on to the ideology of individuality so that we can believe that despite what the sciences say, we too have individual autonomy and also have the possibility of transcending social circumstances and achieving greatness.

Case study: Star–celebrity profile: Angelina Jolie and the transmission of cultural values

An effective way of approaching a star–celebrity profile analysis using methods and conceptual tools drawn from media studies is to begin with general biographical details and professional information about the star and their place in the industry, then move to a specific analysis of one image, interview, or text featuring that star. The broad contextual picture of the star's life and work establishes a relationship between their personal and professional identity and their marketability, as well as suggesting how the media facilitate fan identification. The close textual analysis supports generalisations with a specific example and allows the ideological and cultural values that the star embodies to be decoded. Below we apply this method to analyse the meanings embodied by Angelina Jolie.

It has become fashionable to refer to celebrity couples as a single entity, indicating the extent of public fascination with the love lives of the rich and famous. The media have an ongoing love affair with celebrity couples, reporting every real or imagined bump on the rocky roads travelled by Bennifer (Ben Affleck and Jennifer Garner), Pecks (encompassing Victoria Beckham, née Posh Spice, her breast implants, and the legendary pectoral muscles of her husband David), TomKat (the lopsided partnership of Tom Cruise and former teen television idol Katie Holmes), and KeyHole (the much maligned marriage of Keith Urban and Nicole Kidman). The most newsworthy of them all is Brangelina, the celestial union of two of Hollywood's most attractive and successful stars: Brad Pitt and Angelina Jolie. Brangelina is a darling of the media because one half of the famous couple, Jolie, has a complex and intriguing star persona and a reliable knack for doing things that invoke public shock, outrage, admiration, and compassion. Off screen, Jolie is newsworthy for her humanitarian work as well as for her transgressive sexuality, including kissing her brother James Haven on the lips at the Academy Awards and openly acknowledging her bisexuality. The tattooed, motorcycle riding aviatrix has also exhibited an emotional vulnerability and kindness that makes her particular brand of femininity appealing to mere mortals who mightn't conform to conventional standards themselves, but who also mightn't want to break the mould completely. This means Jolie offers numerous and contradictory points of identification and interest to fans, and to those who love to hate her.

Born 4 June 1975, Jolie is someone whose star image has changed over time, and the film roles for which she is best known roughly parallel shifts in the way her personal life has been represented. Estranged daughter of actor Jon Voight, Jolie was raised mostly by her mother, Marcheline Bertrand, whose death in 2007 sent her daughter into a crisis of weight loss and grief. Jolie worked in the modelling industry and performed in music videos and minor films before her breakthrough role in *Girl Interrupted*, for which she won a best supporting actress Oscar in 1999. In *Girl Interrupted* Jolie played a disturbed young woman, not long after her own rebellious teens saw her struggle with self-harm then plunge headlong into two short, passionate marriages involving the much reported exchange of phials of blood. Jolie wed her *Hackers* co-star Tommy Lee Miller, a union that lasted from 1996 to 1999, then married her screen husband in *Pushing Tin*, character actor Billy Bob Thornton (2000–2003), before hooking up with her *Mr and Mrs Smith* co-star Brad Pitt in 2005.

In addition to her Oscar, Jolie has earned two Golden Globe Awards and three Screen Actors' Guild Awards as well as enormous commercial success as an action star playing intelligent, independent women in blockbusters, including her embodiment of Lara Croft in the *Tomb Raider* films (2001 and 2002), CIA agent Evelyn Salt in *Salt* (2010), and the alluring yet cunning female lead in *The Tourist* (2010). She has also starred in politically engaged films such as *Beyond Borders*, which tackled weighty issues such as *Médecins sans Frontières* (Doctors without Borders) and aid work in Africa, and Michael Winterbottom's 2007 film *A Mighty Heart*, in which she plays Mariane Pearl, wife of journalist Daniel Pearl who was beheaded by terrorists in Pakistan. This not only demonstrates her range as an actor, but also links with her humanitarian work that began soon after shooting on location for *Tomb Raider* when she witnessed impoverished conditions in Cambodia, where she adopted her son Maddox in 2002. She also met with refugees when filming *Beyond Borders* in Namibia in 2003, became a Goodwill Ambassador for the United Nations Refugee Agency, and has donated millions to charitable causes.

Jolie's alliance with Pitt made *Mr and Mrs Smith* her most commercially successful film and signalled a transition in her public image from homebreaker to homemaker. Much of the $478 million box office revenue was attributed to public desire to see the chemistry between the screen couple in the film that allegedly marked the demise of Pitt's marriage to wholesome *Friends* star Jennifer Aniston and the beginning of his volatile relationship with the mercurial Jolie.

Brangelina rapidly began adding to their rainbow family, adopting Zahara from Ethiopia in 2005, Pax from Vietnam in 2007, and celebrating the birth of their biological children in 2006 and 2008. Jolie's strange status as a symbol of the 'united nations' was reinforced by her choice to give birth (by elective caesarean) to daughter Shiloh in Namibia in 2006. Hoping to boost tourism, the Namibian government acquiesced to Brangelina's demands that all paparazzi be refused visas during their stay and even restricted the movements of locals to ensure the couple's privacy. The imperious star power Brangelina wielded to create their birth sanctuary led the event to be called the celebrity colonisation of Namibia—a physical invasion of foreign territory mirroring the omnipresence of media images of the couple that have invaded countries worldwide. Proof that Jolie's value is now located in her identity as a mother and as Pitt's partner could not be more convincing than the record breaking $14 million dollars the couple earned (and reportedly donated to charity) for rights to the first photos of their twins Knox and Vivienne in 2008.

Jolie's unique ability to embody a global identity was further demonstrated when her role as the biracial Mariane Pearl caused barely a ripple of controversy, when most white actors working in blackface to play a person of colour would have faced severe criticism. *A Mighty Heart* was not a big commercial success but it successfully cast Jolie in a role that married political activism with compassion and maternity (Pearl herself was pregnant in the story and demonstrated strength and generosity of spirit in refusing to express vitriol against her husband's murderers).

Jolie's multifaceted star appeal as a feminist, mother of a rainbow family, a bad girl, a fragile and damaged yet strong and independent, glamorous human rights activist make her an extremely lucrative commodity as well as a canvas onto which an enormous range of cultural values have been painted, as suggested in Kate Kretz's 2006 artwork, *Blessed Art Thou* (see Figure 23.1 and Plate 8).

Kretz's painting indicates Jolie had, by 2006, largely transcended her wild child image and, as goodwill ambassador for the United Nations and a mother of adopted children from disadvantaged backgrounds, has been transformed by the media into a virtuous Madonna with child and a saviour of humanity. She is simultaneously revered (for using the power of celebrity in positive ways) and reviled (for the condescending colonial attitude that Westerners can save the people of developing nations when we have so many problems ourselves, and for allegedly 'buying' adopted children and bypassing the lengthy bureaucratic screening and placement process). At the same time, the painting acknowledges and mocks the deification and worship of celebrities as figures blessed with impossibly good looks and good fortune, and situates it within the everyday sphere of consumption. The religious iconography literally depicts her as a heavenly creature far above ordinary mortals, yet she is also shown to be a media commodity and a brand that people buy, much as they purchase Coca-Cola or groceries at the supermarket.

Drawing together semiotic, ideological, intertextual, and political economy approaches to analysis of celebrity, this painting and the media coverage of Jolie to which it refers encompass the star's role as a commodity, a humanitarian, the embodiment of film characters ranging from sanctimonious figures to the legendary sex goddess she plays in *Beowulf*, and as mother to an expanding multicultural family, nurturing the needy and innocent. Jolie's place as an aspirational figure fans may seek to emulate, and a woman whose wealth and beauty is admired or desired,

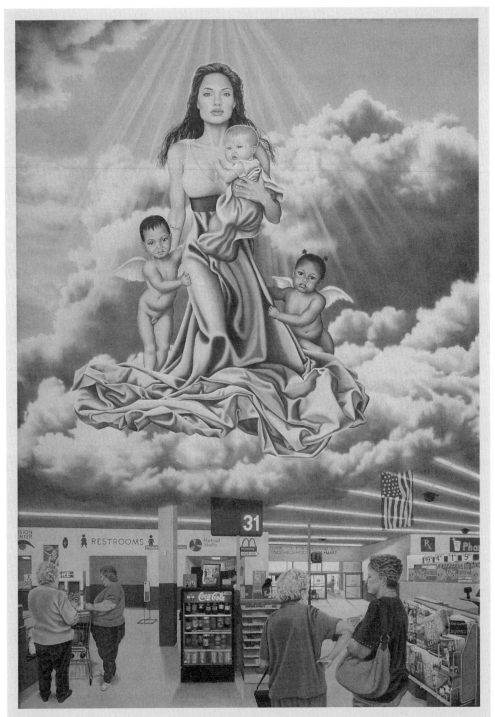

Figure 23.1   *Blessed Art Thou*, 2006, oil and acrylic on linen, 88 x 60cm

Source: Kate Kretz, <www.katekretz.com>

demonstrates the role of celebrity in transmitting cultural values and perhaps usurping the place in our culture once occupied by heroes and saints. To an extent, celebrities have replaced the role once played by heroes in satisfying 'exaggerated expectations of human greatness' (Turner 2004, p. 5). The changes in Jolie's star image might indicate a cultural shift away from meanings of celebrity associated with hedonism, superficial appearances, and materialism, towards valuing things she can now be seen to stand for: feminism, family, multiculturalism, and humanitarianism. It can also be argued though that Jolie's celebrity is simply another aspect of the colonisation of global media culture with Hollywood trivia, products, and values.

Conclusion

This chapter has employed a range of theoretical approaches to explore the role of stars and celebrities in the construction of meanings, identities, desires, and ideologies. Some show stars and celebrities as economic pawns who make media profits in a culture that values notoriety over worthwhile achievements; others suggest how people use stars as a kind of social currency to explore many kinds of social issues, particularly around personal behaviour and relationships. While the media might intrude mercilessly on stars' private lives, the outcome for audiences and fans is that they are given the chance to talk about issues such as love, sexuality, money, body image, and so on. In this way stars and celebrities enable competing discourses and ideologies of achievement and success, of masculinity and femininity, of familial and romantic relationships, of hegemonic and counter-hegemonic social values to be worked through: they are sites for contemporary ideological and hegemonic struggles that you, as media students, can now analyse.

To summarise, the cultural phenomenon of celebrity can be understood as follows: stardom involves the production and circulation of information about charismatic individuals in the media. The power of a star, a celebrity, or a public figure depends to a large extent on their visibility, the employment of spectacle, and their ability to communicate with the public via media images. Narrative, characterisation, identification, merchandising, and image management are some of the ways in which celebrity communicates issues of social value and identity.

This chapter has

- used a political economy approach to analyse stars as bankable financial and industrial commodities
- used an intertextual, semiotic approach to analyse celebrities as texts
- used an ideological approach to discuss stars as the embodiment of social and ideological values
- presented a case study analysing Angelina Jolie's star image.

Discussion points

1   Why are stars and celebrities so popular and what is the difference between them?
2   How are fandom and stardom related?
3   Who is responsible for invasive journalistic practices that entail prying into celebrities' private lives: the press that sells illicit photos, the public who buy them, or the stars themselves?
4   How do media technologies facilitate fandom, and to what effect?
5   What is identification, and how does it work in relation to stars and celebrities? Think of a star with whom you identify on some level. Why do you feel that you can relate to the star and what particular qualities of the star appeal to you? How is your sense of identification expressed?

Summary

You should now be able to

- explain the difference between stars, media personalities, and celebrities
- discuss the contemporary discourse of stardom and celebrity
- show how the star system works through bankability, star image, and the embodiment of social values
- discuss modes of identification with stars
- consider how stars contribute to gender discourses and ideologies
- show an awareness of how media texts function as publicity and marketing devices, image management strategies, and feedback mechanisms linking the industry to the public.

But They Keep Moving the Posts: Postmodern and Global Perspectives ▶

The global reach of the media has the capacity to nourish a sense of responsibility, however fragile, for a humanity that is commonly shared and for a world that is collectively inhabited.

John Thompson, *The Media and Modernity*, 1995

OVERVIEW OF PART 6

In an ever-expanding universe nothing is static. In the past twenty years there have been significant changes in the media, in society, and in media theories. We will examine some of these changes as we conclude our study with a critical overview of postmodernism and globalisation.

CHAPTER 24

Postmodernism

*One listens to reggae, watches a Western, eats McDonald's food for lunch and local
cuisine for dinner, wears Paris perfume in Tokyo and 'retro' clothes in Hong Kong.*
Jean-François Lyotard, *The Postmodern Condition*, 1984

This chapter will

▶ explain the meanings of the prefix 'post'

▶ consider the terms 'poststructuralism' and 'postcolonialism'

▶ examine the concept of postmodernism

▶ discuss the relationship between theoretical positions outlined earlier in the book and these
   newer approaches.

Much of what has been presented so far has been an attempt to pin down the
meanings of texts, to give definitions of concepts, and to outline approaches for
understanding the media. In many ways these methods are fruitful and illuminating,
but they have their limitations. Many of the theories discussed in this book were
developed during the 1970s and 1980s. Since then, there have been significant
changes in media, society, and theory. Some of these changes are encapsulated in
theoretical approaches with the prefix 'post': postmodernism, poststructuralism,
postcolonialism, and postfeminism (which, alongside third-wave feminism, was
discussed in Chapter 20). These words suggest a new era, new ways of being and
understanding.

The prefix 'post'

It is useful to first consider the meaning of the prefix 'post', which literally means 'after', as it is used in all these terms. Using 'modernism' (see p. 447) as an example, the prefix 'post' is used for all the following reasons:

- Postmodernist ideas, beliefs, and feelings are new discourses about art, culture, and society that have emerged *after* earlier, modernist ideas.
- But postmodernism doesn't just come after modernism: it recognises that we live in a world in which modernist ideas and actions were important and are still part of our world; therefore a postmodernist world is one that is built on the theories and practices of modernism.
- Not only are postmodernist ideas built on those of modernism, but in some ways they are also linked to modernism by shared theoretical perspectives. So, you could argue that postmodernism is another version of modernism, not completely new.
- What makes postmodernism different from modernism is that in some ways it challenges, goes against, earlier modernist discourses, and in so doing it breaks new ground.

The use of 'post' as a prefix for 'modernism' has similar implications for the other 'posts'. They are all movements and theories that are new, come after, are built on, are linked to, and yet challenge the previous movements. For the purposes of this discussion, they also point to questions about theories used in media studies.

Poststructuralism and the limitations of structuralist approaches

poststructuralism
Poststructuralism develops and challenges structuralist approaches, taking more account of the way contexts and audiences can produce more fluid meanings and readings of media texts.

Poststructuralism comes after, is built on, is linked to, and challenges structuralism and also semiology and theories of ideology. The main problems with these earlier approaches is that they are too rigid, too limiting in understanding media and culture. In particular, they suggest that people are determined by structures, that they are dominated by them, and, as a result, have little autonomy or freedom. Poststructuralism opens up more possibilities.

Structuralism, which flourished in the 1970s, was opposed to what was called 'culturalism' or theories that drew on 'lived experience' (Hall 1986). This opposition led to a poststructuralist critique of structuralism (Hall 1985). Structuralists argue that people are determined and controlled by the social and aesthetic structures that they live in, for example that dominant ideology is transmitted through these structures to a relatively powerless population; that narrative structures determine how we read and understand texts just as semiology aims to fix the meanings of sign systems. In contrast, culturalists argue that people actually have some say in whether they accept or refuse dominant ideology. According to culturalists, people can challenge dominant ideology and can live it in different ways. Sign systems and signifiers are more fluid and open to different readings and context is a crucial factor. In relation to media, this difference between structuralism and culturalism corresponds with the difference between textual analysis that shows how dominant ideological values are inscribed in a text through its processes of signification, representation, and its narrative structure, and analysis that asks what audiences are actually doing with texts. The stress on audiences and their uses of the texts is crucial to poststructuralist approaches (Weedon 1987).

We have already begun to present poststructuralist analyses in this book in a number of ways: through multiple readings of signs, signifiers, and texts; through the use of hegemony as a conceptual tool; with the view that the media can present a range of ideological positions; through awareness that audiences can make different readings; with our view of the contradictory aspects of the media that we have stressed throughout. Our approach recognises the values of semiology, ideology, and structuralism for analysing the media but goes beyond these—similarly post-structuralism is not dismissing structuralist ideas but is building on them, extending and developing them. Awareness of the changes brought about by globalisation and new technologies are the most recent aspects that need to be taken account of in understanding media and society.

Structuralism uses binary oppositions as a framework for analysing society and the media, and we have used them throughout the book, first, in relation to analysis of language, narratives, and texts, second, as ways of understanding gender, sexual orientation, and ethnicity. We have used binary oppositions to raise the problems of the oppression of women, homosexuals, and people of colour, although the potential danger of this is that using the structure of oppositions helps to maintain and perpetuate these gender and ethnic oppositions—it can help maintain an adversarial framework rather than facilitating the search for different conceptual frameworks. The search for such frameworks is central to queer theory (see pp. 351–2) and the work of Judith Butler, who has suggested that the distinction between male and female may not be a helpful way to understand people (Butler 1990). Many young people today seem less bothered by these differences and can mix easily across gender, sexual, and ethnic divisions.

All these points allow us to move forward in our understanding of media and society, and are relevant in a postmodern view of media and society, which will be discussed below after consideration of the term 'postcolonialism'.

Postcolonialism

What constitutes a postcolonialist view of the world?

postcolonialism
The historical period after colonialism; ways of understanding the (ongoing) effects of colonialism.

'**Postcolonialism**' is a term used in various contexts, and in each context it has a slightly different meaning. It relates to colonialism, the historical relations between Europe and the rest of the world, and the discourses—such as Orientalism—associated with non-Western cultures (see Chapter 22). The term 'postcolonialism' also recognises that the colonialist era, in which European countries established overt control over majority world (colonised) countries, has ended; nearly all the former colonies have achieved political independence. But the reference to colonialism reminds us that the nineteenth century and much of the twentieth century have been colonialist periods and that the influence of colonialism is still being felt throughout the world.

Postcolonialism can operate as an attitude: to be a postcolonialist is to hope and presume that we now have equality between people of different ethnic backgrounds, that old colonial power bases have gone, and that we do not need to dwell on or examine the colonial past (it can be left behind).

Postcolonialism can also be a way of looking at the world, a way that understands the present postcolonial situation in the light of the past colonial situation, and draws attention to this link—not to remind us or make us feel guilty, but to see how this past is still relevant and still has an influence on power relations and social attitudes.

Some argue that we now live in a neocolonialist world. While the traditional forms of colonisation have disappeared, the previously colonised nations are still dominated economically through the powers of multinational corporations and thus a new form of power, neocolonialism, has been established.

Postcolonialism is often used to study literature and media products that come from previously colonised countries or that specifically address postcolonial issues (Rivkin & Ryan 1998). The work of many indigenous writers and filmmakers is interpreted from a postcolonial perspective. In Australia, films made by Tracey Moffat and paintings by Gordon Bennett explore these issues from, among other positions, Aboriginal perspectives. Their work shows how histories of colonialism and discourses of racism are inscribed in present-day Australia. Such discourses and histories are often referred to in their work. Moffat's *Nice Coloured Girls* relates contemporary experiences of Aboriginal women, in particular their relationships to white men, back to a colonial history. Bennett's painting *Altered Body Print (Shadow Figure Howling at the Moon)* (Plate 9) plays on and challenges the binary oppositions (and discourses) around race that were used to construct his identity (McLean &

Bennett 1996). In this painting, Bennett mixes up the oppositions that structure discourses of ethnicity so that they are not neatly paired opposite one another. This breaks the structure of such discourses and also suggests the confusion of an identity positioned within these discourses. He comments:

> There came a time in my life when I became aware of my Aboriginal heritage. This may seem of little consequence, but when the weight of European representations of Aboriginal people as the quintessential primitive 'Other' is realised and understood, within discourses of self and other ... then you may understand why such an awareness was problematic for my sense of identity. The conceptual gap between my sense of self and other collapsed and I was thrown into turmoil.
>
> It is the collapse of the conceptual gap between the binary opposites of self/other, civilised/savage, sophisticated/primitive, or perhaps more appropriately its gradual disintegration and my process of integration, that forms the substratum of my life and work (McLean & Bennett 1996, p. 9).

Bennett's painting is produced out of a knowledge and awareness of cultural theory; it is built on and extends notions of structural binary oppositions, thus linking cultural theory and practice in significant ways.

Essentialism also enters the debate about ethnic identity: this comes up in relation to discussion of people's roots—where they come from in a historical sense. *Roots* is the title of an influential novel, a history of African Americans, by Alex Haley (1976), that was made into a television series. This series celebrated the rediscovery of African American history and saw this history as significant in terms of the identities of modern African Americans. Similarly, many people today seek connection and understanding with their roots, now extended to white Anglo-Celtic ethnic groups seeking to understand their historical and spiritual connections. One of the main issues surrounding this search is whether these roots are cultural–social or genetic–biological (in the blood). Many ethnic groups seem to call on both these understandings of their roots. Roots can be romanticised, as happens when Australians looking at Aboriginal spiritual connections with the land make these connections seem eternal, representative of something beyond culture. Even those who believe only in social construction sometimes lapse into the commonsense view that cultural differences are based on genetics.

Postmodernism

Postmodernism is the most complex and the most inclusive of the 'post' terms: all the others can be seen as part of postmodernism. So what is it? Where did it come from? And where can we find it?

postmodernism
Originally, a style in architecture, the term was later used to describe the late-twentieth-century world and as a style of cultural production.

The origins of the term 'postmodernism'

The term 'postmodernism' was first used as early as the 1960s to describe a style or movement in architecture (Jencks 1986). This style worked by taking various elements of past architectural styles and mixing them together in new buildings. Consequently, there was nothing new or original in it other than the way it combined and reworked past styles.

Frederic Jameson

The term was taken up by political and cultural theorist Frederic Jameson, among others, to describe contemporary Western and global society. Jameson (1991) argues that a shift that began in the late 1960s and which was driven by economic changes is changing the world and its culture. He maintains that society is moving into a phase he describes as 'late capitalism'. By this, he means that the capitalist system—some people investing wealth in the production and distribution of goods and many others selling their labour for wages—that has been evolving since the end of feudalism, is developing a new form. Jameson argues as follows.

- Economic power is increasingly concentrated in multinational companies whose businesses cross national borders, and that through their ability to produce and sell goods globally, these companies are changing the face of production (so that, for example, US-based multinational companies can produce goods much more cheaply in developing countries than they can in the USA) and distribution (see Chapter 25).
- In the drive to sell more goods, emphasis is now placed more on consumption than on production. The emphasis on consumption means that people are becoming more aware of and more concerned with issues of lifestyle, image, and appearance, which leads to a society focused on appearances, on spectacle, a designer-label mentality.

Postmodernism as a style of cultural production

Jameson's focus on spectacle and appearance leads to a definition of postmodernism as a style of cultural production. This is the most common way of using the word, a use you are probably familiar with. When people describe things as postmodern, they are often drawing on this meaning. Postmodernism as a style of cultural production is relevant to aesthetic products (for example, films, advertisements, and television programs) and to lifestyles (how people live, feel, and act in everyday life). Thus 'postmodernism' is a term that can be used to describe the media and the way we live in real life—as demonstrated by the quotation from postmodern theorist Jean-François Lyotard at the beginning of this chapter. Jameson's analysis links postmodern styles of living and cultural production to economic changes. Others see postmodern styles, postmodern cultures, as an aesthetic response to and reflection of at least three other aspects of the world we now live in. These aspects are described below.

New scientific theories

New scientific theories have changed our understanding of the world. Previous theories in the physical sciences (biology, physics, chemistry, and so on) and social sciences (politics, sociology, and so on) aimed to classify and understand the human and physical world; semiology, Marxism, and psychoanalysis, which have informed so much of media studies theory, were part of this project. Scientists have tended to think they can rationally explain the world we live in and how we behave, but current scientific discoveries and theories have undermined these certainties. Developments in nuclear physics, in chaos theory, and in complexity theory suggest that all knowledge about the physical world is relative, partial, and uncertain. The search for ultimate truths, for objective impartiality, is futile. Among social scientists, it has become commonplace to assert that even individual identities are not real, since we are just a collection of constructed social masks. Reality cannot be pinned down. There are no certainties except uncertainty and continual change.

We live in a media-world

The spread of the media, particularly television, has produced a new way of seeing the world. First, people are saturated, as never before, with media-provided images, information, and knowledge. We have an amazing archive of media images available to look at, and we store these and many other images in our brains. Second, media representations and the real world have begun to blur: we see the real world in terms of media images. This is apparent in the way footage of the Gulf Wars, images of the War on Terror, and the collapse of the Twin Towers of the World Trade Center in New York have been compared with footage from an action film (in fact, the 2001 release of an Arnold Schwarzenegger film featuring a terrorist attack on an office building was delayed because it was considered to be insensitive). So much experience, knowledge, and feeling comes by way of media images that the media dominate our ways of seeing the world. Reality TV offers a clear example of this closure of the gap between reality and representation.

Postmodernism as a reaction to politics in the 1990s

Postmodernism is a reaction to post-1960s politics. The 1960s was an important historical moment that crystallised in student uprisings, industrial action, and protests in 1968. This revolutionary period ended the Vietnam War, saw the rise of student and trade union power and the hippie subculture bring about new social liberation, brought down the corrupt Nixon government through the Watergate scandal of the early 1970s, increased freedom and liberation movements throughout the Third World, and, in Australia, led to the election of the Whitlam Labor government in 1972. All this seemed to herald a new beginning, a new optimism in society. But it did not produce a new social utopia. Inequality, war, and social struggle persist, and the postmodernist generations, who know so much about social change, seem to be able to do little but look ironically or dismissively, helplessly or apathetically at the world they live in.

Postmodernism is an expression and response to all the above factors. The big questions about postmodernism as a style or practice are: Does it celebrate this new global, economic, social system? Does it offer a critique and challenge to it? Does it offer a way of coping and surviving in the system? It can do all three, but to explore these questions we need to examine specific instances of postmodernism, since it is not limited to one position.

Postmodernism in context

Postmodernism is built on an earlier movement that has not yet been discussed here: modernism. Since postmodernism is a reaction to and a continuation of modernism, modernism needs to be briefly introduced and, in turn, understood in relation to realism, which preceded it.

Table 24.1 Differences between realism, modernism, and postmodernism

Realism	Modernism	Postmodernism
Nineteenth century onwards: painting, literature, and mainstream film	1900–1960s: modern art and modern architecture, some literature	1960s–present

These three umbrella terms—'realism', 'modernism', and 'postmodernism'—give an overview of aesthetic tendencies in Western culture over the last 200 years. Realism can be described as an attempt to portray things as they really are, as they appear to the human spectator. Realist art often involves portraying humans in their social situations, and realist art and media products tend to reflect and comment on society. Realism dominated painting and literature in the nineteenth century, and it is still common today (see pp. 332–3 for further discussion of realism and pp. 309–12 for a discussion of realism in relation to documentary). In film, realism is characterised by naturalised conventions of representation, acting, and editing that do not draw attention to the process of construction because they resemble normal ways of seeing and experiencing the world. The realist style is thus not unusual or difficult for audiences to read; much mainstream film is still made using realist principles.

Modernism, which marks the beginning of the modern world, describes the art and aesthetic movements of the first half of the twentieth century. These movements were a reaction against realism (Bradbury & McFarlane 1976; Lunn 1985). Modernism grew out of enormous political and social changes that were linked, in many ways, to revolutions in technology and communication. Modernism is characterised by

modernism
Describes Western art and aesthetic movements of the first half of the twentieth century; characterised by optimism in future progress, and ways of seeing or representing the world that challenged realism, including abstraction and focus on the act of representation.

- an optimistic belief in the power and possibilities of machines, technology, science, rationality, and progress
- a range of new art movements that saw and represented the world in new and revolutionary ways (including cubism, dadaism, surrealism, futurism, stream of consciousness writing, and all forms of abstract art)
- an emphasis on the process of experiencing and representing reality.

Many modernist movements were interested in producing art and architecture that draws attention to the processes of construction involved in making the objects and the art. Modernist artists were interested in exploring and foregrounding the very means of representation: paint, the canvas, celluloid, narrative structure, and so on. Modernist artists questioned how they could represent the world, which involved asking how people see and experience reality. They showed that this process is more complicated and fragmented than earlier realist aesthetic styles suggested.

Despite the terrible history of the modernist period—two world wars, and major turmoil in China, the Soviet Union, and throughout the globe—modernism was essentially an optimistic movement. It looked for ways to organise human society that would deliver happiness and fulfilment.

We can see this in the aims of modernist architecture. Its abstractly styled buildings were functional. The angular, box-like constructions with little ornamentation or elaboration that we have come to associate with modernist architecture were designed as utopian housing spaces that would cater for all human needs. People were grouped together in these modernist buildings: housing estates made up of tower blocks are a modernist legacy. But the utopian dream of this sort of housing has rarely been realised, and such housing estates made up of tower blocks are probably the most damning indictment of this dream. In Godfrey Reggio's film *Koyaanisqatsi* (see pp. 240–1) there is an extended sequence that shows the blowing up of one of the most famous modernist housing estates in the USA. Before its demolition, the site had become derelict and deserted because it did not cater for people's real needs. Its destruction can be seen as a metaphor for the death of modernism and the death of the modernist dream. As discussed above, the genesis of postmodernism involves many factors (see pp. 444–6), and one of them is this perceived failure of modernism. While postmodernism is linked to modernism, it also challenges it.

Characteristics of postmodernism

The quotation from Lyotard that opens this chapter gives an excellent flavour of postmodernism; it describes what could be an ideal lifestyle for a global, postmodern individual. It stresses consumption and style, it involves mixing high and low culture, and it involves combining different cultures in one's everyday life. In reading about postmodernism, you will probably come to realise that postmodernism celebrates superficiality, spectacle, and surfaces and that it is associated with various characteristics (Solomon 1988): for example, irony, the blurring of traditional boundaries, fluid identity, intertextuality, pastiche, appropriation, bricolage, hybridity, self-reflexivity, and self-referentiality.

What follows is a discussion of some of the most significant of these. Look for examples of these characteristics in media products: you should be able to find them easily. Many contemporary media products that we have examined—for example, the films *The Thin Blue Line* and *Koyaanisqatsi*, culture jamming examples, and the advertisements illustrating postfeminism—can be classified as postmodern; you can reconsider them in this light.

Irony

Let us start with irony. To be ironic is to mean the opposite of what you say. Something is ironic when it indirectly contradicts its surface meaning. This often involves giving expression to contradictory attitudes and indicating a degree of detachment from a subject. The opening of *American Beauty* is partly ironic. It appears to say 'Here is a beautiful, ideal community', but it sees through this to the dark side of the American dream. Irony is witty and cool, knowing and cynical. Media theorist Todd Gitlin notes that '[the cultural critic] Paul Fussell has made the point that irony became standard in English writing after World War I as a way to navigate around the unspeakable' (Gitlin 1993). Why did irony emerge as such an important form of cultural expression in the late twentieth century? What is unspeakable now? What is this ironic mode built on?

Knowingness

Postmodernism is very knowing and self-reflexive. It is built on knowledge of the world, knowledge of media products, and knowledge of countless theories and critiques of society, modernity, and the media. We have a glut of knowledges, accumulated over twenty centuries and more, with which to make sense of the world, but whereas modernism thought that it was possible to make sense of the world and to rationally organise the future, postmodernism, after modernism's failure, recognises the futility of such a dream. Postmodernism embraces non-rational modes of knowledge: for example, it is open to tarot, astrology, intuition, and so on. Perhaps the most important feature of postmodernism is the way that it is comfortable with lack of certainty. The popular TV series *Supernatural* reflects this pervasive uncertainty; in the show, many things about the supernatural realm remain unknown to the protagonists Sam and Dean, and when answers are revealed, they usually defy rational expectations. As these brothers hunt differing paranormal creatures, they must discover new ways of understanding and overcoming them, and each episode suggests new possibilities. Postmodernism suggests that we can pick up whatever theoretical framework feels right to us at any particular moment to use for a while before moving on to the next one. While we are urged to demonstrate our knowledge, we are reminded that there is no ultimate way of making sense of the world.

Cynicism

Our knowledge has given us the power to see through things. We are no longer naive; we know that the media are all constructions, and that we cannot trust media products to represent reality truthfully, we know that the capitalist world is out to exploit us and that politicians just want power, we know that we are being controlled by family, church, education, and media systems, and we know that Big Brother is watching.

Powerlessness

Despite our knowledge and our ability to see through things, we remain powerless because nothing is certain, everything is relative, and the corporate powers that, to a large extent, control our lives are too strong. What, as individuals, can we do? We can see the world's problems and injustices but they seem too overwhelming for us to do anything about. This apparent intractability of our problems, the fact that the system is too strong, is what is, in Gitlin's terms, unspeakable. As Gitlin says, 'The fear is that what's underneath hurts too much, better repress it' (Gitlin 1993).

Pleasure

What can we do with all our knowledge, uncertainty, and powerlessness? We can at least use it to indulge in humour, wit, and pleasure: we can make ironic jokes about the system, we can live in the moment and celebrate our (limited) power to be what we want to be, we can play, and we can look good. A song called 'Shameless' by the Pet Shop Boys draws on artist Andy Warhol's claim that everyone wants fifteen minutes of fame: we will do anything to get it, to the extent of sacrificing our integrity to attain celebrity.

We can celebrate uncertainty as a freedom from limitations. The feeling that there are no boundaries, that we are in a state of continual change, fluidity, and expansion can lead to excitement and hedonistic experimentation. Postmodern pleasures are also less elitist than modernist ones, as they embrace pop culture.

Aspects of all these constituents are at work in the Biff cartoons (Figures 24.1 and 24.2), and are also evident in much contemporary advertising (see the CAT boots advertisement, Plate 10).

Figures 24.1 and 24.2   Biff cartoons

Source: Mick Kidd, 1988

Biff cartoons are a series of postmodern cartoons, often reproduced on postcards, that were made in the United Kingdom during the 1980s by a company called Biff Products. In a sense, they are a comic and ironic response to media theory and cultural studies theory. In these cartoons we see the inclusion of multiple realities: a 1950s world, in terms of dress and appearance, is juxtaposed with 1980s knowledge. Postmodernism often uses the perceived idealism and naivety of the 1950s (as lived in the West) as an ironic comparison with the cynical, knowing 1980s and 1990s.

Biff cartoons also include different levels of discourse:

- the statements of the characters contrast with their real thoughts
- authorial comments or captions draw our attention to the divide between high and low culture and set philosophical and art theories in low-culture contexts such as the genres of pulp fiction and popular romance
- they use dirty realism (for example, in Figure 24.2 there is dandruff on the man's jacket)
- they comment on commodification and marketing
- they are politically aware
- they demonstrate awareness of narrative theory, feminism, and philosophical movements such as existentialism.

In Biff cartoons, these knowledges and discourses are set in an arena of sexual politics and relationships, in which women's consciousness is usually shown as more developed than that of men. The pleasure that readers derive from these cartoons is partly dependent on recognising the references to such knowledges, time periods, and sexual politics. Biff cartoons are produced by authors and cartoonists steeped in theory and knowledge. But these theories and knowledges are mocked: it is as if the cartoons ask, Where do they get you?

The CAT boots advertisement (Plate 10) displays another element of the post-modern mix. What we find here is the popularisation of theories of the social construction of reality. This time we are not invited to mock knowledge but to take it on board and work productively with it. The caption—'We shape the things we build, thereafter they shape us'—parallels our arguments, presented throughout this book (see, for example, p. 64), about how our society conditions us, how we don't speak language; language speaks us. Cultural studies knowledge surfaces as part of popular discourse in this advertisement, which appeared in the British magazine *The Face* in 1996. The advertisement recognises how we are caught up in urban deserts in which we have become machine-like, and suggests a way through this: the answer is not another course in cultural theory; the answer is to buy a new pair of CAT boots. The advertisement suggests that these boots can give our lives in cities shape, and that our identities are shaped by what we wear and where we live. This advertisement proposes that we can escape from the urban jungle by purchasing stylish commodities. Moreover, the figure in the advertisement is an older, black man. In terms of age and ethnicity, a person from a subordinate group in society is shown as fashionable (clothes and hairstyle add to this): blackness and age become powerful in this advertisement. These advertisements play with signifiers and signification in an exhilarating and pleasurable way, but they do so in the realms of commodification and consumerism.

Blurring the boundaries

Before postmodernism, aesthetic products could be classified into discrete areas—fiction, fact, high culture, low culture, westerns, musicals, documentaries, plays, films, operas, pop music, and so on. But postmodernism knows no such boundaries or rules; it delights in the blurring of cultural boundaries and in hybridisation (see p. 235)—Gitlin cites Australia's Circus Oz, which draws on 'Aboriginal influences, vaudeville, Chinese acrobatics, Japanese martial arts, fireman's balances, Indonesian instruments and rhythms, video, Middle Eastern tunes, B-grade detective movies, modern dance, Irish jigs, and the ubiquitous presence of corporate marketing' (Gitlin 1993). Traditional notions of circuses are blown apart in this mixture or fusion of influences and in the blurring of categories. The inclusion of various non-European elements is an example of the fact that Eurocentrism is coming to an end as postmodern culture embraces other cultural traditions. There is freedom in this loosening of the traditional boundaries between cultural forms.

Within film and television, similar changes have been taking place. The development of music videos and the MTV channel are two of the most important and influential in this respect. The music video has provided a space for visual experimentation in the context of a popular art form (pop music) (Frith et al. 1993; Goodwin 1993). Young audiences have grown up familiar with the wide range of techniques used in these videos: non-narrative structures, experimental editing, the mixing of film formats (Super 8 and 35 mm for example), and so on. This is linked to the freeing up of styles in mainstream film and television. Standard rules of continuity in filmmaking are disappearing, and films are incorporating aspects of other media. *Scott Pilgrim vs the World*, directed by Edgar Wright in 2010, combines traditional narrative with videogame-style sequences, elements of anime, comic book effects, animation, and digital onscreen graphics. It was shot using Super 35, anamorphic 35mm, and a high-speed digital camera for super slow motion. Speed ramping—speeding up or slowing down the action—was added during the editing process to make certain movements appear superhuman. Further extending the boundaries of the film's reality, there are a couple of occasions where a character's fist breaks out of the frame when he punches and becomes visible outside the edges of the screen. At other points, the film brings to life a familiar idea from video games when defeated characters explode into actual coins.[2]

Similar rule-breaking techniques are apparent in many films and in television series such as *Breaking Bad*, *The Office*, and *30 Rock*. Television's realist premises, which dictate the requirement for continuity, have been challenged with great energy, and the innovations in this regard are often well received by the public, particularly by young audiences who have grown up watching television programs and films that use these new styles.

Documentaries have developed significantly in this period (see Chapter 18), and this hybridisation can be seen as a postmodern tendency. Modernism aimed to make people aware of the construction involved in all media products, to make them question the reality effect of media products, and encourage them to deconstruct these products. In this light, documentary's realist premise—that it could innocently, impartially, and objectively record the world—was challenged. But this realisation freed up documentary filmmaking from its link with realism: in its documentation of the real world, it could now use any techniques and could include all manner of representational modes. *The Thin Blue Line* (p. 315) is a great example of a postmodern documentary film.

Intertextuality, pastiche, appropriation, and bricolage

Postmodernism questions the process of signification and the making of meanings. While semiotic analysis seeks meanings and attempts to relate signifiers and representations back to reality, postmodern approaches challenge these aims, seeing texts as simulations (a term popularised by the theorist Jean Baudrillard) rather than representations. In her research on media images, Deirdre Pribram puts it as follows:

> In our culture of information and the mass media, we are inundated with an over-abundance of images and signs that no longer have referential value but, instead, interact solely with other signs. This marks the advent of simulation. Rather than the previous vertical connection, if you

---

[2] http://www.digitalmedia-world.com/index.php?option=com_content&view=article&id=2693: scott-pilgrim-if-looks-could-kill&catid=90:lead-story-of-the-day [Accessed 7 April 2011]

will, between sign and meaning, there is, instead the horizontal relationship of sign to sign (Pribram 1993, p. 201).

A pastiche is an imitation of a style or various styles that is often affectionate and humorous about its sources. **Bricolage** builds on the artistic techniques of collage and montage. While collage involves some form of cutting out and pasting together of images from many different sources, montage refers to the process of editing together images from different spaces and times in film and video. Bricolage means the appropriation and combination of different cultural elements into a new form. It involves appropriation: the original sign or signifier takes on a new meaning or signified in its new context, where it is combined with other signs (for an account of bricolage, see Hebdige 1979). The work of artist Barbara Kruger is an example of bricolage. Intertextuality (see p. 145) involves reference, borrowing (some would say plagiarising), and making links with other texts or sources. Postmodern architecture is a good example of bricolage. Music videos are also notorious for this kind of pop cultural self-referentiality, as are Quentin Tarantino's films, especially *Kill Bill* and *Death Proof*. Tarantino even quotes his own films. In *Kill Bill Volume 1*, The Bride (Thurman) traces a visible square in the air in the fight scene with Vivica A Fox, just as Mia (also played by Uma Thurman) did in *Pulp Fiction* when she told John Travolta's character 'Don't be a square'. *Death Proof* then references *Kill Bill* when a group of young women drive a yellow and black Mustang with a 'Pussy Wagon' icon and one of them has Elle Driver's theme tune, 'Twisted Nerve', as her cell phone ring tone.

> **bricolage**
> The putting together of different, often contradictory, cultural forms, thereby creating new meanings.

Nowadays, the recycling of cultural genres, codes, and conventions, and intertextuality generally, are rife in media products, so you should be able to find many examples. *The Simpsons* frequently adapts mainstream film plots (*Goodfellas*, for example) as the basis for its stories, and it often parodies famous film scenes (such as the shower scene from *Psycho* and the Rosebud sequences from *Citizen Kane*); many music videos recycle old film footage. The Lotteries Commission of Western Australia reworked a famous painting by Edvard Munch, *The Scream* (Figure 24.3), in one of its advertisements.

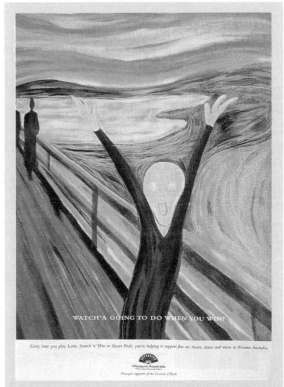

Figure 24.3 Advertisement for Lotteries Commission of Western Australia

Source: Lotteries Commission of Western Australia, published in *Festival of Perth Program*, 1998

This last example shows how irreverent postmodernism can be. The tortured expression on the face of the figure in *The Scream* signifies fear and anxiety; the painting is a commentary on early twentieth-century society, and has, over time, become an icon of high art. In the Lotteries Commission of Western Australia advertisement, however, it is used to make us laugh and buy lotto tickets. For postmodernism, nothing is sacred.

All the above examples draw on and rework known cultural artefacts, producing new meanings through recycling them. They demonstrate how the media–world reflects inwards on itself, looking forward by looking back at other media products. What is the connection between the past and the present in this recycling of images? How do these images and representations relate to reality? Cultural theorist Dick Hebdige argues that

> The past is played and replayed as an amusing range of styles, genres, signifying practices to be combined and recombined at will. The then (and the there) are subsumed in the Now. The only history that exists here is the history of the signifier and that is no history at all (Hebdige 1985, p. 47).

The past is used, but simply for visual play and pleasure. This is what is meant by the disavowal of history: we are not interested in history as a truthful or factual account of the development of our current sociocultural position, or as a way of learning about relationships between different parts of the world over time—history is simply a treasure trove of unconnected, fascinating images and stories. For those in the know, there is the pleasure of spotting the reference; for others there is the simple pleasure of spectacle. You do not need to know all the cultural references to enjoy a postmodern media product. Knowing them is a sign of your cultural knowledge; it indicates that you are a connoisseur of signs and images, not of truth and reality.

In Figure 24.4, cartoonist Judy Horacek draws attention to the mixing of genres, the crossing of boundaries, and the practice of intertextual referencing. This cartoon also signals the way we construct our identities in terms of media images: we picture ourselves as dealing with the world as a hero or heroine in a western or science-fiction movie. Our psyches are being structured in terms of media realities.

Figure 24.4   Judy Horacek cartoon

Source: Judy Horacek ©, first published in *The Australian* magazine

Self-reflexivity and the excess of surface

An understanding of self-reflexivity and surface can help reveal the limitations of both modernism and postmodernism. The self-reflective nature of much postmodern culture represents a strong link with modernism. Self-reflexivity is a modernist technique whereby a text draws attention to its own construction: for example, the characters in a fiction film might talk directly to the camera, or the clapperboard or boom microphone (a microphone on a long pole that hangs over the action) might be shown intentionally. Self-reflexivity means that the audience sees the processes of construction involved in making the media product (see p. 315). We are made aware in such examples that we are watching a film being made, that we are watching constructed representations, not reality. In her critique of film culture and activism in the 1960s, Sylvia Harvey gave an interesting summation and criticism of modernism's tendency towards self-reflexivity:

> Modernist aesthetics induces a reflection upon, a consideration of, the means of representation, and for lovers of art it generates aesthetic pleasure out of a series of 'frame-shifts' (the procedures whereby the work of art playfully refers to itself and its own processes of production). But too often it fails to lead its audience 'through' this first consideration and towards a second, namely, a consideration of the action represented. It is this second area of consideration which opens up the possibility of introduction of knowledge of the social world and its processes, what Brecht would have called 'instruction'. And if there is a sense in which modernism offers the only way forward, there is also a sense in which it constitutes a dead end, a graveyard. Only those who pass through it can learn from it; the rest remain buried within it (Harvey 1978, p. 82).

Harvey's argument is that reflection on representation—self-reflexivity—is not sufficient; it is a potential dead end and we must aim to understand the real world and gain 'knowledge of the social world and its processes'. She is arguing that modernism can tend to forget this project.

How does postmodernism look in the light of her critique of modernism? Postmodernism seems to have extended the self-referential nature of modernism: it remains heavily self-reflective, draws attention to the processes of construction involved in cultural products and knowledges, and derives great pleasure from this. But it has gone further than modernism in seeing that the world has become full of, as Pribram has put it, 'images and signs that no longer have referential value but, instead interact solely with other signs' (Pribram 1993). Does it then become difficult to find instruction about reality in the postmodern world?

While there seems to be a clear political project in modernist self-reflexivity (this project is described by Harvey as 'knowledge of the social world and its processes'), postmodernism often seems content merely to play with processes of production. The following questions address this issue.

- Does postmodernism's focus on surface reality, style, and appearance produce a depthlessness that makes postmodern texts uninterested in understanding the real world?
- Do postmodern texts play with techniques and signifiers merely in order to ensure that their meanings are up for grabs, thereby providing the audience with

the pleasures of decoding the text using their cultural knowledge, or can the postmodern style still produce some Brechtian 'instruction' about the real world? In other words, is postmodernism caught up in consumerism and style, to the detriment of effective critique?

The techniques of postmodernism can be used to provide instruction and new perspectives. Because we now realise that the world is more complex than Brecht and Harvey and their contemporaries could have imagined, the instruction provided by postmodernist texts is inclusive of more possibilities and uncertainties than would have been thought possible from the 1940s to the 1970s. *The Thin Blue Line* and *Koyaanisqatsi* are postmodern texts: the first draws our attention to questions about whether representations can present truth and reality; the second asks us to consider what kind of a world we live in that is so dominated by spectacle. In enabling the inclusion of new modes of thinking, in opening up identity, and in challenging Eurocentrism, postmodernism can be liberating and powerful (Jagtenberg & McKie 1997). There is also an interesting connection between postmodernism, New Age philosophies, and traditional meditation practices, since all these exhort us to live in the present moment: postmodernism problematises grand historical narratives of progress, while Buddhism and meditation stress that what is important is the present moment, that in order to be fully alive we need to bring ourselves into this moment. These philosophies recognise that much contemporary Western life is built around living in the past or the future: at any one time, we tend to be either ruminating about what has happened or planning for what will happen—in other words, we rarely live in the moment.

Conclusion

The danger of postmodernism as a way of thinking about the world is that its view that everything carries a multiplicity of meanings and signs, and its acceptance of the coexistence of different theories and viewpoints, threatens to leave us with no certainties. This is what Baudrillard is describing when he writes: 'All the great humanist criteria of value, all the values of a civilisation of moral, aesthetic, and practical judgements, vanish in our system of images and signs. Everything becomes undecideable' (Baudrillard 1988, p. 128).

The problem with this perspective is that it may deny us some hold on the real world. Finding a connection to and knowledge of the real world through various systems of representation (at the same time as recognising their subjective nature and their partiality) is very important. It is worth repeating (see pp. 75–6) Richard Dyer's view of the relationship between reality and representation: 'Because one can see reality only through representation it does not follow that one does not see reality at all. Partial—selective, incomplete, from a point of view—vision of something is not no vision of it whatsoever' (Dyer 1993, p. 3). Dyer argues that material reality is important and that representations can tell us something about it. This recognises the impossibility of finding absolute truths but insists on the importance of attempting to find some possible truths about the world. Junot Diaz, a writer from the Dominican Republic, puts it even more simply. In his writing he aims to be 'representing as honestly as I can' (1998) his experience and his society from his perspective, and he sees writing (representation) as allowing him this possibility.

This chapter has

- discussed the terms 'poststructuralism', 'postcolonialism', and 'postmodernism'
- considered the historical development and context of postmodernism
- examined key characteristics of postmodernism
- offered a critical overview of postmodernism.

Discussion points

1   Can you find examples of postmodernist characteristics in any contemporary films or television programs?
2   What social and ideological meanings are presented in any postmodern texts?

Summary

You should now be able to

- define the terms 'poststructuralism' and 'postcolonialism'
- define the term 'postmodernism' and relate it to modernism
- describe the central characteristics of postmodernism
- identify postmodern characteristics in contemporary media texts
- offer a critique of postmodernism.

CHAPTER 25

Globalisation

Think local and act global. Think local, as people need to be rooted in their identity, in their interests, and in their institutions of political representation. But act global, via the Internet, connectivity, media politics and international competitiveness, as the powers that be inhabit the global space.

Manuel Castells, *Challenges of Globalisation*, 2001

This chapter will

▶ outline important characteristics and impacts of globalisation

▶ introduce key thinkers who have developed influential theories of globalisation

▶ consider the positive and negative aspects of these changes, questioning why we should care about media globalisation and how can we make the best of it.

globalisation
Globalisation refers to an international community influenced by technological development and economic, political, and military interests. It is characterised by a worldwide increase in interdependence, interactivity, interconnectedness, and the virtually instantaneous exchange of information. Globalisation could lead to the homogenisation of world cultures, or to hybridisation and multiculturalism.

Historically, **globalisation** has been shaped by economic, political, and military interests, and by technological innovation. By the fifteenth and sixteenth centuries trade was already crossing national boundaries. During the time of colonisation and industrialisation, in the seventeenth and eighteenth centuries, global power networks began to form. The nineteenth century saw the introduction of newspapers, the telegraph, and cable systems that enabled the formation of global communication networks. The twentieth century was a time of explosive growth in the media and communication industries as radio and television were popularised. The Pentagon began developing the internet in the 1960s; later, satellite, wireless, and mobile communication technologies proliferated. Each technological development has led to increasing levels of global interrelatedness, ultimately prompting questions about the legitimacy and defensibility of national borders.

Globalisation: positive and negative characteristics

The globalisation of communication is characterised by the following qualities: instantaneity, interconnectedness, interdependence, and a trend towards corporate mergers and conglomeration. It is *instantaneous* in that it effectively bridges time and space, offering almost instant access to distant information and events. In fact, *Business @ the Speed of Thought* is the title of an influential book written by Microsoft mogul Bill Gates (1999) about the economic advantages of ICTs. Globalisation offers a sense of *interconnectedness* by facilitating interpersonal communication and the formation of communities and relationships across geographic, racial, religious, and cultural barriers. People can feel a sense of interconnectedness through communication without physically being together. The global media environment is also characterised by economic and political *interdependence* that transcends national and regional boundaries. Increasingly, it is regulated by global agreements brokered by international organisations (such as the United Nations, the World Trade Organization, the World Bank, the International Monetary Fund, among others) that function in a worldwide capitalist system overarching nation states and national regulations. News and television are dependent on global content, and different media forms are increasingly dependent on one another for content. Corporate convergence is a growing trend in which *mergers and conglomeration* concentrate ownership and control of media production and other forms of corporate activity in a small number of multinational conglomerates, potentially reducing the range of voices and views disseminated in the media.

The cartoon by Laugh it Off artists Alex Latimer and Patrick Latimer (see Figure 25.1) sends up the way multinationals can exercise global economies of scale to silence and outcompete local businesses, thereby reducing diversity in the marketplace.

Utopian views: imagined communities and the global village

The utopian view of globalisation encapsulated in Marshall McLuhan's phrase 'the global village' (see pp. 20–1) suggests that people of the world can be brought closer together by the globalisation of communication, no matter how far apart we may actually live. The global village is an image of a world in which media transcend the nation-state in a democratising process that gives everyone's voice a chance to be heard and enables information to be freely shared. Interactive media facilitates participation in global communication and debates, and offers entry into public space. The globalisation of communication enables us to share in each other's lives as members of internet communities or by means of participation in televised events

Figure 25.1 Thembo's Burger Hut cartoon

Source: Laugh it Off artists Alex and Patrick Latimer, South Africa and so on. In this ideal communication environment, the mass media also play an important role in informing people and generating discussion about events and issues worldwide. The globalisation of communication is seen as an agent of empowerment, education, democracy, and equality. The global dispersal of knowledge facilitates a culture open to sharing responsibility for issues that affect us all and recognising responsibilities to people we may never meet. Media coverage of the horrifying earthquake and tsunami in Japan in 2011 prompted people from all over the globe to give money to help the victims, and encouraged governments to provide personnel and aid to assist Japan in the wake of this tragic natural disaster. These responses and similar altruistic reactions to the floods in Queensland and Mississippi, Cyclone Yasi, the earthquake in Christchurch, New Zealand, and the tornadoes ravaging the United States raise questions about whether the whole world could pull together to deal with issues that affect us all, such as global warming. Global communication and global perspectives mean we can see what is happening across the globe—in the Arctic Circle, Antarctica, Africa, the Amazon and Indonesian forests, anywhere. We could start to work together globally to do something beyond implementing global regulations such as the Kyoto Protocol. This moment presents a unique historical challenge, and global media and communication technologies could be an integral part of educating people about the issue and developing solutions.

The idea that globalisation can unite diverse communities and foster progress is implicit in the HSBC advertisement shown in Figure 25.2. The caption reads:

> An unpredictable bunch. People. Everywhere you go you get a different opinion and a different point of view. What's in, what's out? What is of the moment and what is so 'yesterday'? And when you talk to 125 million people all over the planet you'd be amazed what you learn. We have learned that the more you look at difference as potential, the less it looks like a problem. yourpointofview.com HSBC The world's local bank.

This HSBC advertisement uses a unity in diversity theme that harnesses the concepts of progress and development (being 'of the moment' versus 'so yesterday') as well as multiculturalism (valuing difference and traditional cultures), participation, and democratisation (everyone's point of view can be heard online at yourpointofview. com). These themes converge in the utopian concept of the global village as HSBC's brand identity is 'the world's local bank'.

The HSBC advertisement can also be interpreted in ways that resist the intended meaning. If we take the rhetoric about embracing alternative points of view seriously, we must also consider less positive possibilities of globalisation. In a resistant reading, the distinctive practices of Moko and Mehndi body art signifying identity, status, and initiation rites unique to Maori and Hindu cultures have been commodified, commercialised, decontextualised, and stripped of tradition and cultural meaning as they are popularised and circulated by global media and reduced to trivial, trendy fashion statements. When critically evaluating media texts and media theory, it is important to be aware of both aspects of globalisation and the effects it can have on communities and cultures.

An unpredictable bunch. People.

Everywhere you go you get a different opinion and a different point of view.

What's in, what's out? What is of the moment and what is so 'yesterday'?

And when you talk to 125 million people all over the planet you'd be amazed at what you learn. We have learned that the more you look at difference as potential, the less it looks like a problem.

yourpointofview.com

The world's local bank

Figure 25.2   HSBC traditional/trendy advertisement

A very important effect of the globalisation of communication media is that it has led to the formation of new kinds of 'imagined communities', a term that influential thinker Benedict Anderson uses to describe national identity. Anderson offers a definition of the nation as 'an imagined political community' (Anderson 1991, p. 6). He writes:

> It is *imagined* because the members of even the smallest nation will never know most of their fellow-members, meet them, or even hear of them, yet in the minds of each lives the image of their communion ... in fact, all communities larger than the primordial villages of face-to-face contact (and perhaps even these) are imagined ... It is imagined as a *community*, because, regardless of the actual inequality and exploitation that may prevail in each, the nation is always conceived as a deep, horizontal comradeship (Anderson 1991, pp. 6–7).

The sense of comradeship and common interests characterising the global village arises because of the democratisation of communication technologies. Anderson's work foregrounds the importance of the print technologies, which, he says, 'made it possible for rapidly growing numbers of people to think about themselves, and to relate themselves to others, in profoundly new ways' (Anderson 1991, p. 36). This argument about print media has been extended and applied to new media.

Media and communication technology as a globalising force

The utopian vision of the rewards of globalisation has been eagerly embraced by multinational communication corporations and harnessed to their branding and advertising campaigns. Consider, for example, the advertisements for Nokia's N-series phones in which we see a montage of faces and voices from all over the world, united harmoniously by communication technologies that improve quality of life for one and all, and Microsoft's Unlimited Potential campaign, which claims to focus on 'helping individuals and communities around the globe achieve their goals and dreams with relevant, accessible and affordable technologies'.

While the kind of empowerment that global media products and technologies offer is often the power of consumption, ICTs also have potential benefits for economic and social development. As information flow, speed, and volume increase, decreasing sensitivity to distance and diminishing production costs lead to benefits for local media producers and isolated communities (see Fourie 2001, p. 611). The global media can, therefore, work to create positive social change by facilitating access to valuable information about healthcare, agricultural techniques, and education. The global reach of information also has an impact on transparency and accountability with regard to political policy and practices. This is a factor that some governments see as a boon and others, such as the Chinese government, see as a threat because it prompts the global community to exert political pressure, as was seen when Google protested government control, censorship, and internet surveillance by withdrawing from China in 2010.

Although the development of globalisation has given rise to new forms of community and a sense of global interconnectedness, the quality of life available to many citizens in the global village has been questioned. One of the paradoxes of contemporary life is that the global communication environment is media saturated and offers information overload and access to a virtual global community, but is also characterised by loss of meaningful interpersonal communication and traditional communities, languages, and value systems. These are the 'contradictory trends of integration and fragmentation that characterise information and communication' (Snow 2001, p. 22). It is this darker side of globalisation that theorist Herbert Schiller explores in his work on cultural imperialism, and that are exposed in Castells' theory of the network society; both authors are discussed below.

Dystopian views: cultural imperialism and the network society

Castells counters the utopian view of globalisation described above by pointing out that 'While the media have become indeed globally interconnected, and programs and messages circulate in the global network, *we are not living in a global village, but in customised cottages globally produced and locally distributed*' (Castells 2000, p. 370; emphasis in original). Indeed, the dark side of globalisation is far worse than a tendency towards mass production and homogenisation. The 2005 *United Nations Human Development Report* showed that the richest fifty people in the world have a combined income greater than the total earnings of the poorest 416 million people. Even though world economic output has doubled in the past ten years, the gap between the richest and the poorest has worsened, which is not what you might expect when globalisation is making us increasingly interconnected and interdependent. This disheartening economic reality has spawned a vocal anti-globalisation movement, geared to resist a global system with disproportionate benefits for big business and wealthy individuals. The anti-globalisation movement targets symbols of the global economy such as the World Trade Organization and the World Bank, and corporations such as McDonald's, Nike, and Shell. Ironically, the movement itself is reliant on the technologies and effects of globalisation. In his book *Media, Politics and the Network Society*, Robert Hassan points out that the shared focus of anti-globalisation protesters and the ability to form activist networks 'would have been impossible without the intercommunication made possible by ICTs and through such websites as <www.indymedia.org>' (2004, p. 109).

Castells conceptualises globalisation in terms of a 'network society', which he considers to be the prevailing social structure of the information age. From this perspective, media globalisation has significant financial and cultural ramifications: for instance, the internet is the means by which we access information, power, knowledge, and advantageous networks in many realms of economic, social, and political activity. For those who do not have access to the internet, media globalisation can be a powerful mechanism of social exclusion. It is important to critique the ownership and control of the infrastructure of the network society because:

> There is a systemic relationship between the new, knowledge-based, global network economy, and the intensification of inequality, poverty and social exclusion throughout the world. The trend is not related to technology or to globalisation *per se*, but to the institutional conditions under which globalisation proceeds and the information technology revolution expands (Castells 2001a, p. 157).

The debilitating effect of the digital divide on developing nations in a networked global society has been compared to attempting to make the kind of progress achieved during the Industrial Revolution without electricity: 'Information technology is the electricity of the Information Age' (Castells 2001a, p. 156). In other words, the global economy is powered by the internet, and to be not connected impacts seriously on development. While information poverty and not enough access to digital media are serious concerns, proponents of the cultural imperialism thesis consider that too much access to the media can also be problematic.

Cultural imperialism describes how one culture spreads its values and ideas culturally, such as through the media rather than through direct rule or economic trading. The global reach of Hollywood films and US television is the most obvious example (see p. 468). Economic trading is also important because commodities from toys to tennis shoes, soft drinks to CDs, are carriers of culture. The term 'coca-colonisation' (Klein 2000, p. 131) succinctly expresses the links between colonisation, the global spread of commodities and brands, and cultural imperialism. Cultural imperialism (see p. 23) is, according to Schiller, who coined the term, a form of transnational corporate cultural domination (Schiller 1992, p. 39).

cultural imperialism
Imperial domination of the world maintained partly through the dissemination of cultural products. Argues that the globalisation of communication results in the domination of traditional cultures and the intrusion of Western culture and values such as consumerism.

According to media theorist John Thompson, the cultural imperialism thesis can be summarised as follows:

> The globalisation of communication has been driven by the pursuit of the commercial interests of large US-based transnational corporations, often acting in collaboration with Western (predominantly American) political and military interests; and this process has resulted in a new form of dependency in which the traditional cultures are destroyed through the intrusion of Western values (Thompson 1995, p. 165).

Schiller argues that global monopolies and the proliferation of ICTs bring the threat of cultural imperialism and the loss of cultural diversity. Because the globalisation of communication has been driven by the pursuit of profit, and because new communication technologies are developed to serve the interests of giant transnational media corporations (in ways that often overlap with Western political and military interests), the process of globalisation has, according to Schiller, contributed to the destruction of traditional cultures and dependence on Western value systems. Schiller claims that

> The heaviest cost of transnational corporate-produced culture, however, is that it erodes the priceless idea of the public good and the vital principle of social accountability and the longtime dream of international community. Substituted for these elemental human aspirations is the promise of consumer choice—a choice that is not genuine (Schiller 1998, p. 11).

Even in a state where there appears to be a great deal of choice between television and radio channels, newspapers, and magazines, citizens may not be the recipients of a diversity of content or have access to a range of critical and political perspectives. In an industry dominated by just a few key players, freedom of information and freedom of choice may be a comforting illusion. While citizens are able to choose between many media products, they may all be controlled by one corporation.

Contradictory discourses of globalisation

In *Media Unlimited* (2001) Todd Gitlin claims that 'If there is a global village, it speaks American. It wears jeans, drinks Coke, eats at the golden arches, walks on swooshed shoes, plays electric guitars, recognizes Mickey Mouse, James Dean, ET, Bart Simpson, R2-D2, and Pamela Anderson'. That said, global media flows are not unidirectional: globalisation has also profoundly altered the nature of American popular culture, which is especially evident in the influence of Asian media such as Japanese anime, Bollywood films, and Bhangra music (Jenkins 2006, p. 153).

These different perspectives on globalisation can be discerned on the cover of the Benetton magazine, *Colors* (Plate 11), with the title 'Monoculture'. Bright red liquid is splattered across the page, forming an image recognisable as the Disney character Mickey Mouse. If we read this image as an image of bloodshed, then the question we must ask is: Who, or what, has died, and how is Disney implicated in this death? There are several different responses to this question, many of which point to the positive and negative aspects of globalisation. One answer is that globalisation and cultural imperialism might produce a monoculture, leading to the death of cultural difference and diversity, and the loss of non–American cultural traditions and customs. The other answer, based on the signifier of the internet address turned into a smile on Mickey's mouth, is that the internet and other media have linked people across the globe together into a global village or a virtual community. These positive aspects of globalisation are specifically linked to the ability of communication media to bring people closer together, inform us of issues and events in distant places, and create a sense of unification: one culture shared by all humanity. Schiller's observation that American popular culture is spreading throughout the world, carried by characters such as Mickey and by corporations such as Disney, is incontestable; however, this does not necessarily mean that local cultures will die out as a result. Extensive research into audience reception, including ethnographic studies of audience responses to media texts, indicates that people don't passively absorb media content without resisting, negotiating, and contextualising the message. Communication is a two-way exchange of meaning, and media reception is not so much like absorption as it is appropriation, which suggests that divisions between cultures might die without destroying cultural diversity. Globalisation may leave us smiling after all.

The image in Figure 25.3 is an advertisement for Channel O (Channel 87) on DSTV in southern Africa. This channel addresses a predominantly black audience and the advertisement shows an awareness of the discourse of cultural imperialism by branding the channel as 'uncolonized'. In other words, Channel O is claiming not to be dominated by foreign media products that feature and address white Americans. The image shows an Oreo (a popular brand of American sweet biscuit), but the biscuit doesn't have its usual white filling. The term 'Oreo' is used to describe people who are black on the outside but white inside. In other words, Oreos are black people who have assimilated white culture and adopted the lifestyles and values of white people. In the DSTV advertisement the Oreo is entirely black, which is reinforced by an accompanying advertising slogan, 'Get back to black', meaning that watching the black-oriented programming on Channel O will help the black audience stay in touch with its cultural identity. Ironically, South Africa has been accused of its own form of cultural imperialism because it exports South African culture via film and television to the rest of southern Africa, partly through DSTV's Channel O.

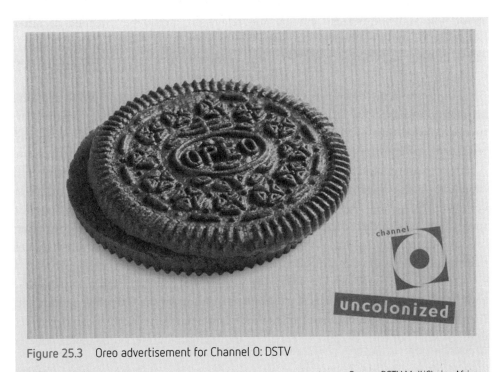

Figure 25.3   Oreo advertisement for Channel O: DSTV

Source: DSTV MultiChoice Africa

Most theorists now acknowledge that the globalisation of communication has not led to straightforward American dominance or to global harmony, but has resulted in a complex process of adaptation, appropriation, hybridisation, and mutual incorporation of different cultural texts and traditions as the media spread knowledge of different cultures around the globe. Power relations of domination and dependency certainly do exist, but the exchange of culture through the media is certainly not one-way or entirely negative. The cultural imperialism thesis is also undermined by the fact that traditional cultures were not pristine or isolated prior to electronic invasion and the influx of American television programs and merchandise. There has been cultural mixing and domination for centuries, as the history of globalisation shows. The global economy has several big players: the USA doesn't control it and should not be held responsible for all of its inadequacies.

Cultural imperialism and Hollywood

While the USA is not the only controlling force in the media world, the global predominance of American films has an economic basis. Commercial film production was established in Hollywood through the studio system and was centrally controlled by a small group of studios such as Warner Brothers and MGM (Cook 1985, pp. 7–8, 10–25). The American film and television industries play a significant part in the American economy, bringing in enormous profits to the USA from many other countries, partly at the expense of local media industries. There are many debates about how much American cinema and television should be screened in other countries. In some countries, it is perceived that there are cultural, economic, and moral benefits and dangers involved in the predominance of American cinema and television.

The positive myths of the USA are that it is a land of opportunity, freedom, prosperity, and equality. It is seen as a melting-pot society in which anyone can succeed, and is thus perceived as a great escape from older, more traditional, and restricted societies. American culture promises energy, sexiness, and freedom, American fashions and style are taken up by young people in every continent, and capitalism and competition have become the new ideals of former communist countries. But some fear this cultural dominance because it glorifies materialist values and because the economic interests with which it is allied seem to be taking over and exploiting the rest of the world. They are apprehensive of the way it erodes traditional values and of its competitive harshness.

One way of considering this issue is to suggest that television and cinema should aim to tell a culture's own stories, for example that Australia, the United Kingdom, and African countries should present stories about Australian, British, or African people set in their own countries. Because of concerns about cultural imperialism, media policies and trade agreements that govern the global flow of cultural products such as film and television, and that restrict foreign media ownership, are very important (see p. 23).

World music

World music is an interesting case to examine in relation to globalisation. World music, particularly African and Latin American music, is now played and marketed around the world, and it influences European and American styles, and invites openness to other cultural influences. Perhaps this demonstrates that Eurocentrism is coming to an end. The spread of world music is not cultural imperialism but a flow of culture back from previously colonised states. World music is also influenced by Western music styles and by Western recording and sampling technology, and the production and marketing of world music is still largely in the hands of a few European and US companies that receive a bigger percentage of profits than do the artists who make the music. In some instances songs include recordings of indigenous music but no money goes to the original artists. 'Wimoweh', also known as 'The Lion Sleeps Tonight', was originally a Zulu song written by Solomon Linda in 1939. Until recently Linda was not credited as the songwriter and received no royalties, even as Western folk musicians such as The Weavers and The Kingston Trio profited handsomely from recording their own versions of the song and Disney made a fortune using it in *The Lion King*. It was not until 2005 when the South African filmmaker Francois Verster made a documentary about the origins of the song and Rian Malan (2000) wrote an article about it in *Rolling Stone* that Linda's family received compensation and acknowledgment for the use of his work.

Although Disney films may not be your preference, chances are, your choices in music have something to do with film soundtracks, music videos, MTV, and the promotional machine surrounding bands signed to large record labels. MTV itself is more than a marketing machine for the products it advertises between songs and the albums it promotes with its music videos; it is also a truly global communication brand in its own right. Music is also used to sell non-music products and to build brand images (Sprite's association with hip-hop is a good example). The implications of this are that there are positive and negative outcomes of globalisation: the media play a positive role in helping us learn about and share in each other's cultures, but they are also implicated in wasteful and exploitative marketing practices that primarily benefit the top tier of corporate executives.

Tactical media responses to globalisation

While there are certainly advantageous aspects of globalisation, it also has its drawbacks and resisting those aspects perceived as negative can seem overwhelming for individuals because globalisation is such a powerful force. French cultural theorist Michel de Certeau suggests in his influential book *The Practice of Everyday Life* (1984) that there are ways in which ordinary people develop tactics for expressing autonomy and struggling against oppressive norms in everyday practices. This conception of grass-roots resistance has been developed by Geert Lovink and David Garcia (1997) in their online essay 'ABC of Tactical Media', which details everyday tactics for using ICTs to hybridise, subvert, innovate, organise, and communicate in ways that take advantage of media globalisation and harness it to serve the interests of civil society and media activism. Building on the idea of tactical responses to globalisation, here are some suggestions that may move us towards a more balanced global society.

- Use the internet to find and disseminate information about ethical consumerism in order to make informed choices about which companies to support and which to boycott.
- Tap into the open source software movement, which shares information instead of using copyright law to serve the interests of companies such as Microsoft.
- Organise online networks of like-minded people and groups to work towards a common cause.
- Encourage self-representation and affirmation of the value of the local.
- Create and support independent media, encourage diversity of content and ownership.
- Lobby media policy designers to serve citizens, not corporate interests.
- Publicise media issues, promote media literacy, provide technological training.
- Use ICTs to promote transparency, accountability, and empowerment.

Whichever tactics you choose, the important thing is to find ways to make the best of globalisation and technological developments and to resist the aspects that you perceive as damaging. As media consumers and as future members of the media industry, you will influence the process of change and development as well as being affected by it.

Conclusion

Although globalisation is not restricted to the media, the most important points for media students to focus on include the relationship between globalisation and technological and economic changes in the media industries. These changes have significant social and cultural impacts all over the world. Critical perspectives on globalisation such as accounts of cultural imperialism, the network society, and imagined communities are attempts to interpret these changes. This chapter has critically evaluated diverse theoretical perspectives on globalisation and revealed a variety of ways in which it has the potential to be empowering as well as disempowering for media producers and consumers.

This chapter has

- outlined key theoretical positions in relation to globalisation
- explained how popular terminology such as 'the digital divide', 'the network society', 'imagined communities', and 'the global village' relates to changes in global media
- discussed the positive and negative impacts of globalisation.

Discussion points

1   Can you think of any other ideas to add to the list of tactical media responses to globalisation?
2   Note down all of the ways in which globalisation affects your daily life. Divide your list into positives and negatives and consider whether, on balance, you favour a utopian or a dystopian view of globalisation.

Summary

You should now be able to

- assess the relationship between new communication technologies and social change
- evaluate how the digital divide impacts on your community and others
- discuss how globalisation has developed historically and how it influences contemporary life
- list the key characteristics, costs, and benefits of globalisation
- distinguish between and debate the merits of Benedict Anderson, Marshall McLuhan, Manuel Castells, and Herbert Schiller's perspectives on globalisation.

Conclusion

This book has been about the media and their relationship with the world. We have argued that there is a series of complex media–world relationships, or media influences, on the world and we have attempted to unravel them. Our focus has been on language, texts, representations, discourses, and ideology: these are the ways in which we apprehend the world, the ways in which we give it shape and form. As Thomas King (2003) says: 'The truth about stories is that that's all we are' (this book is itself just another text). We have looked closely at various media products, taken them apart bit by bit, and mixed appreciation with criticism.

We have also considered how media technologies have developed and are developing. Having read this book, you should be able to draw on a body of theory, past and present, with which you can begin to make sense of the media–world in which you live.

Important social and psychological questions remain: Will late capitalism continue or will we move into a new phase? What directions should we take in the twenty-first century? Can we reach new heights of sophisticated, cultural development, especially through the evolution of new technologies? Will progress be accompanied by new difficulties, such as economic inequalities, social disruptions, and environmental uncertainties? What will the role of the media be in this new era?

We have suggested that we need to look carefully at five important areas in relation to our future lives, areas that cover the personal, the social, and the global.

1 *Gender, sexuality, and the family* How do we live out our gendered and sexual lives? Is the family the place to do it? Does it need to change or should we evolve new forms? How do men and women resolve issues relating to power, oppression, intimacy, sexuality, and love?

2 *Work* What forms of work will be fulfilling for us and provide balanced growth, material and spiritual, for the planet as a whole?

3 *Issues of ethnicity and race* Together these issues form one of the major sources of social division around the world. They are connected directly to issues of economic inequality and global economic imbalance. We have not paid detailed attention in this book to questions of the oppression of Aboriginal Australians and to the way in which the media represent them. However, we hope that the frameworks given, and many of the examples from other countries, will enable you to explore these

issues further. Any ideal of the future has to address and resolve issues of racism and discrimination, and must involve finding ways in which people can live harmoniously together.

4   *Ecological and environmental issues* Media studies has tended to focus on humans. Today, ecological issues relating to all living species, and to the planet as a whole, are pressing. Questions about how we and the planet can survive in the twenty-first century are paramount. While this book has not examined in detail how the media deal with such issues, this question will become even more important in the near future. We hope that you have found, in this book, useful insights about the relationship between the media and our ecological future.

5   *Technology, interactivity, and globalisation* Keeping abreast of technological advances, particularly new forms of interactive communication technologies, is an important aspect of media studies and social change. Being well informed and conscientious consumers of the media and other cultural products can help to make sure that the interconnections linking humans all over the world result in positive influences on other lives, rather than inadvertently widening the gap between the rich and the poor or between those with access to resources, opportunities, and information, and those without.

The media will continue to explore and represent these five broad issues, which will continue to be crucial aspects of the world you live in. We hope that your engagement with the media and with society is enriched by the ideas and insights offered here, and that media studies connects in relevant ways with the interests and ideals that you pursue in your everyday life.

Glossary

After each term, there is a page reference in brackets. This refers to the page in the text on which the term appears.

actual reader (page 97)

> The real flesh and blood individuals who interpret or read texts.

adbusting (page 224)

> Adbusting involves modifying advertisements to undermine their intended meaning (for more information see <www.adbusters.org>).

agenda setting (page 25)

> The process by which media producers set up the issues — the agenda — that the media will focus on and that audiences will subsequently perceive to be important.

alternative/oppositional reading (page 102)

> Audiences interpret a text completely against the preferred reading.

analogue media (page 108)

> Analogue media such as photography, print, and radio use material processes and mechanical modes of representation to transcribe and transmit content in forms such as physical data or electrical signals.

anchorage (page 146)

> Anchorage limits polysemy by articulating the preferred meaning of a text, as a caption labels an image.

angle (page 87)

> In journalism the angle is the central focus or the main idea in the organisation and presentation of a story and its lead.

arbitrary signifiers (page 139)

> Arbitrary signifiers have no logical connection to their signified. The signifier does not look or sound like the signified, nor does it point to the signified in a causal or indexical fashion.

auteur theory (page 93)

> The theory that films are the creative products of film directors and can be interpreted as their personal visions, marked by a unique 'signature style'.

avant-garde (page 264)

> Literally means 'advance guard'; refers to cultural products that are seen as unconventionally new and different from mainstream culture but which will supposedly lead cultural developments forward.

balance (page 85)

Balanced reporting entails the presentation of both sides of an argument, giving them equal space and time.

bankability (page 420)

The stars' potential to guarantee a film's financial box-office success.

binary oppositions (page 282)

A means of cultural classification that splits the world into sets of dualistic opposing categories, such as male and female, black and white.

biological essentialist (page 351)

The belief that the physical body—the hormones, inherent instincts, and genetic predispositions etc.—defines the essence of identity and determines personality characteristics, behaviour, and abilities.

blog (page 109)

A blog (web log) is a website where people can record their diaries or other personal commentaries; often used as an alternative journalistic media outlet.

bricolage (page 453)

The putting together of different, often contradictory, cultural forms, thereby creating new meanings.

broadcast (page 115)

A means of media transmission that makes information available to a broad spectrum of the population.

capitalism (page 8)

The dominant global economic system, organised by workers selling their labour for wages, and investors making profit through interest and economic growth. Capitalism, which gradually replaced the feudal economic system from about 1600, is characterised by private ownership and control of the means of production (capital) by individuals and corporations.

catharsis (page 324)

The expression and release, or purging, of emotions by audiences at the climax of a tragedy or drama.

celebrity (page 417)

A celebrity is a well-known, highly visible public figure whose private life and public appearances frequently attract the media spotlight, often for reasons other than their professional standing or abilities.

cinéma vérité (page 310)

French for 'cinema truth'. A documentary style developed in France in the 1950s and 1960s, cinéma vérité is similar to direct cinema, fly-on-the-wall documentary, and observational documentary, but the filmmakers participate more directly and self-reflexively in the narrative.

cinematography (page 245)

The processes of filming the mise-en-scène—how things are filmed. This includes the angles (for example high or low) and positioning of the camera (for example long-shot or close-up), focus and framing, any camera movements (for example pan, track, zoom, or tilt), any special camera effects (for example slow motion or time lapse), the film stock used, and processing methods.

CMC (page 5)

Computer-mediated communication

code (page 134)

Codes are standardised formulae for communicating meaning.

conclusion (page 161)

The conclusion of an essay should summarise the key points and briefly discuss their significance, with reference to the objectives stated in the introduction.

connotation (page 136)

Operating on the second order of signification, connotation refers to the emotions, values, and associations that a sign gives rise to in the reader, viewer, or listener. The connotative meaning of a sign can be expressed by quickly jotting down what it reminds you of or makes you feel or imagine.

consciousness industry (page 19)

Term used by the Frankfurt School to describe how the media functioned to control the minds and feelings of the masses at the same time as making money.

content analysis (page 21)

Quantitative measurement of media content.

continuity editing (page 250)

A system of editing, established in Hollywood by about 1920, for telling stories smoothly. It uses particular techniques and conventions for filming within a scene such as the use of establishing shot, use of shot-reverse shot, eyeline match, match on action, observance of 180 degree rule, and continuity of action, sound, and lighting.

convention (page 134)

Conventions are methods of organising signs to communicate meaning in ways that become habituated and widely shared over time.

core problematic (page 233)

Central problem or opposition that a genre explores.

counter-hegemony (page 206)

A world view or activity that is in opposition to and challenges the dominant world view.

cultivation (page 100)

The media has a cumulative effect on audiences. Long-term exposure to media cultivates attitudes and beliefs through the persistent repetition of messages and images.

cultural imperialism (pages 23 and 465)

Imperial domination of the world maintained partly through the dissemination of cultural products. Argues that the globalisation of communication results in the domination of traditional cultures and the intrusion of Western culture and values such as consumerism.

culture jamming (page 213)

A form of media activism that subverts and reworks the intended meaning of existing media texts, or parodies major corporations, public figures, and their media images.

defamation (page 223)

Defamation involves publicising information that is untrue and so injures someone's reputation, or if it is deemed to be not in the public interest for that information to be published.

denotation (page 136)

Denotation is what Barthes calls 'the first order of signification'. It is the most obvious level on which a sign communicates and it refers to the commonsense meaning of the sign. The denotative meaning can be expressed by describing the sign as simply as possible.

desensitisation (page 101)

Long-term exposure to media can make audiences progressively less sensitive or responsive to images and messages that made a strong impression when first encountered.

dialectical synthesis (page 284)

Two opposing forces (such as good and evil, or thesis and antithesis) generate conflict or debate that is resolved when the two sides come together in a form of synthesis.

diegetic sound (page 248)

Sound that comes directly from the fictional world (the diegesis) of a screen text.

différance (page 158)

Refers to an endless chain of signification in which each sign or signifier is linked to or associated with something else, so that the complete or final meaning is infinitely deferred.

digital divide (page 5)

The increasing gap between those who have and those who do not have access to technology, access to content, ICT skills, and money to pay for digital services; most often used to refer to the difference between the developed and developing worlds' access to the benefits of digital technology.

digital media (page 108)

Media such as digital videogames, the internet, and other forms of computerised media that mathematically process and convert whatever information needs to be represented into numerical form. The information can then be manipulated, reproduced, converted, shared, and transmitted in versatile, swift, immaterial ways.

digital onscreen graphics (dogs) (page 155)

Dogs or bugs often take the form of station logos or other information added at the bottom of the frame during post production. Such graphics can brand television programs and the networks on which they screen, they can prevent piracy, advertise the next program, or offer viewers extra information.

direct address (page 306)

Direct address to camera is when the person on screen looks straight into the camera as though they are looking at and addressing the audience directly. This breaks the conventions of cinematic realism by acknowledging the process of filming; it also substitutes a different sense of realism, intimacy, and immediacy.

direct cinema (page 310)

The North American corollary of *cinéma vérité*, direct cinema has an observational style, but does not involve interviews or intervention by the filmmakers.

direct effects (page 99)

The direct-effects model of communication (also called the 'hypodermic model') suggests that the media transmits powerful messages to audience members, who absorb the meaning passively and are strongly affected by it.

discourse (pages 69 and 172)

Discourses are paradigms or ways of understanding that are communicated through texts and language use, and that organise knowledge and social power.

discourse analysis (page 172)

Explores the ways in which power and knowledge are communicated through texts, language use, and systems of thought.

disintermediation (page 123)

To bypass intermediaries, such as publishers and distributors, in order to transmit media directly from the creator to the consumer via self-publishing tools and techniques.

documentaries (pages 14 and 307)

Films and television programs about real-life situations.

dominant discourse (page 201)

Contemporary ideas and beliefs shared by a majority of people.

dominant ideology (page 194)

A world view that supports the ruling class as dominant, the status quo, yet is shared by the majority of people.

dominant reading (page 92)

The meaning of a text that is accepted by most audience members and can be determined by examining its textual codes and social/historical contexts.

editing (page 245)

The process of joining or splicing together separate pieces of film, separate shots. Edits may cut directly, dissolve, mix, fade, wipe, etc.

embedded journalism (page 56)

Embedded journalism is when a journalist is allowed to join a group (such as a military troop) to gain access for reporting events; and consequently tends to see events from the group's point of view.

emergent discourse (page 201)

New ideas and beliefs held by a few people at first, and then gradually becoming accepted by more people.

epic theatre (page 327)

A form of storytelling or theatre developed by German playwright Bertolt Brecht that challenged conventional storytelling forms by encouraging audience detachment and understanding rather than emotional identification.

establishing shot (page 247)

A wide or long shot conventionally used to show the whole of a location or set so that we can see and understand the space the action is taking place in. Normally followed by shots that are closer to the action.

Eurocentrism (page 403)

Places European values in a privileged, central position, and sees the world from a European perspective.

expository documentary (page 310)

A voice-over commentary explains what we see, thereby controlling our viewpoint.

extratextual knowledge (page 425)

Knowledge and information taken from sources external to the text.

feminism (page 354)

The movement for women's equality and liberation.

film noir (page 233)

French for 'black film'; black and white thrillers or detective stories made in the 1940s and 1950s conventionally featuring low-key lighting, retrospective voice-over narration, flashbacks, suspicion, intrigue, crime, urban settings, and *femmes fatales*.

flow (page 291)

The continual sequence of television programs, trailers, and advertisements that blend together.

fragmentation (page 291)

The way television often features stories that are broken up over a number of episodes, are full of short separate scenes, and are interrupted by commercials.

freedom of speech (page 223)

The right to express opinions publicly without interference from government or other sectors. This right is subject to legal limitations that restrict the publication of material that incites hatred or violence, or is defamatory.

gatekeeping (page 25)

The process of controlling what gets included and whose voices are heard in the media, particularly in the news.

generic hybridisation (page 235)

Generic hybrids are texts that blend the codes and conventions of two or more genres to produce a new combination.

genre (page 231)

Groups of texts that share a set of conventional characteristics such as content, narrative structure, and visual style, are classified as textual types or genres.

global village (page 20)

The phrase 'the global village' suggests that the globalisation of communication media has brought the whole world closer together, like a village in which everyone is interconnected.

globalisation (page 458)

Globalisation refers to an international community influenced by technological development and economic, political, and military interests. It is characterised by a worldwide increase in interdependence, interactivity, interconnectedness, and the virtually instantaneous exchange of information. Globalisation could lead to the homogenisation of world cultures, or to hybridisation and multiculturalism.

graphic editing or graphic montage (page 253)

The linking of two separate shots through visual similarity or contrast.

hegemony (page 205)

Power and leadership maintained through processes of struggle and negotiation, especially through winning the consent of the majority of people to accept the ideas or ideologies of the dominant group as common sense.

homoeroticism (page 377)

Sexual desire between same-sex couples, though most commonly used to refer to men; also often refers to the pleasure received in gazing at an attractive member of the same sex in sport, film, etc.

homophobia (page 377)

Fear of same-sex intimacy, though most commonly used to refer to men's fear of homosexuality and emotional closeness between men.

horizontal integration (page 112)

This is a form of convergence of media ownership in which a corporation owns several companies involved in the same aspect of media production.

hypertext (page 110)

Chunks of text or data connected by electronic links in a networked database. Hyperlinks enable the user to navigate through information along multiple, non-linear pathways.

iconic sign (page 138)

The relationship between the signified and the signifier is based on likeness or resemblance.

iconography (page 233)

Visual images (icons) associated with a particular genre that are repeatedly used.

ICTs (page 118)

Information and communication technologies, such as computers.

identification (page 428)

A feeling of connectedness to another person. It involves seeing aspects of oneself in that person, experiencing a sense of relatedness or overlapping of identity.

identity (page 36)

Refers to selfhood, to the characteristics and qualities that uniquely distinguish a person, a group, or a thing from others. The meaning of the term 'identity' is connected to difference (being identifiably unique) and sameness (being identical to oneself, having an essence or personality or qualities that do not change over time).

ideology (page 34)

Ideologies are sets of social values, ideas, beliefs, feelings, and representations, by which people collectively make sense of the world they live in, thus constituting a world view. This world view is naturalised, a taken for granted, commonsense view about the way the world works.

implied narrative (page 145)

The story that a picture suggests, including the events that may have happened immediately prior to the moment in the image, and immediately afterwards.

incorporation or recuperation (page 200)

The processes by which dangerous, rebellious, radical ideas and movements are made acceptable, not by banning or criminalising them but by partially accepting them; 'incorporated' means, literally, 'taken into the main body'.

indexical sign (page 138)

The relationship between the signifier is one of indication, direction or measurement, sequence or causation.

inscribed reader (page 97)

An ideal reader who is constructed by the text, or who is imagined/intended by the producers of the text.

intellectual editing or intellectual montage (page 252)

Two images linked together produce an idea or concept.

interpellation (page 185)

A process in which we internalise ideologies as a response to being hailed or addressed.

intertextual knowledge (page 425)

Knowledge and information gained from other related media texts.

intertextuality (page 145)

The process of knowingly borrowing and referring to other texts, or interpreting one text in the light of other related texts.

introduction (page 161)

The introduction of an essay should include an outline of what you aim to achieve (state essay topic, objectives, and the text you are analysing) and how you intend to achieve it (your methodology and structure).

inverted pyramid (page 85)

Information is given in descending order of importance, as in a news report.

ISAs (page 197)

Ideological state apparatuses—the institutions of socialisation and persuasion that societies use to control people, for example religion, family, education, and media.

jouissance (page 332)

A French word, one meaning of which is bliss or ecstasy; much more powerful, and sometimes more disturbing, than *plaisir* (pleasure).

langue (page 159)

Langue is the fundamental structure that underlies and governs language and expression.

liberal pluralism (page 204)

A liberalist pluralist society is one that includes many different social groups with different viewpoints; they all have the liberty and opportunity to speak out.

Marxism (page 189)

The theories developed by Karl Marx, including that the struggle between different groups in society (classes) brings about historical change, that economic needs are the most important factor in determining people's behaviour, and what people think and believe is controlled, often unconsciously, by the dominant social groups.

masochism (page 379)

Pleasure (or perverse sexual gratification) felt when experiencing pain, humiliation, or deprivation. The term is derived from the name of erotic novelist Leopold von Sacher-Masoch.

media activism (page 214)

Activities involving individuals or lobby groups that attempt to change the way in which the media works, or that use the media to make a social or political statement.

media homogenisation (page 24)

Financial pressures and other forces lead all media products to become similar, standard, and uniform.

media studies (page 11)

Media studies analyses the role of the media in society and studies media technologies, media institutions, and the production, consumption, circulation, and content of media texts.

media, the (page 3)

technologically developed communication industries, normally making money, which can transmit information and entertainment across time and space to individuals and/or large groups of people; they are literally in the middle of this process, the means for communication.

metonymy (page 153)

Metonyms are signs in which one part or element stands in for or represents something larger.

metrosexuals (page 387)

Young, stylish, urban men who care about and spend considerable money on their appearance and are attractive to women (and, often, to other men).

mise-en-scène (page 245)

A French theatrical term meaning literally 'placed in the scene'. *Mise-en-scène* refers to *what* has been filmed: settings, objects, costumes, actors, and the way these are visually arranged and lit.

misogyny (page 353)

Hatred of women and femininity (literally, hatred of the womb).

modality (page 141)

A measure of the degree of certainty or realism associated with an instance of communication.

mode of address (page 186)

Refers to the way a text speaks to or addresses its audience.

modernism (page 447)

Describes Western art and aesthetic movements of the first half of the twentieth century; characterised by optimism in future progress, and ways of seeing or representing the world that challenged realism, including abstraction and focus on the act of representation.

montage (page 240)

Montage (the French word for editing) refers to two specific ways of joining together shots from different spaces and times—MTV-style collage of images set to music, and/or Soviet montage or political montage using Sergei Eisenstein's technique of juxtaposition.

motif (page 252)

Any significant element (an object, colour, place, sound, camera movement, or angle) that recurs or is developed throughout a film.

multiculturalism (page 404)

As a policy or a critical concept, multiculturalism celebrates unity in diversity by bringing together a range of cultural groups within a larger identity or community without privileging one culture over another.

multiplatforming (page 111)

A process of media convergence that involves distributing branded content across multiple outlets, for instance, the narrative and characters of a film or television franchise can be distributed as films, novels, games, soundtrack CDs, and as other merchandise, including clothes.

myths (page 328)

Stories that often feature ancient gods or fantasy creatures, that recount how a society evolved. At a rational, scientific level they are fantastic, impossible, and unreal, but they may contain social and psychological truths and insights that offer symbolic resolutions to real issues or questions.

narrative (page 259)

A sequence of events taking place over a given period of time that are linked, mainly through cause and effect.

narrowcast (page 115)

Narrowcast media transmission caters for small groups of people.

negotiated reading (page 102)

Audiences accept only some of what is being presented to them.

news frame (page 87)

The selection and presentation of stories, issues, quotes, headlines, and images influences the way audiences make sense of the news. The processes of inclusion and exclusion, and the use of language, structure, and emphasis convey values, judgments, and perspectives that determine what the audience will consider to be important.

news value/newsworthiness (page 28)

The elements of an issue or event that make it important enough to report on in the eyes of journalists. Newsworthy features include conflict, relevance, locality, prominence, novelty, and magnitude.

non-diegetic sound (page 248)

Sound that comes from somewhere outside the story world, such as the musical score, which the screen characters cannot hear.

normative theory (page 89)

'Normative' refers to assumed norms and standards of correctness; to ideal views about the role the media should play in society, particularly the functions the press ought to perform.

objectivity (page 26)

Perceiving, reporting, or presenting things from an impersonal, neutral, unbiased perspective.

observational learning and cognitive scripts (page 101)

People learn how to behave by observing how their role models act and by remembering the script that was performed so that if, later, they encounter a similar situation they can play the part.

Orientalism (page 406)

The way Europe has perceived, understood, and attempted to control cultures beyond the Oriental line.

paradigm (page 87)

A set of terms, things, or ideas all based on a common theme or unifying system.

parole (page 159)

Parole is a particular instance of language use or expression, when the underlying rules (*langue*) are put into practice.

patriarchy (page 353)

A social structure in which the father or a male figure is the leader and descent is reckoned on the male line. Masculine power and authority dominate social, political, and economic institutions, thereby oppressing women.

plaisir (page 332)

French for pleasure; the kind of enjoyment derived from fictions that do not have a strong or enduring impact.

point of view (page 268)

The positions cameras take and whose viewpoint they show the viewer.

political economy (page 22)

Explains how the media are determined by a combination of economic, social, and political factors, particularly ownership and control of the media.

polysemic (page 102)

A sign that has more than one possible meaning.

postcolonialism (page 442)

The historical period after colonialism; ways of understanding the (ongoing) effects of colonialism.

postfeminism (page 356)

The term can be used to suggest that feminism is in the past, is outdated, no longer relevant to contemporary gender dynamics. Alternatively, postfeminism can refer to a postmodern approach to feminism, and/or contemporary critiques of earlier feminisms.

postmodernism (page 443)

Originally, a style in architecture, the term was later used to describe the late-twentieth-century world and as a style of cultural production.

poststructuralism (page 440)

Poststructuralism develops and challenges structuralist approaches, taking more account of the way contexts and audiences can produce more fluid meanings and readings of media texts.

preferred reading (page 102)

Audiences accept what is being presented without questioning the meaning intended by the media producers.

product placement (page 54)

Companies pay film and television producers to include their products in a story as a subtle form of advertising.

projection (page 103)

People project their own unconscious feelings onto other people or objects; they see in objects and other people aspects of themselves reflected back.

psychoanalysis (page 340)

Psychoanalysis, as developed by Sigmund Freud, argued that people are motivated by their unconscious, that there are several developmental stages people go through as they grow up, and that psychoanalysis can make people aware of their unconscious conflicts, fantasies, and desires (which are attributed chiefly to the development of the sexual instinct) through the free association of ideas, analysis, and interpretation of their dreams.

realism (page 332)

Objects in art—paintings, sculpture, literature—that appear true to real life and the aesthetic methods or styles used to create them. Realism, the dominant aesthetic in painting and literature in the nineteenth century, aimed for verisimilitude and focused on the lives of ordinary people.

reality TV (page 316)

The general premise is that reality-based programs portray people who are not actors saying lines that are not scripted in situations that are drawn from real life but often are constructed and filmed in a manner designed to capture a sense of authenticity, immediacy, and realism.

reception studies (page 97)

The study of how audiences actively receive, read, consume, and interact with media texts.

reinforcement (page 100)

The media reinforces ideas and feelings that other social institutions are already communicating.

repressed desire (page 342)

The act of repression forms the unconscious. Forbidden material (Oedipal desire, for example) is rejected from conscious thought, but not destroyed. It is stored in the unconscious from where it continues to produce effects.

residual discourse (page 201)

Set of ideas and beliefs from the past that are still accepted by some people.

rhythmic editing or rhythmic montage (page 251)

Rhythmic editing means the pace of editing—how long each shot lasts.

RSAs (page 197)

Repressive state apparatuses—the institutions of force that societies use to control people, for example the army, police, law courts, and prisons.

scopophilia (page 340)

From the Greek; love of looking, a basic human drive.

self-reflexivity (page 315)

The process whereby media texts self-consciously refer back to themselves, often drawing our attention to their construction.

semiology (page 131)

Semiology (also called semiotics) is the science of signs, or the study of signs and sign systems.

shadow (page 408)

Parts of our personality that we have hidden, denied, and repressed, also known as the alter-ego.

sign (page 132)

Communicates meaning by standing in for or representing a thing or an idea.

signified (page 132)

The thing or idea that a sign refers to.

signifier (page 132)

The visible, tangible, or audible aspect of a sign that carries the meaning.

social constructionist (page 351)

Sees identity as constructed by external social forces such as the media, family, education, religion, and expectations of community members.

sound bridge (page 254)

Sound is used to link two separate shots.

soundtrack (page 246)

The recorded combination of human voices, sound effects, and music.

star (page 417)

Stardom is an elite type of celebrity based, at least initially, on a person's outstanding professional achievement. Stars play well-publicised leading roles in popular culture and entertainment media. They consistently outshine colleagues and competitors, and their personal and professional lives attract significant attention.

star image (page 424)

The qualities, ideals, and values that a star represents, based on their films and other performances, and on media information circulated about them.

structuralism (page 260)

A method of analysis that involves looking for and examining the underlying structures of meaning in language, social relationships, narratives, and so forth.

subculture (page 13)

People who share cultural activities such as dress, leisure activities, and social beliefs, that are resistant or opposed to mainstream culture; used mainly in relation to youth cultures.

subjectivity (page 189)

Pertains to an individual's personal thoughts and experiences, their own—subjective—way of seeing the world as distinct from general or universal experience, and objectivity.

symbolic sign (page 138)

The relationship between the signifier and the signified is arbitrary (there is no natural link) and is based on culture, context, and convention.

syntagm (page 87)

Syntagm, like syntax, is a term that refers to the structure or pattern of words in a sentence or things in a sequence.

technological determinism (page 116)

The view that technological innovation reshapes social life and drives social change. Technology determines how society functions, rather than society determining how technology should be developed or used.

textual analysis (pages 29 and 91)

The process of interpreting and analysing any media text, typically focusing on its form and content, style, and structure.

thesis statement (page 161)

The part of an essay that outlines the central argument is called the thesis; it should be briefly stated in the introduction, and developed throughout the essay. Writers should also consider possible objections and counterarguments (the antithesis) in order to weigh up different points of view and defend their ideas.

uses-and-gratifications (page 101)

Audiences use the media in unpredictable ways (through selection, interpretation, and integration with other everyday activities) to please themselves, not necessarily as media producers intend it to be used.

Verfremdung **(distanciation, alienation)** (page 328)

Aesthetic techniques that make the audience step back from their emotional narrative involvement to a more critical position, which often enables them to see familiar things in a surprising new way.

vertical integration (page 111)

This term describes a concentration of power when a media company owns various parts of the production, distribution, and exhibition chain, for example printing presses, magazine companies, content providers such as photographic databases, the distribution vehicles, and retail outlets.

References

ABC Radio National 1995 (7, 14, 21, 28 October), 'Talk, Talk, Talk' (originally produced by the Canadian Broadcast Corporation), broadcast as part of *The Science Show*.

—— 1996, *Media Report*, 29 August.

—— 2000a, *Media Report*, 7 December.

—— 2000b, *Media Report*, 21 December.

—— 2007, *Media Report*, 20 December.

Abercrombie, N 1996, 'Television as Text', in *Television and Society*, Polity, Cambridge, pp. 9–40.

Achbar, M (ed.) 1995, *Manufacturing Consent: Noam Chomsky and the Media*, Black Rose Books, Montreal and New York.

Adbusters website, <www.adbusters.org/home/>; accessed 14 February 2008.

Althusser, L 1977, 'Ideology and Ideological State Apparatuses', in *Lenin and Philosophy*, New Left Books, London.

American Beauty (DVD) 2000, Dir. Sam Mendes, USA.

Anderson, B 1983, *Imagined Communities: Reflections on the Origin and Spread of Nationalism*, Verso, London.

—— 1991, *Imagined Communities*, rev. edn, Verso, London and New York.

Ang, I 1985, *Watching Dallas: Soap Opera and the Melodramatic Imagination*, Methuen, London.

—— 1991, *Desperately Seeking the Audience*, Routledge, London.

Armes, R 1971, *Patterns of Realism*, Tantivy, London.

Baker, A & Boyd, T (eds) 1997, *Out of Bounds: Sports, Media, and the Politics of Identity*, Indiana University Press, Bloomington and Indianapolis.

Balogh, S 2007, 'There's a New Tube', *Courier Mail*, 24–25 March 2007, p. 18.

Bandura, A 1994, 'Social Cognitive Theory of Mass Communication', in J Bryant & D Zillmann (eds), *Media Effects: Advances in Theory and Research* (pp. 61–90), Lawrence Erlbaum, Hillsdale, NJ.

Barthes, R 1973, *Mythologies*, Paladin, London.

—— 1974, *S / Z*, Hill and Wang, New York.

—— 1975, *The Pleasure of the Text*, Hill and Wang, New York.

—— 1977, 'The Death of the Author', in R Barthes, *Image, Music, Text*, Fontana, London.

Baudrillard, J 1988, *Jean Baudrillard: Selected Writings*, Stanford University Press, Palo Alto.

Baudry, J-L 1992, 'The Apparatus: Metapsychological Approaches to the Impression of Reality in Cinema', in G Mast, M Cohen & L Braudy (eds), *Film Theory and Criticism: Introductory Readings*, 4th edn, Oxford University Press, New York.

Bell, A, Joyce, M & Rivers, D 1999, *Advanced Media Studies*, Hodder & Stoughton, London.

Benjamin, W 1977, *Understanding Brecht*, New Left Books, London.

Berger, J 1972, *Ways of Seeing*, Penguin, Harmondsworth, and BBC Television, London.

Bettelheim, B 1978, *The Uses of Enchantment: The Meaning and Importance of Fairy Tales*, Peregrine, London.

Biddulph, S 1994, *Manhood*, Finch Publishing, Sydney.

—— 1997, *Raising Boys*, Finch Publishing, Sydney.

Blumler, J & Katz, E (eds) 1974, *The Uses of Mass Communications: Current Perspectives on Gratifications Research*, Sage, Beverly Hills and London.

Bly, R 1990, *Iron John*, Vintage, London.

Bogle, T 1973, *Toms, Coons, Mulattoes and Bucks: An Interpretative History of Blacks in American Films*, Viking Press, New York.

Boorstin, D 2006, 'From Hero to Celebrity: The human pseudo-event', in P D Marshall (ed.), *The Celebrity Culture Reader*, Routledge, New York.

Bordwell, D & Thompson, K 2004, *Film Art: An Introduction*, 7th edn, McGraw Hill, New York.

Bradbury, M & McFarlane, J (eds) 1976, *Modernism, 1890–1930*, Penguin, Harmondsworth.

Brando, M & Lindsey, R 1994, *Brando: Songs My Mother Taught Me*, Random House, New York.

Brohm, J 1978, *Sport: A Prison of Measured Time*, Ink Links, London.

Brown, S 2004, 'Principal Adviser on Technology Issues for United Nations', quoted on ABC's Radio National *News*, 27 July 2004.

Brown, W & Fraser, B 2004, 'Celebrity Identification', in A Singhal, M Cody, E Rogers, & M Sabido (eds), *Entertainment Education*, Lawrence Erlbaum, New Jersey.

Brunsdon, C 1986, 'Women Watching Television', *MediaKulture*, vol. 4.

Bushman, B & Anderson, C 2001, 'Media Violence and the American Public: Scientific Facts Versus Media Misinformation', in *American Psychologist*, 56, no. 6/7, pp. 477–89.

Bushman, B & Huesmann, L R 2001, 'Effects of Televised Violence on Aggression', in D Singer & J Singer (eds), *Handbook of Children and the Media*, Sage Publications, Thousand Oaks, pp. 223–54.

Butler, J 1990, *Gender Trouble: Feminism and the Subversion of Identity*, Routledge, London.

—— 1998, 'Imitation and Gender Insubordination', in J Rivkin & M Ryan (eds), *Literary Theory: An Anthology*, Blackwell, Malden MA.

Cameron, D 2007, *The Myth of Mars and Venus: Do Men and Women Really Speak Different Languages?* Oxford University Press, Oxford and New York.

Campbell, D 1997, *The Mozart Effect*, Hodder Headline, Sydney.

Campbell, J 1972, *The Hero with a Thousand Faces*, Princeton University Press, Princeton.

—— 1988a, *The Power of Myth*, Anchor, New York.

—— 1988b, *Joseph Campbell and the Power of Myth* (video), Mystic Fire Video, in association with *Parabola Magazine*, New York (distributed in Australia by the ABC).

—— 1991, *Occidental Mythology: The Masks of God*, Arkana, New York.

Carter, M 2004, 'Causes for Corporations', in *Mail and Guardian*, 13–19 August, p. 24.

Casey, B, Casey, N, Calvert, B, French, L & Lewis, J 2002, 'Fans', in *Television Studies: The Key Concepts*, Routledge, London.

Castells, M 2000, *The Rise of the Network Society*, 2nd edn, Blackwell, Oxford.

—— 2001a, 'Information Technology and Global Development', in J Muller, N Cloete & S Badat (eds), *Challenges of Globalisation: South African Debates with Manuel Castells*, Maskew, Miller and Longman, Johannesburg.

—— 2001b, 'Think Local, Act Global', in J Muller, N Cloete & S Badat (eds), *Challenges of Globalisation: South African Debates with Manuel Castells*, Maskew, Miller and Longman, Johannesburg.

—— Fernández-Ardèvol, M, Linchuan Qiu, J & Sey, A (eds) 2007, *Mobile Communication and Society*, MIT Press, Cambridge MA.

Caughie, J (ed.) 1981, *Theories of Authorship*, Routledge & Kegan Paul, London.

Cohan, S 2001, 'Judy on the Net: Judy Garland Fandom and "The Gay Thing" Revisited', in M Tinkcom & A Villarejo (eds), *Keyframes: Popular Cinema and Cultural Studies*, Routledge, London.

Cohen, J & Weimann, G 2000, 'Cultivation Revisited: Some Genres Have Some Effects on Some Viewers', in *Communication Reports*, Summer, vol. 13, issue 2, pp. 99–114.

Cohen, S & Hark, I (eds) 1997, *The Road Movie Book*, Routledge, London.

Colors, February/March 2000, vol. 36, Milan.

Connell, R 1987, *Gender and Power*, Allen & Unwin, Sydney.

—— 1995, *Masculinities*, Allen & Unwin, Sydney.

Control Room, 2004, Dir: Jehane Noujaim, USA/Egypt/Qatar, *Control Room* website at <www. controlroommovie.com/noflash.html>.

Cook, P 1985, *The Cinema Book*, British Film Institute, London.

—— & Bernink, M (eds) 1999, *The Cinema Book*, 2nd edn, British Film Institute, London.

Copeland, G 2007, 'A History of Television Style', in J Butler, *Television: Critical Methods and Applications*, 3rd edn, Lawrence Erlbaum and Assoc., Malwah, New Jersey.

Cousins, M 2004, *The Story of Film*, Pavilion Books, London.

Crago, M 2002, 'Just a Spoonful of Grainy Footage: Creating "Realism" and Authenticity Big Brother Style', *Metro Magazine*, no. 133, pp. 108–15.

Creeber, G & Hills, M 2007. 'TV111.' *New Review of Film and Television Studies*, vol. 5, issue 1, pp. 1–4.

Creed, B 2003, *Media Matrix: Sexing the New Reality*, Allen & Unwin, Sydney.

Crow, D 2003, *Visible Signs*, AVA Publishing SA, Crans-près-Céligny, Switzerland.

Culler, J 1976, *Saussure*, Fontana, London.

Cunningham, S & Miller, T 1994, 'The Spectacle of Sport', in *Contemporary Australian Television*, UNSW Press, Sydney.

Cunningham, S & Turner, G (eds) 2009, *Media and Communications in Australia*, 3rd edn, Allen & Unwin, Sydney.

Czitrom, D 1982, *Media and the American Mind: From Morse to McLuhan*, University of North Carolina Press, Chapel Hill.

Davies, J B, Sandström, S, Shorrocks, A & Wolff, E N 2008, 'The World Distribution of Household Wealth' in WIDER Discussion Paper No. 2008/03, at <www.

wider.unu.edu/publications/working-papers/discussion-papers/2008/en_GB/dp2008-03>, accessed 11 October 2011.

De Certeau, M 1984, *The Practice of Everyday Life*, University of California Press, Berkeley.

Department of Health, Western Australia, 2004, 'Fact Sheet on Smoking', Department of Health, Perth.

Diawara, M (ed.) 1993, *Black American Cinema*, Routledge, New York.

Diaz, J 1998, interview on *Arts Today*, ABC Radio National, 14 May.

Dilger, D E 2011 'Apple products appeared in 30% of all top movies in 2010' <http://www.appleinsider.com/articles/11/02/22/apple_products_appeared_in_30_of_all_top_movies_in_2010.html>. Published 22 February 2011; Accessed 1 August 2011.

Dubow, E & Miller, L 1996, 'Television Violence Viewing and Aggressive Behaviour', in T M MacBeth (ed.), *Tuning in to Young Viewers*, Sage, California.

Dyer, G 1982, *Advertising as Communication*, Methuen, London.

Dyer, R 1981, 'Entertainment and Utopia', in R Altman (ed.), *Genre: The Musical*, British Film Institute and Routledge & Kegan Paul, London.

—— 1982, 'Don't Look Now: The Male Pin-Up', *Screen*, vol. 23, no. 3/4, pp. 61–73.

—— 1987, *Heavenly Bodies: Film Stars and Society*, Macmillan, Basingstoke.

—— 1992, *Only Entertainment*, Routledge, London.

—— 1993, *The Matter of Images: Essays on Representations*, Routledge, London and New York.

—— 1998, *Stars*, 2nd edn, British Film Institute, London.

—— 2006, 'Stars as Images', in P David Marshall (ed.), *The Celebrity Culture Reader*, Routledge, New York.

—— Geraghty, C, Jordon, M, Lovell, T, Paterson, R & Stewart, J (eds), 1981, *Coronation Street*, British Film Institute, London.

Edwards, G J 1985, *The International Film Poster*, Columbus Books, London.

Edwards, T 2006, *Cultures of Masculinity*, Routledge, New York.

Ehrlich, S 1995, 'Talk, Talk, Talk', *The Science Show*, ABC Radio National (originally produced by the Canadian Broadcast Corporation).

Eisenstein, S 1992, 'A Dialectic Approach to Film Form', in G Mast, M Cohen & L Braudy (eds), *Film Theory and Criticism: Introductory Readings*, 4th edn, Oxford University Press, New York.

Eliade, M 1963, *Myth and Reality*, Harper & Row, New York.

Faludi, S 1992, *Backlash: The Undeclared War Against American Women*, Chatto & Windus, London.

Fillingham, L 1995, *Foucault for Beginners*, Writers and Readers, London.

Fink, R 2005, *Repeating Ourselves,* University of California Press, Berkeley.

Finke, N 2007, 'Warner's Robinov Bitchslaps Film Women', *Nikki Finke's Deadline Hollywood Daily*, at <www.deadlinehollywooddaily.com>, accessed 5 October 2007.

Fischer, E 1963, *The Necessity of Art: A Marxist Approach*, Penguin, Harmondsworth.

Fiske, J 1987, *Television Culture*, Methuen, London.

—— 1989a, *Reading the Popular*, Unwin Hyman, Sydney.

—— 1989b, *Understanding Popular Culture*, Unwin Hyman, Sydney.

—— 1990, *Introduction to Communication Studies*, 2nd edn, Routledge, London.

Flew, T 2005, *New Media: An Introduction*, Oxford University Press, Melbourne.

Forbes, 2010, 'Celebrity 100' at <www.forbes.com/lists/2010/53/celeb-100-10_The-Celebrity-100.html>, accessed 1 July 2011.

Foucault, M 1979, *Discipline and Punish: The Birth of the Prison*, Penguin, Harmondsworth.

—— 1981, *The History of Sexuality*, Penguin, Harmondsworth.

Fourie, P (ed.) 2001, *Media Studies: Institutions, Theories and Issues*, Juta, South Africa.

Freud, S 1976a, *The Interpretation of Dreams*, Penguin, Harmondsworth.

—— 1976b, *Jokes and Their Relation to the Unconscious*, Penguin, Harmondsworth.

Frith, S, Goodwin, A & Grossberg, L (eds) 1993, *The Music Video Reader*, Routledge, New York.

Gates, B 1999, *Business @ the Speed of Thought: Using a Digital Nervous System*, Grand Central Publishing, New York.

Geen, R 1994, 'Television and Aggression: Recent Developments in Research and Theory', in D Zillman, J Bryant & A Huston (eds), *Media, Children and the Family: Social Scientific, Psychodynamic, and Clinical Perspectives*, Lawrence Erlbaum, Hillsdale, NJ.

Gilbert, C 1988, 'Reflections on *An American Family*', in A Rosenthal (ed.), *New Challenges for Documentary*, University of California Press, Berkeley.

Gitlin, T 1993, 'Style for Style's Sake', *The Australian*.

—— 2001, *Media Unlimited: How the Torrent of Images and Sounds Overwhelms Our Lives*, Metropolitan, New York.

Glantz, S 2004, 'Smoking', *West Australian*, 9 March 2004.

Gledhill, C (ed.) 1991, *Stardom: Industry of Desire*, Routledge, London.

—— (ed.) 2002, *Home is Where the Heart Is*, 2nd edn, British Film Institute, London.

Golden, K (ed.) 1992, *Uses of Comparative Mythology: Essays on the Work of Joseph Campbell*, Garland, New York.

Goodwin, A 1993, *Dancing in the Distraction Factory: Music Television and Popular Culture*, Routledge, London.

Gordon, W T 1996, *Saussure for Beginners*, Writers and Readers, London.

Green, J 2004, 'Playing Dirty', in *Atlantic Monthly*, June, vol. 293, no. 5.

Greer, G 2004, 'Watch With Big Brother', in P Rayner, P Wall & S Kruger (eds), *Media Studies: The Essential Resource*, Routledge, London.

Haley, A 1976, *Roots*, Doubleday, New York.

Hall, S 1980, 'Encoding/Decoding in Television Discourse', in S Hall, D Hobson, D Lowe & P Willis (eds), *Culture, Media, Language*, Hutchinson, London.

—— 1985, 'Signification, Representation, Ideology: Althusser and the Post-Structuralist Debates', in *Critical Studies in Mass Communication*, vol. 2, no. 2.

—— 1986, 'Cultural Studies: Two Paradigms', in R Collins, J Curran, N Sarnham, P Scannell, P Schlesinger & C Sparks (eds), *Media, Culture and Society: A Critical Reader*, Sage, London.

—— 1994, 'The Question of Cultural Identity', in Polity Press (ed.), *The Polity Reader in Cultural Theory*, Polity Press, Cambridge.

—— (ed.) 1997, *Representation: Cultural Representations and Signifying Practices*, Sage, London.

Halloran, J 1970, *The Effects of Television*, Panther, London.

Hammock, B 2004, quoted on *The Science Show*, ABC Radio National, July.

Hartley, J & McKee, A (eds) 1996, *Telling Both Stories: Indigenous Australia and the Media*, Arts Enterprise, Edith Cowan University, Perth.

Hartley, J & O'Regan, M 2000, interview on ABC Radio National, *The Media Report*, 21 December.

Harvey, S 1978, *May '68 and Film Culture*, British Film Institute, London.

Hassan, R 2004, *Media, Politics and the Network Society*, Open University Press, Berkshire.

Hawkes, T 1977, *Structuralism and Semiotics*, Methuen, London.

—— 1996, *Semiotics for Beginners*, Icon, Cambridge.

Hebdige, D 1979, *Subculture: The Meaning of Style*, Routledge, New York.

—— 1985, 'The Bottom Line on Planet One: Squaring up to The Face', *Ten-8*, vol. 19, pp. 40–9.

Henry, M 2002, 'He is a "Bad Mother★$%@!#": *Shaft* and Contemporary Black Masculinity', *Journal of Popular Film and Television*, vol. 30, no. 2, pp. 114–19.

Herdt, G 1989, 'Introduction: Gay and Lesbian Youth, Emergent Identities and Cultural Scenes at Home and Abroad', in G Herdt (ed.), *Gay and Lesbian Youth*, Haworth Press, New York and London.

Hernton, C 1970, *Sex and Racism*, Paladin, London.

Hobson, D 1982, *Crossroads: Drama of a Soap Opera*, Methuen, London.

Hodge, R & Kress, G 1991, *Social Semiotics*, Polity Press, New York.

Hogan, J 1998, personal correspondence with author.

hooks, b 2000, *Feminist Theory: From Margin to Center*, 2nd edn, South End Press, Cambridge, MA.

Hornby, N 2001, 'What Does the New Top Ten List Mean?', *Weekend Australian*, 3–4 November, pp. 4–6.

Hudson, H 2006, 'Universal Access to the New Information Infrastructure', in L Lievrouw and S Livingstone (eds), *The Handbook of New Media: Updated Student Edition*, Sage, London.

Innis, H 1951, *The Bias of Communication*, University of Toronto Press, Toronto.

Jackson, R 1981, *Fantasy: The Literature of Subversion*, Methuen, London.

Jagtenberg, T & McKie, D 1997, *Eco-Impacts and the Greening of Postmodernity*, Sage, Thousand Oaks, CA.

Jameson, F 1971, *Marxism and Form*, Princeton University Press, Princeton.

—— 1977, 'Dog Day Afternoon', *Screen*, vol. 18.

—— 1991, *Postmodernism or the Logic of Late Capitalism*, Verso, London.

Jencks, C 1986, *What is Postmodernism?* Academy Edition, London.

Jenkins, H 1992, *Textual Poachers: Television Fans and Participatory Culture*, Routledge, New York.

—— 2002, 'Interactive Audiences? The "Collective Intelligence" of Media Fans', in Dan Harries (ed.), *The New Media Book*, British Film Institute, London; available online at <http://web.mit.edu/21fms/www/faculty/henry3/collective%20intelligence.html>.

—— 2006, *Fans, Bloggers, and Gamers: Exploring Participatory Culture*, New York University Press, New York.

Johnson, R 1987, *The Psychology of Romantic Love*, Arkana, London.

Johnston, D C 2007, 'Sex sells—just not as fast', *International Herald Tribune*, 4 January, accessed at <www.iht.com/artices/200/01/04/business/sex.php>.

Jung, C G 1923, *Psychological Types, or, The Psychology of Individuation*, Kegan Paul, London.

Kaplan, A (ed.) 1990, *Psychoanalysis and Cinema*, Routledge, New York.

Kee, R 2001, interview with Donna McLachlan, ABC Radio National, *The Media Report*, 28 June.

Keen, A 2007, *The Cult of the Amateur: How the Internet is Killing Our Culture*, Doubleday, New York.

King, G & Krzywinska, T (eds) 2002, *Cinema/Videogames/Interfaces*, Wallflower, London.

—— 2006, *Tomb Raiders and Space Invaders: Videogame Forms and Contexts*, I B Taurus, London.

King, T 2003, *The Truth about Stories*, House of Anansi Press, Toronto.

Kitses, J 2004, *Horizons West*, Thames & Hudson, London.

Klein, N 2000, 'Culture Jamming: Ads Under Attack', in N Klein, *No Logo*, HarperCollins, London.

Koestler, A 1975, *The Act of Creation*, Pan, London.

Langer, J 2006, 'Television's "Personality System"', in P David Marshall (ed.), *The Celebrity Culture Reader*, Routledge, New York.

Lapsley, R & Westlake, M 1989, *Film Theory: An Introduction*, Manchester University Press, Manchester.

Lasswell, H 1960, 'The Structure and Function of Communication in Society', in L Bryson (ed.), *The Communication of Ideas*, Institute for Religious and Social Studies, New York.

Lazarsfeld, P & Stanton, F 1949, *Communication Research*, Harper & Row, New York.

Leab, D 1975, *From Sambo to Superspade*, Secker & Warburg, London.

Leader, D & Groves, J 1995, *Lacan for Beginners*, Icon, Cambridge.

Lévi-Strauss, C 1978, *Myth and Meaning*, Routledge & Kegan Paul.

Lindner, A 2008, 'Controlling the Media in Iraq', *Contexts*, vol. 7, no. 2, pp. 32–8.

Lister, M, Dovey, J, Giddings, S, Grant, I & Kelly, K 2003, *New Media: A Critical Introduction*, Routledge, London.

Lovink, G & Garcia, D 1997, 'ABC of Tactical Media', at <www.nettime.org/Lists-Archives/nettime-l-9705/msg00096.html>, accessed 14 February 2008.

Lowery, S & Defleur, M 1995, *Milestones in Mass Communication Research: Media Effects*, 3rd edn, Longman, New York.

Lumby, C 1997, *Bad Girls: The Media, Sex and Feminism in the 90s*, Allen & Unwin, Sydney.

Lunn, E 1985, *Marxism and Modernism*, Verso, London.

Lyotard, J-F 1984, *The Postmodern Condition: A Report on Knowledge*, Manchester University Press, Manchester.

MacCabe, C 1974, 'Realism and the Cinema: Notes on Some Brechtian Theses', *Screen*, vol. 15, no. 2.

MacDonald, K & Cousins, M 1996, *Imagining Reality: The Faber Book of Documentary*, Faber and Faber, London, pp. 264–70.

Malan, R 2000, 'In the Jungle?', *Rolling Stone*.

Mamet, D 1991, *On Directing Film*, Faber and Faber, London.

Mandela, N 1995, *Long Walk to Freedom*, Abacus, London.

Martin, A 1979, 'Chantal Akerman's Films: A Dossier', *Feminist Review*, no. 3.

Marx, K [1846], 1974, *The German Ideology*, 2nd edn, Lawrence & Wishart, London.

—— [1852], 1948, *The Eighteenth Brumaire of Louis Bonaparte*, Foreign Languages Publishing House, Moscow.

McArthur, C 1972, *Underworld USA*, Secker & Warburg and British Film Institute, London.

McKee, A 1997, 'Images of Gay Men in the Media and the Development of Self Esteem', unpublished paper, Media Studies Department, Edith Cowan University, Perth.

—— 2002, 'Understanding Pornography in Australia', *Eros Journal*, vol. 2, no. 3, pp. 1–21.

McLean, I & Bennett, G 1996, *The Art of Gordon Bennett*, Craftsman House, Sydney.

McLuhan, M 1987, *Understanding Media: The Extensions of Man*, Ark, London.

McQuail, D & Windahl, S 1981, *Communication Models for the Study of Mass Communications*, Longman, New York.

McRobbie, A 2009, *The Aftermath of Feminism: Gender, Culture and Social Change*, Sage, London.

Mendes, S 2000, interview on *The South Bank Show*, ITV.

—— 2004, DVD commentary on *American Beauty*.

Mills, B 2004, 'Comedy Vérité: Contemporary Sitcom Form', *Screen*, vol. 45, no. 1, pp. 63–78.

Mittell, J 2006, 'Lost in an Alternate Reality', in *Flow TV*, vol. 4, issue 7, 16 June, accessed at <http://flowtv.org/?p=165>.

Mizejewski, L 2001, 'Stardom and Serial Fantasies: Thomas Harris's *Hannibal*', in M Tinkcom & A Villarejo (eds), *Keyframes: Popular Cinema and Cultural Studies*, Routledge, London.

Morley, D 1992, *Television, Audiences and Cultural Studies*, Routledge, London.

Mulvey, L 1985, 'Visual Pleasure and Narrative Cinema', in B Nichols (ed.), *Movies and Methods*, vol. 2, University of California Press, Berkley.

—— 1989, 'Visual Pleasure and Narrative Cinema', in L Mulvey, *Visual and Other Pleasures*, Macmillan, Basingstoke.

Murray, W 1964, *Boys and Girls: Key Words Reading Scheme*, Ladybird, Loughborough.

—— 1990, *Read With Me 1: Key Words to Reading*, Ladybird, Loughborough.

Neale, S 1980, *Genre*, British Film Institute, London.

—— 2001, 'Studying Genre' and 'Genre and Television', in G Creeber (ed.), *The Television Genre Book*, British Film Institute, London, pp. 1–3.

Nelson, R 2007, *State of Play: Contemporary "High-end" TV Drama*, Manchester University Press, Manchester.

New Internationalist 1997, 'An Unequal World', <www.newint.org/index4.html>.

New Internationalist 1998 (April), 'Map of the World: Peters Projection', p. 6.

Ngugi, W 1986, *Decolonising the Mind: The Politics of Language in African Literature*, Heinemann, London.

Nichols, B 1991, *Representing Reality*, Indiana University Press, Bloomington.

—— 2001, *Introduction to Documentary*, Indiana University Press, Bloomington.

Nurse, J 2003, 'Black Labour', in *Laugh it Off Annual: South African Youth Culture*, Double Storey Books, Cape Town.

Open University 1981, 'Block 2: Social Aspects of Language', in *E263, Language in Use*, Open University Press, Milton Keynes.

O'Sullivan, T, Hartley, J, Saunders, D & Fiske, J 1986, *Key Concepts in Communication*, Methuen, New York.

—— 1994, *Key Concepts in Communication and Cultural Studies*, 2nd edn, Routledge, London.

Packard, V 1957, *The Hidden Persuaders*, Penguin, Harmondsworth.

Peirce, C S 1958, *Collected Papers, 1931–58*, vols 7–8 (ed. Arthur Burke), Harvard University Press, Cambridge, MA.

Peretti, J 2001, 'My Nike Media Adventure', *The Nation*, 9 April. Available online at <www.thenation.com/doc.mhtml?i=20010409&s=peretti>.

Perkins, V 1990, *Film as Film*, Penguin, Harmondsworth.

Pilkington 2002, 'Saudis Acknowledge Women Exist', *Mail & Guardian*, 19–25 July, p. 18.

Postman, N 1993, *Technopoly*, Vintage, New York.

Powell, C & Paton, G 1988, *Humour in Society: Resistance and Control*, Macmillan, London.

Prensky, M 2004 ABC, Radio National, *The Buzz*, with Richard Aedy, 21 February.

Pribram, D 1993, 'Seduction, Control, and the Search for Authenticity: Madonna's Truth or Dare', in C. Schwichtenberg (ed.), *The Madonna Connection*, Allen & Unwin, Sydney.

Propp, V 1975, *Morphology of the Folktale*, University of Texas Press, Austin.

Rabinow, P (ed.) 1984, *The Foucault Reader*, Pantheon Books, New York.

Radway, J 1987, *Reading the Romance*, Verso, London.

Rayner, P, Wall, P & Kruger, S 2004, *Media Studies: The Essential Resource*, Routledge, London.

Reggio, G 1990, unpublished interview on *Koyaanisqatsi*.

Reid, M (ed.) 1997, *Spike Lee's Do the Right Thing*, Cambridge University Press, Cambridge.

Rivkin, J & Ryan, M (eds) 1998, *Literary Theory: An Anthology*, Blackwell, Malden, MA.

Roscoe, J & Hight, C 1997, 'Mocking Silver: Reinventing the Documentary Project', *Continuum*, vol. 11, no. 1, pp. 67–82.

—— 2001, *Faking It: Mock-Documentary and the Subversion of Factuality*, Manchester University Press, Manchester.

Rouch, J 1995, 'The Camera and the Man', in P Hockings (ed.), *Principles of Visual Anthropology*, Walter de Gruyter, Berlin.

Rousseau, J-J 1974, *Emile*, Dent, London.

Russo, V 1981, *The Celluloid Closet*, Harper & Row, New York.

Rutherford, J (ed.) 1990, *Identity: Community, Culture, Difference*, Lawrence & Wishart, London.

Said, E 1980, *Orientalism*, Routledge & Kegan Paul, London.

Saussure, F 1974, *Course in General Linguistics*, Fontana, London.

Schiller, H 1992, 'A Quarter Century Retrospective', in H Schiller (ed.), *Mass Communications and American Empire*, 2nd edn, Westview Press, Boulder, CO.

—— 1998, 'American Pop Culture Sweeps the World', in R Dickson, R Harindranath & O Linne (eds), *Approaches to Audiences*, Arnold, London.

Schultz, J (ed.) 2004, *Griffith Review: Addicted to Celebrity*, Spring, Griffith University, Brisbane.

Schwichtenberg, C (ed.) 1993, *The Madonna Connection*, Allen & Unwin, Sydney.

Self, W 2000, quoted in *The Media*, February 2003, and online at <www.biz-community.com/Quotes/196/15.html>.

Sexton, J 2003, '"Televerite" Hits Britain: Documentary, Drama and the Growth of 16mm Filmmaking in British Television', *Screen*, vol. 44, no. 4, pp. 429–44.

Skinner, B F 1976, *About Behaviourism*, Random House, New York.

Smith, G 1994, 'When You Know You're in Good Hands: Quentin Tarantino Interviewed by Gavin Smith', *Film Comment*, vol. 30, no. 4, pp. 32–43.

Snow, N 2001, 'Social Implications of Media Globalisation', in Y R Kamalipour & K R Rampal (eds), *Media, Sex, Violence and Drugs in the Global Village*, Rowman and Littlefield, New York.

Solomon, J 1988, 'Our Decentred Culture: The Postmodern View', in *The Signs of Our Times*, St Martins Press, Los Angeles.

Sontag, S 2003, *Regarding the Pain of Others*, Farrar, Straus & Giroux, New York.

Spender, D 1980, *Man Made Language*, Routledge & Kegan Paul, London.

Stacey, J 1991, 'Feminine Fascinations: Forms of Identification in Star-Audience Relations', in C Gledhill (ed.), *Stardom: The Industry of Desire*, Routledge, London.

—— 2006, 'Feminine Fascinations: A Question of Identification?', in D Marshall (ed.), *The Celebrity Culture Reader*, Routledge, New York.

Stam, R & Spence, L 1983, 'Colonialism, Racism and Representation: An Introduction', *Screen* vol. 24, no. 2, pp. 3–20.

Sunday Times 1996, 'Well, Hello Sailors', 3 March.

Tasker, Y 1993, *Spectacular Bodies*, Routledge, London.

Tasker, Y & Negra, D (eds) 2007, *Interrogating Postfeminism: Gender and the Politics of Popular Culture*, Duke University Press, Durham.

Taubin, A 1999, 'So Good it Hurts', *Sight and Sound*, vol. 9, no. 11, November, pp. 16–18.

Taylor, A 2011, *Single Women in Popular Culture: The Limits of Postfeminism*, Palgrave MacMillan, Basingstoke.

'Terror Trap Takes the Cake' 2011, *The Weekend Australian* 'World' section, June 4–5, 2011, page 19, no author – AFP.

Thompson, J 1995, *The Media and Modernity: A Social Theory of the Media*, Polity Press, Cambridge.

Thoreau, H 1973, *Walden or Life in the Woods*, Anchor Press/Doubleday, New York.

Todorov, T 1975, *The Fantastic*, Cornell University Press, New York.

Tulloch, J & Jenkins, H 1995, *Science Fiction Audiences: Watching Doctor Who and Star Trek*, Routledge, London.

Turner, G 2004, *Understanding Celebrity*, Sage, London.

—— 2006, *Film as Social Practice*, 4th edn, Routledge, London.

Ullman, M & Zimmerman, N 1979, *Working with Dreams*, Hutchinson, London.

Vogler, C 1992, *The Writer's Journey: Mythic Structure for Storytellers and Screenwriters*, Michael Weise Productions, California.

von Schoeber, F 2004, quoted on *The Music Show*, ABC Radio National.

Walters, S D 1995, *Material Girls: Making Sense of Feminist Cultural History*, California University Press, Berkeley.

Wark, M 1994, *Virtual Geography: Living with Global Media Events*, Indiana University Press, Bloomington and Indianapolis.

Watkins, K 2005, *UN Human Development Report 2005*, at <http://hdr.undp.org/en/media/HDR05_complete.pdf>, accessed 11 October 2011.

Watkins, P 1997, 'The Dark Side of the Moon: The Mass Media, Media Education, and the Democratic Crisis', n. p. Vilnius.

Watson, P 2003, 'Critical Approaches to Hollywood Cinema: Authorship, Genre and Stars', in J Nelmes (ed.), *An Introduction to Film Studies*, 3rd edn, Routledge, London, pp. 163–83.

Weedon, C 1987, *Feminist Practice and Poststructuralist Theory*, Blackwell, Oxford.

Weekend Australian 2001, 'The Aftermath of September 11th', 13–14 October, p. 1.

Weeks, J 1991, *Against Nature: Essays on Sexuality, History and Identity*, Rivers Oram Press, London.

Wellek, R & Warren, A 1976, *Theory of Literature*, Penguin, Harmondsworth.

West Australian 1997, 'Suicide Alert on Film', 22 February.

—— 1998, 'Cartoon Triggers Illness', 4 February.

—— 1999, 'We Did It', 23 November.

—— 2001, 'Good v Evil', 13 September.

—— 2004, 'Cigarette Smoking', 9 March.

Willett, J (ed. & trans.) 1964, *Brecht on Theatre*, Methuen, London.

Williams, L 1993, 'Mirrors without Memories: Truth, History and the New Documentary', *Film Quarterly*, vol. 46, no. 3, pp. 9–21.

—— 1999, *Hard Core*, University of California Press, Berkeley.

Williams, R 1977a, 'A Lecture on Realism', *Screen*, vol. 18, no. 1, pp. 61–74.

—— 1977b, *Marxism and Literature*, Oxford University Press, Oxford.

Williamson, D 2004, ABC Radio National, *Big Ideas*, 'The Wisdom Interviews with Peter Thompson and David Williamson', 22 February.

Winston, B 1995, *Claiming the Real: The Documentary Film Revisited*, British Film Institute, London.

Winterson, J 1995, *Art Objects: Essays on Ecstasy and Effrontery*, Jonathan Cape, London.

Wolf, N 1990, *The Beauty Myth*, Chatto & Windus, London.

Wollstonecraft, M 1975 (1792), *A Vindication of the Rights of Woman*, Peter Edes, Boston.

Wood, G 2007, 'From the Web to the White House', *The Observer*, 8 July.

Wood, R 1986, 'The American Nightmare', in R Wood, *Hollywood from Vietnam to Reagan*, Columbia University Press, New York.

Woodward, K (ed.) 1997, *Identity and Difference*, Sage, New York.

YouTube 2007, 'Billiam the Snowman', accessed at <www.Youtube.com/watch?v=-0BPnnvI47Q>, 1 December.

—— 2008, 'Hillary Clinton's *Sopranos* Parody: Election Song Video', accessed at <www.Youtube.com/watch?v=9BEPcJlz2wE>, 14 February.

—— 2008, 'The Hire:Star', accessed at <www.Youtube.com/watch?v=QjpKDzVBpzw>, 14 February.

—— 2011, 'Buffy vs Edward', accessed at <Youtube.com/watch?v=RZwM3GvaTRM >, 21 January.

Further Reading

There are many books that are useful for further study of the media and society. The following are particularly recommended as a follow-up to the approaches presented in this book.

Allen, R C & Hill, A (eds) 2004, *The Television Studies Reader*, Routledge, London. This reader contains a good range of approaches to television analysis.

Armstrong, R 2005, *Understanding Realism*, British Film Institute, London. A helpful general introduction to realist traditions of representation in screen culture.

Barthes, R 1974, *Mythologies*, Paladin, St Albans. A seminal media studies text that develops semiology; see especially the chapter 'Myth Today'.

Biddulph, S 1994, *Manhood*, Finch Publishing, Sydney.

Biressi, A & Nunn, H 2005, *Reality TV: Realism and Revelation*, Wallflower Press, London. Biressi and Nunn give an overview of the field, include lots of examples (mainly from the UK), and engage with critical issues.

Bordwell, D & Thompson, K 2008, *Film Art: An Introduction*, 8th edn, McGraw-Hill, New York. An excellent introduction to film studies; particularly useful for introducing the language of film to enhance textual analysis and to deepen technical and aesthetic understandings of cinematography, editing, sound, and *mise-en-scène*.

Brabazon, T 2007, *The University of Google: Education in a (post)information age*, Aldershot. A contemporary perspective on the impact of ICTs.

Branston, G & Stafford, R 2006, *The Media Student's Book*, 4th edn, Routledge, London. An excellent beginner's book on media studies.

Butler, J 2007, *Television: Critical Methods and Applications*, 3rd edn, Lawrence Erlbaum, Hillsdale, NJ. This is an excellent overview of television studies, full of relevant, contemporary examples.

Campbell, J 1991, *The Power of Myth*, Anchor, New York. Along with Campbell's interviews with Bill Moyers from his television series, the best place to start in relation to Campbell's work. The video series, *Joseph Campbell and the Power of Myth* (Campbell 1988b), is also useful.

Cook, P & Bernink, M (eds) 2007, *The Cinema Book*, 3rd edn, British Film Institute, London. An overview of film studies that is particularly useful for understanding genre and narrative.

Cousins, M & Macdonald, K (eds) 2006, *Imagining Reality: The Faber Book of Documentary*, Faber and Faber, London. An anthology covering important writing by documentary film-makers and academics.

Cunningham, S & Turner, G (eds) 2006, *Media and Communications in Australia*, 2nd edn, Allen & Unwin, Sydney. The best analysis of the media in Australia (and the best overview of media studies approaches in relation to Australia). A useful and comprehensive book for all media studies students.

Denzin, N 2002, *Reading Race*, Sage, London. Denzin's book begins with an overview of different theoretical perspectives on race and racism in popular culture from 1900 to 2000.

Durham, M G & Kellner, D 2001, *Media and Cultural Studies KeyWorks*, Blackwell, Malden, MA. This anthology contains extracts from the most influential texts in media and cultural studies along with useful introductions and commentaries.

Dyer, R 1992, *Only Entertainment*, Routledge, London. Discusses popular culture and defines key terms used in cultural studies and media studies.

—— 1993, *The Matter of Images: Essays on Representation*, Routledge, London. Develops many of the issues dealt with in this book. Dyer writes clearly and illuminatingly. Highly recommended.

—— 1998, *Stars*, 2nd edn, British Film Institute, London. Excellent analysis of film stars in terms of ethnicity and sexuality.

Fiske, J 1989, *Reading the Popular*, Unwin Hyman, Sydney. This and the book below by Fiske are collections of fascinating essays that analyse examples of popular culture.

—— 1989, *Understanding Popular Culture*, Unwin Hyman, Sydney.

Gauntlett, D 2002, *Media, Gender and Identity: An Introduction*, Routledge, London. This is an excellent book, written in an accessible and interesting style. The chapter on 'Queer Theory and Fluid Identities' is particularly good; there is also a lot of material dealing with masculinity and femininity in magazines.

Hall, S 1996, *Critical Dialogues in Cultural Studies*, Comedia, London. Hall is one of the most significant cultural studies writers. His work is complex but it offers a brilliant overview of the field.

—— (ed.) 1997, *Representation: Cultural Representations and Signifying Practices*, Sage, London. While this is an introductory textbook, its language and the concepts it explores are more complex. *Representation* also delves deeper into media studies and cultural studies.

Hartley, J 2007, *Television Truths: Forms of Knowledge in Popular Culture*, Wiley-Blackwell, Malden MA, London. This text explores the function of television in contemporary society and discusses television ethics, aesthetics, metaphysics and epistemology.

Holmes, S & Redmon, S (eds) 2006, *Framing Celebrity: New Directions in Celebrity Culture*, Routledge, London. New approaches to studying celebrities.

Kamalipour, Y & Kuldip R R (eds) 2001, *Media, Sex, Violence and Drugs in the Global Village*, Rowman and Littlefield, New York. A collection of essays about the implications of global media flows.

Keane, S 2007, *Cine Tech: Film, Convergence and New Media*, Palgrave, New York. This book and the one below offer perspectives on the impact of new media technologies.

Keen, A 2007, *The Cult of the Amateur: How Today's Internet is Killing Our Culture*, Doubleday/Currency, New York.

Klein, N 2000, *No Logo*, HarperCollins, London. Very readable account of culture jamming and the impact of globalisation.

Lister, M, Dovey, J, Giddings, S, Grant, I & Kelly, K 2003, *New Media: A Critical Introduction*, Routledge, London. This is a well-organised overview of new media issues.

MacKinnon, K 2003, *Representing Men: Maleness and Masculinity in the Media*, Arnold, London. A critical analysis of representations and responses to masculinity in film, television, sport, and magazines.

Marshall, P D (ed.) 2006, *The Celebrity Culture Reader*, Routledge, New York. This anthology offers extensive coverage of key works in star studies and celebrity culture.

McNair, B 2007, *An Introduction to Political Communication*, 4th edn, Routledge, London. McNair's work is clear and intelligent. He is one of the best authors on the relationship between journalism, politics, and the press.

—— 1998, *The Sociology of Journalism*, Arnold, London. This text gives insight into the ideal of objectivity in journalism.

Men and Masculinities. This is a refereed print journal publishing the most recent gender studies on men and masculinities; see <http://jmm.sagepub.com/>.

Montgomery, M 1995, *An Introduction to Language and Society*, 2nd edn, Routledge, London. The best introductory overview of the relationship between language and society.

Neale, S 2000, *Genre and Hollywood*, Routledge, New York. An account of film genres and genre theory from an expert in the field.

Tasker, Y & Negra, D (eds) 2007, *Interrogating Postfeminism: Gender and the Politics of Popular Culture*, Duke University Press, Durham. An accessible and interesting anthology of feminism and postfeminism in contemporary popular culture.

Turner, G 2006, *Film as Social Practice*, 4th edn, Routledge, London. Turner writes clearly and gives good overviews.

—— 2004, *Understanding Celebrity*, Sage, London.

Index